Robert Seymour Conway

The Italic Dialects

Vol. 2

Robert Seymour Conway

The Italic Dialects
Vol. 2

ISBN/EAN: 9783337239664

Printed in Europe, USA, Canada, Australia, Japan

Cover: Foto ©Andreas Hilbeck / pixelio.de

More available books at **www.hansebooks.com**

THE ITALIC DIALECTS

EDITED WITH A

GRAMMAR AND GLOSSARY

BY

R. S. CONWAY, M.A.,

PROFESSOR OF LATIN IN UNIVERSITY COLLEGE, CARDIFF;
LATE FELLOW OF GONVILLE AND CAIUS COLLEGE, CAMBRIDGE.

VOLUME II., CONTAINING PART II.—AN OUTLINE OF THE
GRAMMAR OF THE DIALECTS, APPENDIX,
INDICES AND GLOSSARY.

CAMBRIDGE:
AT THE UNIVERSITY PRESS.
1897.

Cambridge:
PRINTED BY J. AND C. F. CLAY,
AT THE UNIVERSITY PRESS.

CONTENTS OF VOLUME II.

PART II. AN OUTLINE OF THE GRAMMAR OF THE ITALIC DIALECTS.

		PAGE
A.	The Alphabets	458
	Table of Alphabets . . .	*to face* 461
	Notes on the Table of Alphabets	461

B. Accidence of the Osco-Umbrian Dialects.

    I. Noun Inflexion: o- and $\bar{a}$-Stems . . . 469
                           -io- Stems . . . 470
                           Diphthongal and $\bar{e}$-Stems 473
                           i- and u-Stems . . 474
                           Consonantal Stems . . 475

    II. Comparison of Adjectives .   476
    III. Pronouns   . .   477
    IV. Numerals   481
    V. Adverbs   482
    VI. Prepositions and Postpositions .   483
    VII. Verbal Inflexion: In General .   484
            Paradigms of the Active Voice .   486—491
            Passive Forms   492
    Notes on a few points of Phonology   495

C. Notes on the Syntax of the Dialect Inscriptions.
    I. Syntax of Nouns: A. The Cases 497
                           B. Concord 502
                           C. Neuter Adjectives as Abstracta 503

			PAGE
II.	Syntax of Pronouns		503
III.	Syntax of Verbs: A. Person		505
	B. Tense		ib.
	C. Mood		507
	D. The Passive Forms		516
	E. Participles and Gerundive		519
IV.	Order of Words		520

APPENDIX.

I.	The Mensa Ponderaria of Pompeii		521
II.	Alien, Spurious or Doubtful Inscriptions.		
	A. 1*—34*. Etruscan Inscriptions in Italic districts		524
	B. 35*. Gallic Inscription of Tuder		528
	C. 36*—40*. 'East Italic' or 'Sabellic' Inscriptions		ib.
	D. 41*—46*. Doubtful or Spurious Inscriptions		530

INDICES.

I.	Local names of Ancient Italy	535
II.	Modern Local names cited in this work	549
III.	Gentile names from the Dialect-areas	556
IV.	Passages in the Dialect-Inscriptions referred to in the Notes on Dialect Syntax	593
V.	Glossary to the Dialects	595
VI.	Latin words discussed in any part of this work	674

ADDENDA.

Page 681.

ERRATA IN VOL. II.

p. 492 l. 2 *from below read* **Lat. decet** *not* **Lat. de-cet**.

p. 595 *Add at foot:* bis *in e.g.* 232*bis refers to a separate insc.; but* bis, ter *etc. denote the no. of occurrences in the same insc. or line e.g.* 28 8 bis.

p. 596 *s.v.* **aapas** *read* gen. sg. *for* nom. pl.

.. 600 *s.v.* **anaceta** *read* 206*bis not* 206 bis.

.. 601 *s.v.* **Arkiia** (which should be spaced) *read* 80*bis not* 80 bis.

.. 604 *s.v.* **Bivellis** *read* nomen or praenomen.

.. 608 l. 21 *read* 206*bis not* 206 bis.

.. 621 *s.v.* **feḍehtru** *read* *fidē-trum for* *fide-trum*.

PART II.

AN OUTLINE OF THE GRAMMAR OF THE ITALIC DIALECTS.

PART II.

AN OUTLINE OF THE GRAMMAR OF THE ITALIC DIALECTS.

A. *The Alphabets.*

THE alphabets in which the dialect-inscriptions are written are as follows, in their geographical order:

1. Tarentine-Ionic.
2. Oscan.
3. Etruscan (of Campania, p. 96 ff.).
4. Latin, in more than one variety.
5. Faliscan.
6. Umbrian.

The Tarentine-Ionic is identical with the normal Ionic, say of Athens in the IV century, with certain additions, see below (p. 461).

The rest are derived from the Western Greek alphabet of the Chalcidian colonies, e.g. Cumae. Both the Cumaean and Ionic, like the other Greek alphabets, are, by almost universal consent, ultimately derived from the Phoenician. The place of the Faliscan alphabet in the Italic system has not been hitherto determined (see below), but the rest are connected thus [1]:

```
                        Chalcidian
                ┌───────────┴───────────┐
         Latin                    Primitive Etruscan
       ┌───┴───┐              ┌─────────┼─────────┐
  Campano-Etruscan   Oscan       Etruscan       Umbrian
                                (of Etruria)
```

Mommsen once held (*U. D.* p. 25 al.) that the Oscan $a\beta$ was derived immediately from the Umbrian, a supposition always open to obvious geographical objections, and now rendered needless by accumulated evidence, which shows that there were Etruscan settlements in Campania as well as in Latium; see pp. 52, 94, 99 and 148 sup. We can now date the Oscan inscc. from alphabetic and other considerations with sufficient clearness to know that none of them from any part of the Oscan-speaking territory are earlier than the Samnite conquest of Campania between 435 and 420 B.C., but that they begin to appear very soon after it. The close relation of the Oscan to the Campano-Etruscan $a\beta$ will be clear from the table. There appears to be no reason to doubt that the Umbrians learned to write from their Etruscan neighbours across the Tiber; but the date at which they did so, whatever it may have been (p. 464 inf.), has no direct relation to the course of events in Campania.

The annexed Table of Alphabets includes those already mentioned, with the Cumaean $a\beta$ of the VI century, as shown on the surviving inscc. (Roehl, *I. G. A.* 524 ff.),—the oldest direct representative of the mother $a\beta$ of all the Italic group—and also the $a\beta$ of Formello, which is the only complete, and doubtless, save in direction, the most exact presentment of the same type. It is incised on a vase, on which an Etruscan

---

[1] In reply to a request for his opinion Prof. Pauli (April, 1896) was kind enough to express to me his entire agreement with this scheme, reserving only the question of the Faliscan $a\beta$.

syllabary is also written, found at Formello near Veii in 1882, so that there is external as well as internal evidence of its close connexion with the Etruscan. "It is the only complete abecedarium extant which contains the archaic Greek forms of every one of the 22 Phoenician letters arranged precisely in the received Semitic order" (Roberts, *Intr. Gr. Epigr.* p. 20, to whose admirable summary the reader may be referred for all the relations of the Cumaean $\alpha\beta$ outside Italy).

The Campano-Etruscan $\alpha\beta\beta$ in the Table are taken (1) from the two abecedaria incised on paterae from Nola (*U. D.* taf. i. 14) which are now in the Naples Museum, and (2) from the Oscan and Etruscan inscc. in which it is employed (p. 95 ff. and the Appendix).

The order of the letters is directly known to us from the $\alpha\beta$ of Formello, confirmed by the similar $\alpha\beta$ of Caere (Roberts p. 17); from the Etruscan $\alpha\beta\beta$ of Bomarzo (*U. D.* init.) and of Nola (given in the fourth line of the Table) and from the Oscan $\alpha\beta\beta$ of Pompeii (**81**).

In the lines showing the Oscan, Umbrian, Faliscan and Latin $\alpha\beta\beta$ the Table shows the normal forms of each as it is used in the dialect inscc. we at present possess. Where more than one form is given, the first is the earliest, except (1) that *with* between two forms implies that the two are contemporaneous, and (2) that *and* between two forms implies that no opinion is expressed as to their chronological order.

A blank space indicates that the letter was probably wanting in the $\alpha\beta$; but the sign .. that it was probably in use there and is only by accident absent from our inscc.

An asterisk denotes that the sign appears in retrograde writing.

Perigrams (i.e. symbols used singly or in combination as a rough equivalent for some other sound as well as for that which they properly represent in their particular $\alpha\beta$ in that locality) are enclosed in brackets; e.g. in the Tarentine-Ionic $\alpha\beta$ EI represents not only the Oscan diphthong $e\overset{i}{\iota}$ (e.g. in the genitive *hερεκλεις* **17**) but also the simple $\overset{i}{\iota}$ ($\epsilon\iota\sigma\epsilon\iota\delta o\mu$ **15** = $\overset{i}{\iota}si$-*dum* **44** etc.); hence it appears under the $\overset{i}{\iota}$ column in brackets.

To the Tarentine-Ionic and Latin $\alpha\beta\beta$ are added the special signs devised to facilitate their use for the different dialects; the order in this part of these lines is of course arbitrary.

Notes on the Table of Alphabets.

1. *Tarentine-Ionic.*

This αβ appears in **1—10, 13—17, 22—24, 29, 142—3, 145—6, 151—2** and **183—4**.

On the date of its adoption by Oscan-speaking tribes see p. 11, and compare pp. 2—5.

It is written from left to right except in **4 a, 6, 7, 9, 10, 10 bis, 29 d** and **142**, where the retrograde direction is due to the influence of the Oscan αβ.

⊏ *and* ⊢.

The signs ⊏ for *v* and ⊢ for *h* are survivals from the Western αβ used by Lacedaemon and its colony Tarentum before the Ionic αβ was adopted. ⊢ (the origin of the minuscule ') is a modification of H and appears also in inscc. of Tarentine origin at Dodona, while ⊏ is the later form of F. See Roberts p. 271 ff.

E, I, and O sounds.

The representation of the Oscan *e-*, *i-* and *o-* vowels and diphthongs shows, naturally enough, some variation, since the Oscan intermediate sounds $\dot{i}$ and $\dot{u}$ found no exact equivalents in Greek, while the long open vowels η and ω were equally foreign to Oscan. There seems to be at present no evidence that H and Ω were ever used[1] by Oscan writers to denote length, whereas O is clearly used e.g. in **5** to denote *ū*, the Oscan representative of an orig. *ō* (Fερσορει has the same ending as *regaturei* in the Tab. Agnon. **175** a 13, b 15). Osc. $\dot{i}$ is always[2] (save that -*ii*- appears as -*ιε*-) represented by EI, and hence we often find HI written for the Osc. -*ei*- (as in **1**, στατтιηις) though EI also appears (Fερσορει). Osc. $\dot{u}$ is generally *o*, but before -*μ* we have ω at Anzi (**22**), and before -F- at Vibo ου (ΔιουFει, Osc. (*d*)*iůvei*) and at Messana ω (τωFτο)[1]. For Osc. *ū* we have OY regularly, though occasionally O, as we have seen; but -*iu*- is represented by IY on the same inscc. (**1**). Osc. *i* is always I, and Osc. *e* always E except in -*ei*- as we have seen.

---

[1] τωFτο in **1** can hardly represent *tōu-*; it is written *tůvtů* in Osc. αβ and *touto* in Lat. αβ (**28. 15**).

[2] Except in ςεστιες 6 where the first ε must represent a long vowel whether the word be read *Se(h)sties* = L. *Sēstius*, pure L. *Sextius*, or *Festies* = *Fēstius*.

Representation of f.

The sound of Osc. *f* was represented by what in Tarentum, if not everywhere, was the older form of sigma with three strokes, turned in the reverse direction to the rest of the writing, ↱ normally, S in retrograde script, see the notes to **140**, and **6, 7**. Thurneysen put forward the same explanation, conjecturally, in *Idg. Anzeiger* 4. 38.

Representation of final -d.

The sound of Osc. *d* when it was final must have been more like that of Greek *r* than when it was medial; hence final -*d* is always written T in Greek αβ, as was first pointed out by Bugge, *Kuhn's Z.* 22. 385, cf. Conway *Am. J. Ph.* 11. 307 ff.

2. *The Formello Vase.*

To what has been said above (p. 459 f.) I need only add that the variation in some signs is between the two copies of the αβ which are written on the vase one above the other.

3. *Etrusco-Campanian.*

In the abecedaria Mommsen points out (*U. D.* p. 7) that for San and φ the younger of the two vases substitutes 'perigrams' (see p. 460) in the usual Etruscan αβ, while even on the elder vase ꓛ appears as a perigram for κ.

The only authority for ꝗ = *r* and (except the second abecedarium) for ⴭ = *s* in this group is an inscr. published by Von Duhn, see App. II. 6*. But ꝗ appears often on Etr. inscc. elsewhere (Kirchhoff[4] p. 131), cf. p. 464 inf. The only authority known to me for Я = *d* is the inscr. given App. II. 9*.

4. *Oscan.*

For the chief points in the gradual modification of the Oscan αβ on Oscan soil see pp. 56, 107 f. and the notes to **168** ff.

Local variations in development.

It will be understood that where the Table shows older and younger forms this chronological relation is only asserted as between inscc. of the same locality; thus Ƨ is demonstrably older than 8 at Bovianum (p. 184 ff.) and Pompeii (p 56), but at Abella we find the open form in use at the latest period; conversely, the early coins of Fistelia (**184**) show the closed as well as the open form (Dressel, *Beschr. Berl.* p. 96). Again we have many early inscc. (e.g. **101**) in which simply | and V are written for ⊢ and \/; and yet \/ appears (as Y, \/) on the coins of Hyria and Fistelia (**142** and **184**), while their order in the Pompeian abecedaria (**81**) seems to show that the two new symbols were invented at much the same time; since if *ú* had been established long before *í* we should have expected to find *ú* put first.

Representation of Greek Aspirates.

The perigrams given for the Greek aspirates appear in the forms *Santia, thesavrûm, aphinis* (?), *Meelikiieís, kûiníks*.

Signs for f.

The coins of Nuceria Alfaterna (**144**) vary greatly in the signs for *f* even in the third century. Besides 8, Ƨ and ⅋ we have a reversed *b*, theta with the cross strokes omitted (◊ and ○), ⋔ (like Fal. ↑), and a curious sign ꟼ exactly like the koppa of one of the Formello alphabets. This sign occurs also on Etr. inscc., possibly even in the syllabary of Caere (*U. D.* p. 17), with the same value, and Mommsen conjectured (ib. p. 16 n.) that the regular 8 was a modification of the Greek koppa for which Etruscans had no use. Since however there is no similarity of sound between ꟼ and *f* it seems simpler to regard the ꟼ-like symbols as modifications, either of Ⓓ, which we find used to denote *f* at Fistelia (**184**) alone and at Allifae (**182**, according to Garrucci) in a modified form with H (⊖ H), or of B which also represents it at the same place. We have hardly enough evidence to determine the origin of ⅋; it also might be a modified B or Ⓓ; Thurneysen (*Idg. Anz.* 4. 38) points out its resemblance to a fully rounded Ƨ (8), while the early date of the open form, combined with the use of a reversed Ƨ in Tar.-Ionic αβ (see above) and the curious external hook in some of the Nucerine forms (⅋), inclines me rather to suggest that the ⅋ was formed originally by a combination of a four-stroke sigma with itself reversed[1]; and the ↑, which is clearly connected with the Faliscan ↑, might be regarded as a modified three-stroke sigma, though the prevailing view that it is a differentiation of Ↄ is perhaps on the whole more probable; especially if the curious spelling *alavfnum* in 144 (which

---

[1] Cf. the curious symbol ⁇ in **140** *b*.

in any case seems to have lost the syllable -*ter*- by abbreviation) be taken as showing a confusion of the special symbol for *f* with the perigram *vh* which we know (p. 467) was used for it by the Campanian Etruscans.

Signs for d *and* r *in Osc. and Umb.* aβ.

The most noteworthy point in the Oscan and Umbrian alphabets as contrasted with the Chalcidian from which they were ultimately derived lies in the curious changes in value of the symbols Ɑ and Ꝗ (Umb. ꟼ). The course of the process is now, I think, fairly clear. On the Formello vase we have D = *d* and P = *r*, the latter bearing an inconvenient resemblance to Ρ the rounded form of pi which appears beside it. In the Cumaean VI cent. aβ we find ◁ and D = *d*, P, ꟼ and R = *r*. Now the Etruscans had no voiced explosives; hence the symbol Ɑ was to them superfluous, and was treated by them as a by-form of ꟼ, both occurring in Etr. inscc.[1] with the value *r*, though at the date of our Campano-Etr. inscc. the ꟼ has almost completely disappeared. Ɑ was clearly preferable as being less likely to be confused with ꟼ = *p*. Hence

(1) Both Oscans and Umbrians took over Ɑ with the value *r*.

(2) The Umbrians used ꟼ to denote *ḍ*, the special variety of *r*-sound (written RS in Lat. aβ) which they had developed from intervocalic *d*.

(3) The Oscans chose the symbol which between 450 and 400 B.C. was dying out[2] as a symbol for *r* in the Cumaean aβ to denote the sound of *d* for which they found no symbol in the Etruscan aβ. How closely Greek and Etruscan influence were intermingled in Campania may be seen from the coin-legends of the district given in **142** ff.; those of Nola and Cumae do not even appear among them because they were always pure Greek.

5. *Umbrian*.

For the history of the aβ at Iguvium see p. 400 ff.

On the sign ꟼ = *d* see above under 4.

The palatal ᴅ may be regarded as a modified Ƨ, until some definite evidence of its origin is forthcoming; we may hope to find such evidence when the C. I. Etrusc. is complete.

The Etruscan aβ from which the Umbrian was borrowed seems to have been somewhat later than that from which the Oscan was taken, since the

---

[1] E.g. an insc. given by Lepsius in *Ann. Inst. Arch. Rom.* 8. 199; cf. also no. 142 sup.

[2] Roberts, *Intr. Gr. Epigr.* p. 210.

sign for *g* had completely disappeared, though 8 was still present[1], and 8 is always completely closed. The sign ∧ for m^2 of Tab. V appears also in Etr. inscc. of Chiusi and Siena (Fabr. *Pal. Stud.* p. 70).

6. *Faliscan.*

The most striking characteristics of this αβ as compared with its neighbours are
1. The loss of 8.
2. The use of ⟩ for *k* and *g* and the loss of ⋊.
3. The use of ◖ for *d*, Я for *r*.
4. The loss of ⊐.
5. The occasional use of ‖ for *e*.
6. The presence of O.
7. The loss of Ϙ (*cuando*).
8. ↑ = *f*.
9. Its retrograde direction.

Less important but noteworthy is the peculiar modification of the first letter Я.

Now it is clear from even the most cursory consideration of these points that this αβ

(*a*) cannot have been derived from the same Etruscan αβ as the Osc. and Umb. αββ which have 8, ⊐, ⋊ and 8;

(*b*) cannot have been derived directly from the αβ of Cumae, which has 8, ⊐, ⋊ and Ϙ;

(*c*) cannot have been derived directly from the Lat. αβ, even in its retrograde period, which had always the signs for *b* and *g*; nor is it possible to find in the Lat. αβ the origin of ↑, since there we have ⅂ or F from the IV century onwards (Note xxxv) and 8⅂ in the VI (280)[3], while the sign ↑ actually occurs (in the form ↗), as we have seen (p. 142) in the mixed αβ of Nuceria.

---

[1] The sign for *d* had been equally lost, as we have seen, in the original of the Osc. αβ.

[2] The signs for *m* and *n* are unfortunately misprinted on p. 401 sup. in the last line of the fifth paragraph, and should be corrected by those given in the Table (ᴡ and ᴡ, not ᴀᴡ and ᴀ).

[3] It would be a counsel of despair to derive ↑ from the obscure ∣', on which see below.

This last fact points, I think, to more positive conclusions. ↑ at Nuceria can only have come from the neighbouring Etruscan settlements (p. 52 and Note xviii p. 148). The use of Ɔ for both *k* and *g*, the loss of ᛐ, ⋈ and ᛉ, the retrograde direction, and the peculiar form of *a*, which comes simply from an exaggeration of the characteristic Etruscan rounding of the upper half of the left hand stroke, all imply an Etruscan origin, though the mother *aβ* must have (1) varied slightly (↑) from the ordinary Campano-Etruscan, and (2) have been later than that from which the Oscan was derived as is shown by the complete loss of ᛐ and ⋈.

But what of the use of ꓷ, ꓩ, O and the loss of ꓘ? These are all distinctly non-Etruscan, and all clearly derived from one source, namely the influence of the Latin *aβ*, which was always a near neighbour and ultimately drove the Faliscan *aβ* altogether out of use. ‖ is a by-form of E common to both Latins and Faliscans, but on this and its companion sign ꟾ' for *f* see below.

7. *The Latin Alphabet.*

To write a history of the Latin *aβ* is an undertaking which does not fall within the scope of this book[1]. Strictly speaking it had a somewhat separate development in every town in which it was used, as may be seen for instance in the Praenestine inscc. **281—304**; but so far as it is used to write dialect inscc. we need only notice three typical varieties, on the chief characteristics of which a few notes may be added.

(*a*) *The VI century aβ of Praeneste.*

For the evidence of the date see p. 312.

It is curious that *s* shows the form ⟨ in its only two occurrences in the insc. which is otherwise retrograde.

---

[1] For the last two centuries B.C. Ritschl's brief data (*Opusc.* iv. p. 691 ff., esp. p. 765) still hold good, but there is so much variation in details, not only between different localities but even between individual inscc. of the same time and place, as to make any more complete description practically impossible, as later writers than Ritschl have all found. For the earlier centuries, on the other hand, the actual number of inscc., especially of those in pure Latin, is too small to allow of more than a fragmentary account. The *Tafeln* attached to Ritschl's *Opusc.* iv. contain an invaluable selection of representative inscc.

The use of *vh* for *f* explains how the Greek F came to represent the Latin breathed labio-dental spirant. The sign for the voiced labial spirant was first adapted for a breathed sound by the addition of ᗘ, and then, as the old value became forgotten, it was used alone for *f*, forcing upon V a consonantal as well as a vowel value (Darbishire, *Relliq. Philol.* p. 9 f.).

Now *vh* is used for *f* in a Camp.-Etr. insc. App. II. 12*, and this fact, together with the subsequent use of C instead of K in the Latin *αβ* (e.g. in the IV century Duenos insc., p. 330) and the presence of Etruscans in Praeneste (p. 311) raises rather than answers the question how far the Latins were influenced by their Etruscan neighbours in their early attempts at writing. But that the Roman *αβ* as a whole was derived directly from that of the Greeks of the Chalcidian colonies, to which it bears a closer resemblance than does any other *αβ* used by Italians, is altogether beyond doubt.

(*b*) *The 'Colonial' Latin αβ of* 268 B.C.

This title may serve to describe roughly the type of *αβ* which we find in common use at Aesernia (**185**), Sulmo (**209—11**), Teate Marrucinorum (**243** f., **247**), Velitrae (**252**), Marruvium Marsorum (**260** ff.), Praeneste (**287** ff.) and Pisaurum (p. 434) about this date. Its distinguishing features (Λ or ∧, ‖, |' (beside ⱻ ꟻ), ∩, ⌐ and their angular forms ◊, ⌐ with ⟨ for C) were no doubt common at Rome at some period, since they appear sporadically in a great number of inscc. later than 250 B.C.; but they are none of them, nor anything like them, to be found in the official script (e.g. not on the tombs of the earlier Scipios, *P. L. M. E.* p. 31) of the middle of the third century, whereas in the colonies and allied towns just mentioned these forms of the letters were regular down to about 250 B.C., see p. 254.

Of the inscc. in Lat. *αβ* in this volume only the two oldest Praenestine inscc. (**280—1**) and the Duenos-vase, Note xxxv, possibly also the Tabula Veliterna (**252**) are demonstrably older than the invention of the symbol Ꞡ; see p. 254 and Jordan's discussion (in his *Krit. Beitr.* p. 157) of Plutarch's tradition (*Quaest. Rom.* 54. 59) as to its invention by Sp. Carvilius Ruga. On the other hand this 'colonial' type vanished before the acute-angled ⌐ went out of use, which it began to do at Rome soon after 180 B.C. (Ritschl ll. sup. cit.). The coins of Aesernia show that the open ∩ was there disappearing towards the end of the III century B.C.

The origin of the cursive signs ‖ and |' for *e* and *f* has not yet been ascertained. They appear on inscc. from all parts of central Italy[1] from the beginning of the 3rd century B.C., often alternating with E and F, but

---

[1] Picenum, Etruria, Campania, besides the places just mentioned; see the Indices to *Prisc. Lat. Mon. Epigr.*

they never appear in any official Latin inscc. though in the Dialects their use was not so restricted (e.g. 243). At Falerii (325, 328) || is clearly younger than ⱻ and the same seems to hold for the archaic inscc. of Pisaurum. Their form suggests that |' was proportioned to || on the model of F to E in the full Lat. αβ.

A peculiar and isolated variation not inserted in the Table is the use of Ↄ for *g* in one insc. at Praeneste (281).

(c) 'Urban' Latin αβ circa 133 B.C.

There are but few definite marks to distinguish the script of the Gracchan period from simply written inscc. of Ciceronian times. The most noteworthy (Ritschl, ll.c.) are the prevailing but not yet universal use of doubled consonants, and the incipient use of doubled vowels to denote length; the inequality in the arms of *t* (T T); the uprightness of the second hasta of *u* (⋎). These will be found in many dialect inscc., the Tabula Bantina (28) being perhaps the best example. Many of the Paelignian group show careful finials and great exactitude of cutting, features which at Rome are the mark of the best period.

A glance at the last two αββ given in the Table will show how marked a change had come about in the style of Roman writing between 300 and 100 B.C.

On the sign Ə in Paelignian v. note to 206.

B. Accidence of the Osco-Umbrian Dialects.

As in the text of the inscriptions, spaced type represents the local alphabet of the dialect, unspaced the Latin alphabet. No forms are given but those which are actually found, and to those which are rare is added the no. of the inscription in which they occur.

It will be understood that doubtful forms have been intentionally omitted from the paradigms.

I. NOUN INFLEXION.

ā-STEMS.

	Oscan	Umbrian
	Singular	
Nom.	víú, touto Masc. Tanas	muta, toto
Voc.		Prestota (366)
Acc.	eítiuvam	tuta, totam
Gen.	eituas	tutas, totar
Dat.	Anterstataí	tote
Abl.	egmad	tuta-per, tota-per
Loc.	víaí, Bansae	tote

	Plural.	
Nom.	aasas	urtas, iuengar
Acc.	viass	anglaf, angla
Gen.	eehiianasúm, egmazum	urnasiaru, pracatarum,
Dat.	Diumpaís	prusesete(s), -tir
Abl.	kerssnaís	urtes
Loc.	púmperiaís	urnasier

o-STEMS.

	Oscan	Umbrian
	Singular	
Nom.	Masc. Bantins Neut. teerúm	Ikuvins, katel esonom
Voc.		Tefre
Acc.	dolum	Tefro(m), puplu, poplom
Gen.	tereís	katles, popler, agre
Dat.	Abellanúí	pople
Abl.	amnúd	vinu, poplu
Loc.	tereí	uze, onse
Adverb.	amprufid	prufe (Lat. probe)

	Plural.	
Nom.	Masc. Núvlanús Neut. prúftú	Ikuvinus, Iiovinur screihtor veskla, vesklu
Acc.	feíhúss	turuf, toru
Gen.	Núvlanúm N.Osc. hiretum,cerfum	pihaklu [Volsc. Velestrom]
Dat.	Núvlanúís N. Osc. puclois	hostatir
Abl.	feíhúís	veres veris verir snate
Loc.	eídúís	funtlere-e, fondlir-e

It will be seen that in both dialects, as in Latin, the dat., loc. and abl. plur. are the same in all genders. In the subsequent paradigms, therefore, they are not distinguished.

The case-endings in the Campano-Oscan group (p. 95 f.) appear to vary somewhat from the normal Oscan forms; in o-stems we have nom. pl. ending in -*uh* (before the enclitic *sent*); gen. sing. in -*es*; and *viniciiu* appears to be dative.

In 130 *svai puh* seems equivalent to *suae...pod* in 28 (though it need not contain the same case-form) and the adverb *suluh* in 130 was presumably a case-form to start with. Possibly *puh* and *suluh* are both instrumentals, the -*h* denoting their long vowel. (If we are to compare Lat. *sollŏ* Lucil. ap. Fest. 298 M. it would confirm the view which sees in *modŏ* etc. instrumentals, not ablatives, and assumes that the shortening of final -*ō* in Latin (see Brugm. *Grds.* I § 655. 2) took place before the ablatival -*ōd*, -*ād* became -*ō*, -*ā*.)

On *e* and *i* in Umbrian see p. 495 inf.

io-STEMS.

The inflexion of *io*-stems in general follows that of the *o*-stems, but differs in several important respects. Streitberg (*Das Nominal-suffix -io*, Leipzig 1888, cf. Brugmann *Grundriss* II § 63 n.) has shewn that there were two classes of these nouns in pro-ethnic Indo-European, differing only in nom. and acc. sing. which ended respectively in (1) -*is* -*im*, (2) -*ios* -*iom*. These two classes may be called (1) the 'Variable' and (2) the 'Constant'; they are distinct in Old Latin, as in *Clodis alis Cornelis* by the side of e.g. *Manios* (**280**), but the -*ios* forms occur in no Italic dialect outside the Latinian group. This is due to the first syllable accent prevailing elsewhere, by which a short vowel in the last syllable was expelled before -*s*, so that some of the -*is* forms have come from -*ios* just as *húrz* (*z* = *ts*) from *hortos, *Ikuvins* from *Iguvinos. This syncope however did not take place before final -*m*, so that the two classes would be distinct in the acc. masc. and the nom. and acc. neut. We have many examples of masc. and neut. forms in -*im*, all of which therefore show the inflexion of the first of the two declensions just mentioned, but there are none in -*iom* from the simple -*i̯o*- stems, only -*iiom* from the derivative stem -*i̯i̯o*-. This evidence is too scanty to allow of a certain conclusion, but it seems possible that the -*i̯om* forms had been levelled out of use in the Dialects, through the influence of the nom. -*is* which in them was common to the 'Variable' and 'Constant' classes[1]. Conversely, in the derivatives in -*iio*-, if there ever was any 'Variable' flexion, we have no trace left of it in the dialect inscc., since there is only one accus. form from such stems, *Kluvatiium* (130); in the nom. sing. masc. of course -*o*- could not survive the law of syncope.

In the Dialects therefore the distinction between 'Variable' and 'Constant' stems is of little practical importance. But that between -*io*- and -*iio*- stems which has already been mentioned can be very clearly traced, though it was not recognised before Bronisch's essay on *Die Oskischen* i- *und* e-*Vocale* (Leipzig 1892). He shows (p. 67) that the two classes of stems are thus distinguished in Oscan[2].

	A	B
Nom.	*Pakis, Dekis* (neut. *vaamunim*, 70)	*Kluvatiis, Púntiis* (39), Πομπτιες (1), *Ponties* (210)
Acc.	*Pakim, Aesernim* (neut. *memnim*)	*Kluvatiium* (130)
Gen.	*Dekkieís*	*Vírriieís* (109)
Dat.	*Flagiuí*	&c.

The principle of difference is that the names in -*is* are either praenomina, or gentile nomina derived from praenomina which contained no -*i*- suffix; whereas

---

[1] The vowel in the 'Variable' -*is*-forms in Oscan and Umbrian was either (1) long originally (and therefore not expelled by the syncope as -*ĭ*- was from Osc. *ceus*=Lat. *ceiuis*), or (2) restored by the influence of the other cases and of the -*is* which in other nouns had come from -*ios*. In the latter case two paradigms such as, say,
*Paks, *Pakim*, *Pakieís*
Dekis, *Dekiom, *Dekieís*
must have been fused into
-*kis*, -*kim*, -*kieís*.

[2] Some, but not all of the particular examples here given, are taken from Bronisch's list.

those in -*iis* are all nomina and are derived from praenomina in -*i̯o*-. Thus we have

Praenomina	Nomina
(1) *Decmus* (155 B. 2)	*Decimius* (155 A. 1 al.)
Octavus Lat.	*Ůhtavis* (190)
(2) *Mais* (139)	*Mahiis* (179)
Marahis (137 c)	*Maraies* (19)
Στατις (14)	*Staatiis* (173)
Τρεβις (6)	*Trebiis* (47)

The -*kk*- in *Dekkieís* and the like is due to the consonantal value of the following -*i*- (Von Planta, *Osk.-Umb. Gram.* § 243).

A variety of the derivative class in late Oscan shows the spelling -*iís*, -*iíúi* etc. (e.g. *Viínikiís* 42), but it is not yet clear to me whether this is more than a divergence in spelling, cf. *Class. Rev.* 1893 p. 469. Nor is there yet any agreement as to what was the sound of the ending -*iis* -*ies* -*ιες*: if it was identical with -*iís*, it may have been simply a long -*i*- whose second half had rather an opener sound than the first, as in *liímitúm* = Lat. *līmitum*.

In some few cases in Oscan the final -*s* of the Nom. and Gen. is wanting, *Silli* (**89**, cf. **106—7, 112**). But this may be an abbreviation in writing.

In Umbrian in both nom. and acc. we have only the shorter forms, *Trutitis, Atiersir, Fisim, Fisi, Grabovi, Grabove,* cf. *ped̮aem ped̮ae* by the side of acc. pl. fem. *ped̮aia(f)*[1]. Neuter forms are *tertim terti, tehted̮im*. But the distinction between -*i̯o*- and -*ii̯o*- stems can be clearly seen in the other cases, e.g. *Fisiu* (abl. sing.), *Martier* (gen.), *Atiiersiur* (nom. plur.), beside *Kluviier, Kastruśiie(r)* (gen. sing.).

The vocative occurs only in Umbrian, and only from the -*i̯o*- stems; *Grabovie, Sanśie* (also spelt *Saśe* II B 24) &c.

Dat. Sing. and Plur. in Umbr. Sing. *Fisie, Sanśie, Sanśii*, more commonly *Fisi* etc., Plur. *Atiersier, Atiersir, Clauerni* (nom. *Clauerniur*), and *arves arvis arver* if it is from the same stem as the acc. pl. *arviu*.

---

[1] *persae* VI A 58, B 3 may be taken as acc. sing., applying to each successive victim. If it is plural it must be regarded as showing an *i*-declension beside the -*io*-.

NOUN INFLEXION.

DIPHTHONGAL STEMS *diov- rei- bov-*.

Singular Acc. Umbr. *bum.*
Voc. Umb. *Iu-pater.*
Gen. Osc. *Iúveís*, N. Osc. *Ioves.*
Dat. Osc. *Diúveí* Διουfει *Iuveí.* Umbr. *Iuve, ri.*
Abl. Umbr. *bue, ri re.*
Plural Acc. Umbr. *buf.*
Gen. Umbr. *buo.*

ē-STEMS.

Only the following forms occur:

Singular Acc. Umbr. *iouie* (VI B 59, VII A 48) sing. or plur.?
Dat. Osc. *Keri* (130) *Kerrí* (175) (cf. the derivative *Kerrtio-*) probably also N. Osc. *Cerie*[1] (243); cf. Lat. *faciē* etc., the regular forms in old Latin (Gell. 9. 14, Lindsay *Lat. Lang.* p. 386).
Dat. or Loc.? Umbr. *kvestretie* (I B 45), *avie* (VI B 11) sing. or plur.? (Cf. the deriv. *avieklu.*)
Abl. Umbr. *uhtretie* (V i).
Plural Dat. Umbr. *iouies* (VI B 62, VII A 50), never -*r*.

---

[1] If so this name in Umbro-Oscan contained or was altered so as to contain the same suffix as *materiēs* etc., and the Osc. -*rr*- would stand for -*ri̯*- as in *her(r)est* beside Umb. *heriest*; in this respect as in others N. Osc. would show affinity with Umb.

	i-STEMS.		*u*-STEMS.	
	Oscan	Umbrian	Oscan	Umbrian
Nom.	*Singular*		*Singular*	
Masc.	*ceus aídil* (53)	*ocar pacer*		
Fem.	N. Osc. *pacr-si*	*pacer*		
Neut.		*sacre, sehmeniar*		
Acc.	*sakrim, slaagim*	*sakrem, ocre, sevakni*	*manim* (28)	*trifo*
Gen.	*aeteis*	*punes, ocrer* N. Osc. *ocres Tarincris*	*castrous* (28)	*trifor*
Dat.	*Herentatei* (? consonantal)	*ocre*		*ahtu, trifo*
Abl.	*slaagid, praesentid* (28) N. Osc. *fertlid*	*ocri ocre*	*castrid* (28)	*trefi, mani*
Loc.		*ocre*		*manuve* (II B 23)?
Nom.	*Plural.*		*Plural.*	
M.&F.	*trís, aídilis,* N. Osc. *pacris*	*puntes, pacrer*		
Neut.	*teremenniú*	*triia, sakreu*	Neut. *berva pequo*?	
Acc.		*avef ovif ovi*	Masc. *kastruvuf, castruo, manf* (II A 38)?	
Gen.	[*a*]*íttíúm? Tiiatium*	*peracnio*		
Dat. &c.	*luisarifs, sakriiss, fortis* (28)	*aves avis* (never -*r*)		*berus* (never -*r*)

Noun Inflexion.

Consonantal Stems.

Stems without Gradation.		Stems showing Gradation.	
		n-*stems*.	
Oscan	Umbrian	Oscan	Umbrian

Singular.

Nom. *meddíss* N. Osc. *lixs*	Masc. *zedef* 'sedens' Neut. *tuplak*	Nom. Fem. *frukta- tiúf, statif* Neut.	*tribḍiçu, karu* *umen, numem nome*
Acc.	*capirso* (cf. *uhturu*)	Acc. *medicatinom, tanginom*	
Gen. *medíkeis*	*farer*	Gen. *tangineis [kú]m- parakineís*	*nomner*
Dat. *medíkeí*	*kapiḍe*	Dat. *leginei*	*karne, nomne*
Abl. *ligud*, N. Osc. *aetatu*	*kapiḍe, peḍi*	Abl. *tanginúd*	*tribḍiçine, karne, nomne*
Loc.		Loc. N. Osc. *mesene, agine*	*menzne* (? see p. 501)

Plural.

Nom. *meddíss* μεδ- δειξ	[Volsc. *medix*]	Nom. *humuns*	(cf. *frateer*)
Acc. N. Osc. *pes*	*nerf, capif, kapi*	Acc.	
Gen. *liímitú[m]*	*nerum*	Gen. N. Osc. *semunu*	(cf. *fratrom*)
Dat. &c. *ligis*	*nerus, kapiḍus* (never -*r*)	Dat. &c.	*homonus karnus* (never -*r*)

In -*es*- stems the short vowel is expelled in the nominative, Umbr. *meḍs* (cf. *mersto* = Lat. *modesta* instead of *medesta), *erus*. With the acc. compare the infinitive in -*um* Osc. *acum* Umbr. *aferom*.

r-STEMS.

Of the r-stems some words shew gradation, others not. In the former class must be placed, Osc. nom. *patír* dat. *pateref Fuutreí*, Umbr. voc. *pater* dat. *patre* N. Osc. gen. *patres*, Umbr. plur. nom. *frateer* gen. *fratrom* dat. *fratrus*. In the latter class the long vowel of the nom. sing. is carried through all cases. Osc. sing. nom. *kvaístur* dat. *kvaísturei* plur. nom. *censtur*, Umb. sing. nom. *uhtur adfertur*, acc. *uhturu arsferturo* dat. *arsferture*.

NOTE. Two nouns in Umbrian shew confusion between consonantal and o-flexion, *tuder*-, nom. pl. *tuderor* (VI A 12) abl. pl. *tuderus* (the *d* instead of *ḍ* between vowels is also remarkable), and *vas*- nom. pl. *vasor* (VI A 19), acc. pl. *vaso* (VI B 40) apparently antecedent to an acc. relative *porse*, abl. *vasus* (IV 22), cf. Latin *vasi vasa*. *manf* beside *kastruvuf* may shew a confusion between consonantal and *u*-flexion.

II. COMPARISON OF ADJECTIVES.

The following are all the Comparative and Superlative forms that have been recognised in Oscan or Umbrian.

	Comparative		*Superlative*
Osc.	*mais* 'magis'	Osc.	*maimas* 'maximae'
Umb.	*mestru* fem., 'major'		
Osc.	*mins* 'minus,' *minstreis* 'minoris'		
Osc.	*pústro-*, Umb. *pustro-* 'postero-,' Osc. *pústiris* 'posterius'	Osc.	*pustmo-*, *posmo-* 'postremus'
Osc.	*pruter* 'prius'	Umb.	*promo-* 'primus'
N. Osc.	*pritrom-e* 'ultro, recta via,' Umb. *pretro-* 'prior'	N. Osc.	*prismo-* 'primus'
Osc.	*hutro-*, Umb. *hondro-* 'infernus'	Umb.	*hondomo-* 'imus'
Osc.	*supro-* 'supernus,' Umb. *subrā* 'supra'	Umb.	*somo-* 'summus'

Besides these we have Osc. and Umb. *nessimo-* 'nearest,' Osc. *últiumo-* 'furthest,' and *messímo-* (**113**), *valaimas puklum* (**130**), and Umb. *nertro-* 'νέρτερος.'

III. PRONOUNS.

A. Personal.

	Oscan			Umbrian		
	1.	2.	3.	1.	2.	3.
Nom.	*tiium* (**130**)					
Acc.		*siom*			*tiu tiom*	
					teio	
Dat.	*t(i)fei*	*sífeí*		*mehe*	*tefe*	*seso*
	N. Osc. *sefei*					

If N. Osc. *uus* in **216** 6 and 7 is a pronoun it must be equivalent both to Lat. *vōs* nom. and *vōbis* dat.

Possessive. Osc. *suvo-* N. Osc. *suo-* 'suus' Umbr. *touo- tuo-* 'tuus.' On Umbr. *sveso, svesu* see p. 502 footn.

B. Anaphoric.

	Oscan			Umbrian		
	M.	F.	N.	M.	F.	N.
Sing. Nom.	*iz-i-c*	*íú-k*	*íd-í-k*	*er-e*		*ed-e-k*
	ís-í-du	*iiu-k*				*ers-e*
Acc.	*ion-c*				*eam*	
Dat. or Loc.				*esme esmi-k*		
Plur. Nom.	*íus-su*			*eur-ont*		
Acc.		N. Osc. *ioc*		*ef*	*eaf*	*eu*
		iafc				

Umbr. *eo* appears to be masc. acc. pl. in VI A 20.

In Oscan this pronoun is compounded with *-dum*, in Umbrian with *-hont*, in the sense of the Lat. *idem*; and in **39** 5 and 11 the nom. pl. *íus-su* seems to have the same meaning; v. Gloss. s. v. *ekkum*.

In the same sense are used Osc. *eizo-* (*eíso-*), Umbr. *ero- iro-*[1] which are declined in the m. f. and n. as *-o-* and *-ā-* stems, most commonly with the affix *-c* in Umb. also *-hont*. It can hardly be an accident however that the only examples[2] we have are of cases for which we have no form from the simple stem *i-*, which probably was only used in the Nom. and Acc. in all dialects except Umbr., and in Umbr. in the dat. and loc. sing. also.

Thus the remainder of the paradigm is,

	Oscan		Umbrian
	M. and N.	F.	M. and N. F.
Gen. Sing.	*eizeis eiseis*		*erer (ek) erar*
			(once *irer*)
Abl. Sing.	*eizuc* (for *-ōd-ke*)	*eizac* (for *-ād-ke*)	*eru(k) era(k)*
Loc. Sing.	*eizeic*	(cf. *eísaí* demonstr.)	
Gen. Plur.		*eizazunc*	*erom*
Dat.} Abl.} Plur.	*eizois*	*eiza[i]sc* (**28**) ?	{*erer* {*erer* {*erir* {*erir*

C. DEMONSTRATIVE.

The dialects shew a great wealth of demonstrative stems, all apparently declined as regular *-o- -a-* nouns, except that the neut. nom. sing. ended in *-d*, not *-m*, while the nom. sing. masc. has not yet occurred. We have

(i) *eso-* Osc. εσοτ (**22**), nom. neut., *esei* loc. sing. (**95** l. 23, but *eísei* in l. 20). The forms in *es-* should probably be separated from the following stem.

(ii) Osc. *eíso-, eiso-* (sometimes *eizo-*) used as deictic adj.

(iii) Umbr. *eso-, iso-* with Umbr. *issoc* 'ita' *esso* 'ita' or 'hoc' (abl.) perhaps contains a stem *is-so-* parallel to *is-to-* (so Brugm. *Grds.* I. § 568. 2).

(iv) Osc. *ekso- exo-*, neut. nom. *eksûk*.

(v) Osc. *ekho- eko-*, fem. *eka-*, neut. acc. *ekík*, cf. N. Osc. *ecuf* 'ibi,' *ecuc* 'hoc,' 'huc' or 'ita'?

---

[1] Whether Umb. *ero-* is the same word as Osc. *eizo-* is a separate question, but their use corresponds so closely that they can hardly be separated.

[2] As there are no other examples of *-u* for *-ā* in III and IV (p. 404), *eruk csunu futu* (III 14) is not 'ea (kletra) sacra esto' but 'eo (oue, this *ouis* being masc. ib. 31) sacrum fiat.'

(vi) Umbr. *esto- isto-*, neut. nom. *estu*.

(vii) Umbr. *ulu* 'thither,' cf. Osc. *pú-llad-* 'where,' and Lat. *olle*.

(viii) Umbr. *oro- uro-*.

(ix) Osc. and Umbr. *e-tanto-* 'tantus' corresponding to *panto-* 'quantus.'

D. Relative, Indefinite and Interrogative.

Stem *po-* (Gr. πο- Lat. *quo-*)

	Oscan			Umbrian		
Singular.	M.	F.	N.	M.	F.	N.
Nom.	*pui*	*pai paei pae*	*pod* / πωτ	*poi, poe* / *po-rse*		*puḍe*
Acc.		*paam*				
Gen.	(cf. *poiiu?* = Lat. *cuia*)					
Dat.				*pusme*		
Plural.						
Nom.	*pús*	*pas*	*pai*	*puri* / *po-rse* (VI*a* 15, 19)		
Acc.			*pai*		*pafe*	*po-rse* (VI*b* 40)

The true explanation of the use of the form *puḍe porse* as nom. masc. sing. and plur. and nom. acc. neut. sing. and plur. has at length been given by Brugmann (*Ber. Kön. Sächs. Ges. Wiss.* 1893 p. 135) who divides it into the affix *-ḍe* and an adverbial form **quō* which served in Italic as a substitute for any case of the relative, like *wo* in Rhinefrankish and *kur̃* in Lithuanian.

We have compounds of the stem or, as Brugmann plausibly suggests, of this indeclinable form Osc.-Umbr. **pō* (*Grds.* II. § 419) with demonstrative pronouns in Osc. *poizad, púllad,* Umb. *pora,* all abl. fem. sing. Cf. Mod. Gr. ὁ ἄνδρας ποῦ τὸν εἶδα, or ποῦ εἶδα 'the man whom I saw.' Brugmann would find similar compounds in Lat. *quoius, quoiei*; cf. also *Idg. Forsch.* IV. 214.

Stem *pi-* (Gr. τις Lat. *quis*)

	Oscan		Umbrian	
	M. & F.	N.	M. & F.	N.
Nom.	*pis*	*pid*	*pisi so-pir* [Volsc. & N. Osc. *pis*]	*pidi*
Acc.	*phim*			
Gen.	*pieis-um*			
Dat. or Loc.	*piei* (28, 7)			

Plural.   Acc. *pifi*

These forms serve (1) as relatives (e.g. *piei* l.c.) without a definite antecedent, like Lat. *quisquis*, e.g. *Tab. Ig.* VI B 53, and a doubled form also existed in Oscan (*pitpit* 'quicquid' 205 A sup.). (2) They are used as an indef. pronoun in prohibitions (28 passim) and after preceding indefinite relatives or subordinating conjunctions (e.g. Osc. *suae pis* 'si quis,' *pod pis... mins* 'quominus quis'). In Oscan in negative sentences *pisum* = Lat. *quisquam*, e.g. 28 6. Umbr. *pis-her* is closely parallel to Lat. *qui-uis*. (3) The interrogative meaning of Lat. *quis* no doubt also existed in Osc.-Umbr. *pis*, but it cannot be quite certainly identified in the inscc. (cf. **164** and **362** 4).

The Umbr. *sopir* 'quisquis, si quis' has been explained with certainty by Brugmann (*Ber. Kön. Sächs. Ges. Wiss.* 1890 p. 213) as containing, like the Gr. ὅτις (Locr. ϝοτι), the I.-Eu. indeclinable relative *$s\mu od$.

E. Pronominal Adjectives.

From *altro-* 'the other' we have Osc. *altrei* dat. sg. masc. (28. 13) and loc. sing. masc. (175 *b* 21), abl. *a[l]trud*, acc. fem. *alttram*.

F. Pronominal Adverbs.

1. *Common to Oscan and Umbrian.*

Oscan	Umbrian	Latin
inim ini εινειμ 'tum'	(1) einom enom ennom, inum-ek, 'deinde'	
	(2) eine, enem	enim
ifi? (73)	ife, ifont	ibi
svai suae	sve [Volsc. se] no-sve (see below)	si
suae...pod, svai puh cf. p. 470	suepo	'siue'
pam, pan	pre-pa, pane	quam, quamde
pún	puni ponne pone	quom, *quomde
ne-pon	(ar-)ni-po[1]	(dō-)ni-cum
puf	pufe	cf. ubi
puz pús pous	puze pusi puse	cf. ut
cf. pútúrús-píd	podruh-pei	cf. uter-que
nei-p (see below)	nei-p	(ne-)que

2. Found only in Oscan. *ekkum* 'item,' *ekss ex* 'ita,' *pod...mins* Lat. *quodminus*, *púkkapíd pocapit* 'aliquando,' *adpúd* 'quoad.' The *-p* (orig. *-que*) of *íp*, N. Osc. *ip* has lost its generalising force, as in *neip* 'non,' O. Lat. *neque* 'non'; cf. Gr. τό-τε.

3. Found only in Umbrian. *eso iso esoc issoc* 'ita' *isunt* 'itidem' *isek, itek* 'ita,' *inenek* (III 20)? *iepi* (III 21)? *ulu* Lat. *illuc*; *ne-rsa*[1] (VI *a* 6) = Lat. *dō-ne-c*[1] in meaning; *surur*, *sururont* 'itidem' and *sepse* (VI *b* 11)? may contain the stem of the reflexive pronoun. *pu-e* 'quo' cf. p. 479 sup., *-pumpe* = Lat. *-cunque*, *panupei* = *quandoque*, *appei ape ap* (*ad-pe*) 'ἔς τε.' *pidi persei* 'si quomodo, sicubi' cf. Lat. *ride, quicquid amas Cato Catullum* etc.

IV. NUMERALS.

1. Umb. *uno-*, cf. Osc. *úíní-veresím.*
   Ordinal: Umb. *promo-*, N. Osc. *prismo-*.

[1] On this *ne-*, *-ne-*, *-ni-* cf. the Glossary s.v. *arnipo*.

2. Umb. Nom. *dur* (masc.) ⎫
    Acc. *tuf* (masc. and fem.) ⎬ *tuva* (neut.).
    Dat. &c. *tuves, tuver-e*. ⎭
    Ordinal: Umb. *duti(m)* 'iterum'; also *etro-*; Osc. *altro-*.
3. Acc. Osc. fem. *tris*, Umb. masc. *tref*, neut. *triia triiu*, dat. Umb. *tris*.
    Ordinal: Umb. *tertio-, tertim* 'for the third time.'
4. Osc. acc. neut. *petiro (-pert)*, (*petora* according to Festus, 205 A sup.), cf. Umb. *petur-pursus* 'quadrupedibus,' and the name *Petrōn-, Petru-nio-*, common in Osco-Umbrian districts.
5. Osc. adv. *pomtis* 'quinquiens,' cf. Osc. *pŭmperia-*, Umb. *pumpeḍia-*.
6. Cf. Umb. *sest-entasio-* 'sextantarius,' *sehmenier* 'semenstribus,' Osc. *Sehsímbriís* '*Sexembrius' i.e. 'born in August.'
8. Cf. Osc. *Ůhtavis* 'Octauius.'
9. Umb. *nuvis* 'nouies.'
    Ordinal: *nuvime* 'for the ninth time' (II *a* 26), cf. Lat. *proxime* &c.
12. Umb. *desenduf* (i.e. *deś-*) acc. plur.

V. ADVERBS.

Here should be mentioned Umb. *prufe* 'probe,' *rehte* 'recte,' Umb. *subra* 'supra' etc.; Osc. *amprufid* 'improbe, informally,' *úíníveresím* 'uniuersē,' cf. Lat. *statim, passim*, &c. The Pronominal Adverbs have been given above.

Negatives.

The variation between *i, e* and *ei* in Umbrian writing (see p. 495) confuses three forms which are distinct in Oscan and Latin.

(1) Osc. *nĕ*, in *nep* which has the form of Lat. *neque* and the meaning of Lat. *nēue*.

(2) Osc. *ni* corresponds to Lat. *nē* in form and meaning, since *ē* became long *i* in Oscan, written *i* in Lat. *aβ*.

(3) Osc. *nei* corresponds to Lat. *nei, ni* but has the meaning simply of *nōn*; *neip* has the same in **130**.

(4) Umbr. *no-sve* 'nisi' probably contains a negative form *noi*, cf. O. Lat. *noisi* Note xxxv. Brugmann's alternative explanation (*Ber. K. S. Ges. Wiss.* 1890 p. 227 ff.) does not convince me.

VI. PREPOSITIONS AND POSTPOSITIONS.

The postpositions are distinguished by a prefixed hyphen.

A. *With accusative only.*

Osc. *ant* 'ante.'
Osc. *az*, Umb. *-aḍ*, 'apud.'
Umb. *hondrā* 'infra.'
Umb. *-per* 'up to, as far as' (cf. Lat. *parum-per, top-per, paulis-per*); Umbr. *-per* with abl. may be distinct.
Osc. *pert* 'across,' *-pert* 'up to, as far as.'
Osc. *perum* 'without,' cf. Gr. πέραν, πέρα.
Osc.-Umb. *postin* 'according to,' Germ. 'nach.'
Umb. *subrā* 'supra.'
Umb. *superne* 'super.'

B. *With locative only.*

Osc. *contrud*? 'contra,' see p. 502 inf.
Umb. *super* 'super.'

C. *With ablative only.*

Osc. *com* 'cum,' Umb. *-ku(m) -co(m)* 'cum, apud.'
Osc. *dat* 'de.'
Osc. *op* 'apud.'
Umb. *-pe(r)* 'pro.'
Osc.-Umb. *post* 'post.'
Osc. *pru* (? Umb. *-pru*) 'pro.'
Osc. *prai*, Umb. *pre* 'prae' in our inscc. are only found with plural words which may be either abl. or loc.
Umb. *su* 'sub' **354**.
Umb. *-ta -tu -to* 'ab, ex.'

D. *With more than one case.*

Osc. *anter* with acc. and abl. 'inter' (**95**, 14 and 28, passages which do not yet make clear any difference of meaning with the two cases); Umb. *-ander* with acc. VI *b* 47 = I *b* 7 ; *anderuomu* in VI *b* 41 is obscure.

Umb. *trā(f)* with acc. and loc.; here also it is not yet possible to recognise a difference of meaning with certainty.

Finally we have Osc. *-en*, Umb. *-en -em -e*.

(1) With acc. 'into, to, towards' in Umb. sometimes repeated with an adj., *vapefem avieklufe* 'in sellas augurales.'

(2) With loc. 'in, resting in,' Osc. *exaiscen ligis* 'in illisce legibus,' *hŭrtin* 'in horto,' Umb. *arven* 'in aruo,' *fesner-e* 'in fanis,' *testre e uze* 'in dextro umero'; sometimes repeated, *ocrem Fisiem* 'in arce Fisia,' and doubled *tote-m-e* 'in ciuitate.' These interesting forms show us the change of a postposition to a case-ending actually taking place.

(3) With abl. and acc. 'from...up to...'; or with abl. alone 'starting from,' Osc. *eisucen ziculud zicolom* XXX. 'ex illo die usque ad tricesimum diem'; *imaden* 'ex ima (uia).'

Of all these prepositions the only ones that are certainly not to be found in composition in our inscc. are *hondrā, perum, post, postin, super, superne*, and examples of *post* so used are probably only wanting by accident.

Osc. *af-*, Umb. *ā-* 'ab,' Osc. *amfr-* Umb. *ambr-* 'ambi-,' Osc. *eh-* 'ex,' are at present only to be identified in compounds.

One or two so-called 'pseudo-postpositions,' governing an adnominal genitive, may be mentioned here:

Osc. *amnŭd* literally 'in the line of' (Bartholomae, *Idg. Forsch.* 6. 308), hence, 'because of.'

Osc. *ampert* before *minstreis aeteis eituas* 'dum minoris partus (i.e. partis) familias (i.e. -iae) taxsat' as the Latin side of the Tabula Bantina renders it, probably implies, like *dum taxsat*, an acc. *moltam*, 'up to the value of a fine of.'

Umb. *paca* with gen. of gerundive, 'causa.'

VII. VERBAL INFLEXION[1].

The materials for constructing a scheme of Oscan and

---

[1] The following scheme was drawn up and printed for the use of pupils substantially in its present form in 1890, but for the identification of the Imperfect Subjunctive and in many details, I am indebted to Prof. Buck's lucid and almost always convincing discussion of *The Osco-Umbrian Verb-System* (Chicago, 1895).

Umbrian conjugation are unfortunately very scanty. The 1st pers. sing. and the 1st and 2nd pers. plur., and one or two entire tenses, are hardly represented at all. In what follows only those forms are quoted which actually occur, and only those categories which can be recognised with certainty.

We can distinguish with certainty at least six classes of Present Stem, corresponding to six similar classes in Latin.

    I. Non-thematic stems (*sum*-class).
    II. Simple thematic stems (*rego*-class).
    III. *ā*-stems (*amās*-class).
    IV. *ē*-stems (*habēs*-class).
    V. -*ĭ*-stems (*facis*-class).
    VI. *ī*-stems (*finīs*-class).

From the Present Stem are regularly formed the Present and no doubt the Imperfect[1] Indicative, the Present Subjunctive, the Imperative, the Future in -(e)s-, the Infinitive in -o(m), the Present Participle (in -nt-) and the Gerundive (in -nno-).

There are seven forms of the Perfect, of which the last four may be called 'Weak,' as being based upon the Present Stem. One of these however, that in -*tt*-, does not occur in Umbrian, and one, that in -*l*-, has not appeared in Oscan.

    A. Reduplicated class (cf. Lat. *dedit*).
    B. With reduplication absent or lost (cf. Lat. *fĭdit*).
    C. With root vowel strengthened (cf. Lat. *ēgit*, *cēpit*).
    D. -*f*- perfect (Osc. *aikdafed*).
    E. -*tt*- perfect (Osc. *prŭfatted*).
    F. -*nki*- perfect (cf. Umbr. *purdinśiust*).
    G. -*l*- perfect (cf. Umbr. *entelust*).

From the Perfect are formed a Perfect Subj. in -*ē*- (Osc. -*ĭ*-, Umbr. -*i*-, -*ei*-) and an Active Participle in -*us*- (Osc. *sipus*) on which was based the Fut. Perf. Indic. (Osc. *hipust*)[2].

---

[1] In the inscc. we at present possess, only one form of the Impf. Indic. (*fufans* '*fubant*') is known to us, and the tense is therefore omitted (for typographical reasons) in the Tables which follow.

[2] Umb. *sesust* is derived by Brugmann *Grds.* II. § 873 from the -*to*- partc. of the intransitive root *sed*-. If so, the -*u*- instead of the -*ŏ*- of pr. Ital. **sessos* must be, as in -*lust* also, due to the influence of the regular -*ust* forms like *hipust*.

SCHEME OF VERBAL FORMS

i. Active Forms of

Class of Present Stem	Present Indicative.		Present Subjunctive.	
	Oscan	Umbrian	Oscan	Umbrian
I	1 s. *sŭm* 3 s. (1) *est* (2) *ĭst* 3 p. *sent, set*	*est* *sent*		2 s. *si, sir* *si* 3 s. *se, sei, si* 3 p. *sins, sis*
II	3 s. ?N. Osc. *feret* [cf. 3 p. pass. N. Osc. *ferent-er*]	1 s. *sestu* (II *b* 24) 2 s. *seste* (II *b* 22) [cf. 3 s. Pass. *uinct-er*]	3 s. *aflukad* 3 p. *deicans*	 [cf. pass. *emant-ur*]
III	3 s. *faa-mat* [cf. depon. 3 p. *ka-rant-er*]	1 s. *subocau(u)* 3 p. *furfant*	3 s. *deiuaid*	1 s. *aseriaia* 3 s. *portaia* 3 p. *etaians*
IV		3 s. *habe* *ticit*	3 s. *půtíad* *putiiad* 3 p. *půtíans* *putiians*	3 s. *habia* [cf. pass. *tursi-and-u*]
V			3 s. *fakiiad*	3 s. *faśia, feia*
VI	3 s. *sakru-vit* 3 p. *fiiet*			
Add to these, I and II		[cf. pass. 3 s. *teḑte*]		3 s. *teḑa* 3 p. *dirsans*
Doubtful		2 s. *heris, -ri* [cf. pass. *herter*]	3 s. *heriiad*	

IN THE ITALIC DIALECTS.

THE PRESENT STEM.

Imperfect Subjunctive.		Imperative.	
Oscan	Umbrian	Oscan	Umbrian
3 s. *fusíd*		3 s. *estud*	2 and 3 s. *futu, eetu* 2 p. *fututo* 3 p. *etuta, -tu*
3 p. *patensíns*		3 s. *actud*	3 s. *aitu* *ampentu* 3 p. *aituta*
		3 s. *deiuatud*	2 s. *aserio* 3 s. *mugatu* 2 or 3 p. *etato*
	[cf. N. Osc. Pass. 3 p. *upsaset-er*]		
		3 s. *líkítúd*	3 s. {*habetu* / *habitu*} 3 p. {*habetutu* / *habituto*}
		3 s. *factud*	2 or 3 s. *fetu, feitu*
			3 s. *seritu* [cf. depon. *persnih-mu*]
			3 s. {*tedtu, dirstu* / *tetu, ditu*}
3 p. *[h]erríns*			2 or 3 s. {*eretu* / *heritu* / *hereitu*}

	i. ACTIVE FORMS OF THE PRESENT STEM (cont.).		ii. INFINITIVES	
	Future Indicative.		*Infinitive.*	
Class	Oscan	Umbrian	Oscan	Umbrian
I		3 s. *eest, est* 'ibit'	*ezum*	*erom, eru*
II		2 s. *ampenes* 3 s. *ferest*	*acum* *deicum*	
III	3 s. *deiuast* 3 p. *censazet*	3 s. *prupehast*	*censaum* *tribarakavum*	
IV	3 s. '*hafieist*' (28)	*habiest*	*fatíum*	
V				$\begin{cases} façiu \\ façu \end{cases}$
VI	3 s. *sakrvist*			
I and II	3 s. *didest*			
Doubtful	3 s. *herest* 3 p. *hereset*	2 s. *heries* 3 s. *heriest*		

AND VERBALS.

Present Participle.	Gerundive.	Perfect Passive Participle[1].	
Oscan and Umbrian	Oscan and Umbrian	Oscan	Umbrian
O. *praesentid* Abl.			
	U. *anferener* (gen. s. m.)	*scriftas* *ufteis*	*screihtor* *rehte* *spafu*
	U. *pelsans* (nom. s. m.) O. *upsannam* (acc. s. f.)	(1) *staflatas* (2) *censtom*	(1) *pihaz* (3) *muieto* *oseto*
U. nom. sg. {*zedef* *serse*}			*taçez* *virseto*
		facus (28. 30[2])	*aanfehtaf* *feta*
			Depon. *persnis*
[cf. O. *Herentatei*]			

[1] One form has been certainly identified as a supine, Umbr. *aseriato* (*eest*) 'obseruatum (ibit).'

[2] This form does not contain the ordinary -*to*- suffix; see the Glossary.

iii. THE

Class	Perfect Indicative. Oscan	Umbrian	Future Perfect. Oscan	Umbrian
A.	3 s. {*deded* / δεδετ}	*fefure*	2 s. *fifikus* 3 s. *fefacust*	3 s. *tedust* *dersicust* 3 p. *dersicurent*
B.	3 s. *kúmbened* N. Osc. *afded*		3 s. *dicust* *fust*	2 s. *benus* 3 s. *fakust, fust,* *habus* 3 p. *fakurent, fu-* *rent, habu-* *rent*
C.	3 s. *upsed* 3 p. *uupsens*	3 p. *eit-ipes*	3 s. *hipust, urust* *aflakust*	3 p. *prusikurent*
D.	1 s. *manafum* 3 s. *aamanaffed* *aíkdafed* 3 p. *fufens*			2 s. *amprefuus* 3 s. *atedafust* 3 p. *ambrefurent*
E.	3 s. *prúfatted* 3 p. *prúfattens*	[Cf. Volsc. *sis-* *tiatiens*]	3 p. *tríbarakat-* *tuset*	
F.				3 s. *purdinśiust* {*combifianśiust* *combifiansust*}
G.				2 s. *apelus* 3 s. *apelust*

PERFECT ACTIVE.

Perfect Subjunctive.		Perfect Participle Active.
Oscan	Umbrian	
3 s. *fefacid*	3 s. *stiti?* (I *b* 45) 3 p. *steteies?* (*ib.*)	
3 s. *fuid*		On the perf. part. in *-lo-* which is the basis of the fut. perf. in *-lust* v. Brugm. *Gds.* II. § 872 f.
3 s. *hipid*		Osc. *sipus* (**28**) 'sciens' seems to be for **sēp-u̯os* (J. Schmidt *K. Z.* 26, p. 372).
[cf. pass. impers. *sakrafir*]	[cf. pass. impers. *pihafei, herifi*]	
3 p. *tribarakattins*		
	3 s. *combifiansi*	

iv. Passive Forms.

A. Rudimentary passive forms, i.e. forms in which the Passive *r* is *substituted for* the *-nt* of the 3rd pl. Active (*v.* p. 516 inf. and Zimmer *K. Z.* xxx. (1888) p. 224; Conway, *Camb. Phil. Soc. Proc.* 1890, p. 16; Brugmann *Ber. Kön. Sächs. Ges. Wiss.* 1890 p. 214, 1893 p. 134; *Grundr.* II. § 1080; Buck p. 177). These are all impersonal, and when derived from transitive verbs appear in Oscan with an accusative (**113**).

PRESENT. Indic. Osc. *loufi*[*r*] (**28.** 9), Umb. *ier*[1]. Subj. *ferar*.

FUTURE. Ind. Umb. *ise*[1], cf. the act. *eest, est* for **eis(e)t*.

FUTURE PERFECT. Umb. *benuso couortuso*, for *-us-so(r)* or *-us-(e)so-r*, as *benust* for **benusset* or *-us-(e)set*; the second part of the compound containing the Thematic inflexion of *sum* 'I am,' i.e. corresponding to Lat. *ero* and possessing the same future meaning.

PERFECT SUBJUNCTIVE. Osc. *sakrafir*, Umb. *herifi, pihafei*, (p. 517).

B. Developed passive forms, i.e. forms in which the Passive *-r* or *-er* (where either appears) is *added to* the complete forms of the Active or Middle. The great majority, if not all, of these forms are personal[2].

---

[1] Otherwise Brugmann l.c. 1890 pp. 215, 220, whose explanations appear to me to involve serious difficulties. I follow Buck, pp. 163, 178.

[2] The only possible exception which appears to me even plausible is Umbr. *pufe tefte* (V i 7), which Brugmann (*Ber. K. S. Ges. Wiss.* 1893 p. 134) renders 'quae (acc. neut. pl.) datur,' i.e. 'quae homines dant'; see p. 517. Osc. *censamur eituam* (**28.** 19) appears to be a translation of some Latin phrase, such as *censetor pecuniam* (cf. Cic. *Flacc.* § 80 al. 'census es mancipia') and therefore it does not follow in the least that *censamur* is impersonal, whatever the origin of the construction may be. Umbr. *herter* 'oportet' may quite as well be 'optatur (hoc)' as 'optant homines,' i.e. the meaning of the root (cf. Umbr. *tiṣit*, Lat. *de-cet* etc.) must in either case have produced ultimately an impersonal use.

1. *Indicative.*

PRESENT. Osc. 3 s. *uincter*, Umb. 3 s. *herter*[1], *teḍte* (see p. 517).

Osc. 3 s. *sakarater*, 3 pl. (deponent) *karanter*. N. Osc. *ferenter*.

FUTURE. Umb. 3 p. *ostensendi* (p. 506).

FUTURE PERFECT. Osc. 3 s. *comparascuster*.

2. *Imperative.*

(1) With -*r*. Osc. 3 s. *censamur* (see footnote, p. 492).

(2) Without -*r*. Umb. 2 s. *etuḍstamu* (I *b* 16), *persnimu* (e.g. I *b* 21). 3 s. *etuḍstamu* (e.g. VI *b* 53), *persnimu* (passim), *amparihmu, anovihimu, spahmu*. 2 p. *kateramu, arsmahamo*. 3 p. *persnimumo* (e.g. VI *b* 57).

3. *Subjunctive.*

(1) With -*ĕr* added to the Active form (?), or -*r* to the Middle form.

3 s. Osc. *sakahíter* (or is this indic., like *staít*?).

3 p. Umbr. *emantur, terkantur* (?), *tursiandu*.

(2) With the Subjunctive-vowel + *r* added to the Active form.

(*a*) Active Indic. form + Subj.-vowel + *r*.

3 s. Osc. *lamatir* (Buck p. 179), Umbr. *hertei*[1] VII *b* 2 (?), *herte*[1] V *a* 6, 8.

---

[1] Bücheler (*Umb.* p. 194) held that these Non-Thematic or Simple Thematic forms with impersonal use had a different meaning ('oportet, oporteat') from that of the -*ē*- or -*i*- stems seen in Umb. *hereitu* etc. ('uelle, optare, sibi sumere'), but the perf. subj. pass. *herifi(r)* certainly belongs in meaning to *herter*.

(*b*) Active Subj. form + Subj.-vowel + r^1.

Osc. 3 s. *sakraítír* (*amo*-conjug.), *kaispatar, krustatar* (*rego*-conjug.)[2].

C. Periphrastic Forms.

1. With Past Partc. Passive and the verb 'to be.'

Perfect Indic. 3 s. Osc. *teremnatust* (*viú*), Umb. *screhto est.* 3 p. Osc. *staflatas set, upsatuh sent* (Camp.-Etrusc.).

Future Perfect Indic. 3 s. Umb. *pihaz fust.* 3 p. Umb. *sersnatur furent.* Impers. *spafu fust, purditom fust.*

Perfect Subj. 3 s. Umb. *kuratu si.*

Perfect Inf. Umb. *kuratu eru*; on *erom ehiato* see pp. 513 f.

2. *With Gerundive.*

Imperative. Umbr. *pelsans futu.*

3. *Phrases with Supine or a Postposition.*

Umb. Fut. Ind. Pass. impers. *vaṣetumise* (I *b* 8) 'uitiatum ibitur,' i.e. 'uitiabitur.' In the same sense *uasetom-e fust* (VI *b* 47) with which Bücheler compares Lat. *est in mentem* for *uenit in mentem* etc.

There are a few other forms not represented in the scheme.

From the root STA we have Umb. *stahu* (1 sing. pres. indic.), Osc. *staít* (3 s. pres. Ind.) and *stahínt, staíet* (3 p.), Umb. *staheren(t)* (3 pl. fut.), *stahitu stahituto* (Impv. sing. and pl.). In compounds Osc. *eestínt* 3 p. pres. ind., Umbr. *restatu* impv., *restef* nom. sing. pres. partc. Buck explains the simple verb in Oscan as containing the suffix -*i̯o*-, like O.C.Sl. *stoją*; *eestínt* would then be syncopated.

The following forms are at present obscure in conjugation, in inflexion or in both. Most of them have been discussed in one or more of the works cited on p. 492.

Osc. *amfret* (3 p. pl.), *prŭftŭ* (past partc.), *prŭffed* (3 s. perf. ind.).

---

[1] This category was first recognised by Buck l.c.

[2] It is just conceivable that these two should be imperative forms of the *amo*-class; cf. Umb. *aituta* and the doubtful *proieeitad* in Note iv. p. 31.

N. Osc. *asum* (= Umb. *aso*), *lexe*[1], *pedi*.
Volsc. *asif*.
Umbr. *heriei* (see p. 511, footn. 4), *fuia*.

A few remarks are needed to explain the principles of Phonology on which these paradigms have been constructed.

1. i *and* e *in Umbrian*. Bücheler (*Umbrica* p. 179) makes no attempt to distinguish *i* and *e* in flexional syllables. At first sight they appear hopelessly confused in Umbrian, but it will be found that original ī is nearly always written *i* and original ē nearly always written *e*. But, as in Oscan, original ē (=Italic ē) became close, while original ĭ was open, hence these two sounds are represented indifferently by *e* and *i*, as in Oscan both ē and ĭ appear as *i*. (In these cases the earlier tables shew distinct preference for *e*, in the later *i* and *ei* are perhaps commoner than *e*.) Hence verbal forms with varying *i* and *e* should be referred, in default of other evidence, to the *moneo*-class. There is only one word which occurs at all frequently with *i* and only *i*, namely the impv. *persnimu* with its past partic. *persnis* (from **pérsnĭtos*). One or two others that are found only in Tab. VI and VII, as the impv. *seritu* (cf. the derivative verb *aseriaia*), may contain orig. ī, others as *tenito*, Lat. *tenēto*, certainly belong to ē-stems. Umbr. ē = Ital. *ci*, *ai*, *oi*, is far more commonly written *e* than *i* in all the Tables.

2. *Syncope of short vowel*. The Imperative and no doubt other forms of Conj. II (*rego*-class) closely resembled that of the preceding (*sum*-class), since the Italic first-syllable accent has in many cases, if not in all, expelled the short thematic vowel between the root and the imperative termination. Generally however they can be distinguished from true Non-thematic forms by the preservation of the last consonant of the root before the -*to(d)* from the various changes which it has undergone in forms in which it was immediately followed by *t* in the earliest period of the dialects. Conversely, in some words, thematic forms are distinguished by the changes produced on the final consonant of the root by the thematic vowel itself before it was forced out of existence. Thus we have Osc. *factud* Lat. *facito*, Osc. *actud* Umb. *aitu* Lat. *agito*, Umb. *deitu* Lat. *deicito*, by the side of participles like Osc. *saahtum* Umb. *sahta* Lat. *sanctus*, Osc. *ufteis* from *op*- cf. Lat. *optare*, Umb. *rehte* Lat. *recte*. *Deitu*, *aitu*, etc., where *i* perhaps represents a consonant like the Mod. South German *ch* after *i*, show the palatalisation of the final guttural of the root before the theme -*e*-. Similarly Umb. *covertu* Lat. *convertito* contrasts with Umb. *trahvorfi* Lat.

---

[1] *eite uus pritrom-e pacris, puus ecic lexe* clearly means Ite uos porro bona pace freti, qui hoc legistis, and it is tempting to recognise in *lex-e* the same brief 2 pl. suffix as in Skt. *babhūv-a*, *dadắ dadhắ* etc.

transversu, original -*rtt*- becoming regularly -*rf*- in Umbrian, and -*rs*- in Latin. So the past partcc. *mota* Lat. *multa* 'penalty,' and *kumates* from *mol-* 'to grind' shew the regular loss of *l* before *t*; the imperative *comoltu* is a syncopated form, Lat. *commolito*.

To this law of contraction there are definite exceptions, for example a short vowel appears to be regularly kept in the second syllable when it is followed by *ḍ*, *r*, *m* or *n*; hence *staheren haburent*, etc., cf. *tuderus kapide*. There are five words, *dersecor*, *dersicust*, *aḍepes*, *pupḍiçe*, *tribḍiçu*, which unless they are all archaisms (we have *aḍpes*, *pupḍçe* once each) would seem to shew that the short vowel was kept after *ḍ* as well as before it, except when it was followed by *s* or *f* (*mersto*=Lat. *modesta*, *kupif* for **kapĭdef* from **kapĭdens*). If this be so, the impv. *teḍtu* (*dirstu*) cannot have come from **teḍito*. In any case indeed the parallel and fairly frequent form *ditu* (*titu detu*), if it stands, as it probably does, for **dittō* (**did-tōd*, cf. Skt. *dat-tē*) must be an older and certainly Non-thematic form. *Teḍtu* must then be considered a re-formation on the pattern of other parts of the verb beginning with *deḍ-*. Another form of the same kind is seen in *teḍte* (*pue teḍte emantur herte*), on which cf. p. 517.

3. *Future-forms*. The futures of the -*ē*- and -*ĭ*- conjugation seem to be formed alike in -*ies*-, Umb. *habetu* fut. *habiest* Osc. '*hafieist*,' Umb. *purtuvetu purtuvies*, *heritu heriest*. The S. Oscan *herest* no doubt stands for **herrest* from *herjest* by the regular S. Oscan assimilation of *j* to a preceding liquid, as in *Kerrí*, *Keri*=Mruc. *Cerie* (p. 473), *allo*, Lat. *alia*, *famelo* Lat. *familia*, cf. *Bansa* from *Bantia*, *zicolom* from **diëcolom*.

The explanation just given of Umbr. *habiest* assumes that with *habetu*, -*bitu* it has the same conjugation as Lat. *habēre*. The Osc. fut. form just quoted from the Tab. Bant. should no doubt be read *hapiest*, and the most probable explanation of the *p* in this form and in *hipid* has been given by Buck, *Verb-System* p. 165, viz. that two Italic roots of similar meanings, *hab-* and *kap-* (Lat. *capio*), had been fused in usage in Oscan (and Umbrian?). The process must, I suppose, have been that

in Oscan *habē-*+*cap-* (or *cap-t-*) produced *hapē-* or *hapt-*;

in Umbr. *habē-*+*cap-* produced two stems of equivalent meaning;

habē- in *habē*, *habĭtu*, *habiest*, *habia*;

hab- in *ha*(*h*)*tu*, *subator* (-*ā*(*h*)*t-* for -*aft-* for -*ap-t-* for -*ab-t-*), *haburent nei-ḍhabas*, and possibly *eit-ipes* 'sententiam habuerunt,' if *p* here stands for *b* as in *hapina-* beside *habina-* etc.

Buck prefers to refer the fut. in -*iest* and pres. subj. in -*ia* only to -*io* verbs, and therefore starts from Osc.-Umbr. *habĭ-* rather than *habē-*, comparing Anglo-Saxon *hebbiu* rather than Lat. *habeo*.

4. *Final* -*t in Umbr.* Most of the forms of the 3 sg. given in the paradigms show the original -*t*, but in the Iguvine Tables this -*t* is frequently dropped, especially after -*s*-, so that the 2nd and 3rd pers. of the fut. and fut. perf. become indistinguishable.

C. NOTES ON THE SYNTAX OF THE DIALECT INSCRIPTIONS.

A complete account of the Syntax of the Dialects is, of course, impossible until the number of inscc. which we possess is largely increased. The following notes are intended, in the first instance, to record the most noteworthy points of resemblance and contrast to Latin idiom which can at present be observed. Omissions will no doubt be discovered in a first attempt to treat the subject as a whole; but I have preferred to err on the side of brevity by excluding as far as possible merely conjectural matter.

The reader will find in Index IV a list of all the passages discussed in this chapter, which, it is hoped, will to some extent serve as a commentary on the inscriptions.

I. SYNTAX OF NOUNS.

A. *The Cases.*

Nominative and Vocative.

1. On the use of the Nom. with passive forms see 68 and 69 inf.

2. The Nom. is never used for the Voc. in the Iguvine Tables in any paradigm in which there is a distinct form for the two cases, i.e. the Voc. is always used, never the Nom., in the Sing. of *o*-, -*io*- and *ā*-stems.

In the other Dialects no forms have yet appeared in which the ending of the Voc. would be distinct from that of the Nom.

3. In the prayers of the Iguvine Tables the Voc. is only used at the beginning of the sentence, i.e. where the name of the Deity precedes the personal pronoun; where the latter precedes, the name of the Deity is attracted into the case of the pronoun; thus VI *b* 8 *tiom subocau......... Fisoui(m) Sanśi(m)* 'te inuoco Fisovium Sancium,' but ibid. 9 *Fisouie Sanśie tiom*...' Fisovi Sanci, te....' Similarly ib. 27—8, and always.

Accusative.

4. As the External Direct Object after Transitive Verbs[1], e.g. Osc. *toutam censazet* 'urbem censebunt,' Umb. *saluom scritu poplom* 'saluom seruato populum' etc. So also after verbs whose special transitive meaning arises in composition, *appei poplom andersafust* 'cum populum lustrauerit' (literally 'circum-dederit'), so *poplom a(n)ferom* (for *amb-ferom*) 'populum circumferre lustratione.'

In the formal style of the Iguvine liturgy the Object is frequently left to be supplied where its nature is obvious, thus (VII *a* 39) *ennom comoltu, comatir persnihimu* 'tum commolito (integras libas), commolitis (libis) precator.'

5. The omission of the Obj. after such a verb as *tribarakavům* (**95** *b* 10, contrast 15, 16) 'aedificare' shows the 'absolute' use of transitive verbs which is very common in Latin (*damnose bibimus* etc.).

6. The measurements of the roads in 39, *per* X and *perek* III may be abbreviations for forms in the acc. which would be one of extent; or for genitives, like Lat. *fossa trium pedum*. The measure is, probably, in either case that of the breadth of the street or alley (Nissen, *Pomp. Stud.* p. 532).

7. For the acc. with the inf. see 67 inf.

8. For the acc. with pre- and postpositions see p. 483.

Genitive.

9. Possessive Gen. Osc. *kůmbennieís tanginud* 'comitiorum scitu,' Umbr. *erar nomneper* 'pro eius (urbis) nomine.'

So as predicate (Osc.) with *sům* **107**, cf. **102, 108, 28,** 22 etc.

Also with the adj. *můiníkú*- 'communis' in **95** (*a* 22), **101, 115.**

10. The father's praenomen stands in the gen. (with no word denoting 'son'), in Osc. (as in Lat.) placed always after the nomen of the son, e.g. 1 and passim, in Umbr. and Volsc. between the praen. and nomen, though it is almost always abbreviated as in Umb., Tab. Ig. V *a* 15 *uh-tretie K T Kluviier* 'auctoritate Gaii Cluuii, Titi filii.'

11. In the Iguvine liturgy the names of three feminine deities are followed by those of masculine deities in the gen. sg., and the latter are sometimes regarded as the husbands of the former, e.g. I *b* 31 *Tu(r)se Serfie Serfe(s) Marties* 'Tursae Cerfiae Cerfi Martii (uxori)'; cf. Gell. 13. 23 *Luam Saturni, Salaciam Neptuni, Horam Quirini, Virites Quirini, Maiam Volcani, Heriem Iunonis, Moles Martis Nerienemque Martis*, where from what follows (cf. 309 A s. v. *nerio*) it is clear that Nerione is the wife of Mars, but equally clear that some other relation holds between

---

[1] On its use after Passive forms see 68 inf.

I. SYNTAX OF NOUNS.

Heries and Iuno, the Moles and Mars. In the Umb. passages it is probably better to count Tursa and Serfia as daughters, but Vesuna in *Vesune Puemunes* of IV as a wife.

12. Gen. of Origin. Umb. *pisest totar Tarsinater* 'quisquis est urbis Tadenatis,' *far agre(r) Tlatie(r)* 'far agri Tlatii'; Osc. on coins 30, perhaps 185 *a*, 143 *b*, but see p. 144.

13. Partitive Gen. Osc. *idic tangineis* 'id sententiae' (practically meaning 'eam sententiam'); Umb. *mestru karu fratru(m)* 'maior pars fratrum.' So predicatively Umb. VII *b* 4 *motar sins a CCC* 'multae (gen.)[1] sint asses CCC.'

With the governing noun omitted, replacing an acc., Umb. (II *a* 41) *struhṡlas...kumaltu* 'libae (partem) commolito.' So perhaps after *ampert* in Osc. (28, 12) see p. 484 sup.

14. More loosely, equivalent to a locative, Umb. VI *a* 27 al. *orer ose persei...pir orto est* 'illius anni (i.e. illo anno) sicubi...ignis ortus est.'

Here too perhaps, rather than in the last paragraph, should be placed Umb. *esoneir popler anferener* 'sacrificiis populi lustrandi,' cf. 75 inf.

15. The use of the gen. in legal Osc. after *manim aserum* 'manum asserere, sibi lege uindicare' (28, 24), and after *zicolom deicom* (ib. 14) 'diem dicere de,' can hardly be classed save as a predicative use of an ordinary adnominal genitive.

16. For the gen. with quasi-postpositions see p. 484.

Dative.

17. Dat. of Advantage, Osc. 5, 42, 46 etc. Umb. 354 bis after *sacr(um)*, Tab. Ig. passim e.g. *Marte Krapuvi fetu* 'Marti Grabovio facito' etc. So of dedications Osc. 108 *iúvei stahínt* 'Ioui dedicatae sunt.'

So after adjj. Umb. *desva tefe* 'dextram, propitiam tibi' and *pacer* 'propitius, propitia' with dat., passim in VI and VII *a*.

18. Of Disadvantage, Osc. *suaepis altrei zicolom dicust* 'si quis altori diem dixerit' 28, 14.

After the verb 'to be'; Umb. *fratreci motar sins a CCC* (VII *b* 4) 'Let the fratrex have inflicted on him 300 asses for (lit. 'of') a fine.'

19. Of Concord, Agreement etc. Osc. 95 *ligatúís kúmbened* 'legatis conuenit.'

20. With verbs compounded with prepositions, Umb. e.g. VI *b* 44 *proseṡetir fasio arsueitu* 'prosectis farrea aduehito.'

---

[1] Cf. with Bücheler *a CCC moltai suntod* in Note xlii p. 397 and from the XII Tables ap. Gell. 20. 1. 12 xxv *aeris poenae sunto*.

Ablative.

Pure Ablatival Uses.

21. Abl. of Origin, in Osc. on coins, as *Akudunniad* 158, *Benuentod* 159, so 150, 184.

This seems to have developed, in names of towns, something like a locative use *ekík sakaraklúm Búvaianúd aíkdafed* 171, unless *aíkdafed* (which occurs nowhere else) has some meaning which requires an ablative. Bartholomae *Idg. Forsch.* vi 308 takes *slaagid* 95 *a* 12 to mean 'on the boundary' ('an der Grenze,' lit. 'von der Grenze her'), and *eksuk amvíanud* 60 ff. seems to mean 'in, or down this turning.'

Pure Ablatives are hard to find in the Iguvine Tables where this function of the case is mainly discharged by the prepos. *eh* 'ex' (*eetu ehesu poplu* 'ito ex hoc populo') and the postpos. -*ta*, -*to* (*angluto hondomu* 'ex angulo imo'). But after *testru sese* IV 16 'dextronorsus (?)' we have *asa asama(d) purtuvitu* 'ab ara ad aram (libam) porrigito.' The use at all events survives after the adv. (or quasi-preposition) *nesímei* 'nearest' (cf. Lat. *proximus ab*) *nesímei asa deueia* (VI *a* 9 al.) 'proxime ab ara diuina.'

So probably in Osc. (109) *nessimas staíet veruís lúvkeí* 'proxime stant (a) foribus in luco,' though the form *veruís* might of course be dat.

22. After Comparatives; Osc. *mais zicolois* X' 'plus decem diebus' (28, 25).

23. With Pre- and Postpositions (Osc. *dat*, *praí*, -*en*, Umb. *eh*, *pre*, -*to*) see p. 483.

Instrumental Uses.

24. Abl. of Instrument; Osc. *eísak eítiuvad tríibom upsannam deded* (42) 'illa pecunia atrium faciendum locauit,' Umb. *di Grabouie tio(m) esu bue peracrei pihaclu (subocau)* VI *a* 25 al. 'Deus Graboui te hoc boue, optimo piaculo, (supplico),' and passim *puni, vinu feitu* 'posca, uino (sacrum) facito.'

25. Abl. of Accompaniment, Manner, Circumstance; very common in both dialects.

Osc. 28, 11 *pod pis mins deiuaid dolud malud* 'ut quis minus iuret (i.e. ut iusiurandum euitet) dolo malo'; ib. 20 *poizad ligud iusc censaum angetuzet* 'quacunque lege eos censere instituent'; *kúmbennieís tanginud (deded)* 'comitiorum scitu (locauit).'

Here probably belongs the postpositional use of *amnud* p. 484.

Umb. V *a* 12 *felsva adputrati fratru Atiiediu prehubia* '*holusticam materiem i.e. holera (?) arbitratu fratrum Atiediorum praebeat'; I *b* 20 *apretu tures et pure* 'circumito tauris et igne (sacrum faciens).' Note especially V *b* 1 *panta muta adferture si* 'quanta multa (id, i.e. uitiosa curatio) flamini sit (stet, constet)' where in view of *etantu mutu* in l. 6 I cannot think *muta* is the archaic nominative (p. 404). With this abl. compare the recurring formula in the liturgy of the Fratres Aruales, *Iupiter tibi boue aurato uoueo futurum*.

26. The plural forms of Time or Occasion (as Osc. *eidúís Mamerttiaís* 'idibus Martiis') should probably be classed as Locative since that case is regularly used in the Sing., see below[1].

27. In the Abl. Absolute: Osc. **28.** 21 *toutad praesentid* 'praesente ciuitate, coram ciuibus'; with partc. only ib. 22 *amiricatud* '*immercato, i.e. nullius rei pretio persoluto.'

In Umb. the construction seems certain only in one phrase, which is however of frequent occurrence. I *a* 1 *este persklum aves unzeriates enetu* 'istud sacrificium auibus obseruatis (i.e. augurio capto) inito.' For in the common *kumultu, antakres kumates pesnimu* 'commolito, integris commolitis precato' (e.g. I *a* 34, II *a* 42) as in all the phrases attached to *pesnimu*, e.g. *aḍepes arves, klavles* (IV 12), the exact force of the case is uncertain (though the case appears to be fixed as an abl. by *aseśeta karne persnihmu* in II *a* 30). One or two possible examples of the abl. absol. in III and IV are still obscure in meaning.

In the Umbr. examples just quoted, the doer of the action denoted by the Passive Participle is the same as the subject of the main verb of the sentence, as regularly in Latin.

Locative.

28. Of the place where the action occurs, Osc. *staíet lúvkeí* **109** 'stant in luco,' and frequently; rarely on coins, as **195, 196** from the Frentane district. Umb. *destre onse fertu* VI *b* 50 'in dextro umero ferto,' more often with the postposition *-em* or *-em-e(m)*, see p. 484.

So of an assembly in which a thing is done, Osc. *deiuatud comenei* **28.** 5 'iurato pro contione.'

29. Of the time when the action occurs, Osc. *eizeic zicelei* **28.** 7 al. 'illo die,' *Virriieís medikiaí* **106—7** 'Virrii praetura, Virrio praetore,' etc.; Umb. *maronatei Vois. Ner. Propartie(r) T. V. Voisiener* **355** 'magistratu Vols. Propertii Ner. f., T. Volsieni V. f.'; *sume ustite* Tab. Ig. II *a* 15 'summa tempestate (?),' the case being clear though the meaning of the noun is not certain. If *sueso fratrecate* in VII *b* 1 agree together in

[1] But Bücheler supposes the ablative to be used in the phrase *menzne kurślasiu* (II *a* 16) which he renders 'mense circulario, i.e. anni ultimo,' although a clear locative, *sume ustite* 'summa tempestate' has just preceded. This seems prima facie unlikely; and it is easy to conjecture more than one meaning for the adjective which would make the phrase an abl. absol., or *kurślasiu* a gen. plur.

the locative (and it is hard to believe either that *fratrecate* has a different decl. from *maronatei* just quoted, or that, if it were of the third decl. with an *-at-* suffix, it would be masculine, as Büch. supposes, regarding the phrase as an abl.), the first word might be analysed *sue-so*[1], the second half being invariable like Lat. *-met* in *egomet*, *-te* in *tute* etc. Hence plural phrases like *plenasier urnasier* (V a 1 and 16), which denote the time of a meeting, may be loc. rather than abl.; so probably *semenies tekuries* II b 1 'semenstribus decuriis,' though that might conceivably be a dative 'for the meeting of the decuries (choose a pig and a goat).' In Osc. plurals there is the same ambiguity of form, but *eiduis luisarifs* 101, *eiduis ma(merttiais)* 104, *iúviais messimais* 113 etc. are probably locative in function.

30. In a judicial phrase in the place of the Lat. genitive Osc. 28, 20 *suae pis censtomen nei cebnust dolud mallud in(im) eizeic uincter* 'si quis dolo malo in censum non aduenerit et eius uincitur, and is convicted thereof.'

31. In one passage the use of the Locative of place approaches so nearly that of a Partitive Genitive as to suggest that a parallelism of meaning in certain uses was one of the factors in the fusion of the two cases in Latin in *o-* and *ā-* stems. Osc. 95. 17—19 *idík sakaraklúm ínim idík terúm múiníkúm múiníkeí tereí fusíd* '(conuenit ut) id templum et id solum (or 'area') commune in communi solo (communis soli pars) foret.' (On the more formal, 'external' causes of the fusion in Latin see Brugm. *Grds.* II. (III. Eng. Transl.) § 239 b.)

32. The form *ex-eic*, which appears several times in the Tabula Bantina (28. 12, 17, 26) after *contrud*, is clearly parallel to Lat. *illi-(c)* and may be either loc. or dat., cf. Brugm. *Grds.* l. c.

B. *Concord.*

1. *Number.*

33. The Noun of Multitude, Osc. *touto*, takes a plur. verb in the Tab. Bant. (28. 9) where it is used of the body of citizens each swearing for himself (*pous touto deiuatuns*[2] *tanginom deicans* 'ut ciuitas iurati

---

[1] It only occurs elsewhere in the obscure formula which concludes I b and II a; but *-so* appears also in *seso* 'sibi' (see 37 inf.), where it has equally the appearance of an invariable affix; this view of *-so* seems to be preferred to Bücheler's, who takes *sueso-* as an ordinary *o*-stem-adj., by Brugmann (*Grds.* II. (III. Eng. Transl.) § 447.

[2] This form is best regarded as parallel to *cítuus* in 60 ff., as a nom. pl. of a masc. noun or adj. with the suffix of Lat. *edō, bibō* etc. So Buck, *Osc.-Umb. Verb-System* p. 185 (who adds, however, a further conjecture as to its formation)

sententiam dicant'); but where it is used of their collective action it takes the singular (ib. 15 *touto peremust*).

In Umb. we have *sve mestru karu fratru pure ulu benurent prusikurent, pepurkurent* (V *a* 25, 28, *b* 5) 'si maior pars fratrum qui illuc venerint decreuerint, poposcerint.' Bücheler notes also that the three Martian deities (VI *b* 58 ff.) are implored to curse as one person (*tursitu tremitu* etc. all sg.), but to bless as three (*fututo foner* 'estote fauni, i.e. fauentes'). In VI *b* 56 a sg. subject connected by *com* to another noun takes a pl. verb (though the sg. appears in 55); Bücheler compares *S. C. de Bac.* ll. 8, 17 *isque de senatuos sententiad......iousisent*.

34. On *pude tedte* V *a* 10 see 68 inf.

2. *Gender.*

35. As in Latin, an adj. agreeing with both a masc. and a fem. substantive, takes the masc. gender in Umb. e.g. *peiqu peica merstu* VI *a* 1 'pico pica iusto (propitio),' but the adj. is often repeated with changed gender, as ib. 3 al.

C. *Neuter Adjective for Abstract Substantive.*

36. In Osc. *idic tangineis deicum pod ualaemom touticom tadait ezum* (28. 10) 'id sententiae (see 13 sup.) dicere quod quisque optimum reipublicae (or 'optimam publicarum rerum rationem') aestimet esse,' *touticom* appears to have the same substantival force as the Lat. *publicum* in *bono publico* (e.g. Liv. 2. 44. 3), *pessimo publico* id. 2. 1. 1 (*egregium publicum* Tac. *Ann.* 3. 70 shows a similar use with a slightly different meaning, 'a noble reputation for his public acts').

II. SYNTAX OF PRONOUNS.

A. *Personal pronouns.*

37. Note that the use of the reflexive pron. of the 3rd pers. appears, so far as the examples serve us, to be exactly parallel to the Latin use; Osc. 28. 5 *deiuatud siom ioc comono......pertumum* 'iurato se ea comitia dimittere,' so ib. 10 *deiuatuns....siom deicum*[1] 'iurati se dicere.' 95. 9 *pús*

---

[1] See the last footn. Buck (p. 141) strangely takes this inf. clause as depending on *factud*, which, I think, confuses the sentence. *tadait* is of course singular, as the oath would be meaningless unless it applied to each man's vote separately; cf. also 36 sup.

senateís tanginúd suveís pútúrúspid lígatús fufans 'qui senatus sui utrique decreto legati erant' exactly reproduces the distributive use of Lat. *suus* with a following *quisque*. In Umb. VI *b* 51 *stiplatu parfa desua seso, tote Iiouine* 'stipulator (i.e. a dis flagitato) parram propitiam sibi (et) urbi Iguvinae'; *sveso* in VII *b* 1 (see 29 sup.) of course refers to the subject of the sentence; but whether *svesu* in the formula concluding I *b* and II *a* refers to the subject of the sentence, or to the noun which comes first (*kvestretie*), depends on the rendering of the last three words, which is not yet clear.

B. *Demonstrative pronouns.*

38. Note that Osc. *in*(*im*) *idic* has just the force of Lat. *idque*, Gk. καὶ ταῦτα, introducing with emphasis a new phrase (not a new finite verb) in a sentence; **28.** 5 *síom ioc comono...egmas touticas amnud...inim idic siom dat senateis tanginud maimas carneis pertumum* 'se ea comitia reip. caussa (idque de senatus maioris partis sententia) dimittere.'

C. *Relative Pronouns.*

39. These present in general no peculiarity as compared with the Latin uses: on the use of the relative conjunctions Osc. *pon*, *puz*, Umbr. *ponne*, *puze* etc. with the tenses and moods, see 42, 45, 49, 60—62 inf.

40. The antecedent is attracted into the case of the relative and then repeated in its proper case in its own clause in **42.** 1, 3 *eítiuvam paam...deded, eisak eítiuvad* etc.

41. Umbr. *puze, pusei* is often used just as Lat. *quasi* with an adj. or partc. alone, the verb being easily supplied; II *b* 9 *arviu ustetu, eu naratu puze faśefele sevakne* 'fruges ostendito, eas narrato (i.e. uerbis dedicato) quasi sacrificabilem hostiam.' In II *a* 4 the deity is thus entreated to disregard any informality that may have arisen; *fetu puze neip erctu* 'facito, i.e. aestimato quasi non (a nobis) optatum.' In VI *a* 27 al. we have the shorter formula *pusei neip heritu*, which may be an abbreviation of the first, just as VI *a* 25 al. *tio esu bue peracrei pihaclu* 'te hoc boue optimo piaculo (supplico, placo)' has dropped its main verb; or, less probably, I think, *heritu* may be impv. 'optato, sumito, habeto quasi non (factum)' as Bücheler on the whole prefers.

III. SYNTAX OF VERBS.

A. *Use of the Persons.*

42. The only point that seems to call for mention under this head is the frequent ellipse of the subject in religious and legal formulae, where the verb stands in the second or third person and is understood to imply as its subject 'the proper person, the person whose duty it is.' Thus in Umbr. the long string of imperatives in III and IV (from III 15 to IV 25 at least) has no explicit subject. So in I *a* 1—I *b* 7, II *b* (probably 2nd pers. because of *purtiius* in I *a* 30, *purtitius* ib. 33, *benus* II *b* 15 etc.), and almost[1] throughout VI *b*, where the 3rd pers. is used (*peperscust* 5, *combifiansiust* 49). So in Oscan in **101, 102**. The idiom is familiar in legal Latin as in the XII Tables, e.g. ap. Gell. 17. 2. 10 *Ante meridiem caussam coniciunto, cum perorant ambo praesentes. Post meridiem praesenti litem addicito* (sc. *iudex*).

B. *Use of the Tenses.*

43. The Present where it occurs in the inscc., whether in principal or subordinate sentences, has most often, perhaps, the force of a customary, repeated action e.g. Osc. **117** *pas fiiet* 'quae (omnibus annis) fiunt,' Umb. *ponne oui furfant* 'quandocunque oues februant (?).' In main clauses a present stating a rule of action may practically be equivalent to an Imperative, thus Osc. *sakruvit* **102**, N. Osc. *feret, ferenter* 'fert, feruntur' in **243**. But the Present is of course also used to describe an existing fact, as in all the definitions in **95**.

44. From the nature of the inscc. we have little or no evidence showing whether the use of the narrative tenses differed from the Latin; hardly[2] any past tenses in independent sentences are to be found save in builders' inscc. (e.g. **39** ff.) and dedications (e.g. **109**), where the structure of the sentences is very simple. On sequence in subjunctive clauses see below.

45. On the other hand the jussive character of so many inscc. makes the future and fut. perf. indic. extremely frequent, especially in subordinate temporal clauses (see **60—62** inf.) after Osc. *pon* Umbr. *ponne* 'cum, si quando.' The latter tense always describes the act as already completed at some future time, just as in Latin; and when either

---

[1] There are a few exceptions where a special performer is named, e.g. in l. 53.
[2] On N. Osc. *amatens* in **243** see the footn. to 48 inf.

tense is subordinate, the main verb is either an imperative or some other form making a future reference. The difference between the two tenses is marked in almost every line of the Tab. Bantina (28) e.g. 17—18 *suaepis contrud exeic fefacust, ione suaepis herest meddis moltaum, licitud* 'si quis contra haec fecerit, cum si qui magistratus multare uolet, liceto,' and frequently in Tab. Ig. e.g. VI *b* 49 *pufe pir entelust, ere fertu poe perca..habiest* 'in quo ignem imposuerit (?), (id ?) ille ferto qui virgam...habebit.'

Umbr. *uasor..porsi ocrer pehaner paca ostensendi(r), eo iso ostendu* VI *a* 20 'uasa¹..quae arcis¹ piandae caussa ostendentur, ea¹ ita ostendito,' where the form is a perfectly regular² fut. indic. pass. contracted by the regular post-tonic syncope for *ostenn-es-ent-er, as *ostendu* for *ostenn-e-tō, both forms showing the regular Umbr. change of *-nt-* to *-nd-*, and the construction not less regular; and, with Buck (*Osc.-Umb. Verb-Syst.* p. 142 n.), I can see no justification for the view that it could be impf. subj. in such a sentence.

46. Just as in the Latin *bona uenia audies, non me appellabis si sapis* etc., the future sometimes conveys a command: Osc. *sakrvist* 101 'sacrabit (ille quem oportet)'; in the following insc., curiously enough, the present of a customary action (43 sup.) seems used in its place, from the same verb.

47. A somewhat parallel use appears in the fut. perf., denoting an immediate and compulsory consequence, in the Umbr. formula (VI *a* 7) *sve muieto fust...disleralinsust* 'si muttitum erit (i.e. si uox missa erit), irritum (sacrificium) ilico fecerit.'

48. The Sequence of Tenses, so far as our inscc. disclose it, appears to have been in no way different from that observed in Latin. In the various uses of the Subjunctive given below will be found examples of the Pres. Subj. and Perfect Subj. dependent on the Present and Future Indic., on the Impv. and on the Perf. Subj.; of the Impf. Subj. depending on the Perf. (Aorist) Indic., and no others[3].

49. It is interesting to notice that in Orat. Obliq. after a past tense as in Lat., so in Osc., the Fut. Ind. in a dependent clause and the

---

[1] The Umb. forms are masculine.

[2] The only possible doubt would be based on the *-i* for *-ĕ(r)* which (not *-ēr*) we should expect in an indic. form. But cf. *ape, api, appei, seipodruhpei* etc. where the last syllable must surely be identical with the Lat. *-que*, Gr. *-τε* (*ad-pe exactly = ἔς τε), and *tiṣit* = Lat. *decet*. Umbr. *i, ei* = Italic *ē* is rare, but does occur, as these examples show. In this case the syntactical consideration seems to me decisive.

[3] If the mutilated word *nita . a* in 243 contains a present subjunctive, and if it depends upon *amatens*, and if that means 'amauere, i.e. cupiuere, iussere,' then we should have either the retention of the primary tense of the Or. Recta, after a secondary governing verb (like *liceat* etc. in Note xxviii *a* p. 260), or a Present-perfect force 'they *have* decreed' in *amatens*.

Imperative in a main clause, both pass into the Imperf. Subj.: **95** e.g. *b* 23—5 *thesavrům pún patensíns, múínikad tanginúd patensíns* 'thesaurum si quando panderent, communi decreto panderent,' all depending, like *fusíd* in *a* 19 and *[h]errins* in *b* 30 on *kúmbened puz* 'convenit ut,' which introduces the whole Or. Obliq.

50. On the use of the tenses of the Subjunctive in commands and prohibitions see 52—56 below.

C. *Use of the Moods*[1].

1. *In Simple Sentences.*

51. I know of no peculiarity calling for notice in the use of the Indicative in simple sentences, unless the special use of the present, future and future-perfect noted in 43, 46, 47 sup. be so regarded.

The only independent[2] uses of the Subjunctive which appear in the inscc. are (1) in Commands and Prohibitions, and (2) in Wishes, in both of which it shares the functions of the Imperative, so that the two moods must be treated together.

52. In Positive Commands in Oscan our inscc. show generally the Imperative, twice[3] the Present Subjunctive, once the Perfect Subj., all the three latter examples being Passives and in the 3rd pers. or impers.

Impv. Osc. **28** e.g. 9 *factud* 'facito,' **95** e.g. *b* 14 *estud* 'esto,' both 3rd pers. Pres. Subj. **28.** 21 *lamatir* 'ucneat,' see p. 493, **175.** *a* 19 *saahtúm tefúrúm sakahíter*[4] 'sacrum igneum sacretur.' Perf. Subj. **113, 114** *sakriíss sakrafír (iúvilass)* 'sacrificiis (i.e. hostiis) celebret aliquis (has imagines),' see 67 inf.

---

[1] In this section I am greatly indebted to Buck's admirable sketch of the Modal Uses (*Verb-system*, pp. 138—149), for both correction and confirmation of my own notes.

[2] That is to say there are no examples, so far as I know, of either the Potential ('Mild Future') or the Independent Deliberative use, or of the Subj. in the Apodosis of such sentences as *si sciam, dicam; si scirem, dicerem; si sciuissem, dixissem.*

[3] *fakiiad* and *sakraftir* in 117 scarcely belong here, as Buck supposed, since they depend on *kasit* 'decet, oportet' (Lat. *caret*).

[4] From the scanty evidence we have it is conceivable, but not very likely, that this form should be indic. and parallel in stem to *staít* while contrasting with *sakarater*, two certain indicatives on the same insc. If so, cf. 43 sup.

508 NOTES ON THE SYNTAX OF THE DIALECT INSCRIPTIONS.

53. Of Prohibitions in Oscan we have only six examples, but they are all[1] expressed by the Perfect Subjunctive. The resemblance to Latin idiom has often been pointed out; but the Perfect, which is more 'energetic' than the Present, was preferred for all formal prohibitions, and perhaps always, in Oscan, whereas in Latin it is not merely restricted to colloquial use, but to passages where the prohibition is made with some warmth of feeling; see Elmer, *Am. Journ. Phil.* 15 pp. 133 ff. The examples are *nep fefacid* **28**. 10, *ni hipid* ib. 14, 17, *nephim pruhipid* ib. 25, *nep fuid, ni fuid* ib. 28, 29, and *nep tribarakattins* **95**. *b* 21.

54. Of the Construction of Wishes in Oscan we have evidence only in the two curses (**130**, **131**), and the conclusion of the long epitaph of Corfinium (N. Oscan, **216**). Here we have only the Present Subjunctive, in both Positive and Negative sentences.

Positive : **130** *aflukad* 'abigat,' *da[da]d* 'dedat,' *lamatir* 'uencat,' *kaispatar, krustatar* (see p. 494), *turumiiad,* **216** *dida* 'det.'

Negative : **130** *ni putiiad, nip putiians,* **131** *nep putians, nep putiad, nep heriiad.*

---

[1] This assumes the correctness of either Bugge's or Bréal's punctuation in **28**. 15—17. The passage runs as follows, with Bugge's stopping : *suae pis pru meddixud altrei castrous auti eituas zicolom dicust, izic comono ni hipid ne pon op toutad petirupert urust.......in(im) trutum zicolom touto peremust. petiropert neip mais pomtis com preiuatud actud pruterpam medicatinom didest, in(im) pon posmom con preiuatud urust eisucen ziculud zicolom XXX nesimum comonom ni hipid,* 'Si quis pro magistratu (i.e. in his capacity as magistrate) diem alteri de agro aut pecunia dixerit, is comitia (i.e. the vote of the popular assembly trying the case) ne habuerit priusquam apud populum quater orauerit (i.e. pleaded as prosecutor)...et populus quartum (so Bugge; Büch. 'finitum') diem acceperit (i.e. ? heard it fixed). Quater neque plus quinquiens cum reo agito priusquam iudicium dabit (i.e. either 'puts the decision to the vote,' or 'prefers his own formal indictment,' an act repeatedly described by the word *iudicare* in this connexion, see Cic. *Leg.* III. §§ 6, 10, 27; Liv. 26. 3, 43. 16, and Heitland's Introduction to Cic. *pro Rab. Perduell. Reo*), et cum postremum cum reo orauerit, ex illo die in diem tricesimum proximum comitia ne habuerit.' If Büch. were right in placing a full stop before *neip mais pomtis*, we should have two variations from ordinary usage, *neip* being used in the sense of Lat. *nē*, instead of *ni* or *nep*, and the Impv. in a prohibition. Hence I prefer Bugge's rendering (just given), or even Bréal's (see crit. note). In Bugge's the *neip* goes closely with the two following words, and the sense of the whole command is affirmative.

The whole procedure is based on that in the *iudicia populi* at Rome, on which see Heitland l.c. The magistrate here is both prosecutor and president, like the Roman tribune before the Tribes: here as at Rome 30 days' interval is required between the last assembly but one, and the final assembly for voting; but at Rome only three preliminary assemblies were held, here as many as five are allowed and four are required.

III. SYNTAX OF VERBS.

55. In Umbrian we have no such distinctions of idiom. The Impv. and the Pres. Subj. are used side by side in both Positive and Negative sentences with no difference of meaning in any of the Tables in which the Pres. Subj. occurs. Not however quite "indiscriminately" (*pace* Buck p. 138), since the Impv. clearly belongs to the more formal and archaic style. Thus the **Pres. Subj.** does not occur at all in any of the sections of II *a* or *b*, nor in I *a*—*b* 9, and only once in I *b* 10—45 (*kupifiaia* in 36 instead of *kupifiatu* which appears in 35), and there probably by a slip (into every-day idiom) due to the subj. *teḍa* in the dependent clause which both precedes and follows; since in the close reproduction of this passage in VII *a* 43, 44 it is replaced by the **Imperative**[1].

Again, in the whole of the newer liturgy (VI and VII *a*) the Pres. Subj. appears in only one phrase, one of Wish, *fons si(r), pacer si(r)* 'faunus sis, propitius sis' VI *a* 24, *b* 7 and 26. Now all these three lines are in an identical preamble prefixed to the three different prayers to three respective deities. This is especially noteworthy in the first case where the body of the prayer (to Jupiter Grabovius) is repeated with each of three *piacula* (ll. 25, 35 and 45), the preamble occurring only with the first. When we observe that in the body of all these three petitions and of the following two (to Fisovius Sancius and Tefer Jupiter) the form used is *futu fons, pacer*, we can hardly doubt, I think, that we owe the preamble, like the vain repetition of the first prayer it introduces, to the framer of the liturgy, not to the authors of the substance of the prayers; that is to say, that the preamble with its **Present Subjunctive is of later date.** Much the same may be true of the only two (or three?) examples in III and IV of which one (or two?) are close to the beginning (*fuia*, and ? *terkantur* whose meaning and construction are doubtful), the other in the last sentence, *neiḍhabas* 'ne adhibeant,' a Prohibition, and the only example in Umbr. of a negative with an independent

---

[1] There are three parallel clauses, in each of which the chief official is ordered to command his assistant in each of the three spots (*funtlere* 24, *rupinie* 27, *tra sate* 31) where victims have been offered, to consecrate the '*erus*'; thus in I *b* we have

(1) *kaḍetu pufe apruf fakurent* (see l. 24) *puze erus teḍa*.

(2) *pustru kupifiatu rupiname, erus teḍa*.

(3) *ene tra sahta kupifiaia, erus teḍa*.

Now in VII *a* the clauses are reproduced verbatim (to disregard the form *abrons* in place of *apruf*, possibly = *aprōnes instead of *apros*) except that *combifiato* appears in both (2) and (3) equally.

It will be clear, I think, from the parallelism of the clauses that *teḍa* is equally subordinate in all three, the insertion of *puze* in (1) no doubt indicating that *kaḍetu* ('calato, clamato') was less naturally constructed with a (jussive) dependent subj. than *kupifiatu* ('moneto, denuntiato,' or the like). On the parataxis see 63 inf.

Subjunctive. On the other hand in the regulations of V, which are recorded as newly passed, and which are written more in the language of every day life, the Pres. Subj. predominates, while in VII *b*, the latest of all the Tables, the Pres. Subj. is used twice and the Impv. not at all.

The Volscian insc. (253) seems to be on a level with later Umbrian, since it is difficult to see any syntactic difference between *façia* and *estu*.

56. The independent Perf. Subj. in Umbrian occurs only in the obscure conclusion of I *b* and II *a* (*stiti steteies* 'steterit, steterint'), and in the form *pihafei* in the body of the prayers of VI *a*. Whether this is taken as standing for *pihafir* 'utinam piatum sit' (impers. pass.) or for *pihafir* 'utinam piaueris' (2nd pers. sing. act.), the tense is clear.

2. *Complex Sentences.*

(a) *Conditional and General Relative Sentences.*

57. The nature of all the longer inscc. we possess, which are either legal or quasi-legal documents, allows little room for variety in the structure of these clauses. Almost all the hypotheses that occur are General, i.e. they apply to any one of a number of possible occasions, and almost all refer to the future; and only once (I think) have we a statement[1] in the Apodosis which is elsewhere always either a wish or command, expressed by an imperative, a subjunctive present or perfect, or a verb of duty (e.g. Umbr. *fasia tisit* 'faciat decet,' see 63 inf.), the choice between these parallel forms being quite independent of the shape of the protasis, as will be seen from the examples.

Of these Protases referring to the future only two categories can be at present clearly distinguished.

58. The first is what, for want of a better name, may be called the **Non-Committal Class**, implying nothing as to the fulfilment of the supposition, and expressed by the **Indicative**. The tense for a future reference is sometimes (1) the Present, often (2) the Future, most commonly (3) the Fut. Perf. For a past reference we have (4) the Perfect.

(1) Osc. **28 21** *suae pis censtomen nei cebnust in(im) eizeic uincter,... lamatir* 'si quis in censum non uenerit et illius rei conuincitur,... uencat.'

Umbr. IV 6 *svepis heri, antentu* 'siquis uolt, intendito (imponito).'

VI *b* 54. The words to be spoken by the priest in warning aliens away from the city during the lustration are: *nosue ier che esu poplu, sopir habe*

---

[1] Tab. Ig. VI *a* 7, quoted below 58 (3), but cf. also 47.

III. SYNTAX OF VERBS. 511

esme pople, portatu ulu pue mersest etc. 'nisi itur[1] ex hoc populo, si quis habet[2] in illo populo, portato illuc quo ius est (portare) etc.'

(2) Osc. 28 13 al. *suae pis ionc moltaum herest, licitud* 'si quis eum multare uolet, liceto.' Umbr. VII *b* 1 *pisi panupei fratrexs fust, portaia,* etc. 'quisquis quandoque fratrum magister erit, portet etc.'

(3) Osc. 28 11 *suae pis...fefacust, molto etanto estud* 'si quis...fecerit, multa tanta esto.'

Umbr. VI *a* 7 *sue muieto fust... dialeralinsust* 'si muttitum erit, sacrificium uitiatum erit (or 'uitiauerit.').

V *a* 25 *sve prusikurent rehte kuratu eru, edek prufe si* 'si decreuerint recte curatum esse, id bene sit' (i.e. 'esto').

VI *a* 17 *sue anclar procanurent, combifiatu* etc. 'si aues procecinerint, nuntiato etc.'

Of all these examples it is not easy to claim any as being certainly Particular Suppositions except *nosue ier*; for in most, if not all of the others 'si quando' might be put for 'si' in the rendering without injuring the sense.

Whether *heriiei faśiu adfertur,...faśia tiśit* II *a* 16 'si uelit (uolt, uolet?) facere adfertor, facere[3] decet' belongs to this class or the next (59) depends on the view taken of the first word[4], which occurs only in this sentence, and, with the meaning 'uel,' in VI *a* 19 (*herie uinu herie poni fetu,* 'uel uino uel posca facito') and VII *a* 3. On the absence of *sve* see below 63 (3).

(4) Umbr. VI *a* 26 al. *persei...pir orto est...pusei neip heritu* 'sicubi incendium ortum est, pro nihilo ducito' (see 41 sup.). ib. 27 *persei tuer perscler uaseto est...esu bue pihafei* 'quicquid tui sacrificii omissum est,... utinam hoc boue piatum sit' (cf. 56 sup.).

---

[1] See p. 492, and the next footnote.

[2] The meaning of this sentence, and of *habe* in particular, has not yet been made clear; the latest discussion is by Brugmann in *Ber. K. S. Ges. Wiss.* 1890, p. 227. But I feel no doubt that both *ier* (for *ei-er* as Lat. *eunt* for *ei-unt*) and *habe* are present indicative. I am inclined to translate 'Nisi itur (a peregrinis) ex hoc populo, siquis capit, deprehendit (latitantem peregrinum), portato eum etc. (i.e. in poenam or 'extra urbem').' This meaning of *hab-* appears in VII *a* 52; cf. p. 496.

[3] See below 63 (1).

[4] This form has been regarded as a present or perfect subj.; it would be perhaps possible to see in it an old *ē-* subjunctive parallel in form to Lat. *audiēs, audiet*, and surviving in later Umbrian only in this isolated word (which had then as a conjunction fallen 'out of system') when the *ā-* subj. had banished the *-ē-* forms from the present system generally, as in the regular subj. Osc. *heriiad*.

In the present passage, however, an indic. could be defended by common Latin constructions such as Hor. *Sat.* 1. 3. 49 Parcius hic niuit; frugi dicatur, *Epist.* 1. 1. 36 Laudis amore tumes; sunt certa piacula.

59. The second class of Future Protases is that in which the supposition is treated as more or less remote (sometimes called the 'Ideal' class) and expressed by primary tenses of the Subjunctive. This is very scantily represented in the dialects.

Osc. 130 5 *svai neip dadid, lamatir* 'si non dediderit, utinam ueneat.'

In Umbr. the phrase *persei mersei* which always appears before *esu bue pihafei* in the formula just quoted (58 (4) above) is generally (e.g. by Brugmann[1] *Ber. K. S. Ges. Wiss.* 1890 p. 218) rendered 'quod ius sit' 'so far as may be right,' like Lat. *quod opus siet* (Cato *R. R.* c.g. 16, quoted by Buck) 'as far as may be necessary.'

The Oscan example is a Particular supposition, the Umbrian General.

(b) Temporal Sentences.

60. Here again the nature of the long inscc. produces great uniformity in the examples, but there are enough of these, I think, in Umbrian to show that the dialect cannot lay claim to the subtlety or precision of Latin syntax in this department of usage. So far as I know none of the examples have been shown to involve any of the special refinements of meaning by which most of the Latin temporal conjunctions have come to express a good deal more than merely temporal relations (e.g. *dum* and *priusquam* connoting positive and negative Purpose). And the few examples in which the subjunctive is used in the Dialects, if we except those in Or. Obl. (see 65 (2) below), can all be paralleled by others with the indic. without any apparent variation of meaning.

61. The principal sentences on which the temporal clauses depend, refer, I believe, without exception in our inscc. to future time, though sometimes expressed by a generalising Present (Umbr. *parsest* 'par est' VII *b* 2, unless this form be indivisible and future[2]).

In the Temporal Clauses we have:

(1) Present Indic. with General reference; Umbr. e.g. VI *b* 43 *ponne oui furfant, uitlu toru trif fetu* 'cum (si quando) oues februant (?), uitulos masculos tres facito.' So VI *a* 8 etc.

---

[1] He would also count *-se* in I *b* 8 *svepu vakaze vasetumise* (= VI *b* 47 *svepu uacose, uasetume fust*) as subjunctive, but this disregards entirely the indic. *fust* in the same protasis, and *ise* also is far more simply explained as fut. ind., see p. 492. He is clearly right in taking *vakaz uacos* (with the change of *-az* to *-os*, cf. that of *-ā* to *-o* p. 403 sup.) as a noun like Lat. *satias*; but why should not *se* be indicative, the act. sing. corresponding to Lat. *erit* in meaning, and thematic like *erit, sunt* and the Umb. passive impers. *-so(r)* (p. 492)? The sense would then be 'si quod uitium erit, si quod postea uitium ortum erit (repertumue erit)' etc.

[2] If it is a present it must contain a neut. noun, like *meds-est*, cf. L. *secus est*, Gr. χρέος ἐστί. Is the L. neut. noun *par* the same word, for *paros as *uir* for *uiros etc., properly meaning 'an equality'?

III. SYNTAX OF VERBS. 513

(2) Fut. Indic. Osc. 28. 16 *com preiuatud actud, pruter pam medicatinom didest* 'cum reo agito, priusquam iudicium[1] dabit (or dicet)'; so with *pon* ib. 19. Umbr. IV 32 *huntak piḍi prupehast*[2], *eḍek ures punes neiḍhabas* 'fontinale (or 'fonticulum') simul atque (si quando) propiabit, id illis poscis ne adhibeant'; so after *pune* 'cum' I *b* 11, 18 etc., *ap* 'ubi' III 21.

(3) Most frequently with Fut. Perf. Indic. Osc. 28, 14 *izic comono ni hipid ne pon petirupert urust* 'is (magistratus) comitia ne habuerit priusquam (donec) quater orauerit'[3]; so after *pon* ib. 4, 16 etc. Umb. e.g. V *a* 16 *ape apelust muneklu habia numer prever pusti kastruvuf* 'ubi impenderit (i.e. 'sacrificium fecerit'), munusculum sibi habeat nummis singulis secundum fundos' (i.e. 'pro unoquoque fundo'). So after *nersa* VI *a* 6 'donec,' *arnipo* VI *b* 25 (where with Buck supply *fust* after the parte. *uesticos*) 41, *api appei* I *a* 27, 30 etc.

62. With the examples just cited, all of which depend on jussive subjunctives or imperatives, the reader will compare the following cases which are, I believe, all the examples of the use of the Subjunctive in Temporal Clauses (except in Or. Obl., for which see 65 (2) inf.).

Osc. 130 6 ff. *pun kahad...punum kahad,...ni putiiad;...pun far kahad, nip putiiad edum nip menvum limu* 'cum (si quando) incipiat...quandocunque incipiat,...ne possit;...cum far capiat, neu possit edere, neu minuere famem.'

Umbr. VI *b* 50 *pone esonome ferar, pufe pir entelust, ere fertu poe* etc., 'cum in sacrificium feratur, id (?) in quo ignem imposuerit (adfertor), is ferto qui' etc.; ib. 52 *neip amboltu prepa desua combifiansi* 'neue ambulato, priusquam sollemnem (parram) nuntiauerit' (perf. subj.).

To these there is generally added

VII *b* 2 *portaia seuacne desenduf pifi reper fratreca parsest erom ehiato, ponne iuengar tursiandu hertei, appei arfertur poplom andersafust* 'portet uictimas[4] duodecim quas[4] pro re fratrum ius est solui (i.e. let loose for

---

[1] See 53 footnote.

[2] It will be seen that this sentence is parallel to those with *persei* (i.e. *piḍi*) quoted above in 58 (4), but here the temporal signification seems to me more prominent. It is less natural to render 'quicquid fontem piauerit,' and Bücheler's 'fontem quem piauerit' would surely require in Umbrian *puḍe*, not *piḍi*. The object of the command is no doubt to insist on the use of freshly and specially procured water for mixing with the 'posca,' not of water left over from another ceremony; cf. the duties of the Roman Vestals (Warde Fowler in Dict. Antt.[2] s.v. and the authorities there cited).

[3] See 53 sup. footnote.

[4] The gender of *seuacne*(*f*) is indeterminate. If *arṣlataf* in IV 22 agrees with *sevacnef* the latter is there feminine; if it is so here (and *iuengar* certainly is so), the construction of *ehiato* becomes an interesting question. It cannot be

C. 33

the sham sacrificial hunt), quandocunque iuuencae terreantur (fugentur) oportcat (? oportet), ubi adfertor populum lustrauerit' (fut. perf. ind.). If *-ei* in *hertei* represents *-ē(r)* it is a subj. (p. 493), but cf. 45 sup. footn., and observe that between *parsest* and *andersafust* the indic. *hertĕ(r)* would be far more appropriate.

(c) Paratactic uses of the Subjunctive.

63. The inscc. offer us many examples of the use of the Subj. in really subordinate clauses which have no subordinating particle. In nearly all of these the Subjunctive is originally Jussive or 'Volitive,' as in Lat. *uelim facias, fac ualeas* etc., but we seem to have one example of an originally Concessive or Optative use, and perhaps one based on an independent Deliberative.

(1) **Dependent Jussive Subjunctives.** Osc. 117 *a* and *b fakiiad kasit* 'faciat oportet,' N. Osc. 239 *upsaseter coisatens* '(ut) aedificaretur curauere.' Umb. VI *b* 64, 65 *deitu etaia(n)s* 'iubeto itent'=*deitu* '*etato Iiouinur*' 'dicito: itate, Iguvini' in l. 63. So I *b* 35 al. *kupifiatu teḍa* 'nuntiato (ut) det' (cf. 53 sup.), VI *a* 2 *stiplo aseriaia* 'stipulare, flagita (ut) obseruem¹.' V *b* 6 *panta(m) muta(m) pepurkurent herifi(r) eru(m)* 'quantam multam poposcerint (ut) oporteat esse.' II *a* 17 *faśia tiśit* 'faciat decet,' and after *herte(r), -tei(r)* in V *a* 6 *si* 'sit' *sis* 'sint'; V *b* 8, 10, 13, 16 *dirsans* 'dent.' So perhaps in 243 *iafc feret regenai peai Cerie Iouia paersi* 'eas (hostias) fert Reginae Piae, (orans) sit propitia Iouia.'

(2) **Dependent Deliberative?** Umb. V *a* 8 and 9 *revestu…, emantur herte* is rendered by Brugmann (*Ber. K. S. Ges. Wiss.* 1893 p. 134) 'reuisito, i.e. inspicito oporteatne emantur,' on the assumption that *herte(r)* contains the *-ē(r)* of the pass. subj., see p. 493 and 62 sup., and that *emantur* belongs to the class just noticed. If on the other hand Bücheler were right in regarding *herte*, like *heris* 'uel,' as a 'crystallised' indic. which had become a mere adverb, we should render 'emanturne recte,' with the same Deliberative force in *emantur* as that which on Brugmann's rendering would be seen in *herte*. I do not feel that the meaning of the whole sentence is at present quite clear; cf. 69 inf. On Bücheler's view *dirsans* in the passages just quoted from V *b* would be counted an Independent Jussive, but the construction of *si*, *sis* in V *a* 6 would not be clear to me.

acc. pl. fem., though it might be masc. for *ehiato* (*f*), (cf. *uerof-e* 'in fores'); if not, it would then be possible to see in it the dative of the verbal in *-tu-* (cf. *Fiso, trefo* from *Fisu-, trifu-*) and to claim the whole as a precise parallel to Lat. *dicturum* for **dictu erom* (Postgate *Idg. F.* IV. 252) only with a passive instead of an active meaning.

¹ This rendering seems to me (as to Buck p. 141) extremely probable; it is due to Thurneysen *Idg. Anzeiger* 4. p. 39.

III. SYNTAX OF VERBS. 515

(3) Dependent Concessive? Umb. II *a* 16 *heriiei faśiu(m) aḍ-fertur, avis anzeriates faśia tiśit* '(si) uelit (uolt, uolet?) facere adfertor, auibus obseruatis faciat decet' clearly contains a paratactic condition, but the mood of *heriiei* is not yet certain, see 58 (3) footn. sup.

(d) *Final Subjunctive.*

64. This appears, as in Latin, both in pure purpose-clauses and in factitive constructions where the subjunctive-clause contains the direct object of the main verb, or its subject if it be passive or impersonal.

(1) Pure Purpose. Umb. VI *a* 20 *eo iso ostendu pusi pir pureto cehefi dia* 'eos (focos) ita ostendito ut ignem ab igne incendat[1].'

(2) Factitive clauses. Osc. **28.** 9 *factud pous...deicans* 'facito ut dicant'; ib. 11 *nep fefacid pod pis mins deiuaid* 'neue siuerit ut quis minus iuret.' **95.** *a* 10 ff. *ekss kŭmbened,....puz ídík sakaraklŭm...mŭiníkŭm fusíd* 'ita conuēnit, ut id templum commune foret.' Umb. I *b* 34 *kaḍetu puze teḍa* 'clamato ut det.' With these compare the subjunctives quoted in 63 (1) above.

(e) *Oblique Subjunctive.*

65. (1) Indirect Question. Umb. V *a* 24 *ehvelklu feia sve rehte kuratu si* 'consulat (lit. consultum faciat) utrum recte curatum sit'; ib. *b* 1 *ehvelklu feia panta muta aḍferture si* 'consulat (fratres) cum quanta multa adfertori res sit'; cf. 25 sup.

Compare 63 (2) sup.

(2) Subjunctive in subordinate clauses of Oratio Obliqua. Osc. **28.** 10 *siom deicum pod...tadait*[2] 'se dicere quod censeat' (cf. 36 sup.); 95 *b* 23 f. *avt thesavrŭm pŭd eseí tereí íst pŭn patensíns, mŭinikad tanginŭd patensíns* 'sed thesaurum qui[3] in ea[3] terra[3] est cum panderent, communi decreto panderent.' The second *patensíns* depends on *kŭmbened puz*, v. 64 (2) sup. and 49.

---

[1] The mood of *dia*, and the general meaning of *cehefi dia* are clear, but the explanation of the two words separately is doubtful. Bücheler (*Umb.* p. 52) would render either 'accendendo (lit. (ac-)*censu*) inflammet,' or '(ac)censum-det' like *uenum dare*. If the form be compared with *pihafei* (68 inf.), as it must be if it be connected with *kukehes* (III 21), it would be possible to render 'det accendatur' or 'det accendant,' like Cato's *dato bubus bibant omnibus* (*R. R.* 73), *dato edit* (ib. 157. 9).

[2] The -*t* for the regular -*d* of the subjunctive, like the -*t* of *pocapit* ib. 8 and the -τ of the corresponding endings when written in Greek αβ, is due to the difficulty of representing the exact Oscan sound in alien script. Cf. p. 462 and Note xxiv. p. 227.

[3] These words of course are neuter in Osc.

33—2

It is noteworthy that all the definitions in this agreement are taken out of the Orat. Obl. and expressed as direct statements in the present indic., e.g. *púd...íst* in the sentence just quoted; and that the only example of this subordinate subjunctive is in a Temporal clause.

On the Sequence of the Tenses see 48, 49 sup.
On the Acc. and Inf. see below.

(*f*) *Uses of the Infinitive.*

66. As in Latin, the infin. is used as the object of verbs of wish, capability and design. Osc. **28.** 19 *poizad licud* (i.e. *ligud*) *iusc censtur censaum angetuzet* 'quacunque lege illi censores censere (censum facere) statuent'; ib. 24 *suae pis ligud acum herest auti manim aserum* etc. 'si quis lege agere uolet, aut manum¹ asserere etc.' **95** *b* 10 *tribarakavúm líkítud* 'aedificare liceto.' **130.** 8 *nip putiiad edum nip menvum limu* 'utinam neue possit edere neue minuere famem.' Umb. I *b* 10 (= VI *b* 48) *pune puplum aferum heries* 'quandocunque populum lustrare uoles.'

67. The Accusative and Infinitive appears in the latest Osc. and Umb. inscc. and in all the examples that occur is parallel to the Latin use, viz. Osc. **28.** 5, 6 *deiuatud siom...pertumum* 'iuret se dimittere'; ib. 10 *siom deicum pod ualaemom touticom tadait ezum* 'se dicere quod optimum reipublicae censeat esse' (cf. 36, 37 sup.). Umb. V *a* 25 *sve prusikurent rehte kuratu eru* (ib. 28 *neip eru*) 'si decreuerint recte curatum esse' (28 'non esse'). VII *b* 2 *piji parsest crom ehiato* 'quas ius est solui' (or, less probably, 'quos ius est solutos esse,' see 62 sup. footn.).

D. *The Passive Forms.*

68. No part of the Osco-Umbrian verbal system has thrown a more welcome light on that of Latin, both in its morphology and syntax, than Zimmer's discovery in Italo-Celtic of what may be called the 'Rudimentary' class of passive forms with an impersonal active meaning, especially when his theory received the remarkable confirmation of the Osc. construction *sakrafir últiumam* ('consecret aliquis ultimam, ultima consecrata sit') in **113**, an insc. first published almost immediately after his paper. The references to the discussion which has since arisen will be found on p. 492, with all the words which can be certainly regarded as exhibiting the formation. Here it is enough to say that we are warranted in assuming in proethnic Italic, beside the forms which are based upon middle endings, a type of impersonal, or rather, so to speak, of 'tacit-personal' forms in every tense of the finite active verb, which differed from the 3rd pers. plur. only in substituting -*r* for its -*nt* (or -*nti*), and in implying an indefinite, instead of a definite, personal subject, being

---

¹ See 15 sup.

otherwise identical in use. Thus Lat. *ferant* 'they (those persons already mentioned) may carry,' Umbr. *ferar* (VI *b* 50) 'some one or other may carry, man trage, qu'on porte.' Lat. *eunt* 'they, the persons mentioned, go,' Umbr. *ier* VI *b* 54 = Lat. *itur* 'some persons go, any person goes.' The Oscan example with an acc. of the object has been already quoted; beside it are the two Umbr. forms, also in the perf. subj., *herifi*(*r*) 'optauerit aliquis, optatum sit, oportuerit' and *pihafei*(*r*) probably = 'piatum sit,' see 56 sup. In V *a* 7 *sakreu perakneu upetu, revestu puḍe teḍte eru emantur herte* 'hostias agonales (?) optato (?), considerato (?) oporteatne emantur *eru puḍe teḍte*.' Brugmann (see p. 492 footn.) would regard *puḍe* as the object of *teḍte*(*r*), attributing to the latter form an impersonal active meaning, and translate the last three words 'ea,' or 'eorum[1] (aliqua) quae homines dent,' in spite of the fact that *teḍte* is based on a middle or active form, as the -*t*- of the 3rd person shows. This view of the passage is simple and attractive, but unless further discoveries give us examples of words in Osc. or Umbr. formed like *teḍte*(*r*), or Lat. *itur*, and clearly possessing the power of governing an acc. (which forms like *itur* never have in any Latin author[2]), it is safer to take *teḍte*(*r*) as an ordinary 'developed' passive. The antecedent to *puḍe* is contained in the words *eru emantur* and the subject of *emantur* is clearly the *sakreu* or victims mentioned just before; and while it is true that the indeclinable form *puḍe* is used both for sing. and plur. (VI *b* 40, see p. 479), such a form in any case might well take a sing. verb so that we should render 'oporteatne hostiae inde emantur (lit. eorum emantur) quod datur'; but the rendering 'illo (pretio) quod datur' is not impossible. Bücheler's view of *teḍte* as = *teḍente* 'dante' assumes an unparalleled loss of -*en*- (on *libs* for *libens*, v. 272 n.).

Even in the narrow limits of our inscc. it is clear, I think, that this *ferar*-type is no longer a living part of the verbal system. In Oscan, we have only two forms[3], one of which, *loufi*[*r*], has become an adverb, and the other *sakrafir* is only used in the formula of a special ritual, where we find it already superseded in 117 by the 'developed' passive forms (*sakraitir kasit*). Similarly in Umbrian no one of the forms occurs in more than one formula; while the developed passive is far more frequent in both dialects. Add to these considerations the complete disappearance of the

---

[1] If so, cf. 13 sup.

[2] *legitur Vergilium*, quoted by Brugm. from Weisweiler *Das lat. part. fut. pass.* p. 70, is simply one of the many barbarisms of late Latinity like *de* with acc. etc.

The occasional personal use of the periphrastic *itur* in Old Lat. should be mentioned here, though it in no way weakens the argument: Cato ap. Gell. 10. 143 contumelia quae mihi per huiusce petulantiam factum itur, Plaut. *Rud.* 1229 illi istaec uidetur praeda praedatum irier Ut cum maiore dote abeat quam aduenerit.

[3] Three, if the mutilated -*niir* (*kulupu*) of 137 be so regarded, but its meaning is a blank.

ferur-type in Latin, notwithstanding the marked persistence of the impersonal type of construction, and it will, I think, be admitted that this class of forms has a right to be counted decidedly the more primitive in Italic.

Into the history of the -*r* suffix in the Aryan and Latin active 3rd plural forms (e.g. Skt. *dadur*, Lat. *deder-unt* etc.) and in the Celtic passive 3 s. and 3 pl., and the exact process of the development of the personal inflexion in Italo-Celtic, I cannot here enter. But Zimmer's view, which regards the 'rudimentary' forms as originally active and everywhere more primitive than those based on middle forms, still seems to me on the whole (as to Buck p. 180) distinctly more attractive than those of his critics.

69. So far as I know there is no peculiarity to be observed in the use of what I have called the 'developed' forms, as compared with their use in Latin. Their subject is always[1] in the nominative, and they appear both as pure passives (Osc. *uincter* 'uincitur, conuincitur,' Umbr. *emantur* 'emantur, capiantur'), and as deponents (Osc. *karanter* 'uoscuntur, participantur'). The variety of their forms is shown on p. 493.

E. *Participles and Gerundive.*

1. *The Participles.*

70. An example of the Present Participle Active in Oscan may be found in **28. 21** *toutad praesentid* 'praesente civitate'; in this construction the form should be counted a participle rather than an adjective.

In Umbrian the partcc. of one or two verbs occur fairly frequently in the nominative, and, like the Latin partc., always denote an action strictly coincident in time with that of the main verb, which it amplifies or modifies; e.g. I *a* 24 al. *zeḋef fetu* 'sedens facito'; I *b* 9 *restef esunu fetu* 'restituens, instaurans sacrificium facito.'

The concluding sacrifice in II *a* 14 is ordained thus: *aḋetus perakne fetu*, which Büch. would render 'Agentibus sollemne (sacrum) facito,' taking the first word as a participial title, like Lat. *Lactans*, of certain inferior deities whose duty would be to convey sacrifices to the great gods.

72. In the only example of the Perf. Partc. Act. in -*us*, *sipus* 'sciens' **28** passim, it modifies the main verb (*deiuatud*) in precisely the same way as the pres. partc.

73. The Past Partc. Passive, so far as I have observed, presents no peculiarity in use as compared with the Latin: it regularly forms the

---

[1] On *teḋte(r)* V *a* 7 see above.

III. SYNTAX OF VERBS. 519

perfect tenses of the Passive; and once in Umbr., as so often in Latin, the copula, although future, is omitted; VI *b* 25 *arnipo uestisia(m) uesticos* (*fust*) 'donec libam libauerit' (*arnipo* is followed by *pesnis fust* ib. 41).

74. On the Abl. Absol. see 27 sup.

2. *The Gerundive.*

75. No examples of a Gerund occur in our inscc., possibly only by accident. But the Gerundive from transitive verbs, an adj. in -*nno*-, is used in precisely the same way as the Latin -*ndo*-forms with which it is clearly identical.

(1) In agreement with the object of the action it denotes, thereby forming a compound declinable phrase describing the whole action as one which is contemplated.

Osc. *trííbúm úpsannam deded*[1] (39 etc.) 'palaestram aedificandam locauit'; 117 *pas fiiet pústreí iúkleí eehiianasúm* 'quae fiunt (quotannis) postero die (? sacrificio) fugandarum (hostiarum),' i.e. on the next occasion after the sham hunt for the victims, such as is described in Tab. Ig. VII *a* 51—54, I *b* 40—44. The Lat. *kalendae* is a parallel example of a gerundive converted into the title of a day; in it as in *eehiianasúm*, and still more in Umb. *pelsans* in (3) below, the idea of futurity is faint.

Umb. VI *a* 19 *esisco esoneir seueir popler anferener et ocrer pehaner perca(m) habitu* 'in illis sacrificiis omnibus populi lustrandi et arcis[2] piandae, uirgam habeto' (for the genitive cf. 14 sup.); ib. 20 *ocrer pehaner paca* 'arcis piandae caussa.'

(2) As Predicate, a passive participle denoting duty; Osc. 113, 114 *iúvilas sakrannas eíduís mamertt*... 'imagines (hae) celebrandae sunt idibus Martiis.'

(3) Almost as Present Passive participle, cf. Lat. *oriundus*; Umb. II *a* 43 *katel asaku pelsans futu* 'catulus apud aram sepeliendus esto, i.e. sepeliatur.' The word occurs elsewhere only in the impv. *pelsatu* 'sepelito' VI *b* 40, and in the phrase *pelsanu* (plur. fem. -*na*) *fetu*, e.g. I *a* 26, II *a* 6, which Bücheler renders 'pelsandum (sepeliendum) facito,' meaning either 'facito, mactato quod postea sepeliendum est,' in which case the example belongs under (2); or else 'sepeliendum curato,' when it would fall under (1).

---

[1] The Gerundive with *dare* appears also in Latin in this sense, e.g. Tibull. I. 7. 20, Plaut. *Cist.* III. 17, Ov. *Fast.* 2. 36 f., but the Perf. Parte. Pass. (which points to the end of the process instead of the process itself) is of course commoner with *dare*. [J. P. P.]

[2] *ocrer* is of course masculine.

IV. ORDER OF WORDS.

76. The arrangement of the words and subordinate clauses in our inscc. is essentially the same as in the Latin period; that is to say, I doubt if a reader would be conscious of any change of idiom in this respect, even in details, in passing from a chapter in Livy describing an agreement to the Cippus Abellanus (95); or from any of the Latin laws of the first century B.C. to the Tabula Bantina (28), or to the latest Umbrian tables (V and VII *b*); the frigid, strictly balanced asyndeta and the brief clauses of the other Tables, recall rather the sententiousness of Cato's *Res Rustica*. A few points may be mentioned.

77. The main verb, in all periods of both dialects, stands normally at the end, and that of a subordinate clause at the end of its clause, though for special reasons either may be displaced, as by the phrase *aḍepes arves* in Tab. Ig. I, which was no doubt of sacrificial importance; similarly the two adjectives *pernaiaf pustnaiaf* 'anticas posticas, before and behind,' which imply the due completion of the process of augury, are separated from their noun *avef* and put after the verb *anzeriatu* I *b* 11; and there are many similar cases.

78. Adjectives generally follow the substantives they qualify (Osc. *dolud mallud*, Umb. *tote Ikuvine* etc.), but precede if they are contrasted with some parallel adjective, e.g. *Vušiiaper natine* Tab. Ig. II *b* 26, or otherwise emphatic, e.g. Osc. *múiníkeí tereí* 95 *a* 19. Deictic pronominal adjectives invariably precede; Osc. *ídík terúm* 'ea terra,' Umbr. *este persclu* 'istud sacrificium.' On the position of *suo-* 'suus' see 37 sup.

79. The relative generally stands first in its clause, but may be displaced, as in Latin, by an emphatic word, e.g. Osc. *slaagid púd íst* 95. 13 'quod in limite (duarum ciuitatum) est.'

80. The perpetual jingle of antithesis which is the most striking feature of the Iguvine liturgical style need hardly be illustrated. It is occasionally a little relieved by the comparatively playful variation in a repeated phrase which is a familiar device of Latin and other poetry (e.g. Verg. *Aen.* 1. 397, 427—8; 2. 728, 750), as in I *b* 23 *enumek prinuvatus šimu etutu, erahunt vea šimu etutu prinuvatus* 'tum praenouati (?=legati) retro cunto, eadem uia retro cunto praenouati.'

APPENDIX.

I. *The Mensa Ponderaria of Pompeii, now in the Naples Museum.*

The following account of this monument, which has been a standing riddle for 50 years and more, is based entirely on the measurements taken by my friend Mr G. P. Bidder of the Zoological Station, Naples. The sentences in inverted commas are repeated verbatim from notes with which he supplied me, and which he subsequently embodied in a paper read before the Camb. Philol. Soc. on March 7, 1895 (a brief abstract is given in their *Proceedings* XL. p. 5).

The only serious attempt to explain the table hitherto made was that of Mancini in 1871, *Giorn. Scav. Pomp.* I. 143. His conclusion was that the cavities of the block now presented no ratio of size and that therefore when used as standards they must have had metal linings since removed.

The Table was found in a niche beside the forum at Pompei and is now in the Naples Museum (no. 3828) close to the Farnese Bull. It is a block of good Travertine 2·25 m. long by ·552 broad. It contains nine holes arranged thus:

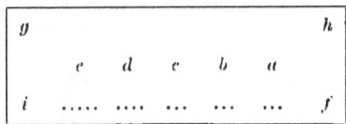

Each of these has or had an outlet hole at the bottom; those of a and d measure ·013 m. in diameter, the rest ·004. a, b and c are each surrounded by a raised rim or lip, but that of c is cut through so as to make three separate slots. The dots indicate the position of Oscan inscc. (57 sup.) which were more than half erased in antiquity. This erasure, as well as the unsymmetrical position of the cavities (v. inf.), was due to a readjustment by duoviri of Pompeii named Flaccus and Arellianus circa 15 B.C. as we learn from a Latin insc. on the side face of the stone (C. I. L. X. 793, quoted p. 68 sup.).

After repeated measurements "made with a flask pouring out $2196·3 \pm 5$ cubic centimetres and a measuring glass graduated to 500 c.c. pouring out

498·5 ± 1 c.c., both being tested by weighing the water actually poured out," Mr Bidder gives the following as the approximate dimensions in cubic centimetres:

Cavity	a	28350 = 28344 +	6 = 48 (590·5) +	6
,,	b	21325 = 21258 +	67 = 36 (590·5) +	67
,,	c	14816 = 14172 + 644 =	24 (590·5) +	644
,,	d	9372 = 9448 −	66 = 16 (590·5) −	66
,,	e	4771 = 4724 +	47 = 8 (590·5) +	47

The smallest cavities are considerably damaged, but their dimensions may be given thus:

f and g	590	= 590·5 − ·5
h ,, i	290	= ½ (590·5) − 5·2

The only noteworthy irregularity is in c, but in measuring this the slots in the rim which were mentioned above were treated as accidental and filled with clay. They may therefore be reasonably regarded as the sockets for some metal ring or flange, an ancient adjustment to correct the volume of the cavity—apparently the units of measure had been miscounted by one. In no other of the cavities does the error exceed 67 c.c., i.e. a wineglassful (or less than 10 in 1000 in e, 7 in 1000 in d, 4 in 1000 in b). This degree of exactitude cannot be accidental, and therefore there can have been no metal linings to the cavities as Mancini supposed.

"The common measure is 590·5 c.c. ± ·5 c.c., more prudently 593 c.c. ± 3 c.c., quite certainly 591·5 c.c. ± 7·5 c.c." This unit corresponds to the sextarius, since from the proportions of the cavities we saw on p. 68 that the seven measures were clearly parallel to the Roman *amphora*, *half-metretes*, *urna*, *modius*, *half-modius*, *sextarius* and *hemina*. How comes it then that while the duoviri used the Roman system of proportions, and presumably the Roman nomenclature (since they erased the Oscan names), they nevertheless adopted or preserved a unit of measure somewhat larger than the Roman sextarius (given by Hultsch (*Metrol.*[2] p. 118 ff.) as approximately 547 c.c., though varying in single specimens from 536 to 576 c.c.)?

The Oscan Pound.

Now we know that at Rome a congius or 6 sextarii of water or wine was supposed to weigh 10 lbs., and the two values of the Roman lb., the commercial pound of about 321 grammes and the coinage-pound of about 327 grammes (i.e. the weight of 321 and 327 c.c. of distilled water at 4° C. respectively) correspond to the 536 c.c. and 547 c.c. values of the Roman sextarius (see Flinders Petrie, *Encycl. Brit.*[9] xxiv. p. 487 b). In the same way the value of the pound corresponding to the Pompeian sextarius of 590 must have been about 354 grammes, i.e. about 8 per cent. heavier than the heaviest Roman pound. On the other hand it is remarkably close to the weight identified with 'the Italic mina,' mentioned by Heron and Priscian as used in Lower Italy, the average of 42 specimens of which (Flinders Petrie *l.c.*) was 349 grammes, while the talent of Herculaneum gives a mina of 357 grammes. With this mina therefore we may reasonably

I. THE MENSA PONDERARIA OF POMPEII.

identify the Oscan or Pompeian pound implied in the sextarius of the Mensa Ponderaria. Hence it appears that the duoviri adopted the local unit though enforcing the Roman proportions as between the different measures; just as [W. R.] the *pes Drusianus* was left by the Romans as the unit of length in North-Western Europe.

Dimensions of the stone.

These are calculated by Oscan feet.

Length 222·5 m. = ¾ in. more than 8 Oscan feet of ·276 m. (see Nissen, *Pomp. Stud.* p. 71).

Breadth ·552 m. = exactly 2 Osc. feet.

Distance of the centre of *a* from rt. hand margin						=	·554 i.e.	2 ft. Osc.
,,	,,	,,	*b*	,,	,,	=	·965 ,,	3½ ft. Osc.
,,	,,	,,	*c*	,,	,,	=	1·332 ,,	4 ft. 10 in. Osc.
,,	,,	,,	*d*	,,	,,	=	1·612 ,,	5 ft. 10 in. Osc.
,,	,,	,,	*e*	,,	,,	probably	=	6½ ft. Osc.

This last estimate is more or less conjectural, since the hole at the bottom is filled up and the edges left by the duoviri cannot be trusted to give a precise indication. The latter greatly enlarged the original content of the cavities, as appears from their bulging shape inside, which between *c* and *d* has left the partition so thin as to have broken into a leak at one point.

Use as a Corn-measure?

Mr Bidder now thinks that even the larger outlet holes of *a* and *d* (·013 m., i.e. ½ in., the rest measuring only ·004 m.) are too small to have allowed the two cavities to be used for measuring corn, and finds the corn-measure-standard in a rougher, black stone, much injured, still *in situ* in Pompei, containing three cavities with (originally) sliding bottoms. This was probably added as an upper storey (as in Mazois' picture, *Ruines de Pompei*, III., Paris 1829), since there are remnants of copper stanchions in the Mensa Ponderaria which would support shelves (to carry the vessels into which the corn was measured) directly underneath the three apertures of the stone still at Pompei.

II. Alien, Spurious or Doubtful Inscriptions.

A. ETRUSCAN INSCRIPTIONS IN ITALIC DISTRICTS.

a. *From Campania.*

These inscc. are all in Campano-Etr. αβ (with A or A rarely ⊲ *a*, ⊣ *v*, ⌶ *z*, ⊬ *m*, ✝ *t*, Ψ *χ*); where the words are divided below there are interpuncts in the original. I give the text as I read it in April 1894, except where other authorities are expressly assigned.

(1) *Incised on vases* a vernice vera *in the Spinelli Collection, Cancello* (*the ancient* Suessula).

1*. *mimatahiianes*

270 in the Spinelli collection; Von Duhn, *Bull. Ins. Arch. Rom.* 1879 p. 157, reads -*taaiianes*, the sign which I take for *h* being ⊲, while *n* is H, *m* ⊬.

2*. *vel χa.epustminas mi*

I do not know whether this has been published before. The sixth sign is ⊥ which I do not know how to read, unless the lower stroke is accidental.

3*. *tinθuracrii na*

Von D. *Bull. Ins. Arch. Rom.* 1878 p. 150 n.

4*. *numes̱ tataiesmi*

Von D. *Mittheil. Dtsch. Arch. Ins. Rom.* 2. p. 266 gave *humes̱ iatniesni*; the first *s* is smaller than the other letters and the second *a* is ⋈, the rest seemed to me clear; some way before the insc. is apparently a first attempt *nuẖ* (?), which von D. gives as |⋕⊃⊂∧H, but the last two signs appeared to me erased.

5*. ⋎⋎ ⋀Ọ
   ⫼∨⋎̇

287 in the Sp. collection. Cf. Note xiv. 2 p. 138.

II. ALIEN, SPURIOUS OR DOUBTFUL INSCRIPTIONS.

6*. (a) *mi putizapu*.....
(b) *miputizaru.iias*

273 in the Sp. collection: (a) Von D. B. *Ins. Arch. Rom.* 1879 p. 157 reads *milutnapu*; the *l* or *p* is ᗧ, the *iz* Ͷ. The text of (b) is from v. D. l.c.; it is on the foot of the vase and escaped my notice. The sign after *u* he gives as ꟼ (whereas *r* is ᗡ) and the final *s* as ⟨.

7*. *minipiiapi miχuliχnacupes*
    alθr nas ei

I do not know whether this has been published before; it is incised in two concentric lines; after *api* is a space of two letters.

(2) *Incised on vases* a vernice vera *from Curti in the collection of Sign. Bourguignon, Naples.*

8*. *saiue*

Under the base of a patera bought in 1892: the *i* has a dot underneath and immediately before it, both probably accidental. Gallozzi, *Not. Scav.* 1877 p. 368 wrongly gave the first letter as *g*.

9*. *miculichnav..uradenelus*

d is Я, *u* V; inside the vase is a clothed female figure of a common Greek type.

10*. *kapemukaθesa kapes sli*

The first *p* is Λ, the second ⊓, *u* is Y, *θ* ⊙. Published by Helbig, *Bull. Inst. Arch. Rom.* 1879 p. 149.

11*. *cupevelieśa*

c is), *u* Y, *ś* ⋈.

12*. *minumisiies vhal mus*

The last two words were given by von Duhn, *Bull. Ins. Arch. Rom.* 1879 p. 157 n., as *vhel mks*, but the text seemed to me clear. *u* is Y.

This insc. is of some importance as shewing the use of *vh=f* as in the *Numasioi* insc. 280 sup.

13*. *mai finastami*

f is Ƃ, *n* N, *m* ᴎᴎ, *t* T.

(3) On other vases, mostly from Nola.

14*. Of uncertain provenance: *U. D.* xii. 33 c p. 189, whence Zvet. *Osc.* xviii. 5, Fabr. 2842.

niifal . us...

This insc. like the preceding is noteworthy as showing 8. It is painted in a ring inside a small vase; *a* has lost its crown (N); after *l* there appears to be an interpunct, but there is no other indication as to where the word or words end or begin. Deecke, *Wochenschr. Class. Philol.* 1887 p. 133 would read *mi fal*[*t*]*us* Etr. for 'hoc Faltonis (est).'

15*. *marhiesa . clemicel*

s is ⟨, *c* ⟩. Mom. *U. D.* xiii. 7, p. 315, who gave it as 1613 in the Berlin Museum.

16*. *mamer ies husinies*

ś is ⋈, *s* ⟨; is the punct after *mamer* accidental? Mom. *U. D.* xiii. 8 p. 315, Berl. Mus. 1614.

17*. *vurelrunahel . . θutumleunue XXII aip*

Greatly injured; the forms of *u* are curiously varied, perhaps only by slips of the stilus and subsequent decay; the first is Y, the second ᛕ, the third and fourth V, the fifth ⟩, the sixth ⌐ (read by Mom. as *i*); the last four might all be *l* (⊲). The last two letters are /\. *U. D.* xiii. 13 p. 315, Berl. Mus. 1618.

18*. *taruś ula mi*

Von Duhn, *Mittheil. Dtsch. Arch. Inst. Rom.* 2. p. 266.

19*. *Not. Scav.* 1877 p. 368 from S. Maria di Capua.

mi munśal (*ś* = ⋈).

No interpunct at *mi*, but : at the end.

(4) On vases of the same class, now lost.

20*. *marvni?*

Inside a cup formerly in the Nolan Seminary; *U. D.* xiii. 10 p. 315 from Remondini, *Dissert. sopra una iscriz. Osca*, tav. iv. (pp. 26, 51, 53); *m* is ᛘ, *n* N, *v* ⊣, *r* D : the text can hardly be correct.

II. ALIEN, SPURIOUS OR DOUBTFUL INSCRIPTIONS.

21*. *miaitilnia*

At the bottom of another cup formerly in the same seminary; *U. D.* XIII. 11 p. 315, from Remondini *op. cit.* tav. III. pp. 51, 53.

22*. *epelatinae*

U. D. XIII. 12 p. 315 from Lanzi tav. III. p. 608 ed. 1, p. 522 ed. 2; 'on a broken cup of the *Museo Borgia*, probably not from Campania' (Mom.).

23*. *ruśiruaimi*??

Practically illegible, on a patera found near *S. Agata dei Goti* (Nola); *U. D.* XIII. 6 from Guarini *Comm.* XI. p. 33. Mom. on p. 315 does not transcribe it.

24*. *mimamerceasklaie*?

Minervini *Bull. Arch. Nap.* 2. 110 'of uncertain provenance': Garrucci ib. p. 164 transcribes it *mi mamerge asklaie*.

25*. *maerceprzieθesmi*??

Garrucci *Bull. Arch. Nap.* nuov. ser. 1. p. 86, 'from Capua,' the last sign but one is ᛞ which G. took to be a compendium for *ae*.

β. *Etruscan inscc. from Falerii and the district, hitherto called Faliscan.*
(For the alphabet see p. 371, and cf. p. 374.)

26*. ɔa : *u*.....*a* | *ca* : ....*ata θannia*. Painted on plaster. Deecke *Falisker* 8, Zvet. *It. Med.* 54, from Garrucci.

27*. *tuconu*. Cut in stone. Deecke 5, Zv. *It. Med.* 49, from autopsy.

28*. *ueltur tetena* | *aruto*. Deecke 57.

29*. *larθ ceises* | *celusa*. Deecke 58.

30*. *larθ* | *urχosna*. Deecke 59.

From Capena.

31*. *a śrpios esχ*. Deecke 66.

32*. *c pscni* | *cel*. Deecke 69.

33*. *apa*. Deecke 72.

34*. ...*śnuśpaurn*.... Deecke 74.

528   APPENDIX.

B. Gallic Inscription of Tuder.

35*. The non-Latin part of the following bilingual insc. which was found at Tuder and taken to the Museo Greg. at Rome, where I saw it in 1894, is now generally counted Gallic; Stokes *Bezz. Beitr.*, xi. p. 113, Pauli *Altital. Forsch.* i. (*Inschrr. in Nordetr. Alph.*) pp. 12 and 84, Büch. *Umb.* p. 175, C. I. L. i¹. 1408.

a.   ....s... | *drutei f frater | eius | minimus locau|it et statuit ateknati trut|ikni karnitu | artuaś koisis t|rutiknos*

b.   ..s]*epulcrum | c]oisis druti f | f]rater eius | m]inimus locauit | st]atuitqu| ..eknati trutikni | ka]rnitu lokan ko|...tiknos*

The Lat. part is in αβ of Gracchan type (cf. p. 468); the Gallic αβ has ᚠ *a*, ⌐ *l*, D *r*, X *t*, ⋈ *ś*, the other signs being like the Latin.

I give the first line of the Latin of (*b*) according to Pauli; but its fragments were to me illegible.

C. The 'East Italic' or 'Sabellic' Inscriptions.

I give simply Pauli's transcription, with the αββ, from *Altital. Stud.* iii. (*Die Veneter*), Leipzig, 1891, pp. 220 ff. and p. 423, to which the reader must be referred for its discussion and defence. Their special mark is that the alternate lines are inverted as well as reversed. Those who desire a 'translation' may turn to Deecke's conjectures at the end of Zvetaieff's *Inscc. Italiae Inferioris Dialecticae*, or Corssen's in *Kuhn's Z.* 10, p. 27. The single puncts in the middle of the line are reproduced from the original; they are not the same as the interpuncts, which are triple (:); a dot at the foot of the line indicates a letter's space, as usual.

36*. Cupra Maritima; Zvet. *It. Med.* 4, *U. D.* p. 333.

peiē | ēn eriáns u? | daoûm esm | ii a·na·a·ié·m a·ê | rēaieimêm hê.

Alphabet: A and A *a*, Δ *d*, E and Ǝ, ||| *h*, | *i*, W and M *m*, И *n*, ⊠ *ś*, ◊ *ô*, Π *p*, P *r*, ξ and ⌠ *s*, Λ *û*, ⋀ *u* (these two Pauli identifies), ⋀ *ê*.

37*. Castrignano; *Notiz. Scav.* 1890, p. 182.

a. *meitimêm | adszaseo seaśs manus | pêpênum estu : k apaiês*

b. *ítéd oapśrśo arśtio śmio puśo | matereśo patereśo o·l :*

Alphabet: A, D, E, ! *z*, | *i*, K, ▸ *l*, M and W *m*, N and И *n*, ⋈ *ś*, ☐ and ◊ *o*, Π, P, ξ, ! and | *t*, Λ *u*, ⋀ and V *ê*.

II. ALIEN, SPURIOUS OR DOUBTFUL INSCRIPTIONS. 529

38*. Bellante; Zvet. *It. Med.* 1.

p·szin siům siretůs | *tetis t·kům alies e|smen* | *sepses sepelen*

Alphabet: A, E and Ǝ, I z, | i, ⊁, ꓶ l, W and M, N and Ʌ, K and ⋈ s, ꓶ and ꓶ p, ▷ r, ⟨ and ⟩ s, T t, Λ and V ů.

39*. Nereto; Zvet. *It. Med.* 3.

petr·o pêpên... | *...r e sêoêo sůdi* | *pis eoůelś re...* | *...nu puêre pepi* | *e*.

Alphabet: Δ d, E and Ǝ, | i, Ɫ l, Ʌ n, ⊠ s, □ o, ꓶ and ꓶ p, D Ɑ and ꓶ r, ⟨ and ⟩ s, T t, Λ u, Λ ů (these Pauli identifies), ⋀ ê.

40*. Grecchio; *U. D.* p. 833, Zvet. *It. Med.* 5.

2 *reiklům z.lpůs pim·* : *i·rim esmenůrstůe·ms upeke* | *...r·m i·rkes iepeien*
3 *esmen ekêsin riuzi·m ru* : *růsim p·i·êetu* | *i·kiperu pru em ·k.kům enei bie* |
4 *mêkes murêm eļhem uei..mes puzies or·i kruhê*

Alphabet: B b, Ɇ e, Ɛ v, [z, ▥ h, | i, K k, ꓶ and ꓶ l, W and M m, Ʌ n, ◇ o, ꓶ ꓶ and ꓶ p, ⊳ and P r, ⟨ s, ꓶ t, Λ and V u, Λ and V ů (Pauli identifies *u* and *ů*), ⋀ and Ψ ê.

To this I perhaps should add that I copied the insc. myself in April 1894 in the Naples Museum, and, assuming that the values given to the signs by Pauli are correct—a question into which I cannot enter here—my reading differs from his in the following points, and those only:

l. 1, 4th word *t·rim*

l. 2, 2nd word ·*rkes* (not *i·rkes*)   3rd word *iepeten*   6th word *růezi·m*

l. 3 I saw no *i* before ·*kiperu*   5th word *enået* (N)

l. 4, 1st word, 4th letter ꓶ (? *li*) not E   3rd word, last letter *tm* (W)

5th word *stůties* (which Lindsay (*brieflich*) would regard as evidence that Λ in this insc.=*a*).

A second stone from Bellante and one from Castel d'Ieri are so damaged that Pauli only transcribes certain letters (*op. cit.* pp. 221, 222), and it would serve no purpose to reproduce them here.

530   APPENDIX.

D. *Doubtful or Spurious Inscriptions.*

41*. Scratched on two sides of a rough red clay circular pot, with handles, now in the Antiquarium at Berlin, found in "*Castellaccio*" in the *Basilicata*, a name unknown to the Italian Postal Guide, and probably therefore misprinted for *Castelluccio*, a small town on the *Lao*, 35 kilom. from *Lagonegro*, that is about 25 miles inland from the Lucanian coast midway between the ancient Pyxus and Laus. *U. D.* xiii. 14, Zvet. *Osc.* xviii. 11 whence the text.

a. ᛘᛉᛡᛉXΟᛉXᛞᛘᛂᛉXᛏVΟᛐ

β. X\X

Mommsen (*U. D.* p. 316 n.) read this ξουτικεμδιποξερεμ, ascribing the letters to the Achaean αβ of Metapontum, Pyxus, Laus etc., and on alphabetic grounds no objection can be offered, as the resemblance is complete (see Kirchhoff[4] p. 163 ff. esp. p. 166, *I. G. A.* 540—545, Roberts *Gr. Epigr.* p. 306), and, if Castelluccio be the place where the pot was found, the appearance of the Achaean αβ is exactly what we should expect in the valley of the Laus in any period before the adoption of the Ionic. As however the insc. is *graffito*, it would be possible to regard the first and thirteenth signs, not as X = ξ, but simply as careless forms of ↑ in which the engraver had begun the hasta too high up (although I can find no parallel irregularity in the Greek inscc. in this αβ or the Tarentine). Further, in Zvetaieff's sketch of the insc. (whence the text above) the ninth sign (from the right) looks more like α than δ.

Corssen however (*Kuhn's Zeitschr.* 22, pp. 304 ff.) read the insc. τουτς κεμρς ποτερεμ, identifying the ninth and fifteenth signs—which can hardly be right—and taking the fifth and tenth as s not ι. There is no difficulty in the second supposition if the αβ be regarded as the Laconian-Tarentine (Kirchhoff[4] p. 149 ff., Roberts p. 271 ff., *I. G. A.* 49—91 and 546—548 b); and it would perhaps be possible, even if the αβ were Achaean, to count the insc. as a solitary exception to Kirchhoff's statement (*l.c.* p. 165) that there is no example of ϛ or Σ=s in any insc. of this district older than the adoption of the Ionic character. The same doubt would apply to X in Tarentine as in Achaean αβ.

Corssen rendered the insc. as Oscan, "Tutus Cemerus (!) poterium (dedicauit)." If the second word be read κεμας (nom. or gen.? masc.), the difficulty of the unparalleled nom. ending *-rs* is removed, and the praenomen might be compared with *km* in **156** and **176** sup., while ποτερεμ might just conceivably represent an Osc. *pütīrīm if ε were used for ĭ as o for ŭ (see p. 461). But the name *touts is at present better known in Dickens than in Oscan and the alphabetic peculiarities just noticed, with the fact that this would be the only Oscan insc. yet known from Magna Graecia earlier than the adoption of the Ionic αβ (see p. 11), make it desirable to suspend judgment for the present.

II. ALIEN, SPURIOUS OR DOUBTFUL INSCRIPTIONS. 531

The letters on the other side of the pot, if they were written at the same date as the rest, must be read ξγξ in Achaean and ξιξ (? τιτ) in Tarentine αβ; but perhaps they are numerals.

Zvet. *Osc.* 145, U. D. *l.c.*

42*. On a broken piece of travertine now in the Naples Museum, seen by me March 1894; said to have been found in 1844 near Larino. First published by Garrucci *Memor. Ercol. d'Arch.* VII. App. p. 26.

NIDA........
LACEAMANAFEDESI
PROFATED

The third line slopes upwards wildly towards the second; the letters are ·068 m. high. Its spurious character is shown (1) by the very irregular formation of the letters, e.g. the curious variation in the length of the arms of E (⅝, ⅜, ¼ in.), and of F (¾ and ₁⁰⁄₁₆ in.), while in the first F the upper arm is the longer, in the second it is the shorter. These peculiarities are doubly strange when occurring in an Oscan (or Frentane) insc. written in Lat. αβ which would point to a late date when any public insc. would be more carefully written; this insc. is a marked contrast to even the earliest of the Paelignian group. (2) It is improbable that the Lat. αβ should be used at all in any Oscan community on a public local monument (the Tabula Bantina came from Rome, see the note to 28). (3) The ending -*ace* is unknown in our insce. (4) The sign ⊢ is either a cursive *l*, or meant for an Oscan ⊢ (⊢ rarely if ever after 300 B.C., see p. 108). (5) The signs for *m* and *a* are frequently half-rounded.

The evidence against its genuineness is cumulative, but, I think, quite convincing to any one who is familiar with the originals of insce. of which there is no doubt.

Zvet. *Osc.* 7, Fabr. 2781.

43*. Now 'lost,' but said to have been found in a vault (a curious place for a dedication to Hercules) at Nesce (= Nersac) in Aequian territory in 1859, along with several Lat. insce.; of the finding of the latter a record has been preserved with no mention of this; *Bull. Arch. Nap.* n.s. VII. 90, *Bull. Inst. Arch. Rom.* 1859 p. 114, and Corssen *Ephem. Epig.* II. p. 185.

pup herenniu | med tuv nuersens | hereklei | prufatted

Observe (1) that there are no other examples of Osc. αβ inter Aequos, (2) the absence of the patronymic, (3) the non-Osc. ending -*niu* in Osc. αβ beside the purely Osc. -*atted*, (4) the unexampled use of *prufatted* with a dative (meaning?), (5) the curious form *nuersens*. Dressel (C. I. L. IX. pp. 388 and 683) decides against it, and states that there have been other forgeries in this district.

Zvet. *Osc.* 1, Fabr. 2732.

44*. Said to have been found near *Collemaggiore* in Aequian territory near Nesce, given by Momm. and Dressel C. I. L. ix. p. 388, the latter deeming it false. Zvet. *It. Inf.* 290.

...*meddis | ners taliud*

45*. According to Garrucci (*Sylloge Inscc. Lat.* 563) the stone is lying in a fountain ('della Villeta' near Collemaggiore), and was copied about 1870 when the fountain was dry by Sign. Caetano Ricci, who explained that the stones of the fountain were taken from ancient buildings; rejected by Dressel and Mommsen (C. I. L. ix. p. 388).

po ca pomposiies medd|iss talii state m dd

In Lat. αβ with /Ʌ and A = a, L = l, but the remaining letters in full classical form, with single interpuncts. Even if the insc. were better attested *talii, m* (and probably *dd* also) must be corrupt. It has a certain resemblance to the Volscian insc. 252 supra.

Zvet. *Med.* 45.

46*. A doubtful insc. in Umb. αβ, said to have been written on two sides of a bronze plate, now 'lost': Büch. *Umbrica* p. 176, who justly adds 'deficit fides examinantem singula.'

(a) ...*ḍuvi ḍun ḍ*... | ..*herinties is*... | ...*tuḍis a s h*.. | *θuθiu t i ven*.. | *ahatrunie*

(b) ..*eḍuvie ḍunu ḍ*.. | ..*herintie istui*... | ..*Hurtentius*.... | ..*etvedis t i u*..

INDICES.

I. LOCAL NAMES OF ANCIENT ITALY.
II. MODERN LOCAL NAMES CITED IN THIS WORK.
III. GENTILE NAMES FROM THE DIALECT-AREAS.
IV. PASSAGES IN THE DIALECT-INSCRIPTIONS REFERRED TO IN THE NOTES ON DIALECT SYNTAX.
V. GLOSSARY TO THE DIALECTS.
VI. LATIN WORDS DISCUSSED IN ANY PART OF THIS WORK.

INDEX I.

THE LOCAL NAMES OF ANCIENT ITALY.

The numbers refer to the numbered sections of the body of the book, but p. indicates a reference to a page. The order is that of the Latin alphabet; θ is treated as th, φ as ph, χ as ch, but ου as ou whether = u or v.

For the Notation the reader is referred to the section on 'Notation and Abbreviations' which follows the Preface.

Neither the quantities nor the ethnica, nor any variant spellings of names are, as a rule, given here, as they may all be found at once by reference to the section in which the name occurs in the body of the book. But where two forms of a name vary considerably, each form will be found in its proper place in the Index. Where a river or mountain belongs to more than one Dialect-area both references are added to it; but where the same name denotes two or more different places the name is repeated in full each time.

Abella, 154 (Camp.) A
Abellinum, 160 (Hirp.) A
Aberrigines, 310 (Sab.) A
Abolani, p. 337 (Lat.) C
Aborigines v. Aberr.
Αβρυστον, 11 (Br.) B
Acalandrum, 26 (Luc.) C
Accienses, p. 337 (Lat.) C
Acerontia, 33 (Peuc.) A
Acerrae, -rranus, 154 (Camp.) A
Acerrae Vafriae, 371 (Umb.) C
Acerronia, 26 (Luc.) C
Acheron fl., -tos, 11 (Br.) A
Acheruntini, 11 (Br.) A
Acherusia palus, 154 (Camp.) A
Ἀχέρραι v. Acerrae 154 A
Aciris fl., 26 (Luc.) A
Acuca, 35 (Dau.) C
Aecae, 35 (Dau.) A
Aeclanum, 160 (Hirp.) A
Aefula, p. 334 (Lat.) A
Aegasus portus, 35 (Dau.) C
Aegetini, 33 (Peuc.) C
Aegilion v. Capraria
Aenaria, 154 (Camp.) A
Aequana, 154 (Camp.) C
Aequi, 275 A
Aequimaelium, p. 340 (Rome)
Aequum Faliscum, 351 (Etr.) A
Aequum Tuticum, 160 (Hirp.) A

Aesarus fl., 11 (Br.) A
Aesernia, 187 (Sam.) A
Aesis, 371 (Umb.) A
Aesis fl., 371 (Umb.) A
Aethalia v. Ilua
Afidena v. Auf-
*Afilae, -anus, p. 335 (Lat.) B, 160 (Hirp.) C
Agrifanus pagus, 154 (Camp.) B
Agylla, -llaei, -llini, 351 (Etr.) A
Aharna v. Arna, 371 (Umb.) A
Alba L., 275 (Aeq.) A
Alba Fucens, 275 (Aeq.) A
Alba (longa), p. 333 (Lat.) A
Albanus pagus, 160 (Hirp.) B
Albinia fl., 351 (Etr.) C
Albiona, p. 336 (Lat.) C
Albula fl., 374 (Pic.) C
Albula fl., p. 334 (Lat.) A
Albulinus riuus, p. 334 (Lat.) A
Albuneae nemus, p. 336 (Lat.) B
Alburnus mons, 26 (Luc.) A
Aletium 31 (Cal.) B
Aletrini, 160 (Hirp.) C
Aletrium, 278 (Hern.) A
Alfaterni, 154 (Camp.) A, cf. 275 (Aeq.) C
Alfellani, 160 (Hirp.) C
Algae, 351 (Etr.) C
Algidus mons, 275 (Aeq.) A
Alia fl., p. 335 (Lat.) A

INDEX I.

Allia fl., p. 335 (Lat.) A
Allifae, -anus, 187 (Sam.) A
Alma fl., 351 (Etr.) C
Almo fl., p. 333 (Lat.) A
Alsium, -ienses, -ietinus, 351 (Etr.) A
Altanum, 11 (Br.) C
Amaranus Iupiter, 160 (Hirp.) B
Amasenus fl., 256 (Vols.) A
Ameria, 371 (Umb.) A
Amerinum Castrum, 351 (Etr.) C
Ameriola, p. 336 (Lat.) B
Ametini v. Amitinum
Aminea (uinea), 33 (Peuc.) B
Amiternum, 187 (Sam.) C
Amiternum, 250 (Vest.) A
Amitinum, p. 337 (Lat.) C
Amitinenses, 351 (Etr.) C
Ampsanctus, 160 (Hirp.) A
Amunclae v. Amyclae
Amyclae, 256 (Vols.) A
Anagnia, 278 (Hern.) A
Ancon, 374 (Pic.) A
Angitula, 11 (Br.) C
Angulum, 250 (Vest.) A
Anien v. Anio
Aniensis, tribus, p. 334 (Lat.) A
Animula (Amin-?), 35 (Dau.) C
Aninus uccus, 270 (Mars.) B
Anio fl., p. 334 (Lat.) A
Annelanum, 351 (Etr.) C
Antemnae, p. 334 (Lat.) A
Antinum, 270 (Mars.) A, 256 (Vols.) B
Antium, 256 (Vols.) A
Anxa v. Callipolis, 31 (Cal.) B
Anxa, 270 (Mars.) B
Anxanum, 35 (Dau.) C
Anxanum, 197 (Frent.) A
Anxia, 26 (Luc.) C
Anxur v. Tarracina, 256 (Vols.) A
Apamestini, 31 (Cal.) C
Apenestae, 35 (Dau.) C
Apeninus mons, 371 (Umb.) A
Aphrodisium, p. 332 (Lat.) A
Apiennates, 371 (Umb.) C
Apinae et Tricae, 35 (Dau.) C
Apiolae, 256 (Vols.) A
Apollinares aquae, 351 (Etr.) C
Appeninus mons, 371 (Umb.) A
Aprilis, 351 (Etr.) B
Aprusa fl., 371 (Umb.) C
Aprustani v. Ἀβρυστον, 11 (Br.) B
Apulia, -ulus (App-), 35 (Dau.) A
Aquae Albulae, p. 334 (Lat.) A
Aquae Apollinares, 351 (Etr.) C
Aqua Claudia, p. 334 (Lat.) A
Aqua Crabra, p. 334 (Lat.) A
Aquae Passerianae v. Passer-
Aqua Petronia, p. 336 (Lat.) C
Aquae Tauri, 351 (Etr.) A
Aqua Virgo, p. 334 (Lat.) A
Aquacrata, 160 (Hirp.) B

Aquenses Taurini, 351 (Etr.) A
Aquileia, 351 (Etr.) C
Aquilonia, 160 (Hirp.) A
Aquilonia, 187 (Sam.) B
Aquilonis mutatio, 35 (Dau.) C
Aquinum, -nas, 256 (Vols.) A
Arcae, 256 (Vols.) A
Archippe, 270 (Mars.) C
Ardaneae v. Herdonia 35 (Dau.) A
Ardea, p. 332 (Lat.) A
Argei, p. 339 (Rome)
Argentanum, 11 (Br.) C
Argentarius mons, 351 (Etr.) C
Argetini, 31 (Cal.) C
Argiletum, p. 339 (Rome)
Argyripa v. Arpi
Ariates, 371 (Umb.) C
Aricia, p. 333 (Lat.) A
Arienates v. Ariates
Ariminum, 371 (Umb.) A
Ariminus fl., 371 (Umb.) A
Ἀρίνθη, 11 (Br.) C, and Note xvii, p. 148
Armenita, 351 (Etr.) C
Arna, 371 (Umb.) A
Arnestum, 33 (Peuc.) C
Arnine, 351 (Etr.) C
Arnus fl., 351 (Etr.) A
Arogas fl., 11 (Br.) C
Arpi, 35 (Dau.) A
Arpinum, -nas, 256 (Vols.) A
Arretium, 351 (Etr.) A
Arsia Silua, p. 336 (Lat.) B
Artena, 256 (Vols.) C
Articulanus pagus, 160 (Hirp.) B
Arusini campi, 160 (Hirp.) B
Asculum, 374 (Pic.) A
Asculum v. Ausculum
Asisium, 371 (Umb.) A
Aspia fl., 374 (Pic.) B
Astura fl. et opp., 256 (Vols.) A
Atella, 154 (Camp.) A, cf. Osc. *Aderl-*
Aternum opp., 250 (Vest.) A
Aternus fl. (Ath-), 241 (Pael.) A, 250 (Vest.) A
Ἄθυρνος v. Aternum, 250 A
Atiedio- v. Attidium 371 (Umb.) A
Atina, 26 (Luc.) A
Atina, 256 (Vols.) A
Atrani, 35 (Dau.) B
Atre, 35 (Dau.) B
*Attidium, 371 (Umb.) A
Aueia, 250 (Vest.) A
Auens fl., 310 (Sab.) A
Auentia fl., 351 (Etr.) C
Auentinus mons, p. 338 (Rome)
Auentinus uicus, 371 (Umb.) B
Auernus, 154 (Camp.) A
Aufentum fl. v. Ufens
Aufidena, 35 (Dau.) C
Aufidena, 187 (Sam.) A

Antidus fl., 160 (Hirp.) A, 33 (Peuc.) A
Aufinates, 250 (Vest.) B
Aufugum, 11 (Br.) C
Aulon, 31 (Cal.) A
Auricus fundus, 26 (Luc.) B
Aurini v. Saturnini, 351 (Etr.) C
*Aurunca v. 258 A and 145
Aurunci, 258 A
Ausculum, 33 (Peuc.) A
Auser fl., 351 (Etr.) A
Ausona v. Ausones
Ausones v. Aurunci, 258 A
Ausonia v. Aurunci, 258 A
Austicula, 154 (Camp.) C
Austranum territorium, 31 (Cal.) C
Auximates, 154 (Camp.) C
Auxumum, -umates, 374 (Pic.) A
Axia, 351 (Etr.) C
Ἀξετινοι, 33 (Peuc.) C

Babia, 11 (Br.) C
Baccanae, 351 (Etr.) B
Βάδιζα? v. Baesidiae, 11 (Br.) C
Baesidiae, 11 (Br.) C
Baotterrae, p. 335 (Lat.) B
Baiae, 154 (Camp.) A
Balabo, 26 (Luc.) C
Βαλεθας (γαλ-) v. Aletium, 31 (Cal.) B
Baletum fl., 11 (Br) C
Bandusia, 33 (Peuc.) B, cf. 310 (Sab.) B
Bantia, 33 (Peuc.) A
Barduli, 33 (Peuc.) C
Barium, 33 (Peuc.) A
Barpana, 351 (Etr.) C
Barra (=Pharos), 31 (Cal.) B
Basta, 31 (Cal.) C
Basterbini v. Basta, 31 (Cal.) C
Βαρία, 310 (Sab.) C
Batinum fl., 374 (Pic.) C
Batulum, 154 (Camp.) C
Batum fl., 11 (Br.) C
Bauli, -lanus, 154 (Camp.) A
Βαῦστα (-στρα) v. Basta, 31 C
Baustranum terr. v. Austranum, 31 C
Bebiana, 351 (Etr.) C
Beneuentum, 160 (Hirp.) A
Beregra, 374 (Pic.) C
Betifulum, 241 (Pael.) C
Βιράκελλον, 351 (Etr.) C
Biturgia, -urza, 351 (Etr.) C
Blanda, 26 (Luc.) A
Blera, 351 (Etr.) A
Blera, 33 (Peuc.) C
Boarium forum, p. 338 (Rome)
Boedinus pagus, 241 (Pael.) B
Bola v. Bolae
Bolae, p. 333 (Lat.) A
Βονδελία, 351 (Etr.) C
Borcani, 160 (Hirp.) C
Βορείγονοι v. Aborrigines
Βορεοντῖνοι, 187 C ad fin., cf. 197 A

Bouianum Undecimanorum, 187 (Sam.) A
Bouianum, -uetus, 187 (Sam.) A, cf. Osc. Búvaiano-
Bouillae, -llenses, -llanus, p. 333 (Lat.) A
Bradanus fl., 33 (Peuc.) B
Brenda, 31 (Cal.) A
Βρεντεσιον v. Brundisium, 31 (Cal.) A
Brittii, -ianus, 11 (Br.) A
Brundisium, -sinus, 31 (Cal.) A
Βρυστακία, 11 (Br.) C
Brutates v. Bruttii
Bruttii, 11 A
Bruttius ager v. Bruttii
Bubetani, p. 337 (Lat.) C
Buca, 197 (Frent.) A
Bulotus? fl., 11 (Brut.) C
[B]usutrani, 250 (Vest.) C
Butrium, 371 (Umb.) A
Butuntum, -tuntini, 33 (Peuc.) A
Buxentum, -entini, 26 (Luc.) A

Cabenses, -bienses, p. 335 (Lat.) B
Caecina fl., 351 (Etr.) B
Καικῖνος fl., 11 (Br.) B
Caecubum, -bus, 256 (Vols.) A
Caedici, -cii, ? 275 (Aeq.) C
Caedicii, 258 (Aur.) B
Caclanus, 160 (Hirp.) B
Caelestini, 371 (Umb.) C
Caelia, 33 (Peuc.) A
Caeliculus, p. 341 (Rome)
Caelimontana porta, p. 341 (Rome)
Caeliolus, p. 341 (Rome)
Caelius mons, p. 341 (Rome)
Caenina, p. 333 (Lat.) A
Καῖνυς prom., 11 (Br.) B
Caere, 351 (Etr.) A
Caeruleus fons, p. 334 (Lat.) A
Caesena, 371 (Umb.) A
Caiatia, 154 (Camp.) A
Caieta, 256 (Vols.) A
Καικῖνος fl., 11 (Br.) B
Calabra curia, p. 339 (Rome)
Calabri, -bria, 31 (Cal.) A
Καλασάρνα, 26 (Luc.) C
Calatia, 154 (Camp.) A
Cale uicus, 371 (Umb.) B
Καλήνη, 197 (Frent.) C
Cales, -lenus, 154 (Camp.) A
Caletranus ager, 351 (Etr.) A
Callicula mons, 154 (Camp.) C
Callifae, 187 (Sam.) C
Callipolis, 31 (Cal.) C
Callita, 241 (Pael.) C
Calor fl., 160 (Hirp.) A, 26 (Luc.) C
Calpurnianus uicus, 154 (Camp.) B
Calypsus, 11 (Br.) C
Camars (Clusium), 351 (Etr.) B
Camere, 11 (Br.) C, Addenda
Cameria, p. 335 (Lat.) A

Camerinum, -mertes, 371 (Umb.) A
Campania, 154 A
Campanus v. Capua, 154 A
Campus Martius, p. 340 (Rome)
Canales, 33 (Peuc.) C
Canales, ad, 187 (Sam.) C
Cannae, 33 (Peuc.) A
Cantorius, 310 (Sab.) C
Canusium, 33 (Peuc.) A
Capena, -enus lucus, -enates, 351 (Etr.) A
Capena, porta, p. 342 (Rome)
Capitolium, -linus, p. 340 (Rome)
Capitulum, 278 (Hern.) A
Caprae palus v. Caprea
Capraria, 351 (Etr.) A
Capraseae, 11 (Br.) C
Caprea palus, p. 340 (Rome)
Capreae, 154 (Camp.) A
Capriculanus pagus, 154 (Camp.) B
Capua, 154 (Camp.) A
Carcinus fl. Carcine urbs v. Καικῖνος
Καρακηνοί, -ρίκινοι, v. Carecina regio
Carecina regio, 187 (Sam.) A
Καρβῖνα, 31 (Cal.) C
Carcine, 351 (Etr.) B
Care(n)tini Supernates et Infernates, 197 (Frent.) C
Carinae, p. 342 (Rome)
Carmeianus ager v. Collatini, 33 (Peuc.) B
Carmentalis (Carmentis) porta, p. 339 (Rome)
Carsioli, 275 (Aeq.) A
Carsulae, 371 (Umb.) A
Caruentana arx, -ντος, p. 336 (Lat.) B
Casilinum, 154 (Camp.) A
Casinum, 256 (Vols.) A
Casperia, -eruli, 310 (Sab.) A
Castrum Inui, 256 (Vols.) B
Castrum Nouum, 351 (Etr.) A
Castrum Nouum, 374 (Pic.) A
Castri Moenium, p. 333 (Lat.) A
Casuentillani, 371 (Umb.) B
Casuentini, 371 (Umb.) B
Casuentum, 26 (Luc.) C
Καταράκτα? 35 (Dau.) C
Cati fons, p. 336 (Lat.) C
Catialis collis, p. 336 (Lat.) C
Catillinus pagus, 160 (Hirp.) B
Catilli mons, p. 336 (Lat.) B
Caudium, 160 (Hirp.) A
Caulinum (uinum), 154 (Camp.) C
Caulon prom., 11 (Br.) A
Celemna, -enna, 154 (Camp.) C
Centum Cellae, 351 (Etr.) A
Ceno, 256 (Vols.) C
Censennia v. Ces., 187 C
Cenus prom., 11 (Br.) B
Κεραυνιλία, 35 (Dau.) B
Cerbalus, 35 (Dau.) B
Cercatae, -atini, 256 (Vols.) A

Cerfennia, 270 (Mars.) A
Cerillae, 11 (Br.) A
Cerionia, p. 342 (Rome)
Κέρκωλοι? 270 (Mars.) C
Cermalus v. Germalus
Germalus uicus, 371 (Umb.) B
Ceroliensis, p. 342 (Rome)
Ceronicnsis, p. 342 (Rome)
Cesennia, 187 (Sam.) C
Cetanus pagus, 160 (Hirp.) B
Χανδάνη, 31 (Cal.) C
Χώνη, Χῶνες, 26 (Luc.) B
Ciceralis fundus, 26 (Luc.) B
Cimetra, 160 (Hirp.) C, 187 (Sam.) C
Ciminius L., Ciminia silua, 351 (Etr.) A
Cimmerium, 154 (Camp.) C
Cingilia, 250 (Vest.) C
Cingulani, 154 (Camp.) C
Cingulum, 374 (Pic.) A
Κίννα, 187 (Sam.) C
Circeius mons, -ceii, opp., 256 (Vols.) A
Κιρραιᾶται v. Cercatae, 256 A
Cisauna, 160 (Hirp.) B
Cispius mons, p. 341 (Rome)
Claimpetia, 11 (Br.) A
Clanis fl., 256 (Vols.) C
Clanis fl., 351 (Etr.) A
Clanis fl., 371 (Umb.) C
Clanius fl., 154 (Camp.) B
Clasia v. Clasis
Clasis fl., 371 (Umb.) C
Claudia, aqua, p. 334 (Lat.) A
Claudia, Praefectura, 351 (Etr.) A
Clibanus mons, 11 (Br.) C
Clitellae, p. 342 (Rome)
Cliternia, 275 (Aeq.) A
Cliternia, 35 (Dau.) C
Clitumnus fl., 371 (Umb.) A
Clocoris fl., 245 (Mruc.) C
Clodi forum, 351 (Etr.) A
Clostra Romae, 256 (Vols.) A
Cluana, 374 (Pic.) C
Cluentensis, uicus, 374 (Pic.) C
Cluilia fossa (Cloeliae), p. 336 (Lat.) B
Clusiolum, 371 (Umb.) C
Clusium, -inas, 351 (Etr.) A
Clustumina tribus, p. 335 (Lat.) A
Cluturnum, 187 (Sam.) C
Cluuiae, 187 (Sam.) A
Cocintus fl., 11 (Br.) B
Collatia, p. 334 (Lat.) A
Collatini, 33 (Peuc.) B
Collina porta, p. 340 (Rome)
Collina, regio, p. 340 (Rome)
Columbaria Veneria, 351 (Etr.) C
Columen? p. 337 (Lat.) C
Cominium, 256 (Vols.) B
Cominium Ocritum (Ceritum), 187 (Sam.) B
Commotiae, lymphae, 310 (Sab.) C
Compiti regio, 154 (Camp.) B

Compsa, 160 (Hirp.) A
Compulteria, 154 (Camp.) A
Concupienses v. Foroiulienses, 371 (Umb.) C
Conini, 275 (Aeq.) C
Consentia, 11 (Br.) A
Consilinum, 26 (Luc.) B
Consuletus riuos, 310 (Sab.) B
Contenebra, 351 (Etr.) C
Copiae, 11 (Br.) A
Cora, 256 (Vols.) A
Corbio, p. 333 (Lat.) A
Corfinium, 241 (Pael.) A
Corinenses, 160 (Hirp.) C
Corinium, 160 (Hirp.) C
Corioli, 256 (Vols.) A
Corne, p. 337 (Lat.) C
Corneta, p. 341 (Rome)
Cornetus Campus, 154 (Camp.) C
Corniculum, -lanus, p. 335 (Lat.) A
Κορσοῦλα, 310 (Sab.) C
Cortona, 351 (Etr.) A
Cortuosa, 351 (Etr.) C
Corythus v. Cortona
Cosa, Cosae, 351 (Etr.) A
Cosae v. Κόσσα, 11 (Br.) C
Κόσας fl., 256 (Vols.) B
Κόσσα, 11 (Br.) C
Κούκουλον, p. 335 (Lat.) B
Crabra, aqua, p. 334 (Lat.) A
Κραμόνες v. Carecina regio, 187 A and 187 C ad fin.
Κρανιτὰ ὄρη v. Carecina regio, 187 A
Crater (Sinus Cumanus), 154 (Camp.)
Crathis fl., 11 (Br.) A
Cremera fl., -ensis, 351 (Etr.) A
Κρίμισσα ἄκρα, 11 (Br.) C
Criniuolum, 371 (Umb.) C
Croto, 11 (Br.) A
Crustumerium, Crustumina tribus, p. 335 (Lat.) A
Crustumium, 371 (Umb.) B
Crustumius fl., 371 (Umb.) B
Cubulteria v. Comp-, (Camp.) A
Κυλιστάρνου γάνος fl., 11 (Br.) C
Cumae, 154 (Camp.) A
Cumerus mons, 371 (Umb.) C
Cunerus prom., 374 (Pic.) A
Cupra Maritima, 374 (Pic.) A
Cupra Montana, 374 (Pic.) A
Cures, 310 (Sab.) A
Curia Calabra, p. 339 (Rome)
Curtius fons, p. 334 (Lat.) A
Curtius lacus, p. 339 (Rome)
Cusuetani, p. 337 (Lat.) C
Κυτέριον, 11 (Br.) C
Cutiliae (Aquae), -iensis, 310 (Sab.) A
Cutina, 250 (Vest.) C
Cuttolonianus Fundus, 351 (Etr.) B
Cyprius vicus, p. 339 (Rome)

Dardi, 35 (Dau.) C
Dauni, -nii, -nia, 35 (Dau.) A, cf. 25 A; 154 (Camp.) C; s.v. Ardea, p. 332 (Lat.) A
Decastadium, 11 (Br.) C
Decennouium, 256 (Vols.) A
Deci Forum, 310 (Sab.) B
Deciani, 31 (Cal.) C
Dianensis uicus, 371 (Umb.) B
Dianensis uia, pagus Dianae Tifatinae, 154 (Camp.) B
Dianium, 351 (Etr.) B
Digentia, 310 (Sab.) A
Δικαιαρχία v. Puteoli
Dioscoron, 11 (Br.) C
Diria, 33 (Peuc.) B
Dolates, 371 (Umb.) C
Doliola, p. 339 (Rome)
Doliolum, 154 (Camp.) C
Δράκοντος ἱερόν, 26 (Luc.) C
Δρίον, 35 (Dau.) C
Duronia, 187 (Sam.) B

Ἥβα, 351 (Etr.) C
Eburum, 26 (Luc.) A
Ecetra, 256 (Vols.) A
Ἐχέτρα v. Ecetra
Egnatia (Ign-) v. Gnatia
Eleutiana, 154 (Camp.) C
Ἐλεύτιοι, 31 (Cal.) C
Ἕλη v. Heles, 26 B
Ἐλίσυκοι v. Volsci
Ἑλλέπορον, 11 (Br.) C
Empulum, p. 337 (Lat.) C
Ἐπειοί, p. 337 (Lat.) C
Epomeus mons, 154 (Camp.) C
Epopus v. Epomeus
Erauusa, 11 (Br.) C
Eretum, 310 (Sab.) A
Ergitium (Egr-), 35 (Dau.) C
Ἐριβάνιος, 154 (Camp.) C
Ἔριμον, 11 (Br.) C
Ἔρρουκα v. Verrugo
Esquiliae, -linus, p. 341 (Rome)
Ἐσῶπις, 11 (Br.) C
Etrusci, Etruria, Tusci, 351 (Sab.) A
Euploea insula, 154 (Camp.) B
Ezetium, 33 (Peuc.) C

Fabaris fl. v. Farfarus
*Fabienses v. Cabenses
Fabrateria, 256 (Vols.) A
Faesulae, 351 (Etr.) A
Fagifulae, 187 (Sam.) A
Fagutalis lucus, p. 341 (Rome)
Falacrinum, 310 (Sab.) A
Falerii, 351 (Etr.) A
Falernus ager etc., 154 (Camp.) A
Falerio, 374 (Pic.) A
Falesia, 351 (Etr.) B
Falinates, 371 (Umb.) C

Falisci, 351 (Etr.) A
Fanum (Fortunae), 371 (Umb.) A
Fanum Fugitiui, 371 (Umb.) C
Farfarus fl., 310 (Sab.) A
Fascianus, 160 (Hirp.) A
Fauentia, -tini, 371 (Umb.) A
Felctes mons, 371 (Umb.) C
Feliginates, 371 (Umb.) C
Fenectani campi, p. 336 (Lat.) C
Fenestella porta, p. 342 (Rome)
Fensernu v. (ad) Veserim, 143
Ferentina porta, p. 339 (Rome)
Ferentium, 351 (Etr.) A
Ferentinum, 187 (Sam.) C
Feretinum, 278 (Hern.) A
Feretrani v. Frentani
Feritrum, 187 (Sam.) A
Feroniae lucus, 351 (Etr.) A
Feroniae lucus, 256 (Vols.) A
Fertor fl., 35 (Dau.) C
Fesconnia, 351 (Etr.) A
Φῆστοι, p. 336 (Lat.) C
Fibrenus fl., 256 (Vols.) A
Ficana, p. 334 (Lat.) A
Ficolea, p. 335 (Lat.) A
Ficolenses, 187 (Sam.) C
Fidenae, p. 334 (Lat.) A
Fificulani, 250 (Vest.) B
Firmum, 374 (Pic.) A
Fiscellus mons, 310 (Sab.) A, 371 (Umb.) A
Fistelia, v. 184
Fisternae, 250 (Vest.) C
Flaminii, Forum, 371 (Umb.) C
Flauina, 351 (Etr.) B
Florentia, 351 (Etr.) A
Flosis fl., 374 (Pic.) C
Flosor, 374 (Pic.) C
Flumentana porta, p. 339 (Rome)
Flusor fl., 374 (Pic.) C
Foederna, 160 (Hirp.) B
*Folianenses, 187 (Sam.) A
Fontinalis porta, p. 341 (Rome)
Forensis pagus, 26 (Luc.) B
For(ensis?) vicus, 371 (Umb.) B
Forentum, 33 (Peuc.) A
Foretii, p. 337 (Lat.) C
Formiae, 256 (Vols.) A
Forobrentani, 371 (Umb.) A
Foroclodienses v. Claudia
Foroiulienses, 371 (Umb.) C
Foropopillienses, 154 (Camp.) A
Foruli, 250 (Vest.) A
Forum Appii, 256 (Vols.) A
Forum Aurelii, 351 (Etr.) A
Forum Cassi, 351 (Etr.) B
Forum Clodi, 351 (Etr.) A
Forum Deci, 310 (Sab.) B
Forum Flaminii, 371 (Umb.) C
Forum Nouum, 160 (Hirp.) C
Forum Nouum, 310 (Sab.) B

Forum Popillii, 154 (Camp.) A
Forum Sempronii, 371 (Umb.) A
Fossa Cluilia, p. 336 (Lat.) B
Fossae Papirianae, 351 (Etr.) C
Fratuentini, 31 (Cal.) B
Fregellae, 256 (Vols.) A
Fregenae, 351 (Etr.) A
Freginates, 154 (Camp.) C
Frentani, 197 A
Frento fl. v. Fertor, 35 (Dau.) C
Frentrum, 197 (Frent.) A
Fresilia, 270 (Mars.) C
Frusino, 256 (Vols.) A
Frusteuiae, 250 (Vest.) C
*Fstaniensis uecus, 270 (Mars.) C
Fucens, Alba, 275 (Aeq.) B
Fucinus lacus, 270 (Mars.) A
Fugifulae, 26 (Luc.) C
Fugitiui Fanum, 371 (Umb.) C
Fulginia, 371 (Umb.) A
Fundi, 256 (Vols.) A
Furfane, 33 (Peuc.) C
Furfo, 250 (Vest.) A

Gabii, p. 334 (Lat.) A
Gabii, aqua Gabia, 310 (Sab.) B
Galaesus fl., 31 (Cal.) A
Gallinaria silua, 154 (Camp.) A
ad Gallinas, 351 (Etr.) A
Garganus mons, 35 (Dau.) A
Garnae portus, 35 (Dau.) C
Gaurus mons, 154 (Camp.) A
Gemoniae, scalae, p. 340 (Rome)
Genusia, 33 (Peuc.) B
Germalus, p. 338 (Rome)
Geronium, -reonium, 35 (Dau.) B
Glanica, 258 (Aur.) C
Glanis v. Clanis, 256 (Vols.) C
Gnatia, 33 (Peuc.) A
Gorgon v. Urgo
In Grani monte, 275 (Aeq.) C
Graviscae, 351 (Etr.) A
Graxa, 31 (Cal.) C
Grumbestini, 31 (Cal.) C
Grumentum, 26 (Luc.) A
Grumum?, 31 (Cal.) C footn.

Hadria, 374 (Pic.) A
Halaesus v. Falisci
Halex fl., 11 (Br.) A
Hamae, 154 (Camp.) B
Helerni lucus, p. 336 (Lat.) B
Heles fl., 26 (Luc.) B
Heluillum, 371 (Umb.) A
Heluina (Ceres), 256 (Vols.) B
Heluinum fl.? 374 (Pic.) C
'Ημιλάμιον, 31 (Cal.) C
Heraclea, 26 (Luc.) A
Ἡρακλεῖον prom., 11 (Br.) B. See also Herculaneum, 154 A
Herbanum, 351 (Etr.) C

Herculaneum, 154 (Camp.) A
Herculaneum, 187 (Sam.) C
Herculaneus pagus Beneuenti, 160 (Hirp.) A
Herculaneus pagus Capuae, 154 (Camp.) B
Herculeae salinae, 154 (Camp.) B
ad Herculem, 351 (Etr.) C
Herculia uia, 160 (Hirp.) A
Herculis petra, 154 (Camp.) B
Herculis portus, 11 (Br.) A
Herculis portus, 351 (Etr.) B
Herdonia, -ea, 35 (Dau.) A
Herianicus fundus, 197 (Frent.) B
Hernici, 278 A
Ἱερὸς λόφος, 35 (Dau.) C
Himella fl., 275 (Aeq.) A
Ἱππώνιον v. Vibo, 11 A
Hipporum, 11 (Br.) C
Hirpi, -ini, 351 (Etr.) C
Hirpini, 160 A, cf. 186 A
Hispellum, 371 (Umb.) A
Histonium, 197 (Frent.) A
Honoratianum, 160 (Hirp.) C
Hormiae, 256 (Vols.) A
Horta or Hortae, 351 (Etr.) A
Hortanum, 351 (Etr.) A
Hortenses, p. 337 (Lat.) C
Horticulanus, 160 (Hirp.) B
Hortona v. Orto-, 197 A
Ὑέλη η. Velia, 26 A
Ὑλίας fl., 11 (Br.) B
Ὕπωρον?, 11 (Br.) C
Ὑρία v. Uria
Ὕριον v. Hyria
Hydrentini, 154 (Camp.) C
Hydruntum, -tinus, 31 (Cal.) A
Hyria, 35 (Dau.) A
*Hyria, 154 (Camp.) B

Ianicolum, p. 340 (Rome)
Ianualis, porta, p. 339 (Rome)
Iapyges, -gia, -gium, 31 (Cal.) A
Igilium insula, 351 (Etr.) A
Iguvium, -vini, 371 (Umb.) A
Ilionenses, p. 336 (Lat.) C
Ilua (Aethalia), 351 (Etr.) A
Imbrinium, 187 (Sam.) C
Imeus mons, 270 (Mars.) C
Inarime v. Pithecussae
Inregillensis v. Regillum
Insteius uicus, p. 342 (Rome)
Instelanus uicus, p. 342 (Rome)
Interamna Nahartium, 371 (Umb.) A
Interamna (Lirenas), 256 (Vols.) A
Interamnia, 374 (Pic.) A
Intercisa, 371 (Umb.) A
Interocrium, 310 (Sab.) A
Interpromium, -promum, 241 (Pael.) A
ad Ioglandem, 351 (Etr.) C
Irini, 160 (Hirp.) C

Isacia, 154 (Camp.) C
Isaurus fl., 371 (Umb.) B
Isia or Ixias, 11 (Br.) C
Issa, 310 (Sab.) C
Italia, 11 (Br.) A
Italicus v. Italia
Italus v. Italia
Ithacesiae insulae, 11 (Br.) A
Iugarius uicus, p. 339 (Rome)
Inturna fons, p. 332 (Lat.) A
Iuturnae fons, p. 339 (Rome)
Iuuanum, -nenses, 197 (Frent.) A
Ἰξίας or Isia, 11 (Br.) C

Λαβανὰ ὕδατα, p. 337 (Lat.) C
Labici, p. 334 (Lat.) A
Labronis portus, 351 (Etr.) B
Lacinium prom., 11 (Br.) A
Lactarius mons, 154 (Camp.) B
Lagaria, 11 (Br.) B
Λαιστρύγονες v. sub Formiae
Λάμης fl., 11 (Br.) B
ad Lamnas, 275 (Aeq.) C
Lanita pagus, 154 (Camp.) B
Lanuuium, p. 332 (Lat.) A
Λᾶος fl. v. Laus, 26 (Luc.) A
Larinum, 197 (Frent.) A, cf. 35 (Dau.) A
Lartidiauus uicus, 154 (Camp.) B
Λατέρνιοι, 187 C ad fin.
Latiaris collis, p. 340 (Rome)
Latinienses, p. 332 (Lat.) A
Latium, p. 332 (Lat.) A
Λάτυμνον ὄρος, 11 (Br.) C
Lauernae, 241 (Pael.) A
Lauernalis porta, p. 338 (Rome)
Lauinium, -inas, p. 332 (Lat.) A
Lauinium, 26 (Luc.) C
Laurentes, -entum, p. 332 (Lat.) A
Laurinienses, 154 (Camp.) B
Laurolauinium, p. 332 (Lat.) A
Laus fl. et opp., 26 (Luc.) A
Lautolae, p. 339 (Rome)
Lautulae, 256 (Vols.) B
Lautulus, locus, p. 340 (Rome)
Lautumiae, p. 340 (Rome)
Leboriae, 154 (Camp.) B, v. also Phlegraei Campi
Leburini campi v. Leboriae
Lemonia, tribus, p. 342 (Rome)
Lepinus mons, p. 335 (Lat.) B
Leuca, 31 (Cal.) A
Λευκανοί, 26 (Luc.) A
Leucopetra, 11 (Br.) A
Leucosia (Leucothea?), 26 (Luc.) A
Λευτερνία παραλία, 31 (Cal.) B
Libicanus pagus, 160 (Hirp.) B
Libitinus pagus, 160 (Hirp.) B
Λίβυρνον ὄρος, 160 (Hirp.) C
Ligures Baebiani, 160 (Hirp.) A
Lincerius } ager? v. Lucerius
Lintirius }

Lirenas Sucasina v. Interamna, 256 (Vols.) A
Liris fl., 270 (Mars.) A, 256 (Vols.) A
Λίστα, 275 (Aeq.) C
Literius ager? v. Lucerius
Liternum, 154 (Camp.) A
Liternus fl., 154 (Camp.) A
Locri Epizephyrii v. Zephyrium
Lollianus fundus, 26 (Luc.) C
Longula, 256 (Vols.) A
Loretanus portus (Laur-), 351 (Etr.) C
Lorium (Laurium), 351 (Etr.) B
Luca, 351 (Etr.) A
*Luca or *Lucanum, p. 310
Lucani, 26 (Luc.) A
Lucanus, 256 (Vols.) B
Luccoli, 371 (Umb.) C
Luceres, -re(n)ses, p. 342 (Rome)
Luceria, 35 (Dau.) A
Lucerius ager?, p. 337 (Lat.) C
Lucoferonenses v. Feroniae lucus
Lucretilis mons, 310 (Sab.) A
Lucrinus lacus, 154 (Camp.) A
Lucus, -a, -um, 26 (Luc.) A
Lucus Angitiae, 270 (Mars.) A
Luna, 351 (Etr.) A
Lupatia, 33 (Penc.) C
Lupercal, p. 338 (Rome)
Lupiae, Lupp-, 31 (Cal.) A
Lusianus pagus, 160 (Hirp.) B
Lutirius ager? v. Lucerius
Lymphaeum, 11 (Br.) C

Maccriatus fundus, 26 (Luc.) B
Macra fl., 351 (Etr.) A
Macrales, p. 337 (Lat.) C
Maccium, -ia tribus, p. 332 (Lat.) A
Maesia silua, p. 336 (Lat.) B
Μαλάνιος, 11 (Br.) C
Maleuentum, 160 (Hirp.) A
Malitiosa silua, 310 (Sab.) B
ad Mallias, 11 (Br.) C
Mamertini, 154 (Camp.) A
Μαμέρτιον, 11 (Br.) C
Mamilia turris, p. 342 (Rome)
Manalis lapis, p. 339 (Rome)
Manates, p. 337 (Lat.) C
Mandela, 310 (Sab.) A
Manduria, 31 (Cal.) A
Manliana (castra?), 351 (Etr.) B
Μαρκίνα, 154 (Camp.) C
Marica, Maricae palus, 258 (Aur.) A
Maritimus circus, 278 (Hern.) B
Marmoreae, 160 (Hirp.) C
Marrucini, 245 A
Marruuium, 270 (Mars.) A
Mars Ficanus, p. 334 (Lat.) A
Marsi, 270 A
Marta, 351 (Etr.) C
Martialis pagus, 160 (Hirp.) A
Martius, campus, p. 340 (Rome)

Martis, uicus, Tudertium, 371 (Umb.) A
Massa Veternensis, 351 (Etr.) C
Massicus mons, 258 (Aur.) A
Mateolani, 35 (Dau.) C
Materina, 371 (Umb.) C
Maternum, 351 (Etr.) C
Ματιήνη, 275 (Aeq.) C
Matilica, -ates, 371 (Umb.) A
Matinus, 35 (Dau.) A
ad Matrem Magnam, 160 (Hirp.) C
Matrini uicus, 351 (Etr.) C
Matrinus fl., 374 (Pic.) A
Medama v. Medma
Medma, 11 (Br.) A
Medullia, p. 335 (Lat.) A
Mefanus pagus, 160 (Hirp.) A
Mefitis, lucus, p. 342 (Rome)
Meflanus pagus, 160 (Hirp.) A
Megaris insula, 154 (Camp.) C
Melae, 160 (Hirp.) C
Melfel v. Melfis, 256 C
Melfis, 256 (Vols.) C
Meloessa, 11 (Br.) C
Melpes fl., 26 (Luc.) C
Μέλπις v. Melfis, 256 C
Menaria, 351 (Etr.) C
Μενεκίνη, 11 (Br.) C
Mensulae, 351 (Etr.) C
Μέντη fons v. Neminiae
Menturnae v. Mint-
Μηφύλα, 310 (Sab.) C
Merinates, 35 (Dau.) B
Mesma v. Medma, 11 (Br.) A
Messapii, -ia, 31 (Cal.) A
Μέταβον v. Metapontum, 26 (Luc.) A
Metapontum, 26 (Luc.) A
Metaurus fl., 11 (Br.) C
Metaurus, Mat-, fl., 371 (Umb.) A
Meuania, 371 (Umb.) A
Meuaniola, 371 (Umb.) B
Milionia, 270 (Mars.) B
Miltopes statio, 31 (Cal.) C
Mineruae Castra, 31 (Cal.) A
Mineruae promontorium, 154 (Camp.) A
Minio fl., 351 (Etr.) A
Minturnae, 258 (Aur.) A
Minutia, porta, p. 338 (Rome)
Miscus fl., 374 (Pic.) C
Misenum, 154 (Camp.) A
Misius fl., 374 (Pic.) C
Misus fl., 371 (Umb.) C
Moera, 154 (Camp.) C
Monades, 35 (Dau.) C
Μοντεφερέτρον, 371 (Umb.) C
Morgetes, 26 (Luc.) B
Mucia prata, 351 (Etr.) B
Mucialis collis, p. 340 (Rome)
Muerae (Nuerno), 187 (Sam.) C
Mugionis, porta, p. 339 (Rome)
Mulfe v. Melfis
Muluius, pons, p. 334 (Lat.) A

LOCAL NAMES OF ANCIENT ITALY. 543

Mundus, p. 339 (Rome)
Munienses, p. 337 (Lat.) C
Muranum, 11 (Br.) A
Murcia uallis (Murtea), p. 338 (Rome)
Murcus, p. 338 (Rome)
Murgantia, 187 (Sam.) C
Murgentia, 26 (Luc.) B
Mustiae, 11 (Br.) B
Mutela mons, 310 (Sab.) C
Mutuesci, -tusci, v. Trebulani

Nacuia silua, p. 332 (Lat.) A
Ναπητῖνος κόλπος v. Λάμης
Nar fl., 371 (Umb.) A
Naranus pagus, 26 (Luc.) B
Nares Lucanae, 26 (Luc.) B
Narnia, 371 (Umb.) A
Nasennianus pagus, 160 (Hirp.) B
Natiolum ?, 33 (Peuc.) C
Nauna, 31 (Cal.) B
Νήαιθος fl., 11 (Br.) A
Neapolis, 154 (Camp.) A
Neapolis, 33 (Peuc.) B
Nelurum ?, 371 (Umb.) C
Neminiae fons, 310 (Sab.) C
Nemus Dianae, p. 338 (Lat.) A
Nepete, 351 (Etr.) A
Nequinum, 371 (Umb.) A
Neretum, 31 (Cal.) A
Nersae } 275 (Aeq.) B
Neruesiae }
Nerulum, 11 (Br.) B
Nesis insula, 154 (Camp.) A
Νήτιον v. Ἀζετινοι, 33 (Peuc.) C
Nicotera, 11 (Br.) C
Νίναια, 11 (Br.) C
[ad] Noceios, 245 (Mruc.) C
Nodinus fl., p. 336 (Lat.) B
Nola, 154 (Camp.) A, cf. Osc. Núrla-
Nomentum, p. 335 (Lat.) A
Norba, 33 (Peuc.) B
Norba, 256 (Vols.) A
Nouana, 374 (Pic.) C
Nouanensis uicus, 154 (Camp.) B
Nouanus fl., 371 (Umb.) C
Nuceria, 154 (Camp.) A
Nuceria, 371 (Umb.) A
Nucrae v. Mucrae, 187 (Sam.) C
Nucriola, -cerulae, 160 (Hirp.) C
Numana, 374 (Pic.) A
Numicus (also -icius) fl., p. 332 (Lat.) A
Numinienses, p. 337 (Lat.) C
Numistro, 26 (Luc.) A
Nurcia, 310 (Sab.) A
Nymphaeus fl., 256 (Vols.) B

Ὀάδμων v. Vadimo
Ocriculum, 11 (Br.) C
Ocriculum, -ani, 371 (Umb.) A
Octulani, p. 337 (Lat.) C
Oenotria, -tri, 11 (Br.) A, 26 (Luc.) A

Oenotrides, 256 (Vols.) A
Oglasa, or -osa, 351 (Etr.) C
Olliculani, p. 337 (Lat.) C
Ὀλσοί v. Volsci, 256 A
Opici, 187 (Sam.) C ad fin. and 153 A
Opino (ad Pinum ?), 33 (Peuc.) C
Oppius mons, p. 341 (Rome)
Orbitanium, 160 (Hirp.) C, cf. 26 (Luc.) C
Orbius cliuus, p. 341 (Rome)
Orestis portus, 11 (Br.) C
Ὀρουίνιον, 310 (Sab.) C
Orta, Horta, 351 (Etr.) A
Ortona, Hort-, 197 (Frent.) A
Ortona, p. 335 (Lat.) B
Osci, 153 A
Oscus locus, 351 (Etr.) C
Ostia, p. 333 (Lat.) A
Ostra, 371 (Umb.) A
Οὐέρητον v. Veretum, 31 B
Οὐερτῖναι, 26 (Luc.) C
Οὐέσβολα, 310 (Sab.) C
Oufentina tribus v. Ufens, 256 A
Οὐιβάρνα v. Vibinum, 35 B
Ouile, p. 340 (Rome)
Οὔξεντον v. Uzentum, 31 A
Οὐολοῦσκοι, Οὐόλσκοι v. Volsci, 256 A
Ὄρειον v. Hyria, 35 A
Οὐρία v. Uria, 31 A

Pactius fl., 33 (Peuc.) C
Paeligni, Pel-, 241 A
Paesinates, 371 (Umb.) C
Paestum, 26 (Luc.) A
Palaeopolis v. Palaepolis, 154 A
Palaepolis, 154 (Camp.) A
Palatina regio, 154 (Camp.) B
Palatium, p. 338 (Rome)
Palinurus, 26 (Luc.) A
Paliouenses, 31 (Cal.) C
Pallanteum, p. 338 (Rome)
Pallanum, 197 (Frent.) B
Pallia fl., 351 (Etr.) C
Palmaria insula, 256 (Vols.) A
Palmensis ager, 374 (Pic.) B
Paludes Pomptinae, 256 (Vols.) A
Palumbinum, 187 (Sam.) C
Pandana porta, p. 340 (Rome)
Pandateria, -aria, insula, 154 (Camp.) A
Pandosia, 11 (Br.) A
Pandosia, 26 (Luc.) C
Pandotira v. Pandateria, 154 A
Πάννα, 187 (Sam.) C
Pantanus lacus, 35 (Dau.) C
Papirianae fossae, 351 (Etr.) C
Παρεούσιος fl., p. 337 (Lat.) C
Parthenope, 154 (Camp.) A
Passeris, -rianae, aquae, 351 (Etr.) A
Paternum, 11 (Br.) C
Pausilypus, 154 (Camp.) A
Pausulae, 374 (Pic.) A

Pecolus fl.?, 11 (Br.) C
Pectuscum Palati, p. 339 (Rome)
Pedum, -anus, p. 333 (Lat.) A
Peligni v. Pael-
Peltuinum, 250 (Vest.) A
Penna v. Pinna, 250 A
Pentri, 187 (Sam.) A
Percennianus fundus, 26 (Luc.) C
Perusia, 351 (Etr.) A
Petelia, 11 (Br.) A
Petelinus lucus, p. 340 (Rome)
Petra v. Leucopetra, 11 (Br.) A
Petra Pertusa, 371 (Umb.) A
Petrinum, 258 (Aur.) A
Petronia, aqua, p. 336 (Lat.) C
Poucetii, -etia, 33 (Peuc.) A, cf. 187 C
  ad fin.
Φάλαι, 31 (Cal.) C
Φαλήρου τύρσις, 154 (Camp.) C
Pharos v. Barra
Φερέντη v. Frentani
Φῆστοι, p. 336 (Lat.) C
Phlegraei campi, 154 (Camp.) A
Φοιβία, 11 (Br.) C
Φρέντανον v. Frentani
Piacularis, porta, p. 339 (Rome)
Picanus mons, 374 (Pic.) C
Picentia, 154 (Camp.) A
Picenum, 374 (Pic.) A
Πίκται πανδοχεῖα, 275 (Aeq.) C
Pinna, 250 (Vest.) A
ad Pinum v. Opino
Pirae, p. 337 (Lat.) C
ad Pirum, 371 (Umb.) C
Pisae, 351 (Etr.) A
Pisandes, 160 (Hirp.) C
Pisaurum, 371 (Umb.) A
Pisaurus fl., 371 (Umb.) A
Pistoriae, 351 (Etr.) A
Pithecussae insulae, 154 (Camp.) A
Pitinum, 310 (Sab.) C
Pitinum Mergens, 371 (Umb.) A
Pitinum Pisaurense, 371 (Umb.) A
Pitulani, 371 (Umb.) A
Planasia insula, 351 (Etr.) A
Plangenses, 371 (Umb.) C
Planina, 374 (Pic.) A
Plestina, 270 (Mars.) C
Plestini, 371 (Umb.) A
Plistia, 160 (Hirp.) B
Ποδαλειρίου ἡρῷον, 35 (Dau.) C
Poediculi v. Peucetii, 33 A
Poetelius lucus v. Petelinus, p. 341
  (Rome)
Πολίειον = Siris, 26 (Luc.) C
Polimartium, 351 (Etr.) C
Politorium, p. 334 (Lat.) A
Pollentia, 374 (Pic.) A
Πολλίτιον, 245 (Mruc.) C
Pol(l)usca, p. 334 (Lat.) A
Pomerium, p. 338 (Rome)

Pomonal, p. 337 (Lat.) C
Pompeii, 154 (Camp.) A
Pomptinae paludes, 256 (Vols.) A
Pontiae insulae, 256 (Vols.) A
Pontinae v. Pomptinae
Popillii forum, 154 (Camp.) A
Populonium, 351 (Etr.) A
Portunium, p. 342 (Rome)
Ποσειδωνία v. Paestum, 26 A
Potentia, 26 (Luc.) A
Potentia, 374 (Pic.) A
Ποτίολοι v. Puteoli
Praeneste, p. 333 (Lat.) A
Praetuttii, 374 (Pic.) A
Prelius or Pri-, fl. v. Prille
Prifernum, 250 (Vest.) C
Prille fl., Prelius, Aprilis, 351 (Etr.) B
Priuernum, 256 (Vols.) A
Prochyta, 154 (Camp.) A
Profianus fundus, 160 (Hirp.) B
Prolaqueum, 371 (Umb.) B
Protropi, 160 (Hirp.) A
Publicius cliuos, p. 338 (Rome)
Puilia saxa, p. 336 (Lat.) C
Punicum, 351 (Etr.) C
Πυξοῦς v. Buxentum, 26 (Luc.) A
Pupinius ager, -ia tribus, p. 334 (Lat.) A
Πυριφλεγέθων fl., 154 (Camp.) C
Puteoli, 154 (Camp.) A
Pyrgi, -gensis, 351 (Etr.) A
ad Pyrum, 187 (Sam.) C

Q[u]aesicianus fundus, 26 (Luc.) C
Quercus sacrata, 275 (Aeq.) B
Querquetulana porta, p. 341 (Rome)
Querquetulani, p. 336 (Lat.) B
Quinctia, prata, p. 340 (Rome)
Quirina tribus, p. 340 (Rome)
Quirinalis collis, p. 340 (Rome)

Ramnes, -nenses, p. 342 (Rome)
'Ρασέν(ν)α v. sub Etrusci
Ratumenna porta, p. 341 (Rome)
Raudusculana porta, p. 338 (Rome)
Rauenna, 371 (Umb.) A
Reate, 310 (Sab.) A
Regia columna, 11 (Br.) A
Regillum, 310 (Sab.) B
Regillus lacus, p. 335 (Lat.) B
Regis uilla, 351 (Etr.) C
Regium, 11 (Br.) A, cf. 186 D
Remona, p. 338 (Rome)
Remuria, p. 338 (Rome)
Respa, 35 (Dau.) C
*Retrices, p. 336 (Lat.) B
Ricina, 374 (Pic.) A
'Ριγνάριον v. Remuria
Roboraria, p. 337 (Lat.) C
Roma, p. 333 (Lat.) A
Roma Quadrata, p. 339 (Rome)
Romanula, porta, p. 339 (Rome)

Romechium, 11 (Br.) C
Ῥῶμος, v. Remuria
Romula Mephitis, 160 (Hirp.) B
Romulea v. Romula, 160 B
Roscianum v. ʽΡουσκία
Rosea, 310 (Sab.) A
Rosulanus v. Rosea
ad Rotas, 154 (Camp.) C
ʽΡουσκία, 11 (Br.) C
Rubi, 33 (Peuc.) A
Rubico fl., 371 (Umb.) A
Rubrae v. Saxa Rubra, 351 (Etr.) A
Rudiae, 31 (Cal.) A
Rufrae, 154 (Camp.) A
Rufri Maceria, 154 (Camp.) C
Rufrium v. Rufrae
Ruminalis ficus, p. 338 (Rome)
Rumon = Tiberis, p. 338 (Rome)
Rusellae, 351 (Etr.) A
Rustunum, 371 (Umb.) C
Rutuli, p. 332 (Lat.) A

Sabata, -batia, 351 (Etr.) A
Sabatini, 154 (Camp.) C
Sabatus fl., 11 (Br.) C
Sabatus fl., -atini, 160 (Hirp.) B
Sabelli, -us, 310 (Sab.) A
Sabini, 310 A, cf. 187 (Sam.) A
Saccumum, 351 (Etr.) C
Sacra uia, p. 339 (Rome)
Sacrani, p. 335 (Lat.) A
Sacrata, 374 (Pic.) C
Sacriportus, p. 333 (Lat.) A
Saeculanus, 160 (Hirp.) B
Saena, 351 (Etr.) A
Saepinum, 187 (Sam.) A
Sagra fl., 11 (Br.) A
Σάγρος fl., 187 (Sam.) B, 197 (Frent.) B
Salapia, 35 (Dau.) A
Salaria, uia 310 (Sab.) A
Salernum, 154 (Camp.) A
Salinae, 35 (Dau.) C
Sallentini (Salent-), 31 (Cal.) A
Sallentini v. Dolates
Salpinates, 351 (Etr.) C
Salutaris, pagus 160 (Hirp.) A
Samnium, -nites, 187 (Sam.) A
Sanqualis porta, p. 341 (Rome)
Sapis fl., 371 (Umb.) A
Sappinates?, 371 (Umb.) C
ad Sapriportem, 31 (Cal.) C
Sarnus fl., 154 (Camp.) A
Sarranates, 371 (Umb.) C
Sarrastes v. Sarnus, 154 (Camp.) A
Sarsina, Sassina, 371 (Umb.) A
Sasina, -ea? portus, 31 (Cal.) C
Sassula, p. 336 (Lat.) C
Saticula, 160 (Hirp.) A
Satricum, 256 (Vols.) A
Saturae palus = Pomptinae paludes, 256 (Vols.) A

Saturium, 31 (Cal.) A
Saturnia, 351 (Etr.) A
Saturnia v. Roma, p. 333 (Lat.) A
Saturnius mons, p. 340 (Rome)
Sauo fl., 154 (Camp.) A
Saxa Rubra (Rubrae), 351 (Etr.) A
Scantia silua, -ianus, -iae aquae, 154 (Camp.) A
Scaptia, p. 333 (Lat.) A
Scatebra fl., 256 (Vols.) C
Sceleratus, campus, p. 340 (Rome)
Σκίδρος, 11 (Br.) A
Scolacium, 11 (Br.) A
Scylaceum, 11 (Br.) A
Scyllaeum, 11 (Br.) A
Σκυλλήτιον v. Scolacium
Sebethus fl., 154 (Camp.) A
Semelae lucus v. Stimulae lucus
Semirus fl., 11 (Br.) C
ad Semnum, 26 (Luc.) C
Sempronii forum, 371 (Umb.) A
Semuncla, 26 (Luc.) C
Semurius ager, p. 334 (Lat.) A
Sena fl., 371 (Umb.) A
Sena Gallica, 371 (Umb.) A
Senna, v. Sena fl.
Sentianum, 35 (Dau.) C
Sentinum, 371 (Umb.) A
Senuisanus v. Sinuessa, 258 A
Senum, 31 (Cal.) C
Seplasia, 154 (Camp.) A
Septem Aquae (Septaq-), 310 (Sab.) A
Septempeda, 374 (Pic.) A
Septimontium, p. 342 (Rome)
Σερεννια v. Cesennia
Serra = Tiberis, p. 340 (Rome)
Serranus fundus, 351 (Etr.) B
Serranus lacus, 197 (Frent.) B
Ser(uitium?), 11 (Br.) C
Sestinum, 371 (Umb.) A
Setia, 256 (Vols.) A
Seuerus mons, 310 (Sab.) B
Sicani, p. 332 (Lat.) A
Σικελία, p. 335 (Lat.) B
Sicilinum, 160 (Hirp.) C
Siculi, p. 332 (Lat.) A
Σιδινοι, 35 (Dau.) C
Σιγλιουρία?, p. 337 (Lat.) C
Signia, 256 (Vols.) A
Sila, 11 (Br.) A
Silarus fl., 154 (Camp.) A
Siler v. Silarus
Siluium, 33 (Peuc.) A
Simbruini colles, 275 (Aeq.) B
Similae lucus v. Stimulae lucus
Sinonia insula, 256 (Vols.) B
Sinope, 258 (Aur.) B
Sinuessa, 258 (Aur.) A
Sipontum, 35 (Dau.) A
Sirenes (Sirenusae insulae), 154 (Camp.) A

Siris fl., 26 (Luc.) A
Sirpium, 187 (Sam.) C
Sisolenses, p. 337 (Lat.) C
ad Solaria, 351 (Etr.) C
Soletum desertum, 31 (Cal.) C
Solinates, 371 (Umb.) C
Solonates, 371 (Umb.) B
Solonius ager, p. 333 (Lat.) A
Sontini, 26 (Luc.) C
Sora, 256 (Vols.) A
Soracte mons, 351 (Etr.) A
Sorrinenses novensides, 351 (Etr.) A
Σούνη, 310 (Sab.) C
Speluncae, 31 (Cal.) C
Σπίνης? fl., 31 (Cal.) C
Spino, -onis fl., p. 336 (Lat.) B
Spoletium, -etinus, 371 (Umb.) A
ad Sponsas, 256 (Vols.) C
Spurianus uicus, 154 (Camp.) B
Stabiae, 154 (Camp.) A
Stafia- v. Stabiae, 154 (Camp.) A
Statanum, 256 (Vols.) A
Statinae, 154 (Camp.) C
Statonia, 351 (Etr.) A
Statuleianus fundus, 26 (Luc.) C
Stellas ager, 154 (Camp.) A
Stellatinus campus, 351 (Etr.) B
Stephane, p. 336 (Lat.) C
Stimulae lucus, p. 338 (Rome)
Στομάλιμνον, 11 (Br.) C
Στοῦρνοι, στυ- v. Stulnini
Strapellini, 160 (Hirp.) C
Streniae sacellum, p. 339 (Rome)
Stulnini, 31 (Cal.) C
Sturna v. Astura
Suana, 351 (Etr.) A
Suasa, -ani, 371 (Umb.) A
Subertum, 351 (Etr.) B
Sublaqueum, p. 333 (Lat.) A
Sublicius pons, p. 338 (Rome), cf. p. 270
Subsecinum, 11 (Br.) C
Suburra, -ura, p. 341 (Rome)
Suburrana regio, p. 341 (Rome)
Succeianum, 11 (Br.) C
Sucinium v. Saccumum
Sucusanus uicus, p. 341 (Rome)
Sudernum, 351 (Etr.) B
Suellianus, 160 (Hirp.) B
Συεσβόλα?, 310 (Sab.) C
Suessa (Aurunca), 258 (Aur.) A
Suessa Pome(n)tia, 256 (Vols.) A
Suessula, 154 (Camp.) A
Suffenates v. Trebulani
Suillates, 371 (Umb.) C
Sulmo, 241 (Pael.) A
Sulmo, p. 336 (Lat.) C
Superaequum, 241 (Pael.) A
Supinas uccus, 270 (Mars.) A
Suriates, 371 (Umb.) C
Surrentum, 154 (Camp.) A
Sutrium, -ria, 351 (Etr.) A

Sybaris, 11 (Br.) A
Syllae, 160 (Hirp.) C

Taburnus mons, 160 (Hirp.) A
Tacina fl., 11 (Br.) C
Tadiates, 275 (Aeq.) C
Tadinum, 371 (Umb.) A
Τάλιον, 35 (Dau.) C
Tanager fl., 26 (Luc.) B
ad Tanarum or Tam-, 160 (Hirp.) C
Τάρας v. Tarentum, 31 (Cal.) A
Tarentum, 31 (Cal.) A
Tarinates, 310 (Sab.) C
Tarineris mons, 243 (Mruc.)
Tarpeius mons, p. 340 (Rome)
Tarquinii, 351 (Etr.) A
Tarracina, 256 (Vols.) A
Tatinic, 35 (Dau.) C
Taurania, 154 (Camp.) C
Taurasia, 160 (Hirp.) A
Tauriana, 11 (Br.) A
Tauroentum, 11 (Br.) C
Taurubulae insula, 154 (Camp.) C
Teanum (Appulum), 35 (Dau.) A
Teanum Sidicinum, 154 (Camp.) A
Teate, 35 (Dau.) C
Teate, 245 (Mruc.) A
Teba v. Sab. Gloss., 309 A
Tebanus pagus, 160 (Hirp.) B
Tegianum, 26 (Luc.) A
Telamon, 351 (Etr.) A
Telesia, 187 (Sam.) A
Tellenae, p. 333 (Lat.) A
Temenis or -itis porta Tarenti, 31 (Cal.) B
Tempsa, 11 (Br.) A
Tepula aqua, p. 340 (Rome)
Teredis fl.?=Tiberis v. Tercutum
Tere(n)tina tribus, p. 340 (Rome)
Terentum = Tiberis, p. 340 (Rome)
Tergilani? v. Tegianum
Terina, 11 (Br.) A
Terracina v. Tarr-
Teruentum, 187 (Sam.) A
Tessinnum fl., 374 (Pic.) C
Τεστροῦνα, 250 (Vest.) C
Tetrica mons, 310 (Sab.) A
Teuranus ager, 11 (Br.) B
Teutanes, 351 (Etr.) C
Thania Sudernia, 351 (Etr.) B
Thebae, 26 (Luc.) B
Thermensium regio, 154 (Camp.) B
Theseunti?, 11 (Br.) C
Thurii, 11 (Br.) A
Tiberis, -erinus, p. 332 (Lat.) A
Tibur, p. 333 (Lat.) A
Tifata, 154 (Camp.) A, cf. p. 221
Tifata, p. 336 (Lat.) C
Tifatinae Dianae pagus, 154 (Camp.) B
Tifernum Mataurense, 371 (Umb.) A
Tifernum Tiberinum, 371 (Umb.) A

Tifernus, -um fl., 187 (Sam.) A, 197 (Frent.) A
Tinia fl., 371 (Umb.) A
Tinna fl., 374 (Pic.) C
Tiretius pons, 258 (Aur.) C
Tirinus fl., 250 (Vest.) A
Tiris insula, 11 (Br.) C
Tities, -enses, p. 342 (Rome)
Τιώρα, 275 (Acq.) C
Tolenus fl., 275 (Aeq.) B, 310 (Sab.) B
Tolerienses, p. 335 (Lat.) B
Tolerus v. Tolenus
Tollentinum, 374 (Pic.) A
Trachas v. Tarracina
Traens fl., 11 (Br.) C
Trasamune... pagus, 26 (Luc.) B
Trasimenus lacus, Tars-, 351 (Etr.) A
Τραύσιον πεδίον?, 351 (Etr.) C
Treba, p. 333 (Lat.) A
Trebia, 371 (Umb.) A
Trebianus ager, 160 (Hirp.) C
Trebium v. Treba
Trebula, 154 (Camp.) A
Trebula, 187 (Sam.) C
Trebula Mutusca, 310 (Sab.) A
Trebulani Suffenates, 310 (Sab.) C
Treia, 374 (Pic.) A
Τρῆρος fl., 256 (Vols.) B
Tres Tabernae, 371 (Umb.) C
Tres Tabernae, 256 (Vols.) A
Tresianus ager, 371 (Umb.) B
Τριβόλα v. Trebula
Tricae v. Apinae
Trifanum, 258 (Aur.) C
Trifolinus ager, 154 (Camp.) A
Trigemina, porta, p. 338 (Rome)
Trinium fl., 187 (Sam.) B, 197 (Frent.) B
Tripontium, 256 (Vols.) A
Triturrita, uilla, 351 (Etr.) C
Triuiae lacus, p. 333 (Lat.) A
Triuicum, 160 (Hirp.) A
Troia ad Lauinium, p. 332 (Lat.) A
Troilum, 351 (Etr.) C
Tromentus, -tina trib., 351 (Etr.) B
Trossulum, 351 (Etr.) C
Truentum, 374 (Pic.) A
Truentus fl., 374 (Pic.) A
Tucianus pagus, 160 (Hirp.) B
Tuder, 371 (Umb.) A
Tudernis uitis, 351 (Etr.) B
Tuficum, 371 (Umb.) A
Turax ager, p. 337 (Lat.) C
Turenum, 33 (Peuc.) C
Turnantini, 160 (Hirp.) C
Turocaelum, 371 (Umb.) C
ad Turres Albas, 256 (Vols.) C
Tuscana, 351 (Etr.) A
Tusci, 351 (Etr.) A
Tuscolum, p. 334 (Lat.) A
Tuscus uicus, p. 339 (Rome)
Tutia fl., 351 (Etr.) B

Tutienses, p. 337 (Lat.) C
Tutini, 31 (Cal.) C
Tyrrheni, 351 (Etr.) A

Vacci prata (in Palatio), p. 339 (Rome)
Vacunae forum etc., 310 (Sab.) A
Vadimon locus, 351 (Etr.) A
Valentia, v. Vibo, 11 (Br.) A
Valentia, v. Roma, p. 333 (Lat.) A
Valesium, -etium, 31 (Cal.) C
Varia, -inum, 310 (Sab.) A
Varia v. Uria, 31 (Cal.) A and 31 (Cal.) C
Vaticanus collis, p. 340 (Rome)
Vecellanus pagus, 241 (Pael.) B
Vecilius mons, 275 (Aeq.) C
Vegetiana, aqua, 351 (Etr.) B
Veheia... pagus, 374 (Pic.) B
Veianus pagus, 160 (Hirp.) C
Veii, 351 (Etr.) A
Velabrensis uicus, 371 (Umb.) B
Velabrum, p. 339 (Rome)
Velecha-, 154 (Camp.) C
Velia, 26 (Luc.) A
Velia, p. 338 (Rome)
Velin, 187 (Sam.) C
Velienses, p. 337 (Lat.) C
Velinianum, 35 (Dau.) C
Velinus lacus et fl., 310 (Sab.) A
Velitrae, 256 (Vols.) A
Vellanus fundus, 197 (Frent.) B
Venafrum, 154 (Camp.) A
Venatrinus fundus, 26 (Luc.) B
Veneria insula v. Menaria
Venetulani, p. 337 (Lat.) C
Ventina aqua, 250 (Vest.) B
Venusia, 33 (Peuc.) A
Vercellium, 160 (Hirp.) C
Veretum, 31 (Cal.) B
Vergae, 11 (Br.) C
Vergellus fl., 33 (Peuc.) A
Verrugo, 256 (Vols.) A
Vertinae v. Οὐερτῖναι, 26 (Luc.) C
Verulae, 278 (Hern.) A
Vescellium, 160 (Hirp.) B
Vescia, -cinus, 258 (Aur.) A
ad Veserim, 154 (Camp.) A
Veseuus v. Vesuuius, 154 (Camp.) A
Vesidia, 351 (Etr.) C
Vesinicates, 371 (Umb.) C
Vespasiae, 310 (Sab.) B
Vestini, 250 A
Vestorianus uicus, 154 (Camp.) B
Vesuuius mons, 154 (Camp.) A
Veteres campi, 26 (Luc.) C
Vettiolum (quod Turocaelum), 371 (Umb.) C
Vettona, 371 (Umb.) A
Vetulonium, 351 (Etr.) A
Ufens fl., 256 (Vols.) A
Via Sacra, p. 339 (Rome)
Vibarna? v. Vibinum

35—2

Vibinum, 35 (Dau.) B
Vibo, 11 (Br.) A
Vicentinum municipium, 187 (Sam.) B
Vicilinus Jupiter, 160 (Hirp.) C
Vidicini, 374 (Pic.) C
Viminalis collis, p. 340 (Rome)
Vimitellarii, p. 337 (Lat.) C
Vindenates, 371 (Umb.) A
Visentium, 351 (Etr.) A
Visolitanus fundus, 26 (Luc.) B
Visuentani, 371 (Umb.) C
Vitellia, p. 333 (Lat.) A
Ulubrae, 256 (Vols.) A
Ulurtini, 160 (Hirp.) C
Umbria, -ber, 371 A
Umbro fl., 351 (Etr.) A
Volana v. Velia, 187 (Sam.) C
Volaterrae, 351 (Etr.) A
Volcei, 26 (Luc.) A
Volci, 351 (Etr.) A
Volsci, 256 A
Volsinii, 351 (Etr.) A
Volsonianus fundus, 351 (Etr.) B

Voltumnae fanum, 351 (Etr.) A
Voltur mons, 39 (Peuc.) A
Volturnum opp., 154 (Camp.) A, v. also Capua
Volturnus fl., 154 (Camp.) A, 187 (Sam. A
Vomanum fl., 374 (Pic.) A
Urbana colonia, 154 (Camp.) B
Urbanus pagus, 197 (Frent.) C
Urbius cliuus, p. 341 (Rome)
Urbs Saluia, -bisaluienses, 374 (Pic.) A
Urgo (Gorgon) insula, 351 (Etr.) A
Uria, 31 (Cal.) A
Uria v. Hyria
Ursentini, 26 (Luc.) B
Uruinum Hortense, 371 (Umb.) A
Uruinum Mataurense, 371 (Umb.) A
Uscosium, 197 (Frent.) C
Usidicani, 371 (Umb.) C
Ustica mons, 310 (Sab.) A
Uzentum, 31 (Cal.) A

Zephyrium prom., 11 (Br.) A

INDEX II.

MODERN LOCAL NAMES.

Abriola, 26 D
Abruzzo, 374 A
Acciano, 197 D
Acerenza, 33 A
Acerra, 154 A
Acqua Sparta, 371 D
Acquaro, 374 D
Affile, p. 335 A
Afragola, 154 D
Agnone, 187 D, cf. 175
Agosta, p. 337 D
Agri f., 26 B
Ajeta, 26 D
Airola, 160 D
Alanno, 250 D
Alatri, 278 A
Albe, 275 A
Albegna f., 351 C
Albero, f. dell', 374 C
Alento f., 11 D
Alento f., 245 D
Alezio, 31 B
Alfedena, 187 A
Alfurno m., 26 A
Alife, 187 A
Aliforni, 374 D
Altidona, 374 D
Alvignano, 154 D
Alvito, 256 D
Amalfi, 154 D
Amaseno, 256 A
Ambra f., 351 D
Amelia, 371 A
Anagni, 278 A
Ancarano, 374 D
Ancona, 374 A
Angitola, 11 C
Aniene f., p. 334 A
Ausidonia, 250 D
Anticoli, 278 D
Antino, Civita d', 270 A
Antrodoco, 310 A
Anzi, 26 C
Anzio, Porto d', 256 A
Apice, 160 D

L' Appennino, 371 A
Appignano, 374 D
Aquilonia, 160 A
Aquino, 256 A
Arbia f., 351 D
Arce, 256 A
Arcevia, 371 D
Archi, 310 D
Archinazzo, Ponza d', p. 337 D
Ardea, p. 332 A
Arezzo, 351 A
Argusto, 11 B
Ariano di Puglia, 160 D
Ariccia, p. 333 A
Arielli f., 245 D
Arienzo, 154 D
Arne, Civitella d', 371 A
Arno f., 351 A
Arnone, 154 D
Arpe, 35 A
Ascea, 26 D
Asciano, 351 D
Ascoli, 374 A
Ascoli-Satriano, 33 A
Aso f., 374 D
Aspio f., 374 B
Aspra, 310 D
Assergi, 250 D
Assisi, 371 A
Asso, Castel d', 351 C
Astura, 256 A
Atella, 35 D
Atena, 26 A
Aterno f., 241 A, 250 A
Atessa, 197 D
Atina, 256 A
Atri, 371 A
Atripalda, 154 D
Attiggio, 371 A
S. Aug. all' Esca, 160 D
Ausente f., 258 A
Avella, 154 A
Avellino, 160 A
Avenza, 351 C
Averno, 154 A

INDEX II.

Baccana, 351 B
Bacugno, 310 A
Badia, 371 D
Balvano, 26 C
Banzi, 33 A
Barete, 250 D
Bari delle Puglie, 33 A
Barletta, 33 C
Basciano, 374 D
Basiento, 26 C
Bauco, 257 D
Bazzano, 250 D
Beffi, 250 D
Belforte, 373 D
Bellante, 374 D
S. Benedetto Ullano, 11 D
Benevento, 160 A
Bettona, 371 A
Bevagna, 371 A
S. Biase, 26 D
Bibina v. *Bovino*
Biccari, 35 D
Bieda, 351 A
Bientina f., 351 D
Biferno f., 187 A
Bisceglie, 35 D
Bisegna, 270 D
Bisenti, 874 D
Bisenzio f., 351 A
Bitetto, 33 D
Bitonto, 33 A
Birona, 11 A
Bocchignano, 310 D
Boiano, 187 A
Bolsena, L. di, 351 A
Bomarzo, 351 C
Bominaco, 250 D
Bonito, 160 D
Bovino, 35 B
Bradano, 33 B
Briano, 154 D
Brindisi, 31 A
Brittoli, 250 D
Brocco, 256 D
Brozzi, 374 D
Bucchianico, 245 D
Buccino, 26 A
Bussi, 250 C

Caggiano, 26 D
Cagli, 371 D
Cagnano, 250 D
Cajazzo, 154 D
Calascio, 250 D
Calitri, 160 D
Callipari, 11 C
Calore f., 100 A
Calore f., 26 C
Calvi, 154 A
Calvi dell' Umbria, 371 D
Calvisi, 187 C

Camerino, 371 A
Campli, 374 D
Campofilone, 374 D
Camporolano, 874 D
Canne, Massa di, 33 A
Canosa di Puglia, 33 A
Cantalupo, 310 D
Capestrano, 250 D
Capo di Chia, 256 D
Capodrise, 154 D
Caposele, 26 D
Caposele, 256 D
Capraia, 351 A
Capri, 154 A
Capricchia, 374 D
Caprodosso, 374 D
Capua, S. Maria di, 154 A
Caraceno m., 187 A
Cariati, 11 D
Carico, S. Giov. in, 256 D
Carife, 160 D, 187 C
Carignano, 371 D
Carinola, 154 D
Carpegna m., 871 D
Carpina f., 371 D
Carpineto, 256 D
Carrara, 351 D
Carsoli, 275 A
Casacalenda, 197 C
Casalbore, 160 D
Casamari, 256 A
Casapesenno, 154 D
Cascano, 154 D
Cascia, 310 D
Cascina f., 351 D
Casigliano, 371 A
Cassino, 256 A
Castel di Lama, 197 D
Castel d' Asso, 351 C
Cataldo, Porto S., 31 D
Catanzaro, 11 D
Caudina, Valle, 160 A
Cavaceppo, 374 D
Cavo, Monte, p. 335 B
Ceccano, 256 D
Cecina, 351 C
Ceglie Messapica, 33 A
Celano, 270 D
Celone, 35 C
Ceprano, 256 D
Cerchio, 270 D
Cerfenna, 270 A
Cerignola, 35 B
Cerreto Sannita, 187 B
Cerro al Volturno, 187 D
Cervaro, 35 B
Cervaro, 256 D
Cerveteri, 351 A
Cese, 250 D
Cesena, 371 A
Cetona, 351 D

MODERN LOCAL NAMES. 551

Chiana, Val di, 351 A
Chiascio, 371 C
Chienti f., 374 C
Chieti, 245 A
Chieuti, 35 D
S. Chirico Raparo, 26 D
Chiusi, 351 A
il Cicolano, 275 A
Cicoli, Stato di, 275 A
Ciggiano, 351 C
Cimino m., 351 A
Cingoli, 374 A
Cintoia, 351 D
Cirella, 11 A
Cirignano, 160 D
Ciro, 11 D
Civita Castellana, 351 A
Civitella d' Arne, 371 A
Clitunno f., 371 A
Collescipoli, 310 D
Comero m., 371 C
Comunanza, 374 D
Conca, 310 D
Conca, 256 D
Conero m., 374 A
Contigliano, L. di, 310 A
Conza, 160 A
Coppito, 250 D
Corato, 35 D
Corcolle, p. 336 B
Coreno Ausonia, 256 D
Cori, 256 A
Corneto Tarquinia, 351 A
Cornia f., 310 D
Correse, 310 A
Corropoli, 374 D
Cortona, 351 A
Cosa, 256 B
Coscile f., 11 D
Coscuza, 11 A
Cotrone, 11 A
Crati f., 11 A
Cucullo, p. 335 B
Cuma, 154 A
Curti, 154 D
Cuvultere, S. M. di, 154 A

Dugenta, 160 D
Durazzano, 160 D
Durone f., 187 B

Eboli, 26 A
Elba Isola, 351 A
Elsa f., 351 D
Entoggi f., 374 D
Era, 351 D
l' Etemarta f., 374 D

Faenza, 371 A
Faeto, 35 D
Fagnano, 250 D

Faifoli, S. M. a, 187 A
Faleria, 351 A
Falerone, 374 A
Falesia, 351 B
Falleri v. Faleria
Falterona m., 351 D
Falvatera, 256 A
Fano, 371 A
Fara, 310 D
Farfa, 310 A
Farma f., 351 D
Farneta, 351 D
Fasano, 33 D
Ferentino, 278 A
Fermo, 374 A
Feronia, 256 A
Fibreno f., 256 A
Fichieri, 374 D
Fiesole, 351 A
Filottrano, 374 D
Fine f., 351 D
Fino f., 374 D
Firenze, 351 A
Fium-esino f., 371 A
Foce, 250 D
Foggia, 35 D
Foglianise, 187 A
Foiano della Chiana, 351 D
Folignano, 374 D
Foligno, 371 A
Fondi, 256 A
Fontanarosa, 160 D
Forenza, 33 A
Formia, 256 A
Foro f., 245 D
Fortore, 35 C
Fossombrone, 371 A
Fragneto, 160 D
Frajoli, 256 D
Frascaro, 310 D
Frascati, p. 337 D
Frasso Sabino, 310 D
Frattocchie, p. 337 D
Fresa Grandinaria, 197 D
Frosinone, 256 A
Fucino, L., 270 A
Fumone, 256 D
Furfona, S. M. di, 250 A
Futani, 26 D

Gaeta, 256 A
Galazze, 154 A
Galeso, S. Mad. di, 31 A
Gallipoli, 31 A
Gargano m., 35 A
Garigliano, 256 A
Gavignano, 310 B
Genazzano, p. 337 D
Genosa, 33 B
Gerace, 11 D
Gerano, p. 337 D

Gesso, 374 D
Gianicolo m., p. 340
Giannutri, 351 B
Giglio, I. del, 351 A
Giovinazzo, 33 C
Gorga, 256 D
Gorgona, 351 A
Grassano, 26 D, 31 C
Grecchio, cf. p. 253
Greve f., 351 D
Grumo, 154 D
Gubbio, 371 A

Ielsi, 35 D
Iesi, 371 A
Imele, 275 A
Indivina, Civita, p. 332 A
Irpino, 160 A
Ischia, 154 C
Isernia, 187 A
Itri, 256 D

Lacedonia, 160 A
Laggia, 26 D
Lagno f., 154 B
Lago di Salpi, 35 A
Lagonegro, 26 B
Laino, 26 C
Lameto or l' Ameto, 11 B
Lanciano, 197 A
Lao f., 26 A
Lapedona, 374 D
Larino, 197 A
Lavinia, Civita, p. 332 A
Lecce, 31 A
Lenola, 256 D
Lepini m., p. 335 B
Lesina, 33 D
Lettere, 154 B
Levanella, 351 D
Leuca, Capo di, 31 A
Licenza, 310 A
Licosa, Capo, 26 A
Limatola, 154 D
Limosano, 187 D
Lioni, 160 D
Liri f., 270 A, 256 A
Lizza, S. M. della, 31 B
Lucca, 351 A
Lucera, 35 A
Luco, 270 A, 250 D
Lugnano, 256 D
Lunghezza, p. 337 D
Luni, 351 A

Macchia, 160 D
Macerata, 374 D
Mad. di Siponto, 35 A
Maenza, 256 D
Magliano, 275 D

Magliano, 310 D
Magra f., 351 A
Manatia Victorina, p. 337 C
Manduria, 31 A
Manoppello, 245 D
Marano m., 160 B
Maroggia, 371 D
Marro, 11 C
Massa di Canne, 33 A
Massico m., 258 A
Massignano, 374 D
Matelica, 371 A
Matera, 33 D, cf. 35 C
Mattinata, 35 A
Mavone f., 374 D
Melfi, 33 D
Melicucca, 11 D
Menocchia f., 374 D
Mentana, p. 335 A
Merino, Torre di, 35 B
Mesagne, 31 D
Mesima, 11 A
Messapica, 33 A
Messenano, 371 A
Meta, 154 D
Metaponto, 26 A
Metauro, 371 A
Mignano, 154 D
Mignone f., 351 A
Mirabella Eclano, 160 A
Misa, 371 C
Miseno, 154 A
Mitino, 351 C
Moggio, 310 D
Molfetta, 35 D
Moline, 241 D
Molise, 187 D
Mollarino f., 256 D
Mompeo, 310 D
Mondavio, 371 D
Montagna del Matese, 187 D
Montalboddo, 371 D
Montaquila, 187 B
Montecosaro, 374 D
Montemale, 160 D
Monte Marano, 160 B
Montepeloso, 33 D
Monteroni di Lecce, 31 D
Monte Rumulo, 160 B
Montesarchio, 160 D
Montorio, 374 D
Montoro, 374 D
Morano Calabro, 11 A
Morcone, 160 D
Morge, 374 D
Morino, 270 D
Moro f., 245 D
Morrea, 270 D
Morrone m., 241 D
Morrovalle, 374 D
Musone f., 374 D

Napoli, 154 A
Narce, 351 D
Nardo, 31 A
Narni, 371 A
Negro f., 26 B
Nemi, 333 A
Nepezzano, 374 D
Nepi, 351 A
La Nera f., 371 A
Nereto, 374 D
Nerola, 310 D
Nesce, 275 B
Neto f., 11 A
Nevola f., 371 D
Nicotera, 11 C
Ninfa, 256 B
Nisida, 154 A
Nocciano, 250 D
Nocelleto, 154 D
Nocera, 371 A
Nocera Tirinese, 11 A
Nocera dei Pagani, 154 A
Nola, 154 A
Norcia, 310 A
Norma, 256 A
Numana, 374 A
Nusco, 160 D

Ofanto, 160 A
Ofena, 250 B
Offida, 374 D
Ombrone f., 351 A
Onna, 250 D
Opi, 250 D
Opi, 256 D
Oppido, 33 C
Ordona, 35 A
Oria, 31 A
Orsogna, 197 D
Ortanova, 35 D
Orte, 351 A
Ortona a mare, 197 A
Ortucchio, 270 D
Osento f., 197 D
Oseri, val d', 351 A
Osimo, 374 A
Ostia, p. 333 A
Otricoli, 371 A

Pacentro, 197 D
Padula, 26 D
Paduli, 160 D
Paglia, 351 C
Pagliara, 275 D
Paglieta, 197 B
Palestrina, p. 333 A
Palinuro, 26 A
Palmarola, 256 A
Palmoli, 197 D
Palombara Sabina, p. 337 D
Paritoli, 374 D

Pastene, 160 D
Patu, 31 D
Paupisi, 160 D
Penne, 250 A
Pennino m., 371 D
Pensilis, S. Mart. in, 35 D
Pentima, 241 D
Perazzo, 35 D
Pergola, 371 D
Pernosano, 154 A
Perugia, 351 A
Pesa f., 351 D
Pesaro, 371 A
Pescara, 250 C
Pescina, 270 D
Pesto, 26 A
Petescia, 310 D
Petilia Policastro, 11 A
Pettorano sul Gizio, 241 D
Piano di Voci, 351 A
Pianosa, 351 A
Pico, 256 D
Pietrastornina, 160 D
Piglio, 278 A
Pignataro, p. 337 D
Pignataro Interamna, 256 A
Pioraco, 371 C
Piperno, 256 A
Pisa, 351 A
Pistoia, 351 A
Pizzorne, 351 D
Poggio Fidoni, 310 D
Poggio Moiano, 310 D
Polesio, 374 D
Poli, p. 337 D
Polignano, 33 B
la Polla, 26 D
Pollena, 154 D
Ponte Molle, p. 331
Ponza, 256 A
Ponza d' Archinazzo, p. 337 D
Popoli, 241 D
Posillipo, 154 A
Potenza, 26 A
Potenza, 374 A
Pozzilli, 154 D
Pozzuoli, 154 A
Prandone m., 374 D
Pratola Peligna, 241 D
Presenzano, 154 D
Presta, 160 B
Preta, 374 D
Preturo, 250 D
Prezza, 241 D
Procida, 154 A
Profiamma, 371 A
Puglie, 35 A
Punta dell' Alice, 11 A
Punta della Ristola, 31 D

Quosa, 256 D

INDEX II.

Ragnola f., 374 D
Rapino, v. 243
Rapolla, 160 C
Ravenna, 371 A
Recale, 154 D
Recanati, 371 D
Reggio, 11 A
Reino, 160 D
Renzano, 371 D
Resina, 154 D
Riccione, 371 D
Ricigliano, 26 D
Ricti, 310 A
Rimini, 371 A
Rionero in Volture, 35 D
Ripabottoni, 35 D
Ripatransone, 374 D
Ristola, Punta della, 31 D
Rocca Pipirozzi, 154 D
Rocca Rainola, 154 D
Rocca Termine, 256 A
Rocca Turchina, 351 A
Rossano, 11 C
Rugge, 31 A
Ruggiano, 31 A
Ruvo di Puglia, 33 A

S. Piet. Vernotico, 31 D
S. Marco de' Cavoti, 160 D
S. Maria di Cuvultere, 154 A
Sabato f., 100 A
Sacco, 256 D
Sala Consilina, 26 B
Salandra, 26 B
Salerno, 154 A
Salpi, Lago di, 35 A
Sambuco, 310 B
Sangro, 197 B
Sapri, 26 D
Sarconi, 26 D
Sarno f., 154 A
Sarsina, 371 A
Sasso Feltrio, 371 C
Saturo, Torre di, 31 A
Savelli, 310 D
Savignano, 371 D
Savignano di Puglia, 160 D
Savino m., 351 D
Savone f., 154 A
Savuto f., 11 C
Scanno, 297 D
Scapoli, 187 D
Scarperia, 351 D
Scoppito, 250 D
Scorrano, 374 D
Scurcola, 275 D
Segni, 256 A
Selci, 310 D
Sele f., 154 A
Senigaglia, 371 A
Sentino, 371 A

Sepino, 187 A
Serchio f., 351 A
Sermoneta, p. 336 C
Serravalle, 371 D
Serrone, 278 D
Sessa Aurunca, 258 A
Sestino, 371 A
Sezze, 256 A
Siena, 351 A
Sieve f., 351 D
Sigillo, 371 C
La Sila, 11 A
Simmari, 11 C
Sinello f., 197 D
Sinni f., 26 B
Siponto, Mad. di, 35 A
Solmona, 241 A
Sonnino, 256 D
Sora, 256 A
Soratte m., 351 A
Soriano nel Cimino, 351 A
Sorrento, 154 A
Sovana, 351 A
Spello, 371 A
Spoleto, 371 A
Squillace, 11 A
Staffoli, 275 D
Staffolo, 374 D
Starza, 160 D
Stimigliano, 310 D
Stroncone, 310 D
Subequo, Cast. Vecch., 241 A
Subiaco, p. 333 A
Sulmona, 241 A
Sutri, 351 A
Suvereto, 351 B

Taburno m., 160 A
Tacina f., 11 C
Talamone, 351 A
Tammaro f., 160 C
Tanagro, 26 B
Tapignano, 374 D
Tappino f., 187 D
Taranto, 31 A
Tavo f., 250 D
Taurasi, 160 A
Teano, 154 A
Teggiano, 26 A
Telese, 187 A
Tenna f., 374 C
Teramo, 374 A
Termoli, 197 D
Terni, 371 A
Terracina, 256 A
Tesino f., 374 C
Tevere f., p. 333 A
Tiriolo, 11 B
Tivoli, p. 333 A
Tocco da Casauria, 197 D
Todi, 371 A

MODERN LOCAL NAMES. 555

Toffia, 310 D
Tolentino, 374 A
Tolero f., 256 B
Topino f., 371 D
Torre d' Egnazia, d' Agnazzo, 33 A
Torre di Merino, 35 B
Torre Treponti, 256 A
Tortora, 26 D
Tortoreto, 374 D
Toscana, 351 A
Toscanella, 351 A
Tossicia, 374 D
Trani, 33 C
Trasacco, 270 D
Trasimeno L., 351 A
Treglia, 154 A
Treglia, 154 D
Treia, 374 A
Tremonti, 241 D
Treple, mediaev. 154 A
Trepuzzi, 31 D
Tresa f., 351 D
Trevi, 371 A
Trevi nel Lazio, p. 333 A
Trevico, 160 A
Tricarico, 26 D
Triflone, 35 D
Trigno, 197 B
Trionti f., 11 C
Triponzo, 310 D
Trisungo, 374 D
Trivento, 187 A
Trocchia, 154 D
Tronto f., 374 A
Turano f., 310 B
Tussio, 250 D
Tuturano, 31 D
Tuzia, 351 B

Uffente, 256 A
Ugento, 31 A
Ullano, 11 D
Umana, 374 A
Urbino, 371 A
Urbisaglia, 374 A

Uso f., 371 D

Vacone, 310 D
Val di Chiana, 351 A
Val d' Oseri, 351 A
Valcaldara, 310 D
Valle Caudina, 160 A
Valle Falacrina, 310 A
Valva, 26 D
Vandra f., 187 D
Varono, 35 D
Vasto, 197 D
Vatolla, 26 D
Veiano, Pago, 160 C
Velino f., 310 A
Velletri, 256 A
Venafro, 154 A
Venarotta, 374 D
Venosa, 33 A
Ventotene, Isola, 154 A
Vereto, S. M. di, 31 B
Vergello, 33 A
Vernotico, S. Piet., 31 D
Veroli, 278 A
Versano, 160 D
Vesuvio m., 154 A Addenda
Vicalvi, 256 D
Vicentina f., 154 A
Vicenza, 154 A
Vicovaro, 310 A
Viggiano, 26 D
Villa Spada, p. 337 D
Visciano, 154 D
Visso, 310 D
Vitulano, 160 D
Volterra, 351 A
Volture m., 33 A
Volturno, 154 A
Volturno f., 187 A
Vomano, 374 A

Zagarolo, p. 337 D
Zannone, 256 B
Zungoli, 160 D
Zuni, 154 D

INDEX III.

NOMINA GENTIUM REGIONES ITALICAS COLENTIUM.

The following abbreviations are used in this Index:

A. Aurunci	H. Hernici	Pi. Picenum
Aq. Aequi	Hp. Hirpini	Pr. Praeneste et Tusculum
B. Bruttii	L. Lucani	S. Sabini
Cl. Calabri	Lat. Latini	Sm. Samnites
Cp. Campania	M. Marsi	Umb. Umbri
D. Dauni	Mer. Marrucini	V. Volsci
F. Frentani	P. Peucetii	Vt. Vestini
Fal. Falisci	Pg. Paeligni	

The reader is reminded that
A after the number implies over six occurrences.
B after the number implies less than six but more than one occurrence.
C after the number implies one occurrence only.

For typographical reasons the abbreviation Lat. has been used alone to refer to the names of the Latini which are to be found in **Note xxxviii**, p. 343 ff.

Where two spellings of the same name are given as such in any list in the body of the book, as a rule only the first is cited in this Index.

Abbia, 155 (Cp.) C
Abeiena, 372 (Umb.) C
Abclasia, 311 (S.) A
Abenia, Lat. B
Abennia, 307 (Pr.) C
Abidia, 161 (Hp.) B, 257 (V.) C, 311 (S.) A
Abiena, 311 (S.) B
Abnatia, 375 (Pi.) C
Abuccia, 34 (P.) A, 155 (Cp.) B, 257 (V.) B, 259 (A.) B
Abucia, 276 (Aq.) C
Abudia, 307 (Pr.) C
Abulenia, 372 (Umb.) C
Abullia, 188 (Sm.) A
Abundantia, 372 (Umb.) C
Aburia, 161 (Hp.) C, Lat. C, 372 (Umb.) B
Aburria, 271 (M.) C
Aburtennia, 311 (S.) B
Abuttia, 257 (V.) B, 279 (H.) C
Acadia, 372 (Umb.) B
Acca, 242 (Pg.) A
Accaa, 212 (Pg.) B

Accaea, 372 (Umb.) C
Accaua, 242 (Pg.) B, 251 (Vt.) C, 375 (Pi.) C
Acceiaua, 155 (Cp.) C, 372 (Umb.) C
Accenna, Lat. C
Accia, 27 (L.) C, 34 (P.) C, 36 (D.) C, 155 (Cp.) B, 161 (Hp.) C, 188 (Sm.) B, 242 (Pg.) A, 257 (V.) C, 307 (Pr.) C, 311 (S.) B, 372 (Umb.) C, 375 (Pi.) C
Accoleia, Lat. B
Acellia, 161 (Hp.) C, 188 (Sm.) B
Aceria, 155 (Cp.) C
Acerra, Lat. B
Acerratia, 32 (Cl.) B, 155 (Cp.) C
Acerratina, 32 (Cl.) C
Acerronia, 12 (B.) B, 27 (L.) B, 257 (V.) B, 279 (H.) B
Acestia, 36 (D.) C, 276 (Aq.) C, 307 (Pr.) C, 311 (S.) C, Lat. C
Achillenia, 36 (D.) C
Acholia, Lat. C
Acidia, 307 (Pr.) C
Acilia, 27 (L.) B, 32 (Cl.) C, 34 (P.) B,

155 (Cp.) A, 161 (Hp.) B, 188 (Sm.) A,
242 (Pg.) C, 257 (V.) A, 279 (H.) B,
307 (Pr.) B, Lat. A, 372 (Umb.) C,
375 (Pi.) C
Aclenia, 161 (Hp.) C
Aclutia, 155 (Cp.) C
Aco, 372 (Umb.) C
Aconia, 155 (Cp.) C, 307 (Pr.) C, 350
(Fal.) B, 372 (Umb.) B, 375 (Pi.) B
Acontia, 161 (Hp.) C
Acrai..., Lat. C
Acria, 188 (Sm.) C, 198 (F.) C, 242
(Pg.) B
Acricedia, 257 (V.) B, 259 (A.) B
Aculena, 251 (Vt.) C
Acuria, 251 (Vt.) C
Acusia, 375 (Pi.) B
Acutia, 155 (Cp.) A, 161 (Hp.) C, 307
(Pr.) B, Lat. C, 375 (Pi.) C
Acutiana, 36 (D.) C
Acuuia, 34 (P.) C
Addia, 672 (Umb.) B
Adia, 155 (Cp.) C
Adiectia, 161 (Hp.) B
Adinia, 161 (Hp.) C
Adurena, 372 (Umb.) C
Aebutia, 12 (B.) C, 27 (L.) C, 155 (Cp.)
C, 188 (Sm.) B, 198 (F.) C, 257 (V.) B,
Lat. A, 372 (Umb.) C, 375 (Pi.) C
Aecia, 155 (Cp.) C
Accilia, 257 (V.) B
Acclania, 155 (Cp.) B, 161 (Hp.) A,
372 (Umb.) C
Aedia, 188 (Sm.) A, 276 (Aq.) B, Lat.
C, 311 (S.) C
Aedinia, 27 (L.) B, 34 (P.) C
Aeficia, Lat. B
Aefria, 357 (V.) C
Aefulana, 155 (Cp.) B
Aelania, 357 (Pi.) C
Aelia, 27 (L.) B, 32 (Cl.) C, 34 (P.) A,
36 (D.) C, 155 (Cp.) A, 161 (Hp.) A,
188 (Sm.) B, 198 (F.) C, 242 (Pg.) B,
251 (Vt.) B, 257 (V.) A, 259 (A.) C,
271 (M.) C, 279 (H.) B, 307 (Pr.) A,
Lat. A, 311 (S.) B, 372 (Umb.) A, 375
(Pi.) B
Aemilia, 12 (B.) C, 27 (L.) B, 32 (Cl.) B,
34 (P.) B, 36 (D.) B, 155 (Cp.) A, 161
(Hp.) A, 188 (Sm.) A, 251 (Vt.) B,
257 (V.) A, 259 (A.) C, 276 (Aq.) A,
279 (H.) C, 307 (Pr.) B, Lat. A, 311
(S.) B, 372 (Umb.) A
Aennia, 307 (Pr.) C?
Aenonia, 161 (Hp.) C
Aequania, 161 (Hp.) C
Aequasia, 372 (Umb.) B
Aequicula, 276 (Aq.) B
Aequisia, 276 (Aq.) C
Aerelia, 155 (Cp.) C
Aerentia, Lat. C

Aeresia, 161 (Hp.) C
Aeria, 155 (Cp.) C
Acronia, Lat. C
Aerullia, 155 (Cp.) B, 161 (Hp.) C
Aerusia, 311 (S.) B
Aerussia, 372 (Umb.) B
Aesernina, 188 (Sm.) B
Aesia, 155 (Cp.) C
Aesqullia, 27 (L.) C
Aestlania, 257 (V.) B
Aeternia, 155 (Cp.) C
Aetia, 372 (Umb.) B
Aetreia, 257 (V.) C
Aetria, 161 (Hp.) C, 372 (Umb.) A
Aetrilia, 257 (V.) B
Afaria, 27 (L.) B
Afiedia, 257 (V.) B
Afilana, Lat. B
Afilia, 307 (Pr.) C
Afillia, 155 (Cp.) B
Afinia, 155 (Cp.) C, 161 (Hp.) A, 188
(Sm.) B, 251 (Vt.) C, 257 (V.) B, 259
(A.) B, Lat. B
Afrania, 32 (Cl.) C, 155 (Cp.) C, 161 (Hp.)
C, 188 (Sm.) B, Lat. B, 375 (Pi.) C
Afrena, 279 (H.) C
Afrenia, 375 (Pi.) C
Afria, 375 (Pi.) C
Afronia, 155 (Cp.) C
Agasia, 276 (Aq.) C
Agidia, 155 (Cp.) C
Agileia, 161 (Hp.) C, 257 (V.) B
Agilia, 307 (Pr.) C, Lat. C
Agilleia, Lat. B
Agnania, 155 (Cp.) C
Agreia, 307 (Pr.) B
Agrestia, 161 (Hp.) C
Agria, 155 (Cp.) A, 161 (Hp.) B, 188
(Sm.) B, 257 (V.) B, Lat. A
Agusia, 307 (Pr.) C, 375 (Pi.) C
Ahernia, 188 (Sm.) C
Ahia, 27 (L.) C, 155 (Cp.) B, 188 (Sm.)
C, 198 (F.) C
Aia, Lat. C
Aiacia, 307 (Pr.) C
Aiadia, 251 (Vt.) C
Aiania, 251 (Vt.) C
Aiasia, 272 (Umb.) C
Aicdia, 257 (V.) B, Lat. C, 375 (Pi.) B
Aiena, 251 (Vt.) B
Aieza, 155 (Cp.) C
Aiezia, 155 (Cp.) C
Aigia, 257 (V.) C
Ailia, Lat. A
Aiopia, 251 (Vt.) B
Aiscidia, 155 (Cp.) C
Alacria, 155 (Cp.) C
Alaria, 161 (Hp.) C
Albana, 188 (Sm.) C
Albania, 161 (Hp.) B, 257 (V.) C
Albeia, 161 (Hp.) C

Albia, 27 (L.) C, 34 (P.) C, 155 (Cp.) A,
  161 (Hp.) B, 251 (Vt.) A, 257 (V.) A,
  271 (M.) B, Lat. A, 311 (S.) A, 350
  (Fal.) C, 372 (Umb.) B, 375 (Pi.) B
Albicia, 36 (D.) C
Albidia, 257 (V.) C
Albiena, 155 (Cp.) B
Albina, Lat. C
Albinia, 32 (Cl.) C, 257 (V.) C, 259 (A.)
  C, 307 (Pr.) B, Lat. C
Albonia, Lat. C
Albucia, 155 (Cp.) A
Aldia, 161 (Hp.) B
Alcin, Lat. B
Alenia, 251 (Vt.) B
Alennia, 372 (Umb.) B
Aletin, 155 (Cp.) B, 161 (Hp.) B, 188
  (Sm.) C
Alfacia, 372 (Umb.) C
Alfedia, 251 (Vt.) C, Lat. C
Alfena, 155 (Cp.) A, 251 (Vt.) C, 271
  (M.) A, 311 (S.) C, 372 (Umb.) C
Alfenatia, 155 (Cp.) C, 307 (Pr.) C, Lat. C
Alfenia, 307 (Pr.) C, 372 (Umb.) C
Alfia, 12 (B.) C, 34 (P.) B, 36 (D.) C, 155
  (Cp.) A, 161 (Hp.) C, 188 (Sm.) B, 242
  (Pg.) B, 251 (Vt.) C, 257 (V.) A, 271
  (M.) B, 276 (Aq.) B, 279 (H.) C, 307
  (Pr.) C, Lat. B, 372 (Umb.) A, 375
  (Pi.) C
Alficia, 155 (Cp.) B, 375 (Pi.) C
Alfidena, 372 (Umb.) C
Alfidia, 12 (B.) C, 155 (Cp.) B, 242 (Pg.)
  C, 257 (V.) B, 271 (M.) C
Alfiena, 375 (Pi.) C
Alfina, 375 (Pi.) C
Alinia, 375 (Pi.) C
Alitia, 188 (Sm.) C
Allodia, 271 (M.) C
Allcia, 155 (Cp.) A, 257 (V.) C, 372 (Umb.)
  B, 375 (Pi.) C
Allenia, 155 (Cp.) C, 375 (Pi.) C
Allia, 27 (L.) A, 32 (Cl.) B, 36 (D.) C,
  155 (Cp.) A, 161 (Hp.) A, 242 (Pg.) B,
  257 (V.) B, 271 (M.) B, 279 (H.) C, 307
  (Pr.) C, 311 (S.) B, Lat. A, 372 (Umb.)
  A, 375 (Pi.) B
Alliana, Lat. C
Alliaria, 251 (Vt.) C
Alliatoria, 155 (Cp.) B
Allidia, 27 (L.) B, 155 (Cp.) B, 161 (Hp.)
  C, 251 (Vt.) B, 257 (V.) C, 276 (Aq.)
  A, Lat. B
Alliedia, 311 (S.) C
Alliena, 155 (Cp.) B, 188 (Sm.) C, Lat.
  B, 372 (Umb.) B, 375 (Pi.) C
Alonia, 155 (Cp.) C (?)
Alpia, 161 (Hp.) C
Alpinia, 155 (Cp.) C, 257 (V.) C, Lat. C
Alsia, 155 (Cp.) C
Amantia, 372 (Umb.) C

Amaredia, 276 (Aq.) A
Amarfia, 311 (S.) C, 161 (Hp.) B
Amatia, 155 (Cp.) B, 188 (Sm.) C, Lat. B
Ambibia, 155 (Cp.) B
Ambilia, 188 (Sm.) C
Ambiuia, 257 (V.) C, 375 (Pi.) B
Ambonia, 155 (Cp.) C (?)
Amdria, 27 (L.) C
Amelia, 257 (V.) C
Ameria, 161 (Hp.) C
Amia, 161 (Hp.) B, 188 (Sm.) C
Amicia, 155 (Cp.) C
Amilia, 372 (Umb.) C
Amiternia, 251 (Vt.) B
Ammaa, 242 (Pg.) C
Ammea, 375 (Pi.) C
Ammia, 32 (Cl.) C, 36 (D.) B, 155 (Cp.)
  C, 257 (V.) B, 350 (Fal.) C
Ammonia, 155 (Cp.) A
Amninia, 198 (F.) C
Amoeniana, 372 (Umb.) C
Ampedia, 155 (Cp.) C
Ampia, 155 (Cp.) B, 242 (Pg.) B, 257
  (V.) C, 307 (Pr.) C, 311 (S.) C, 372
  (Umb.) B, 375 (Pi.) B
Ampiidia, 375 (Pi.) B
Ampudia, 27 (L.) C, 257 (V.) C
Amullia, 12 (B.) C, 155 (Cp.) A
Amunia, 161 (Hp.) C
Amuria, 155 (Cp.) C
Anaiedia, 271 (M.) C, i.e. 266
Ancarsia, 155 (Cp.) C
Ancharena, 311 (S.) B
Ancharia, 155 (Cp.) B, 161 (Hp.) C, 251
  (Vt.) C, 257 (V.) C, 279 (H.) C, 307
  (Pr.) C, 311 (S.) B, 372 (Umb.) B,
  375 (Pi.) B
Anchariena, 257 (V.) C (?), 259 (A.) C
Ancilin, 242 (Pg.) B, 307 (Pr.) C
Andiuia, 311 (S.) B
Angilia?, 36 (D.) C
Ania, 32 (Cl.) C
Anicia, 12 (B.) C, 34 (P.) C, 36 (D.) B,
  155 (Cp.) A, 161 (Hp.) B, 198 (F.) C,
  257 (V.) B (?), 279 (H.) C, 307 (Pr.) A,
  311 (S.) C, Lat. B, 375 (Pi.) B
Aniciana, 372 (Umb.) C
Anilia, Lat. C
Animisia, 257 (V.) B
Aninia, 32 (Cl.) C, 34 (P.) B, 155 (Cp.)
  B, 251 (Vt.) B, 257 (V.) B, 276 (Aq.)
  C, Lat. B, 372 (Umb.) B, 375 (Pi.) B
Anna, 155 (Cp.) C (?)
Annaea, 155 (Cp.) B, 251 (Vt.) B, 257
  (V.) B, 311 (S.) B, 372 (Umb.) B
Annaedia, 251 (Vt.) B
Annalena, 375 (Pi.) C
Annalia, 375 (Pi.) B
Annaua, 242 (Pg.) B
Annea, 307 (Pr.) C, Lat. B, 372 (Umb.)
  B

GENTILE NAMES FROM THE DIALECT-AREAS.

Anneia, 27 (L.) C, 155 (Cp.) B, 161 (Hp.) C, 276 (Aq.) B, 307 (Pr.) C
Annia, 27 (L.) A, 32 (Cl.) C, 34 (P.) A, 36 (D.) C, 155 (Cp.) A, 161 (Hp.) A, 188 (Sm.) B, 242 (Pg.) A, 251 (Vt.) C, 257 (V.) A, 271 (M.) B, 276 (Aq.) C, 307 (Pr.) A, Lat. A, 311 (S.) B, 350 (Fal.) B, 372 (Umb.) A, 375 (Pi.) A
Anniana, 155 (Cp.) C
Annidia, 161 (Hp.) C, 198 (F.) C, 271 (M.) C, Lat. C
Anniena, 251 (Vt.) C, 311 (S.) B
Anniolena, 242 (Pg.) B, 251 (Vt.) B, 257 (V.) C, Lat. C
Ansia, 27 (L.) B, 155 (Cp.) A
Anteia, 155 (Cp.) B, 188 (Sm.) C, 242 (Pg.) C, Lat. B, 372 (Umb.) C, 375 (Pi.) B
Antestia, 188 (Sm.) C
Antia, 155 (Cp.) B, 161 (Hp.) C, Lat. B
Antias, 257 (V.) C
Antilia, 155 (Cp.) C, Lat. C
Antistia, 34 (P.) B, 155 (Cp.) A, 161 (Hp.) A, 251 (Vt.) C, 257 (V.) B, 307 (Pr.) A, Lat. A, 311 (S.) B, 372 (Umb.) A, 375 (Pi.) C
Antonia, 12 (B.) C, 27 (L.) A, 32 (Cl.) A, 34 (P.) A, 155 (Cp.) A, 161 (Hp.) A, 188 (Sm.) C, 242 (Pg.) B, 257 (V.) A, 259 (A.) C, 279 (H.) B, 307 (Pr.) A, Lat. A, 350 (Fal.) B, 372 (Umb.) B, 375 (Pi.) B
Apellia, 276 (Aq.) B
Apertia, 34 (P.) C, Lat. B
Apesia, 243 (Pg.) C, 375 (Pi.) C
Apicata, 155 (Cp.) C
Apicia, Lat. C, 375 (Pi.) C
Apidia, 257 (V.) B, Lat. C, 375 (Pi.) C
Apisia, 155 (Cp.) C, 251 (Vt.) A, 375 (Pi) C
Apitia, 251 (Vt.) C (?)
Aplania, 155 (Cp.) B
Apollonia, 155 (Cp.) C
Aponia, 155 (Cp.) A, 251 (Vt.) A, 257 (V.) B, 307 (Pr.) C, 311 (S.) C, Lat. C, 372 (Umb.) B, 375 (Pi.) C
Appaea, 155 (Cp.) C, 251 (Vt.) B, 311 (S.) B, 372 (Umb.) B
Appaedia, 251 (Vt.) C, 372 (Umb.) C
Appaenia, Lat. C
Appalena, 34 (P.) B
Appalia, 307 (Pr.) B, 375 (Pi.) C
Appeia, 375 (Pi.) C
Appellasin, 257 (V.) C
Appia, 27 (L.) B, 34 (P.) B, 155 (Cp.) A, 161 (Hp.) B, 251 (Vt.) C, 257 (V.) B, 372 (Umb.) B
Appionia, 372 (Umb.) C
Apponia, 155 (Cp.) C
Apponiolena, 251 (Vt.) C
Appuleia, 27 (L.) B, 32 (Cl.) C, 34 (P.) B, 155 (Cp.) A, 161 (Hp.) B, 188 (Sm.) A, 251 (Vt.) B, 257 (V.) B, 276 (Aq.) C, 307 (Pr.) B, Lat. A, 372 (Umb.) B, 375 (Pi.) C
Appusulena, 375 (Pi.) C
Apria, 155 (Cp.) B, 161 (Hp.) C
Aprilia, 372 (Umb.) C
Aprofinia, Lat. C
Apronia, 34 (P.) B, 155 (Cp.) C, 251 (Vt.) B, 257 (V.) B, Lat. C, 372 (Umb.) B
Aproniana, 188 (Sm.) B
Aprucia, 257 (V.) C
Aprufenia, 375 (Pi.) C
Apscillana, 188 (Sm.) B
Apsennia, 257 (V.) C
Apstidia, 257 (V.) C
Aptronia, 307 (Pr.) B
Apusalenia, Lat. C
Apusia, 155 (Cp.) B
Apustia, 279 (H.) C
Aquilia, 27 (L.) B, 155 (Cp.) A, 257 (V.) B, 279 (H.) B, 307 (Pr.) B
Aquillia, 32 (Cl.) B, 34 (P.) B, 188 (Sm.) B, 307 (Pr.) B, Lat. A, 372 (Umb.) C
Aquinia, 257 (V.) C, 350 (Fal.) C
Aqunia, 155 (Cp.) C
Arabia, 257 (V.) C
Aracilia, 307 (Pr.) C
Aradia, 257 (V.) C
Arbaiana, 251 (Vt.) C
Arbustia, Lat. B
Arcaea, 155 (Cp.) C
Areia, 161 (Hp.) B
Arellia, 155 (Cp.) B, 257 (V.) B, Lat. A
Arelliana, 155 (Cp.) C
Arena, 251 (Vt.) C
Arennia, 276 (Aq.) C
Argentaria, 161 (Hp.) C
Aricinia, Lat. C
Aristia, 257 (V.) C, Lat. B
Arlena, 307 (Pr.) C
Armenia, 155 (Cp.) C
Arpagia, Lat. C
Arquinia, 155 (Cp.) C
Arrania, Lat. B
Arrasidia, 307 (Pr.) C
Arrecina, 32 (Cl.) C, 307 (Pr.) B, Lat. B
Arredia, 375 (Pi.) B
Arrena. Lat. C, 372 (Umb.) C, 375 (Pi.) C
Arreniana, 34 (P.) B
Arria, 27 (L.) A, 34 (P.) B, 36 (D.) B, 155 (Cp.) A, 161 (Hp.) A, 188 (Sm.) B, 198 (F.) C, 251 (Vt.) A, 259 (A.) B, 271 (M.) C, 276 (Aq.) C, 279 (H.) B, 307 (Pr.) B, Lat. A, 311 (S.) B, 372 (Umb.) A, 375 (Pi.) C
Arronia, 372 (Umb.) C
Arruntia, 32 (Cl.) B, 155 (Cp.) A, 188 (Sm.) B, 242 (Pg.) B, 276 (Aq.) C, Lat. A, 372 (Umb.) A, 375 (Pi.) C

Arsenia, 155 (Cp.) C
Arsinia, 375 (Pi.) C
Artenna, 198 (F.) C
Articuleia, 34 (P.) C, 161 (Hp.) C, 276 (Aq.) C
Artoria, 27 (L.) B, 34 (P.) B, 36 (D.) C, 155 (Cp.) A, 257 (V.) C, Lat. A, 372 (Umb.) B, 375 (Pi.) C
Aruentia, 36 (D.) C
Arulena, 155 (Cp.) B
Aruttia, 155 (Cp.) C
Asania, 372 (Umb.) C
Ascia, 155 (Cp.) C
Asconia, 307 (Pr.) C
Ascreia, 271 (M.) C
Asellia, 155 (Cp.) B, 188 (Sm.) B
Asicia, Lat. B
Asillia, 161 (Hp.) C
Asinia, 155 (Cp.) A, 161 (Hp.) B, 246 (Mcr.) B, 251 (Vt.) C, 257 (V.) A, 259 (A.) B, 276 (Aq.) C, 279 (H.) C, 307 (Pr.) B, Lat. B, 372 (Umb.) B, 375 (Pi.) C
Aspania, 279 (H.) C
Asubria, 198 (F.) B
Asudia, 372 (Umb.) C
Asuia, 155 (Cp.) B, 161 (Hp.) C
Asuiuia, 36 (D.) C
Asullia, 372 (Umb.) C
Asuuia, 188 (Sm.) C
Ata, 34 (P.) B?
Atafnia, 375 (Pi.) C?
Atalia, 375 (Pi.) B
Atania, 155 (Cp.) C
Atatia, 372 (Umb.) C
Atatina, 251 (Vt.) B
Ataua, 375 (Pi.) B
Atauia, 357 (V.) B
Ateia, 155 (Cp.) A, 242 (Pg.) B, 246 (Mcr.) C, 307 (Pr.) B, Lat. C, 372 (Umb.) C
Ateleia, 155 (Cp.) C
Atelia, 372 (Umb.) C
Atellia, 155 (Cp.) B, 307 (Pr.) B, 375 (Pi.) B
Aternia, 257 (V.) C
Athania, 34 (P.) B
Atia, 276 (Aq.) B, 307 (Pr.) C, 311 (S.) C, Lat. A
Aticia, 12 (B.) C
Atidia, 155 (Cp.) C, 307 (Pr.) B, Lat. C
Atiedia, 271 (M.) C, 276 (Aq.) C, 372 (Umb.) B
Atilena, 12 (B.) B, 34 (P.) B, 36 (D.) C, 155 (Cp.) A, 188 (Sm.) B, 242 (Pg.) B, 257 (V.) A, 271 (M.) B, Lat. C
Atilia, 307 (Pr.) B, Lat. A, 350 (Fal.) C, 372 (Umb.) B, 375 (Pi.) C
Atinatia, 372 (Umb.) B
Atinia, 155 (Cp.) B, 188 (Sm.) A, 257 (V.) B, 307 (Pr.) C, Lat. A

Atisia, 155 (Cp.) C
Atitria, 375 (Pi.) C?
Atleia, 155 (Cp.) C
Atlia, 155 (Cp.) C, 307 (Pr.) C
Atoleia, 32 (Cl.) C
Atreia, 270 (H.) C
Atrin, 155 (Cp.) B, 161 (Hp.) B, 198 (F.) C, 251 (Vt.) B, 257 (V.), C, 311 (S.) B
Atriena, 375 (Pi.) B
Attedia, 375 (Pi.) C
Atteia, 161 (Hp.) C
Attennia, Lat. C
Attia, 27 (L.) B, 34 (P.) B, 155 (Cp.) A, 161 (Hp.) C, 188 (Sm.) B, 198 (F.) C, 242 (Pg.) B, 251 (Vt.) A, 257 (V.) B, 271 (M.) B, 307 (Pr.) C, Lat. A, 372 (Umb.) A, 375 (Pi.) A
Attidia, 242 (Pg.) C, 372 (Umb.) B
Attiedia, 251 (Vt.) B, 242 (Pg.) B
Attiena, Lat. B, 311 (S.) B
Atulena, 155 (Cp.) C, 188 (Sm.) C
Atullia, 155 (Cp.) B, 372 (Umb.) B
Aunea, 251 (Vt.) B, 311 (S.) B
Auchenia, Lat. B
Aucidia, 36 (D.) C
Audacilia, 372 (Umb.) C
Audasia, 155 (Cp.) B
Audeia, 161 (Hp.) B
Audia, 32 (Cl.) C, 155 (Cp.) B, 372 (Umb.) C
Audiena, 311 (S.) C, 375 (Pi.) C
Auedia, 155 (Cp.) C
Aueia, 251 (Vt.) B, 311 (S.) B
Auelia, 242 (Pg.) C
Auena, 188 (Sm.) C
Aufania, 155 (Cp.) C
Aufeia, 155 (Cp.) C, 372 (Umb.) C
Aufellia, 155 (Cp.) B
Aufestia, 155 (Cp.) A, Lat. B
Aufia, Lat. C
Aufidena, 372 (Umb.) B, 375 (Pi.) B
Aufidia, 12 (B.) C, 34 (P.) C, 155 (Cp.) A, 161 (Hp.) B, 242 (Pg.) A, 246 (Mcr.) C, 251 (Vt.) A, 257 (V.) A, 271 (M.) C, 311 (S.) B, Lat. A, 372 (Umb.) A, 375 (Pi.) A
Aufidiena, 251 (Vt.) B, 372 (Umb.) C
Aufillia, 155 (Cp.) B, 161 (Hp.) B, 251 (Vt.) C
Aufustia, Lat. C
Augusia, 155 (Cp.) B
Augustalia, Lat. C
Auia, 155 (Cp.) B, 271 (M.) B, 311 (S.) C
Auiania, 27 (L.) B, 155 (Cp.) A, 257 (V.) B, Lat. B
Auidia, 27 (L.) C, 32 (Cl.) B, 36 (D.) C, 155 (Cp.) B, 161 (Hp.) B, 188 (Sm.) B, 198 (F.) B, 242 (Pg.) C, 246 (Mcr.) C, 251 (Vt.) B, 257 (V.) A, 276 (Aq.) B, 307 (Pr.) C, Lat. B, 311 (S.) B, 372 (Umb.) B, 375 (Pi.) C

GENTILE NAMES FROM THE DIALECT-AREAS.

Auidiacca, 34 (P.) C, 251 (Vt.) B
Auidiena, 161 (Hp.) C
Auiedia, 251 (Vt.) C, 372 (Umb.) C
Auiena, 155 (Cp.) B, 372 (Umb.) B, Lat. C
Auienia, Lat. B
Auilledia, 271 (M.) C
Auillia, 34 (P.) A, 155 (Cp.) A, 161 (Hp.) C, 188 (Sm.) B, 242 (Pg.) B, 257 (V.) A, 276 (Aq.) B, 307 (Pr.) B, Lat. C, 311 (S.) C, 350 (Fal.) C, 372 (Umb.) B, 375 (Pi.) B
Auilliena, 276 (Aq.) B
Auincidia, 251 (Vt.) B
Auittia, 34 (P.) B
Auleia, 12 (B.) C
Aulena, 155 (Cp.) A, 188 (Sm.) B
Aulia, 12 (B.) C, 32 (Cl.) B, 155 (Cp.) A, 257 (V.) B, 307 (Pr.) B, Lat. C, 372 (Umb.) B
Auliena, 155 (Cp.) C
Auonia, Lat. B
Aurelia, 12 (B.) A, 27 (L.) A, 32 (Cl.) C, 34 (P.) A, 36 (D.) A, 155 (Cp.) A, 161 (Hp.) A, 188 (Sm.) B, 198 (F.) C, 242 (Pg.) C, 251 (Vt.) C, 257 (V.) A, 279 (H.) B, 307 (Pr.) A, Lat. A, 311 (S.) A, 372 (Umb.) A, 375 (Pi.) A
Aurellia, 350 (Fal.) B
Aurunceia, 307 (Pr.) B
Aurunculeia, 155 (Cp.) B, 188 (Sm.) C, 257 (V.) B, 276 (Aq.) B
Auscia, Lat. C ?
Ausidia, 155 (Cp.) C, 372 (Umb.) B
Austia, 198 (F.) B
Auteia, Lat. C
Autia, 372 (Umb.) C
Autonia, 155 (Cp.) C, 188 (Sm.) C, 198 (F.) C
Autrodia, 155 (Cp.) C
Autronia, 27 (L.) C, 34 (P.) C, 155 (Cp.) B, 257 (V.) C, Lat. B
Axenia, 251 (Vt.) C
Axia, 32 (Cl.) C, 155 (Cp.) C ?
Axilia, Lat. A

Babbia, 36 (D) C, 155 (Cp.) B
Baberia, 34 (P.) B, Lat. A
Babia, 198 (F.) C
Babidenus, 375 (Pi.) C
Babidia, 161 (Hp.) B
Babiena, 375 (Pi.) C ?
Babinia, 155 (Cp.) C
Babrena, 375 (Pi.) C
Babria, 155 (Cp.) B, 161 (Hp.) A, 311 (S.) C
Babudia, 372 (Umb.) B
Babulia, 257 (V.) B
Babullia, 27 (L.) C, 34 (P.) C, 155 (Cp.) B, 279 (H.) C
Baburia, 155 (Cp.) B, 311 (S.) C

Badeia, 155 (Cp.) C (?)
Badia, 34 (P.) C, 155 (Cp.) B, 161 (Hp.) B, 188 (Sm.) A, 257 (V.) B
Badusia, Lat. C, 372 (Umb.) C
Baebia, 27 (L.) C, 32 (Cl.) C, 34 (P.) A, 36 (D.) A, 155 (Cp.) A, 161 (Hp.) A, 188 (Sm.) A, 198 (F.) A, 242 (Pg.) C, 251 (Vt.) B, 257 (V.) A, 271 (M.) B, 279 (H.) C, 307 (Pr.) B, 311 (S.) C, 372 (Umb.) A, 375 (Pi.) A
Baebiana, 155 (Cp.) C
Baebidia, 276 (Aq.) C, 372 (Umb.) B
Baebutia, Lat. B
Baedia, Lat. C
Baia, 27 (L.) C, 251 (Vt.) C, 311 (S.) B
Baiania, 375 (Pi.) B
Daibilia, 155 (Cp.) C
Baionia, 257 (V.) C
Balbilia, Lat. C
Balonia, 34 (P.) C, 155 (Cp.) B, 257 (V.) B
Bania, Lat. C
Bantia, 372 (Umb.) C
Barbaria, 155 (Cp.) C
Barbatia, 34 (P.) C, 155 (Cp.) C, 251 (Vt.) C
Barbia, 155 (Cp.) B, 161 (Hp.) C, 198 (F.) C, 307 (Pr.) C
Barbuleia, 257 (V.) B
Baria, 155 (Cp.) C
Baronia, 155 (Cp.) C
Barria, 32 (Cl.) C
Barronia, 257 (V.) B
Basilia, 155 (Cp.) C, 375 (Pi.) C
Bassaea, 155 (Cp.) C, 161 (Hp.) A, 188 (Sm.) B
Bassia, 155 (Cp.) B
Bassida, 155 (Cp.) C
Bassilia, Lat. C
Batonia, 155 (Cp.) C
Battia, 34 (P.) C
Bebenia, 155 (Cp.) B
Bebia, Lat. A
Belitia, 155 (Cp.) C (?)
Belleia, 161 (Hp.) C
Bellenia, Lat. B
Bellica, 155 (Cp.) B
Bellicia, 155 (Cp.) B, 271 (M.) C, 307 (Pr.) C, Lat. A
Beneuertia, 155 (Cp.) C
Bennia, 27 (L.) C, 155 (Cp.) A, 242 (Pg.) C, 257 (V.) B
Bentuellia, 155 (Cp.) C
Berbucia, Lat. B
Bergonia, 161 (Hp.) C
Beriena, 155 (Cp.) C, 372 (Umb.) C
Beritia, Lat. C (?)
Beruena, 12 (B.) C
Βηρύτιος, 155 (Cp.) C (?)
Betia, 188 (Sm.) C

C.

Betiliena, 32 (Cl.) B, 155 (Cp.) C, 257 (V.) C, 279 (H.) B, 307 (Pr.) C
Betitin, 34 (P.) B, 161 (Hp.) A
Bettuedia, 372 (Umb.) C
Betubia, 155 (Cp.) C
Betuedia, 257 (V.) C
Betuia, 375 (Pi.) C
Betuina, 276 (Aq.) B, 311 (S.) C, Lat. C
Betulena, 251 (Vt.) B, 276 (Aq.) C
Betulia, 246 (Mcr.) C
Betutia, 155 (Cp.) B, 251 (Vt.) B, 257 (V.) B
Beuila, 155 (Cp.) C (?)
Biallia, 375 (Pi.) C?
Bifonia, 155 (Cp.) C
Billiena, 155 (Cp.) B, 155 (Cp.) C, 198 (F.) C, 307 (Pr.) B
Billucidia, 251 (Vt.) C
Bimla, 34 (P.) C
Biolena, 251 (Vt.) C
Bircia, 257 (V.) B
Birronia, 372 (Umb.) B
Bisellia, 155 (Cp.) C
Bisinia, Lat. C
Bittia, 161 (Hp.) C (?), 242 (Pg) C
Binellia, 34 (P.) C, 155 (Cp.) B
Blaesia, 155 (Cp.) B, 251 (Vt.) B, 271 (M.) B, 279 (H.) B
Blaia, 188 (Sm.) C, 257 (V.) B
Blannia, 375 (Pi.) C
Blasia, 161 (Hp.) B
Blassedia, 34 (P.) C
Blassia, 155 (Cp.) B
Blattia, 188 (Sm.) C
Blossia, 155 (Cp.) A, 257 (V.) C, Lat. C
Boatin, 36 (D) C
Bodia, 276 (Aq.) C
Boelia, 251 (Vt.) B
Boionia, 155 (Cp.) C (?)
Bolana, Lat. C
Bombia, Lat. C
Bottia, 188 (Sm.) C
Boufili[a], 307 (Pr.) C
Bouia, 27 (L.) C, 155 (Cp.) B, 161 (Hp.) C, 188 (Sm.) B
Bouiana, 372 (Umb.) C
Bouiania, 27 (L.) B
Braccia, 257 (V.) B
Braetin, 257 (V.) C, 259 (A) C, 372 (Umb.) C
Brasidia, 155 (Cp.) C
Brenia, Lat. C
Brexia, 155 (Cp.) C
Briunia, 27 (L.) C, 155 (Cp.) A, 198 (F.) C
Britidia, Lat. C
Brittia, 155 (Cp.) A, 161 (Hp.) B, 242 (Pg.) B, 307 (Pr.) B, Lat. B, 311 (S.) C, 375 (Pi.) C
Brotia, Lat. C
Brutsena, 375 (Pi.) C

Bruttia, 27 (L.) A, 34 (P.) B, 198 (F.) C, 251 (Vt.) A, 257 (V.) A, 276 (Aq.) B, 307 (Pr.) C, Lat. A, 311 (S.) B, 372 (Umb.) B, 375 (Pi.) C
Bruttidia, 155 (Cp.) C
Bruttiena, 372 (Umb.) B
Bubbia, 155 (Cp.) C
Buccia, 155 (Cp.) B
Buccidin, 372 (Umb.) C
Buccionia, 155 (Cp.) C
Bucleia, 251 (Vt.) C
Budistin, 276 (Aq.) C
Bullania, 257 (V.) C
Bullatia, Lat. C
Bumbria, 188 (Sm.) B
Burbatia, 34 (P.) B
Burbuleia, 372 (Umb.) C
Buria, Lat. C
Burreia, 161 (Hp.) C
Burria, 155 (Cp.) C
Busia, 36 (D.) C
Busidia, 34 (P.) B
Bussenia, 307 (Pr.) C
Buticeia, 307 (Pr.) B
Butronia, 257 (V.) C
Buttia, 161 (Hp.) C
Buxuria, 375 (Pi.) C

Cabarasia, 307 (Pr.) C
Cabilena, 155 (Cp.) C
Cacelia, 161 (Hp.) C
Cacia, 259 (A.) C, Lat. A
Cacuria, 307 (Pr.) B
Cadin, 242 (Pg.) C, 375 (Pi.) C
Caecia, 161 (Hp.) B
Caecilia, 12 (B.) B, 27 (L.) C, 32 (Cl.) C, 34 (P.) A, 155 (Cp.) A, 161 (Hp.) B, 188 (Sm.) B, 242 (Pg.) B, 251 (Vt.) C, 257 (V.) A, 259 (A.) C, 276 (Aq.) B, 279 (H.) B, 307 (Pr.) A, Lat. B, 311 (S.) B, 372 (Umb.) A, 375 (Pi.) A
Caecina, 32 (Cl.) C, 155 (Cp.) B, 257 (V.) A, 307 (Pr.) C
Caedia, 27 (L.) C, 155 (Cp.) C, 161 (Hp.) C, 188 (Sm.) C, 242 (Pg.) B, 251 (Vt.) B, 311 (S.) C, 372 (Umb.) C
Caedicia, 155 (Cp.) C, 257 (V.) B, Lat. C
Caelia, 34 (P.) C, 155 (Cp.) B, 161 (Hp.) A, 246 (Mcr.) C, 251 (Vt.) C, 257 (V.) B, 307 (Pr.) B, Lat. B, 372 (Umb.) B
Caelidia, 34 (P.) C
Caelonia, 34 (P.) C
Caemia, 257 (V.) C
Caepania, 375 (Pi.) C
Caepia, 155 (Cp.) B, Lat. C, 372 (Umb.) C
Caepionia, 375 (Pi.) C
Caerellia, 12 (B.) B, 32 (Cl.) C, 242 (Pg.) C, 257 (V.) B
Caesaria, 372 (Umb.) C
Caesellia, 32 (Cl.) B, 34 (P.) C, 155 (Cp.) A, Lat. A

GENTILE NAMES FROM THE DIALECT-AREAS. 563

Caesellina, 311 (S.) C
Caesena, 198 (Sm.) B
Caesennia, 155 (Cp.) B, 307 (Pr.) C, Lat. A
Caesernia, 155 (Cp.) C, Lat. C
Caesetia, 155 (Cp.) B, Lat. C
Caesia, 12 (B.) A, 27 (L.) B, 32 (Cl.) B, 36 (D.) C, 155 (Cp.) A, 161 (Hp.) A, 188 (Sm.) B, 198 (F.) B, 242 (Pg.) B, 246 (Mer.) B, 251 (Vt.) A, 257 (V.) A, 271 (M.) C, 279 (H.) C, 307 (Pr.) A, Lat. A, 311 (S.) B, 372 (Umb.) A, 375 (Pi.) A
Caesidia, 27 (L.) C, 271 (M.) C, 276 (Aq.) B, 311 (S.) C
Caesiedia, 251 (Vt.) C
Caesiena, 251 (Vt.) A, 276 (Aq.) C, 311 (S.) B
Caesilia, Lat. B
Caesolena, 276 (Aq.) B
Caesolia, 372 (Umb.) B
Caesonia, 155 (Cp.) A, 257 (V.) B, Lat. A, 372 (Umb.) B, 375 (Pi.) C
Cacsoniana, 36 (D.) B
Caesutia, 161 (Hp.) B
Caetennia, Lat. C, 372 (Umb.) C
Caetrania, 251 (Vt.) C, Lat. B
Caetronia, 34 (P.) B, 155 (Cp.) C, 242 (Pg.) C, Lat. B, 372 (Umb.) C, 375 (Pi.) C
Caeuia, 27 (L.) C
Cafatia, 372 (Umb.) C
Caia, 27 (L.) C, 188 (Sm.) C, 251 (Vt.) C, 257 (V.) B
Caiatia, 155 (Cp.) B, 257 (V.) C
Caicia, Lat. B
Caiedia, 311 (S.) B
Caiolia, 372 (Umb.) C
Calaasia, 155 (Cp.) C
Calatoria, 155 (Cp.) A
Calauia, 32 (Cl.) B, 155 (Cp.) B, 198 (F.) B, 257 (V.) C, Lat. B
Caledia, 155 (Cp.) B, Lat. C
Caleia, 161 (Hp.) C, 307 (Pr.) C
Caleida[na]?, 375 (Pi.) C
Calena, 251 (Vt.) C
Calenia, 155 (Cp.) C
Calestria, Lat. C
Calidena, 375 (Pi.) C
Calidia, 155 (Cp.) B, 188 (Sm.) B, 257 (V.) B, 372 (Umb.) B
Calinia, 155 (Cp.) C
Callaea, 279 (H.) C
Calleia, 279 (H.) C
Callia, 251 (Vt.) B, 372 (Umb.) B
Callistana, 372 (Umb.) C
Callonia, 34 (P.) C
Calpena, 161 (Hp.) C, 375 (Pi.) C
Calpetana, 155 (Cp.) C, 198 (F.) C, Lat. B
Calpurnia, 12 (B.) C, 27 (L.) A, 32 (Cl.) B, 36 (D.) A, 155 (Cp.) A, 161 (Hp.) A, 188 (Sm.) C, 257 (V.) B, 279 (H.) C, 307 (Pr.) A, Lat. A, 311 (S.) B, 372 (Umb.) B, 375 (Pi.) B
Caltia, 307 (Pr.) B
Caltilia, 155 (Cp.) C, Lat. A
Caltinia, 272 (Umb.) C
Caluedia, 276 (Aq.) C, 372 (Umb.) B
Caluena, 251 (Vt.) B, 276 (Aq.) B
Caluentia, 32 (Cl.) B, 155 (Cp.) A, 161 (Hp.) B, 257 (V.) C, 271 (M.) C, Lat. C, 350 (Fal.) C, 372 (Umb.) B
Caluia, 12 (B.) B, 34 (P.) B, 155 (Cp.) A, 251 (Vt.) B, 257 (V.) A, 271 (M.) C, Lat. C, 311 (S.) C, 375 (Pi.) B
Caluidia, 155 (Cp.) B, Lat. C
Caluisia, 155 (Cp.) A, 257 (V.) B, Lat. B, 372 (Umb.) B, 375 (Pi.) B
Calusia, 375 (Pi.) B
Camedia, 276 (Aq.) B
Camelia, 155 (Cp.) C, 307 (Pr.) B
Cameria, 155 (Cp.) C, 271 (M.) B, 276 (Aq.) B, Lat. C, 375 (Pi.) B
Camiana, 32 (Cl.) C
Camidia, 257 (V.) B
Camidiena, 307 (Pr.) C, 372 (Umb.) C
Camilia, 12 (B.) C
Camillia, 34 (P.) C
Camonia, 372 (Umb.) B
Campania, 155 (Cp.) B, Lat. C, 375 (Pi.) C
Campia, 155 (Cp.) C
Campila, 34 (P.) C
Campilia, 155 (Cp.) B, 161 (Hp.) B, 375 (Pi.) C
Campusia, 27 (L.) C
Camudena, 188 (Sm.) B
Camullia, 279 (H.) C
Camurena, 372 (Umb.) B, 375 (Pi.) C?
Camurenia, Lat. C
Camuria, 155 (Cp.) C, 161 (Hp.) A, 251 (Vt.) C, 311 (S.) C, 372 (Umb.) A, 375 (Pi.) B
Camurtia, 27 (L.) C, 32 (Cl.) C, 161 (Hp.) C
Cancria, 372 (Umb.) C
Candilia, 257 (V.) C
Caneia, 155 (Cp.) B
Canena, 251 (Vt.) C, 372 (Umb.) C
Canin, 155 (Cp.) A, 251 (Vt.) C
Canidia, 372 (Umb.) C
Caninia, 32 (Cl.) B, 34 (P.) C, 155 (Cp.) A, 257 (V.) C, 307 (Pr.) B, Lat. A, 375 (Pi.) B
Cannutia, 155 (Cp.) C (?), 372 (Umb.) C
Canonia, 161 (Hp.) C
Cantilia, 155 (Cp.) C
Cantinia, 12 (B.) C, 372 (Umb.) C
Cantria, 155 (Cp.) B, 161 (Hp.) A
Canuleia, 34 (P.) A, 36 (D.) C, 155 (Cp.) B, 257 (V.) B, Lat. B, 372 (Umb.) B
Canusia, Lat. C

36—2

Caparia, 271 (M.) C
Capia, Lat. B, 372 (Umb.) C
Capidas, 372 (Umb.) B
Capiua, 375 (Pi.) B (?)
Capiuas, 307 (Pr.) C
Caprasia, 155 (Cp.) A
Caprelia, 161 (Hp.) C
Capria, 36 (D.) C, 161 (Hp.) B, 242 (Pg.) C, 251 (Vt.) B, 257 (V.) A, 311 (S.) C
Caprilia, 372 (Umb.) C
Captia, Lat. B
Carania, 155 (Cp.) C
Carantia, Lat. C, 311 (S.) B
Carbetania, 257 (V.) B
Carcurin...., 276 (Aq.) C
Cardana, 375 (Pi.) C
Cardona, 375 (Pi.) B
Careia, 161 (Hp.) C, 257 (V.) B
Carfann, 161 (Hp.) B
Carfania, 372 (Umb.) C
Carfia, Lat. C
Carfinia, 375 (Pi.) C
Carinatia, 34 (P.) C, Lat. C
Carisia, 155 (Cp.) A, 259 (A.) C, Lat. C
Caristania, 155 (Cp.) B
Carmeia, 155 (Cp.) B, 307 (Pr.) C
Carminia, Lat. A
Carnia, 155 (Cp.) C
Carol[ia], 307 (Pr.) C
Carpelana, 372 (Umb.) C
Carpiana, 372 (Umb.) C (?)
Carpinaria, 155 (Cp.) C, 375 (Pi.) C
Carpinia, 155 (Cp.) C (?)
Carpitana, Lat. C
Carponin, 155 (Cp.) B
Carrinas, 257 (V.) B
Carsedia, 375 (Pi.) C
Carsicia, 155 (Cp.) C
Cartia, Lat. B
Cartilia, 155 (Cp.) C, Lat. A
Cartoria, 155 (Cp.) C, Lat. C
Caruilia, 155 (Cp.) B, Lat. B
Carulia, 155 (Cp.) A, 372 (Umb.) C
Carullia, 307 (Pr.) C, Lat. B
Carutia, Lat. C
Cascellia, 155 (Cp.) B, 161 (Hp.) B, Lat. C
Cascia, 34 (P.) C
Casellia, 155 (Cp.) A
Caseria, 372 (Umb.) B
Casidaria, 311 (S.) C
Casidia, 188 (Sm.) B, 251 (Vt.) C, 372 (Umb.) A
Casicna, 251 (Vt.) C, 276 (Aq.) B
Casincia, 161 (Hp.) A
Casinia, 27 (L.) B, 251 (Vt.) C, 257 (V.) B
Casnasia, 251 (Vt.) B
Casonia, 155 (Cp.) C
Casperia, Lat. A
Caspertia, 372 (Umb.) B
Caspilana, 36 (D.) C

Cassia, 34 (P.) B, 155 (Cp.) A, 161 (Hp.) B, 188 (Sm.) A, 251 (Vt.) B, 257 (V.) B, 259 (A.) C, 276 (Aq.) B, 307 (Pr.) B, Lat. A, 372 (Umb.) A, 375 (Pi.) B
Cassidaria, 307 (Pr.) C
Cassidia, 375 (Pi.) C
Castricia, 155 (Cp.) A, 161 (Hp.) B, 257 (V.) B, Lat. B, 372 (Umb.) B
Castrucia, 372 (Umb.) C
Casuria, 155 (Cp.) B, 372 (Umb.) B
Cateia, 161 (Hp.) C
Catellia, 188 (M.) C (?), 372 (Umb.) C
Catenia, 155 (Cp.) C
Catia, 155 (Cp.) B, 161 (Hp.) B, 251 (Vt.) B, 279 (H.) C, 307 (Pr.) C, 311 (S.) B, Lat. B, 372 (Umb.) B
Caticania, Lat. C
Catiena, 155 (Cp.) B, 257 (V.) C
Catilia, 36 (D.) C, 155 (Cp.) C, Lat. B, 372 (Umb.) C
Catineia, 161 (Hp.) B
Catinia, 34 (P.) C, 257 (V.) C, Lat. B, 375 (Pi.) C
Cattia, 155 (Cp.) A, 188 (Sm.) A, 271 (M.) C, Lat. B
Catunia, 311 (S.) B
Cauaria, 257 (V.) B, Lat. B
Caucia, 155 (Cp.) B, 161 (Hp.) A, 242 (Pg.) C, 307 (Pr.) C
Caucideia, 257 (V.) C
Caudia, 155 (Cp.) B, 375 (Pi.) C
Cauia, Lat. B, 372 (Umb.) B
Cauilia, 155 (Cp.) C
Cauinnia, 155 (Cp.) C
Caulia, 155 (Cp.) C, 276 (Aq.) C, Lat. B
Cauponia, 161 (Hp.) C, 276 (Aq.) C, Lat. B
Cautina, 32 (Cl.) C
Cebetina, 161 (Hp.) C (?)
Ceciena, 34 (P.) C
Ceia, 34 (P.) C, 155 (Cp.) A, 161 (Hp.) A, 257 (V.) B
Ceionia, 155 (Cp.) B, 279 (H.) C, 307 (Pr.) C, Lat. C, 375 (Pi.) B
Celeria, 155 (Cp.) B, 188 (Sm.) B, 198 (F.) B, 271 (M.) C, Lat. B
Celsia, 155 (Cp.) C, 161 (Hp.) C (?)
Cemoleia, 257 (V.) C
Cennia, 375 (Pi.) B
Centin, 188 (Sm.) B
Cepidia, 155 (Cp.) C, 259 (A.) B
Cepoleia, 307 (Pr.) C
Ceppia, 27 (L.) B
Cerellia, Lat. A
Cernitia, 375 (Pi.) B
Cerrinia, 36 (D.) C, 155 (Cp.) A, 161 (Hp.) A, 188 (Sm.) B, 198 (F.) C, 257 (V.) C
Ceruaria, 257 (V.) C, 271 (M.) C
Ceruia, 155 (Cp.) B, 161 (Hp.) B, 242 (Pg.) B, 251 (Vt.) B, 257 (V.) C, Lat. B

Ceruonia, 32 (Cl.) C, 155 (Cp.) B, 372 (Umb.) C
Cesidia, 372 (Umb.) B
Cessia, 155 (Cp.) C
Cestia, 155 (Cp.) C, 307 (Pr.) A, Lat. A, 372 (Umb.) B
Cestilia, 155 (Cp.) B
Ceternia, 34 (P.) C
Cetria, 251 (Vt.) B
Ciarcia, Lat. C
Ciccreia, 155 (Cp.) B
Cilnia, Lat. C
Ciminia, 161 (Hp.) C (?)
Cincia, 12 (B.) B, 27 (L.) B, 32 (Cl.) C, 155 (Cp.) B, 161 (Hp.) B, 188 (Sm.) C, 257 (V.) C, 307 (Pr.) C, Lat. A, 350 (Fal.) C, 375 (Pi.) B
Cingulana, 375 (Pi.) C?
Cinna, 155 (Cp.) B
Cinsia, 307 (Pr.) C
Cintia, 375 (Pi.) C
Cipia, 12 (B.) C, 155 (Cp.) A, 161 (Hp.) C (?), Lat. A
Ciprinia, 375 (Pi.) C
Circenia, 155 (Cp.) C
Cirpinia, 375 (Pi.) C
Cirria, Lat. C
Cisatia, 27 (L.) C
Cisionia, 155 (Cp.) C
Cispia, 155 (Cp.) C, 276 (Aq.) C, 307 (Pr.) B, Lat. C
Cissonia, 155 (Cp.) B, 372 (Umb.) C
Cissuitia, 372 (Umb.) C
Cisuitia, 257 (V.) B
Classetia, 161 (Hp.) C
Classia, 372 (Umb.) C
Clatia, 34 (P.) B
Claudia, 12 (B.) B, 27 (L.) A, 32 (Cl.) A, 34 (P.) A, 36 (D.) B, 155 (Cp.) A, 161 (Hp.) A, 188 (Sm.) A, 198 (F.) C, 242 (Pg.) A, 251 (Vt.) A, 257 (V.) A, 271 (M.) B, 276 (Aq.) B, 279 (H.) B, 307 (Pr.) A, Lat. A, 311 (S.) A, 350 (Fal.) C, 372 (Umb.) A, 375 (Pi.) A
Clauia, 242 (Pg.) C (?)
Clementiana, 372 (Umb.) B
Clepia, 375 (Pi.) B
Cleppia, 34 (P.) C, 161 (Hp.) C
Clippiana, 161 (Hp.) B
Clodia, 12 (B.) C, 27 (L.) B, 32 (Cl.) B, 34 (P.) A, 155 (Cp.) A, 161 (Hp.) A, 188 (Sm.) B, 242 (Pg.) B, 257 (V.) A, 259 (A.) C, 307 (Pr.) A, Lat. A, 311 (S.) B, 372 (Umb.) B, 375 (Pi.) A
Clodiena, 372 (Umb.) B
Cloelia, 155 (Cp.) B, 257 (V.) C, Lat. A
Clonidia, 34 (P.) C
Clonatia, 155 (Cp.) B, 188 (Sm.) C
Cloulia, 251 (Vt.) C, 307 (Pr.) C
Cludia, 155 (Cp.) C

Cluentia, 155 (Cp.) B, 198 (F.) C, Lat. B
Clusenia, 36 (D.) C
Clusinatia, 372 (Umb.) C
Clutoria, 12 (B.) C, 372 (Umb.) B
Cluturia, Lat. C
Cluuia, 155 (Cp.) A, 161 (Hp.) C, 188 (Sm.) B, 307 (Pr.) B, Lat. B, 311 (S.) B, 372 (Umb.) B, 375 (Pi.) B
Cocceia, 32 (Cl.) B, 155 (Cp.) A, 161 (Hp.) B, 188 (Sm.) B, 251 (Vt.) C, 257 (V.) A, 307 (Pr.) C, 311 (S.) B, Lat. A, 372 (Umb.) B, 375 (Pi.) B
Cocia, 34 (P.) C, 307 (Pr.) C
Cocilia, Lat. C
Codennia, 257 (V.) C, 372 (Umb.) C
Codicaria, 251 (Vt.) B
Codiflania, 161 (Hp.) C
Codonia, Lat. B, 372 (Umb.) C
Coelia, 27 (L.) B, 34 (P.) C, 155 (Cp.) A, 161 (Hp.) C, 198 (F.) B, 251 (Vt.) C, 257 (V.) B, 307 (Pr.) B, Lat. A, 311 (S.) B, 372 (Umb.) A, 375 (Pi.) B
Coesia, 188 (Sm.) C
Cofia, 257 (V.) C
Cogitatia, 155 (Cp.) C
Coiedia, 372 (Umb.) A
Colia, 198 (F.) B
Colionia, 307 (Pr.) B
Comanana, 155 (Cp.) C?
Combarisia, Lat. A
Comia, 307 (Pr.) C
Comica, Lat. C
Comicia, 155 (Cp.) C, 257 (V.) B
Cominia, 27 (L.) B, 34 (P.) B, 155 (Cp.) A, 161 (Hp.) B, 188 (Sm.) B, 251 (Vt.) B, 257 (V.) B, 259 (A.) C, 279 (H.) C, 307 (Pr.) A, Lat. A, 311 (S.) B, 372 (Umb.) A, 375 (Pi.) B.
Cominiena, 372 (Umb.) C
Comnena, 372 (Umb.) B
Concordia, 161 (Hp.) B
Conetania, 372 (Umb.) C
Confuleia, 155 (Cp.) B
Connia, 155 (Cp.) C, Lat. C
Consia, 155 (Cp.) B, 242 (Pg.) C, Lat. B
Considia, 155 (Cp.) C, 251 (Vt.) B, Lat. B, 375 (Pi.) C
Constantia, 155 (Cp.) C
Coponia, 161 (Hp.) C, 198 (F.) C, 375 (Pi.) B
Coranna, 279 (H.) B
Corania, 307 (Pr.) C, 311 (S.) C
Cordia, 32 (Cl.) C, 257 (V.) C, 307 (Pr.) B, Lat. B, 372 (Umb.) C
Cordiuia, 155 (Cp.) C
Corelia, 155 (Cp.) B
Corcliat..., 372 (Umb.) C
Corellia, 307 (Pr.) B, 372 (Umb.) C
Coretin, 372 (Umb.) A
Corfidia, 32 (Cl.) C, 311 (S.) B
Corfinia, 242 (Pg.) C

Coria, 372 (Umb.) C
Coriaria, 307 (Pr.) B
Coricia, 307 (Pr.) C
Corisia, 198 (F.) C
Cornasidia, 375 (Pi.) B
Cornelia, 12 (B.) B, 27 (L.) B, 32 (Cl.) B, 34 (P.) A, 155 (Cp.) A, 161 (Hp.) A, 188 (Sm.) B, 242 (Pg.) A, 251 (Vt.) A, 257 (V.) A, 259 (A.) C, 276 (Aq.) B, 279 (H.) C, 307 (Pr.) A, Lat. A, 311 (S.) A, 350 (Fal.) C, 372 (Umb.) A, 375 (Pi.) B
Cornificia, 155 (Cp.) A, 257 (V.) C, 307 (Pr.) B
Corria, 276 (Aq.) C (?)
Corucania, 307 (Pr.) B
Coruia, 251 (Vt.) C
Cosana, 251 (Vt.) C (?)
Cosconia, 155 (Cp.) B, Lat. C
Cosentana, 307 (Pr.) C (?)
Cosentia, 188 (Sm.) C
Cosia, 161 (Hp.) B, 311 (S.) B
Cosidia, 155 (Cp.) C, 251 (Vt.) C, 276 (Aq.) C, 307 (Pr.) C, Lat. B
Cosinia, 161 (Hp.) A
Cossia, 32 (Cl.) C
Cossinia, 155 (Cp.) A, 257 (V.) C, Lat. B, 375 (Pi.) C
Cossonia, 27 (L.) C, 161 (Hp.) C, 257 (V.) B, 307 (Pr.) C, 372 (Umb.) B
Cossutia, 27 (L.) C, 155 (Cp.) B, 257 (V.) B, 276 (Aq.) C, 279 (H.) B, Lat. B, 311 (S.) C
Cotla, 372 (Umb.) B
Cotria, 155 (Cp.) C
Cottia, 12 (B.) C, 155 (Cp.) A, 246 (Mer.) C
Couia, 155 (Cp.) C, 161 (Hp.) C
Craislia, 307 (Pr.) C
Crasicina, 375 (Pi.) C
Crassa, 161 (Hp.) B (?)
Crassia, 155 (Cp.) B
Crassicia, 155 (Cp.) C, 161 (Hp.) B, 257 (V.) C
Crastina, 372 (Umb.) C
Crathia, 372 (Umb.) C
Cratilia, 155 (Cp.) C
Craudelia, 155 (Cp.) C
Cremellia, 372 (Umb.) C
Cremutia, 350 (Fal.) C
Crepereia, 155 (Cp.) C, 257 (V.) C, Lat. B, 372 (Umb.) C
Creperia, 34 (P.) B
Cresidia, 276 (Aq.) B
Creucentia, 350 (Fal.) B
Crispia, 32 (Cl.) C, 155 (Cp.) C, 161 (Hp.) C, Lat. C
Crispina, 155 (Cp.) B (?), Lat. C
Crispinia, 375 (Pi.) C
Critaria, Lat. C
Critlia, 12 (B.) B, 198 (F.) B, 257 (V.) B

Critonia, 34 (P.) B, 155 (Cp.) B, 161 (Hp.) B, 257 (V.) C, Lat. A
Cronia, 36 (D.) C
Crustidia, 161 (Hp.) C, 257 (V.) C, 276 (Aq.) C
Cufia, 188 (Sm.) B
Culcia, 155 (Cp.) A
Culciscia, Lat. B
Culeia, 161 (Hp.) C
Cumia, 307 (Pr.) C
Cupania, 257 (V.) B
Cuperia, Lat. C
Cupia, 307 (Pr.) B
Cupiennia, 155 (Cp.) B, 257 (V.) B
Cuppiena, 372 (Umb.) B
Curatia, 155 (Cp.) B
Curbisia, 276 (Aq.) C
Curfia, 155 (Cp.) C
Curia, 32 (Cl.) C, 34 (P.) B, 155 (Cp.) B, 161 (Hp.) B, 251 (Vt.) B, Lat. B
Curiatia, 36 (D.) C, 155 (Cp.) B, 188 (Sm.) B, 257 (V.) C, Lat. C, 372 (Umb.) B
Curredia, 155 (Cp.) B
Currelia, 155 (Cp.) C
Curtia, 27 (L.) C, 32 (Cl.) C, 34 (P.) B, 155 (Cp.) A, 161 (Hp.) A, 257 (V.) B, 276 (Aq.) C, 307 (Pr.) B, Lat. A, 350 (Fal.) C
Curtilia, 251 (Vt.) B, Lat. C, 372 (Umb.) C
Curtonia, 257 (V.) B
Curuia, 155 (Cp.) B, 372 (Umb.) C, 375 (Pi.) C
Cusia, 155 (Cp.) C
Cusinia, 307 (Pr.) B, 372 (Umb.) B, 375 (Pi.) B
Cusonia, 155 (Cp.) C
Cuspedia, 372 (Umb.) C, 375 (Pi.) C
Cuspia, 34 (P.) C (?), 155 (Cp.) A, 251 (Vt.) C, 257 (V.) C, 279 (H.) C, 307 (Pr.) C, Lat. B, 311 (S.) C, 372 (Umb.) B
Cutia, 155 (Cp.) C, 257 (V.) C, 307 (Pr.) C, Lat. A, 372 (Umb.) B

Dacria, 155 (Cp.) C
Dania, 257 (V.) C (?)
Dannia, 242 (Pg.) C
Dasia, 375 (Pi.) C
Dasiatia, 155 (Cp.) C
Dasimia, 34 (P.) A, 161 (Hp.) C, 188 (Sm.) B, 242 (Pg.) B
Dassia, 155 (Cp.) C
Dastidia, 36 (D.) C, Lat. B
Dasumia, 155 (Cp.) B, 307 (Pr.) C, Lat. B
Deccia, 155 (Cp.) A
Decciana, 12 (B.) C
Deccitia, 307 (Pr.) C
Decia, 34 (P.) C, 161 (Hp.) B, 188 (Sm.) B, 198 (F.) C, 242 (Pg.) C, 257 (V.) B,

GENTILE NAMES FROM THE DIALECT-AREAS.

271 (M.) C, 279 (H.) B, Lat. B, 311 (S.) B, 350 (Fal.) B, 372 (Umb.) A
Decidia, 155 (Cp.) A
Decimia, 27 (L.) B, 34 (P.) B, 155 (Cp.) A, 188 (Sm.) B, 242 (Pg.) B, 259 (A.) C, Lat. A, 372 (Umb.) B
Deciria, 155 (Cp.) B, Lat. B
Decitia, 188 (Sm.) A
Declia, 251 (Vt.) C
Decria, 188 (Sm.) C, 242 (Pg.) B
Decriana, 257 (V.) C
Decumedia, 251 (Vt.) C
Decumena, 372 (Umb.) C
Decumia, 161 (Hp.) C, 257 (V.) A, 279 (H.) B, 307 (Pr.) A
Decuria, 246 (Mer.) C
Deiia, 188 (Sm.) C
Dellia, 34 (P.) C, 155 (Cp.) B
Demetria, 375 (Pi.) C
Dentatia, 155 (Cp.) B
Dentria, 257 (V.) A, 375 (Pi.) B
Dentusia, 372 (Umb.) C
Dessia, 198 (F.) C
Detelia, Lat. B
Detellia, 375 (Pi.) C
Deuia, 372 (Umb.) C
Dexia, 27 (L.) C, 155 (Cp.) C, 188 (Sm.) C, 372 (Umb.) B
Dexsonia, 155 (Cp.) C
Diania, 375 (Pi.) C
Didia, 34 (P.) C, 155 (Cp.) B, 161 (Hp.) B, 188 (Sm.) C, 198 (F.) B, 251 (Vt.) C, 276 (Aq.) A, 311 (S.) C, 372 (Umb.) B, 375 (Pi.) B
Didiolena, 36 (D.) C
Digitia, 27 (L.) B, 257 (V.) C
Dignia, 257 (V.) C
Diudia, 307 (Pr.) A
Dinnia, 27 (L.) B, 155 (Cp.) A
Dionysia, 155 (Cp.) B, 372 (Umb.) B
Diria, 155 (Cp.) B
Diruitia, 27 (L.) B, 271 (M.) C
Dirutia, 198 (F.) B
Disellia, 375 (Pi.) B
Disinia, 372 (Umb.) B
Dissenia, Lat. B
Diuia, 271 (M.) B
Diuilia, Lat. C
Diuiliena, 372 (Umb.) C
Docetia, 276 (Aq.) C
Doia, 155 (Cp.) C, 372 (Umb.) B
Dolania, 375 (Pi.) C
Dolutia, 155 (Cp.) B, 307 (Pr.) B
Domatia, 155 (Cp.) B, 161 (Hp.) B, 257 (V.) C, Lat. B
Domitia, 27 (L.) C, 32 (Cl.) B, 34 (P.) B, 36 (D.) C, 155 (Cp.) A, 161 (Hp.) B, 188 (Sm.) B, 242 (Pg.) C, 251 (Vt.) B, 257 (V.) A, 259 (A.) B, 276 (Aq.) B, 279 (H.) C, 307 (Pr.) A, Lat. A, 311 (S.) B, 372 (Umb.) B, 375 (Pi.) A

Donatia, Lat. C
Donnia, 27 (L.), Lat. C
Dossennia, 12 (B.) C, 375 (Pi.) C
Dotia, 257 (V.) B
Drusia, 155 (Cp.) C
Drussia, 34 (P.) B, 198 (F.) C
Ducea? 34 (P.) C
Ducenia, 155 (Cp.) A, 279 (H.) C, Lat. C
Duilia, 257 (V.) C
Duillia, 188 (Sm.) C
Dullania, 155 (Cp.) C (?)
Dullia, 242 (Pg.) C
Dupilia, Lat. A
Durdenia, Lat. C
Durmia, 257 (V.) B, Lat. C, 307 (Pr.) C
Duronia, 155 (Cp.) C, Lat. B
Durrachina, 155 (Cp.) C
Dursubia, 372 (Umb.) C
Duruia, 375 (Pi.) B
Duruuia, 372 (Umb.) C
Dusmia, 246 (Mer.) C

Eassidia, 155 (Cp.) C
Ebelana, 375 (Pi.) C?
Eccurncia, 372 (Umb.) B
Edia, 155 (Cp.) B, 257 (V.) C
Edusia, 372 (Umb.) C
Efuria, 155 (Cp.) C
Eggia, 34 (P.) C, 155 (Cp.) C, 161 (Hp.) A, 257 (V.) C, Lat. B
Egnatia, 12 (B.) C, 34 (P.) A, 36 (D.) B, 155 (Cp.) A, 161 (Hp.) B, 188 (Sm.) B, 257 (V.) A, 259 (A.) C, 307 (Pr.) B, Lat. A, 350 (Fal.) B, 372 (Umb.) A, 375 (Pi.) B
Egnatiena, 311 (S.) B, 372 (Umb.) C
Egrilia, 155 (Cp.) C, Lat. A
Egulleia, 279 (H.) C
Egullia, 161 (Hp.) C
Eia, 155 (Cp.) C
Eiedia, 155 (Cp.) C
Eleria, 372 (Umb.) C
Eleuria, 372 (Umb.) B
Elufria, 307 (Pr.) C, 372 (Umb.) B
Elusia, 155 (Cp.) C
Emuslena, 155 (Cp.) C (?)
Ennonia, 32 (Cl.) C
Ennia, 34 (P.) A, 36 (D.) C, 155 (Cp.) A, 161 (Hp.) A, 188 (Sm.) A, 251 (Vt.) B, 257 (V.) C, 276 (Aq.) C, Lat. B, 375 (Pi.) B
Entedia, 311 (S.) B (?)
Enulcia, 155 (Cp.) C (?)
Epidia, 27 (L.) C, 155 (Cp.) A, 161 (Hp.) B, 188 (Sm.) A, 198 (F.) C, 257 (V.) B, 259 (A.) B, 372 (Umb.) B, 375 (Pi.) A
Epillia, 155 (Cp.) B
Epoleia, 307 (Pr.) B
Eppania, 257 (V.) C
Eppia, 27 (L.) C, 34 (P.) C, 161 (Hp.) B, 188 (Sm.) C, 279 (H.) C, 375 (Pi.) B

Eppilia, 155 (Cp.) B
Epria, 155 (Cp.) B, 161 (Hp.) C, 257 (V.) B
Epuleia, 307 (Pr.) B
Epuria, 161 (Hp.) C
Equitia, 27 (L.) B, 155 (Cp.) A, Lat. C
Erecia, 161 (Hp.) C?
Erefria, 251 (Vt.) C
Ereleia, Lat. C
Ermia, 161 (Hp.) C
Ermonia, 372 (Umb.) C
Ernuleia, Lat. C
Eronia, 372 (Umb.) B
Erucia, 36 (D.) B, 155 (Cp.) A, 161 (Hp.) C, 257 (V.) C, 259 (A.) C, Lat. C
Eruciana, Lat. B
Eruia, 155 (Cp.) C
Erullia, 161 (Hp.) C?
Erutia, 372 (Umb.) B
Escionia, 155 (Cp.) C
Esquilia, 34 (P.) B
Essenuia, 155 (Cp.) C
Estania, 251 (Vt.) B
Eteria, 257 (V.) C
Ethereia, 155 (Cp.) C
Etria, 155 (Cp.) C
Etrilia, 161 (Hp.) C, 307 (Pr.) B, 311 (S.) C, Lat. C
Etusia, 372 (Umb.) C
Eumachia, 155 (Cp.) A
Euresia, 372 (Umb.) C
Eututia, 271 (M.) C

Faberia, 257 (V.) C, Lat. C
Fabia, 12 (B.) B, 27 (L.) B, 32 (Cl.) C, 34 (P.) A, 36 (D.) B, 155 (Cp.) A, 161 (Hp.) C, 188 (Sm.) A, 198 (F.) B, 251 (Vt.) B, 257 (V.) A, 259 (A.) C, 279 (H.) C, 307 (Pr.) A, Lat. A, 311 (S.) C, 372 (Umb.) C
Fabraterna, 257 (V.) C
Fabricia, 27 (L.) B, 155 (Cp.) A, 161 (Hp.) B, 307 (Pr.) A, Lat. B, 311 (S.) B, 372 (Umb.) B
Fabullia, 155 (Cp.) C
Fadena, 375 (Pi.) A
Fadia, 27 (L.) B, 32 (Cl.) B, 34 (P.) B, 155 (Cp.) A, 161 (Hp.) C, 188 (Sm.) A, 242 (Pg.) B, 251 (Vt.) B, 276 (Aq.) C, Lat. B, 372 (Umb.) B, 375 (Pi.) B
Faecenia, 188 (Sm.) C, Lat. B
Faecia, 155 (Cp.) B
Faelia, 161 (Hp.) C, 372 (Umb.) C
Faenia, 32 (Cl.) C, 34 (P.) B, 155 (Cp.) A, Lat. A
Faesania, 251 (Vt.) B
Faesasia, 188 (Sm.) C, 198 (F.) C
Faesonia, 375 (Pi.) B
Fafinia, 155 (Cp.) C
Faiania, 311 (S.) B, Lat. C
Falcidia, 311 (S.) C

Falcilia, 161 (Hp.) C
Falconia, 155 (Cp.) C
Faleria, 32 (Cl.) C, 34 (P.) B, 279 (H.) B
Falia, 372 (Umb.) C
Faltonia, 155 (Cp.) B, 161 (Hp.) C, Lat. B, 311 (S.) C, 372 (Umb.) C
Fania, 307 (Pr.) B, 372 (Umb.) C
Fannia, 32 (Cl.) B, 155 (Cp.) A, 161 (Hp.) C, 188 (Sm.) B, 251 (Vt.) B, Lat. B, 375 (Pi.) B
Faracia, 257 (V.) C
Farrania, Lat. C
Farria, Lat. C
Fauonia, 257 (V.) B
Fausi..., Lat. C
Faustia, 155 (Cp.) C, 257 (V.) B, 372 (Umb.) B
Feidenatia, 307 (Pr.) B
Felicia, 372 (Umb.) C
Felsinia, 155 (Cp.) B
Felsonia, 155 (Cp.) C
Ferennia, 161 (Hp.) C
Ferentiana, 372 (Umb.) C
Feridia, 257 (V.) C, Lat. C
Ferlidia, 307 (Pr.) C
Feronia, 155 (Cp.) C, 251 (Vt.) B, 311 (S.) C, 375 (Pi.) A
Ferrania, Lat. B
Ferrena, 34 (P.) B
Ferronia, 257 (V.) C
Fertoria, 257 (V.) C
Feruenia, 155 (Cp.) C
Fescennia, Lat. C
Fescennia, Lat. C
Festiana, 372 (Umb.) C
Festinia, 155 (Cp.) C
Ficellia, 32 (Cl.) C
Ficilia, 155 (Cp.) C
Fictoria, 155 (Cp.) C, 307 (Pr.) B, Lat. C
Fidia, 155 (Cp.) B, 188 (Sm.) B, 257 (V.) B, 271 (M.) B
Fidiclania, 257 (V.) C (?), 307 (Pr.) C
Fidubia, 12 (B.) C
Fiduia, 155 (Cp.) C
Figellia, 27 (L.) B, 198 (F.) B
Figilia, 161 (Hp.) C
Filionia, 372 (Umb.) C
Fillia, 155 (Cp.) B, 161 (Hp.) C, 188 (Sm.) B
Firidia, 257 (V.) C, 259 (A.) C
Firmania, Lat. B
Firmia, 155 (Cp.) A, 161 (Hp.) C, 251 (Vt.) C, 257 (V.) C, Lat. B, 372 (Umb.) C
Firmiana, Lat. C
Firmidia, 372 (Umb.) C
Firmilia, 161 (Hp.) B
Firminia, 257 (V.) B
Firucia, 161 (Hp.) B
Firuia, 155 (Cp.) C, 161 (Hp.) B
Fiscenia?, 36 (D.) C

Fiscilia, 372 (Umb.) B
Fiscuia, Lat. A
Fisia, 155 (Cp.) A, 161 (Hp.) C, 188 (Sm.) B
Fistana, 375 (Pi.) C
Fistia, 155 (Cp.) B
Flaccoia, 161 (Hp.) C, 242 (Pg.) B
Fladia, 188 (Sm.) C
Flaminia, 34 (P.) B, 155 (Cp.) B, 161 (Hp.) C, 257 (V.) C, 279 (H.) B, Lat. C, 372 (Umb.) B
Flatedia, 372 (Umb.) C
Flauennia, 372 (Umb.) B
Flauia, 12 (B.) B, 27 (L.) A, 32 (Cl.) B, 34 (P.) A, 36 (D.) B, 155 (Cp.) A, 161 (Hp.) A, 188 (Sm.) A, 198 (H.) A, 242 (Pg.) B, 246 (Mer.) C, 251 (Vt.) A, 257 (V.) A, 259 (A.) B, 271 (M.) B, 276 (Aq.) B, 279 (H.) A, 307 (Pr.) A, Lat. A, 311 (S.) A, 372 (Umb.) A, 375 (Pi.) A
Flauina, Lat. B
Flauoleia, 307 (Pr.) C
Flauonia, 276 (Aq.) C, 375 (Pi.) C
Florentia, 372 (Umb.) C
Floria, 155 (Cp.) B, 188 (Sm.) A, 257 (V.) B, Lat. B, 372 (Umb.) C, 375 (Pi.) B
Floronia, 350 (Fal.) C
Fluria, 161 (Hp.) B
Fobia, 257 (V.) C
Focnia, 372 (Umb.) C
Foesulena, 372 (Umb.) C
Folia, 155 (Cp.) B, 161 (Hp.) B, 307 (Pr.) C, Lat. A, 372 (Umb.) C
Fonteia, 34 (P.) C, 155 (Cp.) B, 161 (Hp.) B, 257 (V.) B, Lat. A
Foratia, 307 (Pr.) C
Forbeia, Lat. C
Foruiria, 188 (Sm.) A
Fotidia, 155 (Cp.) C
Fraucia, 155 (Cp.) B
Fregania, 161 (Hp.) B, 188 (Sm.) B, Lat. A
Freia, 155 (Cp.) A, 375 (Pi.) B
Fremedia, 372 (Umb.) C
Frensidia, 271 (M.) C
Fresidia, 307 (Pr.) C, 375 (Pi.) B, 257 (V.) C, 271 (M.) C
Fretria, 311 (S.) C
Frigidia, 311 (S.) C
Frontiniana, 372 (Umb.) C
Fudia, 188 (Sm.) C
Fufia, 32 (Cl.) B, 155 (Cp.) B, 161 (Hp.) A, 188 (Sm.) B, 251 (Vt.) C, 257 (V.) C, 276 (Aq.) C, 307 (Pr.) C, 311 (S.) B, 375 (Pi.) B
Fuficia, 155 (Cp.) A, 161 (Hp.) B, 188 (Sm.) C, 242 (Pg.) B, 251 (Vt.) B, 257 (V.) B, Lat. B, 372 (Umb.) A, 375 (Pi.) B

Fuficulena, Lat. C
Fufidia, 34 (P.) C, 155 (Cp.) B, 188 (Sm.) A, 257 (V.) A, Lat. C, 372 (Umb.) C
Fuionia, 375 (Pi.) C
Fulcinia, 155 (Cp.) C, 161 (Hp.) B, 251 (Vt.) B, Lat. C, 375 (Pi.) C
Fulia, 372 (Umb.) C?
Fullia, 155 (Cp.) C
Fullonia, 34 (P.) C, 155 (Cp.) B, 161 (Hp.) C, 251 (Vt.) C, 276 (Aq.) C, Lat. C, 372 (Umb.) A
Fulmonia, 155 (Cp.) B
Fultia, Lat. C
Fuluia, 27 (L.) C, 32 (Cl.) C, 34 (P.) B, 155 (Cp.) A, 161 (Hp.) B, 188 (Sm.) C, 198 (F.) C, 251 (Vt.) C, 257 (V.) B, 279 (H.) C, 307 (Pr.) C, Lat. A, 311 (S.) B, 350 (Fal.) C, 372 (Umb.) B, 375 (Pi.) B
Fuluinia, 155 (Cp.) C
Fundania, 27 (L.) C, 34 (P.) C, 155 (Cp.) B, 161 (Hp.) B, 188 (Sm.) C, 257 (V.) B, Lat. B
Fundia, 257 (V.) C
Fundilia, 155 (Cp.) C, Lat. B, 311 (S.) B, 375 (Pi.) C
Funia, 161 (Hp.) C
Funisulana, Lat. C
Furfana, 372 (Umb.) C
Furfania, 372 (Umb.) C
Furia, 155 (Cp.) A, 161 (Hp.) B, 257 (V.) A, Lat. A, 350 (Fal.) B, 372 (Umb.) A, 375 (Pi.) B
Furnia, 155 (Cp.) B, 155 (Cp.) C, Lat. C
Furuia, 251 (Vt.) C
Fusia, 375 (Pi.) C
Fusinia, Lat. C
Futia, 12 (B.) B, 155 (Cp.) C, 257 (V.) A, Lat. B

Gabbia, 198 (F.) B
Gabinia, 27 (L.) C, 32 (Cl.) A, 155 (Cp.) A, 251 (Vt.) C, 307 (Pr.) B, Lat. B, 372 (Umb.) B
Gagilia, 161 (Hp.) C
Gaia, 307 (Pr.) C
Gaidin, 242 (Pg.) C
Galedia, Lat. C
Galeria, 155 (Cp.) B, 257 (V.) B, 307 (Pr.) B, Lat. B, 372 (Umb.) C
Galgestes, 257 (V.) C
Gallatronia, 251 (Vt.) C
Gallia, 307 (Pr.) C, 311 (S.) C, 372 (Umb.) B
Galliania, 155 (Cp.) C
Gallicia, 155 (Cp.) B
Gallienia, 372 (Umb.) C
Galonia, 155 (Cp.) C
Galuia, 36 (D.) C
Gampulaca, 27 (L.) C

Gargilia, 155 (Cp.) B, 257 (V.) B, 276 (Aq.) B, Lat. B, 372 (Umb.) C
Gargonia, 155 (Cp.) C, 161 (Hp.) C, 372 (Umb.) B, 375 (Pi.) B
Gauedia, 271 (M.) C
Gauelia, 161 (Hp.) C
Gauella, 188 (Sm.) C
Gauenia, 257 (V.) B
Gauennia, 251 (Vt.) B, 372 (Umb.) C
Gauia, 27 (L.) B, 32 (Cl.) C, 34 (P.) A, 36 (D.) B, 155 (Cp.) A, 161 (Hp.) B, 242 (Pg.) B, 251 (Vt.) B, 257 (V.) A, 271 (M.) B, 276 (Aq.) B, 307 (Pr.) B, Lat. A, 372 (Umb.) B
Gauidia, 155 (Cp.) B, 251 (Vt.) B, 257 (V.) C, 307 (Pr.) C
Gauiena, 311 (S.) B
Gauillia, 155 (Cp.) B, 161 (Hp.) C, 188 (Sm.) C, 271 (M.) C, 375 (Pi.) B
Gauinia, 188 (Sm.) C
Gauolena, 188 (Sm.) C (?)
Gegania, 307 (Pr.) B, 257 (V.) C
Gellia, 27 (L.), B, 34 (P.) C, 155 (Cp.) A, 161 (Hp.) B, 188 (Sm.) C, 257 (V.) B, 307 (Pr.) C, Lat. A, 372 (Umb.) A, 375 (Pi.) C
Gelonia, 155 (Cp.) C
Gemellia, 270 (H.) C
Geminia, 32 (Cl.) B, 34 (P.) B, 155 (Cp.) B, 161 (Hp.) C, 257 (V.) A, 307 (Pr.) B, Lat. A, 372 (Umb.) A, 375 (Pi.) B
Genatia, Lat. C
Geneia, 375 (Pi.) C
Genicia, 155 (Cp.) B
Gennia, 257 (V.) B
Gentia, 155 (Cp.) C, 257 (V.) B, 279 (H.) C, Lat. B, 375 (Pi.) C
Genucia, 36 (D.) C, 155 (Cp.) B, Lat. B
Gepidia, Lat. B
Gerellana, 32 (Cl.) A, 34 (P.) C, 155 (Cp.) B
Gerelliana, 32 (Cl.) C
Gergenia, 311 (S.) C
Germania, 155 (Cp.) B
Gerontia, 155 (Cp.) C
Gerulana, Lat. C
Gerusia, Lat. C
Gesatin, Lat. C
Gessia, 155 (Cp.) B, Lat. B, 372 (Umb.) B
Gestiana, 372 (Umb.) C
Gettia, Lat. B
Gifinia, 32 (Cl.) C
Gigania, 155 (Cp.) C
Glitia, 34 (P.) C, 350 (Fal.) B
Gordia, Lat. C
Gracilia, 155 (Cp.) C
Graccalia, 32 (Cl.) C
Graeceia, 155 (Cp.) C, 161 (Hp.) C
Graecia, Lat. B

Graecidia, 34 (P.) B
Graecina, 372 (Umb.) C
Graecinia, 198 (F.) C, Lat. B, 372 (Umb.) B
Graia, 155 (Cp.) C, 257 (V.) C, 372 (Umb.) B
Graicia, 257 (V.) C
Graltia, 155 (Cp.) C
Grania, 32 (Cl.) B, 36 (D.) C, 155 (Cp.) A, 188 (Sm.) C, 257 (V.) B, 271 (M.) C, Lat. A, 372 (Umb.) B
Grassia, 375 (Pi.) C
Gratia, 375 (Pi.) C
Grattia, 155 (Cp.) C, 257 (V.) C, Lat. B
Greia, 311 (S.) B
Grelia, 271 (M.) C
Gresia, 372 (Umb.) B
Gricia, 188 (Sm.) C (?)
Grittia, 34 (P) C
Groesia, 257 (V.) C
Grottonia, 188 (Sm.) C (?)
Grulcia, 27 (L.) C
Grusia, 155 (Cp.) C
Gullia, 188 (Sm.) C (?)
Gungia, 307 (Pr.) B
Gupacia, 155 (Cp.) C
Gustilia, 257 (V.) C
Gutia, 372 (Umb.) B
Gypsania, Lat. C

Haedinia, 27 (L.) B
Haia, 155 (Cp.) B, 161 (Hp.) C, 372 (Umb.) C (?)
Halicia, 311 (S.) C
Harmonia, 155 (Cp.) B
Haruia, 271 (M.) C
Hateria, 27 (L.) B, 155 (Cp.) B, 279 (H.) B, 307 (Pr.) C, Lat. A, 372 (Umb.) C
Hatilia, 155 (Cp.) C
Hatreia, 188 (Sm.) C
Hedia, 155 (Cp.) B, Lat. B, 372 (Umb.) B
Hegia, 155 (Cp.) C
Heia, 34 (P.) C, 155 (Cp.) B, 188 (Sm.) C
Heidia, 155 (Cp.) B, 372 (Umb.) B
Heiolcia, 155 (Cp.) B
Heiulcia, 375 (Pi.) C
Heiulia, Lat. C
Heldia, 372 (Umb.) B
Heleia, 257 (V.) B
Helena, 276 (Aq.) C
Helenia, 155 (Cp.) C
Helfinia, Lat. C
Hellenia, Lat. C
Helmonia, 155 (Cp.) B
Heluacia, 251 (Vt.) B, 276 (Aq.) C
Heluenatia, 372 (Umb.) B
Heluia, 12 (B.) C, 27 (L.) A, 34 (P.) B, 36 (D.) B, 155 (Cp.) A, 161 (Hp.) A,

GENTILE NAMES FROM THE DIALECT-AREAS. 571

188 (Sm.) A, 242 (Pg.) A, 251 (Vt.) B, 257 (V.) A, 271 (M.) C, Lat. A, 372 (Umb.) A, 375 (Pi.) B
Heluidia, 198 (F.) C, 246 (Mcr.) C, 251 (Vt.) C, 307 (Pr.) B, 311 (S.) B, Lat. C, 372 (Umb.) B
Heluisia, 155 (Cp.) B
Heraclia, 372 (Umb.) C
Herbacia, 155 (Cp.) C
Herdonia, 155 (Cp.) C
Hereia, Lat. A
Herena, 372 (Umb.) C
Herenia, 246 (Mcr.) C
Herenncua, 372 (Umb.) C
Herennia, 27 (L.) B, 34 (P.) A, 36 (D.) B, 155 (Cp.) A, 161 (Hp.) A, 188 (Sm.) A, 251 (Vt.) B, 257 (V.) A, 271 (M.) B, 276 (Aq.) A, 307 (Pr.) B, Lat. A, 311 (S.) B, 350 (Fal.) C, 372 (Umb.) B, 375 (Pi.) A
Herennuleia, 311 (S.) C, Lat. A
Hergenia, 372 (Umb.) C
Heria, 155 (Cp.) A, 188 (Sm.) C, 198 (F.) C, 257 (V.) B, Lat. B
Herminia, 34 (P.) C
Hermonia, 155 (Cp.) B, 375 (Pi.) B
Hertoria, 372 (Umb.) C
Heteria, 251 (Vt.) C, 372 (Umb.) B
Hetrilia, 155 (Cp.) B
Hezzia?, 36 (D.) B
Hilariana, 372 (Umb.) C
Hinoleia, 155 (Cp.) C
Hippellia, 155 (Cp.) B
Hippia, 155 (Cp.) B
Hiria, 161 (Hp.) B
Hirnicia, 251 (Vt.) B
Hirpia, 372 (Umb.) B
Hirredia, 276 (Aq.) C
Hirria, 155 (Cp.) B, 161 (Hp.) B, 188 (Sm.) C
Hirtia, (S.) C, 271 (M.) B, 279 (H.) A
Hirtilia, 307 (Pr.) C (?)
Hispella, 372 (Umb.) C
Hispellatia, 155 (Cp.) C
Histria, 155 (Cp.) A
Histumennia, 257 (V.) C
Hoenia, Lat. C, 372 (Umb.) B
Holconia, 155 (Cp.) A
Holstilia, 188 (Sm.) C
Honeria, Lat. C
Honoria, 242 (Pg.) C
Horatia, 34 (P.) C, 155 (Cp.) B, 198 (F.) C, 307 (Pr.) C, Lat. A
Hordeonia, 257 (V.) B
Hordionia, 27 (L.) C, 155 (Cp.) A, Lat. B
Hortensia, 155 (Cp.) B, 372 (Umb.) C, 242 (Pg.) C, Lat. A
Hortesia, 375 (Pi.) C
Hortoria, 257 (V.) B, 372 (Umb.) C
Hoscinia, 32 (Cl.) C

Hosidia, 155 (Cp.) B, 168 (H.) A, Lat. C
Hostia, 27 (L.) C, 155 (Cp.) A, Lat. B
Hostidia, 161 (Hp.) C
Hostilia, 32 (Cl.) C, 34 (P.) C, 155 (Cp.) A, 188 (Sm.) C, 251 (Vt.) B, 276 (Aq.) B, 279 (H.) B, Lat. A, 311 (S.) C, 375 (Pi.) C
Hostiliena, 279 (H.) C
Hostillia, 372 (Umb.) C
Hostria, 155 (Cp.) B, 161 (Hp.) B
Humania, Lat. A
Iallia, 155 (Cp.) C
Ianternina, 271 (M.) C
Iantia, 372 (Umb.) B
Iauolena, 188 (Sm.) C (?), Lat. B, 372 (Umb.) B
Iegia, 276 (Aq.) A, Lat. C
Iegidia, 375 (Pi.) C
Iepriena, 311 (S.) C
Igia, 155 (Cp.) C
Ignatia, 34 (P.) C
Ignia, 161 (Hp.) B
Ilia, (Cp.) B
Ilippia, 155 (Cp.) B
Illyrica, 251 (Vt.) C
Insontia, 161 (Hp.) C
Instacidia, 251 (Vt.) C
Instania, 155 (Cp.) B
Insteia, 27 (L.) A, 155 (Cp.) B, 257 (V.) C, 307 (Pr.) B, Lat. C
Instia, 12 (B) C
Instueia, 155 (Cp.) C
Ipla, 36 (D.) C?
Irpinia, 27 (L.) C
Irria, 198 (F.) B
Iruinia, 161 (Hp.) B
Istaueria, 155 (Cp.) B
Isticidia, 155 (Cp.) A
Istilia, Lat. C (?)
Istiminia, 257 (V.) C
Istoria, Lat. B
Isutia, 375 (Pi.) B?
Iteia, 155 (Cp.) B
Itelia, 307 (Pr.) C
Itia, 198 (F.) B, 372 (Umb.) C
Iuentia, 161 (Hp.) C, 311 (S.) B
Iulenia, 372 (Umb.) C
Iulia, 12 (B.) A, 27 (L.) A, 32 (Cl.) A, 34 (P.) A, 36 (D.) B, 155 (Cp) A, 161 (Hp.) A, 188 (Sm.) A, 198 (F.) B, 242 (Pg.) A, 246 (Mcr.) C, 251 (Vt.) A, 257 (V.) A, 259 (A.) A, 271 (M.) B, 276 (Aq.) B, 279 (H.) B, 307 (Pr.) A, Lat. A, 311 (S.) A, 350 (Fal.) B, 372 (Umb.) A, 375 (Pi.) A
Iunachilia, 155 (Cp.) C
Iunia, 12 (B.) C, 32 (Cl.) B, 34 (P.) A, 36 (D.) B, 155 (Cp.) A, 161 (Hp.) A, 188 (Sm.) C, 198 (F.) C, 251 (Vt.)

B, 257 (V.) A, 259 (A.) C, 276 (Aq.) C, 307 (Pr.) A, Lat. A, 311 (S.) B, 350 (Fal.) C, 372 (Umb.) B, 375 (Pi.) B
Iusta, 155 (Cp.) C
Iustin, 12 (B) C, 155 (Cp.) C, Lat. B
Iustiniana, 161 (Hp.) C
Iustulcia, 155 (Cp.) B, 257 (V.) C, Lat. C
Iuuenia, 372 (Umb.) C
Iuuentia, 27 (L.) B, 32 (Cl.) C, 155 (Cp.) B, 257 (V.) C, 307 (Pr.) C, Lat. A, 372 (Umb.) B, 375 (Pi.) C

Kadia, 155 (Cp.) B
Kania, Lat. C
Karminia, 375 (Pi.) C
Kaulimertia, 155 (Cp.) C?

Laberia, 12 (B.) C, 27 (L.) C, 155 (Cp.) A, 188 (Sm.) C, 257 (V.) B, 271 (M.) B, 279 (H.) C, Lat. A, 372 (Umb.) A
Labia, 161 (Hp.) C
Labicia, 161 (Hp.) C
Labicna, 161 (Hp.) B, Lat. C, 375 (Pi.) B
Lacaenia, 155 (Cp.) C
Laccaca, 372 (Umb.) C
Lacceia, 188 (Sm.) B
Lacia, 257 (V.) B
Laconia, 372 (Umb.) C
Lacutulana, 155 (Cp.) C, 251 (Vt.) B, 257 (V.) B
Laccania, 32 (Cl.) C, 155 (Cp.) A, 307 (Pr.) C, Lat. B, 375 (Pi.) C
Laelia, 155 (Cp.) A, 161 (Hp.) C, 242 (Pg.) C, 251 (Vt.) A, 257 (V.) A, Lat. A, 307 (Pr.) C, 311 (S.) B
Laenia, 32 (Cl.) B
Laetilia, 161 (Hp.) C, 372 (Umb.) C
Laetoria, 155 (Cp.) B, Lat. C, 372 (Umb.) C, 375 (Pi.) B
Lacuia, 155 (Cp.) C, 257 (V.) C, Lat. B
Lafrenia, 372 (Umb.) C, 375 (Pi.) C
Lafria, 161 (Hp.) C
Lainia, 251 (Vt.) C
Lalia, 188 (Sm.) B, Lat. C
Lamia, 372 (Umb.) C
Lampridia, 242 (Pg.) B
Lania, 32 (Cl.) C, 34 (P.) C, 257 (V.) B, Lat. C, 372 (Umb.) C
Laniuia, 372 (Umb.) C
Lantia, 155 (Cp.) C?
Lanuuia, 372 (Umb.) C
Lapillana, 27 (L.) B
Lappia, 155 (Cp.) C, Lat. B, 372 (Umb.) B
Lapscidia, 155 (Cp.) B, 251 (Vt.) C
Lapulcia, 372 (Umb.) C?
Larcia, 34 (P.) C, 155 (Cp.) A, 188 (Sm.) B, 257 (V.) A, Lat. B, 311 (S.) B
Larena, 372 (Umb.) C?

Largia, 257 (V.) B, Lat. C
Laria, 161 (Hp.) C, 372 (Umb.) B
Laricia, Lat. C
Larinata, 372 (Umb.) B
Larinia, 155 (Cp.) C
Laronia, 12 (B.) C, 155 (Cp.) B, 161 (Hp.) C, 242 (Pg.) B, 279 (H.) B
Larsia, 375 (Pi.) C
Lartia, 155 (Cp.) B, Lat. B, 372 (Umb.) B
Lartidia, 155 (Cp.) B, Lat. B
Lartiena, 276 (Aq.) C, 372 (Umb.) C
Lassia, 155 (Cp.) B
Lassuccia, 155 (Cp.) C, Lat. B
Lateria, 32 (Cl.) C, 307 (Pr.) B, 372 (Umb.) B
Laterina, 257 (V.) C
Latia, 12 (B.) C
Laticia, 375 (Pi.) C
Laticli. ., 372 (Umb.) C
Latinia, 27 (L.) C, 161 (Hp.) B, 257 (V.) B, Lat. C, 372 (Umb.) C, 375 (Pi.) C
Latronia, 375 (Pi.) C
Lattia, 375 (Pi.) C
Latuedia, 372 (Umb.) B
Laturnia, 27 (L.) C
Laudicia, 372 (Umb.) B
Laufcia, 257 (V.) B
Lautinia, 34 (P.) C?, 155 (Cp.) C
Lauuia, 372 (Umb.) C
Logaria, Lat. C
Lepania, 257 (V.) C
Lepidia, 34 (P.) B, 155 (Cp.) B, 161 (Hp.) C, 257 (V.) B, 307 (Pr.) B, Lat. C
Leria, 372 (Umb.) B
Lesia, 251 (Vt.) C, 372 (Umb.) C
Lettcia, 372 (Umb.) C
Leuonica, Lat. B
Libertia, 12 (B.) C
Libonia, 161 (Hp.) C
Libuscidia, 34 (P.) B
Liccia, 161 (Hp.) C
Liccuicia, 155 (Cp.) C
Licinacia, 251 (Vt.) C
Licinia, 12 (B.) C, 27 (L.) C, 34 (P.) A, 36 (D.) C, 155 (Cp.) A, 161 (Hp.) A, 188 (Sm.) A, 198 (F.) B, 242 (Pg.) C, 251 (Vt.) B, 257 (V.) A, 276 (Aq.) C, 307 (Pr.) B, Lat. A, 311 (S.) A, 372 (Umb.) A, 375 (Pi.) A
Liconia, 161 (Hp.) B, 372 (Umb.) B
Lictoria, 375 (Pi.) C?
Licustena, 375 (Pi.) C
Licuria, 259 (A.) C
Ligaria, 257 (V.) C
Ligeria, 34 (P.) C, 161 (Hp.) C
Liguria, 307 (Pr.) C, Lat. B, 372 (Umb.) B
Ligustia, 155 (Cp.) C
Ligustinia, 372 (Umb.) C

GENTILE NAMES FROM THE DIALECT-AREAS. 573

Limbricia, 155 (Cp.) A
Lindia, 198 (F.) C, 372 (Umb.) C
Lisennia, 372 (Umb.) B
Lisia, 155 (Cp.) B, 276 (Aq.) B, 307 (Pr.) C?
Lisidia, 161 (Hp.) A
Lissidia, 372 (Umb.) B
Literria, 257 (V.) C
Litoria, Lat. C
Litria, 155 (Cp.) B
Litucia, 155 (Cp.) C
Liueneia, 155 (Cp.) B
Liuia, 34 (P.) A, 155 (Cp.) A, 161 (Hp.) B, 242 (Pg.) B, 257 (V.) B, 279 (H.) C, 307 (Pr.) C, Lat. A, 311 (S.) B, 350 (Fal.) C, 372 (Umb.) B, 375 (Pi.) B
Liuinia, 161 (Hp.) B, 188 (Sm.) B
Lollia, 12 (B.) B, 27 (L.) C, 32 (Cl.) B, 155 (Cp.) A, 161 (Hp.) A, 188 (Sm.) B, 242 (Pg.) B, 251 (Vt.) A, 257 (V.) B, 276 (Aq.) B, 279 (H.) B, 307 (Pr.) B, Lat. A, 311 (S.) C, 372 (Umb.) C
Lollidea, 271 (M.) C
Longana, 257 (V.) B
Longeia, 276 (Aq.) C
Longenia, 372 (Umb.) B
Longia, 161 (Hp.) C
Longidia, 257 (V.) B, Lat. C
Longinia, 155 (Cp.) A, 188 (Sm.) C, Lat. B
Longiniana, 161 (Hp.) C
Longuleia, 257 (V.) C
Longuria, 372 (Umb.) C
Loppia, 155 (Cp.) C
Loreia, 155 (Cp.) B, Lat. C
Lorelana, 307 (Pr.) C
Lorenia, 34 (P.) C, Lat. C, 375 (Pi.) B
Lorentia, Lat. C.
Lotria, 257 (V.) C
Lucania, 155 (Cp.) B, 34 (P.) C
Luccaea, 161 (Hp.) C
Lucceia, 32 (Cl.) C, 36 (D.) C, 155 (Cp.) A, 161 (Hp.) B, 188 (Sm.) B, 198 (F.) C, 242 (Pg.) A, 246 (Mcr.) B, 251 (Vt.) B, 257 (V.) B, 307 (Pr.) C, Lat. A, 311 (S.) C, 372 (Umb.) B
Luccia, 27 (L.) C, 36 (D.) B, 161 (Hp.) A, 188 (Sm.) A, 198 (F.) C, 257 (V.) A, 279 (H.) C, Lat. C, 372 (Umb.) B, 375 (Pi.) C
Lucerina, 161 (Hp.) C
Lucerinia, 36 (D.) C
Lucernia, 257 (V.) C
Lucia, 12 (B.) C, 27 (L.) B, 155 (Cp.) A, 251 (Vt.) A, 257 (V.) A, Lat. B
Lucideia, 279 (H.) B
Lucilia, 32 (Cl.) C, 34 (P.) B, 155 (Cp.) A, 161 (Hp.) C, 188 (Sm.) B, 198 (F.) C, 242 (Pg.) A, 257 (V.) B, 271 (M.) C, 307 (Pr.) C, Lat. A, 350 (Fal.) C, 372 (Umb.) B, 375 (Pi.) B

Lucretia, 27 (L.) C, 32 (Cl.) B, 34 (P.) B, 155 (Cp.) A, 161 (Hp.) B, 188 (Sm.) B, 251 (Vt.) C, 257 (V.) A, 307 (Pr.) C, Lat. A, 311 (S.) B, 375 (Pi.) C
Lucudeia, 161 (Hp.) C
Luculana, 155 (Cp.) B, 307 (Pr.) C
Lucullena, 34 (P.) B?
Lucullia, 251 (Vt.) C
Ludia, 311 (S.) B
Lufinia, 155 (Cp.) B
Lumbia, Lat. C
Lupatia, 155 (Cp.) C
Luria, 155 (Cp.) B, 242 (Pg.) B, 350 (Fal.) B, Lat. A
Luscia, 155 (Cp.) C, 188 (Sm.) B, 307 (Pr.) B, Lat. A
Luscidia, 257 (V.) C
Lusena, 372 (Umb.) B
Lusia, 36 (D.) C, 155 (Cp.) A, 161 (Hp.) C, 188 (Sm.) C, 257 (V.) B, 276 (Aq.) C, Lat. B, 372 (Umb.) B, 375 (Pi.) B
Lusiena, 155 (Cp.) B
Lustuleia, 257 (V.) C
Lutatia, 36 (D.) B, 155 (Cp.) B, 257 (V.) C, 259 (A.) C, 307 (Pr.) C, Lat. B, 372 (Umb.) B
Luttia, 257 (V.) C, Lat. B
Luuiana, 311 (S.) B
Luxilia, 27 (L.) A, 155 (Cp.) B
Lydia, 155 (Cp.) C
Lysia, 34 (P.) B

Maccia, 155 (Cp.) C
Macedina, Lat. C
Maceriana, 372 (Umb.) C
Macia, Lat. C
Maclonia, 311 (S.) C
Macolnia, v. Magulnia
Macrinia, 155 (Cp.) C, 188 (Sm.) B, 257 (V.) C, 307 (Pr.) C, Lat. B
Maculana, 307 (Pr.) C
Macullia, 155 (Cp.) C
Maculonia, 155 (Cp.) C
Maecenas, 155 (Cp.) B, 279 (H.) C, 307 (Pr.) C
Maecenatia, Lat. B
Maecia, 27 (L.) B, 34 (P.) C, 155 (Cp.) A, 161 (Hp.) B, 242 (Pg.) C, 259 (A.) B, Lat. A, 372 (Umb.) C
Maecilia, 27 (L.) B, 155 (Cp.) B, Lat. B
Maeclasia, Lat. B
Maelia, 311 (S.) B, Lat. B
Maena, 372 (Umb.) B
Maenia, 155 (Cp.) B, 161 (Hp.) B, 257 (V.) B, Lat. B, 372 (Umb.) C
Maesia, 27 (L.) C, 155 (Cp.) B, 259 (A.) B, 307 (Pr.) B, 372 (Umb.) A
Maesonia, 155 (Cp.) C
Maetennia, 155 (Cp.) B, 375 (Pi.) C
Maeuatia, 155 (Cp.) B

574   INDEX III.

Maeuia, 161 (Hp.) C, 307 (Pr.) A, 372 (Umb.) C
Magia, 12 (B.) C, 27 (L.) B, 36 (D.) B, 155 (Cp.) A, 161 (Hp.) A, 188 (Sm.) B, 242 (Pg.) B, 257 (V.) B, 271 (M.) B, Lat. B, 372 (Umb.) B, 375 (Pi.) C
Magilia, Lat. C
Magneia, 257 (V.) B
Magnia, 155 (Cp.) B, Lat. B
Magnisia, 155 (Cp.) C
Magolnia, v. Magulnia
Magonia, 155 (Cp.) B
Magria, 155 (Cp.) B, 198 (F.) B
Magullia, 161 (Hp.) C, 257 (V.) C
Magulnia, 155 (Cp.) B, 257 (V.) C, 307 (Pr.) A
Maguttia, 308 (Lat.) C
Mahena, 375 (Pi.) C
Maia, 36 (D.) C, 155 (Cp.) A, 161 (Hp.) C, 198 (F.) C, 242 (Pg.) C, 251 (Vt.) B, 257 (V.) B, 307 (Pr.) B
Maiana, 257 (V.) C
Maiania, 257 (V.) B
Maioria, 161 (Hp.) C (?)
Malia, Lat. A
Mallia, 12 (B.) C, 34 (P.) C, 155 (Cp.) B, 161 (Hp.) C, 276 (Aq.) C, Lat. B, 372 (Umb.) B, 375 (Pi.) C
Mallonia, 155 (Cp.) B
Maltinia, 311 (S.) B
Mamercia, 12 (B.) C, 34 (P.) C, 155 (Cp.) B, 161 (Hp.) B
Mamia, 27 (L.) C, 161 (Hp.) B, 188 (Sm.) C, 257 (V.) A, 307 (Pr.) B, Lat. A
Mamidia, 155 (Cp.) C, 161 (Hp.) C, Lat. A
Mamilia, 34 (P.) C, 155 (Cp.) B, 246 (Mcr.) A, 257 (V.) A, 307 (Pr.) B, Lat. A, 372 (Umb.) C, 375 (Pi.) B
Mamimena, 257 (V.) C
Mammedia, 372 (Umb.) C
Mammia, 155 (Cp.) A, 242 (Pg.) B, 271 (M.) A, 350 (Fal.) C
Mammuleia, 257 (V.) C
Mandorina, 161 (Hp.) C
Mancia, 372 (Umb.) C
Mania, Lat. C
Manilia, 27 (L.) A, 155 (Cp.) B, 161 (Hp.) B, 257 (V.) B, 271 (M.) B, 307 (Pr.) B, Lat. A, 311 (S.) B, 350 (Fal.) C, 372 (Umb.) C, 375 (Pi.) C
Manlia, 155 (Cp.) A, 161 (Hp.) C, 188 (Sm.) A, 251 (Vt.) C, 257 (V.) A, 276 (Aq.) C, 279 (H.) C, 307 (Pr.) B, Lat. A, 311 (S.) B, 375 (Pi.) B
Manllia, 12 (B.) C
Manneia, 27 (L.) C, 155 (Cp.) B, 257 (V.) A, Lat. C
Mantennia, 307 (Pr.) B, Lat. B
Mantia, 271 (M.) C
Manusia, 307 (Pr.) C

Marceia, 276 (Aq.) C
Marcia, 27 (L.) B, 34 (P.) A, 155 (Cp.) A, 161 (Hp.) A, 188 (Sm.) B, 242 (Pg.) C, 251 (Vt.) C, 257 (V.) A, 271 (M.) C, 276 (Aq.) A, 279 (H.) C, 307 (Pr.) A, Lat. A, 311 (S.) A, 372 (Umb.) A, 375 (Pi.) A
Marciana, 12 (B.) C
Marcilia, 188 (Sm.) C, 375 (Pi.) C
Marculeia, 276 (Aq.) B
Maria, 12 (B.) B, 32 (Cl.) C, 34 (P.) A, 36 (D.) B, 155 (Cp.) A, 161 (Hp.) A, 188 (Sm.) A, 242 (Pg.) A, 251 (Vt.) C, 372 (Umb.) A, 375 (Pi.) B
Maridia, 311 (S.) B
Marracia, Lat. C
Marria, 257 (V.) C, Lat. B
Marruca, 372 (Umb.) C
Mars[ia?], 155 (Cp.) B
Marsidia, 372 (Umb.) C
Marsina, 372 (Umb.) C
Martia, 27 (L.) C, 34 (P.) B, 155 (Cp.) B, Lat. B
Martucana, 372 (Umb.) C
Marulcia, 257 (V.) C
Mascnia, 155 (Cp.) C
Masclia, 307 (Pr.) C
Masia, 155 (Cp.) C
Masonia, 257 (V.) C, 372 (Umb.) A
Massellia, 372 (Umb.) B
Massidia, 242 (Pg.) B
Massilia, 372 (Umb.) C?
Masuria, 155 (Cp.) B, Lat. B
Masuuia, 375 (Pi.) C
Mateniana, 372 (Umb.) C
Mateuria, 372 (Umb.) C
Matia, 155 (Cp.) C, 242 (Pg.) C, Lat. C, 372 (Umb.) C?
Maticia, 155 (Cp.) C, 257 (V.) B
Matidia, 259 (A.) B, 307 (Pr.) C
Matiena, 257 (V.) B
Matinia, 307 (Pr.) C, 372 (Umb.) B
Matlia, 307 (Pr.) C
Matria, 257 (V.) C
Matrinia, 372 (Umb.) B, 375 (Pi.) C
Matteia, 155 (Cp.) C
Mattetia, 372 (Umb.) B
Matuccia, Lat. B
Matutina, 155 (Cp.) C
Maximia, 155 (Cp.) B
Maximilliana, 161 (Hp.) B
Mecania, 307 (Pr.) C?
Mecilia, 307 (Pr.) C
Meclonia, 155 (Cp.) B, 307 (Pr.) C, Lat. C, 372 (Umb.) C, 375 (Pi.) C
Meconia, 12 (B.) B
Media, 36 (D.) B
Medioleia, 155 (Cp.) C
Medullina, 155 (Cp.) B
Melissaea, 155 (Cp.) A
Mellia, 375 (Pi.) C

Melsonia, 155 (Cp.) B
Memmia, 32 (Cl.) B, 155 (Cp.) A, 251 (Vt.) C, 257 (V.) A, Lat. A, 311 (S.) A, 372 (Umb.) B, 375 (Pi.) C
Meneia, 27 (L.) C
Menia, 188 (Sm.) C
Menlia, 155 (Cp.) C?
Menturnia, 257 (V.) C
Mercella, Lat. C
Mercellia, 32 (Cl.) C
Mersieia, 307 (Pr.) C
Mescidia, 271 (M.) C
Mescinia, 155 (Cp.) B, 307 (Pr.) C
Mesena, 311 (S.) C, 375 (Pi.) C?
Mesonia, 155 (Cp.) C
Messena, 307 (Pr.) B
Messenia, 155 (Cp.) B, Lat. B
Messia, 32 (Cl.) B?, 36 (D.) C, 155 (Cp.) A, 161 (Hp.) B, 198 (F.) C, 242 (Pg.) B, 257 (V.) A, Lat. A, 311 (S.) B, 350 (Fal.) B, 372 (Umb.) B
Messiena, 307 (Pr.) B
Mestia, 155 (Cp.) C
Mestria, 155 (Cp.) B, 257 (V.) B, 307 (Pr.) C, 372 (Umb.) B, 375 (Pi.) B
Mesulena, Lat. C
Meteia, 155 (Cp.) C, 257 (V.) B
Metella, 372 (Umb.) B
Metidiena, 311 (S.) C
Metilia, 34 (P.) B, 155 (Cp.) B, 161 (Hp.) B, 257 (V.) C, 276 (Aq.) B, 307 (Pr.) B, Lat. A, 375 (Pi.) B
Mettia, 12 (B.) C, 27 (L.) B, 34 (P.) C, 155 (Cp.) A, 161 (Hp.) A, 188 (Sm.) C, 198 (F.) B, 242 (Pg.) B, 246 (Mer.) C, 257 (V.) B, 307 (Pr.) C, Lat. A, 372 (Umb.) C
Mettiena, 36 (D.) C
Meuanas, 372 (Umb.) B
Meuia, 27 (L.) C, 155 (Cp.) B, 188 (Sm.) B, 198 (F.) B, 257 (V.) A, 276 (Aq.) C, Lat. B, 372 (Umb.) C
Mezaea, 308 (Lat.) C
Mgolnia, v. Magulnia
Milasia, 375 (Pi.) C
Milionia, 372 (Umb.) B
Mimesia, 372 (Umb.) B
Mimisia, Lat. C, 372 (Umb.) A
Minasia, Lat. C
Minatia, 27 (L.) A, 34 (P.) B, 36 (D.) B, 155 (Cp.) A, 161 (Hp.) C, 188 (Sm.) B, 257 (V.) B, Lat. B, 311 (S.) B, 372 (Umb.) C
Minculeia, 257 (V.) B
Mincullia, 155 (Cp.) C
Mindia, 32 (Cl.) B, 155 (Cp.) A, 161 (Hp.) A, 271 (M.) C, Lat. A
Mineruia, 372 (Umb.) B
Minia, 155 (Cp.) B, 161 (Hp.) B, 188 (Sm.) C, 257 (V.) B, 372 (Umb.) C
Miniaria, 155 (Cp.) B

Minicia, 12 (B.) B, 155 (Cp.) A, Lat. A, 372 (Umb.) B, 375 (Pi.) B
Minidia, Lat. B
Minisia, 155 (Cp.) C
Mintullia, 155 (Cp.) C
Minucia, 12 (B.) B, 27 (L.) C, 34 (P.) B, 36 (D.) C, 155 (Cp.) A, 188 (Sm.) B, 257 (V.) A, 259 (A.) C, 279 (H.) C, 307 (Pr.) B, Lat. A
Minutia, 155 (Cp.) C
Mitullcia, 34 (P.) C?
Modestia, 155 (Cp.) B, Lat. B
Modia, 155 (Cp.) B, 161 (Hp.) B, 188 (Sm.) C, 198 (F.) C, 242 (Pg.) C, 251 (Vt.) B, 257 (V.) C, 259 (A.) C, 271 (M.) C, 276 (Aq.) C, Lat. A, 375 (Pi.) C
Modiaria, 307 (Pr.) C, 375 (Pi.) C
Modicia, 311 (S.) C
Modiolcia, 188 (Sm.) C
Moccia, 198 (F.) C
Molletia, 375 (Pi.) C
Mollia, 257 (V.) B
Mollicia, 257 (V.) C, Lat. B
Moluia, 161 (Hp.) B
Monnia, 155 (Cp.) B, 198 (F.) B
Montania, Lat. C
Morasia, 155 (Cp.) C
Motilia, 279 (H.) C
Mucia, 34 (P.) B, 155 (Cp.) B, 161 (Hp.) B, 251 (Vt.) B, 307 (Pr.) B, 311 (S.) B, Lat. A
Mufein, 307 (Pr.) B
Muicia, 276 (Aq.) C?
Muileia, 188 (Sm.) C
Mullia, 155 (Cp.) C
Multasia, 36 (D.) C, 375 (Pi.) B
Multillia, 155 (Cp.) C
Muluia, 155 (Cp.) C, 276 (Aq.) C, 311 (S.) C
Mulutia, 155 (Cp.) C?
Mumia, 311 (S.) B
Mummeia, 161 (Hp.) B, 257 (V.) C
Mummia, 27 (L.) C, 36 (D.) C, 155 (Cp.) B, 161 (Hp.) B, 188 (Sm.) C, 257 (V.) B, 307 (Pr.) B, Lat. B
Munatia, 12 (B.) C, 32 (Cl.) C, 34 (P.) B, 155 (Cp.) A, 161 (Hp.) A, 188 (Sm.) A, 257 (V.) A, 307 (Pr.) C, Lat. A, 375 (Pi.) B
Munatidia, 251 (Vt.) C
Munatuleia, 188 (Sm.) C, Lat. B
Mundicia, 257 (V.) C, Lat. B
Munia, 161 (Hp.) A, 188 (Sm.) B, 307 (Pr.) C, Lat. B, 311 (S.) B
Munisia, 372 (Umb.) B
Munnenia, Lat. C
Munnia, 155 (Cp.) A, 257 (V.) B
Murcia, 257 (V.) B
Murdia, 34 (P.) C, Lat. B
Murrasia, 34 (P.) C, 155 (Cp.) B

Murratena, 161 (Hp.) C
Murrenia, 311 (S.) C
Murria, 155 (Cp.) C, 161 (Hp.) B, 257 (V.) C, 372 (Umb.) B
Murridia, 375 (Pi.) C
Murronia, 155 (Cp.) C
Murtia, 155 (Cp.) C
Musaea, 372 (Umb.) C
Musamia, Lat. C
Musana, 372 (Umb.) B
Musania, 155 (Cp.) C
Musedia, 251 (Vt.) C
Muscia, 372 (Umb.) C
Musetia, 372 (Umb.) B
Musidia, 155 (Cp.) B
Mussonna, 375 (Pi.) C
Mussetia, 307 (Pr.) C
Mussia, 257 (V.) B, Lat. A, 372 (Umb.) C
Mussidia, 188 (Sm.) C, 242 (Pg.) C
Mussiena, 32 (Cl.) B
Mustia, 155 (Cp.) C
Musurria, 311 (S.) B
Mutia, 161 (Hp.) C, 372 (Umb.) C
Muticilia, 12 (B.) C
Muticuleia, 155 (Cp.) B
Mutilia, 307 (Pr.) B, Lat. C
Mutronia, 34 (P.) C
Muttia, 155 (Cp.) B, 276 (Aq.) B, Lat. C
Muttiena, 34 (P.) B, 36 (D.) B
Muttina, 311 (S.) B

Naeuia, 27 (L.) C, 36 (D.) B, 155 (Cp.) A, 161 (Hp.) A, 188 (Sm.) A, 198 (F.) B, 246 (Mcr.) C, 251 (Vt.) C, 257 (V.) A, 271 (M.) B, 276 (Aq.) B, 279 (H.) C, Lat. A, 372 (Umb.) B, 375 (Pi.) A
Naeuidiana, 372 (Umb.) C
Naeuolcia, 155 (Cp.) B, 188 (Sm.) B
Nammia, Lat. C
Nanneia, 27 (L.) C
Nanonia, 27 (L.) B
Naria, 34 (P.) C, 155 (Cp.) C, 372 (Umb.) B
Nasellia, 161 (Hp.) B
Nasennia, 155 (Cp.) A, 161 (Hp.) C, 257 (V.) C, Lat. A, 372 (Umb.) C
Nasernia, 257 (V.) C
Nasia, 375 (Pi.) C
Nasidia, 161 (Hp.) C
Nassia, 155 (Cp.) B, 242 (Pq.) C, 307 (Pr.) C, 372 (Umb.) C
Nasuleia, 155 (Cp.) C
Natalis, 155 (Cp.) C
Natria, 161 (Hp.) B
Nauia, 155 (Cp.) B, 257 (V.) C
Nautia, 155 (Cp.) C, 257 (V.) C
Neapolitana, 155 (Cp.) B
Nearcha, 32 (Cl.) C
Negilia, 32 (Cl.) B

Nela, 155 (Cp.) B
Nellia, 257 (V.) C
Nemestronia, 32 (Cl.) C
Nemitia, 161 (Hp.) C (?)
Nemonia, 155 (Cp.) A
Nerasia, 155 (Cp.) C
Neratia, 155 (Cp.) B, 161 (Hp.) A, 188 (Sm.) A, Lat. B
Neria, 34 (P.) C, 36 (D.) C, 155 (Cp.) A, 161 (Hp.) C, 198 (F.) C, 251 (Vt.) B, 257 (V.) C, 372 (Umb.) B, 375 (Pi.) C
Neriana, 307 (Pr.) C
Nerlou..., 307 (Pr.) C
Neronia, 155 (Cp.) B, 307 (Pr.) B
Neruinia, 372 (Umb.) B
Nerusia, 311 (S.) C
Nigidia, 155 (Cp.) A, 311 (S.) B
Nigrinia, 307 (Pr.) C, 350 (Fal.) C
Nimonia, 188 (Sm.) B
Ninn..., 307 (Pr.) C
Ninnia, 155 (Cp.) A, 188 (Sm.) C, 198 (F.) B, 242 (Pg.) B, 246 (Mcr.) C, 251 (Vt.) C, 271 (M.) B
Nipia, 198 (F.) B
Niracmia, 155 (Cp.) B
Nitentia, 307 (Pr.) B
Niturania, 155 (Cp) C
Niuellia, 307 (Pr.) B
Nolcennia, 155 (Cp.) C
Noleia, 155 (Cp.) B
Nonia, 12 (B.) B, 27 (L.) C, 34 (P.) B, 36 (D.) B, 155 (Cp.) A, 161 (Hp.) A, 188 (Sm.) B, 242 (Pg.) C, 251 (Vt.) A, 257 (V.) B, 259 (A.) C, 276 (Aq.) B, 279 (H.) C, 307 (Pr.) C, Lat. A, 311 (S.) B, 372 (Umb.) A, 375 (Pi.) A
Norbana, 155 (Cp.) B, 198 (F.) C, 257 (V.) C, Lat. C, 375 (Pi.) C
Norceiana, 155 (Cp.) C
Nonana, 276 (Aq.) C
Nouanena, 12 (B.) C
Nouelledia, 251 (Vt.) B
Nouellia, 155 (Cp.) B, Lat. B, 375 (Pi.) C
Nouercinia, 155 (Cp.) C
Nouernia, 375 (Pi.) C
Nouia, 32 (Cl.) C, 34 (P.) C, 36 (D.) C, 155 (Cp.) A, 251 (Vt.) C, 257 (V.) B, 271 (M.) A, 279 (H.) B, 307 (Pr.) B, Lat. A, 372 (Umb.) C
Nouicia, 307 (Pr.) C
Nulania, 155 (Cp.) C (?)
Numeria, 34 (P.) C, 155 (Cp.) B, 161 (Hp.) C, 307 (Pr.) C
Numicia, 155 (Cp.) C, 161 (Hp.) C, 276 (Aq.) C
Numidia, 155 (Cp.) B, Lat. C
Numicdia, 271 (M.) C
Numisena, 251 (Vt.) C
Numisia, 12 (B.) B, 27 (L.) C, 32 (Cl.) C, 34 (P.) B, 36 (D.) C, 155 (Cp.) A, 161

GENTILE NAMES FROM THE DIALECT-AREAS.

(Hp.) A, 188 (Sm.) A, 198 (F.) B, 242
(Pg.) B, 251 (Vt.) C, 257 (V.) B, 307
(Pr.) C, Lat. A, 311 (S.) C, 350 (Fal.)
B, 372 (Umb.) A, 375 (Pi.) A
Numistria, 155 (Cp.) B
Numistronia, 257 (V.) C
Numitoria, 12 (B.) C, 32 (Cl.) C, 155
  (Cp.) A, 257 (V.) B, 307 (Pr.) B, Lat.
  A, 375 (Pi.) B
Nummia, 34 (P.) B, 36 (D.) C, 155 (Cp.)
  C, 161 (Hp.) C, 188 (Sm.) A, 198 (F.)
  C, 251 (Vt.) A, 257 (V.) B, 307 (Pr.) C,
  Lat. C, 350 (Fal.) B, 375 (Pi.) B
Numoleia, 155 (Cp.) C
Numonia, 12 (B.) B, 27 (L.) C
Numpidia, 34 (P.) C
Nunidia, 155 (Cp.) B
Nunnia, 155 (Cp.) C, 257 (V.) A, 372
  (Umb.) C
Nunnidia, 155 (Cp.) B, Lat. C
Nunnuleia, 155 (Cp.) C, Lat. C
Nusia, 155 (Cp.) C
Nutria, 155 (Cp.) C
Nymphidia, Lat. C

Obellia, 155 (Cp.) B, 161 (Hp.) C, 188
  (Sm.) B, 242 (Pg.) B, Lat. B
Obideia, 161 (Hp.) B
Obidia, 198 (F.) B, 242 (Pg.) B, 251 (Vt.)
  B, 372 (Umb.) C
Obilena, 375 (Pi.) C
Obilia, 375 (Pi.) B
Obinia, 36 (D.) C (?), 155 (Cp.) B, 188
  (Sm.) B, 257 (V.) B
Oblicia, 276 (Aq.) C
Obulcia, 375 (Pi.) B
Obulnia, Lat. C
Obultronia, 155 (Cp.) C, 257 (V.) B,
  375 (Pi.) C
Ocabia, 155 (Cp.) C (?)
Ocania, 307 (Pr.) C
Ocbrotsinia, 375 (Pi.) C
Occia, 27 (L.) C, 155 (Cp.) B, 188 (Sm.) C
Ocellia, 161 (Hp.) B
Oclatia, 161 (Hp.) B, Lat. B
Oclatinia, Lat. C
Ocratia, 36 (D.) B, 155 (Cp.) B, 251
  (Vt.) C, 257 (V.) C
Ocrinia, 276 (Aq.) C
Octauellia, 251 (Vt.) C
Octauia, 12 (B.) B, 27 (L.) B, 32 (Cl.) A,
  34 (P.) C, 36 (D.) B, 155 (Cp.) A, 161
  (Hp.) A, 188 (Sm.) B, 242 (Pg.) A, 246
  (Mcr.) B, 251 (Vt.) B, 257 (V.) A, 259
  (A.) C, 271 (M.) A, 279 (H.) C, 307
  (Pr.) A, Lat. A, 311 (S.) A, 372 (Umb.)
  A, 375 (Pi.) A
Octauidia, 188 (Sm.) B, 251 (Vt.) A
Oculatia, 155 (Cp.) B
Ofa..., 375 (Pi.) C
Ofania, 155 (Cp.) C, 251 (Vt.) C

Ofasia, 257 (V.) C
Ofatulena, 251 (Vt.) C
Ofdia, 251 (Vt.) C
Ofellia, 161 (Hp.) A, 188 (Sm.) C, 257
  (V.) B, 372 (Umb.) B
Ofia, 257 (V.) B
Ofilia, 27 (L.) C, 34 (P.) C, 161 (Hp.) A,
  242 (Pg.) C
Ofillia, 155 (Cp.) A, 188 (Sm.) A, 257
  (V.) A, 276 (Aq.) C, 307 (Pr.) C, Lat. B
Ofilliena, 155 (Cp.) C
Ofinia, 188 (Sm.) B
Ofitulena, 372 (Umb.) C
Ofonia, 155 (Cp.) C
Ogulnia, 161 (Hp.) C, 257 (V.) C, Lat. A,
  372 (Umb.) C
Olia, 155 (Cp.) A, 276 (Aq.) C, Lat. B,
  375 (Pi.) B
Oliena, 155 (Cp.) C
Ollia, 12 (B.) C
Onussania, 307 (Pr.) C
Opellia, Lat. C, 372 (Umb.) C
Opetreia, 155 (Cp.) C, 257 (V.) B
Opetreiia, 161 (Hp.) C
Opia, 198 (F.) B, 307 (Pr.) A
Opicia, 161 (Hp.) C
Opidiena, 311 (S.) B
Opilia, 307 (Pr.) C
Opimia, 161 (Hp.) B, Lat. C
Oppia, 27 (L.) B, 31 (Cl.) C, 34 (P.) B,
  36 (D.) B, 155 (Cp.) A, 161 (Hp.) A,
  188 (Sm.) B, 246 (Mcr.) C, 251 (Vt.) A,
  257 (V.) A, 271 (M.) B, 276 (Aq.) C,
  279 (H.) B, Lat. B, 311 (S.) B, 350
  (Fal.) C, 372 (Umb.) C, 375 (Pi.) A
Oppianica, 198 (F.) C
Oppidia, 12 (B.) C, 188 (Sm.) A
Oppuneia, Lat. C
Opsia, 27 (L.) C, 155 (Cp.) B, 242 (Pg.)
  C, 251 (Vt.) C
Opsidia, 242 (Pg.) B
Opsilia, 307 (Pr.) C
Opsturia, 251 (Vt.) B
Orania, 155 (Cp.) C, 311 (S.) C
Oraria, 257 (V.) C
Orbia, 12 (B.) C, 188 (Sm.) A, 257 (V.)
  B, 276 (Aq.) C, 307 (Pr.) B, Lat. A,
  372 (Umb.) B, 375 (Pi.) B
Orbicia, 375 (Pi.) C
Orceuia, 307 (Pr.) A
Orcilia, 257 (V.) C
Orciuia, 155 (Cp.) C, 259 (A.) C, 307
  (Pr.) A
Orcuia, 307 (Pr.) A
Oreuia, 155 (Cp.) C
Orestiniana, 372 (Umb.) C
Orfellia, 155 (Cp.) C, 161 (Hp.) C
Orfia, 155 (Cp.) B, 188 (Sm.) C, 251
  (Vt.) B, Lat. C, 372 (Umb.) A
Orfidia, 251 (Vt.) B, 372 (Umb.) C
Orfita, Lat. C

C.

Organia, 155 (Cp.) C
Ortoria, 12 (B.) C, 188 (Sm.) B, 198 (F.) C
Oscia, 311 (S.) C
Ossidia, 34 (P.) C
Ostiensis, 257 (V.) C, Lat. A
Ostilia, 271 (M.) C
Ostoria, 155 (Cp.) B, 242 (Pg.) B, 279 (H.) C
Otacidia, 198 (F.) B
Otacilia, 27 (L.) A, 155 (Cp.) B, 257 (V.) B, Lat. A, 372 (Umb.) B
Otia, 155 (Cp.) C
Otiana, 350 (Fal.) C
Otincia, 155 (Cp.) C
Ottcia, 251 (Vt.) C
Ottiedia, 372 (Umb.) B
Ouania, 161 (Hp.) B
Ouellia, 155 (Cp.) B
Ouia, 12 (B.) C, 34 (P.) B, 155 (Cp.) A, 161 (Hp.) B, 188 (Sm.) A, 257 (V.) B, 307 (Pr.) B, Lat. A
Ouidia, 242 (Pg.) C
Ouiedia, 155 (Cp.) B
Ouilia, Lat. C
Ouilonia, 27 (L.) B
Ouinia, 155 (Cp.) B, 198 (F.) C, 257 (V.) B, Lat. B
Ouiolena, 251 (Vt.) B
Ouitia, 372 (Umb.) C

Paccoia, Lat. C
Paccia, 36 (D.) C, 155 (Cp.) A, 161 (Hp.) B, 198 (F.) C, 242 (Pg.) C, 257 (V.) A, 259 (A.) C, 271 (M.) A, 307 (Pr.) C, 372 (Umb.) B
Pacedia, 271 (M.) C, Lat. C
Pacia, 161 (Hp.) B, 188 (Sm.) C, Lat. C
Pacidaca, 271 (M.) C
Pacideia, 155 (Cp.) A, 188 (Sm.) B, 271 (M.) B
Pacidia, 257 (V.) C
Paciledia, 271 (M.) C
Pacilia, 32 (Cl.) B, 34 (P.) C, 188 (Sm.) B, 307 (Pr.) C, Lat. A
Paconia, 155 (Cp.) A, Lat. B
Pactumeia, 27 (L.) B, 32 (Cl.) C, 155 (Cp.) A
Paculeia, 36 (D.) C
Pacuria, 257 (V.) C
Pacuuia, 34 (P.) C, 155 (Cp.) B, 257 (V.) B, 279 (H.) C, 375 (Pi.) C
Pacxca, Lat. C (?)
Paetia, 372 (Umb.) C
Paetilia, 372 (Umb.) C
Paetina, 372 (Umb.) C
Paetinia, 375 (Pi.) C
Pagia, 271 (M.) C
Pagnia, 251 (Vt.) C
Paicdia, 372 (Umb.) C
Palaa, Lat. B

Palia, 161 (Hp.) C, 372 (Umb.) B
Pal[f]uria, 251 (Vt.) B
Pandia, 155 (Cp.) C
Panentia, 155 (Cp.) C
Pannia, 307 (Pr.) C
Pantilia, 279 (H.) B, 375 (Pi.) C
Pantuleia, 257 (V.) B, Lat. B
Papia, 155 (Cp.) A, 188 (Sm.) A, 198 (F.) C, 251 (Vt.) C, 257 (V.) A, 307 (Pr.) C, Lat. B, 372 (Umb.) B
Papinia, 155 (Cp.) B, 161 (Hp.) C, 257 (V.) B, Lat. B, 350 (Fal.) C, 372 (Umb.) C
Papiria, 27 (L.) B, 32 (Cl.) C, 34 (P.) B, 155 (Cp.) A, 161 (Hp.) B, 188 (Sm.) C, 257 (V.) B, 276 (Aq.) C, 307 (Pr.) C, Lat. B, 311 (S.) B, 372 (Umb.) A, 375 (Pi.) C
Pappedia, 251 (Vt.) B
Paquedia, 271 (M.) C, Lat. C.
Paquia, 12 (B.) C, 155 (Cp.) B, 198 (H.) A, 271 (M.) C
Parconia, 372 (Umb.) C
Paria, 188 (Sm.) C
Pariana, 155 (Cp.) C
Parredia, 372 (Umb.) C
Paruilia, 155 (Cp.) B
Pasidia, 36 (D.) C
Passenia, 32 (Cl.) C, 155 (Cp.) B
Passenna, 372 (Umb.) C
Passidiena, 311 (S.) C
Passiena, 257 (V.) C, 307 (Pr.) B
Passienia, 27 (L.) C
Patercilia, 155 (Cp.) B
Patidia, 155 (Cp.) C
Patoleia, 307 (Pr.) C
Patria, Lat. B
Patronia, 32 (Cl.) C, 307 (Pr) C
Patulacia, 161 (Hp.) A
Patulcia, 155 (Cp.) A, 161 (Hp.) C, 188 (Sm.) B, 257 (V.) C
Paucia, 161 (Hp.) C
Pauillia, 155 (Cp.) A
Pausculana, 251 (Vt.) B
Paxea, 155 (Cp.) C
Pedania, 155 (Cp.) B, Lat B
Pederni...?, 372 (Umb.) C
Pedia, 155 (Cp.) B, 161 (Hp.) C, 198 (F.) B, 242 (Pg.) C, Lat. B, 372 (Umb.) C
Pedicua, 375 (Pi.) C
Pedilia, 372 (Umb.) C
Pedilla, 375 (Pi.) C
Pedisia, 372 (Umb.) C
Peducaea, 155 (Cp.) C, 251 (Vt.) C, Lat. B
Peducaei..., 372 (Umb.) C
Peducaia, 311 (S.) B
Peducea, 34 (P.) C, 161 (Hp.) C
Peilia, 257 (V.) C
Pelacisaua, 155 (Cp.) C (?)

GENTILE NAMES FROM THE DIALECT-AREAS. 579

Pelaginia, Lat. C
Pellia, 257 (V.) C
Pennasia, 372 (Umb.) B
Pensia, 372 (Umb.) C?
Percennia, 155 (Cp.) B, 161 (Hp.) C, 188 (Sm.) C, 257 (V.) C
Perelia, 155 (Cp.) B
Perellia, Lat. C
Perennia, 155 (Cp.) B, 161 (Hp.) C, Lat. C
Perpennia, Lat. B
Perperna, 155 (Cp.) B, 257 (V.) C, Lat. B
Perpernia, 34 (P.) C, 155 (Cp.) B
Perternia, Lat. C
Pescenia, Lat. B, 375 (Pi.) C
Pescennedia, 251 (Vt.) C
Pescennia, 34 (P.) C, 155 (Cp.) A, 161 (Hp.) B, 188 (Sm.) B, 257 (V.) B, 276 (Aq.) B, Lat. B, 311 (S.) B, 372 (Umb.) C
Pesceno...?, 307 (Pr.) C
Pestania, 155 (Cp.) C
Petedia, 271 (M.) C
Petelia, 155 (Cp.) C
Petellia, 161 (Hp.) C
Peticena, 251 (Vt.) C
Peticia, 32 (Cl.) C, 34 (P.) C, 155 (Cp.) B, 242 (Pg.) B, 251 (Vt.) C, 271 (M.) B, 307 (Pr.) C, Lat. B, 375 (Pi.) C
Peticiena, 251 (Vt.) C
Petidia, 242 (Pg.) B, 276 (Aq.) C, 311 (S.) C
Petiedia, 251 (Vt.) C, 271 (M.) B
Petilia, 34 (P.) C, 257 (V.) C, 279 (H.) C, 307 (Pr.) C, Lat. C
Petillena, 375 (Pi.) C
Petillia, 155 (Cp.) B, 161 (Hp.) B, 311 (S.) B, 372 (Umb.) A, 375 (Pi.) A
Petinia, 34 (P.) C
Petisana, 155 (Cp.) C
Petisedia, 375 (Pi.) B
Petisia, 307 (Pr.) C, Lat. C, 311 (S.) C, 372 (Umb.) A
Petreia, 188 (Sm.) C, Lat. B
Petronaea, 271 (M.) B
Petronia, 12 (B.) C, 27 (L.) B, 32 (Cl.) B, 34 (P.) A, 36 (D.) B, 155 (Cp.) A, 161 (Hp.) A, 188 (Sm.) B, 198 (F.) C, 246 (Mcr.) B, 251 (Vt.) B, 257 (V.) A, 259 (A.) C, 271 (M.) B, 276 (Aq.) B, 279 (H.) C, 307 (Pr.) A, Lat. A, 311 (S.) A, 372 (Umb.) A, 375 (Pi.) A
Petruculaea, 271 (M.) B
Petruculcia, 242 (Pg.) B
Petrusidia, 257 (V.) B, 375 (Pi.) B
Petrusulena, 25 (Vt.) B
Pettia, 27 (L.) B, 36 (D.) C, 155 (Cp.) B, 188 (Sm.) C, 242 (Pg.) B, 257 (V.) B, 372 (Umb.) B

Pettidia, 257 (V.) C
Petuellia, 161 (Hp.) C
Petulcia, 375 (Pi.) C
Picidia, 257 (V.) B
Pileia, 155 (Cp.) C
Pilia, 36 (D.) B, 251 (Vt.) C, 307 (Pr.) C, Lat. B
Piliena, 276 (Aq.) B
Pilonia, 155 (Cp.) B
Pinaria, 27 (L.) B, 155 (Cp.) A, Lat. B, 372 (Umb.) B
Pincia, 161 (Hp.) C, 257 (V.) B
Pinnia, 155 (Cp.) C, 307 (Pr.) B, Lat. B
Pipedia, 372 (Umb.) C?
Pipidia, Lat. B
Piricatia, 155 (Cp.) C
Pirria, Lat. B
Piscinnia, 257 (V.) C
Pisena, 372 (Umb.) C
Pisentia, 34 (P.) C, 311 (S.) C, 372 (Umb.) A
Pismatia, 161 (Hp.) C
Pisonia, 155 (Cp.) C
Pisuria, 155 (Cp.) C
Pitia, 155 (Cp.) B
Pituania, 155 (Cp.) C, 311 (S.) A, 375 (Pi.) B
Placentia, Lat. C
Placidiana, 372 (Umb.) C
Placulcia, 307 (Pr.) B
Plaetoria, 27 (L.) A, 155 (Cp.) B, 161 (Hp.) C, 307 (Pr.) B, Lat. B
Plancia, 257 (V.) B, 307 (Pr.) B
Plania, 155 (Cp.) B, 257 (V.) B, 375 (Pi.) C
Plarentia, 155 (Cp.) C
Plaria, 257 (V.) C, Lat. A, 375 (Pi.) C
Platia, 161 (Hp.) B
Platoria, 27 (L.) C, 161 (Hp.) C, 375 (Pi.) C
Plauia, 257 (V.) C
Plausurnia, Lat. C
Plauta, 271 (M.) C
Plautia, 36 (D.) C, 155 (Cp.) A, 161 (Hp.) B, 188 (Sm.) C, 246 (Mcr.) C, 307 (Pr.) A, Lat. A, 372 (Umb.) C, 375 (Pi.) B
Plestina, 34 (P.) B
Pletoria, 375 (Pi.) C
Plinia, 32 (Cl.) B, 155 (Cp.) B, 188 (Sm.) C, Lat. B, 372 (Umb.) C
Plotia, 27 (L.) C, 32 (Cl.) C, 155 (Cp.) A, 161 (Hp.) B, 188 (Sm.) B, 198 (F.) C, 259 (A.) C, 279 (H.) C, 307 (Pr.) B, Lat. A, 372 (Umb.) A, 375 (Pi.) A
Plotidia, 350 (Fal.) C, Lat. C
Plotidiana, 372 (Umb.) C
Plotina, 307 (Pr.) B
Plotulena, 257 (V.) C
Plutia, 155 (Cp.) A, 307 (Pr.) B, 311 (S.) B, Lat. B, 257 (V.) C

37—2

Poinisia, 372 (Umb.) C
Poldia, 307 (Pr.) C
Polia, 188 (Sm.) C
Polit..., 36 (D.) C?
Pollacaspe[na], 251 (Vt.) C
Pollia, 155 (Cp.) A, 161 (Hp.) C, 257 (V.) B, 259 (A.) C, 372 (Umb.) C
Polliena, 372 (Umb.) C
Pollionia, 32 (Cl.) C
Pomeliana, 155 (Cp.) C?
Pompeia, 27 (L.) A, 32 (Cl.) B, 34 (P.) A, 155 (Cp.) A, 161 (Hp.) A, 188 (Sm.) B, 198 (F.) C, 242 (Pg.) C, 251 (Vt.) B, 257 (V.) A, 271 (M.) C, 276 (Aq.) C, 279 (H.) C, 307 (Pr.) A, Lat. A, 311 (S.) B, 372 (Umb.) B, 375 (Pi.) A
Pompilia, 155 (Cp.) C, 251 (Vt.) C
Pomponea, 271 (M.) B
Pomponena, 375 (Pi.) C
Pomponia, 27 (L.) B, 32 (Cl.) A, 34 (P.) B, 36 (D.) C, 155 (Cp.) A, 161 (Hp.) A, 188 (Sm.) A, 198 (F.) C, 242 (Pg.) C, 251 (Vt.) A, 257 (V.) A, 271 (M.) C, 276 (Aq.) B, 307 (Pr.) B, Lat. A, 372 (Umb.) A, 375 (Pi.) A
Pompucleia, 276 (Aq.) C
Pompulena, 251 (Vt.) C
Pompulla, 271 (M.) C
Pompulledia, 188 (Sm.) B, 251 (Vt.) B
Pompullia, 161 (Hp.) B, 242 (Pg.) B, 251 (Vt.) B, 311 (S.) C, 372 (Umb.) B
Pompusia, 276 (Aq.) B, Lat. C
Pompusidia, 372 (Umb.) B
Pontedia, 375 (Pi.) B
Pontia, 12 (B.) C, 27 (L.) B, 32 (Cl.) C, 34 (P.) B, 36 (D.) B, 155 (Cp.) A, 161 (Hp.) A, 188 (Sm.) A, 198 (F.) C, 242 (Pg.) B, 246 (Mcr.) C, 251 (Vt.) B, 257 (V.) B, 259 (A.) A, 271 (M.) B, 276 (Aq.) C, 279 (H.) B, 307 (Pr.) B, Lat. A, 311 (S.) B, 350 (Fal.) B, 372 (Umb.) A, 375 (Pi.) B
Pontidia, 155 (Cp.) B, 188 (Sm.) C, 251 (Vt.) B
Pontiena, 34 (P.) C, 155 (Cp.) C, 375 (Pi.) C
Pontilia, 12 (B.) C, 27 (L.) B, 375 (Pi.) C
Pontiniena, 161 (Hp.) C
Pontuleia, 257 (V.) C
Pontulena, 375 (Pi.) C
Popaedia, 27 (L.) B, 155 (Cp.) C, 246 (Mcr.) B
Popidia, 155 (Cp.) A, 257 (V.) B
Popilia, 155 (Cp.) A, 259 (A.) B, 372 (Umb.) A
Popillia, 12 (B.) C, 161 (Hp.) C, 188 (Sm.) C, 257 (V.) B, 276 (Aq.) B, 307 (Pr.) A, Lat. A, 311 (S.) C, 375 (Pi.) C

Poppaea, 155 (Cp.) A, 257 (V.) B, 307 (Pr.) C, Lat. B
Poppaedia, 198 (F.) C, 271 (M.) C
Poppedia, 251 (Vt.) C
Poppidia, 242 (Pg.) C, 271 (M.) C, Lat. C
Popponia, 372 (Umb.) B
Poppuleia, 276 (Aq.) C
Porcatia, 27 (L.) B
Porceia, 372 (Umb.) C
Porcia, 27 (L.) C, 155 (Cp.) A, 257 (V.) B, 259 (A.) C, Lat. A, 375 (Pi.) B
Porphiria, 155 (Cp.) C?
Portumia, Lat. C
Poseidonia, 155 (Cp.) C
Possidena, 372 (Umb.) C
Postinia, 372 (Umb.) C
Postumia, 27 (L.) B, 34 (P.) C, 155 (Cp.) A, 161 (Hp.) B, 251 (Vt.) B, 257 (V.) A, 276 (Aq.) C, 307 (Pr.) B, Lat. B, 311 (S.) C, 375 (Pi.) B
Postumulena, 34 (P.) C, Lat. B
Potiolana, 155 (Cp.) B
Praecilia, 257 (V.) B, 350 (Fal.) B, 372 (Umb.) B
Praeconia, 372 (Umb.) B
Praesentia, 372 (Umb.) B, 375 (Pi.) A
Prastina, 155 (Cp.) B, 161 (Hp.) C, 307 (Pr.) C, Lat. A, 311 (S.) C
Prausia, 155 (Cp.) C (?)
Preccia, 198 (F.) B
Precia, 257 (V.) C, 372 (Umb.) B, 375 (Pi.) B
Precilia, Lat. C
Prifernia, 276 (Aq.) C, Lat. B, 311 (S.) C
Priscia, 161 (Hp.) C
Priuernia, 257 (V.) C
Procilia, 155 (Cp.) C, 161 (Hp.) B, 257 (V.) B, Lat. C
Proclinia, 307 (Pr.) C
Proculeia, 251 (Vt.) A, Lat. C
Propertia, 155 (Cp.) C, 257 (V.) C, 307 (Pr.) C, 372 (Umb.) A
Proqilia, 307 (Pr.) C
Prosia, 155 (Cp.) B, 188 (Sm.) C, 257 (V.) B, 307 (Pr.) C
Protia, 372 (Umb.) C
Pruculeia, 155 (Cp.) A
Prusinia, 257 (V.) B
Publeia, Lat. C
Publia, 155 (Cp.) B, Lat. C, 372 (Umb.) C
Publicia, 32 (Cl.) B, 34 (P.) A, 155 (Cp.) A, 161 (Hp.) B, 188 (Sm.) B, 246 (Mcr.) C, 257 (V.) B, 276 (Aq.) B, 307 (Pr.) B, Lat. A, 372 (Umb.) A, 375 (Pi.) A
Publilia, 32 (Cl.) B, 34 (P.) C, 155 (Cp.) A, 257 (V.) A, Lat. A, 311 (S.) B, 372 (Umb.) B, 375 (Pi.) B

GENTILE NAMES FROM THE DIALECT-AREAS. 581

Publisidia, Lat. B
Puculcia, 27 (L.) C
Pulfatia, Lat. C
Pulfennia, 34 (P.) C, 155 (Cp.) B, 251 (Vt.) C
Pulfidia, 242 (Pg.) B
Pulfionia, 372 (Umb.) C
Pulia, 307 (Pr.) B
Pullaenia, Lat. C
Pullonia, 27 (L.) C
Pullia, 12 (B.) B, 155 (Cp.) A, 161 (Hp.) B, 188 (Sm.) B, 198 (F.) C, 257 (V.) C, Lat. B
Pullidia, 161 (Hp.) B
Pumidia, 155 (Cp.) B, Lat. C, 375 (Pi.) C
Pummidia, 251 (Vt.) C
Pupia, 155 (Cp.) A, 161 (Hp.) B, 188 (Sm.) B, 251 (Vt.) C, 307 (Pr.) C, Lat. A, 311 (S.) B, 372 (Umb.) B, 375 (Pi.) B
Pupidia, 155 (Cp.) C
Pupiena, Lat. C, 375 (Pi.) C
Pupienia, 155 (Cp.) C
Pupilia, Lat. C
Puplia, 372 (Umb.) C?
Purellia, 188 (Sm.) C
Purpurnia, 257 (V.) C
Purreia, 155 (Cp.) C
Puteolana, 155 (Cp.) B
Puticia, 32 (Cl.) C

Quadronia, Lat. C
Quaelia, 155 (Cp.) C
Quaestoria, 372 (Umb.) C
Quelia, 27 (L.) B
Quinctia, 155 (Cp.) A, 251 (Vt.) B, 257 (V.) A, 276 (Aq.) C, 307 (Pr.) C, Lat. A, 350 (Fal.) C, 375 (Pi.) B
Quinctilia, 257 (V.) A
Quintia, 161 (Hp.) A, 251 (Vt.) A, 350 (Fal.) B, 372 (Umb.) B
Quintilia, 27 (L.) C, 155 (Cp.) A, 161 (Hp.) C, 188 (Sm.) C, 251 (Vt.) C, 307 (Pr.) B, Lat. B, 372 (Umb.) B, 375 (Pi.) B
Quintinia, 257 (V.) C
Quirinia, 155 (Cp.) B, 251 (Vt.) C

Rabilia, 27 (Luc.) C, 155 (Camp.) C
Rabiria, 34 (Peuc.) B, 155 (Camp.) B, Lat. C, 375 (Pi.) C
Rabonia, 257 (Vol.) C, Lat. C
Rabuleia, Lat. C
Racectia, 155 (Camp.) C
Racilia, 257 (Vol.) B, 311 (Sab.) B
Raconia, 155 (Camp.) C
Raecia, 36 (D.) C, 155 (Cp.) B, 257 (V.) C, 307 (Pr.) B, Lat. B
Raeuidia, 34 (Peuc.) B
Rafidia, 155 (Cp.) B

Ragia, 279 (H.) C
Ragonia, 155 (Cp.) B, Lat. A
Raia, 12 (B.) C, 155 (Cp.) A, 161 (Hp.) C, 188 (Sm.) A, 198 (F.) C, 242 (Pg.) C, 251 (Vt.) B, 276 (Aq.) C, 372 (Umb.) B
Raiania, 251 (Vt.) C
Ramennia, Lat. C
Rammia, 155 (Cp.) B, Lat. B, 375 (Pi.) B
Ramnia, 155 (Cp.) C
Rania, 276 (Aq.) C, 372 (Umb.) C
Rantia, 155 (Cp.) B
Rantifana, 372 (Umb.) B
Rantifenia, 372 (Umb.) C?
Rapellia, 155 (Cp.) B, Lat. C
Rapellinia, 155 (Cp.) C
Rapidia, 155 (Cp.) C, Lat. C
Rapinasia, 155 (Cp.) C
Rapurnia, Lat. C
Rasenia, 372 (Umb.) C?
Rasia, Lat. B
Rasidia, 155 (Cp.) B
Rasinia, 12 (B.) C, 27 (L.) C, 155 (Cp.) B, 257 (V.) B, 271 (M.) C, 307 (Pr.) C, 375 (Pi.) C, 372 (Umb.) C?
Rasoria, 161 (Hp.) C?
Rasticania, Lat. C
Ratellia, 161 (Hp.) C?
Ratinia, 155 (Cp.) C
Rattia, 155 (Cp.) C
Rauelia, 34 (P.) C
Rauia, 155 (Cp.) B, 188 (Sm.) C
Raulena, 251 (Vt.) C
Rauonia, 155 (Cp.) C
Reatina, 311 (S.) B
Reccia, 198 (F.) C
Refidia, 242 (Pg.) C
Refria, 257 (V.) B
Refriu .., Lat. C
Remmia, 155 (Cp.) A, 251 (Vt.) B
Rennia, 155 (Cp.) B, Lat. B, 257 (V.) B
Reptinea, Lat. C
Resia, 372 (Umb.) C
Restiana, 372 (Umb.) C
Retula, 32 (Cl.) C
Reutia, 251 (Vt.) C
Rhaesia, 161 (Hp.) B
Ricinia, Lat. C
Ridania, Lat. C
Rimnia, 198 (F.) C
Risnacidia, 25 (Vt.) C
Robilia, 161 (Hp.) B
Rocia, 155 (Cp.) B, Lat. B
Roesia, 257 (V.) C
Rogia, 155 (Cp.) B, 375 (Pi.) C
Romaea, 188 (Sm.) C
Romania, 155 (Cp.) C, 307 (Pr.) B, Lat. B, 372 (Umb.) C
Romatia, 375 (Pi.) C
Ronia, 188 (Sm.) C?
Roscia, 34 (P.) B, 155 (Cp.) B, 257 (V.) A, 307 (Pr.) B, Lat. A, 372 (Umb.) A

Rosiccia, 311 (S.) C
Rossia, 34 (P.) C, 276 (Aq.) C
Rotania, 307 (Pr.) C
Rubbia, 257 (V.) B
Rubellia, 155 (Cp.) B, 307 (Pr.) C, Lat. B
Rubellina, 161 (Hp.) C
Rubrania, 372 (Umb.) C
Rubrena, 257 (V.) C
Rubria, 36 (D.) C, 155 (Cp.) A, 161 (Hp.) B, 188 (Sm.) C, 251 (Vt.) C, 257 (V.) B, 276 (Aq.) B, 279 (H.) C, Lat. A, 311 (S.) B, 372 (Umb.) A, 375 (Pi.) B
Rubrinia, Lat. C
Rudia, 32 (Cl.) C, 307 (Pr.) C
Ruelia, 257 (V.) B
Rufellcia, 155 (Cp.) B, 257 (V.) C, 279 (H.) C
Rufellia, 372 (Umb.) C
Rufena, 307 (Pr.) C
Rufertia, 276 (Aq.) C, 375 (Pi.) C
Rufia, 27 (L.) B, 155 (Cp.) B, 161 (Hp.) C, 276 (Aq.) C?, Lat. C, 372 (Umb.) C
Ruficana, 307 (Pr.) C
Rufinia, 36 (D.) C, 155 (Cp.) C, 161 (Hp.) B
Rufiniana, 372 (Umb.) C
Rufonia, 251 (Vt.) C
Rufrania, 36 (D.) C, 257 (V.) C
Rufreia, 257 (V.) B
Rufrena, 34 (P.) C
Rufria, 36 (D.) C, 155 (Cp.) B, 161 (Hp.) B, 242 (Pg.) C, 251 (Vt.) B, 276 (Aq.) C, Lat. C, 311 (S.) B, 372 (Umb.) B, 375 (Pi.) B
Rullia, 155 (Cp.) B, 188 (Sm.) C, 257 (V.) C
Rumeia, 34 (P.) C
Runtia, 257 (V.) B, 276 (Aq.) C
Rupedina, 276 (Aq.) C
Rupilia, 155 (Cp.) C, 307 (Pr.) C, Lat. B, 375 (Pi.) B
Ruspulcia, 372 (Umb.) B
Rustia, 155 (Cp.) B, 161 (Hp.) A, 198 (F.) C, 257 (V.) B, 307 (Pr.) C, Lat. A, 311 (S.) B, 372 (Umb.) A
Rusticania, Lat. C
Rusticclia, 155 (Cp.) B, Lat. A
Rutedia, 155 (Cp.) C
Rutilia, 32 (Cl.) B, 34 (P.) C, 155 (Cp.) A, 161 (Hp.) A, 242 (Pg.) B, 251 (Vt.) A, 257 (V.) A, 307 (Pr.) A, Lat. A, 372 (Umb.) A, 375 (Pi.) C

Sabbia, 198 (F.) C
Sabellia, 34 (P.) C
Sabernia, 161 (Hp.) C
Sabia, 27 (L.) C
Sabidia, 32 (Cl.) C, 155 (Cp.) A, 161 (Hp.) B, 198 (F.) C, 251 (Vt.) C, 257 (V.) B, 276 (Aq.) C, 307 (Pr.) C, Lat. A, 311 (S.) C, 372 (Umb.) C, 375 (Pi.) B
Sabina, 372 (Umb.) C, 375 (Pi.) B
Sabinia, 155 (Cp.) B, 276 (Aq.) B, Lat. C, 372 (Umb.) B
Saccidia, 161 (Hp.) C
Sacconia, 155 (Cp.) C, Lat. C
Sacella, 375 (Pi.) C?
Sacratoria, 155 (Cp.) C
Sacria, 198 (F.) C
Sadria, 27 (L.) C
Saenia, 34 (P.) C, 36 (D.) B, 155 (Cp.) B, 251 (Vt.) C, 257 (V.) B, Lat. C, 372 (Umb.) C
Saepinia, 188 (Sm.) A
Saeria, 155 (Cp.) C
Saf..., 276 (Aq.) C
Safinia, 155 (Cp.) C, 257 (V.) C, Lat. C, 372 (Umb.) B
Safronia, 161 (Hp.) C, 257 (V.) C
Sagaria, 155 (Cp.) C
Saginia, 155 (Cp.) B
Sagittia, 155 (Cp.) C
Sagura, 372 (Umb.) C
Salania, 242 (Pg.) C, Lat. C
Salaria, 155 (Cp.) B, 372 (Umb.) C
Salcinia, 257 (V.) B
Salena, 155 (Cp.) B, 375 (Pi.) C
Salenia, 155 (Cp.) C
Salenia, 246 (Mcr.) C
Salfeia, 311 (S.) C
Salia, 251 (Vt.) C, 375 (Pi.) B
Saliuatoria, 161 (Hp.) B, Lat. A
Salisia, 34 (P.) C
Sallia, 198 (F.) C, 251 (Vt.) B, Lat. B
Salliena, 155 (Cp.) B
Sallusstia, 271 (M.) C
Sallustia, 12 (B.) C, 27 (L.) B, 155 (Cp.) A, 161 (Hp.) B, 257 (V.) C, Lat. A, 372 (Umb.) B
Salluuia, 155 (Cp.) B, 161 (Hp.) B, 188 (Sm.) B, 259 (A.) C, Lat. B
Salonia, 155 (Cp.) B, 188 (Sm.) C, 257 (V.) B, 279 (H.) B, Lat. A
Salonina, 372 (Umb.) C
Saltoria, 155 (Cp.) B, 276 (Aq.) C, Lat. B
Saludcia, 251 (Vt.) C
Saluena, 372 (Umb.) B
Saluia, 32 (Cl.) C, 34 (P.) A, 155 (Cp.) A, 161 (Hp.) B, 198 (F.) C, 242 (Pg.) B, 257 (V.) B, 271 (M.) C, 276 (Aq.) B, 307 (Pr.) B, Lat. B, 372 (Umb.) B, 375 (Pi.) A
Saluidena, 155 (Cp.) C, 251 (Vt.) B, Lat. B
Saluidia, 242 (Pg.) B, 251 (Vt.) C
Saluidiena, Lat. B
Saluiedia, 271 (M.) C
Saluiena, 251 (Vt.) B
Saluolena, 251 (Vt.) B

GENTILE NAMES FROM THE DIALECT-AREAS.

Samellia, 155 (Cp.) A
Samia, 155 (Cp.) C, 161 (Hp.) B, 307 (Pr.) B
Samianta, 155 (Cp.) C?
Samiaria, 32 (Cl.) C, 155 (Cp.) C, 257 (V.) C, 307 (Pr.) C
Samilaris, 155 (Cp.) C?
Sammia, 161 (Hp.) C
Sandelia, 155 (Cp.) B
Sanguria, 375 (Pi.) C
Sanonia, 198 (F.) C
Sanquinia, 155 (Cp.) C
Sapiena, 251 (Vt.) C
Sappinia, 372 (Umb.) C
Sapsa, 375 (Pi.) C?
Sarciana, 188 (Sm.) C
Sariolena, 307 (Pr.) C
Sarrena, 311 (S.) C
Sarronia, 257 (V.) C
Sassia, 161 (Hp.) B
Satana, 375 (Pi.) B
Satellia, 155 (Cp.) C, Lat. C
Satia, 155 (Cp.) C
Satilia, 155 (Cp.) B
Satrena, 34 (P.) C, 311 (S.) C, 372 (Umb.) B
Satria, 12 (B.) B, 34 (P.) B, 36 (D.) B, 155 (Cp.) A, 161 (Hp.) B, 188 (Sm.) A, 242 (Pg.) A, 257 (V.) A, 372 (Umb.) A
Satricania, 307 (Pr.) B
Satridia, 311 (S.) B
Satriena, 257 (V.) C
Satrinia, 155 (Cp.) A, 372 (Umb.) B
Satriuia, 372 (Umb.) C
Satronia, 311 (S.) B
Sattia, 36 (D.) C, 155 (Cp.) A, 161 (Hp.) B, 257 (V.) C, Lat. B
Satura, 375 (Pi.) C
Saturia, 12 (B.) C, 155 (Cp.) B, 257 (V.) C, 311 (S.) B, 375 (Pi.) A
Saturnia, 155 (Cp.) C, 161 (Hp.) C
Saturnina, 372 (Umb.) B
Saturninia, 155 (Cp.) C
Sauf..., 372 (Umb.) C
Saufeia, 34 (P.) C, 155 (Cp.) A, 188 (Sm.) B, 257 (V.) B, 276 (Aq.) C, 307 (Pr.) A, Lat. B, 375 (Pi.) B
Sauonia, 27 (L.) C, 34 (P.) C, 257 (V.) B
Scaefeia, 372 (Umb.) B
Scaefia, 12 (B.) C, 242 (Pg.) B, 251 (Vt.) C, 375 (Pi.) A
Scalacia, 34 (P.) B
Scalia, 155 (Cp.) B
Scalponia, 27 (L.) C
Scaniania, 161 (Hp.) B
Scannia, 251 (Vt.) C
Scantia, 155 (Cp.) B, 198 (F.) C, 276 (Aq.) C, Lat. A, 372 (Umb.) C
Scaptina, 311 (S.) C

Scatiena, 257 (V.) B
Scaudia, Lat. C, 372 (Umb.) C
Sceidia, 372 (Umb.) C
Scentia, 155 (Cp.) A
Scetasia, 372 (Umb.) B
Scifonia, Lat. C
Scirtia, 257 (V.) C
Scomedia, 257 (V.) C
Scrateia, 161 (Hp.) C
Scribonia, 34 (P.) C, 155 (Cp.) C, 161 (Hp.) A, 188 (Sm.) B, 257 (V.) B, 279 (H.) C, 307 (Pr.) B, Lat. A
Scuppidia, Lat. C
Scurracia, 155 (Cp.) B
Scurrcia, 307 (Pr.) B
Scutaria, 34 (P.) B, 188 (Sm.) C
Scutia, 257 (V.) B
Secia, 372 (Umb.) B
Seculia, Lat. B
Secundia, 161 (Hp.) B
Secura, 155 (Cp.) C
Sedatia, Lat. B
Sedeciana, 34 (P.) B
Segia, 257 (V.) C
Segulia, 12 (B.) B, 311 (S.) C, 372 (Umb.) C
Sehia, 307 (Pr.) B
Seia, 34 (P.) B, 155 (Cp.) A, 161 (Hp.) C, 198 (F.) C, 257 (V.) B, 279 (H.) C, 307 (Pr.) B, Lat. A, 372 (Umb.) B
Seiana, 375 (Pi.) C
Seiena, 251 (Vt.) C, 372 (Umb.) C
Selenia, 271 (M.) C
Selia, 350 (Fal.) C, 372 (Umb.) C
Selicia, 307 (Pr.) A, Lat. B
Sellia, Lat. C
Sellusia, 276 (Aq.) B
Seminiacca, 251 (Vt.) B
Semnia, 161 (Hp.) C
Sempronia, 27 (L.) C, 34 (P.) A, 155 (Cp.) A, 161 (Hp.) A, 257 (V.) B, 307 (Pr.) C, Lat. A, 350 (Fal.) C, 372 (Umb.) C
Senatia, 155 (Cp.) C, Lat. B
Senecia, 155 (Cp.) B
Senenia, 311 (S.) B
Senicia, 155 (Cp.) B
Sentia, 34 (P.) C, 155 (Cp.) A, 161 (Hp.) B, 242 (Pg.) B, 251 (Vt.) B, 257 (V.) B, 307 (Pr.) B, Lat. A, 311 (S.) B, 372 (Umb.) B, 375 (Pi.) A
Sentidia, 307 (Pr.) B, 375 (Pi.) C
Sentinas, 372 (Umb.) B
Seppia, 155 (Cp.) B, 161 (Hp.) A, 188 (Sm.) A, 257 (V.) C, Lat. C
Septicia, 161 (Hp.) B, Lat. A
Septimena, 155 (Cp.) B, 251 (Vt.) B, 372 (Umb.) C
Septimia, 12 (B) C, 155 (Cp.) A, 161 (Hp.) A, 188 (Sm.) B, 242 (Pg.) B, 251 (Vt.) A, 257 (V.) A, 259 (A.) C,

271 (M.) C, 276 (Aq.) A, 307 (Pr.) B, Lat. A, 311 (S.) A, 350 (Fal.) B, 372 (Umb.) B, 375 (Pi.) A
Septimiena, 251 (Vt.) C
Septinena, 375 (Pi.) C
Septueia, 257 (V.) B
Septumia, 198 (F.) B
Septumulcia, 188 (Sm.) C
Septumulena, 32 (Cl.) C
Sepullia, 155 (Cp.) C
Sepumia, 155 (Cp.) C
Sepunia, 34 (P.) C, 155 (Cp.) B, 257 (V.) C
Serania, 375 (Pi.) C
Sereudia, Lat. C
Serenia, 155 (Cp.) C, Lat. C
Sergia, 32 (Cl.) B, 155 (Cp.) A, 161 (Hp.) B, 251 (Vt.) C, 257 (V.) B, 276 (Aq.) C, 307 (Pr.) C, Lat. A, 311 (S.) B, 372 (Umb.) C
Seria, 188 (Sm.) C, 257 (V.) C, Lat. C, 311 (S.) C, 372 (Umb.) B
Serioria, 372 (Umb.) C
Sertia, 36 (D.) C
Sertoria, 155 (Cp.) B, 161 (Hp.) B, 276 (Aq.) C, 307 (Pr.) C, Lat. B, 372 (Umb.) B, 375 (Pi.) B
Sertulla, 372 (Umb.) C
Scruatronia, 155 (Cp.) C
Seruea, 155 (Cp.) C
Serueia, 161 (Hp.) C
Seruenia, 161 (Hp.) C, 372 (Umb.) B
Scruia, 34 (P.) B, 36 (D.) C, 155 (Cp.) B, 257 (V.) B, 307 (Pr.) C, 311 (S.) C
Seruiena, 372 (Umb.) C
Seruilia, 32 (Cl.) B, 155 (Cp.) A, 161 (Hp.) A, 188 (Sm.) B, 242 (Pg.) C, 257 (V.) B, 279 (H.) C, 276 (Aq.) C, 307 (Pr.) B, Lat. A, 372 (Umb.) C, 375 (Pi.) C
Sescenia, 36 (D.) C
Sessia, 372 (Umb.) C
Sestia, 12 (B.) B, 36 (D.) B, 155 (Cp.) A, 257 (V.) B, Lat. B
Sestidia, 161 (Hp.) B, Lat. C
Sestilia, 155 (Cp.) C
Sestullia, 155 (Cp.) C, 257 (V.) C
Setia, 155 (Cp.) C, 307 (Pr.) C
Sctina, 257 (V.) C, Lat. B
Setoria, Lat. B
Setoriana, 350 (Fal.) C
Setria, 307 (Pr.) C, 375 (Pi.) C
Seucia, 307 (Pr.) C?
Seueria, 242 (Pg.) B, 155 (Cp.) B, Lat. B
Seueriana, 246 (Mcr.) C
Seuerinia, 372 (Umb.) C
Seuia, 155 (Cp.) A
Sexo..., 251 (Vt.) C
Sexsaea, 155 (Cp.) C
Sexstilia, 27 (L.) C
Sexti..., 271 (M.) C

Sextia, 12 (B) C, 32 (Cl.) B, 34 (P.) C, 36 (D.) B, 155 (Cp.) A, 188 (Sm.) C, 251 (Vt.) A, 257 (V.) B, Lat. A, 311 (S.) B
Sextilia, 155 (Cp.) A, 161 (Hp.) B, 34 (P.) B, 251 (Vt.) B, 257 (V.) A, 279 (H.) B, 307 (Pr.) C, Lat. A, 375 (Pi.) B
Sextulcia, 161 (Hp.) C, 276 (Aq.) A
Sibidiena, 372 (Umb.) B
Sibilisia, 34 (P.) C
Sicaenia, 12 (B.) C
Siccia, 375 (Pi.) B
Sicilia, 161 (Hp.) C
Sicillia, 155 (Cp.) B
Sicinia, 12 (B.) C, 307 (Pr.) B, Lat. C, 375 (Pi.) B
Siculia, 155 (Cp.) C
Sidonia, Lat. C
Signira, 307 (Pr.) B?
Silana, 161 (Hp.) C?
Silania, 155 (Cp.) C
Sileia, 32 (Cl.) C, 375 (Pi.) C?
Silia, 34 (P.) B, 155 (Cp.) A, 257 (V.) B, 307 (Pr.) B, Lat. A, 372 (Umb.) B
Silicea, 307 (Pr.) B
Silicia, 155 (Cp.) B
Sillia, 32 (Cl.) C, 375 (Pi.) B
Siluana, 251 (Vt.) C
Siluania, 155 (Cp.) B, Lat. C
Siluia, 188 (Sm.) B, 242 (Pg.) C
Similia, Lat. A
Siminia, 155 (Cp.) C
Simnia, 375 (Pi.) C
Simplicia, Lat. C
Sinitia, 251 (Vt.) C
Sinnia, 198 (F.) C, 307 (Pr.) C
Siria, 155 (Cp.) C
Sirinia, 155 (Cp.) C?
Sirtia, Lat. B
Siternia, 155 (Cp.) C
Sitria, 155 (Cp.) C
Sittia, 155 (Cp.) A, 257 (V.) B, Lat. A
Socil[i]a, 155 (Cp.) B
Soconia, 372 (Umb.) B
Socnia, 155 (Cp.) C
Sogellia, 34 (P.) C
Solania, 155 (Cp.) C
Sollia, 375 (Pi.) C
Somnisia, 372 (Umb.) C
Sontia, 161 (Hp.) C, 188 (Sm.) C, 246 (Mcr.) C
Sora, 155 (Cp.) C
Sorana, 257 (V.) B
Sorgia, 36 (D.) C
Sornatia, 375 (Pi.) C
Sornia, 155 (Cp.) A
Sosia, 34 (P.) C, 161 (Hp.) C, 257 (V.) C, 307 (Pr.) C, 311 (S.) C, 372 (Umb.) B
Sossia, 155 (Cp.) A, 188 (Sm.) B, 239 (A.) C, Lat. A

GENTILE NAMES FROM THE DIALECT-AREAS.

Sossulena, 188 (Sm.) C
Sotidin, 34 (P.) B
Sotinia, 257 (V.) C
Soumisia, 372 (Umb.) C?
Spania, 155 (Cp.) A
Spedia, 27 (L.) B, 32 (Cl.) C, 155 (Cp.) A, 161 (Hp.) A, 188 (Sm.) B, 242 (Pg.) C, 257 (V.) B, 271 (M.) C, Lat. C, 372 (Umb.) C
Spelia, 257 (V.) B, Lat. C
Spellia, 311 (S.) C
Spendia, 155 (Cp.) C (p. 157), 161 (Hp.) C
Spetinia, 375 (Pi.) C
Spultia, 257 (V.) C
Spuria, 155 (Cp.) B, Lat. B, 372 (Umb.) B
Spurillia, Lat. C
Staatia, 311 (S.) C
Staberia, 155 (Cp.) B, Lat. B
Stabia, 155 (Cp.) C
Staclena, 251 (Vt.) B
Staedia, 34 (P.) B, 155 (Cp.) C, 257 (V.) A, 271 (M.) C, Lat. C
Stafonia, 161 (Hp.) C
Staia, 12 (B.) B, 27 (L.) B, 36 (D.) B, 155 (Cp.) A, 161 (Hp.) A, 188 (Sm.) A, 198 (F.) B, 242 (Pg.) C, 257 (V.) B, Lat. C
Staiedia, 271 (M.) B
Stalcia, 155 (Cp.) C
Staldia, 257 (V.) C
Stallia, 34 (P.) C, 155 (Cp.) B, 198 (F.) C
Statedia, 271 (M.) C
Stateria, Lat. C
Statia, 27 (L.) B, 32 (Cl.) C, 34 (P.) B, 36 (D.) B, 155 (Cp.) A, 161 (Hp.) A, 188 (Sm.) B, 198 (F.) B, 242 (Pg.) B, 251 (Vt.) B, 257 (V.) B, 271 (M.) C, 276 (Aq.) C, 307 (Pr.) B, Lat. B, 372 (Umb.) A, 375 (Pi.) A
Statidia, 251 (Vt.) B
Statiena, 307 (Pr.) C
Statilia, 12 (B.) C, 27 (L.) C, 32 (Cl.) C, 34 (P.) C, 155 (Cp.) A, 161 (Hp.) C, 188 (Sm.) C, 242 (Pg.) C, 257 (V.) B, 307 (Pr.) C, Lat. A, 372 (Umb.) B
Statioleia, 307 (Pr.) B
Statiolena, 307 (Pr.) C
Statoria, 36 (D.) C, 161 (Hp.) B, 251 (Vt.) C, 307 (Pr.) C?, 375 (Pi.) C
Statria, 155 (Cp.) C
Steia, Lat. B
Stellia, 257 (V.) C
Stenia, 27 (L.) C, 36 (D.) C, 161 (Hp.) B, 257 (V.) B
Stennia, 155 (Cp.) B, 161 (Hp.) B
Sterceia, Lat. C
Stertinia, 155 (Cp.) B, 188 (Sm.) C, 257 (V.) B, 259 (A.) C, 307 (Pr.) B, Lat. B, 350 (Fal.) B, 372 (Umb.) C

Stla..., 375 (Pi.) C
Stlabia, 155 (Cp.) C
Stlaboria, 155 (Cp.) A
Stlaccia, 27 (L.) C, 32 (Cl.) C, 155 (Cp.) A, Lat. B
Stlar..., 36 (D.) C?
Stonicia, 155 (Cp.) C
Storgenia, 372 (Umb.) C?
Strabonia, 271 (M.) C, 276 (Aq.) C
Stremponia, 27 (L.) B
Stritia, 375 (Pi.) C
Stronnia, 155 (Cp.) A
Suallia, 12 (B.) B
Suauitia, 155 (Cp.) B
Suauittia, 155 (Cp.) B
Subidia, 155 (Cp.) B?
Subocrina, 276 (Aq.) C
Subria, Lat. C
Succonia, 372 (Umb.) C
Sudia, 276 (Aq.) B
Suedia, 155 (Cp.) B, 375 (Pi.) B
Sueia, 257 (V.) C
Sueiedena, 372 (Umb.) C
Sueleia, 188 (Sm.) C
Suellia, 155 (Cp.) B, 161 (Hp.) A, 188 (Sm.) C, 251 (Vt.) B, Lat. A
Suernia, 372 (Umb.) B
Suessania, 161 (Hp.) C
Suestidia, 372 (Umb.) C, 257 (V.) C, Lat. B
Suetedia, 242 (Pg.) B
Suetia, 188 (Sm.) C
Suetonia, 257 (V.) C, 311 (S.) B
Suetria, 12 (B.) C, 155 (Cp.) C, 198 (F.) B, 257 (V.) B
Suettia, 155 (Cp.) A, 257 (V.) C
Sufia, 188 (Sm.) C
Suilla, 372 (Umb.) C
Suillia, 155 (Cp.) C, 257 (V.) B, 372 (Umb.) C
Suitia, 188 (Sm.) C
Sulfia, 251 (Vt.) C, Lat. B
Sulgia, 155 (Cp.) C
Sullia, 155 (Cp.) B, 242 (Pg.) C, Lat. B
Sulmonia, 242 (Pg.) B
Sulpicia, 27 (L.) C, 34 (P.) B, 36 (D.) B, 155 (Cp.) A, 161 (Hp.) B, 188 (Sm.) B, 246 (Mcr.) C, 257 (V.) A, 259 (A.) C, 271 (M.) B, 276 (Aq.) B, 307 (Pr.) A, Lat. A, 311 (S.) B, 350 (Fal.) C, 372 (Umb.) B, 375 (Pi.) B
Summocrina, 251 (Vt.) B
Sunturia, Lat. C
Surdinia, 155 (Cp.) C
Surena, 372 (Umb.) C
Suria, 271 (M.) C, 372 (Umb.) C
Sutia, 155 (Cp.) B
Sutisia, 372 (Umb.) C
Sutoria, 155 (Cp.) B, 276 (Aq.) C
Sutria, 375 (Pi.) B
Suttis, 155 (Cp.) B

Tacitia, 161 (Hp.) C
Taddia, 188 (Sm.) C
Tadia, 155 (Cp.) C, 161 (Hp.) C, 198 (F.) C, 251 (Vt.) C, 257 (V.) C, 276 (Aq.) C, Lat. B
Taemulentin, 307 (Pr.) B
Taflenia, 375 (Pi.) C
Tagullia, 34 (P.) C
Taietia, 155 (Cp.) B
Talania, 36 (D.) B
Talasia, 372 (Umb.) C
Taledia, 271 (M.) C
Tallentia, 257 (V.) C
Talonia, 307 (Pr.) C, 372 (Umb.) B
Talpia, 155 (Cp.) C
Tamcia, 372 (Umb.) C
Taminia, 12 (B.) C, 188 (Sm.) C, 311 (S.) C, 372 (Umb.) B
Tampia, 155 (Cp.) C, 257 (V.) B, 307 (Pr.) A, 375 (Pi.) C
Tamudia, 155 (Cp.) B, 188 (Sm.) C, 375 (Pi.) A
Tamulia, 276 (Aq.) C, Lat. C
Tamullia, 36 (D.) C
Tamusia, 155 (Cp.) C
Tannia, Lat. C
Tanonia (-nnon-), 34 (P.) C?, 155 (Cp.) A, 161 (Hp.) B, 257 (V.) C, Lat. C
Tantilia, 155 (Cp.) B, 198 (F.) C
Tappuria, 307 (Pr.) C
Tapsenna, 155 (Cp.) B
Taquia, 372 (Umb.) C
Taracia, 155 (Cp.) C
Taraueia, 161 (Hp.) C
Tarcia, 257 (V.) C
Taronia, 161 (Hp.) C, 276 (Aq.) C
Tarqui..., 307 (Pr.) C
Tarquinia, 155 (Cp.) B, 161 (Hp.) B, 257 (V.) B, 375 (Pi.) C
Tarquitia, 257 (V.) B, Lat. C, 372 (Umb.) B
Tarronia, 155 (Cp.) C, 188 (Sm.) B
Tarrutenia, Lat. C
Tarsinnia, 155 (Cp.) C
Tarulia, 155 (Cp.) B
Tarusia, Lat. B
Tarutia, 34 (P.) B, 375 (Pi.) C
Tataia, 155 (Cp.) C
Tatia, 155 (Cp.) B, 198 (F.) B, 257 (V.) A, 276 (Aq.) C, 372 (Umb.) C
Tattia, 27 (L.) A, 161 (Hp.) C, 242 (Pg.) B, 251 (Vt.) C, 271 (M.) C, 307 (Pr.) B
Tautonia, 161 (Hp.) B
Tebana, 251 (Vt.) B
Tebedana, 372 (Umb.) C
Tedia, 34 (P.) C, 242 (Pg.) B, 257 (V.) B, Lat. C, 375 (Pi.) C
Tedilia, 155 (Cp.) C
Tedusia, 307 (Pr.) C
Teia, 36 (D.) B, 155 (Cp.) B, 188 (Sm.) C

Teidia, 155 (Cp.) B, 161 (Hp.) B
Teiedia, 161 (Hp.) C
Telegenia, 307 (Pr.) C
Telesinia, 188 (Sm.) B
Telonia, 375 (Pi.) B
Teltonia, 27 (L.) B, 188 (Sm.) C
Temonia, 372 (Umb.) C, 375 (Pi.) C
Tenneia, Lat. C
Terebia, 375 (Pi.) C
Terebunia, 307 (Pr.) C
Terentia, 12 (B.) C, 34 (P.) C, 36 (D.) B, 155 (Cp.) A, 161 (Hp.) B, 188 (Sm.) C, 257 (V.) A, 259 (A.) C, 279 (H.) C, 307 (Pr.) A, Lat. A, 372 (Umb.) A, 375 (Pi.) B
Teria, 372 (Umb.) C
Terinnia, 257 (V.) C
Teriuia, 257 (V.) B
Terminia, 375 (Pi.) C
Terpolia, Lat. A
Terraea, 32 (Cl.) B
Tertana, 372 (Umb.) B
Tertullia, 372 (Umb.) B
Teruentinia, 188 (Sm.) C
Tesnea, 155 (Cp.) C?
Testia, 155 (Cp.) B, Lat. A
Tetarfena, 161 (Hp.) B
Tetdia, 271 (M.) C
Tetiana, 155 (Cp.) C
Tetidia, 242 (Pg.) C, 276 (Aq.) C
Tettaca, 161 (Hp.) C, 375 (Pi.) B
Tettaiena, 375 (Pi.) C
Tettedia, Lat. C
Tettein, 155 (Cp.) A
Tettia, 12 (B.) C, 36 (D.) C, 155 (Cp.) A, 161 (Hp.) A, 242 (Pg.) C, 251 (Vt.) C, 257 (V.) B, 271 (M.) C, 307 (Pr.) C, Lat. B, 372 (Umb.) A, 375 (Pi.) C
Tettiana, 251 (Vt.) C
Tettidia, 242 (Pg.) C, 251 (Vt.) C, 271 (M.) B
Tettiedia, 251 (Vt.) C
Tettiena, 155 (Cp.) C, 276 (Aq.) B, 372 (Umb.) B
Tettiolcin, 276 (Aq.) C
Teucidia, 251 (Vt.) C
Thebania, 311 (S.) C
Theia, 161 (Hp.) C?
Thermia, 155 (Cp.) C
Thorania, 155 (Cp.) B, 257 (V.) C
Thorenas, 307 (Pr.) C
Thoria, 155 (Cp.) C, 257 (V.) C, Lat. B, 276 (Aq.) C
Thresia, 155 (Cp.) C?
Thurania, Lat. C
Tiberia, 36 (D.) B, 155 (Cp.) C
Tiburtia, 155 (Cp.) B, Lat. B, 372 (Umb.) C
Ticidia, 155 (Cp.) C
Tidena, 311 (S.) C

GENTILE NAMES FROM THE DIALECT-AREAS.

Tidia, 155 (Cp.) B, 155 (Cp.) C, 161 (Hp.) C
Tidieua, 372 (Umb.) C
Tifania, 372 (Umb.) B
Tifernia, 372 (Umb.) B
Tigia, 161 (Hp.) C
Tigidia, 375 (Pi.) B
Tillia, 155 (Cp.) A, 161 (Hp.) C, 198 (F.) B, 257 (V.) A, Lat. B, 372 (Umb.) C
Timinia, 34 (P.) C, 155 (Cp.) C, 257 (V.) B
Tineia, 155 (Cp.) C, 251 (Vt.) B, 307 (Pr.) C, Lat. B
Tinia, Lat. C, 372 (Umb.) C
Tinnania, 375 (Pi.) C
Tintiria, 34 (P.) C, 155 (Cp.) B, 161 (Hp.) C, 372 (Umb.) C?
Tintoria, 155 (Cp.) B, 161 (Hp.) C, 257 (V.) C, 350 (Fal.) C
Tinucia, Lat. B
Tiresia, 372 (Umb.) C
Tironia, 271 (M.) C
Tirria, 350 (Fal.) C
Titacia, 155 (Cp.) C, 161 (Hp.) B
Titaedia, Lat. C
Titecia, 242 (Pg.) C, 271 (M.) B
Titedia, 257 (V.) B, 271 (M.) B, 276 (Aq.) B
Titellia, 372 (Umb.) C
Titia, 12 (B.) B, 27 (L.) B, 32 (Cl.) C, 34 (P.) A, 36 (D.) C, 155 (Cp.) A, 161 (Hp.) B, 188 (Sm.) A, 198 (F.) B, 242 (Pg.) B, 246 (Mcr.) C, 251 (Vt.) B, 257 (V.) A, 259 (A.) C, 271 (M.) B, 276 (Aq.) C, 279 (H.) A, 307 (Pr.) C, Lat. A, 311 (S.) A, 350 Fal. A, 372 (Umb.) A, 375 (Pi.) A
Titicena, 155 (Cp.) C
Titidia, 271 (M.) C
Titiedia, 276 (Aq.) B
Titiena, 276 (Aq.) C, 350 (Fal.) C
Titienia, Lat. B
Titilenia, 311 (S.) C
Titilia, 155 (Cp.) C, 161 (Hp.) C, 242 (Pg.) C
Titinia, 32 (Cl.) A, 34 (P.) B, 155 (Cp.) A, 161 (Hp.) C, 257 (V.) C, Lat. B, 311 (S.) C, 276 (Aq.) C
Titionia, 307 (Pr.) B
Titiria, 12 (B.) C, 155 (Cp.) C
Titlenia, 311 (S.) B
Titoleia, 307 (Pr.) C
Titratia, 372 (Umb.) C
Titria, 161 (Hp.) C
Titsiena, 251 (Vt.) C
Tittiena, 372 (Umb.) B
Titucia, 155 (Cp.) C, 271 (M.) C, 276 (Aq.) B
Tituleia, 161 (Hp.) A, 276 (Aq.) B
Titulena, 311 (S.) C

Tituria, 32 (Cl.) C, 155 (Cp.) C
Tocia, 259 (A.) C
Tocidia, 271 (M.) B
Tofelana, 155 (Cp.) B, 259 (A.) B
Togia, 161 (Hp.) B
Tondia, 307 (Pr.) A
Tongilia, Lat. B
Tonia, Lat. B
Tonneia, 279 (H.) B
Tonnia, 375 (Pi.) C, 311 (S.) C
Torasia, 372 (Umb.) C
Toratia, 155 (Cp.) C
Torenas, 311 (S.) C
Torinia, 271 (M.) C
Tornasia, 155 (Cp.) B
Torquatia, Lat. C
Toscniana, 307 (Pr.) C?
Tossia, 257 (V.) C, 307 (Pr.) B
Traesia, 27 (L.) C
Traia, 161 (Hp.) B
Traiana, Lat. C
Tranquillia, 259 (A.) C
Trauia, 257 (V.) C, 372 (Umb.) B
Trausia, 155 (Cp.) C
Treb..., 276 (Aq.) C
Trebania, 155 (Cp.) C
Trebatia, 155 (Cp.) C, 161 (Hp.) A, Lat. C, 372 (Umb.) B
Trebellia, 34 (P.) B, 155 (Cp.) C, 161 (Hp.) B, 188 (Sm.) A, 257 (V.) A, Lat. B, 372 (Umb.) C, 375 (Pi.) B
Trobelliena, 188 (Sm.) C
Trebia, 36 (D.) C, 155 (Cp.) A, 161 (Hp.) A, 246 (Mcr.) B, 257 (V.) A, 271 (M.) B, 307 (Pr.) C, Lat. B, 375 (Pi.) C
Trebiena, Lat. C
Trebonia, 155 (Cp.) B, 161 (Hp.) A, 276 (Aq.) B, 307 (Pr.) B, Lat. A
Trebulana, 155 (Cp.) C, 161 (Hp.) B, 307 (Pr.) B
Trebularia, 161 (Hp.) C
Trellena, 251 (Vt.) B
Trellia, 198 (F.) B
Tremelia, 36 (D.) C
Triaria, 155 (Cp.) C
Tribellia, Lat. C
Tricaria, 251 (Vt.) C
Triccia, 34 (P.) B
Tridonia, 257 (V.) C
Trisenia, 155 (Cp.) C
Trisimpedia, 372 (Umb.) B
Trolia, 155 (Cp.) B
Truttedia, 155 (Cp.) B, 259 (A.) C, 307 (Pr.) C, 375 (Pi.) B
Truttidia, 257 (V.) C, 372 (Umb.) B
Tuccia, 12 (B.) C, 32 (Cl.) B, 155 (Cp.) B, 161 (Hp.) C, 188 (Sm.) C, 257 (V.) B, Lat. A, 311 (S.) C
Tullia, 27 (L.) A, 155 (Cp.) A, 161 (Hp.) C, 188 (Sm.) B, 251 (Vt.) B, 257 (V.)

A, 307 (Pr.) A, Lat. A, 311 (S.) B, 350 (Fal.) C, 372 (Umb.) B, 375 (Pi.) A
Tulliana, 34 (P.) B, 161 (Hp.) C
Tullidia, 161 (Hp.) C
Tulliena, 375 (Pi.) B
Tullonia, 161 (Hp.) C
Tuppuria, 155 (Cp.) C
Turcia, 27 (L.) B, 155 (Cp.) B, 188 (Sm.) B, 198 (F.) C, Lat. B, 375 (Pi.) B
Tureia, 155 (Cp.) C
Turellia, 34 (P.) C, 155 (Cp.) B, 161 (Hp.) B, Lat. B
Turia, 155 (Cp.) B, Lat. C, 372 (Umb.) C
Turillia, 12 (B.) B
Turpedia, 372 (Umb.) C
Turpidia, 375 (Pi.) B, 372 (Umb.) C
Turpilia, 34 (P.) C, 161 (Hp.) B, 257 (V.) B, Lat. B, 311 (S.) B, 372 (Umb.) B, 375 (Pi.) C
Turpleia, 307 (Pr.) B
Turrania, 155 (Cp.) A, 161 (Hp.) C, 257 (V.) B, Lat. A, 311 (S.) B, 372 (Umb.) C
Turrena, 372 (Umb.) B
Turrenia, Lat. C
Turronia, 155 (Cp.) B
Tursclia, 161 (Hp.) A
Turturia, 161 (Hp.) C
Turuena, 257 (V.) C
Turullia, 271 (M.) C
Tuscenia, 155 (Cp.) B
Tuscilia, 155 (Cp.) B, 375 (Pi.) B
Tusculanin, 307 (Pr.) B, Lat. C
Tusia, 375 (Pi.) C
Tusidia, 372 (Umb.) B, 375 (Pi.) A
Tussania, Lat. C
Tussia, 155 (Cp.) C
Tussidia, 155 (Cp.) C, 161 (Hp.) B
Tutia, 257 (V.) B, 307 (Pr.) B, Lat. C, 372 (Umb.) B
Tuticia, 155 (Cp.) C
Tutilia, 155 (Cp.) C, 257 (V.) B, Lat. B, 350 (Fal.) C, 372 (Umb.) C
Tutoria, 32 (Cl.) B, 34 (P.) B, 155 (Cp.) B
Tyria, Lat. C

Vaberia, 372 (Umb.) C
Vacaenia, 155 (Cp.) B
Vaccia, 198 (F.) B
Vaccinia, 155 (Cp.) C
Vadia, Lat. C
Vagellia, 12 (B.) B, 27 (L.) A, 155 (Cp.) C
Valentiniana, 372 (Umb.) C
Valeria, 12 (B.) C, 32 (Cl.) B, 34 (P.) A, 36 (D.) B, 155 (Cp.) A, 161 (Hp.) A, 188 (Sm.) B, 198 (F.) B, 251 (Vt.) B, 257 (V.) A, 259 (A.) B, 271 (M.) B, 276 (Aq.) B, 279 (H.) B, 307 (Pr.) A, Lat. A, 311 (S.) A, 372 (Umb.) A, 375 (Pi.) C
Valgia, 155 (Cp.) B, 161 (Hp.) C, 257 (V.) B, Lat. C, 372 (Umb.) C
Valia, 155 (Cp.) C, 372 (Umb.) B
Vallia, Lat. A, 375 (Pi.) C
Valuennia, 188 (Sm.) B
Vania, 372 (Umb.) B
Vannia, Lat. C
Vaonia, 27 (L.) B
Varacia, 155 (Cp.) C
Varatia, 372 (Umb.) C
Varecia, 271 (M.) C
Varena, 251 (Vt.) B, 307 (Pr.) C, Lat. A, 311 (S.) C, 372 (Umb.) B, 375 (Pi.) C
Varenia, 155 (Cp.) A, Lat. B
Varguntein, 257 (V.) C, 279 (H.) B, Lat. B, 311 (S.) C
Varia, 12 (B.) B, 155 (Cp.) A, 161 (Hp.) B, 188 (Sm.) A, 198 (F.) B, 242 (Pg.) A, 251 (Vt.) B, 257 (V.) B, 259 (A.) C, 271 (M.) B, 276 (Aq.) B, 307 (Pr.) C, Lat. A, 311 (S.) B, 372 (Umb.) A, 375 (Pi.) B
Variasia, 251 (Vt.) A
Variena, 155 (Cp.) B, 198 (F.) C, 311 (S.) C
Varin..., 311 (S.) C
Varina, 311 (S.) C
Varinia, 307 (Pr.) C, Lat. B
Varisidia, 188 (Sm.) C, 372 (Umb.) C
Varonia, 372 (Umb.) B
Varredia, 155 (Cp.) C?
Varredinia, 251 (Vt.) C
Varronia, 155 (Cp.) B, 161 (Hp.) B, 257 (V.) B, 307 (Pr.) C?, Lat. C
Varrutia, 372 (Umb.) C?
Varsedia, 372 (Umb.) C
Vasselia, 372 (Umb.) B
Vassia, 161 (Hp.) B, 251 (Vt.) B, 307 (Pr.) C, 311 (S.) B, 372 (Umb.) C, 375 (Pi.) B
Vassidena, 372 (Umb.) B
Vatenia, 372 (Umb.) C
Vateria, 188 (Sm.) C
Vaterria, 161 (Hp.) C
Vatinia, 155 (Cp.) C, 161 (Hp.) B, Lat. C
Vatronia, 307 (Pr.) A, Lat. B
Vauidia, 34 (P.) A
Vauilia, 375 (Pi.) C
Vbonia, 155 (Cp.) B
Vcena, Lat. C?
Vdia, 155 (Cp.) B
Vdisia, 372 (Umb.) C
Vebia, 161 (Hp.) C
Vebidia, 307 (Pr.) C?
Vecilia, 155 (Cp.) B, Lat. A, 375 (Pi.) C?

GENTILE NAMES FROM THE DIALECT-AREAS.

Vecillia, 36 (D.) C
Vectia, 246 (Mcr.) C
Vectiedia, 251 (Vt.) C
Vedia, 155 (Cp.) A, 251 (Vt.) B, 257 (V.) B, Lat. A, 311 (S.) C, 372 (Umb.) A
Vediania, 161 (Hp.) C
Vedina, 276 (Aq.) C
Vedonia, 372 (Umb.) C?
Vegellia, 279 (H.) C
Vegetia, 375 (Pi.) C
Vehilia, 12 (B.) C, 32 (Cl.) C, 307 (Pr.) B, Lat. C
Veia, 155 (Cp.) A, 257 (V.) C, Lat. A
Veiaca, 372 (Umb.) B
Veiania, 161 (Hp.) C, 372 (Umb.) B, 375 (Pi.) C
Veibedia, 242 (Pg.) B
Veidia, 34 (P.) C, 161 (Hp.) A, 375 (Pi.) B
Veiedia, 161 (Hp.) C, 372 (Umb.) B
Veiena, Lat. C, 311 (S.) C, 372 (Umb.) B, 375 (Pi.) B
Veionia, 155 (Cp.) C
Veisia, 271 (M.) C
Velasia, 34 (P.) B, 155 (Cp.) B
Velenia, 311 (S.) B
Velia, 161 (Hp.) C?, 307 (Pr.) B, 372 (Umb.) C
Velina, 155 (Cp.) C
Velineia, 307 (Pr.) C
Vellaea, 34 (P.) B, 161 (Hp.) C
Vellcia, 155 (Cp.) A, Lat. C
Vellenia, Lat. C
Vellia, 155 (Cp.) B
Velonia, 155 (Cp.) B
Veltia, 372 (Umb) C, 375 (Pi.) B
Veluria, 155 (Cp.) B
Vemnasia, 251 (Vt.) C
Venaecia, 161 (Hp.) C
Venafrana, 155 (Cp.) C
Venafrania, 155 (Cp) A, 257 (V.) C
Venecia, 372 (Umb.) C
Venedia, 311 (S.) C, 372 (Umb.) C
Venelia, 155 (Cp.) C, 257 (V.) C, 372 (Umb.) C
Venellia, 34 (P.) C
Veneria, 155 (Cp.) C, 372 (Umb.) B, 375 (Pi.) C
Venetia, 242 (Pg.) B
Venia, 372 (Umb.) B
Venidia, 155 (Cp.) C, 307 (Pr.) B
Venilia, 307 (Pr.) C
Vennia, 155 (Cp.) B, 188 (Sm.) B, Lat. C
Vennonia, 257 (V.) C, Lat. B
Ventidia, 372 (Umb.) B, 375 (Pi.) C
Ventilia, Lat. B
Venuleia, 155 (Cp.) B, 271 (M.) C, 307 (Pr.) C, Lat. B
Veppia, 251 (Vt.) C
Verana, 311 (S.) C

Verania, 155 (Cp.) A, 257 (V.) C, 307 (Pr.) C, 311 (S.) B
Veratia, 32 (Cl.) B, 34 (P.) B, 36 (D.) C, 155 (Cp.) A, 161 (Hp.) B, 198 (F.) B, 257 (V.) B, 307 (Pr.) C, Lat. A, 372 (Umb.) C, 375 (Pi.) C
Vercia, 242 (Pg.) C
Verecundinia, 155 (Cp.) B, 372 (Umb.) C
Veredia, 271 (M.) C
Vergilia, 27 (L.) C, 36 (D.) B, 155 (Cp.) B, 161 (Hp.) B, 188 (Sm.) C, 251 (Vt.) B, 257 (V.) B, Lat. A, 372 (Umb.) C
Verginia, 155 (Cp.) C, 161 (Hp.) A, 375 (Pi.) C
Veria, 311 (S.) C
Veridia, 155 (Cp.) C
Vernasena, 372 (Umb.) C
Vernasia, 372 (Umb.) C
Vernia, 276 (Aq.) C, Lat. C
Veronia, 155 (Cp.) C
Verran..., 372 (Umb.) C
Verrea, 372 (Umb.) C
Verria, 155 (Cp.) A, 257 (V.) A, 279 (H.) C, 307 (Pr.) B
Verronia, 34 (P.) C
Versiculana, 155 (Cp.) B
Versinia, 188 (Sm.) C
Verticia, 155 (Cp.) C
Vertuleia, 257 (V.) B
Verulana, 188 (Sm.) C, 257 (V.) C, Lat. C
Vescinia, 155 (Cp.) B
Vesclaria, 242 (Pg.) C
Vesedia, 161 (Hp.) B
Vesena, 311 (S.) C
Vesennia, 372 (Umb.) B, 375 (Pi.) C
Veserena, 311 (S.) B
Veseria, 155 (Cp.) B
Vesia, 155 (Cp.) C, 198 (F.) C, 372 (Umb.) B
Vesiculana, 155 (Cp.) B
Vesidiena, 372 (Umb.) C
Vesnia, 372 (Umb.) B
Vesonia, 27 (L.) C, 155 (Cp.) A, 161 (Hp.) B, 188 (Sm.) B
Vespasia, 155 (Cp.) C
Vespicia, 188 (Sm.) C
Vespria, Lat. C, 372 (Umb.) A
Vessidia, 372 (Umb.) B
Vesta, 375 (Pi.) C
Vestilia, 155 (Cp.) C, Lat. B
Vestinia, 251 (Vt.) B
Vestiniana, 350 (Fal.) C, 372 (Umb.) C
Vestoria, 155 (Cp.) B, 307 (Pr.) C
Vestricia, 155 (Cp.) C, Lat. B
Vestuleia, 372 (Umb.) C
Vesuedia, 161 (Hp.) C
Vesuia, 155 (Cp.) B
Vesullia, 161 (Hp.) B, 198 (F.) C

Vetedia, 375 (Pi.) C
Vetin, 251 (Vt.) B
Vetidia, 155 (Cp.) C, 188 (Sm.) C
Vetiedia, 271 (M.) C, 375 (Pi.) C
Vetilia, 155 (Cp.) B, 307 (Pr.) C, Lat. B, 375 (Pi.) C
Vetronia, 155 (Cp.) C
Vettedia, 242 (Pg.) C, 271 (M.) C
Vetteia, 307 (Pr.) C
Vettena, 155 (Cp.) B, 161 (Hp.) C, 276 (Aq.) B
Vettenia, 155 (Cp.) B, 307 (Pr.) B, Lat. C
Vettesia, 311 (S.) B
Vettia, 12 (B.) B, 27 (L.) B, 32 (Cl.) C, 34 (P.) A, 155 (Cp.) A, 161 (Hp.) A, 188 (Sm.) B, 198 (F.) B, 242 (Pg.) B, 246 (Mcr.) B, 257 (V.) A, 259 (A.) C, 271 (M.) B, 276 (Aq.) B, 279 (H.) C, 307 (Pr.) B, Lat. A, 311 (S.) B, 372 (Umb.) A, 375 (Pi.) A
Vetticia, Lat. C
Vettidia, 251 (Vt.) C
Vettiedia, 242 (Pg.) C
Vettiena, 155 (Cp.) B, 242 (Pg.) B, Lat. C, 375 (Pi.) C
Vettina, 375 (Pi.) C
Vettlaea, 311 (S.) B
Vettuleia, 155 (Cp.) C
Vettulena, 155 (Cp.) C, Lat. B, 311 (S.) B
Vettulina, 155 (Cp.) C
Vetulania, Lat. C
Vetulena, 251 (Vt.) C
Vetulenia, 307 (Pr.) C
Veturia, 32 (Cl.) C, 155 (Cp.) A, 251 (Vt.) C, 257 (V.) A, 271 (M.) B, 307 (Pr.) B, Lat. A, 311 (S.) C, 350 (Fal.) C, 372 (Umb.) A, 375 (Pi.) B
Vetunia, 155 (Cp.) B
Veucia, 257 (V.) A
Viaria, 257 (V.) C
Vibbia, 161 (Hp.) A
Vibbina, 36 (D.) C?
Vibedia, 271 (M.) C
Vibediena, 271 (M.) C
Vibellia, 155 (Cp.) C
Vibenia, 276 (Aq.) C
Vibenna, Lat. C
Vibennia, 372 (Umb.) C
Vibia, 27 (L.) B, 32 (Cl.) B, 34 (P.) B, 155 (Cp.) A, 188 (Sm.) A, 198 (F.) B, 242 (Pg.) A, 251 (Vt.) B, 257 (V.) A, 271 (M.) B, 276 (Aq.) B, 279 (H.) B, 307 (Pr.) A, Lat. A, 311 (S.) A, 372 (Umb.) A, 375 (Pi.) A
Vibiana, 188 (Sm.) B
Vibidaia, 271 (M.) C
Vibidia, 155 (Cp.) B
Vibiedia, 27 (L.) B, 155 (Cp.) C, 251 (Vt.) C

Vibiena, 34 (P.) C, 36 (D.) B, 251 (Vt.) C, 276 (Aq.) C
Vibina, 27 (L.) C
Viblia, 271 (M.) C
Vibolena, 375 (Pi.) C
Vibpsania, 246 (Mcr.) B
Vibrent..., Lat. C
Vibria, 155 (Cp) A, 161 (Hp.) C, 307 (Pr.) C
Vibronia, 257 (V.) C
Vibulania, 372 (Umb.) C
Vibulca, 161 (Hp.) C?
Vibuleia, 155 (Cp.) A, 161 (Hp.) C, 307 (Pr.) C
Vibulena, 251 (Vt.) B, 350 (Fal.) C
Vibullia, 12 (B.) C, 155 (Cp.) C, 251 (Vt.) B, 257 (V.) A, Lat. B
Vibunia, 161 (Hp.) C
Vibusia, Lat. B, 372 (Umb.) B
Vicasia, 259 (A.) C
Viccia, 155 (Cp.) C, 188 (Sm.) B
Viciria, 155 (Cp.) A, 161 (Hp.) B, Lat. C, 375 (Pi.) C
Vicrena, 251 (Vt.) C, 375 (Pi.) C
Vicria, 251 (Vt.) C, 257 (V.) A
Victoria, 155 (Cp.) B
Vidia, 372 (Umb.) C
Vifia, 375 (Pi.) C
Vigellia, 155 (Cp.) C
Vigilia, 32 (Cl.) B
Vigillia, 311 (S.) C
Viguetia, 155 (Cp.) C
Vilia, 372 (Umb.) A
Villia, 27 (L.) B, 36 (D.) C, 155 (Cp.) C, 161 (Hp.) B, 257 (V.) B, 259 (A.) C, Lat. B, 350 (Fal.) B
Vilon..., 375 (Pi.) C
Vincia, Lat. C
Vindia, 375 (Pi.) C
Vindleia, 372 (Umb.) C?
Vinedia, 27 (L.) B
Vinia, 161 (Hp.) B, 251 (Vt.) C, 257 (V.) B, Lat. C
Vinicia, 27 (L.) C, 155 (Cp.) A, 257 (V.) B, 307 (Pr.) B, Lat. C
Vinnia, 27 (L.) B, 34 (P.) B, 155 (Cp.) B, 188 (Sm.) B
Vintia, 27 (L.) B
Vinucia, 34 (P.) C, 161 (Hp.) B
Vinulei..., 375 (Pi.) C
Vinuleia, 155 (Cp.) C
Vinullia, 155 (Cp.) B
Vipsania, 12 (B.) C, 27 (L.) C, 155 (Cp.) C, 188 (Sm.) C, 251 (Vt.) C, Lat. A
Vipstana, 155 (Cp.) C, 257 (V.) B, 307 (Pr.) C, 311 (S.) C
Virasia, 155 (Cp.) C
Virgilia, Lat. C, 372 (Umb.) C
Virginia, 34 (P.) C, 372 (Umb.) B
Viria, 155 (Cp.) A, 161 (Hp.) C, 257 (V.) B, 279 (H.) B, 375 (Pi.) C

Viriana, 155 (Cp.) C
Virofurcia, 155 (Cp.) C?
Virridia, 155 (Cp.) C
Virtia, 155 (Cp.) C
Virusia, 372 (Umb.) C
Viscaria, 257 (V.) C
Viselia, 34 (P.) C
Visellia, 32 (Cl.) C, 155 (Cp.) A, 161 (Hp.) C, 188 (Sm.) C, 257 (V.) C, 372 (Umb.) C
Visena, 372 (Umb.) B
Visennia, 372 (Umb.) C
Vistilia, 372 (Umb.) B
Vistinia, 372 (Umb.) B
Vistuleia, 188 (Sm.) C
Visuina, 372 (Umb.) C?
Visullia, 257 (V.) C
Vitellia, 27 (L.) C, 155 (Cp.) A, 161 (Hp.) C, 257 (V.) B, 307 (Pr.) B, Lat. C, 372 (Umb.) C
Vitoria, 36 (D.) B, 155 (Cp.) B, 188 (Sm.) C, 279 (H.) C, 372 (Umb.) B, 375 (Pi.) C
Vitrasia, 155 (Cp.) A
Vitronia, 155 (Cp.) C
Vitruuia, 155 (Cp.) B, 257 (V.) A, 372 (Umb.) C
Vittedia, 242 (Pg.) C
Vitteia, 257 (V.) B
Vittia, 155 (Cp.) B, 259 (A.) C
Vitudia, 311 (S.) C
Vitulasia, 251 (Vt.) B
Vitullia, 257 (V.) B
Vituria, 155 (Cp.) C, 161 (Hp.) C
Viuellia, Lat. C
Vlpia, 27 (L.) C, 34 (P.) B, 36 (D.) B, 155 (Cp.) A, 161 (Hp.) B, 188 (Sm.) B, 242 (Pg.) B, 251 (Vt.) C, 257 (V.) A, 279 (H.) B, 307 (Pr.) A, Lat. A, 311 (S.) B, 372 (Umb.) A, 375 (Pi.) C
Vlteia, 155 (Cp.) B
Vmbennonia, 27 (L.) C
Vmbilia, 257 (V.) C, Lat. B
Vmbonia, 161 (Hp.) C
Vmbrena, 276 (Aq.) C
Vmbria, 155 (Cp.) B, 161 (Hp.) A, 188 (Sm.) B, 251 (Vt.) C, Lat. B
Vmbricia, 155 (Cp.) A, 307 (Pr.) C, Lat. C, 372 (Umb.) C, 375 (Pi.) C
Vmennia, Lat. C
Vmettia, 36 (D.) C
Vmidia, Lat. C
Vmmidia, 155 (Cp.) B, 257 (V.) A, 276 (Aq.) C, 307 (Pr.) C, 372 (Umb.) C
Voconia, 27 (L.) C, 34 (P.) B, 155 (Cp.) B, 161 (Hp.) B, 257 (V.) B, 307 (Pr.) C, Lat. A, 375 (Pi.) B
Voesia, 307 (Pr.) C
Voesidena, 372 (Umb.) C
Volaneria, 372 (Umb.) B
Volasenna, 155 (Cp.) B

Volasennia, 155 (Cp.) B
Volcacia, 34 (P.) C, 155 (Cp.) A, 188 (Sm.) C, 257 (V.) C, 307 (Pr.) B, Lat. C, 372 (Umb.) B, 375 (Pi.) A
Volcasia, 372 (Umb.) A
Volceia, 155 (Cp.) C, 188 (Sm.) A, 276 (Aq.) C, Lat. C
Volcia, 155 (Cp.) A
Volesedia, 276 (Aq.) B
Volia, 375 (Pi.) C
Vollia, 311 (S.) B, 372 (Umb.) B
Volsiena, 372 (Umb.) C
Volsonia, 155 (Cp.) C
Volteia, 155 (Cp.) B, 155 (Cp.) C, 279 (H.) C, 372 (Umb.) B
Voltia, 198 (F.) B
Voltidia, Lat. A
Voltilia, 257 (V.) C
Volu..., 375 (Pi.) C
Volumnia, 32 (Cl.) B, 155 (Cp.) B, 161 (Hp.) B, 257 (V.) A, 307 (Pr.) B, Lat. A, 311 (S.) C, 350 (Fal.) B, 372 (Umb.) B, 375 (Pi.) C
Volunseia, 307 (Pr.) C
Voluntilia, 27 (L.) C, 257 (V.) B, 307 (Pr.) A, Lat. C, 372 (Umb.) C
Voluscia, 257 (V.) C
Voluseia, 257 (V.) C, Lat. B
Volusena, 372 (Umb.) B
Volusia, 34 (P.) B, 155 (Cp.) A, 188 (Sm.) C, 257 (V.) B, 259 (A.) C, 307 (Pr.) B, Lat. A, 372 (Umb.) B, 375 (Pi.) B
Volussiana, Lat. C
Volutia, 27 (L.) B
Vonbia, Lat. C
Vorena, 251 (Vt.) C
Vossia, 372 (Umb.) C
Votiena, 375 (Pi.) C
Vottonia, 155 (Cp.) C
Vrania, 372 (Umb.) B
Vrbania, 155 (Cp.) B
Vrbatia, Lat. C
Vrbenea, 372 (Umb.) C
Vrbiculia, 242 (Pg.) C
Vrbinia, 155 (Cp.) C
Vrfi..., Lat. C
Vrgulania, 272 (H.) C
Vrsena, 155 (Cp.) C
Vrsia, 257 (V.) C, 372 (Umb.) B
Vrsidia, 155 (Cp.) C
Vrsilia, 372 (Umb.) C
Vrticia, 372 (Umb.) C?
Vruia, 155 (Cp.) B
Vruina, 311 (S.) B
Vruineia, 155 (Cp.) B, 307 (Pr.) C
Vruinia, 372 (Umb.) C
Vsia, 251 (Vt.) C, 257 (V.) C
Vsidia, 188 (Sm.) C
Vsonia, 307 (Pr.) C
Vsoro (nom. masc.), 307 (Pr.) B

Vssaea, 34 (P.) C
Vssia, 375 (Pi.) B
Vtia, 188 (Sm.) B, 198 (F.) C
Vtiaca, 375 (Pi.) C
Vtiana, 27 (L.) C
Vtilia, 257 (V.) B
Vttedia, 155 (Cp.) C, 257 (V.) C, Lat. B

Vttia, 155 (Cp.) C
Vttiedia, 372 (Umb.) B
Vulcacia, 27 (L.) C
Vulia, 155 (Cp.) B
Vultricia, 155 (Cp.) B
Vuotidia, Lat. C

INDEX IV.

PASSAGES IN THE DIALECT INSCRIPTIONS DISCUSSED IN THE SYNTAX (pp. 497 ff.).

The number of the Inscription is in heavy type; the numbers of lines of the longer Inscriptions are distinguished by l.; the numbers which follow the references are those of the numbered sections of the Syntax.

5	17	**95** *a*	l. 13. 79	**239**	63
22	9		l. 19. 49, 78	**243**	43, 48 footn., 63
28	l. 4. 61	**95** *b*	l. 10. 5		(1)
	l. 5. 28, 37, 38, 67		l. 14. 52	**253**	55
	l. 6. 67		l. 17. 31	**354**	17
	l. 7. 29		l. 18. 31	**355**	29
	l. 9. 33, 52, 64		l. 19. 31		
	l. 10. 36, 37, 53,		l. 21. 53		TABULAE IGUVINAE
	65, 67		ll. 23–25. 49, 65		(**356**—**367**)
	l. 11. 25, 58, 64	**101**	9, 29, 42, 46		
	l. 12. 13, 32	**102**	9, 42, 43	I *a*	l. 1. 27
	l. 13. 58	**104**	29		l. 9. 70
	l. 14. 15, 18, 53,	**106**	29		l. 24. 70
	61	**107**	9, 29		l. 26. 75
	l. 15. 33, 53 footn.	**108**	9, 17		l. 27. 61
	l. 16. 53 footn., 61	**109**	21, 28		l. 30. 61
	l. 17. 32, 53 and	**113**	29, 52, 68, 75		l. 34. 27
	footn.	**114**	52, 75	I *b*	l. 8. 59 footn.
	l. 19. 61, 66	**115**	9		l. 10. 66
	l. 20. 25, 30	**117**	43, 52 footn., 63,		l. 11. 61, 67
	l. 21. 27, 52, 58,		68, 75		l. 18. 61
	70	**130**	ll. 3 ff. 54		l. 20. 25
	l. 22. 27		l. 5. 59		l. 31. 11
	l. 24. 15, 66		l. 6. 62		l. 34. 55 footn., 64
	l. 25. 22, 53		l. 8. 66		l. 35. 55, and
	l. 26. 32	**131**	54		footn., 63
	l. 28. 53	**143** *b*	12		l. 36. 55 footn.
	l. 29. 53	**150**	21		ll. 40–44. 75
30	12	**158**	21		l. 45. 29 footn.,
39	6, 75	**159**	21		37, 55, 56
42	17, 24, 40	**175** *a*	l. 19. 52	II *a*	l. 4. 41
46	17	**184**	21		l. 6. 75
60	33 footn.	**185** *a*	12		l. 14. 70
95 *a*	l. 3. 19	**195**	28		l. 15. 29
	l. 9. 37	**196**	28		l. 16. 26 footn.,
	l. 10. 64	**216**	54		58, 63

C.

II a	l. 17. 63	V a	l. 25. 33, 54, 67	VI b	l. 9. 3	
	l. 30. 27		l. 28. 33, 67		l. 25. 61, 73	
	l. 41. 13	V b	l. 1. 25, 65 (1)		l. 26. 55	
	l. 42. 27		l. 5. 33		l. 27. 3	
	l. 43. 75		l. 6. 63		l. 28. 3	
	l. 44. 29 footn., 37		l. 8. 63		l. 40. 68, 75	
	56		l. 10. 63		l. 41. 61, 73	
II b	l. 1. 29		l. 13. 63		l. 43. 61	
	l. 9. 41		l. 16. 63		l. 44. 20	
	l. 26. 78	VI a	l. 1. 21, 35		l. 47. 59 footn.	
III	l. 14. v. p. 478 footn.		l. 2. 63		l. 48. 66	
			l. 3. 35		l. 49. 45	
IV	l. 6. 58		l. 6. 61		l. 50. 28, 62, 68	
	l. 12. 27		l. 7. 47, 57 footn., 58		l. 51. 37	
	l. 16. 21				l. 52. 62	
	l. 21. 61		l. 8. 61		l. 54. 58, 68	
	l. 22. 62 footn.		l. 17. 58		l. 64. 63	
	l. 32. 61		l. 19. 58, 75		l. 65. 63	
V a	l. 1. 29		l. 20. 46, 64, 75	VII a	l. 3. 58	
	l. 7. 68		l. 24. 55		l. 39. 4	
	l. 8. 63		l. 25. 24, 41		l. 43. 55	
	l. 9. 63		l. 26. 58		l. 44. 55	
	l. 10. 34, 63		l. 27. 14, 41, 58		ll. 51–54. 75	
	l. 12. 25		l. 58. v. p. 472 footn.		l. 52. 58 footn.	
	l. 15. 10			VII b	l. 1. 29, 37, 58	
	l. 16. 29, 61	VI b	l. 7. 55		l. 2. 61, 62, 67	
	l. 24. 65 (1)		l. 8. 3		l. 4. 13, 18	

INDEX V.

GLOSSARY TO THE DIALECTS.

1. *The order of the letters is that of the Latin Alphabet, with a few necessary modifications, viz.*:
a, b, c *and* k *together*, d, ḍ, e, f, g, h, i *and* î *together*, l, m, n, o (*not including* ŭ), p, φ, q, r, s, ṡ, t, θ, ŭ *and both consonant* u (*written* v *in transcribing non-Latin alphabets which possessed a special symbol*) *and vowel* u *together*, z.

2. *Spaced type denotes that the word is transcribed from a non-Latin alphabet, unspaced that it is transcribed from Latin alphabet, as throughout the book.*

3. *Variations of spelling are frequent, and hence while every word is quoted in the form in which it appears in the text, the form chosen for the head-line is that which appeared to represent the actual sound most exactly to the eye,* a n z e r i a t u *rather than* aseriato, andendu *than* a t e n t u, *but in all cases like these, where there is serious divergence, cross-references are given.*

4. *Proper names are printed with initial capitals in the head-lines.*

5. *When a restoration is printed in the text of any inscription, the word should be sought in the Glossary in its restored form.*

6. *The L a t i n w o r d s which immediately follow the dialect forms s i m p l y s t a t e the meaning of the forms and imply nothing as to their etymology (e.g.* kahad *capiat); but the sign* = *implies that two forms are historically identical (e.g.* a v e f = *L.* aues).

7. *The numbers refer to the numbered inscc. etc. in the body of the book; the lines of the particular inscc. are given in italic type; but* p. *denotes a reference to a page.*

8. *A few abbreviations should perhaps be specially mentioned (for the rest, v. Vol.* I. *p.* xxi.):

    L. or Lat. = *Latin*.   *abbrev.* = *abbreviated.*
    O. or Osc. = *Oscan*.   *uel sim.* = *uel simile aliquid.*
    U. or Umb. = *Umbrian*.   *prec.* = *preceding article.*
    Pg. = *Paelignian*.   *foll.* = *following article.*

List Phonet. Pecul. *refers to a list of possibly dialectic peculiarities of sound which is given at the end of the section on Notation, Vol.* I. *p.* xxvi.

a

a Ɲ, first letter of the Osc. αβ,
a, abbrev. of the Umb. word for 'asses';
acc. pl., 364 V *b* *10*, *13*, *15*, *18*, 367
VII *b* *4*
a, ab v. *af*
-**a**, v. -*ad*
A, abbrev. praen., O. 13, Pg. 231
Aadiieis, nomen, gen. sg. masc., O.
164; cf. *gens Adia*, 155 (Camp.) C
Aadirnas, nomen, nom. sg. masc., O.
42
Aadiriis, nomen, nom. sg. masc., O.
60; spelt **aadiriís**, O. 61
aamanaffed, aedificauit, aedificari
iussit, aedificandam mandauit uel
sim., 3 sg. perf. ind. act., O. 43, 45,
47, 50, 52; cf. *manafum*
aanfehtaf, adj. or partic. acc. pl. fem.,
U. 359 II *a* *34*; Büch. renders 'non
factas i.e. non coctas,' but **aan-** need
not be negative, v. *an-* inf.
aapas, subst. fem. probably nom. pl.,
O. 193 q.v.
aasa-, v. *asa-*
dβás, 37 D q.v.
Abelese (si integra uox) cognom., dat.
sg. fem. Fal.-Lat. 336; since the
dative *Polae* appears beside it (with
the diphthong preserved), it would
seem that *Abelese* like *Plenese* ib.
contains not an *ā*-stem but the common -*ensi-*suffix
Abellano-, ethnicon of Abella, O. 95
-*nam* acc. sg. fem. *b* *29*, -*núí* dat. sg.
m. *a* *3*, -*náś* nom. pl. m. *b* *15*, *21*,
-*nám* gen. pl. m. *b* *18*, [-*núís*] dat.
pl. m. *a* *6*; cf. *abro-* and v. s. v. *Aderl*
inf.
abludam or **apl-**, 205 C 8 q.v.
abro-, aper, Osc.-Umb. subst. whence
abrof, acc. pl. masc., U. 366 VII *a* *3* =
apruf 357 I *b* *24*, *33*; cf. Osc. *Abellā-*
from **Abro-lā-*; Lat. *apro-* shows the
more original form, see Brugm. *Grds.*
I. § 499
abrons, acc. pl. m. U. 366 VII *a* *43* are
shown by this passage to be the same
animals as the *abrof* of VII *a* *3*, but
it is not clear to me whether the form
-*ons* is exceedingly ancient and preserved here alone by chance, or should
be ascribed to the following stem
whose nasal might conceivably have
preserved the -*ns* of the acc. from the
usual change to *f*
abrunu, *apronem*, magnum aprum,
acc. sg. masc., U. 358 II *a* *11*; like
Lat. *capo* : *capus*, *pauo* : *pauos*, which

Büch. compares, this word shows the
use of the suffix which gave rise to
the magnificative -*one* in Italian
Acarcelinio (for -*ios*), nomen, nom. sg.
masc. Fal.-L. 325 *b* and 326 *a*, gen.
-*lini*, 324, *Acacelini* 325 *a*
Acca, nomen, nom. sg. f., Pg. 227, and
xxv, p. 249; cf. *gentes Acca*, *Accaua*,
Accaua, all Pg. in Index 4
Akeḍonia-, subst. fem. a locality in
Iguvium, acc. with postp. *Akeḍu-
niam-em*, U. 357 I *b* *16* = *Ace[r]so-
niam-e* 366 VI *b* *52*, loc. *akeḍunie*,
U. 357 I *b* *43*, loc. with postpos. *acersoniem*, U. 366 VII *a* *52*
†ἀκελλεά, 37 D q.v.
akenei̇̊, v. *acno-*
Aciles, Achilles, nom. sg. m. Etr.-Praen.
299, 302, *Acila* 297
aciptum, acceptum, p. ptc. pass. nom.
sg. neut. Fal.-L. 335 *b*
ἀκιρίς, 37 C q.v.
akkatus, adj. or ptc. nom. pl. m.,
describing certain persons cursed,
beside *trstus*, O. 137 *b* *10*
Acmemeno, Agamemnon, nom. sg. m.
Etr.-Praen. 301
acno-, subst. m. or neut., dies festus uel
sim. O. acc. *acunum* (si uera lectio)
28, *31*, loc. *akenei̇̊* 175 *a* *18*, *b* *21*;
U. *acnu*, acc. 364 V *b* *8*, *12*, *14*, *17*;
cf. U. *perakni- serakni-*
akrid = L. *acri*, adj. abl. sg., O. 130 *a* *4*
akrutu, v. *ager*
Actia, Angitiae, dat. sg. M. 267, cf.
Anaqtiai inf.
actud, v. *aġ-*
Akviiai, nomen, dat. sg. f., O. 130 *a*
10; cf. *gens Aquuia*, 155 (Camp.) C
Akudunniad, a Samnite town, abl. sg.
fem., O. 158 q.v. with 160 A. s.v.
Aquilonia; the double -*nn-* is due to
the following -*j-*, see List Phonet.
Pecul. Vol. I. p. xxvi.
acum, v. *ag-*
akun, O. 59
acunum, v. *acno-*
ad, ad prep., Fal.-L. 335 *b*; cf. -*ad* and *ar-*
adasia, 205 C 2 q.v. and *asignas* inf.
Ade-, **Aderl-**, i.e. **Aderlanům* or
*Aderlad, the O. name of the town
called *Atella* by the Romans, 147 *a*
and *b*; O. *Aderlā-* : L. *atro-* as O.
Abellā- i.e. **Abro-lā-* : L. *apro-*. But
Atella 154 A is the Lat. pronunciation
of early Osc. **Adella-* (see *Am. J.
Phil.* xi. 307 ff.), and it has survived
as the name of the town because with
Capua the town ceased to exist as
an Oscan community in 211 B.C.;

whereas Abella remained Oscan probably as long as any Italian town, certainly till the last century B.C. (see 95), and this spelling with the modern form (*Avella*) represents as usual the continuous local development of pronunciation

adpŭd, relative conjn., from *ad* and the neut. rel., perhaps with a temporal meaning, O. 117 *a*

adro-, adj. =L. *ater*, U. only as epithet of *vesklu* unscula (?): 366 VII *a 25 adro* neut. pl. acc.=*atru* 357 I *b 29*, *adrir*, abl. pl., 366 VII *a 9, 10, 21*= *adrer*, ib. 18

-aḍ, ad, U. postp. with acc., often in the form -*a, asamaḍ* 361 IV *6*, *asama* 359 II *a 39*, 361 IV *16*, *ereçlumaḍ* ib. *6*, *ereçluma* ib. III *35*, IV *3, 10, etrama* ib. III *34*, *persklumaḍ* ib. III *21*, *spantimaḍ* ib. III *33*, *spiniama* 359 II *a 37*, *spinamaḍ* ib. *33*, *tertiama* 361 IV *2*; the loss of final -*d* elsewhere in Umb. seems to show that -*a* is the genuine phonetic form, and -*aḍ* a reformate detached from compounds where it preceded vowels and certain consonants: but, in an earlier epoch of Umb., the -*t* of Itlc. *at (Lat. *atauos*, cf. O. *az*) had become *d* before the change of *d* to *ḍ*

adepo-, adj., U. only in pl. as epithet to *arvies* frumentis (for the abl. see the Syntax §§ 25, 27) probably meaning bonis, grandibus, prosperis uel sim.; it is omitted in the later liturgy, possibly because *arvio*- had fallen out of use save in the sacrificial sense, and the distinguishing epithet was no longer necessary; *adepes* 356 I *a 6, 19, 23*, I *b 4*, *adpes*, 356 I *a 13, adepe*, 357 I *b 26, 44*, 358 II *a 8*, and this form was probably intended in 356 I *a 10*; *adeper*, 357 I *b 30, 33*, *adiper*, 356 I *a 27*; on -*es*: -*e*: -*er* cf. p. 402 ff., and on -*ip*-: -*ep*- p. 495, 1. For the stem cf. Lat. *adeps*, Sab. *alipes* 309 B, but the forms -*e*, -*er* show that in U. the word was an -*o*-stem, see the Accidence

adfertur, subst. nom. sg. m. adfertor, i.e. flamen, chief officer of the Atiedian brotherhood, U. 357 I *b 41*, 359 II *a 16*, 362 V *a 3*, *10*=*arsfertur*, 365 VI *a 8*, spelt *arfertur*, 365 VI *a 3*, 367 VII *b 3*; acc. sg. *arsferturo*, 365 VI *a 17*, dat. *adferture*, 363 V *b 3, 5, 6*= *arsferture*, 365 VI *a 2*

adiper, v. *adepo*-

adkani, U. 361 IV *28*; probably acc. sg. neut. for -*nim* 'quod accinitur' (so Büch.)

arsmahamo, i.e. *admāmo, U. 366 VI *b 56*, written *armanu* 357 I *b 19*, ordinamini, sanctificamini uel sim., 2 pl. impv. pass. or depon., denominative from *admo*-

***admatio-**, sollemnis, ad sacra uel ad sacrorum flaminem pertinens, U. only as epithet of *perkam* acc. sg. fem. *arsmatiam*, 366 VI *b 49, 50*, spelt *arsmatia*, 365 VI *a 19*, 366 VI *b 53, 63*, VII *a 46, 51*; from the preceding verb

admo-, subst. masc., ritus uel sim., U. only in pl., nom. *arsmor*, 365 VI *a 26, 36, 46, b 29*, acc. *arsmo* (for -*mof*), 365 VI *a 30, 32, 39, 42, 52, b 13, 32, 34*, 366 VII *a 17, 30*, spelt *asmo*, 365 VI *a 49*

Admune, subst. dat. sg. masc., U. 360 II *b 7*, a title of Iupiter derived from *admo*-, 'rituum sacrorum conseruatori' uel sim.

adpeltu, vb. 3 s. impv. act., U. 359 II *a 32*, 360 II *b 19*, 361 IV *8*; in form =Lat. *adpellito*; it denotes one of a string of movements to be performed towards the close of various sacrifices

adper, adpes, v. *adepo*

adputrati, arbitratu, secundum arbitrium, subst. abl. sg. (cf. the Syntax, § 25), U. 362 V *a 12*; if this word has any connexion with L. *bētere*, whence *arbiter* is usually derived, it can only be that U. -*put*-=-*bot*-, and then U. -*bot*-: L. -*bĕt*- (-*bĭt*- in *arbiter*): L. *bēt*- as L. and U. (*tri*-)*pod*-(*ā*-): *ped*-: Gr. πηδ(άω)

adveitu=L. *aduehito*, 2 and 3 sg. impv. act., U. 358 II *a 12*, 359 II *a 29*, 360 II *b 13*, 361 III *34*, IV *5*,=*arsueitu*, 365 VI *a 56, 59, b 2, 5, 20, 44, 46*, 366 VII *a 4, 8, 42, 54*, spelt *arveitu*, 356 I *b 6*, *arueitu* 365 VI *b 23*, once *aveitu*, 361 IV *1*

adviu, see *arvio*-

Ae[mili] (si sic sanandum), nomen gen. sg. m. Praen. 282

aeraciam, si genuina lectio, uas aereum, acc. sg. fem., Etr.-Camp. 99

aesar, v. *aiso*-

aetat-=L. *aetas*, subst. fem. dat. *aetatei*, Fal.-L. 335 *b*; abl. *aetatu* (for -*tud*) pure Pg. 216, *5*, *aetate* later Pg. 218

aeteis, partis, subst. gen. sg., O. 28, *12, 18, 27*, acc. *aet* for *aetim partem, partitionem uel sim., 117 *a 6*; if a]*ĭttĭŭm alttram* partium alteram is rightly restored in 95 *b 27* the gender of the word at Abella may have differed from its gender at Bantia, where *aeteis* is qualified by *minstreis*, which in form is certainly masculine

Afaries, nomen, nom. sg. m., O. 18; cf. *gens Afaria*, 27 (Luc.) B

af-, the older form of L. *ab*, in Osc. in compounds (v. inf.), and in Old L. v. p. 222, Rem. 1; also perhaps in U. *ahauendu*, *ahtrepuḍatu*, though these may contain a form *ā-* if it existed in Italic

afded = L. *abiit*, 3 sg. perf. ind., Pg. 216, 6, see Thurneysen, l.c. ad loc. On *af-* v. sup.

afer-, v. *anfer-*

afiktu, affigito or ? infigito (if for **anfiktu*), 2 or 3 sg. impv. act., U. 356 I *a 31*; cf. *fik-*

Afillis, nomen, nom. sg. m., O. 71; cf. *gens Afillia*, 155 (Camp.) B, *Afilia* 307 (Praen.) C

aflakus, *ablexeris, abduxeris uel sim., 2 sg. fut. perf. indic. act., O. 130 *a 10, 11*; 3 sg. pres. subj. *aflukad*, ib. 3. On *af-* v. sup.

ag-, agere, O. inf. *acum*, 28, *24*, (perhaps only by negligence for *ag-*) impv. 3 sg. *actud*, ib. 15; U. impv. 3 sg. *aitu*, 357 I b *29, 37*, *aitu* 365 VI b *18* bis, 366 VII *a 40, 45*, 3 pl. *aituta* 361 III 13; perhaps pres. ptc. act. dat. pl. m. *Aśetus* 358 II *a 14*, v. the Syntax, § 70. Aeq.-L. *agat*, agat, 273, Fal.-L. *age(n)d[ae*, agendae, 335 *b*

ager = L. ager, nom. sg. m., U. 355, abl. *akru(tu)*, 362 V *a 9*, loc. *agre*, 364 V b *9, 14*

agine, subst. loc. sg. Mruc. 243 *6, 7*; for formation cf. O. *leginom, tanginud*, etc.

Ahal, praenomen, possibly abbreviated, nom. sg. m., U. 352

ahatripursato, v. *ahtrepuḍatu*

ahatrunie, App. II. 38

ahauendu, i.e. **āvendo* auertito uel sim., 3 sg. impv. act., U. 366 VII *a 27*; on *ā-* see *af-* sup., and for *-ndu* for **-nneto*, cf. *ostendu, ostensendi(r)* etc., and the Syntax, § 46. Not connected with L. *uěnum* which would be *uesno-* or *uisno-* in U., but conceivably with *uěnor*

ahesnes, i.e. *aësn-* = L. *aenis* adj. abl. pl., U. 361 III *18, 19* bis; in Lat. it was the accent *a-és-no-* which prevented the contraction that took place in *aeris* for **á-es-is* etc. (L. *aes* is reformed from the oblique cases instead of **aos* = Skt. *ayas*)

ahti-, subst., U. acc. sg. *ahtim(-em)*, 357 I b *12* bis; abl. pl. *ahtis(-per)*, 361 III *24, 29*; no doubt derived like *Ahtu* (which may be the same stem, see p. 474) from the sacrificial sense of *ag-* q.v.

ahtrepuḍatu = L. **abstripodato*, 2 and 3 sg. impv. act., U. 359 II *a 24, 25, 31*, *38*, = *atrepuḍatu*, 360 II b *18*, *atripursatu*, 365 VI b *16*, *ahatripursato*, 366 VII *a 23, 36*, spelt *atropusatu*, 365 VI b *36*; on *ah-, aha-* (i.e. *ā-*) see *af-* sup.

Ahtu, dat. sg. m. (*u*-stem) title of Iupiter and Mars, U. 358 II *a 10, 11*; "ut Spector (U. *Spetur-* q.v.) spectioni ita hoc numen actioni praeest, i.e. sacrificio rite perpetrando." Büch. *Umb.* p. 126, who compares a *deus Agonius* with similar functions from Paul. ex F. 10 M., s.v. *agonium*

ahvdiuni, O. 59 si unum verbum est

Aiax, Aiax, nom. sg., Etr.-Praen. 295, 299, 300, 301

aidili- = Lat. aedilis, O. nom. sg., possibly abbreviated, *aidil*, 40, 53, 178, nom. pl., *aidilis*, 39

Aiedies, nomen, nom. sg. m., Fal.-L. 346; cf. *gens Aiedia*, Index III

aikdafed, 3 sg. perf. ind. act. governing *sakaraklŭm*, O. 171

αίκλοι, 37 C q.v.

Aisernio- and *Aisernino-*, ethnica of Aesernia 185, Osc. acc. sg. *aiserninm* and *aisernino(m)*, gen. pl. masc. *aeserniom*; on *-no* cf. n. xvi. p. 143, and, for the stem, *aiso-* inf.

αισ, *aisis*, v. *aeso-*

aiso-, subst. masc. deus, res sacra uel sim., αισοί 'θεοὶ ὑπὸ Τυρρηνῶν' 37, αισ, O. 13; *aisos* (*paeris*) Mruc. 243 = *e]sos* Mars. 261 (si uera lectio) pl., probably nom. or acc. 'di propitii (sint)' or 'deos propitios (oramus)' like θεός or τύχη (e.g. Cauer *Delect.*[2] 34, 264, 302—311,—250 is an example of an acc. without θεός beside it—); some prefer to regard *aisos* and Mars. *esos* as dat. pl. like τύχῃ ἀγαθῇ (e.g. Cauer, ib. 232); from what stem is *aisis*, Pg. 206 (possibly abbreviated)? Cf. O. *aisusis* sacrificiis, U. *esōno-* sacrificium and *aesar* 'lingua Etrusca deus' Suet. *Aug.* 97, Vol. *esaristrom* sacrificium, and *Aesernium*, a name which shows that if the word was really used by Etruscans, they had borrowed it from their neighbours

aisusis, abl. (or dat.?) pl. consonantal stem, O. 130 *a 7*; cf. *aiso-*, and for the suffix L. *hon-ōribus, od-oribus* etc.

a]ittíûm, v. *aeteis*, and in any case for the *-tt-* cf. *ḣíttíúf*, and List Phonet. Pecul. Vol. I. p. xxvi.
aitu, aituta, v. *ag-*
aiu, subst. acc., U. 358 II *a 4*; according to Bücheler for *ag-ia* neut. pl. 'agonia, sacra'
ak-, v. sub *ac-*
Alafaternum, Alfaternum, ethnic epithet of the Campanian Nucerines, gen. pl. or acc. sg. masc. (cf. n. xvi. p. 143), O. 144 *b*, abbrev. *Alafternib. c* (probably *a* also), and *Alavfnum* (v. p. 463 f.)
Alafis, nomen, nom. sg. m., Pg. 239; cf. *gens Alfia*, Index III
Albsi, i.e. *Albē(n)si*, Albae (Fucentis) patrono, dat. sg. masc., Aeq.-L. 272, q.v.
Alcumena, Alcmene, nom. sg. fem., Etr.-Praen. 295
alfo- = L. *albus*, U. only as epithet of *vesklu* uascula (?), acc. pl. n. *alfu* 357 I *b 29*, *alfir*, abl. pl., 366 VII *a 25*, *26 = alfer*, ib. 32, 34
Alies, nomen, nom. sg. m., Mruc. 244; cf. *gens Allia* in Index III
alifa, -φa v. Ἀλλιfανων
alipes, adeps, 309 B 2, q.v.
Alixentros, Etr.-Praen. 293, 296, 300; cf. 205 Rem. 9 (1)
ἄλλην, 37 D q.v.
Ἀλλιfανων, Allifanorum, gen. pl. m. of ethnicon of Allifae, O. 183 *e*, written αλλιβανον, ib. *a*, abbrev. αλιφα, ib. *c*, αλλιβα, ib. *b*, αλλει, ib. *d* and *alifa* in Osc. αβ, ib. *a*; on the spelling v. p. 463
allo = Lat. *alia*, nom. sg. fem., O. 28 *22*
Alpes, alpo-, Sab. 309 A q.v.
Alpis, nomen, nom. sg. m., Pg. 210; cf. *alpo-*
Alses, Etr.-Praen. 300, *Alsir*, ib.
altinûm, subst. acc. sg., O. 67, where it appears on an election-appeal beside IIII the sign for the Osc. equivalent of *quattuoruiratum*. In form it = Lat. *altionem* or *-num*
altro- = L. *alter*, O. m. dat. sg. *alttrei*, 175 *a 17*, *b 20 = altrei*, 28. *13*, abl. sg. miswritten *atrud*, ib. 24, fem. acc. sg. *alttram* 95 *b 27*, nom. pl. m. *alttr[ús]* ib.; Gr. -τερο-, Skt. *-tara-* etc., seem to show that the absence of *-e-* in the Osc. form is due to syncope, or, at least, is a purely Osco-Umb. peculiarity
alttram, -*ttrei*, v. *altro-*
am-, prepstn. in O. *amvíanud*, U. *anferom*, *antedafust*; cf. also *ampedia*, *aplenia*; but in all these words the earlier form may have been *amfi-*, or by syncope *amf-*; cf. *amfr-*
amatens, 3 pl. perf. ind. act. governing *eituam uenalinam*, Mruc. 243. *10*; cf. the Syntax, § 48 footn.
amboltu, probably ambulato, 3 sg. impv. act., U. 366 VI *b 52*; the form varies from the Lat. as L. *lauito* from L. *lauato*
ambr-ē-, circum-ire, U. impv. *amprehtu*, 2 sg., 357 I *b 21*, spelt *aprehtu*, 357 I *b 20*, 3 pl. *ambretuto*, 366 VI *b 56*, *63, 64*; fut. perf. 2 sg. *ampreſuus*, 357 I *b 20*, 3 pl. *ambreſurent*, 366 VI *b 56*; contrast Osc. *amfr-(i)e(n)t*, which shows the more primitive form of the prepn., and v. Brugm. *Grds.* I. § 209
amfret, ambiunt, 3 pl. pres. ind. act., O. 95 *b 6, 19*; for *amfr-ient* by analogy of the sg. forms *amfreit* etc. But U. *ambr-etuto*, ambiunto, shows a different form of the prepn.
amiricatud, *immercato, sine mercede, abl. abs. impers., O. 28. *22*; cf. n. xxii. p. 225
Ammai (*kerriíaí*), dat. sg. fem., O. 175 *a 6, 23, b 8*, a Samnite goddess; cf. Hesych. Ἀμμάς ἡ τροφὸς Ἀρτέμιδος καὶ ἡ μήτηρ καὶ ἡ 'Ρέα καὶ ἡ Δημήτηρ. Here at Agnone Ceres has a separate statue, so that the first (or third) of these significations is the most probable
amno-, regio, uia uel sim. Osc. subst. in phrase r[ehtúd] *amnúd*, 95 *a 13*, recta regione, and as postp. *amnud* with gen., caussā, O. 28. *6* bis. So Bartholomae (l.c. ad 95), and rightly, beyond doubt. On the abl. cf. Syntax, § 25
amosio, 205 C 2 q.v.
amparitu, 3 sg. impv. act. governing *kletram*, U. 361 III *14*, pass. *amparihmu*, 359 II *a 42*, where the subject is the sacrificing priest
ampeḍia, subst. or adj. used as subst., abl. fem. sg., U. 359 II *a 29*; no doubt derived from *peḍ-* in *peḍu seritu*, ib. 24
ampen(n)-, impendere, U. in act. impv. *ampentu*, 3 sg., 359 II *a 20*, 361 III *23*, spelt *ampetu* (2 or 3 sg.), 360 II *b 10, 11*, and *apentu* (3 sg.), 361 III *27*, fut. ind. *anpenes*, probably 2 sg., 360 II *b 27*, fut. perf. ind. *apelus*, probably 2 sg. ib., 3 sg. *apelust*, 363 V *a 17*, for *apenn(e)lust*, cf. the Syntax, § 46, and p. 485
ampert, usque ad, non plus quam, prepstn., with gen., but v. p. 484, O.

28. *12*, *18*, also no doubt ib. *3* and *27*; from the negative *an-* and *pert* q.v.
amplius, amplius, Fal.-Lat. 336
ampre-, v. *ambre-*
amprufid, improbe, adv., O. 28. *30*
Amucos, Amycus, nom. sg. masc., Etr.-Praen. 287, *-ces* 288
amurca, 205 Rem. 9 (2), p. 229 q.v.
amvíanud, angiportus, parua uia deuertens, subst. abl. sg., O. 60, 61, 62, 63; cf. the Synt. § 21, and for the meaning Idg. Forsch. 3. 85; from *am-* or (by syncope) **amfi-* and *viā-*
(1) an-, in-, *ἀνά*, prefix denoting inception or approach in Osc. *αναfακετ*, perhaps *angetuzet*, Umb. *ampen-*, *anden-*, *anovihimu* etc., qq.v.
(2) an-=Lat. in-, Gr. ἀ(ν)-, negative prefix, O. *amprufid*, *ancensto* etc., U. *anhostato-*, *ansihito-* etc.
anaceta, sacerdos, antistes uel sim., nom. sg. fem., Pg. 206, 208, *anac* 207 =*anceta* 217, and *anaceta* 206 bis (Addenda); v. note to 206
Anaes, nomen, nom. sg. m., Pg. 218; cf. Etr. Camp. *Anei* 97, and *gens Annaea*, Index III
αναfακετ, dedicauit uel sim., 3 sg. perf. ind. act. O. 7; cf. note ad loc. and p. 462
Anafriss, dat. pl. masc., name of certain Samnite deities, O. 175 *a* 9, *b* 11; often identified with Lat. *imbribus*, quite legitimately so far as the form is concerned; if so, for the anaptyxis compare the foll.
Anagtiai=L. *Angitiae*, Mars. Actia, dat. sg. fem., a Marsian goddess, O. 167; cf. p. 289, and xxviii. *b* p. 261
Anaiedio, nomen, nom. sg. m., Mars.-L. 266
ἀνάρος, 37 D q.v.
ancensto, non censa, O. 28. *22*, nom. sing. fem.; *an-* not and the partc. pass. of O. *censaum* q. v.
anceta, v. *anaceta*
Ancitibu[s, Vest.-L. n. xxviii. *b* p. 261, q.v.
ancla-, v. *angla-*
andendu, intendito, 3 sg. impv. act., U. 366 VII *a* 25=*antentu*, 359 II *a* 20, 361 III 15, 16, 17, 22, IV 21, 27, spelt *atentu*, 360 II *b* 28; from the prepstn. *an-* and U. *tenn-* tendere (on the phonetic changes, cf. Synt. § 46); cf. the parallel *endendu* with which, however, I see no reason to identify it
ander, impv. postp. with acc., U. 365 VI *b* 47, spelt *anter*, 356 I *b* 8, = Osc. *anter*, q.v.
andersafust i.e. **an-dedafust*, circum-

dederit, 3 sg. fut. perf. act. of U. **dedare'* compounded with *am(f)-* 367 VII *b* 3=*atedafust*, 357 I *b* 40, spelt *andirsafust*, 366 VII *a* 46; the change in conjugation (**dedust* : **-dedafust*), as Buck rightly points out, is due to the composition, cf. Lat. *capere* : *occupare*, etc. Büchelor would compare rather Lat. *-tuli*
andersesust, *intersederit, interueniendo caerimonias uiolauerit, 3 sg. fut. perf. ind., U. 365 VI *a* 7; cf. p. 485 footn., and *andersistu*
andersistu, interuenito, 3 sg. impv. act., U. 365 VI *a* 6; in form=Lat. *intersistito*, but its future perfect is *andersesust* q.v.
anderuomu, adv. (or adverbial phrase?), U. 365 VI *b* 41
andirs-, v. *anders-*
Anelia, nomen, fem., Fal.-L. xxxix *a* (7), p. 374
anfer-, circumferre, lustrare, in U. *aferum* pres. inf. act., 357 I *b* 10= *afero*, 366 VI *b* 48, gerundive *anferner*, gen. sg. m., 365 VI *a* 19; from *am-* (q.v.) and *fer-* ferre; the *n* in *anf-* need not, I think, denote more than a nasal colour for the vowel, cf. U. *anpenes*
angetuzet, incipient, instituent uel sim., with inf. 3 pl. fut. perf. ind., O. 28. *20*
anglaf, oscines, i.e. aues omen ferentes, acc. pl. fem., U. 365 VI *a* 5, =*angla*, 365 VI *a* 1, 3, 5, 6, 366 VI *b* 49, spelt *ancla*, 365 VI *a* 18, nom. pl. *anclar*, 365 VI *a* 16
anglo- angulus, U. *anglom(e)*, acc. sg. masc. 365 VI *a* 9, *anglu(to)*, abl. (ex) angulo, 365 VI *a* 8, 10, 10
anhostatu, non hastatos, adj. acc. pl., U 366 VI *b* 60, masc. (for *-tuf*) epithet of *iouie(f)*, spelt *anostatu*, 366 VII *a* 48, dat., *anhostatir*, 366 VII *a* 28, 50, *anostatir*, 366 VI *b* 62, VII *a*, 13, 15
Ania-, v. *Ann-*
Aninus, local adj. nom. sg. masc., Mars.-L. 263
Anniaes, nomen, nom. sg. m. Pg. 237, =*Aniaes*, Pg. 236
Annio-, nomen, *Anniei* (abbrev. for *-ieeís*), gen. sg. masc. O. 107, *Ania*, nom. sg. fem. Pg. 226, cf. *gens Annia* Index III
anost-, v. *anhost-*
anouihimu, induitor, sibi sumito vel sim. 3 sg. impv. pass. U. 366 III *b* 49 bis; from *an-* *ἀνά* and the root of Lat. *ind-uo*, *ex-uo* with an *-i-*suffix
anpen-, v. *ampen-*

anseria-, v. *anzeria-*

ansif, uices, or some plur. word, e.g. pateras, oblationes, carrying with it the idea of succession, acc. pl. U. 359 II *a* 25

ansihito-, i.e. *an-śihto-*, non cinctus, U. acc. pl. masc., *anśihitu* (for *-tuf*) 366 VI *b* 59, spelt *ansihitu*, ib. VII *a* 48, dat. pl., *anśihitir*, ib. VI *b* 62, VII *a* 13, 14, 28, 50; v. *śihito-*

anstintu, distinguito, exornato uel sim. 3 sg. impv. act. U. 361 III 20; a compound of the Umb. for *-stinguere* with *am(f)-* or *an- ḍvá*, spelt *astintu*, ib. 18, 19

anstiplatu = Lat. **in-stipulato*, i.e. a deis flagitato, 3 sg. impv. act., U. 365 VI *a* 3; v. *stiplā-*

ant, ante, of place, prepn. with acc., O. 39 bis

[**ant**] si uerum supplementum, O. 62, abbrev. for *anter* q.v.

antakres, integris, adj. used as subst. abl. pl. (neut.?) only in phrase *a. kumates* integris (libis) commolitis, U. 359 II *a* 42, spelt *antakre*, 357 I *b* 36, 38

ἄνταρ, 37 E q.v.

antentu, v. *andendu*

anteponat, Fal.-L. 336 ubi v. adn.

anter, inter, Osc. prepn. with acc. and abl.: acc. 60, 61 (and probably 62), 63, 95 *b* 28, abl. ib. *a* 14; = U. *ander* q.v.; it is parallel in form, but probably not identical with Lat. *inter*

antermenzaru (for *-rum*), intermenstruarum, adj. gen. pl. fem., U. 359 II *a* 16; v. *mens-*

Anterstatai, deae interuenienti, internuntiae, a Samnite goddess, dat. sg., O. 175 *a* 5, *b* 6, for formation cf. L. *antistita*

anzeriā-, obseruare, U. 2 sg. simple impv., *aserio*, obserua, 365 VI *a* 4 v. Synt. § 63. (1); 2 or 3 sg. impv., *azeriatu*, obseruato, 356 I *b* 8 = *aseriatu*, 3 sg. 365 VI *b* 47; 1 sg. pres. subj. *aseriaia* (v. Synt. l.c.), 365 VI *a* 2; supine *anzeriatu*, obseruatum, 357 I *b* 10 = *anseriato*, 365 VI *a* 6, spelt *aseriato*, ib. VI *a* 1, 6, 366 VI *b* 48; p. partc. pass. abl. pl. fem. (Synt. § 27), *anzeriates*, 356 I *a* 1, 359 II *a* 17 = *aseriater*, 365 VI *a* 1

ap, **ape**, v. *appei*

apehtre, U. 361 IV 15; Büch. ingeniously renders *ἀπέξ* ab extra (cf. Osc. *ehtrād*) comparing for the ceremonial detail 'longe ab templo,' Senec. *De Superst.* fr. 36 Haase; for *ap-* : Lat.

ab v. s.v. *op*, and contrast *af-* which must have a different origin

Apelluneis, Ἀπέλλωνος, Apollinis, O. 52 gen. sg. m., cf. [Α]ππελλουνηι dat. 1 (on the spelling v. p. 461); cf. Praen. *Apolo*

Aphinis, nomen, nom. sg. masc. O. 67

Apidis, nomen, nom. sg. masc. Pg. 210, cf. gens Apidia in Index III

aplenia, impleta uel utraque parte plena uel sim., adj. neut. pl. acc., U. 359 II *a* 23, *aplenies*, abl. (or dat.) ib.

apluda, 205 C. 8 q.v.

Apoli[naris], cognomen seruile, nom. sg. m., Praen.-L. 282

Apolo, Apollo, nom. sg. m., Etr.-Praen. 298, *Apolon[i]*, dat. Praen.-L. 284

appei = *ad-que ἔς τε, i.e. quod ad tempus, quandoque, cum, U. 367 VII *b* 3, more commonly written *ape*, 357 I *b* 34, 358 II *a* 9, 360 II *b* 27, 28, 363 V *a* 17, 18, 20, 22, 365 VI *b* 5, 16, 23, 37, 366 VI *b* 49, 52 bis, 56, 62, 63 bis, 64, VII *a* 5, 8, 39, 42, 43, sometimes *api*, 356 I *a* 27, 30, 33, or *ap*, 361 III 20, IV 31; on *-pei* : *-pe* : *-pi* v. Synt. § 46 footn.

[**Α**]**ππελλουνηι**, v. *Apellun-*

aprehtu, v. *ambrē-*

apruf, v. *abro-*

Aprufclano, Mars. 267, adj. derived from a place not otherwise known (**Aproficulum*?)

Apunies, nomen, nom. sg. masc., Pg. 232; cf. *gens Aponia* in Index III

apur, apud, prep. with acc., Mars. 267; cf. p. 273 Rem. 3

Aquino(m), Lat. pp. 144 and 268

ar = Lat. *ad*, see p. 273 Rem. 3

ara, ara, Praen. 286, nom. sg. fem. *aram*, acc. Mars.-L. 265; cf. *asa-*

Arafiis, nomen, nom. sg. masc., O. 133

aragetud, argento, O. 93, 94, abl. sg.; the first syllable shows the Osc. anaptyxis

ἄρακος, 37 E q.v.

arbilla, O. 37 A 3 q.v.

ἀρβίννη, O. 37 A 3 q.v.

Arkiia, Ἀρχίας (but in what case?), O. 80 bis (Addenda)

Arcio (si sic legendum, non *larcio*), Fal. nomen, 329

Arxvanies, nomen, nom. sg. masc., Etr. Camp. xi. p. 97

Ἀρέντα, Venus, 37 C q.v.

arentika[i], adj. dat. sg. fem., O. 130 *b* 1, epithet of *keri* Cereri in the curse of Vibia, generally rendered ultrici, on the strength of Ἀράντισιν Ἐρινύσι, Μακεδόνες Hesych.; spelt *are-*

tik[ai], ib. *a 12, ar[entikai]*, ib. *a 1, arent[ikai]*, ib. *3*
arfertur, v. *adfertur*
Arghillus, cognom., nom. sg. m., Pg.-Lnt., n. xxvi. p. 249
ἄρμος, 37 E q.v.
Ario, Arion, nom. sg. m., Etr.-Praen. 293
arnipo, donec, with fut. perf. ind, U. 365 VI *b 41*, ib. *25*, where the substantive verb is omitted with the past partic.; from *ar* (see p. 273, Rem. 3) or miswritten for *ars-* (*ad-*)=Lat. *ad*, +-*ne-*, a pronominal particle attaching itself to pronouns and to words denoting locality or direction (e.g. in Lat. *pōne* for *post-ne*, Umb. *perne*, *postne*, Lat. *dō-ne-q(ue)*, *dō-ni-cum*, of which the first syllable is a prepn.= Eng. *to*, Germ. *zu*, Gr. -δῶ (: -δε), etc.) +*pō*, probably the indeclinable relative of Umb. *puḍe*, etc. v. p. 479. The Osc. *ne pon*, 28. *14* 'donec' appears to be precisely parallel to the second part of this word, though as the *ne* is written as an independent word, and as a negative precedes, the common rendering 'nisi quom' might conceivably be right, but the U. *nersa* q.v. strongly favours the connexion with *arnipo*
Aronto, nom. sg., Etr.-Fal. 345
arpatitu, probably 3 sg. impv. act. (conceivably a past parte.) Vol. 252; on *ar-*=*ad* v. p. 273 Rem. 3; the whole word prescribes some particular in the performance of a sacrifice (probably expiatory)
ars-, v. *ad-*, except for *arsie*, *arsier* and *arsir*
arsie, U. adj. in voc. sg. as appellative of Iupiter Grabovius, Fisovius Sancius, and Tefer Iupiter, 365 VI *a 24, b 8, 27*; gen. sg. (or abl. pl.) neut., *arsier*, 365 VI *a 24, b 27*, spelt *asier*, ib. VI *b 8*, only in the phrase *arsier frite(tiom subocau)*, v. s.v. *frite*
arsir, nom. sg. m., U. 365 VI *a 6, 7*; Büch.'s interpretation *alius* gives excellent sense, but it is not yet clear whether U. -*d*- has any phonetic relation to Lat. -*l*-, or, if so, under what conditions; hence even the value of the RS in this word remains doubtful
arślataf, libas alicuius generis, adj. used for subst. acc. pl. fem., U. 361 IV *22*. Büch. compares L. *arculus*, 'circulus capiti impositus ad sustinenda uasa quae ad sacra publica capite portabantur,' Paul. ex F. 16 M. (confirmed by Serv. ad *Aen.* 4. 137),

and *arculata* 'circuli ex farina in sacrificiis facti' id. ib.; the history of the -*ś*- has not yet been certainly explained, but it must be parallel to that in U. *kurślasiu*
Artemo, name of a cook, nom. sg. m., Praen. 282; no doubt from Gr. ἀρτάμος
aruorsu? aduersum, Osc.-L. n. iv. p. 31, v. p. 273 Rem. 3
Arutil..., nomen mutilum, Etr.-Fal. 316
aruvia, v. *arvio-*
arvā-, rus, ager, aruom uel sim., subst. fem. parallel to L. *aruo-*, acc. sg., *arvam*(-*en*), U. 361 III *11*, in aruom, loc. *arve*(-*n*), in aruo, ib. 13, both with postp. -*en*; of course from *ar-* 'arare,' with -*uo-* in its passive meaning; cf. Lat. *pascuos, diuiduos*, etc.
arveitu, v. *adv-*
arvia, arui fruges, subst. neut. pl. acc., U. 356 I *a 3, 9, 26, b 3, 6*, 359 II *a 18, 24*, spelt *aruvia*, 361 III *31*; in later Umb. *arviu*, 356 I *a 12, 16, 23*, 357 I *b 25, 28, 32, 43*, 358 II *a 6, 11, 12*, 360 II *b 8, 29*, once spelt *adviu*, 357 I *b 43*; in Lat. *aβ aruio*, 365 VI *a 56, 58, b 1, 3, 20, 22, 44, 45*, 366 VII *a 4, 7, 42*; abl. pl. *arvies*, 356 I *a 11*, but more commonly *arves*, 356 I *a 6, 13, 19, 23, b 4, 26, 30, 33, 44*, 358 II *a 7*, spelt *arvis*, 356 I *a 27, b 7*; from *arvo-, arvā-*; on final *-a* and *-u* see p. 403 ff.
As, abbrev. praenomen, gen. sg. (Synt. § 10), Mruc. 244
āsā-=Lat. *ara*, subst. fem. O. *aasaí*, loc. sg. 175 *a 16, b 18*, nom. pl. *aasas*, ib. *b 1*, U. dat. sg. *ase*, 359 II *a 19*, 361 III *22*, acc. *asam*(-*ad*), ad aram, 361 IV 6=*asama*, 359 II *a 39*, 361 IV *6, asam*(-*e*), in aram, 365 VI *a 10*, abl. *asa*, 361 III 23, IV *16*, 365 VI *a 9, easa*, ex asa, 359 II *a 38, asa*(-*ku*), apud aram 359 II *a 39, 43*
aseri-, v. *anzeri-*
aserum, infin., in the phrase *manim a. manum asserere*, to lay claim to, with gen., O. 28 *24*; the prepn. is more probably *ad-* than *an-*
aseśeta, insecta, adj., only as epithet of *karne, karnus*, abl. sg. fem., U. 359 II *a 29*; abl. pl. fem. *aseśetes*, 361 IV 7; from *an-* 'not,' and *seśeto-*=Lat. sectus, with slightly varying conjugation, cf. *prusek-*
aśetus, v. *ag-*
asiane, U. 356 I *a 25*
asif, Vo. 252; Bücheler, *arens*, Brealio, 'ones' (acc. pl. cf. *asignas*), mihi prorsus obscurum

GLOSSARY TO THE DIALECTS. 603

asignas, uictimae uel sim., subst. nom. pl. fem. Mruc. 243; Bücheler infers from the gloss *asignae κρέα μεριζόμενα* (Goetz, *C. Gl. Lat.* II., p. 24) that the word means 'natae ad aram,' but compare rather *adasia*, 205 c 2 'ouis uetula recentis partus,' which might mean 'an ewe with a lamb following' (cf. *aduerbium, adulterium*) if an Italic stem *asi-*, 'lamb' be assumed. Bréal (*Mém. Soc. Ling.* VI. 84, 137) would derive from *an-*, 'in' and *sec-are* (comparing L. *dignus* commonly explained as = *dec-nos*), supposing the meaning to be *prosiciae*; this on many grounds seems to me less probable

Asilli, i.e. *-llis*, nomen, nom. sg. masc., O. 77, B; cf. *gens Asillia*, 161 (Hirp.) B

asisua ?, 205 C. 2 q.v., and the Addenda

asnata, sicca, non umecta uel sim. (cf. *snata*), adj. neut. pl. acc., only as epithet to *veskla*, U. 359 II *a 19*, = *asnatu*, ib. 34, abl. *asnates*, ib. 37, 361 IV 9; for *an-snat-*

asom, Praen.-L. n. xxxiii. p. 321 f. = *aso*, U. 366 VI *b 50* = *asum*, Mruc. 243 *8*, in each place with some part of the verb *fero* which in the last example has an unmistakeable object (*iafc *cas-ce), and in the Umb. sentence an object is naturally supplied; hence the phrase at least in Umb. and Mruc. must be parallel to Lat. *uenum do, pessum ire*, etc. Büch. describes *asum* simply as a 'supine' in form = Lat. *assum*, but this is only used as a noun and cannot have the *ā* of *āreo, āra* (Osc. *ūsa-*) as that would have reduced *-ss-* to *-s-* in Classical Latin. Hence *asso-*, whether it be Italic or only Latin, either comes from a distinct root, or has been changed from **asto-* by some analogy not yet pointed out

asta, O. 205, D. q.v.

ἀστάνδης, 37 D. q.v.

asted, ast, quidem, Old L. n. xxxv., p. 330; cf. with Jordan Lat. *antid-, postid-*.

astintu, v. *anstintu*

a[st]utieis, astutiis, abl. pl. fem., Fal.-L. 335 *b*

asum, v. *asom*

At, abbrev. praenomen, Fal.-L. 348

atahus (for *-ust*), 3 sg. fut. perf. ind. act. from some verb denoting an act of sacrilege, Vo. 252; if it be connected with *tango* the same relation of *-ng-*: *-h-* appears in Lat. *fingo*: Osc. *feiho-*, etc. Cf. Mruc. *ta[h]a*

ἀταισόν, 37 E. q.v.

atedafust, v. *andersa-*

Ateleta, i.e. *-enta*, 'Ἀταλάντη, Etr.-Praen. 300; for *-ent-* here = *-αντ-* cf. *Alixentro-, Casentera*

atentu, v. *andendu*

atero, malum uel mala alicuius generis, acc. U. 366 VI *a 11, 27*

aticus, adj. nom. pl. masc. Pg. 219, an epithet of *me(d)dix* magistratūs, denoting some special dignity (*an-ti-co-*, 'foremost, chief'?) or function; the same suffix in O. *mūltas-íko-, toutico-*, etc.

Atiiediate, ethnicon, dat. pl. masc., U. 360 II *b 22* bis), one of the tribes or families summoned to the *sehmenier dequrier*

Atiedius, nomen, nom. sg. m. Mars.-L. 264; cf. the foll.

Atiersio-, v. *Atiiedio-*

Atiiedio-, U. adj., title of the sacred brotherhood (like the Fratres Aruales at Rome) which performed the rites of the Iguvine Tables, and by whom the Tables were written: nom. sg. masc. *Atiersir*, 367 VII *b* 3, nom. pl. *Atiiediur*, U. 362 V *a 1*, 363 V *a 14* = *Atiersiur*, 364 V *b 11, 16*, gen. pl. *Atiiediu*, 359 II *a 21, 35*, 360 II *b 26*, 362 V *a 12*, 363 V *a 25, 27*, *b 4* = *Atiersio*, 367 VII *b 2*; dat. abl. pl. *Atiiedies*, 361 III *24* = *Atiiedic*, 358 II *a 1*, 361 III *29*, later *Atiiedier*, 362 V *a 4*, 363 V *a 16* = *Atiersier*, 367 VII *b 1*, spelt *Atiersir*, 364 V *b 8, 14*

Atila, nomen, nom. sg. f. Umb.-L. n. xlii (1), p. 433

Atiniis, nomen, nom. sg. m., O. 43; cf. *gens Atinia* in Index III.

ato[l]er[o] (si uera lectio), attulerunt, dedicauerunt, 3 pl. perf. ind., Mars. 267 q.v.

atos, probably a name, whether entire or abbreviated, or, quite possibly, miswritten, Etr.-Praen. 297

atrepudatu, *atripursatu*, v. *ahtrepudatu*

atriensis, ad atrium pertinentes, adj. nom. pl. m., Praen.-L. 282 q.v.

Atrno, i.e. Aterno flumini, dat. sg. m., Vest. 248, ubi v. n.

atropu[r]satu, v. *ahtrepudatu*

atru, v. *adro-*

atta, 205 B. 4 q.v.

Au, p. 375 n. xl. β. 20

Aucena, Etr.-Praen. 300

Aukil, cognomen, nom. sg. masc. (possibly abbreviated), O. 87

Avdiis, nomen, nom. sg. m., O. 48, spelt Αϝδειες, O. 14
avef=L. *aues*, acc. pl. fem., U. 357 I *b* *10*=*aueif*, 365 VI *a*, *4*, *18*=*aviſ*, 356 I *b 8*,=*auiſ*, 366 VI *b 47*, *48* bis, spelt *auuei*, ib. VI *a 3*; abl. pl. *aves*, 356 I *a 1*=*avis*, 359 II *a 16*, *aueis*, 365 VI *a 1*
aveitu, v. *adv*·
Avfi (si uera lectio), nomen, abbreviated, O. 38
Avhvσκλι, abbrev. ethnicon of Ausculum, O. 29, αυhυσκλ, αυhυ, αυσκλιν, also αυσκλα, αυσκ... ib.
auiatas, auspicatae, p. ptc. pass. nom. pl. fem., Mruc. 243 *4*; cf. U. *auie*, *auiekate*, etc.
auie in auspiciis, subst. loc. sg. or pl. (p. 473), U. 365 VI *b 11*; an ē-stem, cf. the foll. derivatives; of course from *aui*- 'bird'
aviekate, adj. or ptc., (or subst.?), dat. (or loc.?) sg. U. 358 II *a 1*, *3*; from *auie*-
avieklo-, U. adj. auguralis, abl. sg. fem. -*kla*, 357 I *b 14*, -*cla*, 366 VI *b 52*, acc. pl. m. *aviekluſ*(-*e*), 357 I *b 14*, -*ehclu*, 365 VI *a 10*, -*eclu*, 366 VI *b 51*, abl. pl. *auiecleir*, 365 VI *a 9*, -*clir*, ib. *12*, *13*
auiſ, *avis*, v. *aveſ*
auirseto, i.e. **an-uideto*-, non uiso-, adj., U. 365 VI *a 28*, *38*, *48*, only in the phrase *uirseto auirseto uas est*, where it may be either gen. pl., or more probably nom. sg. fem. agreeing with *uas*
aunom, subst. acc. or nom. sg., the obj. of some verb of dedication to be supplied, or subj. if the verb be supposed passive, Vest. 248, q.v.
Αυσκλ..., v. Αυhυσκλ...
auso-, sol, Sab. 309 A, q.v.
aut, *avt*, sed, praeterea, O. 28 *20*, 95 *a 23*, *b 22*, *26*, *32*, 113, 130 *a*, *5*, *6*, *12*, [*a*]*vt*, 169; cf. Osc. *auti*, L. *aut*, *autem*, U. *ote*
auti=L. *aut*, O. 28 *6*, *11*, *13*, *24*=U. *ote* q.v.
auuei, v. *aveſ*
az, ad, apud, prep. with acc., O. 175 *a 20*; *az*, i.e. *at-s*, cf. Lat. *ab-s*, *sub-s*, Gk. ἐν-s, ἐκ-s, Osc. *ekss* ita beside *ek-kum* item; with *at*-: Lat. *at- ad*, cf. Osc. *op*: Lat. *ob*, etc. and v. U. *ad*
azeria-, v. *anzeria*-

b

b ɡ, second letter of the Osc. αβ, 81
Babiis, nomen, nom. sg. m., O. 156; cf. *gens Babbia*, Index III.
Babr, abbrev. nomen, gen. sg. m., U. 355; cf. *gens Babria* in Index III.
babu, nom. sg. m., Mruc. 243, *9*
baiteis, commonly interpreted 'uenis, aduenis,' O. 164
bananica, U. 370 D. q.v.
βαννάται, 37 D. q.v.
Bansae, Bantiae, loc. sg. fem., O. 28, *19*, *23*, *27* (33 A in the Lat. form); for -*ntia*- by the regular S. Osc. assibilation, as *zicolo*- for **diēcolo*-; cf. the foll.
Bantins, Bantinus, of Bantia, ethnic adj. nom. sg. m., O. 28 *19*
βάστα, 37 D. q.v.
βατάνια, O. 37 A, q.v.
bato, probably a proper name, n. xxv. *d*, p. 249
ben-=Lat. *uen-ire* in O. *kům-bened*, conuēnit, placuit, 3 sg. perf. ind. act., U. fut. perf. act. *benus*, ueneris, probably 2 sg. 360 II *b 16*, 3 sg. *benust* 366 VI *b* 53, 3 pl. *benurent*, 363 V *a 25*, *28*, *b 5*, 366 VI *b 57*, impers. pass. *benuso* (v. p. 492), uentum erit 366 VI *b 64*, *65*, VII *a 2*; Osc.-Umb. *b*- when parallel to Lat. *u*- represents I.-Eu. ɡ, the root being *gem*-
[**be**]**ne**, bene, adv., Fal.-L. 335 *b*
Benuentod (ex) Beneuento, abl. sg. n., O. 159 ubi v. note, and cf. *Beneuentum* 160 A
benust, *benuso*, *benurent*, v. *ben*-
Beriis, nomen, nom. sg. m., Osc.-Etr. 97; cf. *gens Beriena*, Index III.
beru-, subst. neut.=Lat. *ueru*, abl. pl. *berus*, U. 359 II *a 23*, *35*, acc. pl. *berva*, 359 II *a 26*, 33
Betitis, nomen, nom. sg. m., O. 163; cf. *gens Betitia*, Index III.
bia-, subst. fem., cisterna uel sim., nom. sg. *bio*, U. 354, acc. sg. *biam*, Pg. 219
bim, subst. acc. sg., Vo. 252
Bivellis, nomen, nom. sg. m., O. 131; cf. *gens Biuellia*, Index III.
bivus=Lat. *uiui*, adj. nom. pl. m., O. 130 *a 9*; Skt. *jiva*-, I. Eu. ɡi-ɥo-
Blaio?, Mruc. n. xxvii. p. 255; si uera lectio, cf. *gens Blaia*, Index III.
Blaisiis, nomen, nom. sg. m., O. 137 *f 8*; cf. *gens Blaesia*, Index III.
βλένα, **βλεννόν**, **blennos**, O. 37 B. 1 q.v.

Blŭssii, abbrev. of some case, probably gen. (cf. 106) of masc. nomen, O. 109; cf. the note there and *gens Blossia* in Index III.

Bn, abbrev. praenomen, O. 163

Bone, bouae, dat. sg. fem., Umb.-Lat. 370 A

bou- = Lat. *bos*, Umb.-Lat. *bouid* abl. sg. n. xli. p. 397; U. acc. sg. masc. *bum*, 358 II *a 5*, abl. sg. *bue*, 366 VI *a 25, 28, 33, 35, 38, 43, 45, 48, 53*, gen. pl. *buo*, 366 VI *a 54*, acc. pl. *buf*, 356 I *a 3, 11, 20*, 365 VI *a 22*, *b 1, 19*

βούβελα, O. 37 A. 3 γ. q.v.

Bra, abbrev. nomen, O. 77 A; cf. perhaps *brato-*, and *gens Gratia*, Index III.

brais, possibly a mistake for *brats, subst. nom. pl. fem., subject to *datas*, datae, Pg. 209; v. *brat-* inf.

βρασ[σί]κη, 37 D. q.v.

brat-, subst. in the phrase *brat data*, Vest. 247; possibly abbrev. abl. sg. fem. 'beneficio dato,' at the end of a dedication equivalent to Lat. 'merito libens'; cf. *brato-*

brato-, adj. or partc., I believe = Lat. *grāto-*, Skt. *gūrta-*; nom. sg. fem. *Brata* as praenomen, Pg. 206 bis (Addenda); nom. or acc. *bratom*, Pg. 209; neut. βρατωμ, O. 22; neut. used as subst. gen. sg. *brateis (amnud)* gratiae (caussa), O. 28 *6*; both this and *bratom* might be referred to *brat-*gratia, but εσοτ βρατωμ in 22 is clearly neuter. Objections have been raised to the identification with Lat. *grato-* but the resemblance in meaning seems to me far to close to allow of their separation. *brata* in 206 bis is precisely parallel to *saluta* in 206; in both cases the Paelig. adj. in *-to-* is parallel to a Lat. noun in *-t-* or *-ti-*

Βρέττιοι, O. 11 A, 25 A, q.v.

bue, *buf*, *bum*, *buo*, v. *bou-*

bufus, 205 B. 1 Rem. q.v.

burro-, n. xxiv. p. 228 q.v.; cf. βύρρος, 37 E

Burtio, nomen, nom. sg. m., Mars.-L. 268

βυτίνη, O. 37 A. q.v.

buttutti, Hern. 277 B. q.v.

butubatta, 205 B. 4 q.v.

Bŭvaianŭd, abl. (ex, i.e. in) Bouiano, O. 171 see p. 183 and Synt. § 21

c (including *k*)

c C, third letter in Lat. αβ, v. Table of Alphh.

c C, abbreviation in Lat. αβ for praenom. Gaius or its equivalent, Osc.-L. 20, 77 A (10); Pg. 215, 218, 235, 237, 239; Vols.-L. p. 269, n. xxx.; Acq.-L. 273; Fal.-L. 333 *a*, 335 *a*, 336, 347; U. 354, 355. In Fal. αβ, 323

⨯ i.e. *k*, the tenth sign of the Osc. αβ, 81 *b*; cf. 59 bis

K, abbrev. praenom. in Lat. αβ; Praen.-L. 285; Fal.-L. 335 *a*, 346. In Umb. αβ, 363 V *a 15*. Possibly = L. *Kaeso*, Mars. *Caso*, q.v.

Ca, abbrev. praenom., in Lat. αβ, Vo. 252, 253; Umb.-L. 353 *b*; in Fal. αβ, 328 *a*

Ka, abbrev. praenom. masc., O. 93.

Kaal, abbrev. praenomen, O. 190

καβάλλης, 37 C. q.v.

cabriner, caprini, adj. used as subst. gen. sg., U. 364 V *b 12, 17*; cf. *kabro-*

kabro-, caper, subst. masc., acc. sg. *kabru*, U. 360 II *b 17*, spelt *kaprum*, ib. 1, *kapru* ib. 10; gen. sg. *kapres*, ib. 12; for U. *-br-*: L. *-pr-*, cf. *adro-* etc.

cadeis, subst. gen. sg., O. 28 *6*, denoting the opposite of *brateis*, v. *brato-*

kadum (si uera lectio), O. 130 *a 2*; according to Bugge an inf. 'cadere'

kadetu, impv. 2 or 3 p. sg., clamato uel sim.; cf. p. 509 footn., U. 357 I *b 33*, spelt *-itu*, 361 III *21*, and *carsitu*, 365 VI *a 17*, 366 VII *a 43*

kaditu, v. *kadetu*

kahad, capiat, suscipiat, with acc., 3 s. pres. subj. act., O. 130 *a 6* bis, *8*; cf. L. *in-coh-ā-re*, which no doubt owes its *o-*grade of the root and *ā-*flexion to its composition, like *occupare*, *incubare*, etc.

καhας, O. 22 *4*

kaias, O. 193

Caiatino, n. xvi. p. 143 f. q.v.

Cail, nomen aliquod mutilum, Fal.-Etr. xl *a 4* p. 374

ka[i]la, delubrum uel sim., subst. fem. acc. sg., O. 39

cailauit, caclauit, L. or Praen.-L. 291

Caio, i.e. *Gaio(s)*, Fal.-L. 339; cf. the abbrev. C

Caisidis, nomen, nom. sg. m., O.-L. 21; cf. *gens Caesidia* in Index III.

Caisies, nomen, nom. sg. masc., Osc.-Etr. n. xi. P. 98

Kaisillieís, nomen, gen. sg. m., O. 108 a, b; cf. *gens Caesillia* and *Caesellia* in Index III.
kaispatar, 3 sg. pres. subj. or impv. pass., see p. 494, O. 130 a 5
Kalati, i.e. -*tium* or -*tinum*, gen. pl. of ethnicon of Calatia, O. 147 bis, *Kalat*, *Kala*, ibid.
Calauan, abbrev. cognomen, nom. sg. m., Pg. 236
Kalaviís, nomen, nom. sg. m., O. 167; cf. *gens Caluia* and *Calauia* in Index III.
kaleḑuf, frontem albam habentes, adj. acc. pl. m., U. 356 I a 20, spelt *calersu*, 365 VI b 19; in form exactly = Lat. *calido*- (or *callido*-) to which Isid. *Orig.* XII. 1. 52 assigns this meaning
Caleno, n. xvi. p. 143 f. q.v.
calersu, v. *kaleḑuf*
Καλινις, nomen, nom. sg. m., O. 1 *Calin*, Fal.-Etr. xl β 26 p. 375; cf. *Cales*, *Caleno*- and *gens Calinia*, *Calenia* in Index III.; for formation cf. *gens Campania*, etc.
Calitenes, probably gen., Fal.-Etr. 345
callita-, 241 C. q.v.; if it is a common noun it was probably nom. pl. m. 'foot-passengers,' cf. *nau-ita*
Kaluvis, nomen, nom. sg. m., O. 139, gen. *Kalůvieís*, 115, 116
camoro-, *camur*, O. 205 A. q.v,
Kamp..., nomen mutilum, nom. sg. m., O. 52; possibly from a stem *Kampanio-*, cf. *gens Campania*, Index III.
Καμπανομ, Campanum, probably acc. sg. m. (v. p. 144), originally ethnicon of Capua, but applied to the Oscan population of the Campanian plain, O. 146 q.v., καμπανο, καππανο, ib.; the double -ππ- probably represents -*pu̯*- and -*m*- may be unwritten before it, cf. p. 99 footn. 3
κάναδοι, 37 B. q.v.
kanetu, canito uel sim. impv. 3 sg., U. 361 IV 29; but the stem can hardly be the same as in L. *cano*, v. p. 495
cannela, Osc.-L. n. xxiii. p. 226 q.v.
Canopus, Gr. Κάνωβος, p. 230 q.v.
Cantovios, nomen, nom. sg. m., Mars. 267
Kanuties, nomen sg., probably gen. m., Osc.-Etr. n. xi. p. 98
kapiḑ- = L. *capis*, U. subst. fem.; acc. sg. *capirso* i.e. -*om*, 366 VI b 25; dat. sg. *kapiḑe*, 356 I a 29, 32, 358 II a 8, 359 II a 34, 41 = *capirne*, 366 VI b 24, 37; acc. pl. *capif*, 366 VI b 18, VII a 39, 45, spelt, perhaps only by error (ϙ for 8) *kapiḑ*, 356 I a 17, also *kapi*, 357 I b 29, 37; abl. or loc. pl. *kapiḑus*, 359 II a 33, 361 IV 5

καπιδιτωμ, acc. sg. m. or neut., O. 22; deriv. of *capid*- (cf. sup.), no doubt with reference to some sepulchral usage
Kapva, abbrev. Oscan ethnicon from Capua, O. 119, *kapv*, O. 148, 117 b 4; on the date of the form see pp. 99 and 108, and cf. *Capua*, p. 152 (with the Errata)
κάραννος-, **-κάρανο-**, O. 37 B. 2 q.v.
karanter, acdificium, monumentum alicuius generis, subst. acc. sg. with postp. -*e(n)*, U. 365 VI a 13, 14
kartu, partitor, distribuito, 2 or 3 sg. impv. act., U. 359 II a 23; cf. *karanter*, sup.
casco-, uctus Sab. 309 A. q.v.
Kaselate, v. *Casilos*
Casenter, name of woman, probably abbrev. and = Κασσάνδρα as *Alixentro*- = 'Αλέξανδρος, Etr.-Praen. 300 q.v. with p. 229
Casia, woman's name, Etr.-Praen. 297 q.v.
casilam, Sab. 309 B. q.v.
Casiler, local adj. gen. sg. m., U. 364 V b 14
Casilos, ethnicon from preceding, nom. sg., U. 364 V b 13; dat. sg. *Casilate*, ib. 16; dat. pl. *Kaselate*, 360 II b 6, ter
kasit, decet, oportet, with pres. subjunc., 3 sg. pres. ind. act., O. 117 a 7, b 5; identical, I believe, with Lat. *car-ē-t*, for the connection of meaning (want: duty), cf. Gr. χρή, etc.
casnar, subst. nom. sg. m. senex, Pg.

218, O. 205 A, q.v., and cf. Lat. *cascus* and, no doubt, *cānus* for *casno*-
Caso, proper name, nom. sg. masc. Mars. 267; probably identical with L. *Kaeso*, cf. Mars. *actia*=L. *Angitiae*
Casontonio for -*niōm*, gen. pl. masc., Mars. 267, *en urbid C.* in urbe Casuntoniorum, a community not otherwise known
Castor, Κάστωρ, Etr.-Praen. 287, 303
Kastrikiieís, nomen, gen. sg. m., O. 63; cf. *gens Castricia, Castrucia*, Index III.
castrid, *castrous*, v. *kastru*-
kastru-, *fundus uel sim.*, subst. m., gen. sg. *castrous*, O. 28 *13*, abl. *castrid* ib. 8; acc. pl. *kastruvuf*, U. 362 V *a 13*, 363 V *a 18*, spelt *kastruvu*, ib. *20, 22* and *castruo*, 365 VI *a 30, 32, 40, 42, 50, 52*, VI *b 13, 32, 34*, 366 VII *a 17, 30*; cf. L. *castro*- whose meaning has slightly diverged
Kastrušiie, nomen, gen. sg. m., U. 362 V *a 3*; cf. *gens Castricia, Castrucia* in Index III. and O. *Kastrîkiío*-
Catamitus, 205 Rem. 9, p. 229 f. q.v.
katel, v. *katlo*-
kateramu, 2 pl. impv. depon. or pass., in cateruas colligimini uel sim., U. 357 I *b 20*, spelt *caterahamo*, 366 VI *b 56*; no doubt L. *cater-ua* is a deriv. from the same stem
katlo- = Lat. *catulus*, subst. m. nom. sg. *katel*, U. 359 II *a 43*, acc. *katlu*, ib. *18, 20, 29*, gen. *katles*, ib. *22, 27*, spelt *katle*, ib. *15*
cato-, acutus, Sab. 309 A, q.v.
Caucilio, si sana lectio, nomen, nom. sg. m., Etr.-Fal. n. xl. 21, p. 375
Cauio-, i.e. *Gauio*-, a common Fal. praen.; masc. nom. sg. *Cauio* 343, xl. *20*, p. 375, *Caui* 313, xl. *17, 21*, p. 375, fem. *Cauia* 314, 318 *a*, 325 *a, b*, 344, dat. (or gen.?) *Cauiai* 334; cf. Osc. *Gaavio*- L. *Gaio*-
Kavkvis, nomen, nom. sg. m., O. 137 *d 10*
kazi, subst. acc. sing., U. 361 III *16, 18*
Ce, abbrev. praenomen, perhaps=L. *Ceius*, Fal. 316, 323, 326 *b*, U. 353 *b*
cebnust, uenerit, aduenerit, 3 sg. fut. perf. ind., O. 28 *20*; -*bnust* is clearly parallel to U. *benust* q.v., and *ce*- is commonly identified with L. *ce*- in *cědo* 'da,' with which cf. L. -*ce* in *hi-ce* etc., and Gr. ἐ-κε-ῖ, κεῖ-νος
kebu, subst. abl. sg., U. 361 IV *23*; cf. p. 403 f.

cedito = caedito, impv. 3 sg. act., Umbr.- L. n. xlii. p. 397, *cedre*=caedere, ib., showing the Osc.-Umb. syncope; cf. *dedrot* from Pisaurum n. xliii. 4, p. 434
keenzstur (i.e. *kēnts-tur*), censor or censores, nom. sg. or pl. m., O. 169, spelt *censtur*, O. 28 *18* and *20* (pl.), *27* and *28* (sg.). But *kenzsur* (nom. pl.) 190 shows the same absence of the -*t*- in the suffix as L. *censor*; cf. *censaum* inf.; the root syllable shows the regular Osc.-U. -*t*- between -*n*- and -*s*-
cehefi, U. 365 VI *a 20*; cf. p. 515 footn.
Ceilio, nomen, nom. sg. m., Fal. 319 *a*, spelt *Celio* 320 and xl. 1, p. 374 (*celioi*?); cf. *gens Caelia* in Index III.
ceip, abbrev. subst., probably acc. (or. nom.?), Mars. 267
Keis, proper name, apparently praenom., perhaps abbrev., Osc.-Etr. xi. 8, p. 97
Ceisies, nomen, sg. m. nom. (or gen.?) Fal.-Etr. 345, *Cesi* gen. Fal. 318 *a*, fem. nom. *Ceisia* 297; cf. Osc.-Etr. *Keis*, and *gens Caesia* in Index III.
cela, Fal.-Etr. n. xl. 18, p. 375
celio, *celioi*, v. *Ceilio*
kelledehad, if to be read as *kelled ehad*, must mean hac (re aliqua), but if *dehad* is a separate word, it is perhaps a verb, Etr.-O. 132
cenaculum, Tusc. 306 q.v., Fal. 349
censaum, censere, inf. act., O. 28 *20*, *censazet*, ib. *19*, fut. ind. act. 3 pl.; *censamur*, ib. impv. pass. 3 sg. (cf. p. 493); cf. *keenzstur* and *censtom*, which show the natural formation of the -*tor* and -*to*- verbal nouns. L. *census* subst. was, I believe, orig. the simple -*o*- noun from which the verbs L. *censē*-, O. *censā*- were derived; its resemblance to *sensus* etc. drew it into the *u*-stems, and thus drove the orig. verbal noun *censtu*- with the partc. *censto*- out of use in Latin. *censā*- : *censē*- as *densāre* : *densēre*
censo or -*sor*, Fal.-L. 332
Kenssurineís, Ceusorini, cognom. gen. sg. m., O. 109
censtom-en, in censum, O. 28 *20*, acc. neut. sg. of pass. ptc. of *cens*-, O. *censāum* q.v., used as a subst., with postp. -*en*
censtur, v. *keenzstur*
kenzsur, v. *keenzstur*
Cepio, proper name, Fal. 340; cf. *gens Caepia* in Index III., and L. *Caepio*
ceres, subst. fem. sg. panis? v. 309 D. and cf. *Cerie, Kerrî*- inf.; if the name of the goddess in Sabine had the -*iē*- suffix, it is intelligible that the

form with the -*es*- suffix (cf. Lat. *cererem* for *ceres-em) should take or keep a more concrete meaning
Cerfum, subst. gen. pl. m., name of deities with the appellative *semunu* (Semonum) added, Pg. 216 *4*; cf. Umb. ꟼerfo-
Keri, v. *Kerri*
Cerie, Cereri, dat. sing., Mruc. 248 *10*, v. pp. 473 and 514
Kerrí, Cereri, dat. sg. fem., O. 175 *a 3, b 7*, spelt *Keri*, 130 *a 1, 3, 12, b 1*; v. p. 473 footn., and cf. *Ceres* sup.
Kerriio-, ad Cererem pertinens, Osc. adj., m. sg. dat. -*ííńí* 175 *a 13, b 15*, loc. (with postp. -*en*) -*íiín* ib. *a 2*, pl. dat. -*íińís* ib. *a 9, 10*; fem. sg. dat. -*íiaí* ib. *a 4, 6, 22, 23, 24, b 10*, pl. dat. -*íiaís* ib. *a 7*. Spelt *Cerria* fem. nom. sg., Pg. 248 = *Ceria*, Pg. 206, abbrev. *Cerri*, Pg. 217, *Ceri* 206 bis (Addenda), and *Cerr*, Pg. 207; from *Kerri*- q.v., the Paelig. treatment of -*ri*- resembling the Osc. not the Umb. and Mruc. (*Cerie* q.v.)
kersnā- = Lat. *cēna* (Sab. *cesna*- 309 D.), subst. fem. abl. pl. *kerssnaís*, O. 118, perhaps nom. sg. *kersnu* 137 *d 5*; cf. U. ꟼersnā-, ꟼesnā-, the Osc. form being as usual the most primitive
kerssnasias, cum cena celebratae, adj. nom. pl. fem., O. 115, 117 *b 10*; from *kersnā*- q.v.
Cesi, v. *Ceisies*
Cesilia, nomen, sg. fem., Fal. 315; cf. *gens Caesilia*, Index III.
cesna, Sab. 309 A q.v., and cf. O. *kersnā*- etc.
Cesula, fem. praenomen, Fal. 329, Umb.- L. xliii. 1, p. 433
cetur, Vols. 253
ceus, ciuis, subst. nom. sg. m., O. 28 *19*; for *ceiuis (Old L. *ceiuis*) by regular syncope, on which cf. p. 470
Char, abbrev. cognomen, Pg. 237
cia, uox mutila aut corrupta, Pg. 209
Kiípiís, nomen, nom. sg. m., O. 68; cf. *gens Cipia*, Index III.
cipro-, bonus, Sab. 309 D. q.v. and *cubrar* inf.
Cisi, nomen aliquod mutilum, Fal.-Etr. xl. *a* 11, p. 375
cisterno, cisterna, subst. nom. sg. fem., U. 354; that the word is borrowed from Lat. appears from the retention of *c* before *i* (pure Umb. ꟼ)
citrus, from Gr. κέδρος?? 205, Rem. 9, p. 229

Klar..., cognomen (an nomen?) mutilum, O. 173 *a*
Klaverniio-, Clauernius, local adj., nom. pl. m. *Clauerniur*, U. 364 V *b 8*, dat. pl. *Klaverniie* (for -*iier*), 360 II *b 3* bis, and *Clauerni* (for -*nir*), 364 V *b 10*
klavlaf, subst. acc. pl. fem., U. 359 II *a 33*, abl. *klavles* ib. *36*, 361 IV *11*; in form = Lat. *clauolae* (i.e. a graft, scion), but interpreted by Büch. to mean 'clunes', comparing Germ. *Keule*
kletra-, subst. fem. abl. sg. *kletra*, U. 361 III *13*, IV *24*, loc. *kletre* III *14*, acc. *kletram* III *13*; Büch. plausibly compares L. *clitellae*, but renders 'lectica': it denotes some implement of the sacrifice by or with which the sheep is carried *aruamen*
Klí, nota praen. masc. Osc. 48, fortasse = Lat. *Clemens*
Clipiai, v. *Clipeario*, Fal.-L. 331
Clipeario, nomen, nom. sg. m., Fal. 332 *b*, 333 *a*, probably abbrev. or mutilated in *Clipiai* 331
Cloil, abbrev. nomen, n. xxx. p. 269; cf. *gens Cloelia*, Index III.
Kluv..., nomen uel praen. mutilum, O. 135 *c*, 137 *b 5*; cf. the foll.
Kluvatiio-, nomen of a Capuan gens, nom. sg. m. *Kluvatiis*, O. 130 *a 9*, acc. sg. -*tiium* ib. *10*; gen. pl. -*tiium* 105 *a, b*, and probably -*tium* 130 *a 2*, abbrev. 111 *a, b*, 108 *a, b*
Kluviier, nomen, gen. sg. m., U. 363 V *a 15*
Km, abbrev. praen., O. 156 bis, 176; cf. p. 530. Zvet. compares *Comius* a praen. ap. Fest. 326 M. (si integra lectio)
Cmecio, probably = *C. Mecio*, C. Maecius, Fal. 315
Cnaive, si sic legendum, praenomen or nomen, O.-Etr. xi. 9, p. 98; cf. the following
Cnaiviies, Gnaeuii, nomen, gen. sg. m., O.-Etr. 98
cnatois, i.e. *gnatois, gnatis, dat. pl. m., Pg. 209
coenalia, subst. or adj., Praen.-L. xxxiii. p. 322 q.v.
cofeci, confeci, Praen.-L. xxxiii. p. 322
coiraueront, curauerunt, Fal.-L. 335 *a*
coisatens, curauerunt, 3 pl. perf. ind. act., Pg. 239; *coisā*- = Old Lat. *coirā*-, L. *cūrā*-
com, cum, prep. with abl., O. 28 *15, 23*, spelt *con* ib. *16*, U. 366 VI *b 52, 55, 56, 57*. As a postp. in Umb. spelt -*kum*, -*ku*, -*com*, -*co*, it takes the same case

and denotes a looser connexion, like Lat. apud, ad, secundum : 356 I *a 29, 32*, I *b 1, 4*; 357 I *b 19*; 359 II *a 39, 43*; 361 III *28, 31*, IV *29*; 362 V *a 5, 11*; 365 VI *a 18*, VI *b 37, 39, 40, 43, 45*; 366 VI *b 50, 53, 55, 57*; in some of these passages, e.g. VI *b 50*, the meaning 'in company with' would be, perhaps, admissible, but as the pre- and postpositional uses are juxtaposed and clearly contrasted in VI *b 57*, it is safer at present to assume only the looser meaning for the postp. in all passages.

It is noteworthy that the word is preposed only in later Umb. and only in one phrase.

comatir, v. *comol-*

combifia-, nuntiare uel sim., the regular Umb. term to denote announcements made by one priest to another engaged in another part of the same ceremony, act. impv. 2 or 3 sg. *combifiatu*, 365 VI *a 17*; 366 VI *b 48, 51*, VII *a 43, 44,* = *kumpifiatu*, 357 I *b 14*, *kupifiatu* ib. *35*; fut. perf. ind. 3 sg. *combifiansiust*, 366 VI *b 49*; *-ansiust* ib. *52*; *-ansust* VII *a 5*; pres. subj. 3 sg. *kupifiaia*, 357 I *b 35*; perf. subj. 3 sg. *combifiansi*, 366 VI *b 52*; the root is probably that of Gr. πείθω, Lat. *fides*; U. *-mb-* may = Ital. *mp-*; cf. U. *ander* and List Phonet. Pecul.; on its construction cf. p. 509

comenei, v. *comno-*

comestores, Mars.-L. 269 A. q.v.; probably from *ed-* to eat, meaning *conuiuae*, *sodales*

commircium, 205 n. xxii. p. 225 q.v.

comno-, populi comitium, subst. neut., in Osc. with anaptyctic vowel varying with the vowel of the case suffix; loc. sg. *comenei*, 28 *5, 21*, acc. sg. *comonom* ib. *17*, acc. pl. *comono*, 28 *5, 7, 8* bis, *11, 14, 17* (on the meaning of *comono hipid*, v. p. 508 footn.); U. loc. sg. (after *super*), *kumne*, in foro, 357 I *b 41*

comohota, commota, uel sim., p. parte. pass. abl. sg. fem., U. 365 VI *a 54*; *-oho-* = *-ō-* v. p. 401 footn.

comol- i.e. *com-mol-*, commolere, tundere, pinsere, the regular term in Umb. for preparing the grain etc. for sacrifice, only appearing in impv. act. and p. parte. pass.: impv. act. 2 or 3 sg. *comoltu*, U. 365 VI *b 17, 41*; 366 VII *a 39, 44, 45* = *kumultu*, 356 I *a 34*; but there seems some variation of stem in the spelling *kumaltu*, 358 II *a 9*; 359 II *a 41*; 361 IV *28*,

(for which see s.v. the uncompounded *maletu*); p. parte. pass. abl. pl. *kumates*, 356 I *a 34*; 359 II *a 42*; 361 IV *29*; spelt *kumate*, 357 I *b 37, 38*; 358 II *a 10*; later *comatir*, 365 VI *b 17, 41* bis; 366 VII *a 39, 44, 45*; on the loss of *-l-* in the parte. v. p. 495 f.

comono, *comonom*, v. *comno-*

comparascuster, deliberata, decreta erit uel sim., 3 sg. fut. perf. indic. pass., O. 28 *4*; for *comprasc-* by regular anaptyxis; cf. Lat. *po(r)sco*, which, like this form and the corresponding Skt. *prach-*, retains the inceptive suffix in the perfect tenses

comuiuia, conuiuia, Fal.-L. 335 *b*

con, v. *com*

conegos, conixus, genu nixus, U. 365 VI *b 5, 16*; 366 VII *a 37*, = older *kunikaz*, 361 IV *15, 18, 20*; the parte. of an *-ā-* deriv. of the same root as Lat. (*g*)*nixus*

conea, ciconia, Praen. 305 A, q.v.

confice, Praen.-L. n. xxxiii. p. 322

contrud, prepn. with dat. (or loc.?), O. 28 *11, 17, 25, 32*

coques, coqui, nom. pl. m., Praen. 282

Corano, n. xvi. p. 143 f., q.v.

coraueron[t], curauerunt, Praen. 284; on *cōr-* for *coer-* cf. p. 287

Coredier, proper name, gen. sg. m., U. 365 VI *b 45* = older *Kureties*, 356 I *b 4*

Cosano, n. xvi. p. 143 f. q.v., also n. xix. p. 171

cosmis, comis, beneuola, nom. sg. fem., Old L. n. xxxv. p. 330

cossim, retro, in coxas, 205 B. 3 q.v.

Cosuties, Cos(s)utius, nomen, nom. sg. m., Vo. 252; cf. *gens Cossutia*, Index III.

Cotena, proper name, nom. sg. m., Fal. 321

cotonia mala, 205 Rem. 9. 3, p. 230 q.v.

Κοτταιηις, probably = *kattieis, nomen, gen. sg. m., O. 8, abbrev. κοττει 9, κοττι 10; cf. *gens Cottia*, Index III.

couehriu, *co-uirium*, curia, Vo. 252; *toticu couehriu*, publica curia; the Volsc. word is probably neuter, cf. *sepu*; if *-eh-* = *-ē-*, the stem differs from Lat. *utro-*; cf. rather Skt. *vira-*, Umb. *ueiro-*

couert-, conuertere, intrans., act. impv. 3 sg. *couertu*, conuertito se, U. 365 VI *b 47*; 366 VII *a 44, 45*; spelt *kuvertu*, 356 I *b 9*; 357 I *b 36, 38*; 359 II *a 39*; fut. perf. 2 sg. *kuvurtus*, 357 I *b 11*, 3 sg. *courtust*, 365 VI *a 6*, spelt *couortus*, 366 VII *a 39*; pass.

impers. *couortuso*, 366 VI *b 64*, v. p. 492
Kpι?=*kiipiís*, O. 157
cra, cras, Fal. 312 *a, b*
Craboule, *Krapnvi*, v. *Grabovio-cratia*, i.e. gratia, Praen. 281 q.v.
crefrat, O. 205 C. 1 q.v.
Creisita, Criscis, nom. sg. fem., Etr.-Praen. 302, spelt *Crisida* ib. 300; on -*t*-=Gr. -δ-, cf. 205 Rem. 9. 1, p. 229
krematra, ucrūs uncos, uel sim. subst. acc. pl. neut., U. 359 II *a 23*; clearly from the stem of Lat. *cremāre*, cf. the foll.
krematruf, subst. acc. pl. masc., U. 359 II *a 26*; spelt -*tru* ib. 28. Bücheler admirably distinguishes the meaning of this masc. form as 'ucruinas,' i.e. carnes ucru adfixas; the double meaning appearing both in L. *ueruina* and Gr. ὀβελίσκος
krenkatrum, insigne aliquod sacerdotis lustrum facientis, in umero portandum, subst. neut., U. 357 I *b 11*; spelt *krikatru*, 360 II *b 27, 29*, *cringatro*, 366 VI *b 49*; Büch. regards it as a garment, comparing Old Lat. *clingere* 'cingere' Paul. ex F. 56 M.
crepero-, Sab. 309 A. q.v.
crepusco-, Sab. 309 A. q.v.
krikatru, *cringatro*, v. *krenkatrum*
Crisida, v. *Creisita*
krustatar, 3 p. sg., pres. subj. (or impv.) pass., O. 130 *a 5*, perhaps *b 1*; cf. p. 494. The word denotes some penalty invoked by the curse
-**ku**, v. *com*
kvaisstur, quaestor (cf. p. 51), Osc. nom. sg. m. 42, 43, 49, 53, 52, dat. *kvaisturei*, 95 *a 2*; nom. pl. *kvaizturr* 48 (v. note); probably sg. [κƒ]αιστορ 16, κƒαιϛ 14. U. *kvestur*, nom. sg. m., 363 V *a 23, b 2*
cuando, quando, quandoque, Fal. 321, ubi v. not. and cf. p. 261
cubat, cubat, Fal.-L. 333 *b*; in Fal. αβ written *cupat*
Cubrar Matrer, Bonae Matris, "Ηρας (an Bonae Deae?), U. 354; the epithet is clearly identical with Sab. *cipro-bonus* 309 D, q.v., and cf. the Picentine (earlier perhaps Umbrian, p. 395) towns Cupra Maritima and Montana (p. 450); this Fulginian goddess is no doubt the same as *Dea Cupra* of Cupra Marit. (*C.I.L.* ιχ. 5294) whom Strabo 5. 4. 2 identifies with Hera; Umb. -*br*- beside L. -*pr*- is regular
kukehes, vb. 2 or 3 sg. ind. act. probably fut., U. 361 III *21*; cf. p. 515 footn., and on -*ke*- p. 403
Cudido, miswriting for *Cupido*, Etr.-Praen. 289
-**cue**, -que, et, Fal. 314
kvestretie, quaesturae, subst. fem. dat. or loc. sg., U. 357 I *b 45*; 359 II *a 44*, cf. p. 504, 502 footn.; from the stem of *kvestur* (q.v.) as *uhtretie*- from *uhtur*
kvestur=L. quaestor, U. 365 V *a 23*, V *b 2*. The *kv*- of this word=L. *qu* appears in Osc.-Lat. αβ as *q*-, and with -*kv*- in *ekvine* seems to show that I.-Eu. *k̑u* was distinct in sound and treatment in Osc.-Umb. from I.-Eu. *q*
kŭinik-, χοῖνιξ, Osc. 57, the name of a measure of capacity at Pompeii, superseded about 14 B.C., v. note, ad loc. and Append. I.; of course borrowed from the Greek
Kuiirinis (or *Kuir*-), Quirinius, nomen, nom. sg. m., O. 85
kulupu, O. 137 *e 3, f 4*
-**kum**, v. *com*
kumaltu, v. *comol*-
kumate, -*tes*, v. *comol*-
cumba, Sab. 309 A, q.v.
kŭmbened, conučnit, perf. ind. act. 3 sg. O. 95 *a 10*; cf. *ben*- sup.
kŭmbennieis, conuentus, gen. sg., probably neut., the name of a Pompeian assembly, O. 42, 43, 52; the L. equiv. would be *conuĕnium*, i.e. the -*nn*- is due simply to the following -*i*-, cf. *List Phonet. Pecul.*
kumiaf, v. *gomia*
kumnahkle, in comitio, in collegio uel sim., subst. loc. (or dat.) sg. neut., U. 361 III *7, 8*; 363 V *a 15*; from *comno*- q.v.
kumne, v. *comno*-
Cumnios, Comenius, nomen, nom. sg. m., Vol.-Lat. 253
[kŭ]mparakineis, subst. gen. sg., probably fem., the name of some Pompeian deliberative body other than the *kŭmbennio*-, O. 50; equiv. to a Lat. *comprecio* or *compracio*; cf. *comparascuster*, and for the declension *leginei*, etc.
kumpiṙ-, v. *combif*-
kumultu, v. *comol*-
cuncaptum, conceptum, Fal. 321, ubi v. not.
kunikaz, v. *conegos*
cupa, κώπη, handle, 205 B. 5 q.v.
cupa, Fal. v. *cupat*

cupat, cubat, used on sepulchral inscc., Fal. 325 *b*, 327, 328=*cupa* 324; pl. [*cupa*]*nt* 314

Kupelternum, -*nãm*, Compulterinum, O. 149 *a*, *b*; ethnicon from Compulteria (later Comb-, v. p. 153); the change from -*mnul*- to -*mbul*- is regular in Lat. and probably in Osc.; on the case v. n. xvi. p. 143 f.

cupenco-, Sab. 309 A, q.v.

kupif-, v. *combif-*

kura-, curare, impv. act. 3 sg. *kuratu*, U. 363 V *a 24, 26, 29*, pres. subj. 3 sg. *kuraia*, 362 V *a* 5

Kureiate, Curiatibus, dat. pl. m., name of a tribe or gens invited (?) to certain ceremonies, U. 360 II *b 3*, bis

Kureties, v. *Coredier*

Curia, nomen, fem. sg. nom., Umb.-Lat. n. xliii. 9, p. 434; cf. *gens Curia*, Index III.

curis, hasta, Sab. 309 A. q.v.

curnac-, cornix, subst. fem. acc. sg. *curnaco*, U. 365 VI *a 2, 4, 15, 17*, abl. *curnase*, i.e. -*ase* ib. *1*; on the relation of -*c*- to -*s*-, v. p. 405 f.

kurŝlasiu, U. 359 II *a 17*; v. p. 501 footn.

kŭru, O. 164

kutef, silens, uel sim., pres. partc. nom. sg., U. 356 I *a 6, 10, 13, 19, 23, b 7*, spelt, no doubt by error, *kutep*, 356 I *b 3*; the meaning is fixed by *taśez* (tacitus) which replaces it in the later Tables; possibly from *caudens* (=L. *cudens*; cf. p. 448 footn. 2) in the sense of 'beating time, making dumb show'

kuveitu, conuehito uel sim., impv. act. 2 or 3 sg., U, 359 II *a 32, 40*

kuvert-, *kuvurt-*, v. *couert-*

---

d

d Я, fourth letter of the Oscan *aβ*, 81 *a—d*, v. Table of Alphb.

d, abbrev. for *Dekis* q.v.

d=donum, Praen. 283

d nota incerta, Praen. 286

da[da]d, si uera lectio, dedat, 3 sg. pres. subj. act., 130 *a 3*, cf. the foll.

dadid, dediderit, perf. subj. act. of Osc. equivalent of L. *dare* (v. s.v. *dato-*) compounded with *dā*, 'de,' O. 130 *a 4*; if it be regarded as present indic. for *dadet* it is the only example (on *kahad* v. s.v.) of -*d* in a primary tense of the indic. in Osc., in Osc. *aβ*

da-dikatted, dedicauit, perf. ind. act. 3 sg., O. 174; from *dā*, 'de' and Italic *dīcā-*, 'dicare'

daetom, demptum, omissum uel sim., p. partc. pass. of some vb. compounded with *dā*-, 'de,' U. 365 VI *a 28, 37, 47*, 364 VI *b* 30; U. -*etom* may be equivalent to L. *emptum*, *itum*, or even other forms

daliuo-, O. 205 A, q.v.

δάμεια, *damium*, *damiatrix*, 37 D, q.v.

damia..., uox mutila, O. 130 *a* ?

δάμνος, 37 E, q.v.

damsennias, adj., or adj. used as subst., nom. or acc. pl. fem., O. 117 *b 6*; as the word occurs in connexion with the sacrificial hunt (v. s.v. *eehianasom*) it would be tempting to compare Gr. *δαμάω*, *δαμασ-θῆναι*, etc., and to see in *damuse...*, the -*os*- form of the noun stem on which the deriv. adj. is ultimately based; but until further evidence shows whether the -*un*- is gerundival or merely for -*n*- before -*i*-, further conjectures are unsafe

damuse..., uox mutila, O. 103 *a*, *b*; cf. the preceding

dat, de, prepn. with abl., O. 28 *6, 8, 9, 10*; its connection with Lat. *dē*, U. *dā*- is obvious, but the exact relations of the forms are not yet clear

dato-, datus, p. partc. pass. of the root 'to give'; Pg. *datas*, nom. pl. fem. 209, *data*, fem. sg. probly abl. 247. Fal. *datu*, nom. sg. neut. 321 (v. note ad. loc.), Fal.-L. *datus*, nom. sg. m. 336. Under this heading may be grouped the various forms of the finite verb: (A) Reduplicated present stem: Italic stem *dido-*, *did*- appearing in Osc.-Umbrian dialects only: (1) N. Osc. *dido-*: Pres. act. ind. 3 sg. Vest. *didet* 247, subj. Pg. 3 sg. *dida*, 216 7; (2) Osc. Fut. ind. act. 3 sg., *didest*, 28 *16* (on *da-did*, v. s.v.); (3) Umb. *diḍo-*, *diḍ-*: Pres. subj. act. 3 sg. *ḍirsa*, 364 V *b 13*, 366 VII *a 46*, spelt *dersa*, 366 VII *a 43, 44*=*teḍa*, 357 I *b* 34, 3 pl. *dirsans*, 364 V *b 11*, *16*=*dirsas*, ib. 8; Pres. ind. pass. 3 sg. *teḍte* for -*ter*, 362 V *a 7* (cf. p. 519). Impv. act. 2 or 3 sg. *ditu* (i.e. **dit-tu*, cf. p. 496), 365 VI *b 10, 16, 25*, 366 VII *a 38*=*titu*, 356 I *a 34* and *tetu*, 358 II *a 9*, 360 II *b 21*;

612 INDEX V.

with the same meaning but probably distinct in formation (cf. p. 496) is *tedtu*, 359 II *a 40* bis, spelt *tertu*, 361 IV *28*, and *dirstu*, 365 VI *b 17, 38* bis, *39*, 366 VII *a 5*. (4) Umbro-Lat. *deda*, xliii *9*, p. 434 must be indic. act., but must be anomalous, indeed unique in Italic, to whatever tense and number it is assigned.
(B) Unreduplicated present, only in Latinian; ind. act. 3 sg. *dat* Praen. 286, Umb.-Lat. xliii. *1*, p. 434; 3 pl. *dant*, Mars.-Lat. 263.
(C) Reduplicated perfect *ded-*, common to Osco-Umbr. and Latinian: (1) Osc. Lat. *ded-*, Perf. ind. act. 3 sg., O. *deded*, 42, 44, 49, 167, 170 = δεδετ 6, abbrev. *ded* 172. So Vol.-L. *ded* 253, Mars.-L. *dedet* 266, *ded* 268, Praen. *dedi* (? 1st p.) 281, Praen.-L. *dedet*, n. xxxiv. p. 323, *dedit*, 304, Fal. *dedet* 321, Umbro-L. *dede*, xliii. *2*, p. 433. 3 pl. [*d*]*edero*, Praen. 285, *dederunt*, Fal.-L. 335 *a b*, Umb.-L. *dedrot*, xliii *4* p. 433, *dedro* ib. *8* (for the syncope cf. *cedre* = caedere, n. xlii, p. 397). (2) Umb. *ded-*; Fut. perf. ind. act. 3 sg. *teḍust*, 357 I *b 34* = *dirsust*, 366 VII *a 43*. (3) *ḍeḍe*, dedit, U. 352, with *ḍunum*, ibid., from Tuder, either shows a change of initial *d-* to *ḍ-* unknown in Iguvium, or else has q simply for *d*, so that the form would fall under the Latinian-Oscan group above

de, uncertain abbrev., O. 106
de, de, propn. with abl., Fal. 321
de, abbrev., probably nomen, O. 177
decatae, dicatae, Umb. L. 370 A; *ē* for *ī* is clearly a provincialism, cf. p. 495
deketasiûī, v. *degetasis*
decimatrus, Fal. 349 A, q.v.
Dekis, praen. nom. sg. m. O. 48, 137 *c. 3, 4, 7*, mutilated ib. *a 7, b 1, 4*, abbrev. 77 A *3*, gen. sg. *Dekkieis*, 137 *c 9, j 7*; = L. *Decius*, cf. gens *Decia*, *Deccia*, Index III, and for -*kk*- before -*i*- v. List Phonet. Pecul.
dekkviarím, subst. neut. acc. sg., name of an official resort of the *meddix* of Pompeii, O. 39; cf. U. *tekvia-*, *degurier*, L. *decuria*, and for the suffix, L. *aerarium*, *tabularium*, etc.
Declune, dat. sg. (m. or f.?), a deity of Velitrae, Vol. 252; the ending may be that of either L. *Semo*, or *Pomona*, or *Portunus*, or *Fortuna*; U. *Puemune* (dat. masc.) is equally ambiguous
Dekmanniuís, subst. or adj. used as subst., pl. (m. or neut?, dat. abl. or loc.?), O. 175 *b 22*, *hūrz D. staít*; if it be taken as dat. cf. *Iuveí stahínt* 108, but if the Dekm. are deities at all, they must be affiliated to *Kerres*, to whom the garden belongs (175 *a 1*); 'deities of the sacred tithes' (πολύχρυσα λατρεύματα σχόντες, Eur. *I. T.* 1275) would be no more strange to Italic sentiment than the *Ašetus* (dat. pl. v. sup.) of Iguvium, or *Porrima Postuerta*, *Robigus*, and a host more in Latium
Decries, nomen, nom. sg. m., Pg. 214, cf. *gens Decria*, Index III
decrit, for *decret(o)*, Umb.-L. 370 A; on *í* for *ē* cf. p. 495
deda, v. s.v. *dato-*, A 4
dede, *deded*, δεδετ, *dedet*, *dedit*, *dedero*, etc., v. s.v. *dato-* C
dedro-, *dedrot*, v. s.v. *dato-* C
dee, deae, dat. sg. f., Umbro-L. 370 A
degetasis, adj. epithet of *meddís*, nom. sg. m. O. 94, nom. pl. -*síús*, 93; dat. sg. spelt *deketas-iûī*, 95 *a 5*. Büch. connects the word with L. *digitus*, in the sense of ὁ πεμπάζων, aerario praefectus, and this may well be. If so, Lat. *digitus* probably owes its first -*i*- (instead of -*e*-, cf. Germ. *zehe*, etc.) to the influence of *dicare*, *indicare*: in any case the later Osc. -*k-* instead of -*g-* is no doubt due to a popular connexion with *decem*, *dekvia-*
degvinum, O. 144 *b*
dehad, v. *kelledchad*
dei, deus, voc. sg. m., U. 365 VI *a 23, 24, 25, 26, 27*, but far more frequently (29 times) spelt *di* in the same insc. (ll. 25—55 passim)
dei, probly abbrev. for *deiuā*, dat. sg. fem., Umb.-L. n. xliii. *6*, p. 434
deic-, dicere, (1) Pres. stem *deico-*: pres. subj. act. 3 pl., *deicans*, O. 28 *9*, pres. inf. act. *deicum*, ib. *10*, = *deíkum*, 131 *6, 8*. Impv. act. 2 or 3 sg., U. *deitu* (cf. p. 495), 366 VI *b 56, 63, 64, 65*, VII *a 1, 20, 51*, spelt *teitu*, 359 II *a 26*; 360 II *b 7, 25*; 361 III *9, 25*. (2) Perf. stem, *dic-*: fut. perf. act. 3 sg. *dicust*, O. 28 *14*. (3) Perf. stem *dedic-*: U. fut. perf. act., 3 sg. *dersicust*, 366 VI *b 63*, 3 pl. *dersicurent*, 366 VI *b 62*
deina, dinina, nom. sg. f., Umb.-Lat. n. xlii. p. 397, dat. *dinai*, ib.
deitu, v. *deic-*
deiu, deo or deis, abbrev. dat. U. n. xliii. *10*, p. 434

deívā-, diua, *deivai*, dat. sg. f., O. 175 *a 15, b 17*, cf. Vol. *deue* inf.; the stem *diir-* is distinct, v. *diiviai*, inf.

deiuā-, iurare; act. fut. ind. 3 sg. *deiuast*, O. 28. *3*, pres. subj. 3 sg. *deiuaid*, 28 *11*, impv. 3 sg. *deiuatud*, ib. *5*; on *deiuatuns* ib. *9*, v. p. 502 footn.

deivinais, diuinis, adj. pl. fem. (dat. or abl.?), O. 110: v. p. 110; probably this is the word abbrev. *deiv*, 122

deiuos, Old L. n. xxxv. p. 329 f.; see the authorities cited on p. 331

delicatus, 309 B., Rem. p. 360 q.v.

dequrier, Decuriis, subst. fem. pl., probly loc. (but cf. p. 502), U. 364 V *b 11, 16 = tekuries*, 360 II *b 1*; in both passages the word denotes the day of some solemn assembly, no doubt orig. being the name of some tenfold group of families

dersa, v. s.v. *dato-* A (3)

dersecor, adj. nom. pl. m., only as epithet of *arsmor*, U. 365 VI *a 26, 36, 46, b 29*; Bücheler renders debiti, iusti

dersic-, v. *deic-*

dersua, bona, secunda, adj. fem., only as epithet of *parfa* and *curnac-*; U. abl. 365 VI *a 1*, acc. ib. *2* bis, *4* bis, *15* bis, *17* bis, spelt *desva*, 366 VI *b 51, 52* bis = *tesvam*, 357 I *b 13*; the stem may be *de-d-uo*, meaning 'dans, permittens, secundans'; if so for the suffix cf. *assiduos contiguos deciduos*, etc.; for the form of the root Gr. τέ-θ-μος, Skt. 3 pl. *dad-ati*, perhaps U. *dirs-tu* (v. p. 495); for both L. *ui-d-uos* = Skt. *vi-dh-ava-*

des, Pg. 218; cf. *deti*

desenduf = *decem-duos*, i.e. duodecim, acc. pl. m., U. 367 VII *b 2*; *desen* of course stands for *desen*, L. *decem*, etc.; for *-duf* v. s.v. *dur*

destro-, Osc.-Umb. = L. *dextro-* ; sg. nom. fem. *destr-st*, i.e. *destruest*, O. 101; U. acc. fem. with postp. *destram-e*, 366 VI *b 49*; loc. (perhaps as fem. subst.; so Büch.) *destre*, 365 VI *b 4*; loc. m. (as adj.) 366 VI *b 50* = *testre*, 360 II *b 27, 28*, where the postp. *e* is added; abl. m. with postp. *-co*, *destruco*, 365 VI *b 24, 28* = *testruku*, 356 I *a 29*. The construction is not clear in the phrase *testru sese*, which takes an abl., 361 III 23, IV 15, cf. p. 500

deti, adj. (or subst.?) sg. neut., probably acc., Pg. 216. *7*; commonly compared with L. *d(e)init-*, *dit-*, but the vocalism requires explanation

deue, deae (or deo?), dat. sg., Vol. 252

deueia, diuina, adj. abl. sg. fem., U. 365 VI *a 9*, acc. ib. *10*; cf. either O. *deivā-* or O. *diiviā-*

di, v. *dei*

dia, 3 sg. subj. act., U. 365 VI *a 20*, v. p. 515 footn.

diama, miswriting for *Diana*, Etr.-Praen. 298

Diane, Dianae, dat. sg., Umb.-L. n. xliii *1*, p. 433

dicator[ei], dat. sg., denoting some official of the sacred grove near Spoletium, Umb.-L. n. xlii. p. 397 (v. Errata)

dicust, v. *deic-*

dida, *didest*, *didet* v. s.v. *dato-* A

dies, dies acc. pl., Fal.-L. 335 *b*

diesptr, i.e. *-pater*, Iupiter, Etr.-Praen. 229; on the abbrev. cf. 272 n.; this form is of course the true Lat. nom., Iupiter being properly voc.

difue, U. 365 VI *b 4*; Büch. renders διφνές, biforme, as adj. acc. sg. neut.

[d]iíkŭlŭs, v. *iikŭlŭs*

diiviai, diuinae, adj. (or subst.?) dat. sg. fem., O. 167; from the stem *div-io-*, cf. Skt. *divya-*, Lat. *diui-no-*, etc.

Dindia, nomen, nom. sg. fem. Praen. 282, 304; cf. *gens Dindia*, Index III

diou-, old form of *Iou-*, Iupiter, Osc. dat. sg. διουfει 5, *diŭvei* 175 *a 11, 12, b 13, 14*; Praen. gen. sg. *diouo*, i.e. *-os*, 281

dira, mala, U. 370 D., Sab. 309 D, q.v.

dirsa, *dirsans*, *dirsas*, *dirstu*, *dirsust*, v. s.v. *dato-* A and C

disleralinsust, i.e. *Sust*, uitiauerit, uitiatum erit ucl sim., 3 sg. fut. perf. ind., U. 365 VI *a 7*, cf. p. 506; for the formation cf. *purdiuŝnst*, *-siust*, p. 485; Büch. connects with L. *lira* [pr. It. *loisā-*, Germ. *Geleise*, etc.]

dispennite, Plautine for dispendite, n. xxiii., p. 226, q.v.

ditu, v. s.v. *dato-* A

diumpaís, lymphis, Nymphis, subst. dat. pl. fem., O. 175 *a 7, b 9*; on the Lat. form see p. 361; Osc. *-iu-* for *-u-* after dentals is regular, cf. *Niumsis* etc.

diŭveí, v. *diou-*

diuvilā-, older form of *iŭvilā-* q.v., nom. sg. *diuvil*, i.e. *-ilu*, O. 102 (i), acc. *diuvilam*, 101

diuvia, O. 103 *a, b*; clearly derived from *diuv-*, but its meaning is doubtful, esp. as the form may be mutilated

dkuva, forma mutila, O. 137 *c 5*

dolo-, dolus, acc. sg. *dolom*, O. 28, 5, 14, *-lum*, 21, abl. *-lud* 11, 20

donum, acc. sg. neut. Mars.-L. 263,

-*nom* 267, -*no* 264, acc. or abl. 266, 268; Praen. acc. -*nom* 281, -*nu* 285, acc. or abl., -*no* 286; Fal.-L. acc. -*num* 335 *a*; Umb.-L. acc. -*nu* xliii. *1*, p. 433, acc. or abl. -*no* ib. *4, 8*

doxa, δόξα, personified Etr.-Praen. 301

δροῦνα, 37 E q.v.

duenos, nom. sg. Old L. n. xxxv. p. 329, dat. *duenoi*, ib. probably a proper name

duvo-, duo, declinable in Umb. m. nom. pl. *dur*, 366 VI *b 50*, VII *a 46*, acc. *tuf*, 357 I *b 41*, neut. acc. *tuva*, 359 II *a 27*, 361 III *32, 34*, abl. *tuves*, 361 III *19*, with postp. *tuver-e*, 359 II *a 33*, later spelt *duir*, 364 V *b 10, 15*

dunte, uox mutila, O. 130 *a 4*

dunum, Osc.=L. dōnum, 167, *dūnûm* 176, *dunom*, Vol. 253, acc. or abl. *duno*, Vest. 247; perhaps *dunum* 352 in Umb. *aβ* merely = *dunum*

dupla, duplas, duplices, adj. acc. pl. fem., U. 365 VI *b 18* bis

dupursus, i.e. -*d us*, bipedibus, dat. pl. adj. used for subst., U. 365 VI *b 10*; for the form of the root cf. Lat. *tripodare, tripudium*

dur, v. *duvo*

duti, i.e. -*tim*, iterum, acc. sg. n. of ordinal of the number 2, used as adv., U. 366 VI *b 63*; cf. *tertim*

[d]uunated, donauit, 3 sg. perf. ind. act., O. 169 (if Pauli's restoration of the first letter be correct)

d̨

dedę, v. s.v. *dato-*

dunum, donum, U. 352; on *d̨*- cf. *dedę*, s.v. *dato-* and *dunum* sup.

e

e Ǝ, earlier Ꙅ, fifth letter of the Osc. *aβ*, 81, v. the Table of Alphb.

e, abbrev. incertae signif., O. 64, 69, possibly, not probably, 106 *4*

e = L. *ē*, prepn. with abl. spelt *ch*, U. 366 VI *b 54* (*chesu* = *eh esu* ex illo), *casa ex arn*, 359 II *a 38*. In compp. usually *ee-* or *eh-* v. inf.

-e, postp. v. *en*; after a locative, it is sometimes written as a separate word, *rupinie e*, U. 357 I *b 27*, *tafle e*, 366 II *b 12*, cf. *testre euze*, i.e. *e uze*, ib. *27*

eaf, *eam*, v. *eo-*

eb, BƎ? nota incerta, O. n. xx. p. 182

ebetraf-e, subst. acc. pl. fem. with postp. -*e(m)*, U 365 VI *a 12*, spelt *hebetafe*, 366 VI *b 53*, which Büch. would regard as a miswriting, HEB- for EHB-; it is the name of the first point of the lustral circuit after the 'augural seats,' so that Büch.'s connexion with *eh-* ex and *baetere* gives a plausible meaning, 'exitūs'

ebrios, ebrius, Etr.-Praen. 301

Ec, nota praenominis, fortasse *Egnato-*, Vol. 252; cf. *gens Egnatia*, Index III

ek, abbrev. for the fem. of *ekho-*, 'haec', O. 102 (i), 115, v. *ekho-*

ek, 132, si sic interpungendum

eka-, v. *ekho-*

ἑκατογκάρανοι, O. 37 B. 2 q.v.

ekho-, *eko-* hic, v. p. 478: Fem. acc. sg. *ekak* (i.e. -*am-k*), O. 39, 42, 44, 172; abl. *ekhad* 40, -*kad* 51, nom. pl. *ekas*, 108 *a b*, 109, probably 119, *ekask*, 175 *b 1*, acc. pl. *ekass* 39. Neut. acc. sg. *ekík* 171; Pg. *ecic* 216 *6*; uncertain *eko*, O. 13

ecic, *ekík*, v. *ekho-*

ekkum, item, adv., O. 95 *b 5, 19*; instead of *ek-dum*, cf. *eks* ita, *ísidum* idem, etc., just as *ífís-su* instead of *ífís-du(m)*. Probably the double consonant (instead of the etymologically correct -*k-d-*, -*s-d-*, etc.) started from the neut. *íd-dum*, and the ablatives *íud-dum*, *íad-dum*

ecla, adj. abl. sg. fem., epithet of *uia* in the curse and blessing, U. 366 VII *a 11, 27*; cf. *Ingoldsby Legends*, p. 131: 'He cursed him in sitting, in standing, in lying;
He cursed him in walking, in riding, in flying,
He cursed him living, he cursed him dying.'

ekso-, hic (cf. p. 478), O. sg. neut. abl., *eksuk*, 60, 61, 62, 63; loc. or dat. *excic*, O. 28, 17, 26, and no doubt *11*; fem. abl. *exac*, ib. *8, 23*, pl. loc. fem. with -*c* and postp. *exaisc-en*, ib. *25*

ekass, ita, adv., O. 95 *a 10* = *ex*, 28 7

ecuc, i.e. *ek-(h)ûc* for *ek-hôd-ce*, Pg. 216 *3*; see *ek-ho-*, p. 478; observe that *ō* always becomes *ū* in Osc. and N. Osc.

but not in Lat., hence Lat. *hūc* does not belong here, but probably = **hoic*, cf. *Idg. Forsch.* 4, p. 213

ecuf, ibi, adv. from *ekho*-, Pg. 218, cf. p. 478; for suffix cf. *puf*

ekvine, subst. or adj. used for subst. loc. sg. after *tra*, U. 358 II *a 13*. Büch. plausibly renders 'trans equinum,' i.e. 'in circo equestri' (Mars, who is here worshipped, being the patron of horses), comparing Lat. Equirria, *quae deus in campo prospicit ipse suo*, Ov. *Fasti*, 2. 859 with the October *equos*, etc.; on *kv*- in Umb. v. *kvestur*

eculia, nomen fem. initio fortasse mutilum, Fal. 314

ede, eisdem, abl. pl. fem., Praen. 286

ed-e-k, id, v. *is*

edum, edere, inf. act., O. 130 *a 8*

ee-hiiā-, *ex-hiare, i.e. emittere, used of the sacrificial 'hunt' in which the victims were released in order to be chased and captured (described 357 I *b 40* ff., 366 VII *a 51* ff.), as probably in the *ludi Taurei* (Serv. Dan. ad *Aen.* 2. 140) of the Sabines, and perhaps the *Poplifugia* at Rome (Varro *L. Lat.* 6. 18): gerundive gen. pl. fem. used as subst. (cf. p. 519) *eehiianasām*, O. 117 *a 5* and no doubt *b 8* (ubi incisum *veh*-); on U. *ehiato*, 367 VII *b 2*, v. p. 513 footn.; L. *hiare* is occasionally transitive, and the word could naturally be applied to the opening of the doors of a den, as is pointed out by Mr Horton Smith, *Class. Rev.* 10 (1896), p. 196

eeson-, v. *eson*-

ee-stint, exsistunt, exstant, 3 pl. pres. ind. act., O. 175 *b 1*; according to Buck's almost certain explanation (*Osk. Vokalism.* 24) a syncopation of *ee-stahint, cf. *stahint*, s.v. *stā*- inf.

eest, ibit, *eetu*, ito, v. *etu*

ef, v. *is*

effañlare, 205 C. 1 q.v., with *sufafias*, inf.

efurfatu, 3 sg. impv. act. trans., only in phrase *purom-e efurf*. U. 365 VI *b 17*, 366 VII *a 38*; cf. *furfant*, inf.

egmo, res, subst. nom. sg. fem., O. 28 *4*, gen. -*m[as]* ib. *5*, abl. -*mad* ib. *10*, gen. pl. -*mazum* ib. *24*

ehad, v. *kelledehad*

ehesu, v. *eh* and *eso*-, Umb.

ehe-turstahamu, exterminato, exeant moneto, 3 sg. impv. depon., U. 366 VI *b 55* bis = *eturstahmu* ib. 53 bis, spelt *etuḍstamu*, 357 I *b 16*; from *tudes*- q.v.

e-hiato, v. *eehiiā*-

eh-peilatasset, i.e. -*tas set*, sunt statutae, collocatae uel sim., 3 pl. (fem.) perf. ind. pass., O. 109; as the word is used of the erection of the heraldic statues (v. pp. 101 ff.) it is clearly connected with L. *pila*, 'pillar'

eh-preivid, re familiari (illo quod ex priuato sumitur), uel sim., subst. abl. sg. (if the reading of the last letters is correct), O. 168; cf. *preivo*- inf., and for the formation L. *exsomnis subtilis*, etc.

eh[stit], exstat, O. 95 *b 26*, si quidem recte se habet uolgare supplementum ad formam pluralem *eestint* (q.v. sup.) satis exacte efflctum (cf. *staiet*, *stahint*)

ehtrad = L. *extra(d)*, O. 95 *b 5*, perhaps *a 14*

ehvelklu, i.e. -*lum*, relationem, consultum, subst. acc. sg. neut. only in phrase *chvelklu feia*, relationem faciant, i.e. fratres consulant, U. 363 V *a 23*, *b 1*; perhaps from *uel*-, uelle, with -*klu* = Gr. -τλον, L. -*clum*, in the sense of an 'exercise of authority'; but if so the usual connexion of *uelle* with Gr. βούλομαι δήλομαι, I.-Eur. *gel*-, must be given up, since *g*- becomes *b*- in Osc.-Umb. (O. *bivo*-, U. *berue* etc.); cf. the foll.

ehueltu, edicito, iubeto uel sim., 3 sg. impv. act., U. 365 VI *a 2*; cf. the prec.

eikvasese, subst. or adj. used as subst., pl. loc. with postp. -*e* or dat., U. 362 V *a 4, 16*; if it is dat. it is either an -*io*- stem (-*asesio*- or -*asensio*-; hardly -*aseso*-) or a second doubtful example (cf. *sevakne*, IV 9) of the loss of the -*ss* of the dat. abl. pl. of the *i*-stems (-*asesi*- or -*asensi*-, the latter is Büch.'s view); if it is loc. with -*e* the stem will be (not -*aso*- or -*asio*- which would give -*aser-e*) but -*asi*- (?-*ansi*-). Büch. renders *pagis*; cf. the foll.

eikvasatis, adj. abl. pl. only in phrase *ahtisper eik*, U. 361 III *24, 29*; Büch. renders 'pro sacris paganicis'

eiduis, Idibus, loc. pl. fem. (-o- stem), O. 113 = *eiduis*, 101, 104; cf. Lat. and Sab. *idus* 309 A.; the word must be Italic, and the 'Tuscan' *itus* (ib.) borrowed from it, but the Osc. form creates more than one difficulty in the old connexion with Gr. αἴθω, L. *aestus*, *acstas*

eine, v. *enem*

[ειϝε]ιμ, v. *iním*

einom, et, Old L. n. xxxv. p. 329; if this word is equiv. to U. *enom* and related to Lat. *enim*, the *ei-* must be a form of writing a short close *e*; cf. Pg. *inom*

eiscurent, comportauerint, attulerint; 3 pl. fut. perf. ind. act. trans., U 364 V *b 10, 15*; Büch. plausibly regards the vb. as a causative in *-sc-* from *ei-*, ire; in any case cf. L. *poposci*, O. *comparascuster* for the retention of a pres. stem in *-sc-* in the perf. tenses

eisei, v. *eiso-*

ειστεδομ=*isídům*, v. *is*

eiso-, *eiso-* hic, Osc. demonstr. often with *-c (-k)*; *eiso-* is also anaphoric 'is' (cf. *eizo-* inf.): acc. sg. masc. *eisunk*, 137 f. *11.*, gen. sg. n. *eiseis*, 95 *a 20*, m. or n., 130 *a 4*; abl. n. *eisůd*, 95 *a 13*, with postp. *eisuc-en*, 28 *16* (cf. p. 484); loc. sg. *eisei*, 95 *b 20*; abl. fem. *eisak*, 42; loc. sg. [e]*ísai*, 95 *b 31*

eite, ite, Pg. 216 *6*, v. *etu*

eitipes, i.e. *-pens*, censuere, decreuere uel sim., 3 pl. perf. ind. act., U. 362 V *a 2*, 363 V *a 14*, sometimes explained as a contraction (like *neiḑhabas*) for **eitim *hipens* 'partem ceperunt,' but it would be the only form of this root showing *-p-* in Umb. and needs further support (contrast *habē-* inf. with fut. perf. *habus-*) v. p. 496

eitiuvā-, pecunia, res familiaris, Osc. subst. fem.: gen. sg. *eituas*, 28 *13, 18, 27*; acc. sg. *eituam*, 28 *19*, Mruc. 243 *11*=*eítinvam*, O. 42, abbrev. *ei* 28 *22*; abl. sg. *eitiuvad* 42, 43, *eitiu*[*vad*] 52, abbrev. *eitiv* 177. *cituas* 28 *9* is probably acc. pl. after *en*, in; probably from *ei-*, ire in the sense of 'reditus,' 'income'

eitua-, v. *eítiuvā-*

eituns=Lat. **ētōnes*, subst. nom. pl. m., O. 60, 63, abbrev. *eítu* 62, *eít* 61; perhaps=*cisiaria*, vehicula leuia alicuius generis, as they are advertised at the corners of turnings all leading towards the walls of the town (Pompeii), and we know that *cisiarii* etc. were as a rule stationed just outside the walls of Italian towns, v. note ad loc.

eizo-, is, Osc. anaphoric and demonstr. often with *-c*, in both senses, gen. sg. m. *eizeis*, 28 *22*, loc. *eizeic*, ib. *7, 21*; fem. sg. abl. *eizuc*, ib. *29, 30*; abl. pl. *eizois*, ib. 23, abl. *eizac*, ib. 10, gen. pl. *eizuzun-c*, ib. 24, loc. pl. *eizas-c* (an corrigendum *-aisc*?), ib. 9; the spelling with *-z-* in Lat. *αβ* may be a mere variation for *-s-*, since both appear as *-s-* in Osc. *αβ*. For another view v. *Verner's Law in It.*, p. 32 ff. In any case it shows that *-s-* between vowels in Osc. of the 1st cent. n.c. was in some forms at least a voiced sound (Eng. and Fr. *z*)

[e]lisuist, probably=[e]*lisu ist*, perf. ind. pass. 3 fem. sg., elata, sepulta est uel sim., Pg. 216, ubi v. nn.

emo-, emere: *emantur*, emantur, parentur, 3 pl. pres. subj. pass., U. 362 V *a 8*, spelt *-tu* ib. 10; *emps*, emptus (est), p. part. pass. nom. sg. m. 355

empratois, abl. (or dat.) pl., Pg. 216 *3*, probably neut. partc. used as subst., generally identified with Lat. *imperata*

emps, v. *emo-*

en, in, Osc.-Umb. prepn. and postp., v. p. 484. In Umb. spelt also *-em*, *-e*, showing the final nasal was weak. Osc. with acc. *en eituas*, in pecuniam, i.e. ex pecunia alterius aliquantum sibi uindicaus; *censtom-en* in censum, ib. *20*; with acc. and abl. *eisuc-en zieulud zicolom* xxx. ex illo die in diem tricesimum, ib. *17*; with loc. *exaisc-en ligis*, in illis legibus, ib. *25*. Umb. only as postp.: Acc. sg. *ahtimem* 357 ib. *12*, *akeduniamem* ib. *16*=*acesoniame* 366 VI *b 52*, *anglome* 365 VI *a 9*, *arvamen* 361 III *11*, *asame* 365 VI *a 10*, *destrame* 366 VI *b 49*, *esonome* ib. *50*=*esunume* 357 I *b 14 esunumen* 361 III 20, *ferime* ib. *16*, *carsome* 365 VI *a 13, 14*, *ooserclome* ib. *12*, *pedume* 359 II *a 27*=*persome*, 365 VI *b 38*, *pertome* 365 VI *a 14*, *purome* 365 VI *b 17*, *randeme* 365 VI *a 14*, *ruseme* 366 VII *a 8*, *rubiname* ib. *44*=*rupiname* 357 I *b 35*, *satame* ib. *38*, *smursime* 365 VI *a 13*, *termnome* 366 VI *b 57, 63, 64*, *tertiame* 365 VI *a 13*, *tettome* ib. *13, 14, 14*, *todcome* ib. *10, 10*, *uasirslome* ib. *12*, *vukumen esunumen* in aedem sacram aut in aedem ad sacrum 361 III 20. Acc. plur. *ebetrafe* 365 VI *a 12*=*hebetafe* 366 VI *b 53*, *fesnafe* 360 II *b 16*, *presoliafe* 365 VI *a 12*, *uerofe* 365 VI *b 47*=*verufe* 356 I *b 9*, *vapefem avieklufe* in sellas augurales 357 I *b 14*=*uapefe auichclu* 365 VI *a 10*. With loc. sing. *acersoniem* 366 VII *a*

GLOSSARY TO THE DIALECTS. 617

52=akeḍunie 357 I b *43*, *arvem* 361 III *13*, *ocrem Fisiem* 365 VI *a 46* (alias *ocre Fisie*), *toteme Iouinem* ib., *toteme Iouine* ib. 26 *(tote Iouine* ib. 36) (cf. *destra me* for *destrame*), *rupinie e* 357 I b *27=rubine* 366 VII *a 6*, *tafle e* 360 II b *12*, *testre euze* dextro in umero ib. *27, 28, destre onse* 366 VI b *50, destr e* 365 VI b *4*, *manuve* 360 II b *23*, *etre* et *tertie sviseve* ib. *14, 15*. Loc. pl. *fesnere* 360 II b *11, funtlere* 357 I b *24=fondlire* 366 VII *a 3, tuvere kapiḍus* 359 II *a 33*. Latinian: with acc. Old L. n. xxxv. p. 329; with abl. Mars. 267

endendu (from **entenn-(e)-to=L. intendito*) imponito uel sim., 2 or 3 sg. impv. act., U. 365 VI b *40* bis, *49*; spelt *ententu*, U. 357 I b *12*, 361 III *15*; fut. perf. ind. 2 or 3 sg. *entelus*, U. 357 I b *12*, 3 sg. *-lust*, 366 VI b *50*, on which v. p. 491

endo, in, erga, postp. with acc. Old Lat. n. xxxv. p. 329, cf. p. 331; cf. Lat. *induperator, ind-uere*, Gr. ἔνδον; no doubt a compd. of *en*, in and *dō*, for which v. s.v. *arnipo*

enem, deinde, deinceps, U. 366 VII *a 44* bis=*ene*, 357 I b *35*; spelt *eine*, 365 VI *a 10, 11*, but *ei* does not imply a long vowel, v. p. 506 footn. 2; it is exactly equiv. in form to Lat. *enim*, Osc. *inim*, but in each dialect the particle has taken a slightly different meaning; cf. the cognate *enom*

enetu, inito, 2 or 3 sg. impv. act., U. 356 I *a 1*, 365 VI *a 1*; v. *etu* inf.

enom, tum, deinde, U. 365 VI b *17, 38* bis, *39, 40* bis, 366 VI b *53, 64*, VII *a 5, 8, 9, 23* bis, *36, 45* bis, *51*, spelt *eno*, 365 VI b, *16, 17, 46*, 366 VI b *56* bis, *62, 65*, VII *a 1*; and *enu*, 357 I b *36, 37, 38* bis, 358 II *a 9*, 360 II b *21*; with *-nn-, ennom*, 366 VI b *51*, VII *a 20, 24, 34, 39, enno*, 366 VII *a 38*. With *-k* or *-ek*: *enuk*, 356 I *a 30, 33*, 363 V *a 29*; *enumek*, 357 I b *11, 13, 16, 19, 20, 21, 22*

entelus, *entelust*, v. *endendu*

ententu, v. *endendu*

entraï, internae, i.e. gentili, patriae, dat. sg. fem., epithet of Samnite goddess, O. 175 *a 8, b 10*

eo-=L. *is* in certain Cases (v. p. 477 f.); Masc. Osc. acc. sg. *ionc* (with *-c(e)* affixed), 28 *12, 17, 26*, nom. pl. *iús-su* (with *-su*) 142. Umb. nom. pl. *eur-ont* (with *-hont*), 366 VI b 63, acc. pl. *eo*, 365 VI *a 20*. Neut. O. acc. pl. *ioc*, 28 *4*, U. *eu*, 358 II *a 2*, 360 II b *9*.

Fem. O. nom. sg. *íú-k*, 95 *11, 16, ioc*, 28 *4*, *iiu-k* 101; acc. sg. pl. *iak* 169, Mruc. *iaf-c* 243 *8*; U. acc. sg. *eam*, U. 365 VI b *16, 24*, acc. pl. *eaf*, 357 I b *42*, 366 VII *a 52*

epid, probably nomen abbrev. O. 55, ?*ep* 180, cf. *gens Epidia* in Index III.

era-, *era*, v. *ero-*

ere, *erec, erihont, eront*, all U., nom. sg. m.=*is+-e, -ec, e-hont, -hont* respectively, v. p. 477 and *is*. It would be conceivable that nom. *ere*: *ero-* (q.v.) as L. *ille*: *illo-*, but the neut. *eḍ-ek*, *ers-e* as well as the forms under *eo*sup. point to *is*

ereȝlo-, arae uel arae instrumenti pars, Umb. subst. acc. sg. *ereȝlu*, 361 IV 13 bis, with postp. *-aḍ ereȝlumaḍ* ib. 6=*ereȝluma*, 361 III *35*, IV *3, 10*; loc. *ereȝle*, ib. V *17, 19*

eretu, v. *heri-*, and p. 504

Ἐριύντης, 37 C q.v.

erietu, arietem, acc. sg. m., U. 358 II *a 6*

Erine, si uera lect., dat. sg. m., the name of some deity, *Erine patre*, Mars. 264; v. the foll.

Erinie, si uera lect. dat. sg. fem., epithet of *Vesune*, the consort of the preceding, Mars. 264; from the order of the names in the insc. she was clearly counted the better half

ero-, *iro-*, ille, U. anaphoric and demonstr. =Osc. *eiso-* often with *-c (-k)* and *-hont* (with the latter, meaning 'idem'), probably distinct from the nom. m. *ere* q.v. The spelling *ir-*, though it only occurs once, makes O. *eiso-*, a more likely equiv. than O. *eso-*. Masc. *ero-*, gen. sg. *erer*, eius, 365 VI *a 23, 24, 31, 33, 34, 35, 40, 43, 45, 50, 53, 54, 55*, VI b *7, 7, 10, 12, 14, 15, 26, 27, 28, 33, 34, 35*, 366 VII *a 10, 18, 19, 22, 26, 31, 32, 35, ererek*, 361 III *32*, spelt *irer*, 365 VI *a 25*, *crir*, ib. 31 (v. crit. note), abl. *eruhu*, 360 II b *22*; with postp. *-ku(m)*, *eruku*, 361 III *31=erucom*, 366 VI b *50*; on *eru*, 362 V *a 8*, v. p. 517; on *eruñ*, 361 III *14* v. p. 478 footn.; gen. pl. m. *erom*, 366 VII *a 14, 50=ero* 366 VI b *62* bis, VII *a 13, 28*, abl. pl. m. *eriront*, 366 VI b *48*, written *erererunt*, 361 IV 5: Fem. *erā-*: gen. sg. *erar*, 365 VI *a 23, 24, 26, 31, 33, 34, 35, 40, 43, 44, 45, 50, 53, 54, 55*, VI b *7, 8, 10, 12, 14, 15, 26, 27, 28, 33, 35* bis, 366 VI b *62*, VII *a 11, 14* bis, *18, 19, 22, 26, 28, 31, 32, 35, 50, 51, erarunt*, 361 IV *1*, abl. sg. *erak*, 361

III *12, erahunt*, 357 I *b 23*, written, no doubt by error (F for H), *erafont* 366 VI *b 65*

erom, *eru*, osse v. *es-*

erse, i.e. *ed-e*, id, v. s.v. *is*

erus, *erus*, 'quod dis datur peractis sacris' (Büch.), Umb. subst. acc. sg. neut., nearly always the object of *ditu, dirstu* dato (*kuveitu* 359 II *a* 33 conuchito), and after sacrifices of flesh; but also (1) as an internal acc. after *umtu* (*putrespe erus*), IV 14, where *ereslu* appears to be the external acc. (Büch. would render 'utriusque dei gratiā,' but I see no reason why *erus* should not have its usual meaning and *putrespe* be neut., referring to the two portions of *klavlas* just mentioned; (2) as a part of *vestisia*, VI *b 16*, 28 al., *ezariaf* IV *27*, 356 I *a 33*, 357 I *b 34* bis, *35*, *36*, 358 II *a 9*, *28*, *32*, *40*, 360 II *b 21*, 361 IV *14*, *27*, 365 VI *b 16* bis, *25*, *38* bis, 366 VII *a 5*, *38*, *43* ter, *44*; since the *-s* is never omitted and never became *-r*, it must be double, i.e. it must stand for *-ss*, *-cs*, *-fs* or the like, and since it is acc. it must be a neut. *-s-* or *-es-* stem. I formerly identified it with Gr. ἔρευθος, rendering 'red embers,' or 'red blood,' but further justification is needed for the assumption of a disyllabic form in Italic of the common root *rouf-*.

es- esse, to be (for forms from *fu-* v. s.v.), cf. pp. 486 ff. Osc. Pres. ind. 1 sg. *sům*, 87, 107, 128; *sum*, O.-Etr. 98, O. 136 *a*, perh. 189 *b*; 3 sg. *ist*, 95 *a 12*, *15*, *b 5*, *8*, *23*, *30* (cf. Plautine 2 sg. *ĕs*), but *est*, 115, 116 (this is a distinct, possibly dialectic form), 3 pl. *set*, 109, 115, 116, 175 *a 1*, *set* 28. *25*; *sent*, O.-Etr. 97. Impv. 3 sg. *estud*, O. 28 *12*, *23*, *26*, *30*, *estud*, 95 *b 14*, *18*, Inf. pres. *czum* esse, 28 *10*. Mruc. Pres. subj. 3 sg. *si*, 243 *11*, v. p. 514. Vols. Impv. 3 sg. *estu*, 252. Umb. Pres. ind. 3 sg. *est*, *est*, 357 I *b 18* bis, 359 II *a 15*, 365 VI *a 8*, *9*, *10*, *26*, *27* ter, *28* ter, *36*, *37* quinquiens, *38*, *46*, *47* quinquiens, *48*, VI *b 29*, *30* quinquiens, *31*, 366 VI *b 50*, *53* bis, *55* bis, VII *a 46*, *51*, *52*, 367 VII *b 3*, 3 p. *sent*, U. 365 VI *a 15*, *27*, *36*, *46*, VI *b 3*; on *-se* in *vakaze*, *uacose*, v. p. 512 footn.; on *-so(r)* in *benuso* etc., p. 492. Pres. subj. 2 sg. *sir*, U. 365 VI *b 7* bis, *26*=*si* ib., *sei* ib., VI *a 23* bis, 3 sg. *si* 362 V *a 6*, 363 V *a 24*, *27*, *b 3*, *7*; in *mersi*, 365 VI *a 38*, *48*, *mersei* ib. 28 (cf. p. 512), 3 p. *sins*, U. 367 VII *b 4*, spelt *sis*, 362 V *a* 6. Impv. 2 or 3 sg. *estu*, 358 II *a 2*, 360 II *b 23*=*esto*, 365 VI *a 15* bis. Inf. pres. *erom*, 367 VII *b 2*=*eru*, 363 V *a 26*, *29 b 5*. Latinian: Old-Lat. pres. subj. 3 sg., *sied*, n. xxxv. p. 329, cf. p. 331; Fal.-L, *sunt* sunt, 335 *a*

e-salicom (si uera lect.), acc. sg. masc. Mars. 267, ethnicon of a town or tribe not elsewhere known, unless we follow Büch.'s conjecture (*Rh. Mus.* 38, p. 490) and derive it from Ἴσσα, an island in L. Fucinus (Dion. Hal. I. 14)

esaristrom, sacrificium, piaculum, acc. sg. neut., Vo. 252; cf. *aiso- aesar* sup.

esidum, probably=*isidům*, the Osc. equiv. of Lat. *idem*, v. *is*; but the word may conceivably have been based, or re-derived, from O. *eso-* q.v.

eskamitu for *-tum*, acc., adj. or parte. used as subst., probably neut., U. 361 IV 1; it is the part of the sacrificial cake or cakes offered to a masculine deity contrasted with the part offered (*strusla(m) petenata(m)*, ib. 4) to his divine consort, and hence explained by Büch. ad loc. as a phallic image (or which as offered to Liber see Augustine *Civ. Dei* G. 9); he connects the word with L. *scamillum* and *scamnum* in the agricultural sense of a projecting unploughed clod

esme, *esmei*, *esmik*, v. *is*

eso-, *eso-* hic, Osc. demonstr. (cf. p. 478): nom. sg. n. *εσορ* 22, loc. sg. n., *esei*, 95 *b 23*, perhaps *25*; abl. sg. m. *esuc*, Mruc. 243 *8*

eso-, *eso-*, hic, Umb.: nom. sg. fem. *eso*, 354; abl. fem. *esa*, 365 VI *b 9*, *14*; abl. m. or n. *esu*, 365 VI *a 25*, *28*, *33*, *35*, *38*, *45*, *48*, *53*, VI *b 28*, *31*, *35*, 366 VI *b 54* (*chesu*) *54*, *essu* VI *a 43* (but this may be 'ita'), *esuku*, 361 IV 29, abl. pl. *esis-co*, 365 VI *a 18*, *esir*, 366 VII *a 10*, *18*, *26*, *32*, *isir* ib. *34*; *eso* sic 365 VI *a 2*, *3*, *8*, *16*, *22*, VI *b 6*, *9*; 366 VI *b 53*, *57*, VII *a 9*, *20*, *25*, *34*, *46*, *iso* 365 VI *a 20*, *esu*, 358 II *a 3*, 362 V *a 14*. With *-ck* or *-k* acc. sg. n. *esumek*, 356 I *b 8* = *esome*, 365 VI *b 47*, *esoc* sic, 365 VI *b 25*, *issoc*, 366 VII *b 3*, *esuk*, 362 V *a 1 isek*, item, 361 IV 4, *isec*, 365 VI *b 25* is not clear. With *-hont*: *isunt* itidem, 359 II *a 28*, *36*; 361 III 16, 17. On the stem *eso-*, *esso-* v. p. 478

esono-, sacer, diuinus, Umb. adj. and in neut. as subst. Adj. dat. sg. f. *esone*,

362 V *a 4, 6*; abl. sg. fem. *esuna*, ib. 5, acc. pl. fem. *eesona* (for -*af*), 365 VI *a 18*=*esona* ib. *3, 5*; abl. pl. agreeing with *vepurus*, *csunes-ku*, 362 V *a 11*. As subst. neut.: nom. and acc. sg. *esono*, 365 VI *a 57*, VI *b 47* bis=*esunu*, U. 356 I *b 8, 9*, 357 I *b 38*, 358 II *a 2* (ubi incisum *esum*), 359 II *a 20, 21, 42*, 361 III *1, 14* (cf. p. 478 footn.), IV *30*, acc sg. with postp. *esonom-e* in sacrum, 366 VI *b 50, 52, esunume*, 357 I *b 14*=*esunumen*, 361 III *20*; probably loc. sg. n., 365 VI *b 11*; abl. pl. *esoneir*, 365 VI *a 18*; a deriv. from *aiso-*, deus, sacer, q.v. sup.

e]sos, v. *aiso-*
essu, hoc (abl.) or ita, U. 365 VI *a 43*, v. *eso-*, Umb. and p. 478
essuf, ipse, pron. nom. sg. m., O. 169 = *esuf*, 25 *19, 21* and Umb. *esuf*, 359 II *a 40*, 361 IV *15*; the meaning of this word can hardly be disputed if all the passages be carefully compared; the only explanation yet suggested which accounts for the form is that it is a partc. of sum; if so, for both form and meaning cf. L. *sons*= 'ipse qui in re est,' 'rei ipse actor,' 'reus.'
est, est, v. *es-*
est, ibit, U. 365, VI *a 6*, v. *etu*
esto-, *esto-*, iste, Umb. demonstr. and anaphoric: masc. acc. sg. *estu*, 360 II *b 24*, pl. (m. or n.) *esto*, 366 VI *a 15* bis; neut. acc. sg. *este este*, 356 I *a 1*, 365 VI *a 1*, 366 VI *b 62, 63*, VII *a 51*; neut. acc. pl. *estu* 358 II *a 2*, 360 II *b 23*
esuf, v. *essuf*
esumek, *v. eso-*, Umb.
et, et, Pg. 206; Mars. 264; Fal.-L. 336; Umb. 355, 357 I *b 20*, 361 IV *7, 12*, 362 V *a 6, 8, 13*, 363 V *a 18, 20, 22*, 364 V *b 9, 13, 15, 17*, 365 VI *a 19*, VI *b 5, 24*, 366 VII *a 37, 44, 46, 51*. It is noteworthy that the particle is not found in pure Oscan
eta-, Umb.=Lat. *itā-re*: 3 pl. impv. *etato* (i.e. -*nto*), 366 VI *b 63*=*etatu*, 357 I *b 21, 22*, 3 pl. pres. subj. *etaians*, 366 VI *b 64*=*etaias*, ib. VII *a 1, 65*
e-tanto-, tantus, O. *etanto*, nom. sg. f. 28 *26*, and no doubt *11*=U. *etantu*, 363 V *b 6*; for the *e-* cf. L. *e-quidem*, etc.
etat-, v. *eta-*
etro-, alter, Umb. adj.: abl. sg. neut. *etru*, 365 VI *a 35, 38, 43*; loc. sg. *etre*, 360 II *b 14*; dat. pl. m. *etres*, 361 III *18*=*etre*, 360 II *b 2, 3* bis, *4* bis, *5* bis, *6* bis; fem. acc. sg. with postp. -*a(d)*

etrama, 361 III *34*, acc. pl. *etraf*, 356 I *a 18* bis; the stem is no doubt related to that of L. *iterum*, whether U. *e-*=*i* or some stronger form of the pronom. root
etu, *etu*, ito, 2 or 3 sg. impv., U. 37 I *b0 10, 14*; 358 II *a 6*; 359 II *a 335 36*; II *b 12*; 361 III *20*, 1V *21*; 366 VI *b 48*, VII *a 39*; spelt *ectu*, 366 VI *b 54*, plur. *etuta*, U. 361 III *11*=*etuto*, 366 VI *b 51, 52, 65*, VII *a 1*, spelt *etutu*, 357 I *b 15, 23* bis. Other tenses are: *ier itur*, pres. ind. pass. impers., 366 VI *b 54*; *ise* for **iser* fut. ind. pass. impers., 356 I *b 8* (on these forms v. p. 492); fut. act. ind. 3 sg. *eest*, 365 VI *a 2*, spelt *est* ib. *6*; fut. perf. ind. act. 3 sg. *iust* ib. *7*; this last form shows like Pg. *afded* that the Italic perf. of the verb corresponded to Lat. *iit*; *iuit* is a late analogy form
etudstamu, *eturstahmu*, v. *eheturst-eu*, v. *eo-*
eveietu, euincito uel sim., 2 or 3 sg. impv., U. 360 II *b 8, 11*; U. -*veie-* may=either It. ụeịē-, ụiē-, or ụic-ē-
Evklûî, Εὐκόλῳ, i.e. Ἑρμῇ, dat. sg. m., O. 175 *a 3, 25, b 4*; v. Εὔκολος, 37 D
euront, v. *eo-*
euze, v. *eu* and *onso-*
ex, v. *ekss*
exac, *exeic* etc., v. *ekso-*
exelct, v. *exeic*, s.v. *ekso-*
ἐξομπλον, 37 C, q.v.
ezariaf, subst. or adj. used as subst. acc. pl. f., U. 361 IV *27*; Büch. would render 'escas,' but the -*z-* requires explanation; if it were regarded as the earliest Umb. representation of proethn. It. -*t*+*t*- (L. -*ss-*), the form would be of considerable interest in its bearing on a difficult question
ezum, Osc. esse, v. *es-*

f

f 8, nineteenth letter of the Osc. αβ, 81 *a*, cf. p. 463
f, abbrev. for *filius* or *filia*, Pg.-Lat. 213, 229, 233, 234; Mars. or Mars.-Lat. 262, 266, 268; Acq.-Lat. 273; Praen. 285, 286; Tuscul. xxxiv. p. 323; Fal. 318 *a*, 321, 323, 326 *b*, 329, 333 *a*, *c*; Fal.-Lat. 335 *a*, 336; Umb.-Lat. xliii. *10*, p. 434

f. p. = Fortunae Primgeniae, Praen. 283

faamat, habitat, 3 sg. pres. ind. act, O. 60, 61, 63 and no doubt 62; clearly containing a strong form of the root of O. *famel*, L. *famulus*, etc.

faber, Pg. 218; if it is used as a common noun = L. *faber*, as is generally assumed, and is native to Paelignian, the medial *-b-* cannot be taken to represent an I.-Eu. aspirate (as e.g. Brugm. *Gds*. II. § 77), without further justification

fabres, fabri, nom. pl. m., Praen. 283

fac-, facere: Osc. Impv. act. 3 sg. *factud*, 28. 9; pres. subj. 3 sg. *fakiiad*, 117. *a* 7; fut. perf. ind. 3 sg. *fefacust*, 28. *11, 17*, perf. subj. 3 sg. *fefacid*, ib. 10 (ubi aes *fepacid*). On *facus* v. s.v. Vol. *facia*, pres. subj. 3 sg., 252. Umb. Fut. perf. ind. 3 sg. *fakust*, 361 IV *31*, 3 pl. *fakurent*, 357 I *b 34*, *facurent*, 366 VII *a 43*, pres. subj. 3 sg. *faśiu*, 359 II *a 17*; inf. pres. *faśiu*, 359 II *a 16=faśiu*, 360 II *b 22*. On *feia, fetu, feitu* see under *fē-*. Latinian: perf. ind. 3 sg. *fefaked* (written ϝheϝhaκeδ), Praen. 280; *feced*, Old L. n. xxxv. p. 329, *fecid*, Praen.-Lat. 304. The agreement of Osc. with 6th cent. Praen. indicates that the Perf. stem *fefac-* is as old as proethnic Italic

facus, factus, creatus, of magistrates, nom. sg. m., O. 28. *30*: for **facuos*, with which compare the pass. sense of L. *relicuos, aruom*, etc., and the verbal force of *deciduos, mortuos, saluos*; if this formation was common in pr. Ital. it must have exercised some influence, even if only dissimilatory, upon the *-us-* perf. partc. act.; cf. Volsc. *sepu*.

fahe, U. 364 V *b 13*; contrasted with *toco* (q.v.) in the phrase defining the gift of flesh to be made to the Clauerniaus by the Brotherhood

fal, *fale* (or *faler*?), O. 106, an abbrev. and probably gentile epithet; it seems probable that the *r* in this line really belongs to the *pümpe* in the line before it: if so, *fale* is simply an abbrev. of the foll.

faleniaas, adj. nom. pl. f., O. 107, a probably gentile epithet of a set of *pümperias*, v. pp. 101 ff.

Falesce, Falisci, nom. pl. m., Fal.-L. 335 *a*

famedias, nom. pl. fem., adj. or subst.?, U. 360 II *b 2*; from root of L. *famulus*, O. *faamat*, the suffix being equivalent in meaning to that of L. *familia*, as that of U. *pumpedia-* is to that of O. *pümperia-*

famel, famulus, subst. nom. sg. m., O. 205 (q.v.), Pg. 208 *bis* (where it may be an abbrev.), written *fml*, O. 181; from the root of Osc. *faamat*, habitat

famelo, i.e. *-ello* (cf. p. 496), familia, res familiaris, nom. sg. fem., O. (Bantine) 28. *22*; cf. p. 496 *3*; from *famel*, cf. the foll.

famila, U. 370 A, if it is not a miswriting, would seem to stand for **familla*, and show the same assimilation as O. (Bantine) *famelo*

far = L. *far*, subst. neut., acc. sg., O. 130 *a 8, far*, U. 364 V *b 10, 15*; gen. sg. *farer*, ib. *9, 14*; cf. *farsio* inf.

farferus, 205 C 1, q.v.

fariolus, Sab. 309 B, q.v.

farsio, farrea, subst. or adj. used as subst., acc. n. (pl. or sing.), only in the phrase *f. proseseter adueitu*, U. 365 VI *b 2*, spelt *fasio* ib. *44=fasiu*, 358 II *a 12*

fasefele, *facibile, sacrificabile, adj. acc. sg. n., U. 360 II *b 9* (ubi aes *fasefate*)

fasena, Sab. 309 A, q.v.

fata, si sic legendum, Etr.-Praen. 297, ubi v.n.

fatium, loqui, inf., O. 181 *6, 8*; *fati-* clearly = L. *fatē-(ri)*, both probably connected with the root of L. *fāri*

fato, probably acc. of subst. or parte. used as subst., only in phrase *f. fito*, which appears to denote some kind of blessing (Büch. 'prouentum euentumque prosperum'), U. 365 VI *b 11*; Büch.'s explanation of the forms as = *factum* and φῖτυ respectively offers no phonetic difficulty; cf. U. *Ahtu-* for *Actu-* etc., but cf. *feta* s.v. *fē-*

fē-, θεῖναι, facere, is clearly preserved in Umb.: Impv. act. 2 or 3 sg. *feitu*, U. 356 I *a 4, 5, 7, 29, 30, 32* ter, I *b 5, 7, 9*; 357 I *b 18, 24, 28, 31, 32*; 359 II *a 20*; 361 III *31* bis, *32*; 365 VI *b 3, 22, 47*; 366 VII *a 3, 4*; spelt *fetu*, I *a 3, 9, 11, 12, 13* bis, *14, 16, 17* bis, *20, 22, 24, 25* bis, *26* bis, *28* bis, I *b 2, 3* bis, *6*; 357 I *b 25, 27, 29, 32, 43, 44* bis; 358 II *a 2, 4, 6, 7, 8, 9, 11* bis, *12, 13* ter, *14*; 360 II *b 7, 10, 26* (aes *feiu*), *29*; *fetu*, 365 VI *a 22, 56, 57* bis, *58* ter, *59*, VI *b 1* ter, *2, 3* ter, *5, 19* bis, *20* bis, *22* ter, *23, 24, 37, 43* bis, *44* ter, *45* ter, *46* bis; 366 VI *b 55*, VII *a 3, 4* bis, *6, 7* ter, *37, 41* bis, *42* bis, *53* bis, *54* bis, *feetu*, 366 VII *a 41*. Pres. subj. 3 sg. *feia*, 363 V *a 23*. *feta* in 360 II *b 14* is rendered by Büch. 'facta,' but the meaning is not clear; the stem may be identified with *fito-*, cf. 365 VI *b 11*, v. s.v. *fato*. The origin of the *-i-* in *feitu* is doubtful: it may come from the *-c-* of *fēc-*, Gr. θηκ-, as *deitu* for *deicetod*

februo, Sab. 309 A, q.v.

fedehtru, subst. acc. sg. neut., U. 361 III *16, 18*; a part or appurtenance of the *kletra*, q.v.; possibly for **fidetrum* from *fid-*, L. *findo*, meaning a 'chopping-board'

fedo-, Sab. 309 A q.v.

fefac-, v. *fac-*

fefure, uitiauit, turbauit uel sim., perf. ind. act. 3 sg., U. 358 II *a 4*

feia, v. *fē-*

feiho- = Gr. τεῖχος, but in the *-o-* declension, acc. pl. *feihúss*, O. 95 *b 5*, loc. pl. *feihúis* ib. 19; Osc. *feiho-*: L. *fingere* as Gr. νειφο-: L. *ninguere*; cf. *fifikus* inf.

fel, probably abbrev. of **felio-* filius, Etr.-Umb. 353 *b*

feliuf, lactantes, adj. acc. pl. m., U. 356 I *a 14=filiu*, 365 VI *b 3*; it can hardly be doubted that the Umb. usage gives the original meaning of L. *filius* (which must therefore be connected with Gk. θῆλ-υ-, Skt. *dháyati*), but unfortunately the Umb. spelling gives no certain clue to the original Italic vocalism

felsva, subst. or adj. used as subst., acc. fem. (sg. or pl.?), U. 362 V *a 11*; since the word denotes material for *vepurus*, 'fireless' sacrifices, Büch. reasonably connects *fels-* with L. *holus-*, *holer-*, Sab. *folus* 309 B

ϝενσερ, *fensernu*, acc. sg. or gen. pl. m., ethnicon of the 'Fenserines,' O. 143, v. ad loc.

fer-, ferre: Mruc. 3 pl. pres. ind. pass. *ferenter*, 243 *3*, cf. p. 505, *feret*, 3 sg. ind. act., probably present, ib. *9*. Umb. Impv. act. 2 or 3 sg. *fertu*, 359 II *a 17, 19, 26, 27, 33, 94*, 360 II *b 12* bis, *13, 14* bis, 15 ter, *16* bis, 366 VI *b 50* bis, 3 pl. *feriutu*, 361 III *13*. Fut. ind. *ferest*, 359 II *a 26*. Pres. subj. impers. pass. *ferar*, 366 VI *b 50* (v. p. 516 f.). Latinian: *fero*, Praen.-Lat. n. xxxiii. p. 322, probably = L. *fero*

feri, doubtful form in Praen.-Lat. n. xxxiii. p. 322

ferime, U. 361 III *16*; it appears from 366 VII *a 4* that in 357 I *b 25* the form is a mistake for *ferine* q.v.

ferine, *ferine* only in the phrase *vatuva* (*uatuo*) *ferine feitu*: Umb.

subst. abl. sg. 356 I *a 4, 13, 22*, I *b 3, 6*; 357 I *b 25* (acs *ferime*); 361 III *31*; 365 VI *a 57*, VI *b 1, 19, 43, 45*; 366 VII *a 4*. Büch. renders **ferione*, i.e. cultro

ferom, Vol. 252, perhaps inf. = ferre, others render *ferrum*; it appears to be subject to *pihom estu*, pium esto

Feronia, dea Sabina, Sab. 309 A q.v.; dat. sg. *feronia*, xliii. *2*, p. 433

fertalis, adj. loc. (or dat.?) pl. fem., O. 109, v. p. 110; the *-a-* is probably long, cf. *Vestalis*, *Cerealis* etc., and contrast L. *fertilis* and the foll.

fertlid = L. *fertili*, adj. abl. sg. fem., agreeing with *aetatu*, Pg. 216

Fertrio, nomen, nom. sg. m., Fal.-L. 348

fēsnā-, *fanum* uel sim., Osc.-Umb. subst. fem. Umb. acc. pl. with postp. *fesnaf-e* in fana, 360 II *b 16*, loc. pl. with postp. *fesner-e* in fanis, ib. *11* (but it is clear that if this pl. denotes more than one object, the objects are close together). Pg. *fesn*, 239, abbrev. probably for **fesno*, nom. sg. f. Osc. *fīsnā-*, *fīisnā-* : nom. sg. *fīisnú*, 95 *b 4*, acc. sg. *fīisnam*, ib. *6*, *fīsnam* ib. *19*; mutil. *fīi[su..]*, 95 *a 24*, *fīis...* 169. The word is cognate to O. *fīisia-* = L. *fēriae*, L. *fēs-tus*; and also to *fānum* if that stands for **fās-nom*

ϝεστιϛ, Festius, si sic legendum nomen, nom. sg. m., O. 6, v. n. ad loc. and p. 461

festos, festos, Fal.-L. 335 *b*

fi, O. 121, v. *fīsio-*

fi, probably = the Fal. equiv. of *filius*, Fal. 326 *b*, 338

ficlā-, *fiklā-*, the Umb. equiv. of L. *fitilla*, librum alicuius (fortasse uarii) generis, acc. sg. fem. *ficlam*, 366 VII *a 42=fikla*, U. 359 II *a 18, 29, ficla*, U. 365 VI *a 56, 59, b 2, 4, 20, 23, 44, 46*, 366 VII *a 4, 8, 54*; gen. sg. *fiklas*, U. 359 II *a 41* (on the construction cf. p. 499). Umb. *-kl-*, like Lat. (Plaut.) *-cl-*, represents Italic *-tl-* regularly; in this word perhaps Italic *-ctl-*, and Lat. *fitilla* can hardly be separated

fiktu, impv. act. 2 or 3 sg., U. 356 I *a 28*, cf. *fifikus* inf.

fif-, uerbum mutilum, O. 169, ubi v. n.

fifikus, perhaps fixeris, 2 sg. fut. perf. ind. act., O. 130 *a 5*; the root must in Italic at least be distinguished from that of Osc. *feiho-*, murus, with which go Skt. *dēha-*, Gr. τεῖχος, θιγεῖν, Lat. *fingo*, *figlina*, Osc. *figlo-* etc. If L. *figo* contains an orig. *g*, then Osc. *fik-* : L. *fig-* as *pāc-(em)* : *pāg-(us)* etc., v. Brugm. *Grds.* I. § 467; but if the *g* of Lat. *figere* is based on a velar, as it must be if it is connected with U. *fiktu* (and Old L. *fiuere*), then it would be easy to suppose that the analogy of *finxit* : *fingo* produced in Lat. *figo* in place of *fiuo*; but the connexion of Osc. *fifikus* would be doubtful

figel, figulus, nom. sg. m., 205 B. 7, q.v.; stem *figlo-* from *dheigh-*, see the rule in Brugmann, *Grds.* I. § 509. 2 and cf. the preceding art.

fiiet, fiunt, 3 pl. pres. ind. act., O. 117 *a 3, 10, b 7*; contrast the Umb. *fuia*, *fueist*, which present a slightly different stem *fu-io-* instead of *f(u)iio-*, which the Osc. and Lat. forms show

fiisna-, v. *fēsnā-*

filio-, filen-, Latinian=*filius*, *filia*; nom. sg. m. *filios*, Etr.-Praen. 294; nom. sg. f. *filea*, Fal. 334; dat. sg. *fileia*, Praen. 281, later *fileai*, Praen. 304; cf. *felio-* sup.

finem, finem, acc. sg., Mars. 267

firata, p. parte. pass. abl. sg. fem., agreeing with *aetatu fertlid* as abl. absol.=finita, consumpta uel sim., Pg. 216 5; *-d* is written in only one of the three abl., and was therefore probably no longer pronounced, but retained occasionally as a poetic spelling

firco-, Sab. 309 A q.v.

Fīsanis, Fisanius, nomen, nom. sg. m., O. 62

fīis... v. *fēsnā-* sup.

fīis v. *fīisiais*

fīisīais, loc. pl. fem., probably adj., O. 116, *fiisiais* 115, *fisiais* 101, abbrev. *fiis* 120; v. *fēsnā-* and p. 110, and note that the use of *i* in 115 and 116 is too uncertain to allow us to conclude that *fii-* represents an orig. *fi-* rather than *fē-*, for which we should expect *fii-*

Fisio-, *Fisio-*, Umb. adj., sacred epithet of the citadel of Iguvium (cf. the deity *Fisu-*): Sg. Masc. Abl. *Fisiu*, 356 I *a 5, 8, 12, 15, 17, 21, 25, 29, 31*, 365 VI *a 23, 25, 34, 35, 45, 53, 55, 58*, VI *b 1, 3, 6* bis, *9, 14, 19, 22, 26, 28, 35*, *Fissiu*, 365 VI *a 43*. Acc. *Fisim*, 365 VI *a 41, 49, 51*, *Fisi*, 365 VI *a 31, 39*, VI *b 12, 31, 33*, *Fisei*, 365 VI *a 29*. Gen. *Fisier*, 365 VI *a 30, 32, 39, 41, 49, 51*,

VI *b 13, 32, 33*, *Fisie*, 365 VI *b 10*. Dat. *Fisie*, 365 VI *a 40*, *Fisi*, VI *a 30, 33, 42, 50, 52*, VI *b 7, 10, 11, 14, 26, 32, 34*, *Fisei*, 365 VI *a 23*, VI *b 10*. Loc. with postp. *Fisiem*, 365 VI *a 46*, *Fisie*, 365 VI *a 26, 36*, VI *b 29*, *Fise*, dat. sg., probably masc., name of the patron deity of the citadel of or a hill adjacent to Iguvium, U. 356 I *a 15*; this implies an ordinary *-o-* stem, but the later form *Fiso*, dat. sg. m., 365 VI *b 3* comes from an *-u-* stem; cf. *Trebe* and *Trebo*

Fisouio-, another deity whose name is derived from the preceding; voc. sg. m. *Fisouie*, U. 365 VI *b 9, 10, 12* bis, *14*; acc. *Fisoui*, 365 VI *b 6, 8* bis; dat. sg. *Fisoui*, U. 365 VI *b 5*, 366 VII *a 37*=*Fisuvi*, 356 I *a 17*

Fisouina, adj. abl. sg. fem., U. 365 VI *b 9, 14*; from the preceding

Fistelū, the true Osc. form of Fistelia, nom. sg. 184 *b* fem.=Φιστελια; ethnicon *Fistlo-*, nom. pl. *fistlus* ib. *a*, dat. or loc. *-luis* ib. *c* and *e*, *-lůis* ib. *d*: v. note ad loc.

fito, U. 365 VI *b 11*, v. *fato* sup.

fiuusasiaīs, O. 175 *a 20*, miswriting for *fluus-* q.v.

flagiui, dat. sg. m., epithet of Jupiter, O. 108 *b*; cf. p. 109 f. and footn.

fluusaī, Florae, a Pompeian and Samnite goddess, dat. sg. f., O. 46, 175 *a 24*

flusare, Quinctili, Vest. 248, loc. sg. m., the Vestine name for July, v. xxviii. *a*, p. 260 f. Clearly derived from the preceding

fluusasiaīs, Floralibus, loc. pl. fem., O. 175 *a 24*, and no doubt *20*; clearly the name of a feast in the loc., not of Floral nymphs in the dat., who could not (with any propriety) include Father Hermes in their number (*evklūi pateret*, l. 25, v. s.v.)

foied, hodie, Fal. 312 *a*, *b*; the meaning is beyond doubt; on the *f-* see 349 Rem. p. 385; *-i-* for *-di-* is parallel to Pg. *afited* for *af-ied, Bantine *zic-* for *diec-*, Umb. *hoio-* for *hodio-*

Folcozeo, Faliscan nomen, nom. sg. m., Fal. 338, *-cuz-* 339, 340, *Fulczeo* 337

folus, Sab. 309 B q.v.

fondlo- (or *-la-*?), used in pl. as the name of a spot in the peregrination of the Iguvine lustrum, *fondlir-e*, loc. pl. with postp., U. 366 VII *a 3*=*funtlere*, 357 I *b 24*; Büch. equates the word with L. *fontulus*

GLOSSARY TO THE DIALECTS.

fons, faucns, adj. nom. sg. m. and f., U. 365 VI *a 42, 50, 52,* VI *b 7, 11, 13, 26, 32, 34,* 366 VII *a 13, 17, 31, 49*; spelt *fos,* 365 VI *a 23, 30, 38, 40,* plur. nom. *foner,* 366 VI *b 61.* In the sentence *Prestotar Serfer fouer frite tiom subocauu* which occurs four times, 366 VII *a 20, 23, 33, 36,* the gender, number and case of *fouer* are to me doubtful (cf. *frite* inf.). The word clearly = L. *faunus* (from *fauēre*) declined as an *i*- stem
fordeum, Sab. 309 B q.v.
forte, Pg. 218
fortis, i.e. *-iss* (earlier *-ifs*), abl. pl. *fortibus*, i.e. forte, casu, O. 28. *12*
Fortuna, Fortuna, nom. sg. f., Etr. Praen. 298, dat. sg. *Fortuna*, Praen. 281, *-ne* Tusc.-Lat. xxxiv. p. 323
fostia ?, 309 B q.v.
fostis, 309 B q.v.
Fougno, Fucino, dat. sg. m., Mars. 265, the god of Lake Fucinus
Fourio, Furius, nomen, uom. sg. m., Tusc.-L. n. xxxiv. p. 323
fratr- = L. *frater*, Osc. gen. pl. *fratrûm,* O. 115, 116. Umb. nom. pl. *frateer,* 364 V *b 16,* and probably ib. *11,* spelt *frater,* 361 III *5,* 362 V *a 1,* 363 V *a 14, 22,* gen. pl. *fratrum,* 361 III *10* = *fratru*, 359 II *a 21, 35,* 360 II *b 26,* 361 III *6,* 362 V *a 12,* 363 V *a 25, 27, 29,* V *b 3* and *fratrom,* 367 VII *b 1*; dat. pl. *fratrus*, fratrus, 358 II *a 2*, 361 III *23, 28,* 364 V *b 8, 13,* 367 VII *b 1*
fratreca, fratrica, adj. abl. sg. f., U. 367 VII *b 2*
fratrecate, in fratrum magisterio, loc. sg., U. 367 VII *b 1,* v. p. 501
fratreks, fratrum magister, nom. sg. m., U. 363 V *a 23,* V *b 1* = *fratrexs,* U. 367 VII *b 1*; dat. sg. *fratreci,* U. 367 VII *b 4*
frehtef, U. 359 II *a 26*; Büch. renders 'frigidans,' supposing a verb of the 3rd conj. (such as *plectere*, etc.); cf. the foll.
frehtu, acc. sg. n., adj. or partc., epithet of *pune*, U. 361 IV *31*; Büch. plausibly renders 'frigidum,' supposing a p. ptc. pass. *fricto-* from *frigeo*
frentrei, *Frentri, loc. sg. n., O. 196, ethnicon *f[rete]rnum*? ib., v. n. ad loc. and contrast *Frent(r)ani*, q.v. 197 A
frif, subst. acc. pl., probably = L. *fruges* (cf. for the contraction *capif* = *capides*), U. 365 VI *a 42, 52,* VI *b 13,* 366 VII *a 17, 30,* spelt *fri,* 365 VI *a 30, 32, 40, 50,* VI *b 32, 34.* *i* for *ū* is certainly

regular in Umb. in monosyllables (*pir* = Gr. πῦρ, *sim* = ὕν, etc.)
frip, perhaps an abbrev., Etr.-O. 132
frite, U. 365 VI *a 24,* VI *b 8, 15, 27,* 366 VII *a 20, 23, 33, 36*; always preceding *tiom subocau(u)*, 'te supplico' and following either *arsier* or *fouer*. Büch. takes it as a loc. and renders 'fretu,' 'fiducia,' i.e. 'per fiduciam,' 'confisus,' regarding the preceding words as gen. neut., comparing Plaut. *Aul.* 678 *ibo ad te fretus tua, Fides, fiducia*
Frondisiae ?, U. 370 D q.v.
frontesia, 205 C 2 q.v.
frosetom, uitiatum, defrudatum uel sim., p. partc. nom. neut. impers., U. 365 VI *a 28, 37, 47,* VI *b 30*; probably a deriv. from the root of L. *fraus*; if so cf. the partc. *muieto, -seseto* from *mugā-, sekā-*
fruktatiuf, fruitio, usus fructus, O. 95 *a 21*
frunter, O. 165
fruti, *frutinal, frutilla*, 205 Rem. 9, p. 230 q.v.
fu-, *fu-*, esse, forming part of the verbal system of *sum* in Osc. and Umb., though varying somewhat from the L. distribution. Osc. Impf. ind. 3 pl. *fufans* 95 *a 10.* Perf. ind. 3 pl. *fufens,* 115, 116; perhaps *fuf* in 113 is an abbrev. for some part of this tense; Büch. would interpret *staieffuf* as a perf. partc. nom. sg., but it is hard to believe this without another example of the perf. *-ff-* preceded by the thematic vowel. Fut. perf. ind. 3 sg. *fust,* 28. *19,* 22 bis, *23,* 28 bis, *29* bis, *30*; *fust* 113, 114; this form is properly fut. perf., and is so used (e.g. 28. *28* clearly), but no other form appears as the fut. simple of *sum*; it seems probable that the fut. perf. did double duty since an Osc. and Umb. form corresponding exactly to L. *erit* would be indistinguishable from *est* the pres. ind., through the regular syncope (cf. however p. 492). Impf. subj. 3 sg. *fusíd,* 95 *a 19.* Perf. subj. 3 sg. *fuid* 28. *28* bis, *29.* Umb. Fut. perf. 3 sg. *fust* 356 I *b 7,* 357 I *b 39,* 361 III *6,* 362 V *a 4, 11, 19, 20,* 365 VI *a 7,* VI *b 39, 41, 42, 47* bis, 366 VII *a 45,* 367 VII *b 1, fus* 365 VI *b 40,* 3 pl. *furent,* 363 V *a 22.* Impv. 2 or 3 sg. *futu,* 359 II *a 22, 43* bis, 361 III *14,* IV *32,* 365 VI *a 30, 33, 40, 42, 50, 52,* VI *b 11, 13, 32, 34,* 366 VII *a 13, 17, 31, 49,* 2 pl. *fututo* 366 VI *b 61.* Cf. the foll.
fuio-, Umb. verbal stem = L. *fio-* : *fuia,*

fiat, pres. subj. 3 sg., 361 III *1, fuiest,*
fut. ind. 3 sg., 362 V *a 9;* cf. O. *fiiet*
sup.
fulczeo, v. *Folcozeo*
Fulonie for *-ier,* nomen, gen. sg. m., U.
354
fundatid?, Osc.-L. n. iv. p. 31; a doubtful form which might just conceivably
be an Osc. perf. subj., if *fundo,* 'I
cast' was conjugated as an *-ā*-stem
in Osc.
funtlere, v. *fondlire*
furfant, pres. ind. act. 3 pl., U. 365 VI
b 43, spelt *furfa-θ,* 356 I *b 1,* denoting some part of the sacrificial performance upon the sheep; cf. *efurfatu*
furo = Lat. *forum,* acc. sg. n., U. 366
VII *a 52=furu,* 357 I *b 42*
futreí, genetrici, dat. sg. fem., title of
a goddess in the Cereal cycle, O. 175
a 4=fuutreí ib. *b 5,* cf. *futre* 162;
the masc. seems to be preserved in a
Grecised shape in φύτροπες, nom. pl.,
37 D. What was the nom. sg. of the
fem. word?

g

g ⟩, third letter of the Osc. αβ, 81 *a, f*
g, abbrev. Osc. praen. **Gaavis,* 77 B,
83, 89 bis, 168, 201; cf. C in Lat. αβ
Gaav, abbrev. praen. gen. sg. m. (giving
the father's name), O. 190
Gaviis, nomen, nom. sg. m., O. 93, 131.
6
γᾴπος, 37 E q.v.
γίλα, 205 D q.v.
Gemenio, nomen, nom. sg. m., Praen.
286
genetaí, Genetrici, dat. sg. fem., a
Samnite goddess, O. 175 *a 15, b 17*;
cf. L. *Māna Geneta,* and for the act.
use of the *to-* parte. L. *ausus, potus,*
Gr. συνετός, τλητός, etc., Brugm. *Idg.
Forsch.* 5. 110 ff.
glito-, 205 B *6* q.v.
Gn, abbrev. for praen. *Gnaivs,* O. 77 B,
137 *b 2,* 157 (here in the gen.)
Gnaivs, Gnaevos, praen. nom. sg. m.,
O. 137 *d 3*
γνᾴρει, 37 C q.v.
γολύριον, 37 D q.v.
gomia, adj. acc. pl. fem., U. 365 VI *a
58=kumiaf,* 356 I *a 7,* no doubt meaning 'granidas', from root of Gr. γέμειν

gondecorant, written by false archaism
for *condecorant,* Fal.-L. 335 *b*
gonlegium, archaistic writing for *conl-,*
Fal.-L. 335 *b,* cf. prec.
Grabouio-, epithet of Mars, Jupiter and
Vofion at Iguvium: dat. sg. m. *Grabouie,* U. 365 VI *b 19,* spelt *Grabouei,*
365 VI *a 22,* VI *b 1=Krapuvi,* 356
I *a 3, 11, 21;* acc. *Graboui,* 365 VI *a
23=Graboue,* ib. *24, 25;* voc. *Grabouie,*
365, 31 times between VI *a 25* and *55,*
spelt *Crabouie,* 365 VI *a 27, 37*
γραιβία ἡ γραιτία (i.e. γραιφία), 37 D q.v.
grunnire, xxiii. p. 226 q.v.

h

h, Ⓗ, the seventh letter of the Osc. αβ,
81
haba=L. *faba,* Fal. 349 A q.v.
habē-, Umb.=L. *habēre.* Pres. ind. act.
3 sg. *habe,* habet uel sim., U. 357 I *b
18=habe,* 366 VI *b 54* (on these passages cf. p. 511 footn. 2). Fut. ind.
3 sg. *habiest,* habebit, 366 VI *b 50, 53,*
VII *a 46, 51.* Pres. subj. 3 sg. *habia,*
363 V *a 17, 19, 21* (but contrast *neiq-
habas,* 361 IV *33,* commonly rendered 'ne adhibeant (or adhibeas?)'.
Impv. 2 or 3 sg. *habetu,* 360 II *b 23
bis, 27, 28,* 361 III *28,* IV *30, 31=
habitu,* 365 VI *a 19,* VI *b 4:* 2 or 3 pl.
habetutu, 357 I *b 15=habituto,* 366
VI *b 51.* Fut. perf. ind. 3 sg. *habus,*
365 VI *b 40,* 3 pl. *haburent,* meaning
'ceperint,' 366 VII *a 52;* on the meaning of the verb v. p. 496, and note
that the Umb. *-b-* shows that the
Italic root is *hab-* not *haf-*
habina-, uictima alicuius generis (fortasse ouilis) Tefro Iouio in urbe lust-
randa mactata: acc. pl. *habina,* 356
I *a 27, habina,* 365 VI *b 22, 23, 24=
hapinaf,* 356 I *a 24;* gen. pl. *hapi-
naru,* 356 I *a 33.* Büch. compares
the Campanian cognomen *Habinnus*
(gen. *-nae*) in Petron. *Sat.* 65
hac, haec, acc. pl. n., Osco-Lat. n. iv.
p. 31
'**hafiest,**' lege hapiest et v. **hape-*
hahtu, capito, impv. act. 2 or 3 sg., U.
359 II *a 22* bis=*hatu,* 357 I *b 11,
hatu,* 366 VI *b 49;* 3 pl. *hatuto,* 366
VII *a 52=hatutu,* 357 I *b 42.* From
hab- or *hap-,* v. p. 496

Halaesus, Fal. 349 A q.v.
ηαμπανομ, misreading of καμπ-, O. 146 b q.v.
hanula, fanula, 349 Rem. q.v.
hanustu, adj. or ptc. nom. sg. fem. (or acc. sg. neut.?), Pg. 216. 7; for formation cf. Lat. on-us-tus etc.
*****hap-** (or *hapē-?), Osc.=L. habēre, v. p. 496; fut. ind. act. 3 sg. ha[p]iest, 28. 8 (ubi aes hafieist); fut. perf. ind. 3 sg. hipust 28. 11; perf. subj. 3 sg. hipid, O. 28. 8, 14, 17. The perf. belongs to the ēgi- type
harac, uox mutila, Fal. 333 a, perhaps rather a cognom. than a title
harisp, uox mutila, Fal. 332
Hat, abbrev. name of Hatria, 373 q.v. with Hadria p. 450. The coin and the modern name together prove the local pronunciation
he, hic, in the formula he cupa(t), Fal. 324, 325 b, 327, 328
hebetafe, v. ebetrafe
Ἥβων, 153 C q.v.
hebris, febris, 349 Rem. q.v.
Ἑκτόρειοι κόμαι, 37 D q.v.
Hegi, nomen mutilum, O. 77 B
Heirennis, Osc. nomen, nom. sg. m. 93, abbrev. heiren, 140 a
Helena, Helena, Etr.-Praen. 300, 302
Helevio-, nomen, Osc., nom. sg. m. helleviis, 131. 4, heleuis, Pg. 235, 238, abbrev. helevii 141 b, helevi 106. Gen. sg. heleviieis, 107; doubtful helv-, n. xiv. p. 138. Cf. gens Heluia, Heleuia in Index III
her, O. 176 abbrev. either for Herklúi or Herentatei
Hercle-, -cele-, -cole-, Latinian stem, Hercules. Nom. sg. hercles, Etr.-Praen. 299, spelt hercele, ib. 290; hercle, ib. 298. Dat. hercole, Praen. 285, 286. Cf. the Osc. form inf.
herclit, abbrev. cognomen, Pg. 238
Hereklo-, Hercules; Osc. gen. sg. herekleis, 95 a 24, b 4, 6, 7, ηερεκλεις, 17, dat. sg. hereklúi, O. 175 a 13, b 15. Vest. dat. herclo, 247, probably also the abbrev. herec, Pg. 239 represents the same stem; cf. sup. and Ἡρύκαλον, acc. sg. 37 A p. 46 q.v.
Herenni, i.e. -nis, nomen, abbrev. nom. sg. m., O. 64, perhaps here... 137 c 7. Cf. gens Herennia Index III
Herentas, Venus, nom. sg., Pg. 216. 7; gen. herentateis, O. 87, dat. -tei ib. For -enti-tas from herent- partc. of her-, uelle, cupere, v. heri-
hereitu, herest, v. heri-

heri- or her-, uelle, optare, sumere (cf. p. 484 ff.). Osc. Act. Pres. subj. act. 3 sg. heriiad, 131. 9. Fut. ind. 3 sg. herest (see below and p. 496), 28. 12, 18, 24, 26. Impf. subj. 3 pl. [h]erríns, 95 b 27. Umb. Act. Pres. ind. 2 sg. (always as a conjunction meaning 'uel') heris, 356 I a 4, I b 6 bis, spelt heri, 356 I a 4, 22 bis, 360 II b 9, 10, heri, 365 VI a 57 bis, 366 VI b 46 bis, 3 sg. heri (uolt), 361 IV 26. Impv. 2 sg. heritu, 365 VI a 27, 47, VI b 29, spelt hereitu, 365 VI a 37, and probably eretu, 358 II a 4, always in the phrase pusei neip her., v. p. 504. Fut. ind. 2 sg. heries, 357 I b 10, 360 II b 21; 3 sg. heriest, 366 VII a 52, spelt heries, 366 VI b 48. Perf. subj. 2 sg. act. or impers. pass. herifi, 363 V b 6 (v. pp. 514, 517). The form heriiei, 359 II a 16=heriei, 366 VII a 3 bis, and herie, 365 VI b 19, 20 is difficult to class (cf. p. 511 footn. 4), but it means 'uel.' The following forms show a shorter stem: ind. pass. 3 sg. herter, optatur, i.e. oportet, 359 II a 40, 361 III 1; with this may be identical (v. pp. 493, 513) herte, 362 V a 6, 8, 10, spelt herti, 364 V b 8, 11, 13, 16, and hertei, 367 VII b 2. The Osc. herest, herentas may show this shorter stem also
heriam, perhaps subst. acc. sg. f., O. 130 a 1
Herine, nomen, uel cogn., Osc.-Etr. xi. 5, p. 97
*****herinties**, uox spuria, 46* p. 532
herna, Mars. 269 A, Sab. 309 A qq.v., and cf. Hernici, 278 A
herte, hertei, herti, herter, v. heri- sup.
Ἡρύκαλον, 37 A, p. 46 q.v., with Hereklo- sup.
herukinai, dat. sg. fem., epithet of Herentas, O. 87 b
hetta, 205 B 4 q.v.
hipid, hipust, v. *hap-
hiretum, captorum, optatorum, uel sim., pass. ptc. gen. pl., depending on aunom, Vest. 248
Hirmio, nomen, nom. sg. m., Fal. 323; cf. p. 385
hirpo-, lupus, O. 186 A, Sab. 309 D, qq.v., and cf. Hirpini, 160 A
huc=hoc, acc. sg. n., Fal.-L. 335 b
Hoier, v. Hudie
holtu, impv. 2 sg., U. 366 VI b 60, VII a 49, one of the malignant acts of the deities invoked against the enemies of Iguvium; Büch. plausibly suggests a connexion with Lat. fallere
homon-=Lat. homo, dat. pl. homonus,

C. 40

U. 364 VI *b 10, 15*, nom. pl. spelt *humuns*, O. 130 *a 9*
Honde, dat. sg. m., name of a deity, U. 365 VI *b 45=Hunte*, 356 I *b 4*; but *Hunte Iuvie* in 359 II *a 20, 34* might be feminine. The word is clearly connected with *hondra* (q.v.) and means 'Infernus,' uel sim.
hondu for -*n-d(e)tu*, or -*n-n(e)tu* impv. 2 sg., U. 366 VI *b 60*, VII *a 49*, one of the malignant acts of the deities invoked against the enemies of Iguvium; if it is connected with *hondra* (q.v.) the meaning would be *pessum dato*. Büch. compares L. *fundere*
hondomu, adj. superl. abl. sg., U. 365 VI *a 9, 10*, cf. the foll.
hondra, infra, prepn. with acc., Umb. 365 VI *a 15*, 366 VII *a 52=hutra*, 357 I *b 42*; the same stem appears in Osc. adj. *huntro-* q.v. inf. The preservation of *-ā* (not changed to -*o*) shows that -*d* is lost, as in the Lat. forms in *-trā(d)*
-**hont**, -*hunt*, Umb. affix, v. p. 477
horcto-, 349 Rem. q.v.
horda, 349 Rem. q.v.
Hordicidia, 349 Rem. q.v.
Horse, v. *Hudie*
hostatu (i.e. -*tuf*) probably=Lat. *hastatos*, adj. acc. pl. m., U. 366 VI *b 59*, VII *a 48*, dat. pl. *hostatir*, ib. VI *b 62*, VII *a 13, 15, 28, 50*
Hudie, dat. sg. m., epithet of Mars, 356 I *b 2*, spelt *Horse*, 365 VI *b 43*. The gen. sg. *Hoier*, 365 VI *a 14* probably belongs to this word (or a derivative?); if so cf. S. Osc. *zic-* : L. *diēc-*, Pg. *Vibdu*=L. *Vibia*
Hule, deae uel deo, inter inferos, dat. sg., U. 361 IV *17*; Büch. points out that *Hule* probably contains the root of *holtu* as *Honde* that of *hondu* (v.s. vv.)
huntak, subst. (or adj. used as subst.?) acc. n., U. 361 III *3*, IV. *32*; Büch. would render 'puteus,' cf. p. 513. If so, and if this contains the root of L. *fons*, what is the relation between *h-* in this word, and *f-* in Umb. *fondlir-e*? For the variation in Lat. (due to borrowing) cf. 349 Rem.
Hunte, v. *Honde*
Huntia, probably subst. fem., U. 359 II *a 15* (perhaps abl.), *17* (perhaps acc.); from *hond-* in *hondra*, etc., meaning 'inferiae,' uel sim.
huntro-, inferus, Osc. adj.: nom. or acc. pl. m. *huntrus* (si sic diuidendum), 130 *a 11*, and *huntrus(teras)* ib., abl. pl. *hu[n]truis* ib. *a 7*. Cf. Umb. *hondra, hondomo-, huntia*

HVDIETES, ὑριήτης, ethnicon of *Hyria, O. 142 q.v. and cf. *urina* inf.
Hūrtiis, nomen, nom. sg. m., O. 176
hūrto-=L. *hortus*, but in sense rather 'lucus, τέμενος': nom. sg. *hūrz*, O. 175 *b 22*, acc. *hūrtūm* ib. *a 20*, dat. *hūrtūi* ib. *b 2*, loc. with postp. (cf. p. 484) *hūrtīn* lb. *a 1*
Hūsidiis, nomen, nom. sg. m., O. 190, cf. *gens Hosidia* in Index III
hutra, v. *hondra*

i and *ī*

| i, eighth letter of the Osc. αβ, obliterated from the abecedaria in 81
⊢ **ī**, twentieth letter of the Osc. αβ, 81; its sound was that of an "open *i*," half-way between *i* and *e*, cf. p. 461
Iabusco-, name of a tribe (*nomen*) hostile to Iguvium (cf. p. 407 footn.): acc. sg. neut. *Iabuscom*, U. 366 VI *b 58*, *Iapusco*, 366 VII *a 47=Iapuzkum*, 357 I *b 17*; gen. sg. n. *Iabuscer*, 366 VI *b 54, 59*, VII *a 12*, spelt *Iapuscer*, 366 VII *a 48*; dat. sg. n. *Iabusce*, 366 VII *a 12*. The -*z-* of the older spelling betrays the -*d-* of the *Iapydes*, for whom see p. 16
iaf-e, eas, v. *eo-* and p. 477
iak, eam, v. *eo-* and p. 477
iacor, nomen aliquod, Etr.-Praen. 209
icasilio, Fal. 317; possibly the *i-* belongs to the preceding *seielio*, but the fragments allow of no certainty
Ikuvi-, *Iiuvi-*, *Iioui-*, v. *Iguvi-*
idīk, *idik*, v. *is* and p. 477
idus, Sab.=L. *idus*, 309 A q.v.
Ielis, nomen, nom. sg. m., O. 204, the name of a leader of the allies in the Social war, v. the notes to 203, 204
iepi, U. 361 III *21*
iepru, U. 359 II *a 32*; Büch. is probably right in taking *ie-* for *ies* abl. pl. and rendering 'pro eis,' 'ante ea'; for *ies* v. *eo-*
ier, itur, v. *etu*
ife, eo, ibi=Lat. *ibi*, U. 366 II *b 12, 13*, *ife*, 365 VI *b 39, 40*, with *-hont*, *if-ont* ibidem 366 VI *b 55*; cf. the foll.

GLOSSARY TO THE DIALECTS. 627

iñ, O. 28. *29* perhaps=L. ibi; whether the fragment *ifi* in 73 is a complete word is still more doubtful

ἰγγρουσία, 205 C *2* q.v.

Iguvino-, Iguvinus, ethnicon of Iguvium: Umb. Masc. nom. sg. *Ikuvins* 369; nom. pl. *Ikuvinus*, 357 I *b 21, 22, Ikuvinu*, ib. *20*, later *Iiouinur*, 366 VI *b 63, Iouinur*, ib. *56*. Fem. acc. sg. *Iiouinam*, 365 VI *a 49, 51*, VI *b 33* 366 VII *a 16, 29, Iouinam*, 365 VI *b 12, Iiouina*, 365 VI *a 31, 41*, VI *b 31, Iouina*, 365 VI *a 29, 39*; gen. *Iiuvinas*, 356 I *b 2, 5, Iiouinar*, 365 VI *a 32, 39, 42, 49, 52*, VI *b 32, 43, 45*, 366 VI *b 61*, VII *a 3, 6, 10, 14, 15, 16* bis, *17, 19, 21, 24, 26, 27, 28, 29, 30* bis, *31, 32, 35, 37, 41, Iouinar*, 365 VI *a 30*, VI *b 10, 13, 34*, 366 VII *a 9, 27, 50, 53*, dat. *Ikuvine*, 357 I *b 13, Iiouine*, 365 VI *a 18, 24, 31, 40, 43, 50, 53*, VI *b 7, 11, 14, 33, 34*, 366 VI *b 51, 62*, VII *a 14, 18, 27, 31, Iioueine*, 365 VI *a 5, Iouine*, 365 VI *a 33*, VI *b 10, 27*, 366 VII *a 50*, loc. *Iiouine*, 365 VI *b 29, Iouine*, 365 VI *a 26, 36*; with postp. (p. 484) *Iouinem*, 365 VI *a 46*, abl. *Ikuvina*, 356 I *a 5, 8, 12, 15, 19, 21, 25, 29, 31*, I *b 2, Iiuvina*, 356 I *b 5*, 361 III *24, 25, 30* bis, *Iiouina*, 365 VI *a 23, 45, 54, 55, 58*, VI *b 1, 3, 7, 9, 15, 19, 22, 26, 28, 35, 43, 45*, 366 VII *a 4, 10, 22, 26, 32, 35, 37, 41, Iouina*, 365 VI *a 25, 34, 35, 43*, VI *b 6*, 366 VII *a 7, 9, 19, 24, 53*. For the pious fraud to which, I believe, the spelling *Iiuv-, Iiou-, Iou-* was due v. p. 405 footn. In any case the Latin *Iguvium* and modern *Gubbio* show that the -*g*- was never wanting in the spoken language of the town, and all the attempts hitherto made to explain the "change" of -*g*- to -*i*- as phonetic have been signally unsuccessful

iikŭlŭs, uox fortasse mutila, nom. uel acc. pl. m., O. 189 *a* q.v.

iiv, O. 164

iiuk, ea, v. *eo-* and p. 477

imad-en, ex ima (uia) usque ad..., adj. abl. sg. fem. with postp. 39 *10* (v. p. 484). Unless the Oscan of Pompeii differed from that of all its neighbours in dropping -*s*- before -*m*-, the identity of form between this word and L. *imo-* makes it difficult to derive the latter from **insmo-* as is commonly done, or indeed from anything but an orig. (pronominal?) *i-mo-* (? cf. L. *iterum* and Gr. δεύτατος : δεύτερος)

..imeisunk, v. *eiso-*

immusulus, 205 C *1* q.v.

impelimenta, 309 B q.v.

in, Osc., v. *iním*

in, in, Fal.-L. 335 *a*, cf. *en* sup.

incitega, 205 xxiv. p. 227 f. q.v.

incubat, incubat, 3 sg. pres. ind. act., Pg. 218

inenek, adv. or pron., U. 361 III *20*, cf. *iním, enem*

inferior, inferior, Mars.-L. 273

iním, Osc. et (v. U. *enem*, and cf. L. euim), 95 *a 3, 6, 7, 12, 18, 20*; *b 11, 13, 17, 25, 29*, 109, 115, 169, 170. Spelt [ειν]ε]μ 1; *iní* 39. 8 bis, 60, 61, 62, 63; *iním*, 28. *6*, 116, 130 *a 2, 4, 5* bis, *11* bis, 137 *a 6, b 10, c 11*; Pg. 208 bis, abbrev. *in*, O. 28. *12, 15, 16, 19, 21, 22* bis, *26, 28* bis

innulgen?, xxiii. p. 226 q.v.

inom, et, Pg. 209, cf. Old Lat. *einom*, U. *enom*

i]nperatoribus, Fal.-L. 335 *b*, used as a divine appellative of Jupiter, Juno and Minerva

inuk, v. *inumek*

inuiteis, inuitis, pl. abl. absol., Fal.-L. 336

inumek, U. 361 III *9, 11, 26, 34*, IV *2, 17, 18, 20, 21, 24, 26, 27, 28*; shorter form *inumk*, 361 IV *29*, spelt *inuk*, 356 I *b 7*, 361 III *4, 7, 15, 16*, IV *13, 14*. From *enom (inom)*, q.v.

io, fortasse=*Ioupiter*, voc. sg. m., xxxv. p. 329 f. (si recte uerbum diuisit Deecke)

ioc, ea, v. *eo-* and p. 477

ione, v. *eo-*

Iou-=L. *Iou-*, Iupiter, Osc. gen. sg. *iñveis*, 39, 191; dat. *iuveí*, 108 *a, b*. N. Osc. Mruc. gen. *ioues*, 243. *5*. Latinian: Mars. perhaps *ioue*, dat. sg. (?) 260 *a*, certainly *ioue*, xxxi. *b*, p. 295, *iue* 268. Fal.-L. *iovei*, 335 *a* 7; on Etr.-Praen. *iouei* 290, *iouos* 298 v. n. ad locc. Umb. voc. sg. *Iupater*, 360 II *b 24*; dat. *Iuve*, 356 I *a 3, Iuue* 365 VI *a 22, Iuvepatre*, 358 II *a 5*, 360 II *b 17, 22, 26*, 361 III *22*, separated *Iuve patre*, 360 II *b 7*, abbrev. *Iuvip*. 358 II *a 10*. The older form *diov-* is preserved in Osc. v. s. v.

Iŭvkiiŭí, nomen Oscum dat. sg. m., 95 *a 4*: cf. *gens Iouicia* in Index III

iouent, iuuent, 3 pl. pres. subj. act., Fal.-L. 335 *b*

iouie, iuuentutem, peditatum uel sim., acc. sg. or pl., U. 366 VI *b 59*, VII *a 48*, dat. pl. *iouies* ib. VI *b 62*, VII *a 13*,

40—2

628   INDEX V.

14, 28, 50. See p. 473; no doubt from the root of L. *iuuenis*.
iouio-, adj. ad Iouem pertinens, Ioue natus, et sim. Osc. Fem. acc. sg. *iŭviia* (for -*am*) 39, loc. pl. *iŭviaís* as subst. 'festis Iouis diebus' 113. N. Osc.: Mruc. Fem. nom. (or dat.?)*iouia* 243. *10*, gen. sg. *iouias* (adj. or subst.?) ib. 7; Vest. dat. sg. m. *iouio*, i.e. Iouis filio, 247; Pg. dat. pl. m. *iouiois* 210, Latinian: Mars. dat. pl. *i]ouies* 260 *b*. Umb. Masc. abl. sing. *Iouiu*, 365 VI *b 43=Iuviu*, 356 I *b 1*. As a divine appellative masc. sg. voc. *Iouie*, 366 VI *b 28, 29* bis, *31* ter, *33, 36*, *Iiouie* (p. 405 footn.), 365 VI *b* 35, acc. *Ioui*, 365 VI *b 26, 27* bis, dat. *Iuvie*, 356 I *a 24*, also I *a 8* perhaps=*Iouie*, 365 VI *a 58*, the gender in both being uncertain, as it is in 359 II *a 20, 35*, and in 358 II *a 6, 8*; *Iuvi*, 356 I *a 28=Ioui*, 365 VI *b 22* is certainly masc. Fem. sg. voc. *Iouia*, 366 VII *a 47, 49*; dat. *Iuvie*, 357 I*b 43=Iouie*, VII *a* 53, and cf. sup.
ip, adv., O. 95 *b 8=ip*, Pg. 216. *2*; the meaning must be 'ibi,' 'iuxta,' 'e regione,' or some similar local relation, but the word cannot be directly identified with Lat. *ibi*=Umb. *ife* but perhaps stands for **if-pe* v. p. 481
irer, eius, v. *ero-*
irnθ, *irnθi*, *irnθr* (Etr. αβ), n. xviii. p. 148, q.v.
irtiola, U. 370 D, q.v.
is, is, O. *iz-ic*, etc., U. *er-e*, anaphoric and demonstr. pron. (for the inflexion v. p. 477 f. and cf. *eo-* sup.), Nom. sg. masc. O. *iz-i-c* (with -*ĭ-* and -*c*), O. 28. *1, 7, 14, 29, 30*; with -*ĭ-* and -*dŭm*, *isidum*, 42=*ísidu*, 44, 45= εισειδομ, 15. With this is sometimes identified *esidum*, -*du* q.v. Umb. *er-e* (from **is-ī*), 362 V *a 4*, *ere*, 366 VI *b* 50; with -*c*, *erec*, 367 VII *b 1*; with -*hont*, *erihont*, 366 VI *b 50*, *eront*, 365, VI *b 24*. Nom. acc. neut. Osc. *íd-í-k*, 95 *a* 17, *18=idik*, 130 *a* 3, 5, and *idic*, 28. *6, 9, 30*; perhaps *id* if Büch. is right in reading *id-ad*, 'ad id' in 113. Umb. *erse*, i.e. *eḍ-e*, 365 VI *a 6, 8*, *eḍe-k*, 356 I *a 30*, 361 III *33, 35*, IV *3, 21, 32*, 363 V *a 26*. Loc. sg. Umb. [*e*]*sme*, 365 VI *b 55*, spelt *esmei*, 365 VI *a 5, 18*, with -*k*, *esmik*, 356 I *a 28, 31*. Acc. pl. masc. Umb. *ef*, 365 VI *a 4*
ise, ibitur, v. *etu*
isek, pronominal adv., U. 361 IV *4*= *isec* 365 VI *b* 25; cf. perhaps U. *issoc*.

iseseles=Lat. **insectilibus*, i.e. intro sectis, sectilibus, adj. or adj. used as subst. abl. pl., U. 361 IV 7; for the formation cf. *faṡefele*, *facibile
isidu, -*dŭm*, -*dum*, v. *is*
isir, v. *eso-*, Umb.
iso, v. *eso-*, Umb.
issoc, v. *eso-*, Umb.
ist, est, v. *es-*, esse
istui, uox spuria 46 p. 532
istor, nomen aliquod, Etr.-Praen., 301 q.v.
isunt, eisdem, v. *eso-*, Umb.
Italia, name of the capital of the allies in the Social war, probably Mars. (=Osc. *vítelliú*), 201 *c*. On the history of the word elsewhere cf. 11 A and p. 48
ἰταλός, Greek form of *uitulus*, v. p. 48
itek, pronoun or pronom. adv., U. 361 IV *31*
ittiŭm, v. *aet-*
itur, itur, Mars.-L. 273
iŭk, ca, v. *eo-* and p. 477
iuka, preces, dedicationem uel sim., subst. acc., probably neut. pl., U. 361 III *28=iuku*, acc., 360 II *b 23* (though this might be sg.). Büch. compares L. *iocus*, but as it was uttered *uvikum cum oue*, i.e. super hostiam, it was clearly of a serious character, at least from the sheep's point of view
iŭkleí, subst. loc. sg., O. 117 *a 4, b 8*, denoting some point of time
iue, Ioui, v. *Iou-*
iuengar, iuencae, nom. pl. fem., U. 367 VII *b 2*, acc. *iuenga* (for -*gaf*), 366 VII *a 51=iveka*, 357 I *b 40, 42*; the Umb. and Lat. words are clearly identical, and it is generally assumed that Italic *juu-* became Umb. *iu-*, but contrast U. *iou-ie* beside L. *iuu-enis*; this difference, however, may be due to accent if the Umb. like the Lat. and Osc. acc. became ultimately bound by the quantity of the penultimate syllable
iufahis, uel *diufahis*, nomen aliquod, ut uidetur, Etr.-Osc. xi. *8*, p. 97
Iuieskanes, dat. pl., name of a tribe or gens, U. 360 II *b 6=Iuieskane*, ib. *5*
Iuna, a Faliscan name, 316; xxxix. *19*, p. 375
Iuneo, nomen Faliscum, 327
Iunio, nomen aliquod Etr.-Praen. 297
Iuno, Iuno, nom. sg., Etr.-Praen. 290, 298, 299; Osc.-Lat. 153 A q.v.; dat. *iunonei*, Fal.-L. 335 *a*, *innone*, Umb.-L. xliii. 3, p. 433, 4 p. 434
iu[s]su, v. *eo-*, and p. 477

GLOSSARY TO THE DIALECTS. 629

iust, ierit, v. *etu*
iuve-, v. *Iou-*
iůvkiiůí, nomen, dat. sg. m., O. 95 *a 4*; commonly compared with a supposed Lat. nomen *Iouicius*
iůvila-, imago gentilis, subst. fem., v. p. 101 ff., nom. sg. *iuvilu*, O. 118 *a*, *b*, abbrev. *iůvil* 115; acc. sg. *iůvílam* 107, abbrev. *iuvil* 106; nom. pl. *iůvilas*, 108 *a*, *b* (ubi *iuvilas*), 109, 113, abbrev. *iůvil* 114. If the -*í*- of 107 be trusted the second syllable will be regarded as short; but the letter is doubtful, and the pair of inscc. as a whole is inconsistent on this point with *iůvil* in 106, and *sepíeís* beside *medikkiaí* (not -*dík*-) in 107. Hence Buck and others have regarded the -*i*- in -*vil*- as long. Its connexion with Jupiter in 108 and *Iůviaís* in 113 favours the derivation from *Iouizic*, v. *is*

k, v. sub *c*

l

1 √, tenth letter of the Osc. *aβ*, 87
l, nota praenominis Lucii (v. Osc. *Lůvkio*-). Osc. 3, 63 bis, 65, 69, 76, 77 A 2 bis, 86 bis, 115, 116, 173 *a*; Pg. 215, 224, 225, 232 bis, 233, 235, 239. Mruc. 244. Praen. 286 bis. Fal. 329, 331, Fal.-Lat. 335 *a*, 336 quater. Umb. 354
l = libertus (cf. Pg. *loufir*-): Pg. 230, 231, 232, 232 *bis*
l = libens, Mars. 261
La, nota praenominis, Fal. 321 bis, Etr.-Umb. 353 *d*; perhaps = *Lars* or *Lartio(s)*
labiku, O. 67
lacrima, 309 B, Rem. q.v.
Ladumeda, herois aliqua, Etr.-Praen. 301
Laí, nomen abbrev., O. 166, cf. *gens Laeuia*, Index III
lamatir, ueneat, pres. subj. pass. 3 sg., O. 28. *21 = lamatir*, 130 *a 4*. On the form v. p. 493, for the construction p. 507, and for the meaning p. 331

lapit?, 309 B, Rem. q.v.
Λαπονις, nomen, nom. sg. m., O. 13, commonly compared with *M. Lamponius* 27 C 1 *a*
larcio (or *arcio*?), Fal. nomen, 329
Larinei, Larini, loc. sg., O. 195 *a*, -*nom*, acc. sg. or gen. pl. 195 *b*, cf. Note xvi. p. 143 f.
larix, 309 B, Rem. q.v.
Lartio, Etr.-Fal. nomen, 345
λάταγες, O. 205, Rem. 9. *2*, p. 229 f. q.v.
latrio, nomen mutil. Fal. 313, nom. sg. m., fortasse *Flatrio*.
lauis, nomen aliquod Etr.-Praen. 301
lautia, 309 B, Rem. q.v.
Lebasius, Sab. 309 D q.v.
Lebro, Libero, dat. sg. (scil. dedicatum), Umb.-L. n. xliii. 5, p. 434, cf. Praen. *Leiber*
leces, leges, Etr.-Praen. v. *lēg-*
lectu, lectus, i.e. discretus in sepulcro mortui locus, nom. sg., Fal.-L. 336
lēg-, lex, subst. fem., Osc. *lig*-, abl. sg. *ligud*, 28. *24*, spelt *licud*, ib. *19*, abl. pl. *ligis*, ib. *25*. Mruc. *lixs*, nom. sg., 243. 2. Latinian: Praen. abl. pl. *leigibus* 286, Etr.-Praen. nom. pl. *leces* 301
legin-, legio, or perhaps cura, prouincia, imperium uel sim., Osc. subst. fem. dat. sg. *leginei*, O. 130 *a 4*, *11*, *12*, acc. *leginum*, ib. *3*; mutil. *legin* ib. *a 1*, *b 1*, where the case is not certain. The word is undoubtedly identical with L. *legio*; for the stem-gradation v. the paradigms, p. 475
le[gio]nibus, legionibus, abl. pl., Mars. 267
Leiber, Liber deus, Etr.-Praen. 298
λεικειτ, 3 sg. indic. act. (pres. or perf.?), O. 22
leígůss, subst. acc. pl. m., palos, ligna, tigna uel sim., O. 169
lepesta, Sab. 309 A q.v.
Leueli, nomen, perhaps gen. masc. Fal. 334, cf. *Leiueli* or *Leiuelio* in xxxix. *15*, p. 375
leuenna, xxiii. p. 226 q.v.
Leuieis, nomen, abl. pl. m., Fal.-L. 336, cf. *gens Liuia* Index III
leuir, 309 B, Rem. q.v.
lexe, Pg. 216. *7*, cf. p. 495 footn.
libs, i.e. *libē(n)s*, Mars. 264, on the spelling v. 272 n.
licitud = L. *liceto*, impv. impers. 3 sg., O. 28. *13*, *18* bis, *26*, *27 = líkítud*, 95 *b* 10
lifar, Pg. 216. *7*, probably acc. sg. n. (adj. or subst.?)

Līganakdíkeí, dat. sg. fem., a Samnite goddess, O. 175 *a 8, b 10*; no doubt the last part is identical with that of Osc. *med-dic-*, Lat. *iu-dic-* etc., and the first syllable must = either L. *lēg-* or *-līg-* in *relligio* etc.

līgatūís = L. *legatis*, subst. dat. pl. m., O. 95 *a 6, 7*, nom. pl. *līgat[ú]s* ib. *9*

līímítú.. = some case of L. *limes*, v. cr. not., O. 95 *b 3*

líís, uox Osc. mutila 169, cf. fortasse Pg. *elísu ist*

limu, famem, acc. sg. masc., O. 130 *a 8*

lingua, 309 B, Rem. q.v.

λιοκακειτ, si sic legendum et diuidendum, uerbum aliquod 3 sg. act. esse uideatur

lisuist, v. [*e*]*lisuist*

Liuia, nomen, nom. sg. f., Umb.-L. xliii. *9*, p. 434; v. *gens Liuia* Index III, and cf. Fal. *Leuio-*

líxs, *ligud* etc. v.s.v. *lēg-* sup.

līxulae, Sab. 309 A q.v.

locatin, probably 'locauerunt,' 3 pl. perf. ind. act., perhaps abbrev. Pg. 219

loferta, liberta, nom. sg. f., Fal. 324, cf. Pg. *loufir*

loidos, ludos, Fal.-L. 335 *b*

losna, luna, Etr.-Praen. 288

Λουκανομ, Lucanum, O. 23, on the case v. p. 143 f.

loucarid?, luco sacro, Osc.-L. iv. p. 31; cf. Lat. *lucaris* and the neut. subst. *lucar*, which has different meanings in sg. and pl. but in neither means 'lucus'

Loucetio-, epithet of Jupiter, O. 205 Aq.v.

louci, luci, cf. *lúvkeí*

Loucio- = L. *Lucio-*: nom. sg. f. *Loucia*, Pg. 212, 232 *bis*, masc. Pg. *Loucies* 211, 213, Osc. *Luvkis*, 131. *7*, spelt *Luvikis* ib. *5*, abbrev. *Lúvkí* 203, mutil. *Luv* 137 *b 3*; nom. pl. (as common adj.) *lucií*, Sab. 309 A. Gen. sg. m. *Luveies*, O.-Etr. 98. Used as nomen except in 131 (and probably 137) where it is a praenom. On its meaning v. 309 A

Loucilia, nomen, fem. Etr.-Praen. 297, cf. *gens Lucilia*, Index III

louff[r], uel (si uera lect.), O. 28. *8*; lit. '*libetur*,' pass. impers., see p. 492

loufir, liber-, Pg. 208 bis; probably abbreviated for some case of **loufirto-*(?) libertus (cf. Fal. *loferta*, Osc. *lúvfreís*) if we may assume the same change as in *amiricatud*, *stircus*, *commircium* etc., for which see p. 225

lr, Etr.-Fal. n. xxxix. *a* 10, p. 375; perhaps equiv. to *la* q.v.

lubent[es], libentes, Fal.-L. 335 *b*

lubs, i.e. *lubē(n)s* = L. *libens*, Mars. 266, Praen. 286, cf. *libs*, and the note to 272

lucii, Sab. 309 A q.v., and cf. *Loucio-* sup.

lumpa, 309 B, Rem. q.v.

Lúvkanateís, Lucanatis, ethnicon, gen. sg. fem.[1], see note ad loc. O. 193; for form cf. L. *Arpinas* etc.

luisarifs, adj. loc. pl. fem., epithet of *eiduis*, probably the name of an Oscan month, O. 101. The old Oscan ending *-fs* is a step nearer the orig. Italic *-bhos* than the later *-ss, -s*. The root of the word may conceivably be that of Slav. *lěcha* = I. Eu. **loisā-* (Brugm. *Gds.* I. § 588. 2) beside Lat. *lira*, Germ. *Ge-leise*, so that it would mean 'the ploughing-month'

Luqorcos, heros aliqui, Etr.-Praen. 294, commonly identified with Gr. Λυκοῦργος.

lúvfreís = Lat. liberi, gen. sg. m., epithet of Jupiter, O. 191; Lat. *libero-* = Italic *loufro-* = I. Eu. *leudhro-*, Gr. *ἐ-λεύθερος*

lúvkeí, in luco, loc. sg., O. 109 = *louci* gen. or loc., Umb.-L. xlii. p. 397

m

m ⋈, twelfth letter of the Osc. αβ, 81 *a*

m, abbrev. praenomen, O. 39 bis; Pg. 231. Latinian: Tusc. xxxiv. p. 323, Fal. 323, 332, 333 *a*

m. t., *meddíx tůvtíks*, O. 109, 171

m, lapidarii signum aliquod, O. 59 bis

m = *mereto*, Mars. 261

m', i.e. ⋏⋏ = Mania, Umb.-L. n. xliii. 9, p. 434

ma, abbrev. praenom. Osc. 50, 63, 64, perhaps 141; Vol. 252; perhaps Fal. 326 *b*, Umb.-Etr. 353 *a, b, c*. It need not necessarily represent the same praenomen in the different localities

Maak-, v. **Mak-**

maamieise, uox Etrusca aut corrupta O. 75

Maatúís, dat. pl. m., Samnite deities, O. 175 *a 10, b 12*; clearly akin in stem to L. *mater Matuta*, *Pales Matuta*, *maturus*

maatr-, v. *matr-*

Mací, praen. m. gen. sg., Fal. 325 *a*, probably = L. *Marci*, as in the same insc. we have *Acacelini* and *Acarcelinio* side by side

---

[1] *aapas* ib. is probably in the same case; hence its description on p. 596 should be corrected.

Makkiis, nomen, nom. sg. m., name of a magistrate at Naples, O. 145 *a*, *b*, and no doubt *Makkiis* was intended in *c*; cf. n. ad loc.

Macolnia, i.e. *Magolnia*, Praen. nomen, nom. sg. f. 304, cf. *gens Magulnia*, Index III

made?, mndet, si uera lect., Praen.-L. n. xxxiii. p. 322

maden[t? madent, si uera lect., Praen.-L., n. xxxiii. p. 322

Maesio-, *Pappus Maesius*, O. 205 A q.v.

Magio for *-ios*, nomen, nom. sg. m., Mars. 266, cf. *gens Magia*, Index III

magiste, magister, nom. sg. m., Umb.-L. 370 A; the loss of final *-r* is a mark of Umb. pronunciation, but the word is not wholly Umbrian, as else *-g-* would have been palatilised

mag[i]steratus, i.e. magistratus, Osc.-L. n. iv. p. 31

magistreis, old Latinian form of nom. pl. magistri, Fal. 335 *a*, Praen. *-tres* 282, *-tere[s]* 284

Mahiis, v. *Maiio-*

Magiium, nomen, gen. pl. m., O. 101, cf. *gens Magia*, Index III

Maiio-, Osc. nomen, nom. sg. m. spelt *mahiis* 179 and (probably) μαιιες 152; dat. *maiiui*, O. 95 *a 1, 3*, abbrev. gen. *mai* ib. *1, 4*; cf. *Mais* and p. 472, and deus *Maius*, Tusc. 306 A

maimas, maximae, adj. superl. gen. sg. f., O. 28 *3, 7*; cf. *mais* and p. 476, and note that Osc. and Umb. have carried the form *mah-* through both degrees of comparison while Lat. has done the same with *mag-*. It is clearly a case of the frequent I. Eu. variation of *-g* and *-gh* as the final sound of root-syllables

μαιφίην, 37 D q.v.

Mais, Maius, praen. nom. sg. m., O. 139 *Mais* 96; cf. the derivative *Maiiomais*, magis, Osc. adv. 28 *5, 15, 25*, cf. *maimas* sup.

malaks, adj. or subst. nom. pl., O. 130 *a 2*; in formation parallel to L. *mendac-* etc., and means acc. to Bugge 'maleuolos'; the meaning seems probable, but we have as yet no other acc. pl. from a consonantal stem in Osc.

maletu, molito, pinsito, U. 359 II *a 18*; contrast *kumaltu, kumultu*; there would seem to be two verbal stems, *mol(o)-* = L. *molere*, a simple thematic, and a deriv. of the same root, *male(i̯o)-*; *kumaltu* shows the two confused as L. *lauēre* and *lauāre*, *feruēre* and *feruēre*, *uertere* and *uortere*. The stem *malē-* presumably represents I. Eu. *ml̥-ē-*, cf. Gk. μύλη

mallo-, malus, Osc. adj., acc. sg. m. *mallom* 28. 5, 15, 22, abl. *mallud* ib. 20, *malud* ib. 11; perhaps for *mal-i̯o-* as O. *allo* = L. *alia*

malo, Old L. n. xxxv. p. 329, I believe for *malom*, nom. sg. n.

mam, O. 104, 123 = *Mamertiais*, v. inf.

mame, uncertain abbr., O.-Etr. 100; in O. 129 it is probably for *mamertiais*, v. inf.

Mamerco-, classical cognomen, cf. *Mamers* 205 A and the foll.; of this *mamurkes*, O.-Etr. xi. 7, p. 97 may be the gen. sg.

Μαμερεκιες, nomen, nom. sg. m., Osc. 7, cf. *gens Mamercia*, Index III, and *Mamerco-* sup.

Mamers, Mars, O. 205 A q.v. The word is clearly a reduplicated form of L. *Mars* (Umb. *Mart-*), and probably neither has any etymological connexion with L. *Mauors*

Mamertino-, name taken by the Campanian mercenaries who seized Rhegium, nom. sg. fem. μαμερτινο, O. 1, gen. pl. m. on their coins, etc., *-ρτινουμ* 2, 4 *a*, *-ετιν- 4 b*

mamerttio-, Martius, adj., name of a month [v. Addenda], loc. pl. fem. *mamerttiais*, O. 115, 116, mutil. *mamertt-* 113, *mamert* 124, abbrev. *mam* 123, *ma[m]* 104, probably 126

mamurkes, v. *Mamerco-*

manafum, mandaui uel sim., 1 sg. perf. ind. act., O. 130 *a 3*, and no doubt orig. *1*; the Osc. stem is *manā-*, and at present it is impossible to determine its exact relation to L. *mandā-*, to which it is generally counted at least akin

mandraclo, mantele manibus tergendis uel tegendis, subst. acc. sg. n., U. 365 VI *b 4* = *mantrahklu*, 359 II *a 19*, *mantraklu*, 360 II *b 16*. The word is clearly parallel to some extent with L. *mantellum*, which e.g. Plaut. (*Capt.* 519) uses to mean 'inuolucrum,' but I do not yet see my way to identifying the words. The use in the sacrifice to Fisus Sancius directed in VI *b 4* is generally compared with the types of some of the cast trientes of Tuder (368), in which a right hand held upright with fingers outstretched is swathed by bands which first surround the wrist, cross one another on the back of the hand, and then surround the base of the fingers. Büch. calls it *fidei insigne*, from this passage

mane, Lanuv. 308 A q.v.

manf, manus, acc. pl., U. 359 II *a 38*,

where the stem appears to vary from *manu-*, q.v. and cf. p. 474

mani, *manim*, v. *manu-*

Mavιος = L. *Manius*, Praen. 280, nom. sg. m., fem. *Mania*, Fal. 328 *b*, where it is a nomen, cf. *gens Mania*, Index III

manom, acc. sg., probably a proper name, Old L. n. xxxv., p. 330, cf. *Manius*, and 308 A

mantra-, v. *mandra-*

manu- = Lat. *manus*, U. loc. sg. (perhaps with postp.), *manuve*, 360 II *b* 23, abl. *mani*, 359 II *a* 32, *mani*, 365 VI *b* 24 (where from the foll. *nertru* it appears to be masc., and this is the only passage with any indication of its gender); the Osc. acc. sg. *manim* 28. 24 probably also belongs to this stem, cf. p. 474; Osc.-L. gen. pl. *manum*, iv. p. 31

Mar, abbrev. praen. (gen. sg. m.), Pg. 226

Maraiio-, Osc. nomen (derived from the praen. *Maraio-* q.v. inf., as that from *Marā-*, v. p. 471 f.), nom. sg. m. Osc.-L. *marales* 19, gen. sg. m. O. *maraiieís* 169 = *marahieís*, O.-Etr. xi. *13*, p. 98

Maraio-, Osc. praen., nom. sg. m. *marahis* 137 *c 6*, gen. sg. *maraheís* ib. *e 1*, abbrev. *marai* 94 and probably *marah* ib. *d 9*, mutil. *mara* ib. *d 6*, but ib. *b 6, 8, f 8* the case is not clear. μαραι quoted in the note to 8, p. 4 may belong either to this praen. or to the preceding nomen. *Maraio-* is of course derived from *Marā-*

Maras, Osc. praen. m. sg. (nom. or gen.?), 137 *c 8*, and the nom. ending *-as* in 1 should no doubt be restored Μαρας from the ms. copies. The common abbrev. *Mr.* probably represents this name

Markas, O. 82, fortasse meritricis nomen, gen. sg. fem. O. 82

Marcio-, nomen Faliscum, nom. sg. fem. *marcia* 330, nom. m. *marcio* 314, 325 *b*, gen. *marci* 324, spelt *maci* 325 *a*. Cf. *gens Marcia*, Index III

Marhio, nomen Faliscum, nom. sg. m., probably = L. *Marius*, 341, cf. O. *Maris*

Marica, Maricae, dat. sg. f., a goddess at Pisaurum, Umb.-L. n. xliii. 6, p. 434; the same name appears in Auruncan territory at the mouth of the Liris 256 A

Maris, praen. nom. sg. m., O. 137 *f 8*, cf. *gens Maria*, Index III

maron-, uir magistratu praeditus, Umb.-L. quoted in n. to 355; compare the cogn. *Maro*, and for its derivation from *mas-* 'masculine' cf. Sab. *Nero* 309 A, with the use of *ner-* as a title of honour (v. inf. s.v.)

maronato, magistratu; abl. sg., U. 354, loc. *maronateí* 355

Maroucai, Marrucinae, ethnicon, dat. or loc. sg. fem., Mruc. 243. *2, 5*

Mars, Umb. and Etr.-Praen. = L. *Mars*, Etr.-Praen. nom. sg. 298, dat. Umb. *Marte* (*Krapuvi*), 356 I *a 11* = *Marte Grabouei*, 365 VI *b 1*, *Marte* (*Huḍie*), 356 I *b 1* = *Marte Horse*, 365 VI *b 43*, *Ahtu Marti* (beside *Ahtu Iuvip*), II *a 11*

Marsi, v. 270 A and p. 289; for the form cf. *Martses*

Marsuas, Marsyas, Etr.-Praen. 291

Martio-, Martius, ad Martem pertinens, in Umb. always as epithet of *Šerfo-* (a masc. deity) except in 364 V *b*, where it is applied either to *Piquier* (q.v.) or (Büch.) to *agre*: voc. sg. m. *Martie*, 366 VII *a 3*, gen. *Marties*, 357 I *b 28, 31* = *Martier*, 364 V *b 9, 15*, 366 VI *b 58* bis, VII *a 6, 9, 10, 11, 13, 15, 16, 18, 19, 20, 21, 22, 23, 24, 25, 27, 29, 30, 32, 33* bis, *34, 35, 36, 41*, dat. *Martie*, 366 VI *b 57, 61*, spelt *Marti*, 357 I *b 24*; cf. *Mamers* sup. and the foll.

Martses, Marsis, abl. pl. f. 267; this spelling makes it hard to doubt the common deriv. of *Marsi* from *Martii*, assuming the same assibilation of *-ti-* in Marsian as in S. Osc. (*Bansa-* from *Bantia-*) parallel to Pg. *ꞇ* (a sound no doubt similar to French *j*) from *-di-* (*Musesa: Mussedia*, *Petieḍu* from *Pet-i*(*i*)*edio-*)

mascel = L. *masculus*, adj. nom. sg. m., 205 B 7 q.v.

mātr- = L. *mater*, Osc. gen. sg. *maatreís* 162 = U. *matrer* 354; Fal. nom. sg. *mate* 324; Umb.-L. dat. sg. *matre*, n. xliii. *8*, p. 434

matrona, matronae, nom. pl. Umb.-L. xliii. *4* and *8*, p. 434; commonly the *-na* is identified with L. *-nae* as *Maricae* ib. = *Maricae*, but on this insc. it may equally well stand for *-nas*.

M[a]tusia, epithet of Minerua, Umb.-L. 370 D; cf. O. *maatúís*, Umb.-L. *mater Matuta* etc.

Matuta, Matutae, dat. sg. fem., Umb.-L. xliii. *8*, p. 434; cf. the preceding artt.

maxomo = L. *maximus*, Fal. 327

Meania, nomen, nom. (or abl.?) sg. f., Fal. 328 *a*

μεδ, me acc. sg., Praen. 280, *med* 304,

Old L. xxxv. *1* bis, p. 329, but, I think, abl. in l. 3; cf. Gr. με, Skt. *mat, madiya*- etc. although of course in the αβ of 280 the ∃ may be equally short or long

meddikiaí, sub magistratu, O. 115, subst. loc. sg. fem. -*kiai* 116, *medikkiai* 107, -*ikia*[í] 106, and probably the *medikkia* 117 *b 3* and *medikk* 117 *a 8* represent the same case mutilated and abbreviated respectively. So *m* in 109. *7*

meddix, in ciuitatibus Oscis summus magistratus, in Latinised form 205 A q.v., and for the office cf. p. 51; Osc. nom. sg. *meddíss* 87, 163 = *meddis* 94, *meddis* 113, *meddis*, O. 28. *8, 12, 18, 26,* abbrev. *med*, O. 44, 45, 47, probably also 119; *medd* 114, *metd* 174 (v. ad loc.), gen. sg. *medíkeís* 39, dat. sg. *medíkeí* 95 *a 5*; *medik* 117 *b 9* probably is some case of this word, but possibly of the preceding, nom. pl. μεδδειξ 1, *meddíss* 98; Pg. *medix* 219. Vo. nom. sg. *medis* 253, nom. pl. *medix* 252. From *med*- (Lat. *medēri, medicus*) = U. *med*- mos, ius, and -*dic*-, dicere as in L. *iudic*- etc.

meddixud, v. *medicim*

medicatinom, iudicium, iudicationem, acc. sg. fem., O. 28. *16*, cf. p. 508 footn.

medicatud, magistratu, subst. abl. sg., O. 28. *24*, where from the context it is clear that *pru m.* is not equiv. to *pru meddixud* of l. 14 (= magistratus munere fungens), but, probably, 'apud magistratus, apud praetorem praefectumue'

medík-, v. *meddix*

medicim (i.e. *medd*-) iudicium uel sim., subst. n. nom. or acc., O. 28. *30, 31, 33.* If -*ci*- in S. Osc. was palatalised (cf. -*s*- from *tí*- in *Bansa*-), the abl. *meddixud* ib. *13, 21* will come from this word. Else we should have to suppose a stem **meddictio-*

medidies, Praen.-L. 305 A q.v.

medix, v. *meddix*

meds, ius, fas, mos, subst. neut. nom. sg., U. 357 I *b 18* bis = *mers* in *mersest*, ius est, 365 VI *b 31*, 366 VI *b 55* bis, and *mersei* (-*si*), ius sit, 365 VI *a 28, 38, 48*; cf. Osc. *med-dix* sup. The same word is really contained in L. *modes-tus* altered from **medes-to-* (= U. *mersto*-) by the influence of *modus*, which contains the -*o*- form of the root

meelíkiieís, μειλιχίου, O. 39 adj. gen. sg. m., epithet of Jupiter, clearly derived from the Greek title

meersta, v. *mersto*-

mefa = L. *mensam*, i.e. libam sacram, subst. acc. sg. fem., U. 356 I *a 16*, 361 IV *14*, *mefa* 365 VI *a 56*, VI *b 17, 20*, 366 VII *a 4, 38*, abl. *mefa* 360 II *b 13*, *mefa* 365 VI *b 5, 9* bis, *14*, 366 VII *a 37*; dat. *mefe*, 360 II *b 28*; the word is based on the partc. stem = L. *menso*-, 'measured,' meaning 'the thing made in a fixed shape.' Proethnic -*n-tt*- regularly becomes -*f*- in Umb., cf. *spefa, spafu*; and also *trahuorfi* (-*r-tt*-)

mefio-, Osc. = L. *medio*-, Gr. μέσο-; nom. sg. fem. *mefí*[ú] 95 *b 4*, loc. (or dat.?) *mefiaí* ib. *31*

mefitaiiaís?, O. 75

mehe = L. *mihi*, U. 365 VI *a 5*, cp. p. 477

Melerpanta, Bellerophon, Etr.-Praen. 293

melica, 309 B, Rem. q.v.

meliissaii..., O. 74, v. n. ad loc.

memnim, memoriam, monumentum, uel sim., acc. sg. neut., O. 131. 9, cf. p. 471

Menerua, Minerua, nom. sg. f., Etr.-Praen. 298, dat. sg. *menerua*, Fal. 321. *1*, but *uineruai*, Fal.-L. 335 *a*; cf. *minerua*, Pg. 209 where the case is doubtful, and *Minerua* s.v. *Feronia* 309 A. On the formation v. s.v. *mersus*

menes, uenies (or ueniet), uel sim. 2 or 3 sg. fut. ind., U. 357 I *b 15*; the meaning is clear, but not the root; some have wished to correct to *benes*

menvum, minuere, inf. act. depending on *putiiad*, O. 130 *a 8*; if the word comes from *minus* the -*e*- needs explanation

menzne, mense, subst. loc. sg., U. 359 II *a 17* (on the case v. p. 501 footn.) = N. Osc. *mesene* 248; the orig. Italic stem is *mens*-, as in L. gen. pl. *mensum*, *sē-me*(n)*s-tris*, Gr. Dor. μείς for **μενς; this became in Umb. *menz*-, i.e. *ments*- by the regular Osc.-Umb. change of orig. -*ns*- (not orig. -*n-tt*- which became -*f*-) to -*nts*- as in *uze*, i.e. *ontse*, Ital. **om*(*e*)*sei* in umero, Osc. *keenztur*, etc. From this stem was formed U. *antermenzo*-, but instead of the simple noun we have the stem extended by the suffix -*en*- : -*n*- in certain dialects, a secondary use common in many languages, v. Brugm. *Gds.* II. § 114

Mercuris = L. *Mercurius*, Etr.-Praen. 298, *Mircurios* ib. 299, *Mirq*- 292, cf. Osc.-L. *Mircurius*, u. xxii.

mereto, merito, adv. Mars.-L. 266, 268, abbrev. *meri* 264 and Praen. *merto* 286

meri, v. *mereto*

mersto-, i.e. *med(e)sto-*, iustus, sollennis, prosperus, of omens : masc. acc. sg. *mersto*, U. 365 VI *a 3, 4, 16*, abl. *merstu* (on concord cf. p. 503), 365 VI *a 1*; fem. acc. sg. *mersta*, 365 VI *a 3, 4, 16*, spelt *meersta* ib. *17*; acc. pl. *merstaf*, 365 VI *a 4*, spelt *mersta*, ib. *3* bis, *4, 18* bis; cf. *meds*

mersuvo-, iustus, Umb. adj. masc. nom. sg. *mersus*, 361 III *6* (for *-uos* as Osc. *sipus* for **sēpuos*, *facus* for **facuos*), fem. abl. sg. *mersuva*, 361 III *11*, acc. pl. probably neut., ib. *28*. Brugmann's explanation of the form *pude* as equiv. to any case (p. 479) makes the endings of these forms intelligible, but the stem is not so clear. Bücheler would cut the knot by assuming that *-rs-* here in Umb. *aβ* is put for -*ds*-, but I think it more likely that the *-uo-* suffix is added to the stem of *med(e)s-*, and that *-rs-* is put for *-ds-*. L. *Minerua*=**menes-nā-* (cf. Gr. μένος, -μενής) offers a precisely parallel formation, indeed the orig. meaning of the two must have been so parallel that it is quite conceivable that the one was formed on the pattern of the other in proethmic Italic

merto, v. *mereto*

messimais, adj. superl. loc. pl. fem., either 'maximis' or 'maxime mediis,' O. 113; the Bantine superl. *maimo-* (28) favours but does not, I think, necessarily establish the latter view

mestru, maior, adj. compar. nom. sg. fem., U. 363 V *a 24, 27*, V *b 4*; v. p. 476, and for suffix cf. Gr. -ιστερο-, L. *magister*, with which the Umb. stem is identical save for the form of the root (Osc.-U. *mah-* : L. *mag-*, v. *maimo-, mais* sup.) if we assume that the Umb. *ē* here is based on *-ahi-*. But it would be just possible to compare Osc. *messimo-* if that were analysed **meg-symo*

Metilio, nomen mutilum, Praen. 284, cf. *gens Metilia*, Index III

Metlis, nomen, nom. sg. m., O. 181, cf. *gens Metiia*, Index III

Metio, Etr.-Praen. 297, uox dubia; si uera lect., cf. uoc. praeced.

Mh, abbrev. praenomen, O. 174, 181, cf. probably *Mahio-*, *Mais*

Mi, abbrev. Osc. praenomen, 107, 109 bis, 204 bis, n. iii. p. 15; for *Minaz* or *Minis* or some other ?

micos, puer aliqui (? Gr. Dor. μικκός), Etr.-Praen. 299

miletinar, subst. gen. sg. fem., commonly regarded as a proper name, U. 365 VI *a 13*

militare, abl. sg. fem., Tusc.-L. xxxiv. p. 323

Min, abbrev. praen., O. 20, Pg. 230; cf. *mi* sup.

Minato-, praen. Osc., masc. nom. sg., *Minaz*, 137 *b 7*, gen. *minateis* 108 *a, b*, abbrev. *mina* 112

Minio-, Osc. praen., m. nom. sg., *minis*, O.-Etr. 97, gen. *minieis*, O. 108 *b* = *minnieis*, ib. *a* and *miinieis*, 134; spelt *minies*, and abbrev. *min* ib. *b*

minive, possibly a corruption due to the engraver or to the friable stone for *ñinive*, i.e. *ñiniveresim* (114); in any case the form is probably an abbreviation, O. 117 *b 9*

min[s], adv.=L. *minus* (or **minis*?), O. 28. *10*, where it practically means 'non,' cf. the Syntax, §§ 25 and 64

minstreis, minoris, adj. compar. gen. sg. masc., O. 28. *12, 27*, spelt *mistreis* ib. *18*; of course=L. *ministro-*, cf. p. 476 and U. *mestru*

mire? Praen.-L. n. xxxiii., p. 322 q.v.

μίρον, 37 D q.v.

misc? for *miscē*, Praen.-L. n. xxxiii., p. 322

mitat=*mittant* rather than *mittat*, since on the same insc. *sied*=*sit* shows the regular Old L. *-d* in the 3 sg. of secondary and subjunctive tenses, Old L. n. xxxv., p. 330

Mitl, cognomen, nom. sg. m., perhaps complete, O. 181

Modies, nomen, nom. sg. m., Vest.-Lat. n. xxix., p. 261; cf. *gens Modia*, Index III

μοῖτον, O. 37 A q.v.

moltā-, *multā-*, subst. fem., Osc. and Sab.=Lat. *multa* (cf. 186 A), Umb. *motā-*, q.v. Osc. nom. sg. *molto*, O. 28. *11, 26*, acc. sg. *-tam* ib. *2*, acc. pl. *-tas* ib. *13, 27*. Sab. v. 309 A

moltaum, multare, verb inf. act. (with cognate acc.), O. 28. *12, 13, 18, 26, 27*; from the preceding

motā-, Umb. subst. fem.=Lat. *multa*, gen. sg. *motur*, 367 VII *b 4* (on case cf. p. 499); nom. sg. *mutu*, 363 V *b 6*, acc. *muta* ib. 3, abl. *muta* ib. *1* (v. Syntax, § 25); cf. Osc. *moltā-*

Mr, nota praenominis, O. 42, 43 bis, 54 bis, 56, 60, 61, 63, 67, 77. *26*, 203, no doubt=*Maras* or its genitive

mufrius, 205 C 1 q.v.

mugatu, muttito, sonum facito uel sim. impv. 8 sg. act., U. 365 VI *a 6*; the neut. p. parte. pass. corresponding is *mueto* ib. 7; cf. L. *mugire* with variations like *sonāre* : *sonitum*, *densāre* : *densēre*; and on -*i*- : -*g*- v. pp. 401 footn., 403, 495

múíníkú-, communis Osc. adj.: neut. sg. nom. *múíník[úm]*, 95 *a 18*, loc. -*keí* ib. *19*; fem. nom. sg. *múíníkú* ib. *22*, abbrev. *múíník* 115, *múiník* 116, acc. *muinikam*, 101, abl. *múíníkad* 95 *b 24*, and orig. 95 *a 15*. Derived from the same stem as L. *com-muni-s*, *moenia*, *munia* etc.

mulcifer, 205 C 1 q.v.

multasiko-, multaticius, ex multis constans, Osc. epithet of *eituā*- etc.; abl. neut. sg. *multas[íkud]* 94, fem. *múltasíkad* 43

Mulukiís, nomen, nom. sg. m., O. 94

Mumm..., nomen mutilum, O. 86, cf. *gens Mummia*, Index III

muneklu=L. *municulum in the sense of *munusculum* 'fee,' subst. acc. sg. m., U. 363 V *a 17, 19, 21*

Museiate, dat. pl. m., name of a gens or tribe, U. 360 II *b 5* bis

Musesa, nomen, nom. sg. fem.=L. *gens Mussidia*, *Musetia*, Pg. 206, ubi v. n.

muta, *mutu*, v. *motā*-

Mutíl=Μότυλος, cognomen, O. 200, 201 *a* (nom. sg. m.) of C. Paapius, the 'consul' of the allies in 90 B.C., the Greek form being given e.g. by Diod. Sic. l.c. ad loc.

Muttillieís Osc., nomen, gen. sg. m., 137 *f 9*; derived from the prec.

Mz, nota praenominis, O. 48 (ubi v. n.), 176

n

n Н, thirteenth letter of the Osc. αβ, 81

n, nota praenominis: Osc. αβ (Osc.) 39, Lat. αβ (Osc.) 19 bis, 77 7 bis, Pg. 210, 223; at Pompeii we have also the abbrev. *ni* commonly taken for *Niumsis*=L. *Numerius*, so that there it would seem *prima facie* that *n* stood for some other name, perhaps=L. *Nouius* (=*nv* 171); but the Lat. use of N=*Numerius* may have begun to influence the Osc. fashion.

n, abbrev. equiv. of nummos, nummis, O. (Lat. αβ) 28. *12, 26*, Osc.-L. iv p. 31, perhaps 66 (Osc. αβ), U. (Lat. αβ) 354

n, nota dubia (Osc. αβ), O. 64

Naharko- Nartius, ethnicon of some tribe hostile to Iguvium (v. p. 395 footn.): neut. acc. sg. *Naharkum*, U. 357 I *b* 17; =*Naharcom*, 366 VI *b* 58, VII *a 47*; gen. *Naharcer*, 366 VI *b 54, 59*, VII *a 12, 48*; dat. *Naharce*, ib. *12*

nanfurae? 205 C. *1* q.v.

nar, Sab. 309, D. q.v.

naraklum, narratio, pronuntiatio (haruspicum?), subst. neut. subject (or object?) to *vurtus* q.v., U. 358 II *a 1*

naratu=L. *narrato*, pronuntiato uel sim., U. 358 II *a 3*, 360 II *b 8, 9, 11, 25*, 361 III *27*; *naratu* 365 VI *a 22, 56, 59*, VI *b 2, 20, 23, 44, 46*, VII *a 5, 7, 38, 42, 53*

νάρω, νάρειν, 37 C q.v.

Naseni, abbrev. nomen, O. 112; probly. for the gen. sg., cf. *gens Nasennia* Index III, and L. (Paelig.?) *Nasōnuatine*=L. *natione*, gente uel sim. abl. sg. fem., U. 359 II *a 21, 35*, 360 II *b 26*; for the inflection v. p. 475

nationu, subst. gen. sg. (or pl.?), Praen. 281 ubi v. n.

ne, in *ne phim* O. 28. *25*; commonly rendered 'nē quem.' But (1) in none of the 12 other sentences in the Tabula beginning with *suaepis* is the indef. pronoun used in the apodosis referring to the person defined by the *suaepis*-clause, the pronoun used, if any, being *izic* (7, *14*, etc.); (2) we have no other example of Osc. *ne*=L. *nē* in meaning, but only *nep* and *ni* (v. p. 482), nor would it help us to suppose *ne* here written for *nei* as *ceus* for *ceius since Osc. *nei*=L. *non* in meaning; (3) I distrust an explanation of the -*h*- which I once offered, and, so far as I know, no other has been since put forward. Hence I am inclined to suggest the reading *nep him* 'nē hunc' (supposing *him* to be acc. masc. corresponding to the neut. *ek-(h)ík* p. 478) as offering fewer difficulties.

ne in *ne pon*, Osc. 28. *14*; v. s.v. *arnipo* sup.

ne, nē, Fal.-L, 336, Old Lat. xxxv. p. 320

nebrundines, νεφροί, Latinian (Lanuv.), 308 q.v. with 305

nefrones, νεφροί, Praen. 305 A q.v. and cf. the foll.

nefrundines, 205 B 1 q.v. and cf. the preced.
nei, non, Osc. adv. 28. *20, 28* bis; v. p. 482
nei, Old L., xxxv. *1*, p. 329 = *nē* in meaning; but in view of *einom* = Umb. *ĭnom*, and *nē* = *nē* in l. 3 it is difficult to be sure which of the forms of the negative (cf. p. 482) it represents.
neiḍhabas, Umb. 361 IV *33*; for *nei* 'nē' (v. p. 482, and cf. *neip*) and *aḍhabas*, for which v. Umb. *ha b ē-* sup.
nei-p, neque, Osc. 28. *15*; non (old Lat. *neque*), 130 *a 4, 5, 6*; Umb. *neip* non 358 II *a 4*, 363 V *a 29*, *neip* 365 VI *a 27, 36, 46*, VI *b 29*, 367 VII *b 3*; meaning 'nŏue' 366 VI *b 51* (cf. *neiḍhabas*); *neip...nep* = neque...neque, 365 VI *a 6*. On the form v. p. 482
n[ene]rnum (si uera coniect. Buggii), O. 130 *a 6*; either adj. nom. sg. neut. 'aliquid uirilitatis expers,' or acc. sg. neut. adverbially 'sine uirilitate'; from *ner-* q.v.
νεο[πο]λ, Νεοπολιτῶν uel sim. 145 *a* q.v.
nep, Osc. nŏue, 28. *10, 28*; *nep* 95 *b 19, 20*; 131. *6* bis, *8* bis, *9* bis; v. p. 482
nep, Umb., v. *neip*
nepitu, impv. act. 2 sg., U. 366 VI *b 60*; VII *a 49*; the word denotes some penalty invoked on the enemies of Iguvium and is coupled with *ninctu* 'ninguito'; hence Büch. reasonably compares L. *Neptunus*, so that we should render 'imbribus (uel fluuiis?) mergito,' uel sim.
nequs, i.e. nequis, Umb.-Lat. n. xlii p. 397
ner- = Gr. (ἀ-)νέρ-, uir; used as a title of rank; Osc. gen. pl. *nerum* 28. *29* (cf. 31), 108 *a, b*; in 67 we have the abbrev. *IIIIner* = L. *IIIIuir*—the collective term for the highest offices in Italian municipalities v. p. 55; Umb. *ner* 355. *3* as praenomen of the '*ohtor*,' 5 as that of the father of the '*maro*' may stand for *Nero* or *Nerius*, but the acc. pl. *nerf* 365 VI *a 30, 32, 39, 42, 49, 52*, VI *b 13, 32, 34*, 366 VI *b 59*, VII *a 17, 30, 48*, and the dat. pl. *nerus* 366 VI *b 62*, VII *a 13, 14, 28, 50* clearly mean much the same as the Osc. word. Cf. the foll. derivv.

Neria-
nerica-
nerien- } Sab. 309 A, q.v.
nerioso-
neron-

nersa, donec, U. 365 VI *a 6*; I have no doubt that this stands for *ne-ḍā* or *neḍa(m)* in which *ne-* = Osc. *nc* in *ne pon* and Umb. *-ni-* in *arnipo* (q.v.), while the second half is a parallel particle to *dum, dō-*, L. *dō-ne-que*
nertru, sinistro, adj. abl. sg. m., U. 365 VI *b 25*; with postp. *nertruku* 356 I *31, 43*; = *nertruco* 365 VI *b 37, 39*; the word is clearly equal in form to Gr. νέρτερος
nesei, nisi, Umb.-Lat. xlii p. 397; this archaic spelling happens to represent what is, of course, the origin of the first syllable of *nīsi*, i.e. the negative *nĕ* (not *nei*); the change of *nĕ-* to *ni-* is no doubt due to the fact that *nisi* was a proclitic in actual pronunciation, cf. *igitur* from *agitur*, *simul* unemphatic beside *semel* emphatic etc.
nes(s)imo-, proximus, adj. superl., Osc. acc. sg. *nesimum* 28. *17, 31*; abl. pl. *nesimois* ib. *25*; nom. pl. fem. *nessimas* Umb. adv. *nesimei* 365 VI *a 9* bis with abl. cf. L. *proximus ab*. Brugmann would derive from *nedh-* (νήθω, Skt. *nadh-*, Eng. *needle*), quoting with approval Osthoff's conjecture that the stem of L. *nectere* was altered from *net-to-* in proethnic Italic by the influence of *plecto* (*Ber. k. Sächs. Ges. Wiss.* 1890, p. 236)
ni = L. *nē*, particle of prohibition (for its constructions v. p. 507 f.); Osc. 28. *8, 14, 17, 29, 33*; Mruc. 243. *11, 12*; v. p. 482
Ni, nota Osci praenom., 41, 47, 72 bis(?), 77. *1, 17*, ix *c* p. 81 (?), 203
ni, O. 120, uox mutila, fortasse gentilicii nominis pars, 110
ninctu = L. *ninguito*, 2 sg. impv., but with transit. force 'niue oppleto,' U. 366 VI *b 60*, VII *a 49*; what is the reason for the variation here as compared with *umtu* beside L. *unguito*?
Ninium, nomen gen. pl. masc., O. 123, cf. *gens Ninnia* Index III, and for the construction v. pp. 101 f.
nip, nŏue, O. 130 *a 7* bis, *8* bis; v. *ni*, and p. 482
nipis, i.e. *ni pis* (qq.v.), nēquis, Mruc. 243. *11*
niquis, nēquis Mars.-L. 273
niru, subst. acc. sg. (or pl.?), U. 360 II *b 15*, 'herbam frumentumue quod pinseretur,' Büch. Some compare Gr. νήριον 'oleander'
nistrus, adj. nom. pl. masc., O. 130 *a 2*; perhaps 'nostros' (Büch. 'propiores'); if the former (so Bugge) then *nis-* is for *nēs-* whose vowel would show the quantity of *nōs(-tro-)* though adapted in quality to *nes-tro-*. On Büch.'s view, its relation to the *e* of Osc. *nessimo* is hard to explain
Niumeriis, nomen nom. sg. m., O. 165;

cf. *gens Numeria* Ind. III.; the pure Osc. praenomen which follows shows that this particular family came from some rhotacising dialect

[N]**ium[s]is**, Osc. praenomen nom. sg. m. 93, gen. *niumsieís* ib.; spelt νι-υμσδιης 1 (what was the sound of -σδ-?); cf. *gens Numisia* (where -*mīs*- is from -*mēs*- as *attineo* from -*teneo* etc.) Ind. III. and Νυμψίου in the Osco-Greek insc. quoted on p. 84. L. *numerus* vouches for a stem **nomeso-* (later **numeso-* as L. *humo*: Gr. χθομ- in χθών), but Sicilian νούμμος, whence L. *nummus*, whence U. *numo-*, attests equally the stem **nomso *numso-*; if we possessed the Osc. word corresponding to L. *umerus* Umb. *uze*, i.e. **ontse* 'in umero,' we should know to which Italic stem to refer the Osc. equiv. of L. *numerus*

No, nota praenominis, in Lat. αβ, perhaps = L. *Nouii*, Pg. 221; cf. *No Comni No* quoted in the note to 21, and *Nv* inf.

noisi, Old L., n. xxxv p. 329; I believe with Jordan that the first part of this word is the same as that of U. *nosue* 'nisi,' both containing a form **noi* non, which stands in an ablaut relation to *nei*, q.v.

nome = L. *nomen*, natio, populus uel sim., U. acc. sg. n. 365 VI *a* 30, *32, 39, 42, 49, 52*, VI *b 13, 32, 34*, 366 VI *b 58*, VII *a 17, 30, 47*; spelt *nu-mem* 357 I *b 17* bis, gen. *nomner* 365 VI *b 54, 59*, VII *a 12, 48*; dat. *nomne* 365 VI *a 24* bis, *31* bis, *33* bis, *40* bis, *43* bis, *50* bis, *53* bis, VI *b 7, 8, 12* bis, *14* bis, *27* bis, *33* bis, *35* bis, 366 VI *b, 62* bis, VII *a 12, 13, 14* bis, *18* bis, *28* bis, *31* bis, *51* bis; abl. *nomne* 365 VI *a 17*; with postp. *nomneper* pro nomine 365 VI *a 23* bis, *25, 26, 34* bis, *35* bis, *44* bis, *45* bis, *54* bis, *55* bis, VI *b 7* bis, *10* bis, *15* bis, *26* bis, *28* bis, *35, 36*, 366 VII *a 10, 11, 19* bis, *22* bis, *26* bis, *32, 33, 35* bis

noniar, subst. or adj. gen. sg. fem., used as subst., perhaps a proper name, U. 365 VI *a 14*

nosue, nisi, U. 366 VI *b 54*, probably for **noi-suae*; cf. Old L. *noisi* sup.

nouesede, Mars. 261, Umb.-Lat. xliii. *10* p. 434, both either dat. sg., or, perhaps more probably, abbrev. for the dat. pl. cf. L. *Di Nouensides* and the foll.

nouensiles, Sab. 309 A, q.v.

Nouios, praen. nom. sg. m., Old Lat., 304

Nounis = L. *Nonius*, nomen, nom. sg. m., Pg. 239

Nv, nota praenominis in Osc. αβ, O. 171, perhaps = L. *Nouius*; cf. *No.* sup.

nudpener, U. 362 V *a 13*; Büch. plausibly regards this as an abl. pl. agreeing with the following *preuer (pusti kastruvuf)* 'singulis (secundum fundos),' but his explanation of the form as = Lat. **nullipondiis* ('nummis minimis') needs further defence on phonetic grounds. Brugmann would analyse *et nudpener* as *et nu ad-pener* 'et quidom (ad)pendebitur' (*Ber. k. S. Ges. Wiss.* 1890, p. 217) and would compare this rather meaningless use of **nŭ* (?) with Gr. καί νυ and the Skt. and O. Ir. *nu*

[**nu]h[ti]r[n]as**, nocturnae, Osc. adj. fem., si uera coniectura Buggii 130 *a 12* ***nuersens**, *43, p. 531

Νυμασιοι, Numasio, dat. sg. m., Praen. 280. At the date of this insc. it is indifferent whether this be called a nomen or praenomen; the *a* shows that it is a distinct formation from *Numerius*, but no doubt from the same root, cf. *Numa Pompilius*

numer, nummis, subst. abl. pl., U. 363 V *a 17, 19, 21*

Numeri, Praen. 281, either abbrev. for *Numeria* or gen. sg. masc. = Numerii filia; cf. Osc. *Niumeriis, Niumsis* sup.

nurpier, Umb. subst. gen. sg., perhaps a proper name, 365 VI *a 12*; cf. p. 408

nutr, probably abbrev. for *nutrix*, Pg.- L. 228; for so contrast the ending of *saca-racirix* in 216 which is pure Paelignian

Nŭv, abbrev. nomen, O. n. viii *a* p. 78

Nŭvellum, acc. sg. or gen. pl. m. of some proper name, O. 131. 7; is it the simple -*o*-stem from which the *gens Nouellia* formed its name? Or is it miswritten for -*elium*? Or should we assume the phonetic change which appears in S. Oscan *allo* = L. *alia*?

Nuvkirinum, O. 144 *a*; *nuvkrinum*, ib. *b*; *nuvirkum*, ib. *c, d*; all different forms of the Osc. ethnicon of Nuceria. On the case v. p. 144

nuvim-e, in nonum, usque ad nonum, nouics, U. 359 (II *a 26*); acc. sg. n. of ordinal stem *nov-io-* (cf. p. 470 ff.) with postp. -*e(n)*

nuvis, nouics, U. 359 II *a 25*; but as the sounds which appear in Lat. as -*ns* are regularly represented by Umb. -*f*, the two forms should not be directly identified; cf. Osc. *pomtis*

Nŭvlano- = L. *Nolanus*, Osc. ethnicon of Nola; nom. pl. masc. *núvlanús*, 95 *b 12, 21*, probably *a 23*; gen.

-*nŭm* ib. *14*; dat. -*nŭis a 7*; dat. sg. *nuvl*[*anŭí*] *a 5*; doubtful *nuvlan*- ib. *25*; fem. acc. sg. *nŭvlanam b 29*. The Osc. form shows the etymon 'New-town' more clearly than the Latin

O

ŏ is represented in the full Osc. αβ by V, transcribed *ŭ* in this book; as in the older Osc. and in Umb. αβ it is written simply *u*, the symbol *u* has been treated as *u* in the arrangement of the Glossary

Ob, nota praenom. uirilis, Pg. 213, 225
Obelies, nomen nom. sg. m., Pg. 221; fem. abbrev. *obel* 222; cf. *gens Obellia* Ind. III.
Obsci, *Opici*, *Osci*, v 153 A
ocri-, mons, arx, Mruc. gen. sg. *ocres*, 243. *6*; Umb. sg. nom. (the gender is masc.); *ocar* 365 VI *b 46*, =*ukar* 356 I *b 7*; gen. *ocrer* 365 VI *a 8, 19* bis, *29, 32, 39, 41, 49, 51*, VI *b 10, 13, 32, 33*, 366 VI *b 48*; dat. *ocre* 365 VI *a 23, 30, 33, 40, 42, 50, 52*, VI *b 7, 10, 11, 14, 26, 32, 34*; =*ukre* 363 V *a 16*; acc. *ocrem* 365 VI *a 49, 51*, VI *b 12*; *ocre* 365 VI *a 29, 31, 39, 41*, VI *b 31, 33*; loc. *ocrem* in arce with postp. VI *a 46*, alone *ocre* VI *a 26, 36*, VI *b 29*; abl. with postp. *ocriper* pro arce 365 VI *a 23, 43, 45, 53, 55, 58*, VI *b 1, 6* bis, *9, 14, 19, 22, 26, 28, 35, ocreper* 365 VI *a 25, 34, 35*; =*ukriper* 356 I *a 5, 8, 15, 17, 21, 25, 28, 31*; *ukripe* 356 I *a 12*. The word no doubt stands in an ablaut-relation to L. *acri*-; cf. Ocrem montem confragosum Fest. 181 M q.v.
Ocrisiua, M. 370 C q.v.
ὀδάχα, 37 D, q.v.
Ofentina, U. 370 A, q.v.
Ofturies, Paelig. nomen nom. sg. m., 231
oht, U. 355, abbrev. for *ohtretie* auctoritate, the name of a magistracy at Asisium and among the Fratres Atiedii, subst. loc. sg. m., spelt *uhtretic* 362 V *a 2*, 363 V *a 15*; from *ohtur*-, spelt *uhtur*, q.v.; the L. form would be *auctr-itia* or -*ities*; cf. U. *kvestretie*
Oilios, i.e. Οἰλιάδης, Etr.-Praen. 301, q.v.
Oinumama, i.e. unimamma, name of an Amazon Etr.-Praen. 300; cf. Verg. *Aen.* 1. 492 etc.

Oinomauos, heros aliqui, Etr.-Praen. 293
oisa, partc. abl. sg. fem., Pg. (or Pg.- Lat.) 218, commonly regarded as =L. *usā* in pass. sense 'consumpta, exacta'
olere, *oletum*, *olfacere*, 309 B Rom. q.v.
olna, Etr.-Fal., xl. *16*, p. 375
omnitu, probably adj. or partc. nom. sg. fem. or gen. pl. m. Pg. 216
onse, in umero loc. sg. m. U. 366 VI *b 50*; =*uze* 360 II *b 27, 28*, i.e. *ontse*, -*t*- being inserted between -*n*- and orig. -*s*- in Umb. and Osc. (*kenzur*=I*u*. censor), v. s.v. Osc. *Niumsis* sup. Is this word based on Italic *omso- = Gr. ὦμος, or on *omeso-=L. *umerus*?
ooserclom-e, subst. acc. sg. with postp. U. 365 VI *a 12*; Büch. very reasonably derives from *au(i)ser-clom*, i.e. auium obseruaculum; cf. U. *scritu* 'obseruato'
op, apud, prepn. with abl., O 28. *14, 23*, and no doubt *33*; =*ŭp* 95 *a 13*; cf. Gr. ἐπί, Skt. *api*, and L. *ob*, which seems to stand in the same relation to O. *op* as L. *sub* to Gr. ὑπό, L. *ad* to O. *az*, i.e. *at-s* with L. *at-auos*; the form *op* is probably to be seen in *operio* (cf. *herē*- sup.), *oportet* (cf. perhaps *hort-ari*)
ope, opi, ope, or opem? Old L., n. xxxv. p. 330
opertis (or *pertis*?), nomen aliquod, Etr.-Fal. n. xl *15*, p. 375
opeter delecti, optimi, partc. or adj. gen. sg. neut., U. 364 V *b 9*; clearly containing the root of L. *op-t-āre*, *op-(i)-tumus*, O. *ufteis*. Cf. perhaps also U. *upetu* inf.
Opici, 153 A, q.v.
opid ope, Fal.-Lat. 335 *b*
Ὄπιες=L. *Oppius*, Osc. nomen nom. sg. m. 13=*Ŭppiis* 131 *4*; v. *gens Oppia* in Index III
opiparum, opulentiam pariens, adj. probably sg. neut., Fal. L. 335 *b* (conceivably gen. pl. m.)
Ὄψι, abbrev. nomen, iii. p. 15; cf. *gens Opsia* and *gens Opsidia* in Index III
optantis, i.e. optantes, Fal.-L. 335 *b*
Orceuia, nomen, nom. sg. fem. Praen. 281, *Or[ceui- 282
Orestes, Etr.-Praen. 302
oriunna, xxiii, p. 226, q.v.
oro-, ille, Umb. pronoun, perhaps gen. sg. *orer* in *over ose* 365 VI *a 26, 36, 46*, VI *b 29*; probably abl. sg. *uru* 357 I *b 18*,=*uru* 366 VI *b 55*; abl. fem. with postp. *uraku* 362 V *a 5*; dat. (or abl.) pl. neut. *ures* 361 IV *33*
ὀρούα, O. 37 A, q.v.

GLOSSARY TO THE DIALECTS. 639

Ορτιηις, nomen, gen. sg. m., O. 10*bis*;
cf. *gens Hortia*, Ind. III, Osc. *Húrtiis*
orto-=L. *ortus*, perf. partc. pass. nom.
sg. n. *ortom*, U. 365 VI *a 46*; spelt
orto ib. *26, 36*, VI *b 29*; acc., perhaps
neut. pl. *urtu* 358 II *a 4*, nom. pl. fem.
urtas 361 III *10*; abl. (or dat.?) pl.
urtes ib. 4
osatu, impv. act. 3 sg., U. 365 VI *b 24*,
37; in the phrase *cupirse perso osatu*;
commonly derived from *op(e)sa*- Osc.
úpsā- =L. *operā*-, but the history of
-*ps*- in Umb. is not yet clear; cf. *oseto*
ose, U. 365 VI *a 26, 36, 46*, VI *b 29*;
Büch. would regard it as standing for
oses, gen. sg. meaning 'auni,' connecting it with L. *hornus* for *ho-os-ino*-, and U. *ustite, usase* (qq.v.) and
for the root with Sab. Aus-elii (309 A,
s.v. auso-); the only other evidence for
this word *os*- or *oso*- is in *amosio*
'annuo' 205 C.
oseto facta, instaurata, excauata uel sim.
p. partc. pass. nom. sg. fem., U. 354;
commonly regarded as heteroclite
partc. to U. *osā-tu*, q.v.
osi..., uerbum mutilum, O. 28. *4*
ostendu for *ostenn(e)to*=L. *ostendito*,
impv. 2 or 3 sg., U. 365 VI *a 20*; =*us-tentu* 356 I *a 3, 9, 12, 16, 23, 26*, I *b 3,
6*, 357 I *b 25, 28*, 358 II *a 6, 11*; spelt
ustetu 356 I *a 17*, 357 I *b 32, 43*, 358
II *a 12*, 360 II *b 9, 29*; pl. *ustentuta*
361 III *5*; fut. ind. pass. 3 pl. *osten-sendi* 365 VI *a 20* (cf. p. 506 with
footn.)
ote, Umb.=Osc. *auti*, L. *aut*, 364 V *b
10, 13, 15, 18*, 365 VI *a 7*, 366 VII *a 6*;
=*ute* 357 I *b 24, 27*, 363 V *a 23*, V *b 2*
Ou, nota praenominis, perhaps=L.
Ouius, Osc. 18 bis, 21 bis, Pg. 222,
230, perhaps Etr.-Fal. xl. *19*, p. 375
ouflllo, Etr. Fal. xl. *19*, p. 375; cf. the
preceding
Ouiedis, nomen nom. sg. m., Pg. 225;
cf. *gens Ouiedia* in Index III
ουπσενς, operauere, fecere, O. 1; 3 pl.
porf. of *úpsā-*, q.v.
oui=L. *ouis*, acc. pl., U. 365 VI *b 43*;
=*uvef* 356 I *b 1*; acc. sg. *uvem* 361 III
8, 10, 12, 26, 31; =*uve* 358 II *a 10*;
loc. or dat. *uv[e]* 356 I *a 31*; abl. with
postp. *uvi-kum* 361 III *28*

p

p ⊓, fourteenth letter of the Osc. *αβ*, 81
P, nota praenominis, Osc. 40, 41, 68,
71, 85 (in 77. *26* it probably stands for
a nomen); Pg. 219; Fal. 344. Commonly regarded as equiv. to Lat.
Publius (Pg. *Poef* inf.); but it is
equally possible that it may represent, in Osc. and Pg., the equiv. of L.
Quinctus, i.e. the original stem from
which the Osc. and Pg. nomen
Púntiis, Ponties was derived. It is
probably not *Pakis*, for which v.
Pg. *Pa*, Osc. *Pak*
p, abbrev. Umb. equiv. of L. *pondo* (or
**pondos, pondera*?), 361 V *b 9, 14*
p, in *f. p*. Praen. 283=Fortunae Primigenine
Pa, nota praen. Paeligni, Volsci, Falisci;
Pg. 206, Vol. 253, Fal. 346
pā-, Osc.-Umb. fem. stem (*paam,
pae(i), pafe, paí, pai, pam, pas*) of
the relative pron. *po*- q.v. with p. 479
Παα, abbrev. nomen, O. 3
Paakul, praenomen, perhaps complete
(stem *Pākullo*-) nom. sg. m., O. 94,
cf. the deriv. nomen *Pakulliis*
paam, v. *po*- qui
Paapii for -*piis*, abbrev. nomen, nom.
sg. m., Osc. 201 *a*, -*pií* ib. *b*, -*pí* ib. *c*;
C. Papius Mutilus leader of the Allies
in 90 B.C.
paca, causā, abl. (or acc.) of some noun,
used as postp. with gen., U. 365 VI *a
20*
Pak, nota praenominis Osci 113, 114
(*Pakis* or **Pakvis*, or even *Paakul*), cf. Mars. *Pac*. 266. O. *Pak* 77.
18, 137 a 5 may represent either a
praen. or nomen
pacari, Old Lat. xxxv., p. 329; commonly identified with L. *pacari* and
interpreted either *pacem facere, reconciliari*, or *stipulari, implorare*
Pakio-, *Pacio*-, Osc. and Pg. praenomen, nom. sg. m. *pakis*, O. 130 *a
9*, 194; Pg. *paci* 214; acc. *pakim* 130
a 10; gen. pl. (or abl. sg.?), *pakiu*
130 *a 2* (v. crit. note). Nom. sg. fem.
pacia, Pg. 209
pacri-, propitius, N. Osc. Mars. and
Umb. adj. Umb. nom. sg. masc. and
fem. *pacer*, 365 VI *a 23, 30, 33, 40,
42, 50, 52*, VI *b 7, 11, 13, 26, 34*, 366
VII *a 14, 17, 31, 50*; nom. pl. *pacrer*,
366 VI *b 61*. Mr uc. *pacr* nom. sg. fem.
243. *11, pacris*, probably nom. or acc.

pl. ib. *1*, v. s.v. *aiso*. Pg. *pacris* probably nom. pl. Mars. *pacre* 261, which may be abbrev., and whose case is not clear

Πακϝηις, si uera lectio, gen. sg. praenominis, O. 13; the stem *pacuo*- occurs nowhere else, though it is implied in the foll. nomen

Pacuies=L. *Pacuuius* 253, nomen, nom. sg. m., Vol. 253

Pakulliis, nomen nom. sg. m., O. 137 *d 4*; from *Paakul* q.v.

padellar, subst. gen. sg. fem., U. 365 VI *a 14*; cf. p. 408, and *pertome* inf.

pafo, Fal. 312 *a* = *pipafo* ib. *b* q.v.

Pagio, nomen, nom. sg. m., Mars 265, no doubt miswritten for *Pacio*(*s*), as it occurs nowhere else (271 C of course represents only this insc.)

Παιδοκόρης, i.e. παίδων ἐράστης, 37 D q.v.

painiscos, nom. sg., Etr.-Praen. 291, v. note

Παιστανο, ethnicon of Paestum, Osc. 24, for the case v. p. 143 f.

Palanud, ex Pallano, abl. sg. neut., O. 193 ubi, v. adn.

pam, Osc. v. *pan*

πάμπανον, O. 37 A q.v.

pan, quam, adv. of comparison, O. 28. *6*, and with *pruter prius*, ib. *4*, spelt *pruter pam* ib. 16; if any stress could be laid on the spelling of the Tab. Bant. we might take *pam*=L. *quam*, and *pan*=Umb. *pane* as *pon*=*punc*, but cf. the foll.

pane, quam, adv. of compar., U. 357 I *b 40*=*pane*, 366 VII *a 46*; no doubt rightly identified with L. *quamde*, *quande*, since L. -*nd*- is regularly parallel to Osc.-Umb. -*nn*-; Osc. *pan* has lost the short final vowel as *pŭn* beside U. *ponne*, *pune*. The uncompounded *pam survives in U. *prepa*. Should this Italic -*de* be called a postposition, or a purely pronominal particle? Cf. -*ne*, *ne*- in U. *arnipo*, *nersa*, O. *nepon*, qq.v. and L. *done-c*

panis, 309 D q.v.

panta=L. *quantā*, fem. sg. abl. (p. 500 f.), U. 363 V *b 2*, acc.=*quantam* ib. *3*

panupei, i.e. *pannō-pe=L. *quandoque*, quolibet tempore, U. 367 VII *b 1* with a preceding *pisi*, quisquis. On the -*dō* v. s.v. *nersa*, and on -*pei* = -*quē* cf. p. 506 footn.

Papo-, praen., Osc. gen. sg. m. *papeis* 137 *d 8*, cf. Osc.-Etr. *papes* or *pape* 38, and *pap* 137 *f 6*. Cf. the deriv. gens *Pa*(*a*)*pia* sup.

parentaret, parentauerit, fut. perf. ind. 3 sg., Fal.-L. V 336 ubi v. n.

parentatid? (si uera lect.), conceivably an Osc. perf. subj. 3 sg. 'parentauerit,' cf. *fundatid*, n. iv. p. 31

parfā-, parra, uel sim., an Umb. bird of omen, acc. sg. *parfam*, 357 I *b 13*, spelt *parfa*, 365 VI *a 2*, *4*, *15*, *17*, 366 VI *b 51*; abl. *parfa* 366 VI *a 1*. The form has been explained by Brugm. (*Ber. k. Sächs. Ges. Wiss.* 1890, p. 210) as containing the -*bho*-, -*bhā*- suffix common in names of animals, Gr. κάλαφος, Old Ir. *heirp erb*, 'capra' (beside Gr. ἔριφος), so that *parfā*- (for *parro-fā) : *parrā*- as Gr. ἔλαφος (for *eln-bho-s*) : ἐλλός (for *eln-os). The second half of the old equation Lat. -*rr*-=Italic -*rs*-=U. -*rf*- is disproved by U. *farsio*=L. *farrea*, *tursa*, *tu*(*r*)*setu* : L. *terrere*

parsest, U. 367 VII *b 2*; either 3 sg. fut. ind. of the simple thematic verb from which Lat. *pāret*, *parret*, *appārēre* are derivatives, or for *pars est* ius est, v. p. 512 with footn.

pase, i.e. *paše*=L. *pace*, abl. sg. fem. only in the phrase *pase tua* of deities, U. 365 VI *a 30*, *33*, *40*, *42*, *50*, *52*, VI *b 11*, *13*, *32*, *34*, 366 VI *b 61*, VII *a 14*, *17*, *31*, *50*

passtata, i.e. -*tam*, παστάδα, porticum, acc. sg. fem. O. 44; probably borrowed from the Gr., and Oscanised, cf. *catamitus*, p. 230

Patanaí, Pandae, dat. sg. fem., a Samnite goddess, O. 175 *a 14*, *b 16*; certainly akin to the Lat. form, and identical if Italic -*tn*- became Lat. -*nd*-; cf. O. *patensins* beside L. *panderent*; the more so that the epithet here is *piistiaí*, Πιστῳ, while Panda acc. to Arnob. 4. 128 and Gloss. Philox. (*C. Gl. L.* 2, p. 141) was a goddess of peace (Aelius ap. Non. 44. Merc. identified her with Ceres, but wrongly, see the lexica). But v. s.v. *patensíns* inf.

πατάνια, O. 37 A q.v.

πάταχνον, O. 37 A q.v.

patensíns=L. *panderent*, 3 pl. impf. subj. act., O. 95 *b 28*, *29*; for *paten(*e*)*sēns*, and if Italic -*tn*- became -*nd*- in Lat. we should further refer O. *paten- to Italic *patn-, which we should see directly in L. *pand*-. But *paten- or *patyn*- ; *patn- may be regarded simply as an I. Eu. doublet like Gr. -*avw* : -*vw* (the change of -*tn*- to -*nd*- in I. Eu. cannot be doubted,

L. *fundus* : Gr. πυθμήν etc.) and the same explanation would apply to *Patanaí* q.v.

patr- = L. *pater*; Osc. nom. sg. *patír* (perhaps as cognomen) 134, cf. 77 B; dat. sg. *patereí* (as epithet of *Evklo-*) 175 *a 25*. Mruc. gen. *patres* 243. *6* (epithet of Jove). Mars. dat. *patre* 264 (epithet of *Erine*). Aeq. dat. *patre* 272 (also a deity). Etr.-Praen. nom. sg. *pater* 303. Umb. dat. sg. *patre*, epithet of Jove, 360 II *b 7*

patt- probably represents a 3 pl. perf. ind., O. 190; cf. *pat* 40 and the note

Pk, nota praenominis (perhaps = *pak* q.v.), O. 166 bis, 177 bis

pd, Osc. abbrev. perhaps = L. *pedēs*, ix. p. 81. Cf. *p[a]d* or *p[e]d* in 168

Pe, nota praenominis, Mars 265, ? 260 *a*

pe, Umb. = *-per* q.v.

peai = L. *piae*, as divine epithet, dat. sg. f. Mruc. 243. *10*, cf. Vol. *pihom*, U. *pehā-*, piare, and Osc. *piíhiuí*, an epithet of Jupiter

pecus = L. *pecus*, acc. sg. n. Mars.-L. 273

peḍ-, Umb. = L. *pes*, foot, m. abl. sg. *peḍi*, 356 I *a 29, 32* = *persi*, 365 VI *b 24, 37, 38, 39.* To this word also (rather than to *peḍo-* q.v.) Büch. refers the acc. *peḍu*, 359 II *a 24* (*p. seritu*, 'pedem conseruato'), comparing the primaeval practice 'membrum abscidi mortuo...ad quod seruatum iusta fierent' Paul. ex F. 148 M

peḍaio-, Umb. adj. describing the manner or character of sacrifice; Büch. renders 'pedaneus, humi stratus'; acc. pl. fem. *peḍaia*, 357 I *b 28, 32, 44* = *persaia*, 366 VII *a 7*, spelt *persaea*, ib. *41, 54*. It is, I think, as Büch. says, impossible to make any separation between these feminine forms and the following; acc. sg. m. *peḍaem*, U. 358 II *a 11*, 361 III *32*, spelt *peḍae*, 358 II *a 13*; nom. sg. neut. *peḍae*, 359 II *a 22*; these might be all regarded as having *-em, -e* = the regular *-im* of *-io-* stems (p. 471), but the following seem more anomalous: *persae*, apparently acc. pl. fem., 365 VI *a 58*, and *persae*, apparently acc. pl. masc., 365 VI *b 3*; but cf. p. 472 footn. Except in II *a 22* (*esunu p. futu*) the word only occurs in agreement with the object of *fetu*, and its position before *f* may account for the absence of *-f* in all the fem. forms

peḍe, v. *pis*

pedi, Mruc. 243. *12*; ingeniously rendered 'pendat' by Deecke ap. Zvet.

Inscc. It. Inf., p. 175; if this be thought probable, *-di* must be taken (like L. *edim, sim*) as a non-thematic subj. from the root of *dare*; if so Osc. *dadid* might possibly be a pres., not a perf. subj.

peḍo- = Gr. πέδον, fossa, terra ad sacrum accipiendum cauata, acc. sg. *peḍum*, U. 356 I *a 29, 32*, spelt *peḍu*, 358 II *a 9*; *perso*, 365 VI *b 24, 37*. With postp. *peḍume*, 359 II *a 27*, 361 III *33* = *persome*, 365 VI *b 38, 39, 40*. Bücheler's interpretation of the word appears to be established by the numerous examples he quotes (e.g. Hom. *Od.* 11. 25, Ovid *Met.* 7. 243, Stat. *Theb.* 4. 451) of the use of trenches in the way here prescribed

peessl[ûm?], O. 178, commonly identified with *pestlúm* (q.v. inf.) in 173; seeing how little distance separates Pietrabbondante from Alvito, if the forms are identical in origin, their present difference may perhaps be chronological (rather than dialectic); indeed it is perhaps scarcely more than a matter of spelling, cf. *kenzsur* beside *censor*. The *-ee-* as usual in Osc. (cf. *Meelikio-, teero-*) is non-original—here as 'compensation for' the loss of *-rc-*, the root no doubt being that of L. *prec-or, posco*, Osc. *comparascuster*

peha-, *peiha-*, v. *piha-*

peica = L. pica, abl. sg. fem., U. 365 VI *a 1*, acc. 365 VI *a 3, 4, 16, 17*, cf. *peico*

peico = L. *picum*, a bird of omen, acc. sg. m., U. 365 VI *a 3, 4, 16, 17*, abl. spelt *peiqu*, 365 VI *a 1*. The U. *-c-* (not *-p-*) confirms the derivation from *pic-* (ποικίλος, *pingere*) and the meaning 'pied.' For the part the bird played in Italic times v. p. 450

Peiediate, dat. pl., U. 360 II *b 4* bis, name of a tribe or gens

peiu, Umb. adj. denoting colour (not red), acc. pl. masc., 357 I *b 24* = *peiu* 366 VII *a 3*; acc. pl. fem. *peia*, 357 I *b 27* = *peia* 366 VII *a 6*. In view of the use of *e* in Umb. writing = orig. Italic *ĭ* I can see (pace von Planta *Osk. Umb. Gram.* p. 370) no reason to doubt the usual identification of this word with **pic-io-* parallel to L. *piceus*, Gr. πίσσα. *-i-* is written for *-ě-* as in *usaie* I *b 45*

pel or **pelt**, Praen. 286, apparently an abbrev. abl. of the donor's place of origin (? Peltuinum)

πελένα, O. 37 A q.v.

pelmner, pulmenti, subst. (or adj.) gen. sg., U. 364 V *b 12, 17*; this rendering, which is Bücheler's, is no doubt substantially correct

pelsā-, sepelire; Umb. impv. act. 3 sg. *pelsatu*, 365 VI *b* 40 bis; gerundive (v. p. 519), nom. sg. masc. *pelsans*, 359 II *a 43*; acc. sg. m. *pelsanu*, 358 II *a 6*, 361 III *32*, acc. pl. fem. *pelsana*, 356 I *a 26*=*pelsana*, 365 VI *b 22*. It would be natural to compare L. *sĕ-pel-io*, *sĕ-pul-crum* if any explanation could be found for *sĕ-*

peperscust, *pepescust*, v. *perstu*

pepurkurent, poposcerint, decreuerint uel sim. 3 pl. fut. perf. ind. act., U. 363 V *b* 5; if this is based on the stem of L. *posco*, the form is interesting as showing that in the perfect tenses Umb. has discarded the -*sc*- which runs through the verb in Lat. and Osc.; but on the whole it is perhaps better to compare the simpler stem of L. *precari, proc-u-s*

pequo=L. *pecua*, acc. pl. n., U. 365 VI *a 30, 32, 40, 42, 50, 52*, VI *b 13, 32, 34*, 366 VII *a 17, 30*, only in a string of things blessed (*saluom scritu...uiro, pequo, castruo, fri*), cf. L. *pastores pecuaque salua seruassis*, etc. Cato *R. R.* 141. The *q* is a mere orthographic variant before -*u*-, cf. *peiqu* beside *peico*

per=*perek* q.v., O. 39

per, Umb. postp. with acc. =Osc. *pert*, L. -*per* in *parum-per* etc. meaning 'up to, as far as'; *triiuper*, 357 I *b 21*, *22* bis, 360 II *b 25* bis=*trioper*, 366 VI *b 55*, VII *a 51*. Contrast the foll.

per, Umb. postp. with abl.=L. *prō*: *ahtisper* pro actibus, 361 III *24, 29*, *fratrusper*, 358 II *a 2*, 361 III *23*, *fratruspe* ib. *28*, *nomneper* passim, *ocriper ocreper ukriper* passim *ukripe*, 356 I *a 12*, *Petruniaper*, 359 II *a 21, 35* (ubi aes -*pert*), *popluper*, *pupluper* passim, *reper*, 367 VII *b 2*, *totaper*, *tutaper* passim *tutape*, 361 III *24*, *trefiper* pro tribu, 361 III *25, 30*, *Vuŝiiaper*, 360 II *b 26*

peracni-, Umb. adj. describing particular victims: acc. sg. *peraknem*, 358 II *a 10*=*perakne*, 358 II *a 5 bum perakne 12*, 360 II *b 7, 10*; as subst. neut. acc. 358 II *a 5 perakne restatu, 14*, acc. plur. neut. adj. *perakneu*, 362 V *a 7*, gen. pl. subst. *peracnio*, 365 VI *a 54*. The derivation of this word from *acno-* (q.v.) and its general sense are clear; it is often used side by side with the parallel *sev-akni-*, but it is not clear whether they have equivalent or contrasted meanings

perakri-, Umb. epithet of victims, opimus, ἀκμαῖος uel sim., abl. sg. *peracri*, 365 VI *a 34, 35, 38, 43, 45, 48, 53*, spelt *peracrei*, 365 VI *a 25, 29*; acc. pl. fem. *perakre* 357 I *b 40*; probably gen. pl. (as subst.) *peracrio*, 366 VII *a 51*, abl. pl. *peracris*, 366 VI *b 52, 56*. Brugmann's derivation (*Ber. k. Sächs. Ges. Wiss.* 1893, p. 144) from *acri-* in the sense of ἐν ἀκμῇ ὤν, ἀκμαῖος, maturus, can hardly be doubted

Peraznanie, dat. pl., name of a tribe or gens, U. 360 II *b 7*

perkā-, uirga, caduceus, acc. sg. *percam*, U. 366 VI *b 53*=*perca*, 365 VI *a 19*, 366 VI *b 49, 50, 63*, VII *a 46, 51*; acc. pl. *perkaf*, 357 I *b 15*, *perca*, 366 VI *b 51*. No doubt the same word as Osc. *perek* q.v., and cf. *perstu* inf.

Perkedne[is], gen. sg. m. cognominis Osci 93, nom. *Perkens* ib., cf. *gens Percennia* and the foll.

Perkhen, abbrev. nomen, O. 67, no doubt equiv. to *gens Percennia*; cf. the praen. *Perkedno-* whose unassimilated *d* points, perhaps, to a somewhat earlier date

perek, abbrev. probably of **perekas* (cf. Syntax § 6), perticas, *p. iii* being the breadth of a road in Pompeii, O. 39. Cf. U. *perkā-*, which no doubt shows the simplest meaning of this word, and *perstu* inf.

peremust, perceperit, promulgatum acceperit uel sim., 3 sg. fut. perf. ind. act., O. 28. *15*; the meaning of *emere* was orig. rather 'take' than 'buy,' as appears in Lat. *adimere, perimere, eximere*, though the simple verb has the same meaning in Umb. (355) as in Lat.

per-etom, peremptum, uiolatum, interruptum, p. parte. pass. neut. sg. nom. impers., U. 365 VI *a 27, 37, 47*, VI *b 30*, v. *daetom* sup.

perfa[kium]? perficere O. 130 *a 6*.

perfines, perfindes, n. xxiii. p. 226 q.v.

Pernai, dat. sg. fem., a Samnite goddess, companion of Flora, and connected with Ceres, O. 175 *a 22*. Büch. would derive it from *pro-*, comparing U. *perne, pernaio-*, and for the meaning, *Anteuorta*, a maieutic goddess

perne, Umb. adv. πρόσω, 365 VI *b 11*; on -*ne* v. s.v. *arnipo*, and the foll.

pernaiaf, anticas, ex aduerso conspectas, adj. acc. pl. fem., augural epithet of *aveƒ*, U. 357 I *b* 10, abl. *pernaies*, 356 I *a* 2. Derived from *perne*; cf. *pustnaiaƒ*; both words show the ease with which postpp. (or case-endings) may become converted or absorbed into suffixes forming stems. No doubt L. *prōnus* has a parallel origin

persae, v. *peḍaio*

persklum, supplicationem, acc. sg. neut., U. 356 I *a* 1 = *persclo*, 365 VI *a* 1, with postp. *persklumaḍ*, 361 III 21, gen. sg. *perscler*, 365 VI *a* 27, 28, 37, 38, spelt *pescler*, 365 VI *a* 47, 48, VI *b* 30 bis ; abl. sg. *persklu*, 361 III 12 = *persclu*, 365 VI *b* 36, 366 VII *a* 20, 24, 34 (possibly acc.), and *pesclu*, 365 VI *b* 15, 366 VII *a* 8. From *per*(c)-, 'precari,' v. sub *persnimu*

perse, *persi*, pede, v. *peḍ*.

perse, *persei*, v. *pis*

Perseponas = L. *Persephonae*, gen. sg. fem., Pg. 216. 5

persnimu, precamino, supplicato, Umb. impv. 2 or 3 sg. deponent, 357 I *b* 7, 21, 361 IV 8, 10, persnimu 365 VI *a* 55, 59, VI *b* 2, 4, 6, 9, 20, 25, 37, 41, 44, 46, 366 VII *a* 4, 7, 25 bis, 34, 42, 44, 54, persnihmu 359 II *a* 27, 29, 30 bis, 31, 36 bis, 37, 38, 39, 42, 361 IV 11, 23, 25, 29, persnihimu 365 VI *b* 17, 366 VII *a* 9, 39, 45, persnimu 356 I *a* 6, 10, 13, 19, 23, 26, 34, I *b* 3, 357 I *b* 22, 26, 30, 32, 37, 38, 44, 358 II *a* 7, 10, 360 II *b* 18 bis, 20, 3 pl. *persnimumo* supplicanto, 366 VI *b* 57, *persnihimumo*, 366 VII *a* 47, *pesnimumo* 366 VI *b* 64, 65, VII *a* 1, p. parte. nom. sg. m. *persnis* precatus 365 VI *b* 39, pesnis 365 VI *b* 40, 41. Cf. *prepesnimu*. Commonly regarded as standing for *perc-sc-ni-*, connected with L. *poscere* for *porc-scere*, O. *comparascuster*, U. *persclom* (from *perscilo-*, Osc. *pestlúm*, or simply from *persc-* + *-lo* ?), but I am not sure that the changes of the final group of consonants have yet been fully explained

persondro-, *persuntro-*, Umb. adj. always used to describe a secondary and presumably complementary offering, sometimes only of confectionery; applied only to *suḍum* (*sorsom*) and *staflare* qq.v., but used also as a subst. alone. As adj.: acc. sg. m. *pesuntru*, 356 I *a* 27, pesuntrum, ib. 30, pesutru, 358 II *a* 8, pesondro, 365 VI *b* 24, 37, 39, p. *staflare*, 40; abl. sg. *persontru*, 365 VI *b* 28, persondru ib. 31, 35. Alone as subst. ;

acc. sg. *persutru*, 360 II *b* 13, *persuntru*, 361 IV 17, 19; dat. sg. *persuntre* ib. 21; plur. acc. *pesondro*, 365 VI *b* 37, abl. with postp. *pesondris-co*, 365 VI *b* 40. On *-dr-* for orig. *-tr-* v. s.v. *adro-* : Bücheler's view of the *-tr-* as the comparative suffix would suit the meaning, but the instrumental *-tro-* would do so even better, especially if his comparison of *person-* with *persnimu* could be maintained (as it is difficult to do if *persn-* is for *persc-n-*). But it would be possible to compare Skt. Ved. *sanóti*, 'he offers,' *sanitṛ-*, 'sacrificer'

perstico, U. 365 VI *b* 25; Bücheler regards this as neut. acc. of an adj. derived from *peḍ-*, *pers-* as L. *rusticus* from *rus*, meaning *pedestre*, or *terrestre*, and agreeing with *erus*, which however nowhere else has any epithet, though often governing a genitive (in form *perstico* itself might be a gen. pl.)

perstu, impv. act. 2 or 3 sg., Umb. 359 II *a* 32 = *pestu* 360 II *b* 19, fut. perf. ind. act. 3 sg. *peperscust*, 366 VI *b* 5, pepescus, 366 VII *a* 8. Only with the adj. *postro* (n. pl.), the object being three times *supo* (*-pa*), once *vesklu*. Büch. renders '(re-)ponere,' comparing L. *compescere*, *dispescere*, 'to mark off, limit,' and Umb. *praco*(m)-, to which I would add U. *perkā-*, Osc. *perek-*, L. *per*(c)*tica*. His further suggestion that we should see in these words an Italic root *perc-* (+ *-sco-* in the verbs) which gave rise to the widely spread Romance *perco-* (Low Latin *parcus*, *parricus*, Italn. *parco*, Fr. *parc*, Eng. *park* and the Dutch *perk*; Germ. *pferch* appears to be borrowed from this) is extremely attractive. For other Romance words taken from the dialects cf. pp. 218, 222, 226 and especially 227—9, and for the Germ. derivv. Klüge, *Etym. Wtb.*[4] s.v. The relation of meaning between U. *percā-* and this supposed *perco-* is exactly illustrated by the meanings of Eng. 'rod, pole, or perch,' the last being of course Fr. *perche*, L. *pertica*, and all three having been transferred as measurements from length to area

persuntr-, v. *persondro-*

pert as prep. with acc. meaning 'trans, supra,' O. 95 *b* 7, U. 359 II *a* 36. But as postp. in Osc. it means 'usque ad,' *petiropert* 28. 14 'non amplius quater,' cf. *ampert*, and Umb. *-per*

pertemest, *-must*, v. *pertumum*

pertentu, protendito uel *sim.*, 2 or 3 sg. impv. act., U. 359 II *a 31*, 361 IV *8*; cf. *antentu, entendu*

pertome, subst. acc. sg. with postp. describing some building, place or visible object belonging to Padella, U. 365 VI *a 14*; Büch. renders plausibly 'peruium ianum,' deriving *Padella* from *pat-* in *patēre* (if so cf. Osc. *Aderlo-, Abellā-,* from *atro-lo-, *apro-lā-.)

pertumum, perimere, intercessione (comitia) dimittere, inf. act., O. 28. 7; fut. ind. 3 sg. *pert-emest* ib. *7*, fut. perf. *pert-emust* ib. *4.* With this compare Cincius (*De uerbis priscis*) 'peremere idem quod prohibere,' apud Fest. 214 M., who adds 'at Cato in lib. de re militari pro *uitiare* usus est, cum ait cum magistratus nihil audent imperare ne quid consul auspici peremat'; this is very near the Osc. use of *pertumum,* the second half of which contains the stem of L. *emo* modified by the influence of forms which came under the Oscan rules of anaptyxis, some of them perhaps in the paradigm of the verb itself. Cf. *peremust* and *pert*

perum, sine, prepn. with acc., O. 28. *14, 21*; its close connexion with Gr. πέραν etc. is obvious; for the change of meaning cf. L. *praeter,* Gr. χωρίς, ἐκτός, etc.

pes, Pg. 218; commonly explained as = L. *pedes,* acc. pl.; if so for the contraction cf. Umb. *uef, kapif*

pesclo-, v. *persklum*

pesco, Mars. 261; Büch. regards this as a neut. (or m.) subst. meaning 'offering, piaculum'; if so cf. U. *persklum,* etc. It might conceivably be a verb meaning 'precor, oro'

pesetom, pessum datum, peremptum p. parte. nom. sg. neut., U. 365 VI *a 27, 37, 47,* VI *b 30*; quite possibly U. *pesetom est* = L. *pess(um) itum est*; Bücheler's comparison with *peccare* is hard to justify in point of phonetics

pesondr-, v. *persondro-*

pestlici sacerdoti, U. 370 A, cf. the foll.

pestlūm templum, fanum uel sim., O. 173 *b*; cf. *peessl-* sup. and U. *persklum,* which is perhaps the same word, though with a different meaning

pestu, v. *perstu*

pesuntr-, *pesutr-,* v. *persondro-*

πίτακνον, O. 37 A q.v.

petenata, i.e. *pe(h)tīnatam* (= *pectinatam*) constructam in pudendorum muliebrium formam, U. 361 IV *4*, cf. *eskamitum* ibid.

Peticis, nomen, nom. sg. m., Pg. 215, cf. *gens Peticia* in Index III

Petiedu, nom. sg. fem. = *Petiedia* or gen. pl. m. *Petiedium,* Pg. 216. *2*; on this (Thurneysen's) interpretation of the sign Ə v. 206 n.

petiolus, 205 Rem. 9, p. 230 q.v.

petiru-pert, O. 28. *14, petiropert* ib. 15, usque ad quattuor, non amplius quater, from *petiru-,* neut. pl. 'quattuor,' and *-pert* q.v. Whence comes the difference in the second syllable between this and *petora* 'quattuor,' O. 205 A? (That the *-u* or *-o* should be Latinised into *-a* is a matter of course in the Glossographers.) Cf. U. *peturpursus.* The first syllable is, of course, regular: I.-Eu. *qet- = Skt. *cat-,* Gr. τετ-, Italic *quet-,* Osc.-Umb. *pet-,* and Lat. presumably at first *quet-*

Petrunes, nomen, perhaps nom. sg. m., Etr.-Fal. 326. *b*; cf. *gens Petronia* in Ind. III, and the foll.

Petrunia-per, name of a 'natio,' in the abl. with postp., U. 359 II *a 21, 35.* The same name (or its parent stem?) is written *Ptrunia,* Pg. 234. The word is no doubt derived from *petr-* = Italic *quetr-,* 'four'

Pettieis, nomen, gen. sg. m., O. 115 = *Pettieis* 116, v. *gens Pettia* in Ind. III

peturpursus = L. *quadrupedibus,* dat. pl., U. 365 VI *b 11,* cf. Osc. *petiru-, petora*

phim, O. 28. *25,* v. s.v. *nephim*

Pikŭf, res aliqua uenalis, O. 66

piei, *pieisum, piʃi,* v. *pis*

piha-, Umb. = L. *piā-re*: impv. 3 sg. *pihatu* 365 VI *a 29* ter, *30, 39* ter, *40, 49* ter, *50,* VI *b 31* bis, *32,* spelt *pehatu* 361 III *3.* Perf. subj. 2 sg. act. or impers. pass. (v. pp. 510, 517), *pihafi,* U. 365 VI *a 38, 48,* VI *b 31,* spelt *pihafei* 365 VI *a 29.* P. parte. pass. nom. sg. m. *pihaz* 356 I *b 7* = *pihos* 365 VI *b 47.* Gerundive gen. sg. m. *pehaner* 365 VI *a 20,* spelt *peihaner* ib. *8, pihaner,* 365 VI *a 19, b 48.* Cf. *prupehast* and Osc. *pithio-*

pihaclu = L. *piaculo,* Umb. subst. neut. abl. sg., 365 VI *a 25, 29, 34, 35, 38, 43, 45, 48, 53,* VI *b 28, 31, 35*; abl. sg. or more probably gen. pl. *pihaclo* VI *a 54,* certainly gen. pl. *pihaklu* 362 V *a 8*

pifhiŭi pio, pios protegenti uel sim., dat. sg. m., O. 175 *b 14,* an epithet of Jove in Samnium; v. the foll.

pihom, pium, legitimum factum, fas, adj. neut. sg. nom., Vol. 252; it seems probable that this stem with that from which U. *pihā-* (and Osc. πιω?) are derived, should be distinguished from the preceding which looks like a derivative in *-io-*. To which of them Lat. *pius* belongs it is hard to say; possibly *pīus*, *pīare* to this, and *pius* so frequent on inscc. (with the I longa) to *pīh-io-*, though of course L. *pius* may be simply an archaism preserved in written formulae. Mruc. *peai* is applied to a deity like Osc. *piihiúí*. The spelling with *h*, invariable in Umb. as in the Osc. and Vol. forms, is noteworthy, though it has been commonly taken to be a mere indication of divided syllables

piistíaí, dat. sg. fem. adj., epithet of Patana, O. 175 *a 14, b 16*; probably borrowed (like *evkláí* ib. *a 3, 23, b 4* from Εὔκολος) from Gr. Πλάτιος, which is the regular translation of L. *Fidius*, e.g. Dion. Hal. 4. 58

pilipus, Φίλιππος, Praen.-L. 291

pilonicos, Φιλόνικος, pueraliqui fabulosus, Etr.-Praen. 294

πιω, uox obscura et fortasse mutila, O. 13; if the following αισ has anything to do with *aiso-* deus, this word might be plausibly referred to *piho-*, v. Vol. *pihom*. It has been commonly compared with U. *bio* cisterna (nom.), but the acc. would be required here (Pg. *biam*) since a nom. Λαπονις precedes

pipafo, bibam, Fal. 312 *b*, 1st sg. fut. ind. act. (absol.) of *pipā-*, the redupl. pres. stem inflected as an *a-* verb. Note that Fal. *p* may represent either orig. *p* or orig. *b*. On the parallel insc. we have the shorter form *pafo*, and as the whole sentence is clearly proverbial, it is possible that the longer form had gone out of every day use

pipatio, O. 205 A q.v.

Piquier, gen. sg. m., U. 364 V *b 9, 14*; Büch. regards this as an adj. describing certain lands, but as *P. Martier* follows equally *agre Tlatie* and *agre Casiler*, and as *Martio-* elsewhere in Umb. is only used as an epithet to the deity *Serfo-*, it is at least to be considered whether *Piquier* is not a similar deity equally patronized by the Brotherhood and claiming dues from certain 'Tlatian' and 'Caselatian' lands. He would be thoroughly at home on the borders of Picenum (374 A), if his name is connected with the *peico-* (*peiqo-*), whom the Iguvine augurs observed (VI *a* init.)

pir = Gr. πῦρ, ignis, Umb. subst. neut. nom. *pir* 365 VI *a 26, 36, 46*, 366 VI *b 29*, acc. *pir* 357 I *6, 12*, 359 II *a 19*, 360 II *b 12*, 361 III *12, 21*, *pir* 366 VI *b 49, 50* and no doubt 365 VI *a 20*. abl. *pure* 357 I *b 20*, with postp. *pure-to* 365 VI *a 20*. *ū* becomes *i* in Umb., in monosyllables at least, but not so *ŭ*. Cf. *purom-e*, and O. *purasiaí*

pis, Osc.-Umb. pron. = L. *quis*, v. p. 480. Osc. (1) As indefinite non-relative = L. *quis*, after subordinating conjunctions introducing general protases, nom. m. sg. *pis* 28. *4, 10, 11, 12, 13, 17, 20, 23, 25, 26, 29, 30*, pío 114. *6*, possibly 113. *6*; dat. *piei* ib. 7; neut. acc. *píd* 95 *b 15*. (2) As indefinite relative *pis* quisquis, nom. sg. m., 28. *8, 19* (possibly *pís* 113. *6* si sic legendum), neut. nom. *píd* 95 *b 25*. (3) *pis* in 164 is commonly counted interrogative (*pis tiú*(*m*) quis tu?). (4) Doubled like L. *quisquis*, nom. sg. m. (?) *pispis* 80, neut. *pitpit* 205 A. (5) With *-um*, meaning quisquam, in negative sentences : acc. sg. *pídum* 95 *b 21*, *pidum* 130 *a 7*; in ib. 8 *pi*(*dum*) is generally restored as an abl. neut., gen. sg. *pieisum* (as adj. 'ullius') 28. *6*. Pg. *pid* 209 is doubtful. Vol. as indef. non-relative, nom. sg. m. *pis* (after *se* = L. *si*) 252. *1* bis, *3*. Umb., the form *pis* only survives in *svepis* (cf. *sopir*), and in the old formula *piscet totar Tarsinater* etc. 366 VI *b 53* (where orig. perhaps it was interrogative). Else it is augmented by *-i, -e, -ei* or *-her*, (1) As indefinite non-relative after *sve, -pis* 357 I *b 18*, 361 IV *26*, *pisi* 365 VI *a 7*, and in the form *sopir* (v. p. 480), 366 VI *b 54*. With *-her*, like L. *quinis*, 365 VI *b 41*. (2) As indefinite relative: nom. sg. m. *pisi* quisquis, 362 V *a 3, 10*, 366 VII *a 52*, 367 VII *b 1*, so in effect *pis*(*est*) 366 VI *b 53* (v. sup.); acc. pl. (on the gender v. p. 513 footn.), *piji* quoscunque or quascunque, 367 VII *b 2*; neut. nom. and acc. *piḍe* quicquid, 362 V *a 5*, spelt *peḍe* 357 I *6, 18*, 358 II *a 3* = *persi* 365 VI *a 38*, perse ib. *47*, VI *b 30, 31*, persei VI *a 27, 28, 36*, pirsi ib. *48*, pirse 366 VI *b 55*.

But in the pair of phrases *pirsi mersi*, *pirsi mersest* (365 VI *a 28, 38, 48*, VI *b 31*, 366 VI *b 55*) the meaning of the pron. can hardly be distinguished from its uses under 3. (3) Brugmann has pointed out (in *Idg. Forschungen* 5. 150) that the neut. acc. is used as a conjunction meaning 'si, si quando,' cf. p. 481: *perse* 365 *b 29*, *persei* 365 VI *a 26*, *pirse* ib. 46, *persi* ib. 37. (4) Further in two passages (361 IV *32 pidi* and 365 VI *a 5 pirsi*) this word comes second in its clause and is followed by *edek* (*erse*) in the apodosis, and in both cases I would render ἕως...τέως, i.e. *dum... interea*

Pisaurese = *Pisaurenses*, nom. pl., Umb.-L. n. xliii. 4, p. 434

piscim, piscem, Praen.-L. n. xxxiii., p. 322

pistu, i.e. -*tum* = L. *pistum*, U. 363 II *b 15*, acc. sg. pass. parte.

pl., plebis, O. 28. *29*; a most tantalizing abbreviation!

Plasis, si uera lectio, praen. nom. sg. m., O. 131. *3*

Plauties, nomen, nom. sg. m., Pg. 220, Old Lat. *Plautios* 304; cf. *gens Plautia, Plotia* in Ind. III

Pleina, doubtful, perhaps abbrev. (or Etr.) name, Fal. (or Fal.-Etr.) 314

plenasier, adj. loc. or abl., U. 362 V *a 2*. pl., in phrase *pl. urnasier* denoting some point of time, contrasted with *sestentasier urn*. Convivial potations were part of the Atiedian as of the Arval assemblies (*Acta Arv.* 218 A.D.), but at one season the full measure seems to have been allowed to the Atiedians, at another only 'sextantarial,' i.e. presumably a sixth part. Cp. Horace's special celebration of the new moon and of midnight (*Od.* 3. 19. 9)

plener = L. *plenis*, adj. abl. pl. n., U. 366 VII *a 21, 34*

Plenese, apparently dat. sg. fem. (nom. or cogn. ?), Fal.-Lat. 336, cf. *Plenes* 333 *c* and *Abelese* sup.

plostru(m) = L. *plaustrum*, acc. sg. n., Mars.-L. 273

ploto- = L. *plautus*, planipes, U. 370 A, q.v.

po-, Umb.-Osc. relative pron. = L. *quo-*, v. p. 479. Osc. masc. nom. sg. *pui* 130 *b 1*, probably *a 1*; nom. pl. *pûs* 95 *a 8, b 11*, *pû[s] b 15*, 175 *a 1*; neut. nom. and acc. *pod* 28. *10* (*pod todait*), *32* = *pûd* 95 *a 12, 13, 14*, *b 2, 23* = πωτ 22; nom. and acc. pl. *paí* 95 *a 15*, 130

a 9; fem. *pã-* nom. sg. *paei*, 28. *22*, spelt *pae* ib., *pai* 130 *a 1, b 1, paí 95 b 8*; acc. sg. *paam* 42, [*p*]*aam* 169, *pam 95 b 12*; nom. pl. *pas* 28. *25*, *pas* 115, 116, 117 *a 3, b 7*, probably *b 3*; on the adv. uses of *pod* v. s.v. Pg. Masc. probably nom. pl. *puus* 216. *6*; probably fem. acc. sg. *pam* 209. Umb. Masc. nom. sg. *poe* 366 VI *b 50*, spelt *poei* 365 VI *a 1, poi* 365 VI *a 5, b 24*, 366 VI *b 53*; dat. sg. *pusme* 359 II *a 40*; nom. pl. *pur-e* 362 V *a 6*, 363 V *a 25, 28, b 4, puri* 364 V *b 10, 15*. Fem. acc. pl. *paf-e* 366 VII *a 52*. On the origin of the form *puḍe, po-rse* v. p. 479; it is used (1) as masc. nom. sg. 361 III *5* (*puḍe*), 365 VI *a 6* (*por-si*), *9* bis (*-sei*), 366 VI *b 63*, VII *a 46, 51* (*-se*), (2) as masc. nom. pl. 365 VI *a 15* (*-sei*), *19* (*si*), (3) as neut. (or masc.?) acc. pl., 365 VI *b 40*, (4) in *puḍe tedte*, 362 V *a 7*, v. p. 517, (5) in *puḍe nuvime ferest krematruf sumel fertu*, 359 II *a 26*, where it may be 'quod' (Büch.), or 'quae,' or, I think more probably, equiv. to *pune*, 'cum.' On the adv. *-pu*, *-po* in *svepu* v. s.v. Compare further the relative advv. O. *pûn*, U. *poune*, O. *pûz*, U. *puze*, O. *puf*, U. *pufe*, U. *pue* etc, and the compounds O. *poizad*, *pûllad*, U. *pora*, s. vv.

pocapit, Osc. indef. adv. quandoque, 28. *8*, and orig. *30*, *pûkkapíd* 95 *b 26*

pod, Osc. rel. adv.: (1) in *pod...mins quominus*, 28. *10*; (2) in *suae...pod* sine ib. *23*, cf. *-puh*, Umb. *-pu* inf.

Poef, abbrev. nomen, nom. sg. fem. Pg. 206*bis* (Addenda); no doubt equivalent to some Lat. name beginning with *pûb-*.

poimunien, loc. sg. with postp. Vest. 248; perhaps 'in *Pomonio,' i.e. 'in horto, luco Pomonali'

poizad quâcunque, compd. relative abl. sg. fem., O. 28. *19*, v. p. 479

Pola = L. *Paulla, Polla*, feminine praen., nom. sg. f. Fal. 330, *Pola*, Umb.-Lat. xliii. 9, p. 434, dat. *Polae*, Fal.-Lat. 336

poleenis, uox fortasse mutila, Mruc. 243. *9*

πολλαχρόν, 37 C, q.v.

Polouces, Πολυδεύκης Pollux, Etr.-Praen. 287, *-oces* 288

πομποβόλῳ, 37 B, q.v.

***Pomposiies**, *45, p. 532

Πόμπτιες, v. *Ponties*

pomtis, quinquies, O. 28. *15*; the nature

of the ending is not clear, but of the Lat. *-ens* no clear evidence has yet appeared in Osc. or Umb., v. s.v. *nuvis*.

pon, Osc.=L. *quom* (v. inf.) 28. *14, 16, 18=pún* 95 *b 24*, 114, *pun* 130 *a 6, 8*. Shortened for *pon-ne*, which appears in Umb. (v. inf.), as *púz* beside U. *puze*, *pan* beside U. *pane* etc. Cf. *punum* and *ne pon*

pone, posca, an inferior wine (or vinegar), Umb. subst neut. abl. sg., 365 VI *a 59, poni* ib. 57 VI *b 1, 3, 9, 20, 22, 44, 46*, 366 VII *a 4, 7, 41, 54=puni* 356 I *a 4, 9, 13, 16, 22, 26, 32*, I *b 3, 7*, 357 I *b 25, 29, 32, 44*, 358 II *a 7, 11, 13*, 359 II *a 20, 24, 25*, 360 II *b 9, 20, 29*, acc. *pune* 359 II *a 18, 33, 40*, 360 II *b 14, 16*, 361 IV *30*, gen. *punes*, 359 II *a 41*, plur. dat. (or abl.?) *punes*, 361 IV *33*. Closely akin to Gr. πώνι-ον, from the root *pōi-*, 'bibere,' cf. L. *pōculum* etc.

ponisiater, apparitoris sacri (uirgam portantis), U. 366 VI *b 51*, subst. gen. sg. m.=*puniśate* 357 I *b 15*. Perhaps derived ultimately from the prec. word; if so, the meaning is 'uini sacri promus.' The suffixal part is like that of L. *pannuceatus*

pon-ne, Umb.=L. *quom* (v. inf.), 366 VI *b 43*, 367 VII *b 2=pone* 366 VI *b 48, 49, pune* 356 I *b 1*, 357 I *b 10, 11, 12, 15, 19, 33*, 358 II *a 1, 7*, 360 II *b 16, 21, 22, 27*, 362 V *a 8, puni*, 357 I *b 20*. Almost certainly derived from *quom-de like *pane* from *quam-de*, which survives in Lat. The shorter *pom may perhaps be seen in *arnipo* as *pam in *prepa*

Ponties, nomen, nom. sg, m., Pg. 210= Osc. *Púntiis* 39, and the probably older spelling Πομπτιες 1. Cf. *gens Pontia*, Ind. III; the name is of course derived from the 5th ordinal, cf. L. *Quinctius*

Pop, abbrev. nomen or praenomen, Fal. 326 *b*, Umb.-L. xliii. *10*, p. 434; cf. *Poplio-*, *Popaio-*, etc.

Popaio, nomen, nom. sg. m., Umb.-L. xliii. *10*, p. 434; cf. *gens Poppaea* in Ind. III

Popdis, nomen, nom. sg. m. N. O. 219. =O. *Púpidiis*, 44, 45, 54, *Pupdiis* 138; cf. *gens Popidia* in Ind. III

Popia, nomen, sg. f. Etr.-Fal. 345

Poplia, Fal. 339, xl. *19, 21*, p. 375 and cf. perhaps *pop* 326 *b*, and *Popia* 345

poplo-, Umb. subst. m. = L. *populus*; acc. sg. *poplom* 366 VII *a 15*, 367 VII *b 3*, *poplo*, 366 VI *b 48*, VII *a 29, 46=*

puplum 357 I *b 10*, *poplu* ib. *40*, gen. *popler* 365 VI *a 19*, 366 VII *a 16, 27, 30*, dat. *pople* 366 VI *b 55, 61*, VII *a 14, 17, 27, 31, 50*, abl. *poplu* 366 VI *b 54* bis, with postp. *popluper* pro populo ib. *43, 45*, VII *a 3, 6, 9, 10, 18, 21, 24, 26, 32, 35, 37, 41, 53=pupluper* 356 I *b 2, 5*

Populona, epithet of Iuno in Campania, 153 A q.v.

pora, quā, Umb. abl. sg. compound relative (perhaps identical with O. *poizad*), 366 VI *b 65*, v. p. 479

porca, i.e. *-caf* porcas, acc. pl. fem. U. VII *a 6=purka* I *b 27*

porculeta, Mars. 269 A q.v., and U. 370 A

porod, Praen.-L., n. xxxiii p. 322; possibly=L. *porro*, but as adv. or subst. neut. abl. sg.?

porse, *-sei*, *-si*, v. *po-*

portatu = L. *portato*, U. 366 VI *b 55*, =*purtatu*, 357 I *b 18* impv. 2 or 3 sg. act.; *portaia*, 3 sg. subj. 367 VII *b 1*; *portust*, 3 sg. fut. perf. ind., ib. *3*

posmom, v. *postmo-*

post, Osc.-Umb. adv. and prepn. = L. *post*: Osc. Adv. *pússt*, 95 *b 7*. As prepn. with abl., 28 *8* (errore sculptoris iteratum), *23* (with *exac*), *29* (*eizuc*, neut. sg.); 95 *b 19*; in 180 *a 5* (*pust*) the object is lost. Umb. prepn. with abl. *postertio*, 366 VII *a 46*, =*pustertiu*, 357 I *b 40*; *post*, 365 VI *a 58 b 3, 22*, 366 VII *a 38, 46* (*pos*), =*pus*, 356 I *a 7, 14, 24*

postin, secundum, Germ. 'nach,' Osc.-Umb. compound prepn. with acc.: Osc. *pústín*, 95 *b 8*. Umb. (in distributive sense with plur. object), *pustin*, 359 II *a 25*, 361 IV *13*, spelt *pusti*, 362 V *a 13*, 363 V *a 18, 20, 21*, =*puste*, 356 I *a 25* and *posti*, 364 V *b 8*

postmo-, Osc. adj. superl. = L. *postumus*, nom. pl. fem., *pustm[as]*, 105 *a, b*; acc. sg. neut. used as adv. *posmom*, 26 *16*

postne, a tergo, adv., U. 365 VI *b 11*, cf. *perne*, and on *-ne* v. *arnipo*, *nepon*

postro-, Osc.-Umb. adj., = L. *postero-*: Osc. loc. sg. m. *pústreí*, 117 *a 4*, and governing gen. *b 7*; and *pus-* 102 (i). Umb. acc. pl. fem., *postra*, 364 V *b 13*; acc. neut. ip. *pustra*, 359 II *a 32* =*pustru*, 360 II *b 19*, *postro* 365 VI *b 5*, 366 VII *a 8*; cf. the foll. and *pústiris*

postro, retro, Umb. adv., 366 VII *a 43*, *44=pustru*, 357 I *b 34, 36*
*ποτερεμ, *41 p. 530
poumilionom, Πυγμαλεόντων, gen. pl. masc. Etr.-Praen. 303
pous, v. *puze*.
Pr = the Osc. equiv. of L. *praetor*, 28 *23, 27, 28* bis
Pr abbrev. praen. O. 77 A
pr = *pru* in O. 28 *21* (cf. *13*)
pracatarum, *praco uel *prace praeditarum, adj. used as subst. gen. pl. fem., U. 365 VI *a 13*, v. the foll.
praco, subst. fem. acc., U. 365 VI *a 13*; *tertia* *prax was one of the points in the lustral peregrination of Iguvium; cf. also [*p*]*racom* Pg. 216 *1*; for the probable meaning v. s. v. *perstu*.
Praefecti Capuam Cumas, v. p. 100
praefucus, praefectus, O. 28 *23*, from *prai-* and *facus* q.v.
praesentid, praesente, adj. or parte. abl. sg. fem. O. 28 *21*
praesilium, 309 B q.v.
prai, Osc. prepn. with abl. (of time), 115, 116; = Umb. *pre*, *pre* with abl. (of place), 356 I *a 2, 11, 20*, 365 VI *a 22, 59*, VI *b 1, 2, 4, 19, 20*, 366 VII *a 7*. The apparent restriction of meaning in our inscc. in both dialects is no doubt accidental, cf. U. *prepa*.
praicim-e, in potentiam, regnum, regionem, uel sim., subst. acc. sg. probably neut. with postp., Pg. 216 *5*
pre, v. *prai*.
prebaiam (si sic uox finienda), O. 130 *a 3*, is compared by Büch. with L. *praebia* (n. pl.) 'amulet,' a connexion which can only, I think, be allowed if the Lat. word is mis-spelt for *prebia in order to suit *praebeo* from which its sponsors strangely derive it, v. the Lexica
precario, precario, Mars.-Lat. 273
prehubia = Lat. *praebeat*, pres. subj. 3 sg. U. 362 V *a 12*, spelt *prehabia* ib. *5*; *-hub-* is no doubt the phonetic, *-hab-* an etymologising spelling
preiuatud = Old L. *priuato*, i.e. reo, abl. sg. O. 28 *15, 16*, cf. p. 508 footn.
prepa, priusquam, lit. = *praequam, U. 366 VI *b 52*, cf. *pane* sup.
prepesnimu, prius precator, 2 or 3 sg. impv. depon., U. 360 II *b 17*, v. *prai* and *pesnimu*.
preplohotatu, 2 sg. impv. act., U. 366 VII *a 49*, i.e. preplotatu, 366 VI *b 60*, one of the verbs of the curse; no doubt from *pre-* and *ploto-*, planipes, meaning 'impedito, claudum facito.'

presoliaf-e, Umb. subst. acc. pl. fem. with postp. 365 VI *a 12*; perhaps = tribunalia, rostra, sedilia publica
Prestotă-, a Umb. goddess connected with Šerfus Martius (spelt once *-tat-*): voc. *Prestota* 366 VI *b 57, 61*, VII *a 9, 11, 13, 15, 16, 18, 19, 21, 22, 25, 26, 28, 29, 31, 33, 34, 35*, dat. *Prestate* 357 I *b 27*, *Prestote* 366 VII *a 6, 8, 24*, gen. *Prestotar* ib. *20, 22, 33, 36*. For the formation cf. L. *antistita*, where the verbal is active, as here. If *-o-* be the real sound, cf. *prehubia* from *prehabia*
pretod (before a following *d-*) = L. *praetor*, Fal. 321, abbrev. *pret* 323
pretra, posteriores, adj. compar. acc. pl. fem., U. 364 V *b 12*; either for *praetr-* or *prītr-*; if the latter cf. N. Osc. *pritrom-e*
preuendu, aduertito, inserto, uel sim., 2 sg. impv. act., U. 366 VII *a 11*; v. *ahauendu*.
preuislatu, 2 sg. impv. act., U. 366 VII *a 49*, spelt *preuilatu* 366 VI *b 60*; Büch. derives from *uinco-* or *uincio-*, meaning either 'utterly overcome,' or 'bind hand and foot.' The Lat. *uinclum* rather favours the latter
prevo-, Umb. adj. = L. *pr(e)iuos*, i.e. in plur. 'singuli'; abl. pl. m. *prever* 362 V *a 13*; adv. *preve* separatim 356 I *a 28*, 358 II *a 9*
primogenea, primigeniae, dat. sg. fem., epithet of Fortuna, Praen.-L. 281
prinuvatus legati, uel sim., Umb. adj. or parte. used as subst. masc., nom. pl., 357 I *b 19, 23* bis, *prinuvatu* ib. *15, 41*, = *prinuatur* 366 VI *b 50, 65*, VII *a 1, 46, 52*; abl. com *prinuatir* cum legatis 366 VI *b 55, 56, 57*. Since they are clearly persons of dignity (sons of noble parents or the like) Büch. would explain the word as *prae-nouati, i.e. 'recens, ad hoc creati,' or 'noui magistratus,' etc.
prisnu, prima, adj. nom. sg. fem., Pg. 216 *2*
pristafalacirix, *praestabulatrix, i.e. antistita, sacerdos uel sim., nom. sg. fem., Pg. 216 *2*
pritrom-e, in id quod porro iacet, in iter, in futurum uel sim., Pg. 216 *6*; for this form of the stem cf. L. *pri-us*, *pri-s-tinus*, Gr. πρί-ν, etc., and perhaps U. *pretro-*
pro = L. *pro*, prepn. with abl., Mars. 267, Praen.-L. 286; = O. *pru* 28, *13, 24*; in U. perhaps as postp. in *ie-pru* 359

GLOSSARY TO THE DIALECTS. 649

II *a 32*, if the first part is for **ies*
abl. pl.
procanurent, *procecinerint, 3 pl. fut.
perf. ind., U. 365 VI *a 16*
*profated, meant for *prŭfatted*, *42
p. 531
proiecitad? (si uern lect.) proicito, Osc.-
L. n. iv, p. 31; beside Umb. *fertuta*,
etc. it would be possible to regard
this as showing an impv. form in
-tad, but no stress can be laid on the
text, v. crit. note
proles, 309 B Rem. q.v.
promom, primum, adv., U. 366 VII *a 52*,
=*prumum* 361 III *3, prumu* ib. *3,
23*; cf. Gr. πρόμος, Goth. *fram*, etc.
Propartie, for *-er*, nomen gen. sg. m.,
U. 355, cf. the *gens Propertia*, whose
home was in Asisium, and to which
the Roman poet belonged
propom, probum, acc. sg. masc., Osc.-
L. 159; scil. nummum uides, cf. the
note to 159, and Note xvi p. 143; for
the *-p-* cf. ropio
pros, Pg. 218; *pes pros* is commonly
rendered 'pedes *paros, i.e. paucos,'
but the supposed adj. stem *pro-*
appears to me to need further justification
prosecā-, Umb. vb.=L. *prosecare*, i.e. to
cut off the parts of the victim to be
offered to the gods: 2 or 3 sg. impv.
act., *prusekatu* 359 II *a 28*, 361 III
33, 35, IV *2*, spelt *prusektu* 359 II *a
28*; p. partc. pass. acc. n. pl. *pruseŝetu*
360 II *b 12*,=*proseseto* 365 VI *a 56*,
gen. *proseseto* 365 VI *b 16, 38*; dat.
prusesete 358 II *a 12*,=*proseŝetir*
365 VI *b 44, 46, prosesetir* 365 VI *a
56, 59*, VI *b 2, 4, 23*, 366 VII *a 4, 8,
42, 54, proseseter* 365 VI *b 20*. The
variation of the stem in the partc. is
parallel but not identical with that in
the Lat. vb. On '*prusektu*' v. the
crit. note ad loc.
Protus, praen. nom. sg. m. Praen.-L.
282
pru, and compds. with *pru* not given
below v. sub *pro, pro-*
prŭfā-, Osc. vb.=L. *probare*, regularly
used of the formal sanction given to
public works by the magistrate concerned, stating his approval of the
contractor's work (in a parallel sense
of a jovila erected on behalf of a
corporation 107): 3 sg. perf. ind. act.
prŭfatted, 42, 44 (abbrev. *-ttd*), 45,
49, 51, 170, 172; 3 pl. *prŭfattens* 39,
probably [*p*]*rŭfat*[*tens*] 178, abbrev.
prŭfts 107. From Osc.-Umb. *profo-*

=L. *probo-*, Italic **pro-fuo-*, cf. Skt.
prabhu-
prufe=Lat. *probē*, adv., U. 363 V *a 27*;
used as predicate like L. *bene est, male
est*, etc.
prŭffed, 3 sg. perf. ind., O. 87, 163; in
87 the meaning of *prŭfatted* would
be hardly suitable, as the insc. contains
merely a dedication; in 163 we have
only a block of stone left which tells
us nothing of the nature of the insc.
But Allen's suggestion (*Class. Rev.*
1896, p. 18) that this perf. and the
perf. pass. *prŭftŭ* (n. pl.) *set 95 a
16* should be referred to an Osc. equiv.
of L. *pro-dere* (containing the root
dhē-) as representing orig. *pro-fe-f-ed,
ἀνέθηκε, *pro-fe-ta, προθετά, is most
attractive
prŭfts, v. *prŭfā-*
prŭftŭ, v. *prŭffed*
pruhipid, prohibucrit, 3 sg. perf. subj.,
O. 28 *25, pruhipust*, 3 sg. fut. perf.,
ib. *26*, v. *hap-*
prumu, v. *promom*
prupehast, propiabit, piabit, 3 sg. fut.
ind. act., U. 361 IV *32*; cf. *piha-*, and
p. 513
prupukid, adv. or adverbial phrase
modifying *sverruneî* q.v., O. 95 *a
2*; from *prō-* and *pāc-* or *pāc-* (cf. L.
pāx, pāciscor); for change of vowel
cf. O. *praefucus* : O. *facus*
pruseŝia, prosicias, i.e. partes hostiae
primum sectas, acc. pl. fem. (or neut.?
cf. p. 404), U. 359 II *a 23*. From
prosecā- q.v.
prusikurent, pronuntiauerint, decreuerint, uel sim., 3 pl. fut. perf. ind.,
U. 363 V *a 26*
pruter, prius, Osc. adv. 28, *16, p*[*rut*]*er*
ib. *4*; cf. of course Gr. πρό-τερ-ος, U.
pro-mo-, etc.
pruzude, U. 361 IV *23*; Büch. regards the word as an adj. abl. sg.,
derived from *prō-(d)* and *sed-*, meaning 'praesente, praesto parato'
ptruna, v. *Petrunia-*
pukalatŭí, cognomen masc. dat. sg.,
O. 95 *a 4*, from *puclo-*, apparently
meaning 'prole felix ' 'Mr Quiverful'
puclo-, filius, puer, subst. common
gender, Osc. *valaimas puklum
optimae puerorum*, i.e. Εὐμενίδες,
Ἐρινύες, in the Curse of Vibia (130):
gen. pl., *puklum* 130 *a 4* (and ib. *3*
Büch. would read *pu*[*k*]*ulum* also
as gen. pl., but not referring to the
Eumenides), so no doubt ib. *2*,

puklu ib. *12*, *puk* ib. *9*. The form *puklui*, ib. *8* and *10*, if it be correctly written, may conceivably stand for the dat. pl. (*-uis*), but the dialect of this insc. is probably not pure Oscan
Pg. *puclois iouiois*, i.e. Διοσκόροις, dat. pl. m. 210, so also Mars. *pucl* 260 *b*
The correspondence in form and meaning with Skt. *putra-* 'son' is so close as to make this (Bücheler's) view of the word extremely probable; nor would it be easy to suggest another meaning which would suit the Mars. as well as the Osc. passages. The root is of course that of L. *puer* for *pou-er* (earlier **poues-*, probably a neut. noun like *genus*, made masc. to suit the sense)
puḍe, v. s.v. *po-*
pue, *pue quo*, rel. adv., U. 357 I *b 18*, 365 VI *b 38, 39, 40*, 366 VI *b 55*; i.e. **pu+-e* as *pafe=*paf+-e, pis-i= pis+-i* (on the variation *-e, -i, -ei*, cf. p. 495 and 506 footn.)
Puemune, Pomono, an Iguvine deity, dat. sg. m. 361 III *26, 35*, IV *5, 10, 12, 24*, gen. *Puemunes* 361 IV *3, 11, 12, 26*. He can hardly be separated from the L. *Pōmōna*, nor she from her *poma*, and as the Umb. form vouches for an orig. diphthong, we should refer *pōmum* to the root *pōi-* (cf. *pōculum*) in the sense of the 'juicy fruit.' The name only occurs in these, the most archaic, of the Tables (p. 400 ff.), and therefore I feel no difficulty in supposing that the later Umb. form would have been *Pōm-*, like *pone* from the same root
puf=L. *-cubi* (in *si-cubi, ne-cubi*), of place, O. 60, 61, 62, 63, 79; cf. the foll.
pufe=L. *-cubi*, of place, U. 357 I *b 33*, *pufe* 365 VI *a 8*, 366 VI *b 50*, VII *a 43*. On L. *ubi* etc. v. s.v. *pūtro-*
-**puh**, Osc. indef. affix in *svai puh* siue, 130 *a 10, 11*=U. *svepo* 365 VI *b 47*, *svepu* 356 I *b 8*; cf. p. 470
pũiu, perhaps = Lat. *cuio-*, interrog. adj. (nom. sg. fem.?), O. 164
p]ũllad, ubi, O. 95 *b 34*, si sic legendum, v. p. 479
Pũmpaiians = L. *Pompeianus*, Osc. ethnicon of Pompeii, nom. sg. m. 42 *4*, gen. *-neís* 39 *9*; acc. fem. *-na*, ib. *5*, dat. *-naí* 42 *2*
-**pumpe**=L. *-cunque* in *pisi pumpe* quicunque, nom. sg. m., U. 362 V *a 3*

pumpeḍias, quinctiles, nom. pl. fem. subst. or adj., U. 360 (II *b 2*); parallel to Osc. *pũmperias*, both words denoting some group of families, and also the days of their solemn assembly (? on the Nones, as the fifth day of the month); cf. p. 110. The case of the following numeral is doubtful; possibly XII means 'mensis duodecimi'
pũmperias, Osc. subst. fem. pl., cf. p. 110 and the preced. q.v.: nom. pl., *pumperias* 105 *a, b*; abl. *pũmperiais*, 114, 115, 116, abbrev., *pũmpe* 106, *pũmper* 107, *pumperi* 123
pun, *pũn*, v. *pon*
pune, *puni*, v. *pone* and *ponne*
puntes, Umb. subst. fem. nom. pl., 361 III *9, 10*; abl. (or dat.?) *puntis* ib. *14*: the word denotes some groups or parts or order of the *fratres*, and Büch. hesitates between identifying the word with L. *pons* in its comitial meaning, or referring it to **pompe* 'quinque' (cf. πεμπάζειν). In point of the form the first explanation should perhaps be preferred
pũnttram, uiam, pontem uel sim., acc. sg. fem., O. 39
punum, unquam (cf. *pid-um*), O. 130 *a 6*
pupḍiko-, Umb. adj. epithet of *Puemun-*: dat. sg. m. *pupḍike* 361 III *27, 35*, IV *10, 12*, *pupḍiše* IV *24*, gen. *pupḍikes* IV *11, 13*, *pupḍišes* IV *4*, *pupḍšes* IV *26*. Büch. would identify the word with L. *poplicus* (later *pūblicus* from association with *pūbes*), but the evidence for the relation of orig. *-l-* to U. *-ḍ-* is not clear. On the variation *-k-, -š-* v. p. 403 f.
Pupdiis, *Pũpid-*, v. *Popdis*
Pupie, nomen, probably nom. sg. m., O. 77 *17*
Puplece, nomen aliquod Etr.-Umb. 353 *a, b, c*, cf. *d* ib.
puplu-, v. *poplo-*
Puponio, nomen, masc., Etr.-Fal. xl β 23 p. 375
pupu, Osc. or Etr.-Osc. 132
purasiaí, ignease, igneis sacrificiis proprinae, adj. dat. sg. fem., O. 175 *a 16*, *b 18*; cf. U. *pir*=Gr. πῦρ (but not, of course, borrowed from it)
purka, v. *porca*
purdi-, *purdoue-* (*purti-*, *purtue-*), porricere, deis sollemni modo offerre, the Umb. vb. denoting the consummation of the sacrifice (cf. the Elevation

of the Host in the Roman Catholic ritual); impv. act. 2 or 3 sg. *purtuvitu* 359 II *a 24, 29*, 361 III *33*, IV *1, 4, 6, 16, 18, 20, 22, purtuvetu* 360 II *b 17, purtuetu* ib. *11, purdovitu* 365 VI *a 56*; ind. fut. 2 (or 3) sg. *purtuvies* 360 II *b 28*, fut. perf. 2 or 3 sg. *purtiius* 356 I *a 27, 30*, 358 II *a 7, 9, purtitius* 356 I *a 33*; *purtinšus* 357 I *b 33, purdinšiust* 366 VII *a 43, purdinšus* 365 VI *b 23, 37, 38, purdinsust* ib. *16, 24*. P. partc. pass. nom. sg. neut. *purditom* 366 VII *a 45*, =*purdito* 365 VI *b 42, purtitu* 357 I *b 39*, 359 II *a 43*, 361 IV *31*, 363 V *a 18*, acc. pl. fem. *purtitaf* 356 I *a 18* bis, =*purdita* 365 VI *b 18*. There is no doubt whatever that all these forms belong in use to one verbal system, but they are variously explained. If it were allowed that Umb. -*ū*- became -*i*- in unaccented syllables (i.e. in all syllables but the first), and that -*i*- may represent -*š*-, the difficulties would be greatly lightened; but neither of these theories has been freed from all objection, though both still seem to me attractive

pure, igne, v. *pir*

pure, *puri*, qui, v. *po-*

purom-e, εἰς πυρόν, U. 365 VI *b 17*, acc. sg. with postp. 366 VII *a 38*; derived from *pur-* (U. *pir*), but its meaning is hardly distinguishable and Büch. suggests that the words were practically fused

[p]urtam, portam, acc. sg. f. O. 169, si uera coniect., v. ad loc.

purtifele, *porricibile, quod dis porrigi potest, adj. acc. sg. masc. (agreeing with *vitlu*) or neut. (with *totum sacrificium*), U. 360 II *b 25*; cf. U. *faśefele* and *purditom, purdouitu*

Purtupite, U. 361 IV *14*; Büch. renders, with great probability, *Porricipoti, i.e. 'numini omnibus porricientium ministeriis praeposito,' like *Ašetus* sup., and L. *Adolenda*, etc. in the *Acta Arval.*; cf. the prec., and, for the vowel change in the second half, L. *hos-pit-em* beside *potis*, Gr. δεσ-πότης

pus, v. *post*

puse, -*sei*, -*si*, v. *puze*

pūstiris, posterius, compar. adv., O. 169; cf. *postro-* and for the ending Osc. *mais*, L. *magis*, but the treatment of -*ī*- in *ceus*, 'ciuis' shows either that Osc. -*is* contains ī (cf. Gr. -ῑο(σ)-, πρῑν)

or that -*is* has been restored by some analogy; cf. *mins* supr.

pustmas, v. *postmo-*

pustnalaf, posticas, a tergo spectatas, Umb. epithet of the birds of augury, acc. pl. fem., 357 I *b 11*; abl. *pusnaes* 356 I *a 2*; from *postne* q.v.

pūst, *pūstin*, v. *post-*

pustra, *pūstreī, pustru*, v. *postr-* πυτίνη, 37 A q.v.

pūtereipid, etc. v. *pūtro-*

pūtiad, possit, 3 sg. pres. subj., O. 131 *8*, =*putiiad* 130 *a 6, 7, 8, 3* pl. *putīans* 131 *6*, =*putiians* 130 *a 7* bis. Cf. L. *potens, potui*

pūtro- = Gr. πότερος, L. *uter* indef., in derivv. with -*pid* in Osc. and -*pe* in Umb. both meaning 'uterque.' Osc. loc. sg. m. (or neut.?) *pūtereipid* 175 *a 18*, *put-* *b 20*; nom. pl. m. *pūtūruspid* 95 *a 9*, gen. pl. *pūtūrū[mpid]* ib. *23*. Umb. *putrespe* 361 IV *14* Büch. regards as gen. sg., but v. s.v. *erus*. The absence of the *c-* (earlier *qu-*) in Lat. *uter, ubi, unquam* etc. beside *si-cubi, ne-cubi* etc. has been explained plausibly by Zubatý (Berichte d. Böhmischen Gesellsch. d. Wissensch. 1892) as due to a wrong division of *ne-cuter*, *necunquam* etc. into *nec-uter* etc. Cf. Eng. *orange, eft* (beside *norange, newt*) etc. Possibly also *sicuti* was orig. *si-cuti*, and then divided *sic-uti* because of *sic*, which of course contains the pronominal -*ce* added to **si* 'so.'

puz, v. the foll.

puze (*puse, pusi, pusei*), Umb. particle =L. *ut*: (1) introducing clauses of purpose or object, *puze* 357 I *b 34, puse* 366 VII *a 43*; (2) introducing comparisons (with and without a finite verb, cf. p. 504): *puze* 358 II *a 4*; 360 II *b 9*; *pus-e* (-*i*, -*ei*) 365 VI *a 20, 27, 36, 46, 59*, VI *b 2, 4, 20, 23, 29, 37, 44, 46*; 366 VI *b 48*, VII *a 5, 7, 38, 42, 53*; 367 VII *b 3*. Osc. (in final clauses) *puz* 95 *a 17*, spelt *pous* 28 *9*; *puz*: *puze* as *pan*: *pane, pon*: *ponne* etc. On the initial sound of *ut* v. s.v. *putro-* sup.

pvt 130 *a 12* v. *avt* and crit. not. ad loc.

φ

Ⓟ φ, a sign of the Tar.-Ion. αβ occasionally but very rarely written for Osc. *f* v. p. 462, 463

Ⓟ, mille (in L. αβ), O. 28 *12, 26,* cf. the list of numeral signs ad fin. With the rest of the Lat. letters this no doubt comes from the Chalcidian αβ
Φαῦνος, i.e. Faunus, 37 D q.v.
φιστελια, v. *Fistelu*
φύτορες, O. 37 C, v. *futrei*

q

q in Lat. αβ = the Osc. equiv. of L. *quaestor*, U. *kvestur* (q.v.), O. 28 *28* bis, perhaps ib. *2*
q, in Latinian = Quintus, Quinti, Praen. 282, 285, Fal. 333 *c*; in 333 *a*, *q* is ambiguous (does *q.cue = quaestorque*?)
qoi = *cui* (or *qui*?), Old L. xxxv p. 329
queistores = L. quaestores, nom. pl., Mars. 266
quolundam, archaism for *colendam*, gerundive acc. fem., Fal.-L. 335 *b*
ququei, archaism for *coqui*, nom. pl. m., Fal.-L. 335 *b*

r

Ⓡ r, fifteenth letter of the Osc. αβ 81 *a*; v. the Table of Alphh.
r, abbrev. name, O. 77 A
racom, Pg. 216 *1*, v. *praco*
rahiis, nomen fortasse mutilum (*Marahiis?*), O. 137 *f 6, 9,* sed cf. *Rah...* ib. *c 4, 5*
ranu, abl. sg. masc. or neut. U. 360 II *b 19*, where it is parallel to *puni, vinu* and *une* and therefore denotes some kind of liquid; Büch. would compare L. *summa rana* which in an insc. of imperial date (*Eph. Epig.* III. p. 167), denotes a mark of depth fixed in the side-wall of a bath, but probably the *rana* here was simply named from the likeness of the mark to a frog. Gr. ῥαίνω is commonly referred to *rad-*, but the *-d-* may be merely a 'root-determinative'; cf. *randeme* inf.
ra[val]nnnum, [*ra*]*valnnum*, O. 144 *b, c*
randem-e, subst. acc. sg. with postp., U. 365 VI *a 14*; note that *-nd-* in pure Umb. can only represent an older *-nt-*; if a root *ra-* were recognised in *ranu* sup. this word might be referred to its partic. in *-nt-*; cf. U. *spantim* beside L. *spatior*
re, abbrev. for *regina*, dat. sg. fem., Umb.-L. xliii 4, p. 434
rē-, Umb. subst. fem. = L. *rēs* : dat. sg. *ri* 362 V *a 4, ri* abl. ib. 5, with postp. *reper* 367 VII *b 2*
rected = L. *recte* adv. Fal. 321; cf. *rehto-*
regaturei, rectori, dat. sg. masc., epithet of Jupiter in Samnium, O. 175 *a 12, b 14*
regen[ai], reginae, dat. sg. fem., a divine epithet, Mruc. 243 *10*
ῥέγες
ῥῖγες } reges, 186 D q.v.
regia oliua, 309 D q.v.
regie ?, regie adv., splendide, Praen.-L. xxxiii p. 322
rehto-, Osc.-Umb. = L. *rectus*, Umb. *rehte*, recto, adv. 363 V *a 24, 26, 29*; Osc. abl. sg. (si uera coniectura) 95 *a 16 r[ehtud]*
reloqui, Sab. 309 A q.v.
reluuia, reduuia, 309 B q.v.
remeligines ?, 309 B Rem. q.v.
restatu, reddito, instaurato (of a supplementary sacrifice), 2 or 3 sg. impv., U. 358 II *a 5*; cf. the foll., and observe the transitive sense
restef, iterans, restaurans, pres. partc. nom. sg. m., U. 356 I *b 9,* = *reste* 365 VI *b 47*; in form perhaps = L. *resistens*, and for the meaning Büch. happily compares L. *ager restibilis*, 'land that can be sown every year or twice in the same year.' Whether this partc. was felt to belong to the same paradigm as the prec. impv. we have not yet evidence to decide
ret, uox curta et dubia, Etr.-Praen. 297 bis; the same is true of *rit* Etr.-Praen. 289, though this does appear to be the name of a youth
retūmaf, i.e. *-afed*, denuo caelauit, 3 sg. perf. ind. act., O. 88; no doubt from τομή, which belongs to a class of words, those relating to art, constantly borrowed. Cf. the equally borrowed L. *lantumiae*
revestu, 3 sg. impv., U. 362 V *a 7, 9*; Büch. renders 'reuisito, i.e. inspicito'; v. pp. 514, 517
rit, v. *ret*
Rodo, nom. sg. name, Praen. 282, of a slave, perhaps abbrev., probably = Ῥοδῶν

rofo-, Umb. adj.=Old L. *rōbus*, and Osc.-Lat. *rūfus*, Ital. **roufo-* acc. pl. m. *rofu* 366 VII *a 3*, fem. *rofa* ib. *6*
ῥουοί, 37 A γ. q.v.
Romai, loc. sg., Old L. 304
Romana (porta), Sab. 309 A q.v.
ropio, Osc.-L. 205 C 8 q.v.
rubinā-, Umb. subst. denoting one of the halting-places in the lustration of Iguvium: acc. sg. with postp. *rubinam-e*, 366 VII *a 43, 44*, =*rupinam-e*, 357 I *b 35, 36*; loc. sg. *rubine* 366 VII *a 6*. If this is connected with *rubus*, *rubus* has no connexion in Italic with L. *rubēre* from *ruf-*
Rufries, nomen, nom. sg. m. Pg. 230, cf. *gens Rufria* in Index III
rufro-, Umb.=L. *rubro-*; acc. pl. m. *rufru* 357 I *b 24*, fem. *rufra* ib. *27*; gen. sg. m. as proper name, *Rufrer*, 365 VI *a 14*, whom Büch. would identify with L. *Robigus*, the god of rust and mildew
rupinie e, loc. sg. (with postp.), U. 357 I *b 27*, =*rubine* q.v.; possibly to be read -*nie*, i.e. -*nē(i)-e*, so that the *i* would be merely the final diphthong of the locative, remaining syllabic and developing a 'glide-consonant' before the postp.; if not, we must suppose two forms of the noun-stem (-*nā-* and -*niā-* or -*nio-*)
rusem-e, subst. acc. sg. with postp., U. 366 VII *a 8, 9, 23*; it denotes a spot to or on which *vestiϑia* is put in the neighbourhood of *rubinā*
rustix=L. *rusticus*, nom. sg. masc., used as a cognomen, Pg. 235

S

s ϟ, sixteenth letter of the Osc. αβ, 81 *a*
S, nota praenominis, fortasse Sexti, Pg. 211, cf. Osc. 6
s=seruos, Praen.-L. 282
s, nota incerta, Osc. 59 bis
Sa, nota praen., N. Osc. and Mars.: Pg. 207, 211, 212; Mruc. 244; Mars.-L. 261, 266, 268. Perhaps the equiv. of L. *Saluius*, but cf. the common Pg. fem. praen. *Saluta*
saahtūm, v. *sahto-*
Sabdia, nomen, nom. fem. sg., Pg. 228, cf. *gens Sabidia* in Index III
Sabini 310 A q.v.
Sabinis, nomen, nom. sg. m., O. 78, cf. *gens Sabinia*, Index III

sak, O. 169 v. *sakaraklo-*
sakahiter, sacratur (or sacretur?), 3 sg. pres. ind. (or subj.?) pass., O. 175 *a 19*; cf. p. 493
sacaracirix, sacratrix, antistita uel sim., subst. nom. sg. fem., Pg. 216
sakaraklūm, sacellum, templum, Osc. subst. neut. sg. nom. 95 *a 11, 17*, acc. 171, probably 162, 169, perhaps *sakrak* 118 *a*; gen. *sakarakleis* 95 *a 20*; abl. -*klūd* ib. *13*
σακορο, v. *sacro-*
sakra, Umb. v. *sacro-*
sakra-=L. *sacrare*, consecrare, feriis celebrare: Osc. pres. ind. pass. 3 sg. (or pl.?) *sakarater* 175 *a 21*; perf. subj. impers. *sakrafir* with acc. (v. p. 516 f.) 113, 114; pres. subj. pass. 3 sg. *sakraítir* 117 *b 5* (cf. p. 494); gerundive nom. pl. fem. *sakrannas* 113, abbrev. *sakranu* 114
sakrak.. v. *sakaraklūm*
sakrasias, sacrificio (non cena) celebrandae, adj. nom. pl. fem., O. 116, cf. p. 102
sacri-=L. *sacri-*, sacer, sacrificandus, Osc.-Umb. adj., and in neut. as subst.: Osc. acc. sg. m. or f. *sakrim* 130 *a 11*, 117 *a 6*; abl. as subst. *sakrid* 104, 114, 118 *b*, and no doubt 125; abl. pl. *sakriiss* 113. Latinian *sacri* doubtful xxvi *b* p. 295. Umb. neut. subst. acc. *sakre* hostia 358 II *a 5*; *sakre* acc. or dat. 361 III *8, 9, 12, 22, 30*, *sacre* nom. sg. 355; *sakre* acc. in 358 II *a 6*, 359 II *a 21*, may be adj. or subst.; acc. pl. neut. *sakreu* 362 V *a 6*, fem. *sakref* 356 I *a 18, 19*, abl. *sacris* 366 VI *b 52, 56*
sacro-=L. *sacer*, Osc.-Umb. adj. Osc. nom. sg. f. (or neut.?) σακορο 1. Fal. nom. sg. n. *sacru[m]* 321. Umb. nom. sg. abbrev. *sacr* 354 bis, acc. pl. fem. *sakra* 357 I *b 29, 37*, =*sacra* 365 VI *b 18*, 366 VII *a 40, 45*
sakruvit, consecrat uel sim., 3 sg. pres. ind. act., O. 102 (i); 3 sg. fut. ind. act. *sakrvist* 101, cf. pp. 505 f.; the future form seems to show that the verb belongs to the -*i-* stems
Sadiriis, nomen, nom. sg. m., O. 53 =*Sadries* Pg. 219, cf. *gens Satria*, *Sadria* in Index III
Safinim, ad Samnites pertinens, Osc. ethnic adj. probably acc. sg. 169 (where for this reason I doubt Pauli's restoration), 200, cf. p. 144
sahiis, nomen, fortasse initio mutilum, nom. sg. m. 137 *d 7*
sahto-, Osc.-Umb. adj.=L. *sanctus*:

Osc. nom. sg. n. *saahtům* 175 *a 17, b 19*, cf. *saa* 41: Umb. in fem. as subst. denoting a place in the lustral peregrination, acc. sg. *sahta* 357 I *b 35*, with postp. *satam-e* ib. *38, sahatam* 366 VII *a 39, 44, 45, sahata* ib. *5, 39*; loc. *sate* 357 I *b 31, sahate* 366 VII *a 41*

Saidiieis, nomen, gen. sg. m., O. 102 (i)

saipinaz, Osc. appellative adj. = L. *Saepinas*, nom. sg. m. 137 *f 7*, from *Saepinum* 187 A, cf. the foll.

Σαιπινς, Osc. appellative adj. nom. sg. m. 7; perhaps connected with *Saepinum* 187 A

sai[pi]sume, saepissime, Fal.-L. 335 *b*

salauatur = L. *saluator*, nom. sg. masc., apparently a proper name, Pg.-L. n. xxvi p. 249

Salaviis = L. *Saluius*, nomen, nom. sg. m., O. 135 *a*, cf. Index III

Salavs (= L. *saluos*), Osc. cogn. nom. sg. m. 90, = Σαλαϝς 13

Salier, Umb. subst. gen. sg. m., 365 VI *a 14*, cf. p. 408; Büch. counts the word as the name of a deity to be compared with the gen. sg. *Salisubsali* Catull. 17. 6; the Roman *Salii* themselves were priests, not deities

salu = L. *salem*, acc. sg. masc., U. 359 II *a 18*

Salu[e]na, used as nomen, nom. sg. m., Fal.-L. 335 *a*; *-na* is an Etruscan ending, cf. *Porsena, Caecina* etc.

Saluiedi, nomen, nom. sg. m., Mars. 265; cf. *gentes Saluidia, Saluidiena* etc. Index III

saluo- = L. *saluos*, Umb. adj., only as secondary predicate with the obj. of *seritu* 'saluom, -uam etc. seruato': acc. sg. m. and n. *saluom* 365 VI *a 51, b 33, 41*, 366 VII *a 15, 29, 30* = *saluuom* 365 VI *a 41, saluo* ib. *31, 32, 41, 51, b 12* bis, *33*, 366 VII *a 16*; fem. *saluam* 365 VI *a 51* = *salua* ib. *31, 41*, 366 VII *a 15, 29. salua* in 365 VI *a 32, 52, b 13, 34*, 366 VII *a 17, 31* = *saluua* 365 VI *a 42*, which Büch. regards as neut. pl., I prefer to count fem., agreeing with the immediately preceding word *frif*

salut- = L. *salus*, gen. sg. *salutus*, Praen. 280, dat. *salute*, Umb.-L. xliii 11, p. 434

Saluta, Pg. feminine name, nom. sg. 206, 217, 222, 227

samentum, Hern. 277 A q.v.

samíp......, uox composita mutila, O. 169; Pauli ingeniously identifies *samí*-

with L. *sēmi-*; if so, cf. *sē-men* : *sátus* etc.

Sancus, Sab. 309 A q.v.

sane, Praen.-L. n. xxxiii p. 322

sanes, Umb. adj. abl. pl. fem., epithet of *vempesuntres*, or, if that be an adj., of *karnus*, 361 IV *8*; Büch. renders 'sanīs,' i.e. 'integris, nulla religione contactis'

Sanqualis (porta, auis), Sab. 309 A q.v.

Sansio-, Umb. subst. masc., name of a deity: voc. *Sansie* 365 VI *b 9, 10, 12* bis, *14, 15* = *Saše* 360 II *b 24*; acc. *Sansi* 365 VI *b 8* bis, *Sansi* ib. *6*; dat. *Sansie* 365 VI *b 3, Sansii* 366 VII *a 37, Sansi* 365 VI *b 5, Saši* 356 I *a 15*, 360 II *b 10, 17, Saçe* 358 II *a 4*

Santia = Ξανθίας, nom. sg. m., Gr.-Osc. n. xiii p. 138; the omission of *-s* can be paralleled in Osc. inscc. of Campania, cf. 89, 106, 107

Sardinia, abl. sg. fem., Fal.-L. 335 *a*

sarnnu, si uera lect., Osc. name of a gate in Pompeii (now called Porta Herculanensis) acc. sg., probably masc., O. 60, 61

sarsite, adv. from p. ptc. pass., U. 365 VI *b 11*; Büch. renders with great probability '*sarcite, sarte*,' i.e. *uniuersim*, supposing *-s-* written for *-s-* as often, and comparing the Lat. augural phrase *sane sarteque audire et uidere*

sat, Old-L. xxxv, p. 329, possibly an abbrev. for *Saturnus*

Satanes, U. 360 II *b 4*, = *Satane* ib., dat. pl. m. name of a tribe, gens or family

sato, perhaps abbrev., Pg. 206

sauitu, 2 sg. impv. act., U. 366 VI *b 60*, VII *a 49*; combined with *sonitu* in the curse; Büch. compares Gr. σεύομαι, σοῦσθαι, but the Gr. initial σ- cannot be equated with Italic *s-* without explanation

Scaifia, nomen, nom. sg. fem., Pg. 217, cf. *gens Scaefia*, Index III

scalsi-, patera uel sim., Um. subst.: abl. sg. with postp. *skalše-ta*, 361 IV *15, 18, 20*, = *scalse-to*, 365 VI *b 16*; loc. sg. with postp. *scalsie*, 365 VI *b 5*, 366 VII *a 37*

scapla = L. *scapula-*, umerus, subst. fem. acc., U. 366 VI *b 49*

*Skiru, nomen dubium, Osc. vii p. 75

σκλαβενς, claui, subst. nom. pl., O. 17, with decl. of L. *homo* or *Anio*, and with the root L. *scalp-, sculp-*; the meaning appears to me to be indicated by the design upon the object, v. n. ad loc.

screhto-, Umb. ptc. = L. *scriptus*, O.

scrifto-: nom. pl. masc. *screihtor* 365 VI *a 15*, nom. sg. neut. *screhto* 367 VII *b 3*
scriftas=L. *scriptae*, p. ptc. pass. nom. pl. fem., O. 28 *25*, cf. the prec. and p. 495
scripulum, 205 Rem. 7 p. 226 q.v.
se, Vol. 252 *2*: according to Deecke= Umb. *sim*, L. *suem*, but the phonetic changes are not clear. Others identify this with *se*- 'si' in *sepis* ib. *1*
Se, abbrev. praen., Vol. 252 *4*
seciolucus, si una uox est, Etr.-Praen. 302 ubi v. n.
seculae, 153 A q.v.
sed, se, pron. abl. sg., Praen. 286
sed-, Umb. vb.=L. *sedēre*, impv. 3 sg. *sersitu* 365 VI *b 41*, pres. partc. nom. sg. *zedef* 356 I *a 25, 33, 34* = *serse* 365 VI *a 2, 16, b 17, 22, 41* in *serse comoltu* and *serse persnimu*; Büch. takes the first *serse* in VI *b 41* and *sersi* in VI *a 5* in the same sense. 3 sg. fut. perf. ind. *sesust* 365 VI *a 5* v. p. 485 footn. 2. For the sacrificial custom v. Macrob. *Sat.* 1. 10. 21
seemun[ar(-iss)], si uera lectio, ad Semones pertinentibus, O. 168 q.v.
sefi, v. *siom*
sehemeniar, v. *sehm-*
sehemu, v. *semu*
sehmeniar, adj. acc. sg. n., U. 357 I *b 42* = *sehem-* 366 VII *a 52*; connected by Büch. with *mensis*, U. *menzn-* and rendered 'semenstre,' but the phonetics are difficult, and the simpler connection with *sēmen* gives a better name for a market-place (*furu, furo*); but cf. the foll.
Sehsímbríís, si uera lectio, nomen, nom. sg. m., O. 63, which I would conjecturally render *Sexembrius* 'mense sexto natus'; if the sixth Pompeian month was called *Sehsímber*, the name would be a natural one for a freedman since the fashion of naming slaves after the months (of their birth, no doubt) was common all over Italy, cf. the Cognomina passim. With *Sexember* might be compared Old Fr. *Octembre, Witembre* v. Ducange (ed. le Favre) s.v.
sei, sis, v. *es*-
Seiclio, apparently nomen, Fal. 317
Seinq, Mars. 266, an abbreviated name of a *uicus* not elsewhere mentioned
seipodruhpei, adv., U. 365 VI *a 11*; the last three syllables=L. *utroque* (v. *pûtro-* sup.), and Büch. reasonably identifies the first with L. *sē(d)-*, rendering 'separatim utroque,' 'seorsum'
Seís=L. *Seius*, nomen, nom. sg. m., O. 67, cf. Index III
σέλπον, 37 B 3 q.v.
semenies, Umb. adj. loc. or dat. pl., 360 II *b 1*, = *sehmenier* 364 V *b 11, 16*, only in the phrase *s. dequrier* (*-es*) which Büch. renders 'semenstribus decuriis,' and which certainly denotes some periodical festival
semu, U. 365 VI *b 16*, = *sehemu* ib. *36*, only after *pesclu* and therefore either an adj. or postp. Büch. would compare L. *sēmi-*, mediaev. Lat. *semum, sematum* meaning 'half,' and render here 'precibus nondum finitis'
Semunu, appellative subst., attached to the deities *Cerfum*, gen. pl. m., Pg. 216 *4*, cf. L. *Semo Sangus* p. 357
senateís=Old L. *senati*, senatūs, O. 95 *a 8, b 9*, *senateis* 28 *3, 6*
sent, sunt, v. *es-*
sententiad, sententia, abl. sg., Fal. 321
sepis=L. *siquis*, Vol. 252 *1, 3*, cf. *pis* sup.
Sepis, Osc. praen. nom. sg. m. 106, gen. *Sepíeís* 107
seples, simpulis, pateris sacris, abl. pl. masc., U. 361 III *17*; clearly identical with the Lat. word, the first part of which may be the root of *simul, semel*, Gr. ὁμο- etc.
Seppiis, nomen, Osc. nom. sg. m. 48, cf. the praen. *Sep(p)is* (p. 472) and *gens Seppia* Ind. III.
sepse, adv., U. 365 VI *b 11*; Büch. analyses *sē-pse* comparing L. *sē(d)-* and *i-pse, reapse* etc., and rendering 'separatim'
Septematrus, Tusc. 306 A q.v.
sepu, Vol. 252 *3*; commonly rendered 'sciente' as abl. of the Vol. equiv. of Italic *sēpuos* Osc. *sipus*, q.v.
serevkid, Osc. subst. abl. sg. 39 *10*; if it agrees with *imad-en* it must have a local meaning, but it is commonly connected with L. *seru-ā-re* and rendered 'auctoritate, auspicio' etc., as governing the preceding *medíkeís*
seritu, servato, 2 or 3 sg. impv. act. U. 359 II *a 24*, *seritu* 365 VI *a 11, 15, 16, 31* bis, *32, 33, 41* ter, *42, 51* ter, *52, b 12* bis, *13, 33* bis, *34*, 366 VI *b 49*, VII *a 15, 16, 17, 29* bis, *30, 31, -tuu* 366 VII *a 15*. Cf. *anzeriā-* sup.
serse, *sersi*, *sersitu*, v. *sed-*
sersiaru, subst., or adj. used as subst., gen. pl. fem., U. 359 II *a 16*; the

name of a festival, no doubt connected with O. *kersnā-*, U. *śersnā-*, L. *cēna*

sese, U. 361 III *23*, IV *15 (testru s. asa)*, IV *3 (supru s. ereślum-a)*; Büch. regards it as abl. of a masc. or n. subst. denoting place or direction; it is clear that in combination with *testru* and *supru* it makes up a phrase denoting direction

sesed, sese, acc. pl., Fal.-L. 335 *b*

seso, sibi, pron. dat. sg., U. 366 VI *b 51*; cf. p. 502 footn.; *se-* perhaps stands for *sei or *soi (*suoi) like Gr. οἱ, μοι, σοι, L. *mi* (gen. and dat.)

sestaplens, lectio corrupta, Pg. 210 ubi v. n.

sestentasiaru, sextantem continentium, adj. of measure, gen. pl. fem., U. 361 III *2*, cf. *plenasier* sup.

sestoi?, Fal. 337, must contain some case of the praen. = L. *Sextus*

sestu, sisto, 1 sg. pres. ind. act., U. 360 II *b 24*; 2 sg. *seste*, sistis ib. *22*; 2 or 3 sg. impv. act. *sestu* ib. *22*; perf. subj. 3 sg. and 3 pl. in an ancient combined phrase 'let him or them offer(?)' (cf. Osc. *paí puí*, L. *si deus, si dea es* etc.) *stiti steteies* 357 I *b 45*, spelt *stiteteies* 359 II *a 44*. Cf. *sistu* inf. and for the sacrificial use, Verg. *Aen*. 8. 85

sesust, v. *seḍ-*

set, *set*, sunt, v. *es-*

setio, Etr.-Praen. 297

sevakne, sollemne, victimam, Umb. adj. or subst.; "in acc. sing. haud facile distinguas sitne ut *sakre* substantivum nomen neutri generis an adiectivum masc. aut fem. ut III *25 et 27*, si adiectivum est, utrum plur. an sing." Büch. 359 II *a 21*, 360 II *b 8* bis, *9, 10*, 361 III *22*, IV *16, 18, 19*, *sevakni* 361 III *25, 26, 27*; abl. sing. *sevakni* 359 II *a 38, 39*, *sevakne* 361 IV *23*; acc. plur. *sevaknef* ib. *22*, *seuacne* (subst. masc. or fem.) 367 VII *b 1*; abl. pl. *sevaknis* 359 II *a 36, 37*, 361 IV *25*, *sevakne* ib. *9*. Rightly derived by Büch. from Italic *sēuo-* 'totus' and *acno-* q.v.

seuo-, totus, omnis, acc. sg. n. used as subst., U. 356 I *a 5*, *sevum=seuom* 365 VI *a 56*; abl. pl. *seueir* 365 VI *a 18*; the word is identical with Osc. *siuom*, nom. sg. neut. (in apposition to *eituo*) or, better, acc. used as adv. = 'funditus' 28 *22*

Sexatrus, Tusc. 306 A q.v.

si, *si*, v. *es-* and *sim*

Sidikinud, Sidicino, ethnic adj. abl. sg. n., O. 150 *a, b*, cf. *Teanum Sidicinum* 154 A [and Pref. p. ix footn.]

sifei, v. *siom* and p. 477

siflare, 205 B 1 q.v.

sihitu, v. *śihitu*

Silanus, nomen Satyri, Etr.-Praen. 301

Silie (or *-es?*), *Silli*, nomen, nom. sg. m., O. 90, 89; cf. *gens Silia*, Index III

sim, Osc.-Etr. xi *10, 11, 12*, p. 98; von Planta would count this a parallel form to L. *sum*, O. *súm*, but it may be an abbrev. of some Osc. or more probably Etrusc. word

sim, suem, subst. acc. sg. m. and f., U. 360 II *b 1*, *si* ib. *7*; acc. pl. *sif* 356 I *a 7, 14*, *sif* 365 VI *b 3*, *si* 365 VI *a 58*. Italic *ū* became *i* in monosyllables in Umb.

Simos, Etr.-Praen. 302, ubi v. n.

siom, se, pron. acc. sg., O. 28 *5, 6*, and no doubt *9*, dat. *sifei* 131 *9*, spelt *seffi* (lege *sefei*) Pg. 209; cf. p. 477

sipus, sciens, nom. sg. masc. perf. ptc. act. (p. 491), from the Osc. equiv. of L. *sapere*, O. 28 *5, 14*; the inflection in Osc. is uncertain, and can hardly be that of the Volsc. *sepu* abl. sg. The word can hardly be separated from Old L. *sibus, persibus*: Varro *L. L.* 7. 6. 107 Multa apud poetas reliqua esse uerba quorum origines possint dici non dubito, ut apud Naeuium...in Demetrio persibus a perite, itaque sub hoc glossema 'callide' subscribunt. Similarly Festus 217 M. 'persicus' with corrupt quotations from Plautus ('nisi qui persicus sapis') and Naevius, and Paul. ex F. 336 M.

The relation between the forms admits of more than one explanation and I do not think *sibus* can be a borrowed word. See Stolz *Hist. Gram. Lat. Spr.* I. 140, Von Planta *Osk.-Umb. Gram.* p. 193; nor should the variation *hap-*: *hab-* be forgotten (p. 496).

sir, sis, v. *es-*

sir, O. 95 *a 1*; probably an abbrev., but of a title rather than of a cognomen

sis, sint, v. *es-*

sistiatiens, statuerunt uel sim., 3 pl. perf. ind. act., Vo. 252 *4*; we do not know enough of Volsc. to explain the ending *-tiens* or the curious stem *sistia-*

sistu, 3 sg. impv. act., U. 361 III *8*; Büch. renders 'sidito' i.e. 'sedeto,' but in form it is far easier to explain if it be identified with *sestu* = L. *sis-*

tito, and regarded as showing here an intrans. use as in L. *re-sisto*
siuom, v. *seuo-*
Siuttiis, nomen, nom. sg. m., O. 39, cf. *gens Sutia, Suttia* in Index III
Slaabiis, nomen, nom. sg. m., O. 87, cf. *gens Stlabia*, Index III
slāgi-, regio, limes uel sim., Osc. subst. acc. sg. *slagím* 95 *b* 8, 28, abl. *slaagíd*, commonly taken adverbially 'e regione' but v. p. 500
Smintiis, nomen, nom. sg. m., O. 136 *a* bis, *b*
smursim-e, Umb. subst. acc. sg. with postp., 365 VI *a 13*; Büch. compares *ad murcim*, a name of *intimus circus* at Rome, Varro *L. L.* 5. 154 (ubi Spengel *ad Murciae*) who adds, however, 'ibi est sacellum etiam nunc Murteae Veneris,' and the latter title must surely be connected with Gr. μύρτον which is rather far from *smursim*
snata, umecla uel sim., Umb. p. ptc. pass. acc. pl. neut. only in phrase *sn. asnata* as epithet of *veskla* uascula(?) 359 II *a 19*, =*snatu* ib. *34*, abl. *snate* ib. *37*, *snates* 361 IV *9*; Büch. p. 131 is no doubt right in connecting this word with Lat. *nāre* and comparing the name of the *pagus Arusnatium* near Verona, and of their chief priest *manisnauius* (*C. I. L.* v. 3931 —2); the word was probably not used outside this phrase
socie, socii, nom. pl. masc., Mars. 267
sociennis, xxiii p. 226 q.v.
Soies, nomen, nom. sg. m., Osc.-L. 20
sol, sol, Sab. 309 A q.v.
solium, 309 B q.v.
sollo-, totus, Osc. and Pg. adj., cf. 205 A; Osc. nom. (or acc.?) pl. m. *sullus* 137 *c 11*, gen. *sullum* ib. *12*=*sulum* 101; *sŭll* 114 is perhaps for **sŭllaís* loc. pl. fem.; adv. (perhaps instrum.) *suluh penitus* 130 *a 9*. Pg. *solois* 218 is commonly regarded as abl. pl. neut. used as subst.; cf. of course L. *sollicitus, soll-ers* etc.
sommo-=L. *summus*, Umb. adj. acc. sg. masc. *somo* 365 VI *a 9*, abl. *somo* ib. *10*; loc. sg. *sume* 359 II *a 15*, 361 III *1*
sonitu, sonato, intonato uel sim., 2 sg. impv. act., U. 366 VI *b 60*,=*sunitu* 366 VII *a 49*
sopir, siquis, pron. nom. sg. m., U. 366 VI *b 54*, v. p. 480
sopo- (*soppo-*?)=L. *suppus*, supinus, Umb. adj.: acc. sg. fem. *sopam* 366 VII *a 38*, *sopa* 365 VI *b 17*; acc. sg. m.

supu 361 IV *17* where it seems to govern a locative; acc. pl. fem. *supaf* 359 II *a 22*; neut. *supa* 356 I *a 9, 16*, 359 II *a 22, 30, 32*, =*supo* 366 VII *a 8*, *sopo* 365 VI *b 5*; abl. pl. *supes* 361 IV *8*. The word denotes the posture and parts of the victim appropriate to the infernal deities
Soresios, nom. sg. m., Etr.-Praen. 301; Büch. compares L. *susurrus*, Osc. *sverrun-*, and explains as 'fetialis, legatus sacro sanctus (sollemnia uerba muttiens)'
sorex, Fal. 333 *a*, perhaps a cognomen σοροϝμ, O. 22, probably a subst. acc. sg., commonly compared with Gr. σόρον, but the σ- of the latter is difficult (unless σόρον (for *σορϝον) be really an Osc. word introduced into Greek through Sicilian comedy, cf. p. 45)
sorsalem, Umb. adj. acc. sg. 365 VI *b 39*, gen. *-lir* ib. *38*, derived from *sorso-* q.v.
sorso-, *sudo-*, Umb. subst. masc.: acc. sg. *sudum* I *a 27, 30*, *sudu* 358 II *a 8, 9*, *sorsom* 365 VI *b 24*, *sorso* ib. *38*; gen. *sorser* 364 V *b 12, 17*; abl. *sorsu* 365 VI *b 28, 31, 35, 37*; acc. plur. *suduf* 356 I *a 33*. The word denotes some animal victim (in V *b 12, 17* it is on a level with a goat), of secondary importance (see I *a*); and Büch. would derive the first syllable from *su-*, Lat. *sus*, Umb. *si-*, comparing the abundant use of *porciliares* in Roman ceremonies
Sp, nota praenom., O. 115, no doubt= L. *Spurius*, cf. the nomen [*S*]*pŭriís* (?) in 50
spafu, spahamu, v. the foll.
spahatu, tendito, trahito, iacito uel sim., 3 sg. impv. act., U. 365 VI *b 41*, 3 sg. impv. pass. *spahmu* 365 VI *b 17*, *spahamu* 366 VII *a 39*, se iacito, saltato uel sim., p. ptc. pass. neut. nom. impers. *spafu* 363 V *a 20*. Brugmann has explained this partc. (U. *spafo-*= earlier **spansso-*) with L. *menso-*, *mensā-* (U. *mefā-*), no doubt rightly, as formed on the pattern of **tensso-*=L. *tensus* from the root *ten-* or *tend-* (L. *tend-*, Umb. *tenn-*), through the similarity of meaning (*Ber. k. Sächs. Ges. Wiss.* 1893, p. 143). The root appears in L. *spa-tium* and in the form *span-* in *spanti-* q.v., and *spon-* in L. *sponte* (on the *-o-* with that of *mons* v. Brugm. l.c. 144 footn.), perhaps also *sponda*, and is no doubt akin to that of Gr. σπᾶν, σπάσ-σαι

spantea, lateralia, adj. neut. pl., U. 359 II *a 30*, from the following, q.v.

spanti-, latus, subst. fem. acc. sg. *spantim (-ad)*, U. 361 III *33*, *spanti* 361 III *34*, IV *2*. Since all these forms are in Umb. *aβ* the *-t-* no doubt represents the sound of *-d-* after the *-n-* as regularly in Umb. (e.g. in *ostensendi*), but the original form was the common *-ti-*; the root is *span-*, an extension of *spa-* (v. *spahatu*), cf. Mod. Germ. *spannen* etc.

Σπεδις, praen. nom. sg. m., O. 7, cf. n. iii *a*, p. 15, and *gens Spedia*, or *gens Spendia* in Index III

spefa, Umb. adj. or partc. only as epithet of *mefa-*: acc. sg. 365 VI *a 56*, VI *b 20*, 366 VII *a 4, 38*; abl. 365 VI *b 5, 9* bis, *14*, 366 VII *a 37*. It is difficult to understand whether Büch. approves of the connexion with Gr. σπένδεσθαι (L. *spondeo*), which seems prima facie probable enough

speture, deo Spectori, dat. sg. masc., U. 358 II *a 5*; the deity supposed to assist the augurs (*karu speturiu*) at the Atiedian ceremonies

speturie, adj. dat. sg. fem., U. 358 II *a 1, 3*; from the prec., q.v.

spina, subst. acc. sg. fem., U. 359 II *a 38*, with postp., *spinam(-ad)* ib. *33*, denoting some object near the altar, to be anointed in the course of the ceremony. No doubt=L. *spina*, but in what sense?

spinia, subst. or adj. used as subst. acc. sg. fem., U. 359 II *a 36*, with postp. *spiniam-a* ib. *37*; derived from the preceding

[s]pŭriis, si sic restituendum, nomen, nom. sg. m., O. 50; cf. Osc. praen. **sp.** and L. *Spurius*, and the foll.

Spurneis (or *-riieis*?), nomen, gen. sg. m., O. 63

St, abbrev. Pg. and Mars. praen. (perhaps for *Stenis* or *Statis*), 210, 232, 265, 266 bis

st, O. 88, perhaps abbrev. for *staflatū* uel sim., cf. 109

Στα, *Sta*, v. *Statis*

Staatiis, v. *Statiis*

stakaz, statutus, permissus uel sim., p. partc. pass. nom. sg. m., U. 359 II *a 15*

Staf[i]anam=L. *Stabianam* 39, Osc. ethn. adj. from *Stabiae* (154 A), acc. sg. f.; the Osc. form of the name perished at Stabiae because the town did, see p. 51 and cf. *Aderl* sup.

staflare=L. *stabularem*, epithet of victims, acc. sg. m., U. 365 VI *b 37, 40, staflarem* ib. *39*, cf. the corruption *stafli inve-* 356 I *a 30*

staflatas, *stabulatae, i.e. dicatae, erectae uel sim., p. partc. pass. nom. pl. fem., O. 109

staflii, si sana lect., stabularem, adj. acc. sg. masc., U. 356 I *a 30*; but possibly a syllable is omitted or miswritten so that we should read *staflari(m)*, q.v.

stahint, *stahu*, v. *staio-*

stahmei, augurio, rituum ratione uel sim., subst. loc. sg. (m. or n.?), U. 365 VI *a 5, 18*; of course from *sta-* 'stare, instituere'

stahmito, augurale, sollemne uel sim., adj. or partc. nom. sg. n. (perhaps as subst.), U. 365 VI *a 8*, loc. *stahmitei*, *-meitei* ib. *5, 18*; from the prec.

Staiedi, nomen, nom. sg. m., Mars. 265, cf. *gens Staiedia*, Index III

staiet, *stait*, v. *staio-*

Staiis, nomen, nom. sg. m., O. 174, cf. 172, and *gens Staia* in Index III

staio-, Umb.-Osc. vb.=L. *stāre*: Osc. pres. ind. act. 3 sg. *stait* 'dedicatus est' uel sim., 175 *b 22*, 3 pl. *staiet*, stant 95 *b 32*, 109, *stahint* 108 *a, -hint* 108 *b*; if *staief* in 113 is a complete word, it will be the present partc. act. nom. sg.; cf. also *statūs* inf. Vol. *statom* dedicatum nom. sg. n. 252. Old Lat. *statod*, 3 sg. impv. ('stato' or 'sistito'?) xxxv. p. 330. Umb. pres. ind. act. 1 sg. *stahu*, sto, dedicor, U. 355 (cf. Addenda); fut. ind. 3 pl. *staheren(t)*, stabunt 357 I *b 19*; impv. 3 sg. *stahitu* 366 VI *b 56*, pl. *stahituto* ib. *53*. Cf. *sestu*

statif, statua, Osc. (Samnite) subst. nom. sg., no doubt fem., 175 *a* passim; in form the word is parallel to L. *statio*, cf. Abellan *ńíttiúf* etc., which show a more original form of the stem in the nom.

Statis, praen. στατις, nom. sg. m., Osc. 14, Osc.-Gr. στα, iii. p. 15, Osc. *stat* 137 *b 9*, gen. σταττιης 1. Vol.-L. *Statis*, nom. sg. xxx. p. 269, Umb.-L. *Sta* xliii. *2* p. 433; cf. the foll. and p. 472

Statiis, nomen, nom. sg. m., O. 131 *6*, 141 *b*, *Staatiis* 173 *a*; cf. *gens Statia* in Index III and p. 472

statita, adj. or partc. pass. acc. pl. neut., U. 359 II *a 42*; Büch. renders 'supellectilem quae arae prius imposita est.' It is at least closely parallel with L. *statūtus*, cf. *purditom* sup.

statitatu, statuto uel sim., impv. 2 or 3 sg. act., U. 359 II *a 32*, 360 II *b 19*, 361 IV *9*; always in the formula *persnimu (ahtrepuḍatu) adpeltu stat*. From the prec.

statŭs, erecti, stantes (scil. lapides), i.e. statuae, effigies sacrae, p. partc. pass. used as subst. nom. pl. masc., O. 175 *a 1*; from *stā*-, cf. *staio*- sup.

Stenis, Osc. praen. nom. sg. m., 167, 138, cf. 170 and 1

Steniklum, O. 131 *1*; perhaps acc. sg. m. of a praen. with the same construction (sc. *denuntiat*) as *nůvellum* in l. 8

step, nomen dubium, O. n. viii. p. 78

stiplā-, Umb. act. vb.=L. *stipulari*, i.e. a dis flagitare; 2 sg. impv. act. *stiplo* 365 VI *a 2* (cf. p. 421 crit. note), 3 sg. *stiplatu* 365 VI *a 3*, 366 VI *b 48*, *51*

stircus, stercus, Osc.·L. iv. p. 31, cf. xxii. p. 225

stiteteies, v. *sestu*

stitisteteies, v. *sestu*

stlatta, 205 B 4 q.v.

strebula, U. 370 A q.v.

strena, Sab. 309 A q.v.

strittabilla, 205 B 4 q.v., but the form is commonly corrected to *strictiuilla*, a pure Latin word

strittare, *strittilare*, 205 B 4 q.v.

struhṡla, struem, libum alicuius generis, acc. sg. f., U. 359 II *a 18*, *28*, 361 IV *4*, *struṡla* 361 III *34*, *struṡla* 365 VI *a 59*, VI *b 5*, *23*, 366 VII *a 8*, *42*, *54*; gen. *struhçlas* 359 II *a 41*, 361 IV *1*. Cf. Fest. 310 M. strues genera liborum sunt, digitorum coniunctorum non dissimilia, qui superiecta panicula ('tuft') in transuersum continentur

struppearia, Fal. 349 A, v. *struppus* 306 A

struppus, Tusc. 306 A q.v.

su, Umb. prep. with abl.=L. *sub* (as in *sub rege Tullio*) 354

svai̇̊, si, Osc. 95 *b 15*, *svai* 130 *a 4*, *5* bis, *6* (*svaipid*), *10*, *11*, *suae 28 4*, *11*, *12*, *13*, *17*, *23*, *25*, *26*, *28* quater, *29*, *suaepis 17*, *20*;=Umb. *sve* q.v. If Lat. *sei*, *si* is parallel to this form (as Gr. εἰ to αἰ) its *s*- must be compared with that of old L. *sos* (Umb. -*so* in *sve-so*)=*suos*, *salum* with *in-solescere*, *in-solens* (Pokrowskij *Kuhn's Z.* 35, 230) beside Germ. *schwellen*, Gr. κονίσαλος, etc.

subator, omissi, neglecti uel sim., partc. or adj. nom. pl., U. 365 VI *a 27*, *36*, *46*, VI *b 29*; the meaning is fairly clear; Büch. and Buck are perhaps right in explaining it as *sub-hah-to*- from -*haf-to*-, -*hap-to*-; cf. *hapē*- sup. and p. 496

subahtu, 2 or 3 sg. impv. act., U. 359 II *a 42*; Büch. renders summoueto, amoueto, deriving the word from -*ha(h)tu*, i.e. **haptu*, 'capito'; cf. the prec.

subocau, supplico, probably 1 sg. pres. ind. act., U. 365 VI *a 22*, *24* bis, *34*, *44*, *55*, VI *b 6*, *8* bis, *15* bis, *26*, *27* bis, *36*, *subocauu* 366 VII *a 20* bis, *22*, *23*, *33*, *34*, *36* bis; cf. *stahu*

suboco, U. 365 VI *a 22*, *24*, *25*, VI *b 6*, *8* bis, *26*, *27* bis; only in the formula *tiom subocau suboco*, and as *suboco* is sometimes omitted, *subocau* would seem to be the verb of the phrase. Hence the simplest explanation of *suboco* is to regard it as a cognate acc. 'precem, preces,' being neut. if pl.

subotu, 3 sg. impv. act., U. 365 VI *b 25*, governing the acc. *capirso*(*m*)

subra, subra, U. adv. and prepn. with acc.=L. *supra*: adv. 363 V *a 20*, 365 VI *a 15*, *b 17*, *41*, 367 VII *b 3*; prepn. 365 VI *a 15*; cf. *supro*-

sukatu, 3 sg. impv. act., U. 361 IV *16*; Büch. renders 'declarato,' supposing it tantamount to *naratu*, which occurs elsewhere with *sevakne* (e.g. II *b 8*) in much the same context, and comparing U. *prusikurent* and L. *insece*, *insequis*, etc.

suḍum, v. *sorso*-

sve, si, U. 363 V *a 24* bis, *27*, *sue* 365 VI *a 7*, *16*, 366 VII *b 3*; *svepis*, siquis, 357 I *b 18*, 361 IV *26* (cf. *sopir* sup.), *svepo*, εἴτε, p. 481, 365 VI *b 47*=*svepu* 356 I *b 8*; *sve*=O. *svai̇̊* q.v. and cf. U. *nosue* sup.

svepis, *svepo*, *svepu*, v. *sve*

sverrunei̇̊, subst. dat. sg. masc., O. 95 *a 2*; Büch. compares L. *susurrus* and renders 'fetiali,' i.e. 'whisperer of sacred formulae,' and the word appears to denote some public official. For the form cf. Umb. *maro -onis*, 'magistratus'

Suesano, Suessanum, probably Lat., v. n. xvi. p. 143 f.

svesu, U. 357 I *b 45*, 359 II *a 44*, *sueso* 367 VII *b 1*; v. p. 501 f.

sufafiaf, partes quasdam hostiae, subst. acc. pl. fem., U. 359 II *a 22*, gen. sg. (for constr. v. p. 499) *sufafias* ib. *41*; Büch. renders 'subligacula cor-

42—2

poris,' i.e. testiculos uel glandulas similes corpori subligatas, comparing *effafillare* q.v. sup.

sufeḑaklu, acc. sg. neut., U. 361 III *16, 18*; a part or appurtenance of *feḑehtrum* (q.v.) and no doubt from the same root, with *sub-*

sviseve, in sino, capide uel sim., U. subst. loc. (perhaps with postp.? cf. *manuve*), 360 II *b 14* bis, *15*. L. *sesunium,* the name of a plant (Opillius Aurelius ap. Fest. 343 M.) may conceivably be a derivative, cf. Eng. *pot-herb*

sŭll, *sullu-, sulu-,* v. *sollo-*

sum, *sŭm,* v. *es-*

sume, v. *somo-*

sumel, adv., probably = Lat. *simul* (so Büch.), U. 359 II *a 27*; these words cannot be separated from L. *semel, similis.* How far was their variety produced by changes (under sentence-accent?) in Italic?

summeis, summis, adj. dat. pl. masc., Fal.-L. 335 *b*

sumtu = L. *sumito* (in some sacrificial sense), 2 or 3 sg. impv. act., U. 356 I *a 9, 16*

sunitu, v. *sonitu*

Suntia, praenom. nom. sg. fem., Pg. 228 (for **sum-to-lā* 'nursling'?)

suo-, v. *săvo-*

supa, v. *sopo-*

super = L. *super,* prepn. with loc., U. 357 I *b 41,* 361 IV *19*

superne, super, U. 366 VII *a 25,* probably prepn. with acc. (so Büch.); cf. U. *postne, perne,* L. *supernē,* whence *supernus*

Supn, i.e. *Supinas,* local adj. nom. sg. m., Mars. 266, ubi v. n.

supparo-, O. 205 A., q.v. with the foll.

supro-, Osc.-Umb. adj. = L. *supero-:* Osc. abl. (or dat.?) pl. *supruis* 130 *a 7; supr...* ib. *10*. Umb. *supru* possibly abl. sg., 361 IV *3,* v. *sese* sup.

Supunne, dat. sg. m. (or fem.?), clearly the name of some local deity of Fulginia, U. 354 *bis*; for the form perhaps cf. Lat. *rotundus, uoluenda dies,* etc. Is it to be connected with *somnus, ὕπνος,* etc.? More probably it contains *sup-* = L. *sub*; cf. the Lat. deities *Adolenda, Commolanda, Deferunda* (Act. Arval. 183 A.D.)

surur, item uel sim., U. 365 VI *a 20* bis, *56, 59,* VI *b 2, 4, suror* ib. *37*. With *-hont, sururont* 365 VI *b 39,* 366 VI *b 48, 51, 64* bis, *65* bis, VII *a 1* bis, *sururo* 366 VI *b 48, suront* 365 VI *b 8,* *20, 23, 37, 44, 46,* 366 VII *a 5, 7, 37, 43, 53*

sus, cognomen aliquod, perhaps abbrev., Fal. 330

sutentu, subtendito, supponito, 3 sg. impv. act., U. 359 II *a 23*; cf. *andendu,* etc.

sŭvo- = L. *suos,* Osc.-Umb. pron. poss. adj.: Osc. gen. sg. m. *suveís* 95 *a 9, b 9,* acc. sg. fem. *suvam* 130 *a 1,* probably *b 1*; abl. *sŭvad* 177, perhaps 168; *suv* 58 is doubtful. N. Osc. Pg. dat. pl. m. *suois* 209, abl. sg. f. *sua[d]* 216 *4,* perhaps *suad* 208 *bis.* Mruc. acc. sg. f. *suam* 243 *13*; cf. σFα 22. Also Latinian: Praen. abl. pl. *sue- (-que)* 286, *soueis,* Fal.-L. 335 *b*

Ś

ś, ḑ in Umb. *αβ,* **Ś** in Lat. *αβ,* often simply *S,* cf. pp. 464 and 495

Śefi, v. the foll.

Śerfo-, *Śerfo-, Serfo-,* a god of Iguvium: voc. sg. *Serfe* 366 VI *b 58, 61*; dat. *Śerfe* 357 I *b 24,* *Śerfe* 366 VII *a 3,* gen. *Śerfer* 366 VI *b 57, 58,* VII *a 6, 9, 10, 13, 15, 18, 19, 20, 21, 22, 23, 24, 25, 27, 29* bis, *32, 33* bis, *34, 35, 36, 41, Serfer* 366 VI *b 61* bis, VII *a 16, Śerfe* 357 I *b 28*

Śerfio-, *Śerfio-, Serfio-,* Umb. adj., ad **Cerfum pertinens:* masc. dat. sg. *Śefi,* Cerfio 356 I *b 4,* *Śerfi* 365 VI *b 45*; fem. dat. sg. *Śerfie* 357 I *b 28, 31,* *Śerfie* 366 VII *a 6, 8, 24, 41*; gen. *Serfiar* 366 VII *a 20, 23, 33, 36*; voc. *Serfia* 366 VI *b 57, 58, 61,* VII *a 10, 11, 13, 15, 18, 19, 21, 22, 25, 27, 28, 29, 32, 33, 34, 35, Serfia* 366 VI *b 61,* VII *a 16*

śersiaru, feriarum, subst. fem. gen. pl., U. II *a 16*; from *śers-,* cf. *śersnā-*

śersnatur = L. *cenati,* partc. depon. nom. pl. m., U. 363 V *a 22*; from the foll.

śesna, i.e. *śe(r)sna(m),* = L. *cenam,* subst. acc. sg. f. (for **cersna-),* U. 364 V *b 9, 13, 15, 18*; cf. O. *kerssnā-*

śihitu = L. *cinctos,* ptc. pass. acc. pl. m., title of a class of citizens or soldiers, U. 366 VI *b 59, sihitu* 366 VII *a 48*; dat. *śihitir* 366 VII *a 14, 28, 50,* sihitir 366 VI *b 62*, *šitir* 366 VII *a 13*; cf. p. 401 footn. 1

šihšeḍa, subst. acc., U. 361 III *15*; Büch. renders κιγκλίδας, i.e. the fencing or railing of the *kletrā-*, comparing also L. *cing-ere*

šimu, retro, adv., U. 357 I *b 23* bis, = *šimo* 366 VI *b 65*; cf. *šive*

šitir, v. *šihitu*

šive, U. 360 II *b 11*, *šive ampetu*, *fesnere purtuetu* which Büch. very plausibly renders 'citerius', i.e. citra uel extra templum impendito, in templo porricito,' comparing U. *šimu* retro, and Lat. *ceu*, which will therefore be equivalent to 'iuxta'

t

t T, seventeenth letter of the Osc. αβ, 81 *a*

t, nota praen. (=L. *Titus*?): Osc. 62, 141 *b*, cf. 172. Pg. 219, 224, 238, 239. Mruc.-L.? xxvii. p. 255. Latinian; Mars. 273; Fal.-L. 347 (cf. also *Tito*). Umb. 354, 355 *bis*, 362 V *a 3* bis, 363 V *a 15*

t = *tůvtiks* after *m.* = *meddiss*, Osc. 109, 171, 174

t, nomen, abbrev., O. 77 A *4, 8*

-ta, later *-tu*, *-to*, ex, ab, Umb. postp. with abl. *skalše-ta* ex patera 361 IV *15* = *scalseto* 365 VI *b 16*; *akrutu* ex agro 362 V *a 9*; *angluto* ab angulo 365 VI *a 8*, *pureto* ab igne ib. *20, tefruto* de rogo, 366 VII *a 46*, *uapersusto* 365 VI *a 12*

The postp. may well be akin to the L. *-tus* in *caelitus*, etc., Skt. *-tas* in *dēvatas*, etc.

tadait, aestimet, credat uel sim., 3 sg. pres. subj., O. 28 *10*; for the ending compare what is said on *-τ*, p. 462, and for the root cf. perhaps Gr. Dor. ἐπι-τᾱδες, κ.τ.λ.

Tadinate, Tadinatem, Umb. ethnicon from Tadinum (q.v. 371 A) acc. sg. 357 I *b 16, 17*, = *Tarsinatem* 366 VI *b 58* bis, VII *a 47* bis; gen. *Tarsinater* 366 VI *b 54* bis, *59* bis, VII *a 12* bis, *48* bis; dat. *Tarsinate* 366 VII *a 11* bis

Tafanies, nomen, nom. sg. m., Vol. 252 *4*

Tafidins, adj., apparently ethnicon of a town not elsewhere known, nom. sg. m., O. 174

tafle, in form=L. *tabulae*, in tabula, loc. sg. f. (with the foll. postp. *e*), U. 360 II *b 12*

ta[h]a, si uera coniectura, 3 sg. pres. subj., Mruc. 243 *11*; cf. Volsc. *atahus* and Synt. § 48 footn.

Talenate, name of a gens or tribe, dat. pl. m., U. 360 II *b 4, 5*

tammodo, Praen. 305 A q.v.

Tanacu, praen. fem. Fal.-Etr. xxxix. *7*, p. 374, cf. Θ*anacuil*, ib. *20*

Tanas, praen. nom. sg. m., O. 165, v.p. 469

tangin-, decretum, consultum, Osc. subst. probably fem.; acc. sg. *tanginom* 28 *9*; gen. *tangineis* ib. *9*; most common in abl. *tanginud* ib. *7* and *3*, *-nůd* 95 *a 8, 16, b 9, 25, -nud* 42, 49, cf. 43, 50, 52. Cf. for the root *tongitio*, inf.

Tantrnnaium, Tanternaeorum, nomen Campanum, gen. pl. m., O. 113, 114.

tapistenu, subst. acc., U. 361 IV *30*; some sacrificial requisite used after the fire is kindled and before it is extinguished by '*pune frehtu*': Büch. compares *tapis-* with L. *tepor* ('quasi tepestinum')

Tarincris, local adj., epithet of a hill, gen. sg., Mruc. 243 *6*

Ταρπίνιος? 37 B 4 q.v.

Taseos, Θήσευς? Etr.-Praen. 294, gen. *Tasei* ib.

tašez, Umb. adj., tacitus, nom. sg. m. 356 I *a 26*, 357 I *b 26, 30, 32, 44*, 358 II *a 7*, 359 II *a 39*, 361 IV *27*, = *tases* 365 VI *a 55, 59, b 2, 4, 20, 44, 46*, 366 VII *a 4, 7, 42, 54*, *tasis* 365 VI *b 23*; nom. plur. m. *tasetur* 366 VI *b 57*, VII *a 46*; the *-e-* of this last form must either be long by nature (so that the word would correspond to L. **tacētus*, *monēta*), or (?) have been restored after syncope by some analogy

Taties, nomen, nom. sg. m., Pg. 229, cf. *gens Tatia*, Ind. III

Taurei. ludi, Sab. 309 D q.v. and cf. the foll.

ταυρομ=L. *taurum* (and U. *toro-* q.v.), acc. sg., O. 5

Te, nota praen., Fal. 329

tebae, Sab. 309 A q.v.

τήβεννα, n. xxiii. p. 226 q.v.

tekvias, decuriales, nom. pl. fem. subst. or adj., U. 3C0 II *b 1*, cf. *pumpeḍias* sup.

tekuries, v. *dequrier*

ted, te, acc. sg. (governed by *endo* in) Old Lat., n. xxxv. p. 329

teḑa, *teḑte, teḑtu*, v. s.v. *dato-*
tedur, si sic legendum, adv., O. 95 *b* 30; commonly rendered 'ibi' and compared with Skt. *tatra*, but the ending has not been explained
teḑust, v. s.v. *dato-*
teer[ům], v. *terům*
tefe, v. *tiom*
tefrali, ad Tefrum pertinenti, Umb. adj. abl. sg. 365 VI *b 28, 35*; probably from *deus* *Tefer, but cf. the subst. *tefro-*
Tefre, Tefro deo, dat. sg. m., U. 356 I *a 24, Tefri* ib. *28, Tefrei* 365 VI *b 22*; acc. *Tefro* 365 VI *b 26, 27* bis; voc. *Tefre* 365 VI *b 27, 28, 29, 31* ter, *33* bis, *35, 36*. Cf. the foll.
tefro-, Osc. Umb. subst. = Gr. τέφρο-, in sacrificial sense: Osc. nom. sg. n. *tefůrům*, igneum sacrificium 175 *a 17, b 19*, Umb. abl. sg. with postp. *tefru-to*, ex rogo, 366 VII *a 46*; acc. pl. *tefra*, carnes cremandas (always as object of *prusekatu*), 359 II *a 27*, 361 III *32, 34*, IV *2*
tehtedim, subst. acc. sg., Umb. 361 IV *20*; Büch. would compare *teht-* with Lat. *tect-*
teio, te, Umb., v. *tiom*
teitu, v. *deic-*
Telis, i.e. *-isiad* ex Telesia, O. 182; cf. *Telesia* 187 A
Telis for Οέτις, Etr.-Praen. 295 ubi v. n. τελλίην, 37 D q.v.
tenitu = L. *teneto*, 3 sg. impv. act., U. 365 VI *b 25*
tennitur, *distennite*, rustic (possibly Umbro-) Lat. for *-tend-*, v. n. xxiii. p. 226
tenzitim, subst. acc. sg., U. 356 I *b 6*, = *tesedi* 365 VI *b 46*; from the context Büch. infers it is a kind of cake; the name may then be derived from the shape, which opens a wide field for conjecture
Ter, nota praen., Pg. 232 *bis*, fortasse Tertia
terkantur, 3 pl. pres. subj. (or ind.?) pass., U. 361 III *9*; Büch. renders doubtfully 'suffragentur,' i.e. 'assentiant,' conjecturing that *terk-* : L. *te(r)stă-ri*, O. *tristamento-* as L. *prec-* : *post-ulare*
Terede, Teretinates, 205 Rem. 9 (5) p. 230, but cf. also *Terentum*, p. 340
teremen-, terminus, Osc. subst. (neut. at Abella); τερίμη 37 C is perhaps a masc. nom.; nom. pl. n. *teremenniă* 95 *a 15, b 31, 32*; abl. pl. *teremniss* 95 *a 14*; the word is closely parallel, if not identical, with Old L. *termen*, Gr. τέρμα; we have no other Osc. pl. from a stem in *-n*, so that *-nniă* may be the regular acc. ending, the *-i-* having, if so, invaded the nom. acc. and dat. abl. pl. (*-niss*) of some or all neut. nouns of this declension, just as it has invaded the gen. pl. of many consouantal nouns in Lat., and all the neut. adjj. in nom. and acc.
teremnā-, v. *termnā-*
tereno-, 309 D q.v.
termnā-, Osc.-Umb. = L. *terminare*: Osc. perf. ind. act. 3 pl. *teremnattens* 39 *2, 5*, probably 40; perf. ind. pass. 3 sg. fem. *te[r]emnatu-st* 39 *4*; from this stem Bartholomae would also derive the mutilated *term* 95 *b 3*, restoring as 3 sg. pres. ind. pass. *term[nater]*, in spite of the absence of anaptyxis. Umb. p. ptc. pass. nom. sg. m. *termnas* 355; of course from *termno-*
termno- = L. *terminus*: acc. sg. with postp. *termnom-e*, U. 366 VI *b 57, 63, 64*; abl. sg. with postp. *termnu-co* 366 VI *b 53, 55, 37*; abl. pl. with postp. *termnes-ku* 357 I *b 19*
Tertineo, nomen, nom. sg. m., Fal. 323; cf. also *Tertinei* xli. p. 382
tertio-, U. ordinal = L. *tertius*: neut. acc. sg. used adv. *tertim* 366 VI *b 64*, *terti* 359 II *a 28*; abl. sg. after prep. as subst. *-tertiu* 357 I *b 40*, = *-tertio* 366 VII *a 46*, with subst. *tertiu* 365 VI *a 45, 48, 53*; loc. *tertie* 360 II *b 14*; dat. pl. *tertie* 366 II *b 6*, fem. acc. with postp. *tertiam-a*, ad tertiam, 361 IV *2*, *tertiam-e* 365 VI *a 13*
tertu, v. s.v. *dato-*
terům, area, terra, Osc. subst. neut. nom. 95 *a 18*, spelt *teer[ům]* ib. *12*; loc. sg. *tereí* ib. *a 19, b 23, 24*; gen. sg. *tereís* ib. *a 21*. The *-ee* shows that the first syll. was long but that it does not contain an Italic ē (Osc. í); hence there can be little doubt of the usual identification of the word as the neut. corresponding to L. *terra* for **tersā-* 'the dry land'
Tesenakes, adj. abl. pl., name of a gate of Iguvium, U. 356 I *a 11, 14*; = *Tesenocir* 365 VI *a 20, b 1, 3*, 366 VII *a 38*; the relation of the *-a-* and *-o-* is not clear to me
tesqua, Sab. 309 A q.v.
tetet = Osc. *deḑed*, O.-Etr. 99, v. s.v. *dato-*
Tettia, nomen, nom. fem. sg., Pg. 207;

GLOSSARY TO THE DIALECTS. 663

Tetio nom. masc., Umb.-L. xliii. *2*, p. 483; cf. *gens Tettia*, Index III

tettom-e, subst. acc. with postp., U. 365 VI *a 13, 14* bis

tetu, v. s.v. *dato-*

thesavrūm, subst. = Gr. θησαυρός, acc. sg. 95 *b 22*, loc. *thesavrei* ib. 26

Tianud, ex Teano (Sidicino), sg. abl., O. 150 *a, c* (on the case v. p. 500), *tianud* 150 *b*; on the case of *tiano* ib. *d* cf. xiv. p. 143 f.; loc. sg. *tiianei*, O.-Etr. 97

Tiati, O. 30, either abl. sg. ex Teate or abbrev. for *tiiatium*, ib. gen. pl. Teatium (Teanorum Appulorum)

tikamne, U. 358 II *a 8*; Büch. would transcribe *dicamne* = a Lat.* *dicamine*, dicatione, inuocatione, a loose abl. of accompaniment; mihi non liquet

tifata, 205 B 1 q.v. with Ind. I s.v.

t[i]fei, v. *tiiom*

tiia-, v. *tia-, tia-*

tiiom, Osc.-Umb. pron. = L. *tu* : nom. Osc. *tiium* 130 *a 5*, probably *tiū* 164; acc. Umb. *teio* 365 VI *a 22, tiom* 365 VI *a 43, 44, 45, 53, 55, b 8* bis, *9, 14, 15* bis, *25, 27* bis, *28, 35, 36*, 366 VII *a 10,18,19,20,21* bis, *22, 23, 25, 32, 33* bis, *34* bis, *35, 36, tio* 365 VI *a 24* bis, *25, 33, 34, 35, 54, b 6, tiu* 359 II *a 25* bis; dat. O. *t[i]fei* 130 *a 3* = U. *tefe* 357 I *b 13*, 360 II *b 24*, *tefe* 365 VI *a 18,* = L. *tibi*; v. p. 477

Tintiriis, nomen, nom. sg. m., O. 194, cf. *Tint* 88 and *gens Tintiria*, Index III

Tiperilia, nomen, nom. sg. f., Fal. 329; for *Tib-* as Fal. *p* often stands for L. *b*, cf. *Vipia*

tir, uox curta et dubia, O. 77 B

Tirentium, nomen, gen. pl. m., O. 101, cf. perhaps *gens Terentia*, Index III

tišlo-, dicatio uel sim., U. subst. m., nom. sg. *tišel* 359 II *a 15*; acc. *tišlu* 361 III *25, 27*; abl. *tišlu* 360 II *b 22*; Büch. reads *dišlo-* and derives from *dic-* in L. *dicare* etc., cf. *tikamne* and *tišit*

tišit = L. *decet*, 3 sg. pres. ind. impers. with subj. (p. 514), U. 359 II *a 17*. On the *-i-* of the first syll. cf. p. 506, footn. 2

Tito, praen. nom. sg. m. = L. *Titus*, Fal. 326 *a*, 341; cf. the abbrev. T supr.

titu, v. s.v. *dato-*

tiurri = L. *turrim*, acc. sg., O. 60, 61, aud no doubt 62

Tiatie, local adj. gen. sg. m., U. 364 V *b 9*; Büch. renders 'Latii,' perhaps correctly so far as the sounds are concerned, but it seems unlikely that the geographical Latium should be meant, cf. *Casiler*

toco, acc. masc. pl. (or acc. sg. masc. or neut.?), tuccos, i.e. sale conditos, or tuccum, U. 364 V *b 13*

todco-, v. *toutico-*

Toitesiai, si sic legendum, dat. sg. f., Old Lat. n. xxxv. p. 329

Tondrus = Τυνδαρεύς, Etr.-Praen. 302

tongitio, Praen. 305 A q.v.; perhaps connected with O. *tangin-*, consultum, scitum

τόροvος, 37 A q.v.

toru = Lat. *tauros*, acc. pl. m., U. 365 VI *b 43, 45,* = *turuf* 356 I *b 1*, spelt *turup* ib. 4; abl. *tures* 357 I *b 20*. Cf. Osc. ταυροµ, Sab. *Taureo-* sup.

totā-, **totco-**, **totico-**, v. *tout-*

touo- = L. *tuos*, pron. poss. adj., Osc. dat. sg. fem. *tuvai* 130 *a 11*, Umb. gen. sg. n. *touer* 365 VII *b 30* bis, = *tuer* 365 VI *a 27, 28, 37* bis, *47*; abl. sg. fem. *tuua* 365 VI *a 42, tua* 365 VI *a 30, 33, 40, 50, 52, b 11, 14, 32, 34*, 366 VII *a 14, 17, 31, 50*

toutā-, ciuitas, Osc.-Umb. subst. fem., Osc. nom. sg. *τωfτo* 1, *touto* 28 *9, 15*; acc. miswritten *tautam* ib. *19*; abl. *toutad* ib. *14, 21*; Mruc. dat. or loc. *totai* 243 *1, toutai* ib. *3*; Umb. acc. *totam* 365 VI *a 41, 49, 51, b 12, 33*, 366 VI *b 58*, VII *a 16, 29, 47, tota* 365 VI *a 29, 31, 39, b 31,* = *tuta* 357 I *b 16*; gen. *totar* 365 VI *a 30, 32, 39, 41, 49, 52, b 10, 13, 32, 34, 43, 45*, 366 VI *b 53, 59, 61*, VII *a 3, 6, 9, 10, 12, 14, 15, 16* bis, *17, 19, 21, 24, 26, 27* bis, *28, 29, 30* bis, *31, 32, 35, 37, 41, 47, 50, 52, 53,* = *tutas* 356 I *b 2, 5*; dat. *tote* 365 VI *a 5, 18, 24, 31, 33, 40, 42, 50, 53, b 7, 10, 11, 14, 26, 32, 34*, 366 VI *b 51, 62*, VII *a 11, 14, 18, 27, 31, 50,* = *tute* 357 I *b 13*; loc. with postp. *toteme* (cf. p. 484) 365 VI *a 26, 46*, alone *tote* 365 VI *a 36, b 29*; abl. with postp. *tota-per* 365 VI *a 23, 25, 34, 35, 43, 45, 53, 55, 58, b 1, 3, 6, 7, 9, 15, 19, 22, 26, 28, 35, 43, 45*, 366 VII *a 3, 6, 9, 10, 19, 21, 24, 26, 32, 35, 37, 41, 53,* = *tutaper*, 356 I *a 5, 8, 12, 15, 19, 21, 25, 29, 31, b 2, 5*, 361 III *29, tutape* ib. *24*

toutico-, publicus, Osc.-Umb. adj. from *toutā-*; Osc. masc. nom. sg. *tūvtiks* 87, 170, abbrev. *tūv* 44, 45, 47, *t* 109, 171, 174; Latinised *tuticus* 205 A q.v.; neut. acc. *touticom* 28 *10*; fem. nom. sg. *toutico* 28 *23*; gen. *touticas* ib. *5*; loc. abbrev. *tuvtik* 117 *a 8, tūvtikb 4, tūv* 107. Vol. abl. sg. (m. or n.?) *toticu* 252 *3*.

Umb. masc. nom. pl. *totcor* 365 VI *a 12*; neut. acc. sg. with postp. *todcom-e* 365 VI *a 10* bis; abl. pl. *todceir* 365 VI *a 11*; cf. the name *Totco* 370 C q.v.

*****τουτς**, uox dubia, p. 530

tr, nota praen., probably = Τρεβις C (L. *Trebius*): Osc. 47, 109, 131 *2*, 171; Pg. 210

tr, = the Osc. equiv. of L. *tribunus*, 28 *29*

tra, v. *traf*

trabea, τραβαία, 309 D q.v.

traf = L. *trans*, U. prep. with acc. and loc.: (1) with acc. *tra sahta kupifiaia* 357 I *b 35*, *traf sahatam etu* 366 VII *a 39*, *traha sahata combifia-* 366 VII *a 5, 44, 45*, t. *sahata couortus* ib. 39: (2) with loc. (the main verb is in all three places *fetu*): *trahaf sahate* 366 VII *a 41* = *tra sate* 357 I *b 31*, *tra ckvine* 358 II *a 13*. Its affection for *sahta-* seems to suggest that it had died out of use in later Umb. except with that word. The Umb. form in *-f* establishes the current explanation of *trans* as a crystallised nom. sg. of an active ptc. (cf. *superans, intrans*, etc.), since only an Italic *-nts* becomes at once *-ns* in Lat. and *-f* in Umb.; its combination with a loc. in Umb. shows that it was completely established in its new value

trahuorfi = L. *transuorsu*, adverbial abl. of verbal noun, U. 366 VII *a 25*: for U. *-rf-* from *-rt+t-* cf. U. *mefa*, L. *mensa* from *ment+tā-*, and contrast O. *ϝερσορει*, uersori

transenna, n. xxiii. p. 226 q.v.

Tre, abbrev. nomen, perhaps = *Trebiis* O. 77 A *3*, C 27

tre, Umb. = *tref*, v. *trei-*

Trebe, deo deacue cuidam, dat. sg., U. 356 I *a 8*, spelt *Trebo* 365 VI *a 58* in the same formula; it is on the whole more likely that this deity should have changed his declension (*-o-* to *-u-*) than his sex (*-ā-* to *-u-*) between the two recensions of the liturgy

trebeit, uersatur, considit uel sim., 3 sg. pres. ind. act., U. 365 VI *a 8*; cf. the deriv. *tremnu*; Büch. compares also Osc. *triíbom*, L. *trab-*

Τρεβις, Osc. praen., nom. sg. m., 6, probably abbrev. *tr* q.v. sup.

Trebiis, nomen, nom. sg. m., O. 47, cf. *gens Trebia* in Ind. III and *Tre* sup.

Treblano-, name of a gate at Iguvium, adj., acc. pl. m. *treblano* U. 365 VI *b 47*, = *Treplanu* 356 I *b 9*; abl. *Treblanir* 365 VI *a 19, 58, 59, b 2, 4,*

21, 23, 44, 46, 366 VII *a 5, 7, 53, Treblaneir* 365 VI *a 22*, 366 VII *a 42*, = *Treplanes* 356 I *a 2, 7.* For towns called *Trebula, Treba, Trebia* v. Index I, but they are all far from Iguvium

Trebo, v. *Trebe*

tref, *tre*, v. *trei-*

trefu-, Umb. subst. fem. = L. *tribus*: abl. sg. with postp. *trefi-per* 361 III *25, 30*; acc. *trifu* 357 I *b 16*, *trifo* 366 VI *b 58*, VII *a 47*; gen. *trifor* 366 VI *b 54, 59*, VII *a 12, 48*; dat. *trifo* 366 VII *a 11*

trei-, Osc.-Umb. numeral = L. *tres*: Osc. nom. pl. fem. *trís* 109, perhaps *tris* 119. Umb. acc. pl. m. and f. *tref* 356 I *a 7, 14, 20, 24, b 1, 4*, 357 I *b 31*, *tre* 356 I *a 3, 11*, 357 I *b 27, 43*, *trif* 357 I *b 24*, *trif* 365 VI *a 58, b 1, 3, 19, 22, 43, 45*, 366 VII *a 3, 6, 41, 52*, *treif* 365 VI *a 22*; acc. pl. n. *triia* 361 IV *2*; with postp. *triiuper* ter 357 I *b 21, 22* bis, 360 II *b 25* bis, *trioper* 366 VI *b 55*, VII *a 51*; abl. pl. *tris* 361 III *18* bis

trem or **terem**, uox corrupta, O. 96

tremitu, tremefacito, 2 sg. impv. act., U. 366 VI *b 60*, VII *a 49*; the *-eio-* suffix has its causative force as in Gr. φοβέω, L. *terreo*, etc.

tremnu, sede augurali, abl. sg. (for the case cf. p. 500), U. 365 VI *a 2, 16*; from *treb-*, v. s.v. *trebeit*

Treplan- v. *Treblan-*

Triatrus, Tusc. 306 A q.v.

tribḍisu, ternio, subst. nom. sg. fem., U. 362 V *a 9*; abl. spelt *tribrisine* 365 VI *a 54*; Brugmann (*Ber. K. Sächs. Ges. Wiss.* 1890, p. 207) plausibly explains the form as = a Lat. **tripedicio*, i.e. 'tres (hostiae) una pedica uinctae,' cf. Eng. 'a leash of hounds,' 'a brace of hare,' etc.

tribarakā-, aedificare, Osc. vb. trans., act. pres. inf. *tribarakavúm* 95 *b 10*, *triíbarak[avúm]* ib. 2; 3 pl. perf. subj. *-akattíns* ib. *21*; 3 sg. fut. perf. ind. *-akattust* ib. 15, 3 pl. *-akattuset* ib. 13; from *triíb-* q.v.

tribarakkiuf, aedificatio, subst. fem. nom. sg., O. 95 *b 11, 16*; from the prec., the ending corresponding to L. *-cio* (not to L. *-tio*) and the double *k* being due merely to the following *-i-*

trif, *trif*, v. *trei-*

trifax, 205 B 1 q.v.

trifo, *trifor, trifu*, v. *trefu-*

triíb-, aedes, aedificium uel sim., acc. sg. fem. *triíbúm* O. 42, cf. 62. Probably a root noun = L. träb-; for the ablaut cf. sēmen : sātus, etc.

Triib, si uera lectio, nomen mutilum, O. 168; cf. the prec.

trimodia, 309 D q.v.

tripler, triplicibus, adj. abl. pl. m., U. 363 V *a 21*

trĭs, tris, v. *trei*-

trĭstaamentud = L. *testamento*, subst. abl. sg., O. 42. The first syll. shews that L. *test-* stands for **terst-* from **trĭst-* as *certus* from *critus = Gr. κριτός

triumphus, borrowed from Gr., 205, Rem. 9, p. 230 q.v.

trstus, ptc. adj. or subst., m. pl., probably nom., O. 137 *f 10*; the choice for an etymon lies prima facie between L. *testis* (v. *trĭstaamentud*) and *tristis*

Trutiknos, Gallic, p. 528

Trutitis, nomen, nom. sg. m., U. 352, cf. *gens Truttedia* in Ind. III

trutum, adj. acc. sg. neut., O. 28 *15*; see p. 508 footn.; *trutas* fem., gen. sg. (or nom. or acc. pl.?) 130 *a 12*

tu, doubtful abbrev., O. 123

tua (*tuua*), *tuer*, v. *touo-* sup.

tuder, finem, U. subst. n. acc. sg., 365 VI *a 10, 11*; abl. pl. *tuderus* 365 VI *a 11*, 366 VI *b 48*. But we have also as masc. nom. pl. *tuderor* 365 VI *a 12*; acc. pl. *tudero* 365 VI *a 15, 16*; cf. p. 476 and the town *Tuter, Tuder*

tuderato, finitum, U. adj. or partc. nom. sg. n. 365 VI *a 8*

tuf, v. *dur*

tŭmaf, see *retŭmaf*

tuplak, i.e. *duplak*, subst. n. acc. sg., furcam uel sim., part of the *kletrā-*, U. 361 III *14*; cf. L. *duplex*, Gr. δίπλαξ

tupler, duplicibus, adj. abl. pl. m., U. 363 V *a 19*; cf. *tripler*

Tupleia, nomen uel praen., nom. sg. fem., Etr.-U. 353 *c*, cf. *Tvpei* ib. *d*

tures, *turuf*, v. *toru*

Tursa, dea Iguvina, voc. sg., U. 366 VI *b 58, 61*, VII *a 47, 49*; gen. *Tursar* 366 VII *a 46*; dat. *Turse* 361 IV *19*, 366 VII *a 41, 53*; spelt *Tuse* 357 I *b 31, 43*; probably connected with the foll.

tursitu = L. *terreto*, 2 sg. impv. act., U. 366 VI *b 60*, VII *a 49*, spelt *tusetu* 357 I *b 40*; 3 pl. *tursituto* 366 VII *a 51*; 3 pl. pres. subj. pass. *tursiandu* 367 VII *b 2* (on the constr. v. p. 513, 514); the Umb. word has the vocalism of the root proper to the causal in -*eio-*; the L. *terreo* must owe its first -*e-* to the influence of other words with the *e*-form of the root, perhaps *terror* if that is the older of the two

Turskum = L. *Tuscum*, ethnicon acc. sg. n., U. 357 I *b 17, Tuscom* 366 VI *b 58*, VII *a 47*; gen. *Tuscer* 366 VI *b 54, 59*, VII *a 12, 48*; dat. *Tursce* 366 VII *a 12*. On the historical value of these references (only an excommunication and a curse) cf. p. 407

turumiiad, langueat, tormentetur, conterreatur, uel sim., 3 sg. pres. subj. act. intrans., O. 130 *a 9* in a cursing formula

tută-, tuticus, v. *tout*-

Tutere, ex Tudertium urbe, name of an Umbrian town, abl. (cf. p. 500) sg., U. 368 *a*, cf. *Tuder* 371 A p. 438; abbrev. (or nom.?) *Tuter* 368 *b*, *Tut*, *Tu* ib. *c, d*. Cf. the subst. *tuder* supra; the unusual medial -*d*- (not -*d̦-*) marks the two words as identical

tuva, *tuves*, v. *dur*

tuvai, v. *touo*-

u û v

u V, eighteenth letter of the Osc. αβ, 81 *a, b*

û V, twenty-first and last letter of the Osc. αβ, 81 *a*; v. p. 463

v], sixth letter of the Osc. αβ; cf. p. 108

û, nota Osci praen., 52, 62, 141 *b*, and n. viii. p. 78

v], in Osc. αβ nota praen., probably for *vibis* q.v., Osc. 44 bis, 45 bis, 53 bis, 60, 61, 63, 71, 77 *5, 11, 16* = *u* V in Lat. αβ; Pg. 210, 212, 213, 220, 221, 234, 236, 244, and n. xxvii. p. 255; Mars. 261, 264, 268; Umb. 354 bis, 355 bis

vaamunim = L. *uadimonium*, subst. nom. sg. neut., O. 70

Vaaviis, nomen, nom. sg. m., O. 77 B *11*; cf. *gentes Vauidia, Vauilia*, Ind. III

vakaz-e, uacatio, uitium sit (or erit?), U. 356 I *b 8* = *uacos-e* 365 VI *b 47*; a subst. nom. sg. like L. *satias, -atis*, containing the orig. -*ti-* of verbal nouns superseded generally in Lat. by -*ti-ōn-*, with a part of the verb *es-*, v. p. 512 footn. The verbal stem of course is that of L. *uacā-re*, which is thus shown to be as orig. as the parallel Plautine *nocā-re*, which is an ablaut-variant like *notare* beside *uetere*, U. *tursi-* beside *L. terrē-* etc. No doubt *uacare* outlived its competitor because it saved confusion with *nocare*, 'to call.' The root appears in Umb. also in *uas, vaśetom* qq.v.

Vacuna, Sab. 309 A q.v.

Vahies, nomen, nom. sg. m., Osc. (Lat. *aβ*) 77 A *10*

valaimo-, optimus, Osc. superl. adj., neut. acc. sg. *ualaemom* 28 *10* (on the constr. v. p. 503); fem. dat. pl. *valaimais* 130 *a 12*, spelt *valamais* ib. *2*, but the proper restoration of this form and of *valaims* ib. *9*, and the construction and case of *valaimas* ib. *4, 8, 10* are uncertain through the fragmentary condition of the text. On the persons denoted v. s.v. *puklo-*. Büch. reasonably compares the L. *pira uolaema*, a large kind of pear

ϝαλε, O. 13

Valentia, U. 370 A q.v.

Valesies, nomen, nom. sg. m., Pg. 224 = L. *gens Valeria*, q.v. in Ind. III

Valetudne = L. *Valetudini*, a Marsian goddess, dat. sg. f., Mars.-L. 261, 263; it is not easy to say whether the penult was syncopated in sound or only in writing (for the latter cf. the note to 272); but *Fougno* and *Actia* 'Angitiae' seem to show post-tonic syncope in this dialect

vapeḑ-, solium aliquod augurale, U. subst. masc.: loc. sg. *vapeḑe* 361 III *7*; abl. pl. with postp. *uapersus-to* 365 VI *a 12, 13*, alone ib. *9*; acc. with postp. *vapef-em* 357 I *b 14, uapef-e* U. 365 VI *a 10*, 366 VI *b 51*. Büch. ingeniously derives from *vak-*, the root of U. *uas, vakaz,* and *-peḑ-*, rendering 'σκίμπους, solium sine pedibus, αὐτόξυλον,' which gives an excellent meaning since a Roman in taking auspices in the morning sat in *solida sella* (Fest. 347 M. with 348 s.v. *silentio surgere*). Such a use of the root-noun *vac-* seems to need further illustration in Italic, but it might easily arise from the pattern of such stems as *sim-plex*, U. *duplak, dupoḑ-* etc.

vaputu, Umb. subst. acc., probably pl. 360 II *b 10, vaputu* probably abl. sg. ib. *17, vaputis* abl. pl. ib. *13*; Büch. renders *tus*, connecting the word attractively with L. *uapor*, as *arbuta* with *arbor*

uas, uitium, Umb. subst. nom. sg., 365 VI *a 28, 38, 48*, VI *b 30*, probably fem., as it only occurs in the phrase *persei...tuer persoler uirseto auirseto uas est*, and the preceding adjj. have never final *-m*; hence the noun is parallel in form rather to L. *uox, lex*, than to L. *genus*, Umb. *meḑs* etc. Cf. *vakaz-e* sup.

vaśetum, uitiatum, in uitium, a supine (of the verbal stem *vakā-*, v. *vakaz-e* sup.) in the phrase *vaśetum ise*, U. 356 I *b 8*, replaced in 365 VI *b 47* by the equiv. *vasetome fust*, see p. 494. Nom. sg. neut. of the corresponding partc. pass. *uaśetom (est)* 365 VI *a 37*, spelt *uusetom* ib. *47*, VI *b 30, uaseto* VI *a 27*

uasirslom-e, subst. acc. sg. with postp., U. 365 VI *a 12*; Büch. would interpret *uaśirślom *uacellum* (i.e. *uacri-clum*), locus uacuos; it is a point in the *tuderor totcor*

uaso = L. *uasa*, acc. pl., probably neut., U. 365 VI *b 40*, abl. pl. *vasus* 361 IV *22*; but masc. nom. pl. (by attraction to the relative) *uasor* 365 VI *a 19*; *uaso* might be masc. for *uasof* since the following *po-rsc* is intermediate (p. 479), but it seems likely that the Lat. variation (*uas* neut. sg., *uasis* abl. pl., *uasus* nom. sg. Petron. 57) springs from an Italic doublet, cf. p. 476

vatra, adj. abl. sg. fem., U. 361 III *31*; this view (Büch.) is proved by the following *cruku*, which shows that the object of *feitu* is the sing. masc. or n. *sakre*, not *vatra*

vatuva, 'extorum cocturae idonea' (Büch.), Umb. subst. acc. pl. n., only in the phrase v. *ferine fetu*: U. 356 I *a 4, 13, 22, b 3, 5, vatuvu* 357 I *b 25, uatuo* 365 VI *a 57, b 1, 19, 43, 45* (ubi aes *uatue*), 366 VII *a 4*

ukar, *ukre, ukri*, v. *ocri-*

udetu, adoleto incendito uel sim., 3 sg. impv. act., U. 361 III *12*, IV *30*; the various uses of L. *adolēre* point to more than one origin; possibly the meaning 'inflame' really contains a Sabine word with *-l-* = pure Lat. *-d-* (p. 359 f.), Umb. *-ḑ-*. Whether this root were identical with that of *odor olēre* (p. 361) would be a further question. Cf. the foll.

udf[akium] (si uera est coniectura Buggii uerisimillima) olfacere, inf. act., O. 130 *a 7*; cf. L. *odor*, Sab. *ol-*, p. 361

ve, v. *Vesulliā-*

ϝε, abbrev. for ϝελεχ- q.v.

vea, v. *viā-*

GLOSSARY TO THE DIALECTS. 667

Vecilio, nomen, dat. sg. m., Fal.-L. 336 *1, 4*; cf. *gens Vecilia*, Index III
Vecineo, nomen, nom. sg. m., Fal. 327, 328 *a, b*; fem. -*ea* 325 *a, b*
uecos=L. *uicus*, Gr. ϝοῖκος, Mars.-L. 266, *necus* 263
uef, partes, acc. pl., U. 364 V *b 12* bis, *17* bis; from *ued-, as *kapif* from *kapiḍ*-; the root is that of Umb. *vetu*, L. *di-uid-ere*, *uid-uos*, Skt. *vidh*- (ultimately no doubt=*vi*-+*dhē*; but the Italic forms may come from *vi*-+*dō*-)
ueia (probably for *veh-ia), O. 205 A q.v.
vehiian, miswritten for *eehiian*- q.v.
Vehiies, U. 356 I *a 20*, *24*=*uehier* 365 VI *b 19, 22*, *uehieir* 365 VI *a 21*, adj. abl. pl. m., name of a gate of Iguvium, possibly=L. *Veiis*, referring to the South Etruscan town
Vei, si sic uerba diuidenda, Old Lat. xxxv. p. 329; perhaps for *Veiovis*, nom. or voc. sg.
Ϝει, Ϝειπ, abbrev. Greek name of Vibo, n. i. p. 4 q.v.
ueiro, i.e. *uirof*, uiros, acc. pl., U. 365 VI *a 30, 32, 39*, spelt *uiro* 365 VI *a 42, 50, 52, b 13, 32, 34*, 366 VII *a 17, 30*; the Umb. form (and cf. Vol. *co-uehr-iu*) has the quantity of Skt. *vira*-, not of L. *uīro*-
ueitam, uitam, Fal.-L. 335 *b*
uel, Etr.-Fal. praenominis nota incerta, n. xl. β *16*, p. 375
veleh, uox mutila, O. 137 *d 5*
ϝελεχα, ϝελεχ, ϝελε, ϝε, abbrev. Osc.-Gr. name of a vanished Campanian town, 151 q.v.
Velestrom, gen. pl. masc. Veliternorum, Vol. 252: for *Velet-tro*-, showing the same dissimilation as Lat. *pedestris*, *tonstrix*, etc.
Veliiesnipe, si uera lectio, O.-Etr. xi *4*, p. 97, perhaps contains a nomen in the gen.
Veliteis, si uera lectio, nomen, Etr.-Osc. probably gen. sg., xi *12*, p. 98
velliam, O. 131 *7*; if this is a subst. it must be a masc. name, acc. sg. (cf. Etr. *Porsena*, Fal. *Satuena* etc.)
Veltinei (or -*neis?*), O.-Etr. xi *10*, p. 98, perhaps a genitive
veltu, capito, deligito uel sim., 3 sg. impv. act., U. 361 IV *21*; so Büch., comparing L. *uelle*, but the precise meaning is uncertain; v. *ehveltu, ehvelklu*
ve[r]na, uox mutila et abbrev., O. 118 *a*, cf. p. 138
uenalinam, adj. or subst. acc. sg. fem., Mruc. 243 *12*

Venilei, praenom. masc., apparently dat. sg., O.-Etr. 99, *venileis* (possibly gen.), O.-Etr. xi. *2*, p. 97; cf. the foll.
Veneliis, nomen, nom. sg. m., O.-Etr. 99, cf. *Venlis* (perhaps praen.), O.-Etr. xi. *3*, p. 97
Venos=*Venus*, Etr.-Praen. 289, *Venus* 300
venpersuntra, Umb. subst. fem. abl. sg., 359 II *a 30*, *vepesutra* 360 II *b 18*; acc. sg. *vepesutra* 360 II *b 15*; abl. pl. *vempesuntres* 361 IV *7*; Büch. renders 'caro semidiuina,' i.e. those parts of the victim remote from the *prosicia* or choice parts cut off for offering, ascribing to *vem*- the meaning of L. *uē*- (in *uēcors*, etc.); cf. *persoudro*-
Ventarc, nomen, uel cogn. mutilum, Fal. 314
uepitus, uox corrupta, Etr.-Praen. 299, ubi v. n.
vepuratu, 2 or 3 sg. impv. act., U. 359 II *a 41*; Büch. renders 'restinguito,' which is quite possible; cf. the foll.
vepurus, subst. abl. or dat. pl., U. 362 V *a 11*; Büch. renders 'uisceribus,' i.e. 'demptis ex sacrificio carnibus quae praebere in cenam flaminem oporteat.' Gr. ἄπυρα ἱερά means 'sacrifices that need no fire,' but apparently something more in Aesch. *Ag.* 70
uerecunnus, n. xxiii. p. 226 q.v.
verehasiū́i, adj. dat. sg. m., O. 175 *a 11, b 13*; epithet of Jupiter derived probably from the foll. q.v.
vereias, subst. fem. gen. sg., O. 193, dat. *vereiiaí* 42; it clearly denotes some corporation of men (the *ver. pûmpaiianû* has property left it and with this the town-quaestor builds it a palaestra at the request of *kûmbenniefs*); Buck (*Osk. Vokal.* p. 76) rightly approves Büch.'s suggestion that the word is derived from *vero*-, 'gate' in the sense of 'Landwehr,' 'guards of the gates,' 'military reserves'
uerfale, the sacred augural enclosure (between imaginary lines), nom. sg. n., U. 365 VI *a 8*; cf. L. *uerbum*; the spot is 'finitum conceptis uerbis,' cf. Varro L. L. 7. 8; cf. the L. *effata*, id. 6. 53 'fines qui ab auguribus effantur'
vernisera ?, 205 C 2 q.v.
vero-, porta, Osc.-Umb. subst. m.: Osc. acc. sg. *veru* 61, abbrev. *ver* 60, abl. pl. *veruis* 109. Umb. acc. pl.

with postp. *veruf-e* 356 I *b 9=
uerof-e* 365 VI *b 47*; abl. pl. *veres
(pre-veres)* 356 I *a 2, 11, 20, (pus-)
veres* ib. *7, 14, 24*, with postp. *ueris-
co* 365 VI *a 19, 20, 21, b 23, 44, 46*,
366 VII *a 5, 42, 53*; *uerir* 365 VI *a
58, 59, b 1, 2, 3, 4, 19, 20, 22*, 366
VII *a 7, 38, uereir* 365 VI *a 22.*
Brugm. *Grds.* ii. § 706 abandons altogether the old connexion with L. *fores*
ϝεϱσοϱει,Versori,Victori,dat. sg. masc.,
epithet of Jupiter, O. 5; on the *-op-*
cf. p. 461
versus, 153 A q.v. and 370 D
veskla, vascula uel sim., Umb. subst.
n. pl. acc., 359 II *a 19, vesklu* 357 I
b 29, 37, 359 II *a 34*, 360 II *b 19*; abl.
veskles 359 II *a 31, 37*, 360 II *b 18*,
361 IV *9, 24, uesclir* 366 VII *a 9, 10, 18,
21, 24, 26, 32, 34.* The Umb. and Vol.
words can hardly be connected with
Lat. *uascula* unless one or other has
been changed to suit some resemblance of meaning in a different word
uesclis, subst. abl. pl., Vol. 252 *3*; commonly rendered 'uasculis,' cf. the
prec.
vesi, uox corrupta, fortasse pars nominis, O. 96
uesperna, Sab. 309 A q.v.
vestikā-, libare, Umb. depon., 2 or
3 sg. impv. *vestikatu* 359 II *a 24, 31,
35, 37=uesticatu* 365 VI *b 16*, 366
VII *a 8, 23, 24, 36.* P. parte. nom.
sg. m. *uesticos* 365 VI *b 25* (cf. p. 519);
cf. *uestis, vestiśia-*
Vestirikiiâi, nomen, dat. sg. m., O.
95 *a 1*, cf. *gens l'estricia* in Ind. III
uestis, cum libatione, uel sim., U. 365
VI *b 6* (where *uestisia* precedes it), *25,
uesteis* VI *a 22.* Büch.'s explanation
of the word as a contraction for '*ues-
ticans*' can hardly be defended on
phonetic grounds; the word may conceivably be (1) an adv. like Osc. *fortis,*
orig. an abl. pl. (or even like L. *mor-
dicus?*), or (2) a perf. parte. in form =
L. *uestitus*, but with the sense of
libans
Vestiśe, deo libationis, dat. sg. m., U.
358 II *a 4*, gen. *Vestisier* 365 VI *a 14*;
so Büch. *Umb.* p. 56, but on p. 125
he appears to prefer to connect the
word with L. *Vesta*
vestiśiā-, libamentum, U. subst. fem.
acc. sg. *vestiśia* 361 IV *14, 19, ves-
tiśam* 356 I *a 28, vestiśa* ib. *17, 31,
vesteśa* 361 IV *17, uestisiam*, 365 VI *b
39, uestisia* ib. *6, 17, 24, 25*, 366 VII
a 38; abl. *vestiśia* 359 II *a 27, vis-
tiśa* 360 II *b 13, uestisia* 365 VI *b 5,*

uestisa 366 VII *a 37*; gen. *uestisiar*
365 VI *b 16, 38*, 366 VII *a 38*
uestra=L. *uestrā*, abl. sg. fem., U. 366
VI *b 61*
Vesulliaís, nomen, nom. sg. m., O.
171; the ending is quite regular, =
L. *-aeus*, and the whole is of course
derived from the foll.
vesulias, subst. nom. pl. fem., O. 111
b, abbrev. *ves* 111 *a,* perhaps *vesu*
120, *ve* 121; dat. or loc. *vesuliais*
110, *-ulliaís* 109; v. p. 110
Vesune, deae Marsicae, dat. sg. f., Vol.
253, Mars. 264, Umb. *Vesune* (wife or
daughter of 'Pomonus'), 361 IV *3, 6,
10, 12, 25*. In view of the Mars. and
Umb. syncope, the *-u-* is probably
long; cf. *Fortuna, Pomona*, etc.
Vetio, nomen, nom. sg. m., Vest. 247 =
Vetius, Mars.-L. 261, cf. *gens Vettia*
in Ind. III
uetu, dividito, 2 or 3 sg. impv. act., U.
357 I *b 29, 37*; for the root v. *uef* sup.
Vetulio, nomen, nom. sg. m., Fal.
343, fem. *-lia* 344; cf. *gentes Vetilia,
Vettuleia,* etc. in Ind. III
Vezkeí, dat. sg., a Samnite deity, O.
175 *a 2, b 3*, associated with *Evklúí,*
and hence perhaps masc.
ûf, nota praenominis mutila, O. 190
ufestne, U. 361 IV *22*; Büch. would
regard this as an adj. abl. pl. derived
from a parte. parallel to L. *manu-
festus*, in the sense of 'uinculo coopertis,' but he is doubtful, and quite
rightly so, of deriving *-stno-* from a
parte. in *-sto-*
Ufiís, nomen, nom. sg. m., O. 91; cf.
gens Ofia, Index III
ufteis, gen. sg. p. ptc. pass., O. 130 *a
7*; Bugge compares U. *opeto-*, optatus,
optimus; *uhftis* 137 *f 11* would seem
to be derived from the same verbal
stem (?an acc. pl. from an *-i-* stem,
meaning '*spes, uota*')
ϝhεϝhακεδ, fecit, 3 sg. perf. indic.,
Praen. 280, ubi v. n.; cf. *fac-* sup.

uhftis, v. *ufteis*

ûhtavis=L. *Octauius*, nomen, nom.
sg. m., O. 131 *5, 7*, 190; cf. *gens
Octavia*, Index III. The *-ā-* in Italic
octāuos and the *-o-* in Gr. ὄγδοος I
believe to be equally the result of
levelling in different ways two I.-Eu.
forms of the stem, (1) *-āyos*, and (2)
-ǝyos becoming *-ǝyos* in proethnic Gr.
and proethnic Italic. For the change
in quality but retention of quantity
in Gr. cf. δοτός in place of *dǝtos*

GLOSSARY TO THE DIALECTS. 669

uhtretie, auctoritate, U. subst. loc. sg.
f., 362 V *a 2*, 363 V *a 14, oht* 355, n
probably eponymous office of the Atiedian brethren; from the foll., for the
suffix cf. *kvestretie*

uhtur (i.e. *oht*-)=L. *auctor*, nom. sg.
m., U. 361 III *7, 8*, acc. *uhturu* ib. *4*;
the word denotes an officer of the
Atiedian brethren. Hence *ohtretie-*
(*uht*-) q.v.

vIă-, Osc.-Umb. fem. subst.=L. *uia*:
Osc. nom. sg. *riú* 39 *4*, *40*, 95 *b 30*;
acc. *viam* 39 *2*, *via* ib. *5, 8*, 95 *b 7*;
loc. *viaí* ib. 31; acc. pl. *viass* 39 *7*.
Mars.-L. nom. *uia* 273. Umb. abl.
sg. *vea* 357 I *b 14, 23*, *via* 361 III *11*,
uia 366 VI *b 52, 65*, VII *a 1, 11, 27*

Vibđu, v. *Vibio-*

Vibedis, nomen, nom. sg. m., Pg. 223;
cf. *gentes Vibidia, Vibiedia, Veibedia*,
Index III

Vibiio-, nomen Osc.: dat. sg. fem.
Vibiiai 130 *a 5, 10*; masc. abbrev.
probably nom. sg. *Vi* 113, 114, and
probably *Ϝιβι*, O.-Gr. iii. *e*, p. 15; cf.
gens Vibia, Index III. Derived from
the foll., as *Trebiis* from *Trebis*,
p. 472

Vibio-, common praen.: Osc. nom. sg.
m. *Vibis* 133, 136 *a* bis, 136 *b*, spelt
Vilbis 190 (Frent.); Pg. (pure) nom.
sg. fem. *Vibđu* 216 *3* (v. Thurneysen
l.c. ad loc., and 206 n.); Pg.-L. *Vibia*
233, abbrev. *Vib* 226, 234; Vol. *Vi*
253; perhaps Mars. *Vip* (*Vib?*) 260;
Praen.-L. masc. *Vibis* 291; Fal. fem.
Vipia 324 (for the *-p-* cf. Fal. *Tiperilia*); commonly abbrev. *v*] in Osc.,
u √ in Lat. *aβ*, v. sup. *v*. Cf. the prec.

Victoria, Νίκη, Etr.-Praen. 296, 298,
299, spelt *Vit-* 289; dat. *Victorie Seinq*, Mars. 266

uiđa-, uia, acc. with postp. *uiđa-du*, ad
uiam, Pg. 216 *2*; *-du*=L. *dō-* in
dō-ne-c. For *-đ-* from *i* in Pg. cf.
Vibđu etc. and Thurneysen l.c. ad
loc.

Villis, si initio integrum, nomen, nom.
sg. m., O. 137 *d 2*; cf. *gens Villia*,
Index III

uincter, uincitur, conuincitur, 3 sg.
pres. indic. pass., with gen. of offence,
O. 28 *21*; see p. 516 f.

Viínikiís, nomen, nom. sg. m., O. 42,
cf. *Viniciiu*, apparently dat., O.-
Etr. 99, *gens Vinicia*, Index III and
vino- inf.

uín, uox mutila, O. 169, ubi Pauli
conicit *uín[itá]* 'unita'

uíniveresím, uniuerse, adv., O. 114

vino-=L. *uinum*, subst. n., Vol. abl.
(or acc. ?) sg. *uinu* 252, *2*; Fal. acc.
vino 312 *a, b*; Umb. acc. *vinu*
359 II *a 18, 40*, 360 II *b 14*; abl. *vinu*
356 I *a 4, 22, b 6*, 359 II *a 25* bis,
39, 360 II *b 10, 20*, *uinu* 365 VI *a 57*,
VI *b 19, 46*. The Fal. and Umb.
forms show that if this word=Gr.
ϝοινο- the change from *voi-* to *vei-*
must have happened in proethnic
Italic. It is unfortunate that we
have not the Osc. equiv.; but if
Viinikiis is based on this stem, the
Italic form was simply *uino-*, not
ueino-

Vinuchs, praen. nom. sg. m., O.-Etr.
99; cf. perhaps Osc. *Viínikiio-*

uiolasit=L. *uiolassit*, i.e. uiolauerit,
3 sg. fut. perf. ind. act., Umb.-L. xlii.
p. 397

Vipia, *Vip*, v. *Vibio-*

Vipleis, Etr.-Osc. name, probably gen.
sg. xi. *12*, p. 98

uirco, i.e. uirgo, nom. sg., Old Lat. n.
xxx. p. 329, I believe=Κόρη, Proserpina, v. n. ad loc.

ϝιριν∈ις or *Vipineis?*, gen. sg. masc.,
Osc.-Etr. n. v. p. 53 q.v.

Virriis, nomen, nom. sg. m., O. 131 *1*;
gen. sg. *Virriieís* 106, 109; gen. pl.
Viriium 110; the form *Virriiis*
131 *2*, if it is correctly written, must
be nom. sg. to a parallel stem in *-ēio-*;
cf. *gens Viria* in Ind. III

uirseto, uisa, p. partc. pass. nom. sg.
fem., U. 365 VI *a, 28, 38, 48*, VI *b 30*,
v. s.v. *uas* sup.

Visidianus, U. 370 D q.v.

Visni, nomen aliquod, Etr.-Fal. xl. β
16, p. 375

Vistinie for *-ie*(*r*), nomen, gen. sg. m.,
U. 355; cf. *gens Vestinia*, Index III

vistiša, v. *vestišia*

Vitelliú, Italia, Osc. subst. nom. sg. f.
199, *-eliú* ib., 201 *a, b*, *-eliu* 203.
Italia is really the form this word took
when borrowed into Greek, the initial
ϝ- being lost in the Greek dialects of
S. Italy soon after 400 B.C. v. p. 4; on
the derivation (L. *uitulus*=Umb.
vitlo-, Gr. ἰταλός) v. p. 48; and cf.
Addenda

vitlaf=L. *vitulas*, acc. pl. fem., U. 357
I *b 31*,=*uitla*, U. 366 VII *a 41*

vitlu=L. *uitulum*, acc. sing. m., U.
360 II *b 21, 24*; acc. pl. *vitluf*, 356 I
b 1, spelt *-lup* ib. *4*

uíttiuf, usus, subst. fem. nom. sg., O.

95 *b 14, 17*; variously explained as equiv. to Lat. *usio*, *utio, or *utitio

ûlam, subst. fem. acc. sg., O. 131 *9*, gen. *ulas* 130 *a 4, 12*; commonly interpreted 'sepulcrum, funus,' but it cannot be identical with the L. *aula*, *olla*, except as a borrowed word from (rustic?) Lat. into Osc.

Ulixes, v. 309 B Rem. p. 361

ullas, O. 137 *f 12*

ulo, illuc, U. 366 VI *b 55*, = *ulu* (in *purtatulu*) 357 I *b 18* (cf. p. 511 footn.), 363 V *a 25, 28, b 4*; for the stem cf. L. *olli*, *ŏlim* etc., and O. *pů-llad*

ûltiumam = L. *ultimam*, adj. superl. acc. sg. fem., O. 113; for the constr. v. p. 516

ûmbn, uox mutila, O. 169, ubi Pauli *ûmb̥n[i̥m]* = L. *omnem*

Umbreni, nomen, gen. sg. m., Aeq.-L. 273

umen = L. *omen* (or *unguen*?), acc. sg. n., U. 359 II *a 19, 34*; abl. *umne* ib. *38*, spelt *une* 360 II *b 20*

umtu, unguito, 2 or 3 sg. impv., U. 359 II *a 3*, 361 IV *13*. Is the resemblance of U. *um(b?)-* to L. *ungu-* in this word and in *umne* accidental or historical? V. s. v. *fiktu* sup.

une, v. *umen*

ungulo-, O. 205 A q. v.

unu = L. *unum*, adj. acc. sg. m., U. 358 II *a 6*; cf. Osc. oini-veresîm

Vo, nota praen., Fal.-L. 336; perhaps = *Volta*

uoco-, aedes uel sim., Umb. subst. (m. or n.?): abl. sg. with postp. *uocu-com* 365 VI *b 43, 45*, = *vukukum* 356 I *b 1, 4*; acc. with postp. *vukum-en* 361 III *20*, alone *vuku* ib. *21*; gen. *vuke* ib. *3, 21*. Commonly compared with L. *uicus*, Gr. ϝοῖκος (cf. *nosue* for *noisnae), and if this be correct, *vinu* cannot be the Italic equivalent of ϝοῖνος, v. s. v.

Vofione, deo uotorum, dat. sg. m., U. 365 VI *b 19*, = *vufiune* 356 I *a 20*; v. *vufetes* inf.

Vois, abbrev. praen., U. 355, no doubt the base of the foll. nomen, q. v.

Voisiener, nomen, gen. sg. m., U. 355, = L. *Voisienus*, v. n. ad loc.

Volcanom, Volcanum, acc. sg. masc., 185, cf. n. xvi. p. 143 f.; gen. spelt *Volgani* (by false archaism) Fal.-L. 335 *b*

uollia, nomen aliquod, Etr.-Fal. xl. β *24*, p. 375

Φολλοhωμ, Osc. 22

Voltai, proper name (m. or f.?) gen. sg., Fal.-L. 335 *a*

Volti, cogn. perhaps abbrev., Fal. 328 *a*, xl. β *15*, p. 375; cf. the prec. and foll.

Voltilio, nomen, nom. sg. m., Fal. 341, 342; fem. *Voltilia* 314, *Vot-* 325 *a*. Cf. the foll., and *gentes Voltidia*, *Voltilia*, Index III

Voltio, praen. nom. sg. m., Fal. 327, 338; cf. *gens Voltia* in Index III

Vomanio, nomen, nom. sg. m., Fal.-L. 347

uomu, subst. in *anderuomu*, U. 365 VI *b 41*; Büch. guesses 'rogos,' but the position of *ander* seems to show the ending is the adverbial -*mum*

uootum = L. *uotum*, subst. acc. sg. n., Fal. 321; cf. *vufetes*

vorsus, 370 D and 153 A q. v.

uouse, in uotis uel sim., loc. sg., U. 365 VI *b 11*; cf. *vuvsi* (according to Büch. = *uouicium, i. e. *uotum*), U. 357 I *b 45*, 359 II *a 44*, if so, the change in the final consonant of the root (I.-Eu. ṷogh-) may have been from -ghu- to -χu- to -hu- to -u- (so von Planta Osk.-Umb. Gr. p. 451). See *vufetes* inf.

ůp, v. *op*

upetu, 2 or 3 sg. impv. act., U. 360 II *b 1, 8, 11*, 361 III *22, 26*, 362 V *a 7*; 3 pl. *upetuta* 361 III *10*; variously explained as (1) the pres. stem corresponding to the perf. partc. pass. *opeter* (q. v.) and meaning 'optato'; (2) as = L. *obito*, i. e. arcessito

Upfals, praen. nom. sg. m., O. 134, 135 *a*; gen. sg. *upfaleis* 102 (i), -*lleis* 137 *f 5*; abbrev. ůpf ib. *d 7*, 48. The -*ll*- suggests a deriv. from the Italic equiv. of Gr. φαλλός, cf. Gr. Πόσθων

Ůpil, praen. nom. sg. m., perhaps abbrev., O. 113, 114, cf. *upils* 91

ůppiis, *uppieis*, v. Ὄπιες

ûpsă-, Osc. and Pg. = L. *operare* in the sense of 'aedificare': Osc. perf. ind. act. 3 sg. *upsed* 140 *a*, 177; cf. *ups* 172, 181; 3 p. *uupsens* 39 *10*, *upsens* 48, ουπσενς 1; gerundive acc. sg. fem. *ůpsannam* 42, 170; masc. or n. [*ůps*]*annu* 52, cf. 44, 51, 173 *b*; Osc.-Etr. nom. pl. m. perf. ptc. pass. *upsatuh (sent)* 97; Pg. 3 sg. (or pl.?) impf. subj. pass. *upsaseter* 239; cf. perhaps U. *osatu*, *oseto(m)*

Upsiis, nomen, nom. sg. m., O. 184 *d*, cf. *gens Opsia* in Ind. III, and *Upsiie*, O.-Etr. xi. *6*, p. 97 (perhaps gen.)

ûpsim, O. 92; if the text is to be trusted the word is either a neut. subst. nom. or acc. or, more probably, 1st sg. perf. subj. of some verb; v. ad loc.

ura-, *ures*, *uru*, v. *oro-*

Uranias, Οὐρανίας, gen. sg. fem., Pg. 216 *3*; Büch. interprets 'Veneris' (*Rh. Mus.* 33, pp. 285, 280), but the epithet is also applied to Demeter, Kore and Hera, v. the Lexica

urbid, urbe, abl. sg., Mars. 267

Urena, *Urinai*, abbrev. ethnicon of Hyria (contrast the Greek form Τριαvos), O. 142 ubi v. n.

urfeta=L. *orbitam*, i.e. a cake in the shape of a wheel, subst. acc. sg. fem., U. 360 II *b 23*; Büch. compares *summanalia*, Fest. p. 348 M., which were cakes of the same shape

ures, v. *oro-*

urina, *-nai*, v. *Urena*

urnasiaru, feriarum ab urnis appellatarum, subst. fem. gen. pl., U. 361 III *3*; abl. or loc. pl. *urnasier*, U. 362 V *a 2*, 363 V *a 15*; cf. *plenasier* sup.

urseïs, gen. sg., fortasse initio mutilum, O. 189 *a*; but *Ursus* was a common cognomen in Italy

urtas, *urtes, urtu*, v. *ortom* sup.

urust (causam) orauerit, 3 sg. fut. perf. ind. act., O. 28 *14, 16*; for the meaning cf. p. 508 footn. If the word is not borrowed from L. *orare* (as it may be), it would seem to show that *orare* is not connected with *ōs, oris* since the *-s-* would have remained in Osc.

uruvū=L. *urua*, curua, adj. nom. sg. fem., O. 95 *b 34*

usaṣe, Umb. 359 II *a 44*, spelt *usaie* (in the same formula) I *b 45*, loc. (or dat.?) sg. Büch. would render *kvestretie u.* quaesturae annuae, v. *ose*

ustentu, *ustetu, ustentuta*, v. *ostendu*

ustite, tempestate uel sim., loc. sg., U. 359 II *a 15*, 361 III *2*; Büch. derives from *os-*, v. *ose*; but a neut. subst. *obstitum* meaning 'a point to stop at' would be conceivable

usur, probably=L. *uxor*, Pg. 216 *2*, nom. sg. fem.

usurs, nisi curta lectio, subst. nom. pl., O. 130 *a 2*; Bugge renders 'osores, malevolo-'; Bréal 'uxores,' which seems to be favoured by the context; since if *Pakiu Kluvatiium* be gen. pl. as it probably is, some noun is required to govern it, and as Pakis Kluvatiis is the person cursed later on, it would not be his enemies that were cursed at the beginning. Cf. also the prec.

ute, v. *ote*

utei, uti, Fal.-L. 335 *b*

utur, subst. acc. sg. n., U. 360 II *b 15*;

Bücheler's rendering ὕδωρ is too attractive to be doubted; if so cf. of course L. *unda*, Skt. *udan-*, Gr. ἁλοσύδνη

uve-, v. *oui-*

vufetes, partc. or adj. abl. pl., uotiuis, U. 359 II *a 31*, 361 IV *25*; cf. *Voſione, vufru*. The root is *uogh-* which appears quite regularly in L. *uou-ere* (*-gh-* between vowels becoming *-u-*, as e.g. *niuem*) and a parallel form *eugh-* may be seen in Gr. εὔχομαι; cf. *uouse* sup., and for the participial stem *uirseto*

Vufiune, v. *Vof-*

ũvfrĭkũnãss, adj. mutilum, acc. pl. masc., O. 169, where Pauli conjectures *rufri-*, *roborignos, roboreos

vufru, uotiuom uel sim., adj. masc. acc. sg., U. 360 II *b 21*; v. *vufetes* sup.

vurtus=Lat. *uorterit*, intrans. like *couert-* q.v. (or *uorteris*, trans.?), U. 358 II *a 1*. If I have understood Bücheler's view rightly he would render *pune karne speturie naraklum vurtus* 'si quando in extis (or as dat. incommodi 'extis') quae inspiciuntur ominum narratio male uerterit, i.e. infausta fuerit.' This makes excellent sense, but it is a little harsh to give to the simple *vurtus* the sense of *male uertere*, though not impossible (the *extorum mutatio* to which he alludes in Cic. *de Divin.* § 35 means something quite different and is not a technical phrase at all)

uus=L. *uos*, 2 p. pron., voc. pl., Pg. 216 *6*; ib. *7* it appears to be dat.=*uōbis*; if so it stands for *uōſs*, *uōſ(i)s*, and the syncope would show that the *-i-* of *uobis* was orig. short (cf. Skt. *-bhĭs*) and owed its length to the influence of the dat. pl. of *o*-stems (*illis, eis*, etc.)

Vuẹiia-per, adj. abl. fem. sg. with postp., name of a tribe, U. 360 II *b 26*

vutu, lauito, U. 359 II *a 39*; hence some have plausibly concluded that Italic *l-* became *v-* at Iguvium, but the other evidence is slight, save the absence in Umb. of any words beginning with *l-* (except the praen. in 354, but that comes from Fulginia, and the owner of the name may have taken it from anywhere)

vuvẹi, v. *uouse*

uxo=L. *uxor*, Fal. 325 *a*, *uxor*, Etr.-Fal. 345

uze, v. *onse*

Z

z Ɪ, seventh letter of the Osc. αβ, 81 α
zeḍef, v. *seḍ-*.
zenatuo (for *-uos*) = L. *senatūs* or rather **senatuis*, gen. sg. m., Fal. 321; observe that the next word begins with *s*
Zertenea, nomen, nom. sg. fem., Fal. 324
Zextoi, Fal. 338; is this = *Sexti*, gen. sg. m.? And if so should we compare the Gr. Thess. gen. in -οι (whence probably the apparently plur. place name Φίλιπποι like 'Αθῆναι from a loc.)?
zicolom, diem, subst. (m. or n.?), acc. sg., Osc. 28 *14, 17*, abbrev. *zico* ib. *15*; abl. sg. *ziculud* ib. *16*; loc. sg. *zicel*[*ei*] ib. *7*; abl. pl. *zicolois* ib. *25*. The variation of the vowel in the anaptyxis with that of the foll. syllable is of course regular, cf. *comenei* : *comono*, etc. The word no doubt stands for **djēclo-*, a diminutive of *diēs*; how far north and west the assibilation of dentals before *i* spread is not clear, cf. Pg. *Vibātu*, etc.

NUMERAL SIGNS IN INSCRIPTIONS NOT WRITTEN IN LATIN ALPHABET.

(The arabic numerals refer to the inscriptions.)

|| 'two' xxi. p. 217
||| 'three' 39, xxi. p. 217
|||| 'four' vii. p. 75, 64, 67 bis (where it denotes the Quattuorvirate of Pompeii)
Λ 'five' xxi. p. 217
|Λ 'six' ib.
||Λ and ||V 'seven' ib.
|||V 'eight' ib.
X| 'nine' ib.
X 'ten' 39, 62, 66, perhaps 87, xxi. p. 217

|X 'eleven' 62, xxi. p. 217
||X 'twelve' 60, 61, 360 II *b* 2
|ΛX 'sixteen' xxi. p. 217
||ΛX 'seventeen' ib.
|||ΛX 'eighteen' ib.
||||ΛX 'nineteen' ib.
||XO 'a hundred and twelve' 59
⊙⊙⊙ (? si uera lectio) 'three hundred' 168
∞ ∞ (? si uera lectio) 'two thousand' ix. *f*, p. 81

Among the signs occurring in inscc. in Lat. alphabet may be noted: V||Ƨ 'seven and a half' 364; ↓ 'fifty' 354; ⊕ 'a thousand' 28 *26*; ⊕⊕ 'two thousand' 28 *12*.

FRAGMENTA ET CORRUPTELAE.

abuk··dn, p. 81
alpnupuz, p. 98
arasne, O. 144 *e*
arnn, p. 138
aurunkim, falsa lectio, 145 *b*
avieĭs, O. 178
αχερητ, O. 22
but, O. 137 *c*
cdimi and costf, p. 295
cela, p. 375
dare, O. 189 *a*
·e·renem, O. 192
erk, O. 69
fdiis, O. 137 *f 8*
hann, p. 5
·iasiis, O. 57
ig·paarigtĭs, O. 74
imr, Fal. 319 *b*
ist, O. 88
lare, O. 77 A
legib, 208 bis
mat, Osc. 40, Pg. 208*bis*
main, O. 96
μεται, O. 22
mirik...ui, p. 97

nied, O. 65
niel, O. 67
nutr, p. 375
pask, O. 77 B
pisu, O. 76
·poleenis, Mruc. 243 *9*
pperci, Pg. 209
pŭl, O. 77 B
puntaisa, p. 98
rah, O. 137 *c*
rex, Fal. 319 *a*
rezo, p. 375, β 26
sei, Pg. 209
sicu, 208*bis*
terem, O. 96
tita, p. 97
tura, p. 255
tus......, O. 130 *a 12*
veat, O. 76
uelzu, p. 375
verna, p. 138
uezθi, p. 375
uoc, Fal. 319 *b*
utpos, p. 374
vue, p. 98

INDEX VI.

INDEX OF LATIN WORDS.

'Gloss.' refers the reader to the Glossary which precedes this Index.

ā, ab, Gloss. s.v. *af*
abluda, 205 C, q.v.
acer, Gloss. *ocri-*
ad, Gloss. *-ad*
adeps, 309 B 2, q.v.
Adolenda, *dea*, Gloss. *Supunne*
adolere, Gloss. *uṛetu*
aenus, Gloss. *ahesnes*
aes, Gloss. *ahesnes*
aesar, Gloss. s.v.
aetas, Gloss. *aetat*
af for *ab*, p. 222, Rem. 1
af, Gloss. and p. 222, Rem. 1
albus, Gloss. *alfo-*
Alixentrom, 205, Rem. 9 (1)
Alpes, 309 A
amurca, 205 Rem. 9 (2), p. 229
Angitia, Gloss. *Anagtiai*
angulus = U. *anglo-*
antistita, Gloss. *praestotā-*
ap, Gloss. s.v. *op*
aperio, Gloss. s.v. *op*
apluda, 205 C 8, q.v.
apro-, Gloss. *abro-*
apur, cf. Mars. *apur*, and p. 273, Rem. 3
aqua, cf. 193 n.
ar = *ad*, p. 273, Rem. 3
ara, v. Gloss.
arbiter, Gloss. *adputrati*
arena, 309 A, s.v. *fasena*
arfuisse, p. 273, Rem. 3
aries, cf. U. *eriet-*
aruina, 37 A 3
aruom, Gloss. *arvā-*
aruorsum, p. 273, Rem. 3
asserere, cf. O. *aserum*
assum, Gloss. *asom*
atauos, Gloss. *-ad*
auctor = U. *ohtur*, v. Gloss. s.v. *uhtur*
auis = U. *avi-*, Gloss. *aveſ*

ausus, Gloss. *genetai*
autem, cf. O. *auti, aut*

b in Lat. = Osc.-Umb. *b* = Italic *b* (not *f*),
v. Gloss. s.vv. *hab-, triib-, Vibio-*
baetere, *bĕtere, arbiter*, etc., Gloss. *ebetraf-e*, and *adputrati*
bibo, cf. Fal. *pipafo*
bos, Gloss. *bou-*
bufus, 205 B 1
burrus, p. 228

Caecina, Gloss. *Saluena*
calidus (of horses), Gloss. *kaleḍuf*
callita, Gloss. s.v.
camur, 205 A
canus, cf. Gloss. *casnar* and 205 A
caper = U. *cabro-*
capis = U. *capiḍ-*
careo, Gloss. *kasit*
caro, Gloss. *karanter, karn-*
cascus, Gloss. *casnar*
Cassantra, p. 229 and Gloss. *Casenter*
castrum, Gloss. *kastru-*
catamitus, p. 229 f.
caterua, Gloss. *kateramu*
catulus = U. *katel*
catus, 309 A
cēdo, *cette*, Gloss. *cebnust*
Ceius, praenomen, Gloss. *Cc*
cena, Gloss. *kersnā-*
cenatus = U. *ſerſnato-*
census, Gloss. *censaum*
Ceres, 309 D and Gloss. s.v.
certus, Gloss. *tristaamentud*
ceu = Umb. *ſive*, 'citra, iuxta'
cibus ? = U. *kebu*, p. 403 f.
cinctus = U. *ſihto-*
cisterna, borrowed in U., 354

INDEX OF LATIN WORDS. 675

citrus, p. 229
ciuis = O. *ceus*
clauos, cf. U. *klavlaf*
clingere, Gloss. *krenkatrum*
clitellae, cf. U. *kletrā-*
clucidatus, 205, Rem. 9. 4, p. 230
clunes, cf. U. *klavlaf*
comis, Gloss. *cosmis*
commircium, Gloss. s.v.
Commolanda, *dea*, Gloss. *Supunne*
communis, cf. O. *mūiniko-*
compescere, Gloss. *perstu*
conger, 205, Rem. 9. 3, p. 230
contra, cf. O. *contrud*
cornix, cf. U. *curnac-*
cossim, 205 B 3
cotonia mala, 205, Rem. 9. 3, p. 230, q.v.
cracentes, 205, Rem. 9. 4, p. 230, q.v.
cras = Fal. *cra*
crefrat, 205 C 1
cremare, cf. U. *krematra*
crepusculum, v. *crepusco-*, 309 A
cudo, cf. U. *kutef*
cuia, Gloss. *pūiiu*
cum (prepn.), Gloss. *com*
-cunque, Gloss. *-pumpe*
cupa, 205 B 5
cupencus, 309 A
cura, *curare*, Gloss. *coisatens*
curis, 309 A

dacrima, 309 B, Rem.
damnum, 309 B, Rem. s.v. *lapit*
dare, Gloss. *dato-*
decem = U. *dešen-*
decet = U. *tišit*
decuria, cf. U. *dequrier*
dedrot, xliii. 4, p. 434 and Gloss. s.v.
Deferunda, *dea*, Gloss. *Supunne*
delicatus, 309 B, Rem.
dexter, Gloss. *destro-*
dicare, cf. O. *dadíkatted*
dicere, cf. Gloss. *deic-*
dies, Gloss. *zicolom*
digitus, Gloss. *degetasis*
dingua, 309 B, Rem.
dispennite, n. xxiii., p. 226
dispescere, Gloss. *perstu*
distennite, n. xxiii., p. 226
diua, cf. Gloss. *deiuā-* and *diivia-*
diuidere, Gloss. *uef*
diuinitus, *caelitus*, etc., Gloss. *-tā*
diuinus = O. *deivino-*
domare? cf. O. *damsennias*
donec, *donicum*, Gloss. *arnipo*
donum = O. *dunum*
dumtaxat, p. 484
duo = U. *duvo-*
duplex, cf. Umb. *duplak, duplo-* (written *tup-*)

e- in *equidem*, Gloss. *etanto-*
e, prepn. = Osc. *ee-, eh-*, U. *eh-*, qq.v. in Gloss.
edo, cf. O. *edum*
emere, Gloss. *emo-* and *peremust*
endo, Gloss. s.v.
enim, Gloss. *enem, einom*
equos, Gloss. s.v. *kvaísstur*
esse, Gloss. *es-*
extra = O. *ehtrad*
exuo, Gloss. *anouihimu*

faber, Gloss. s.v.
facio, oldest perfect of, Gloss. *fac-*
fallere, Gloss. *holtu*
fanum, Gloss. *fēs-nā-*
far = U. *far*
farferus, 205 C 1
fateor, Gloss. *fatíum*
faunus, Gloss. *fons*
februare, 309 A *februo-*
fēriae, Gloss. *fēsnā-*
fero = Osc.-U. *fer-*
feronia, 309 A, xliii. 2, p. 433
fertilis = Pg. *fertli-*
festus, Gloss. *fēsnā-*
fides, Gloss. *combifla-*
figlina, Gloss. *fifikus*
figo, Gloss. *fifikus*
filius, Gloss. *feliuf*
findo, Gloss. *feḍehtru*
fingere, Gloss. *feího-*
fingo, Gloss. *atahus* and *feího-*
fio, Gloss. *fiiet*
fitilla, Gloss. *ficla-*
Flora = O. *Fluusā-*
fons, Gloss. *huntak*
fores, Gloss. *vero-*
frater = Osc.-U. *fratr-*
fraus, Gloss. *frosetom*
fretus, Gloss. *arsie*
frigidus, Gloss. *frehtu*
fruges = U. *frif*
fruor, cf. O. *fruktatiuf*
fundere, Gloss. *hondu*

Gaius, *praenomen*, Gloss. *Gaauio-*
geneta, Gloss. s.v.
Gnaeus = O. *Gnaivs*
gnatus, Gloss. *cnatois*
gnixus, cf. U. *co-ncg-os*
Graeci, *Graecia*, orig. of name, p. 361
gratus, *grates*, Gloss. *brato-, brat-*
grunnire, xxiii., p. 226

haba, 349 A
habere, Gloss. *habē-*, and p. 496
haedus = Sab. *fedo-*, 309 A
hanula, 349 Rem.
hasta, Gloss. *hostatu*
hebris, 349 Rem.

43—2

INDEX VI.

hiare, Gloss. *cehiiā-*
hodie, Gloss. *foied*
holus, Gloss. *felsua*
homo, Gloss. *homon-*
horcto, 349 Rem. q.v.
horda, *Hordicidia*, 349 Rem.
hortus = O. *hŭrto-*
hospes = Pg. *hospus* (Addenda)
huc, Gloss. *ecuc*

-ia, in neut. pl. of consonantal adjj. v. Gloss. s.v. *teremen-*
ibi = Osc.-Umb. *ife*
idus, Gloss. *eíduís*
imber, Gloss. *anafriss*
imus, Gloss. *imaden*
in, Gloss. *en*
in- (negative), cf. O.-U. *an-*
inchoare, v. *incohare*
incohare, Gloss. *kahad*
ind-uere, *indu-perator*, Gloss. *endo*
induo, v. Gloss. *anouihimu*
inter, cf. O. *anter*
ipse, Gloss. *sepse*
ire, Gloss. *etu*
is, eum = Osc.-U. *is, eo-*, cf. p. 477
iste, p. 477
Italia = O. *Vítelliú*
itare, Gloss. *etaí-*
iterum, Gloss. s.v. *etro-*
Iupiter, Gloss. s.v. *diesptr*
iuuenca = U. *iuengā-*
iuuenis, cf. U. *iouie*

lacrima, 309 B Rem.
lapit, 309 B Rem.
larix, 309 B Rem.
latices, p. 229
Latium, Gloss. *Tlatie*
lauare, Gloss. *vutu*
lautia, 309 B Rem.
lautumiae, Gloss. *retŭmaf*
legatus = O. *lígato-*
legio = O. *legin-*
lego, cf. Pg. *lexe*
lepesta, 309 A
leuenna, xxiii., p. 226
leuir, 309 B Rem.
lex, Gloss. *lēg-*
liber, cf. O. *lŭvfro-*, Fal. *loferta*
libet, cf.? O. *loufir*
licět, cf. Osc. *likítŭd*, 'liceto'
limes = O. *liímit-*
lingua, 309 B Rem.
lira, Gloss. s.v. *luisarifs* and *dislera-linsust*
lixulae, 309 A
locare, cf. Pg. *locatin*
Loucetius, 205 A
lucus = O. *lŭvko-*

ludus = Fal.-L. *loido-*
luna = Etr.-Praen. *losna*
lympha, *lumpa* = Osc. *diumpā-*, and cf. 309 B
lympha, lumpa, 309 B Rem.

magis, Gloss. *maimas*
magnus, Gloss. *maimas*
malus, Gloss. *mallo-*
Mana Geneta, Gloss. *Genetai*
mantellum, Gloss. *mandraclo-*
manisnauius, Gloss. *snata*
manus, Gloss. *manu-*
Mars = U. *Mars*, cf. O. *Mamers*
mas, masculus, Gloss. *maro*
mater, Gloss. *maatr-*
maturus, cf. Gloss. Osc. *maato-*
matuta, Gloss. O. *maato*
Mauors, Gloss. *Mamers*
mederi, *medicus*, Gloss. *meddix*
medius = O. *mefio-*
melica, 309 B Rem.
mensa = Umb. *mefa*, q.v.
mensis, Gloss. U. *menzne*
mi, Gloss. *seso*
Minerva, Gloss. *mersus*
modestus, Gloss. *meḍs*
molere, *mola*, Gloss. *maletu*
molere, Gloss. s.v. *comol-*
moneta, Gloss. *tažez*.
mons, beside *men-tum*, *e-mineo*, Gloss. *spahatu*
motus = U. *(com)-mohoto-*
mugire, Gloss. *mugatu*
multa, Gloss. *moltā*.

nare, Gloss. *snata*
narrare, Gloss. *naratu*
-ně, nč, nei, p. 482
Neptunus, cf. U. *nepitu*
ninguere, cf. U. *ninctu*
nisi, Gloss. *nesei*
nix, Gloss. *ninctu*
nixus, Gloss. *conegos*
-no, *-nom*, on coins, p. 143 f.
nomen = U. *nome*
nouensides = Sab. *-siles*, 309 A
numerus, Gloss. *Niumsis*
nummus, Gloss. *Niumsis*

ob, Gloss. *op*
occupare, conjugation of, Gloss. *andersafust*
octauos, Gloss. *ŭhtavis*
odor, 309 B Rem. and Gloss. *uḍetu, uḍfakium*
olere, *oletum*, 309 B Rem.
olfacere, 309 B Rem.
olla, Gloss. *ŭlam*
olle, Gloss. *ulo*
omnis, Gloss. *omnitu, ŭmbn*

INDEX OF LATIN WORDS. 677

-on-, suffix, v. Gloss. *abrunu*
operare = O. *úpsā-*
operio, *aperio*, Gloss. *op*
oportet, Gloss. *op*
optare, *optumus*, Gloss., U. *opeter*, Osc. *ufteis*
orare, Gloss. *urust*
orbita = U. *urfeta-*
ortus = U. *orto-*
osor, Gloss. *usurs*

pandere, v. Gloss. s.v. *patensíns*
panis, cf. 309 D
par (a pair), p. 512
parcus, *parricus*, Low L., Gloss. s.v. *perstu*
parra, Gloss. *parfā-*
parret, *paret, apparere*, v. Gloss. s.v. *parsest*
parum-per, p. 483
pater = Osc.-Umb. *patr-*
paullis-per, p. 483
pax, Gloss. *pase*
pecten, cf. U. *pehtenata*
pedestris, formation of, Gloss. *Velestrom*
pedica, cf. Gloss. s.v. *tri-bḍišu*
pertica, Gloss. s.v. *perstu*
pes = U. *peḍ-*
pessum, Gloss. *pesetom*
piare = U. *pihā-*
piceus = U. *peiu*
picus = U. *peico-*
pila, Gloss. s.v. *ehpeílatas*
pistus = U. *pistu*
píus, Gloss. *pihom*
plenus = U. *pleno-*
poculum, Gloss. *pone*
Pomona, cf. U. *Puemune*
pomum, v. Gloss. s.v. *Puemune*
pone, cf. U. *postne*
pons, cf. O. *púnttram*
populus = U. *poplo-*
porca = U. *porcā-*
Porsena, Gloss. *Saluena*
portare, Gloss. *portatu*
posco, Gloss. s.v. *comparascuster*
post = Osc.-Umb. *post*
posterius = O. *pústiris*
posterus = Osc.-Umb. *postro-*
postulare, Gloss. *terkantur*
postumus = Osc. *postmo-*
potens, *potui*, cf. Osc. *pútíad*
potis, Gloss. *purtupite*
põtus, Gloss. s.v. *genetaí*
prae = Osc. *praí*, Umb. *pre*
praebere = U. *prehub-*
praesens = Osc. *praesent-*
praesilium, 309 B, Rem.
precor, Gloss. *pepurkurent*
primus = Pg. *prismo-*

priuatus = Osc. *preiuato-*
priuos = U. *prevo-*
pro, Gloss. s.v.
probus, *probare*, v. Gloss. s.v. *profā-, prufe*
proles, 309 B, Rem.
pronus, Gloss. *pustnaiaf*
publicus, Gloss. s.v. *pupḍiko-*
puer, v. Gloss. s.v. *puclo-*
pulmentum, cf. U. *pelmner*

quaestor = O. *kvaísstur*, U. *kvestur*
quamde, probably = Osc.-Umb. **panne, pan(e)*
quattuor, etc., v. Gloss. s.v. *petirupert*, and *Petrunia-*
-que, p. 506 footn., p. 481
quis = Osc.-Umb. *pis*
quisne, Gloss. *arnipo*
quo- = Osc.-Umb. *po-*, q.v. and p. 479
quō, cf. U. *pue*

reapse, Gloss. *sepse*
rectus = Osc.-Umb. *rehto-*
rego, Gloss. *regatureí*
res, Gloss. *ri*
resistere, cf. U. *restef*
restare, U. *restatu*
reuisere, Gloss. *revestu*
rex, 186 D
rōbus = U. *rofo-*
ropio, 205 C, 8
ruber = Umb. *rufro-*
rubus, Gloss. *rubina*
rufus, Gloss. *rofo-*
rusticus = Pg. *rustix*

Sabinus, cf. Gloss. *safinim*
sacer = Osc.-Umb. *sacro-*
sacrare = Osc.-Umb. *sakrā-*
sacris = Osc.-Umb. *sacri-*
sal, Gloss. *salu*
saluos = O. *salavs*
sanctus = O. *sahto-*
sanus, cf. U. *sanes*
sarcio, cf. U. *sarsite*
satias, *-atis*, Gloss. s.v. *vakaze*
scalpere, Gloss. σκλαβενς
scapula = U. *scaplā-*
scriptus = O. *scrifto-*, U. *screihto-*
scripulum, p. 226
sed, Gloss. *seipodruhpei*
sedeo, cf. U. *seḍ-*
semen, Gloss. *sehmeniar*
semi-, Gloss. *samíp*
Semo = Pg. *Semun-* and p. 357
semum, Gloss. *semu*
senatus, cf. O. *senato-*, Fal. (gen. sg.) *zenatuo*
seruare, Gloss. *anzeriā-*

*sessus, p. 485 footn.
sextans, cf. U. *sestentasiaru*
sibus, Gloss. *sipus*
simpulum, Gloss. *seples*
sistere, intrans. cf. U. *andersistu, sestu*
sociennis, p. 226
sollus, v. 205 A
sonare, cf. U. *sonitu*
sons, Gloss. s.v. *essuf*
spatior, Gloss. *spantim*
spatium, Gloss. s.v. *spahatu*
spectare, cf. U. *spehtur*
spelunca, p. 229
spina, Gloss. s.v.
sponda, -*ēre*, Gloss. s.v. *spahatu, spanti-, spefa*
sponte, Gloss. s.v. *spahatu*
spurius, Gloss. *Spŭriis*
stabularis = U. *staflari-*
stipulor = U. *stiplā-*
-str- in *pedestris*, etc., cf. Vol. Velestrom
sub, Gloss. *Supunne*
summus = U. *sommo-*
suos = O. *suvo-*
supero-, Gloss. *supro-*
superare, Gloss. *traf*
superne, Gloss. s.v. and cf. *perne*
suppus = U. *sopo*
sus, Gloss. *sim*
susurrus, Gloss. *sverrunei*

tabula = U. *tafle* (loc. sg.)
taeda, 205 Rem. 9 (5), p. 230
tango, Gloss. *atahus, tanginud, tongitio*
tantus, cf. Osc.-U. *e-tanto-*
taurus = Osc. ταυρο-, U. *toro-*
tectus? cf. U. *tehteḍim*
Telis for Thetis, 293
tendo, Gloss. *andendu*
tennitur, n. xxiii. p. 226
tepor, Gloss. *tapistenu*
termen, cf. Osc. *teremen-*
terminus = U. *termno-*
terra, Gloss. s.v. *terŭm*
terreo, *terror*, Gloss. s.v. *tursitu* and *tremitu*
tertius = U. *tertio-*
tesqua, 309 A
testamentum = O. *tristaamento-*
testis, testor, cf. O. *trstus*, and ? U. *terkantur*
thesaurus, thensaurus, cf. O. *thesavro-*
-ti- suffix, Gloss. s.v. *vakaz-e*
tibi = O. *tifei*, U. *tefe*, p. 477
-to- partcc., active use of, Gloss. s.v. *geneta-* and Addenda
tongitio, Gloss. s.v.
tonstrix, -*str-* in, Gloss. *Velestrom*
topper, p. 483

tormentum, cf. O. *turum-iad* -trā, Gloss. *hondra*
trabs = O. *trīib-*
trans = U. *trāf*
transenna, p. 226
transuersu = U. *trahuorfi*
tremere, cf. U. *tremitu*, 'tremefacito'
tres, p. 482
tribus = U. *trefu-*
triplex, cf. U. *triplo-*
tripudare, -*dium*, cf. U. *dupursus*
triumphus, p. 230
tuccus = U. *toco*
tuos = O. *tuvo-*, U. *touo-*
turris = O. *tiurrí-*
-tus in *diuinitus*, etc., cf. Umb. postp. *-tā, -to*
Tuscus = U. *Tursko-*

uacare, *uocare*, Gloss. s.v. *vakaze*
uacatio, Gloss. *vakaz-e*
uadimonium = O. *vaamunim*
uapor, cf. U. *vaputu*
uasa = U. *uaso*, }
uasi = U. *uasor*, } v. Gloss. s.v. *uaso*
uascula, v. Gloss. s.v. U. *vesklu*
uasus, nom. sg. Gloss. *uaso*
ubi, Gloss. *pufe, pŭtro-*
uehere, cf. U. *kuveitu*
uelle, Gloss. *ehvelklu, veltu*
uenio, Gloss. *ben-*
uenor, cf. Gloss. *ahauendu*
uenum, cf. Gloss. *ahauendu*
uerbum, cf. U. *uerfale*
uerecunnus, xxiii. p. 226
uersor = O. ϝερσορ-
uertere, cf. U. *kuvertu*
ueru = U. *beru-*
uester = U. *uestro-*
uetere, *uetare*, Gloss. s.v. *vakaze*
uia = Osc. *vía-*, U. *veā-, viā-*
uicus = Mars. *uěcos*, ? cf. U. *uoco-*
uideo, cf. U. *uirseto*
uiduos, Gloss. s.v. *dersua* and *ucf*
uiěre, *uimen*, Gloss. s.v. *eueietu*
uinculum, cf. Umb. *pre-uišl-a-tu*
uinum = U. *vinu*, q.v.
uir, v. Gloss. s.v. *ueiro* and *couehriu*
uitulus = U. *vitlo-*
uiuos, Gloss. *bivus*
Ulixes, p. 361
ultimo = O. *últiumo-*
umerus, Gloss. *onse*
unda, Gloss. *utur*
unde, Gloss. *pŭtro-*
unguere, *unguen*, v. Gloss. s.v. *umtu*
unus = Osc. *úino-*, Umb. *unu-*
-uo- suffix in *aruom, deciduos*, etc., Gloss. s.v. *facus*

uolema (better *-aema*) *pira*, cf. Osc. *valaimo-*
uos, *uobis*, v. Gloss. s.v. *uus* and p. 477
-uos, suffix, Gloss. s.v. *dersua*
uotare, *uetare*, Gloss. s.v. *vakaze*
uouere, Gloss. s.v. U. *vufetes* and Fal. *vootum*

urbs, cf. Mars. *urbi-*
urna, cf. Umb. *urnasia-*
uruos = Osc. *uruvo-*
ut, Gloss. *puze, pŭtro-*
uter, Gloss. *pŭtro-*
utor, cf. O. *ŭittiuf*, Pg. *oisa*
uxor = Pg. *usur*, ? cf. O. *usurs*

ADDENDA.

Page 7. Add to 11 C. Cămĕrŭ Ov. *Fast.* 3. 582.

Page 25, l. 4 of 28. Von Planta reads **osins** 'adsint' (*obsint*).

Page 28, l. 31 of 28. I am glad to find that Von Planta now also reads **acunum** or **agunum**.

Page 50. Add to αισοι the gloss from Suet. *Aug.* 97: **aesar** *Etrusca lingua deus*.

Page 69. In **59** Mr Walter Dennison, Fellow of the American School of Archaeology at Rome, writes to me that he recognised the square interpunct after **ahvdiu** and would separate it from **ni**.

Page 70. Von Planta (*Osk. Umb. Gram.* II. p. 609) rightly objects to the argument advanced by me in *Idg. Forsch.* l.c. and repeated in the note to **60** (as to the date of these inscc. painted on the tufa-blocks), urging that when Pompeii was first uncovered these inscc. were underneath a coating of stucco[1]; hence they probably were not written immediately before the destruction of the town. I regret that I overlooked the loss of the stucco, and so far as it goes Von Planta's criticism is perfectly just; but that the inscc. were advertisements of some kind, as Mommsen held (*U. D.* p. 185), still seems to me abundantly clear, and Nissen's theory inherently improbable. The position of the 4 inscc., all close to the ends of side streets leading from the centre of the town to spots along the walls, appears to me to fix the meaning of **amvĭanud** beyond a doubt (v. Glossary), whatever meaning be given to **eítuns**.

Page 72 f. **65** and **67**. Von Planta conjectures (II. p. 611 f.) that **nie** are the initial letters of words corresponding to the Lat. *u. b. o. u. f.* = *uirum bonum, oro uos faciatis* (*aedilem* etc.) and the like. Fiorelli (*Mon. Epigr. Pomp.* 11) renders **altinûm** plausibly 'alimentorum,' supposing a Pompeian office like the Lat. *praefecti alimentorum* etc. (*C. I. L.* IX. 699 al.).

---

[1] Fiorelli, *Descriz. di Pomp.* 83, 103, 153, 436.

Page 78. **78.** Von Planta (II. p. 615 footn.) suggests that the line through the last *i* is meant to erase it so that **Sabins** should be read.

ib. **80 bis.** **arkiia** on plaster-work of the Nolan gate (*C. I. L.* IV. ad 1608).

Page 93. **95 *b* 33.** Von Planta (II. p. 625) following Bugge in part (*Kuhn's Z.* 5. 8) conjectures plausibly s]**ullad** ('omnino' uel sim.) **víú uruvú íst p̱edu X̱**.

Page 96. **98 bis.** Von Planta (II. p. 527) gives an insc. of this class which I had overlooked from his own copy of a patera in the Naples Museum (Fabr. 1 Suppl. 512).

cnaives flaviies p

Page 117. **114. 7.** Von Planta (II. p. 633) thinks **úíníveresím** impossible from the original, and reads with confidence **iním vereẖias**.

Page 118. **115, 116.** The curious description of the date of this sacrifice **filsíais púmperiais pas prai mamerttiais set** may well be intended to cover the case of an intercalary month. If so, it is tempting to compare Plut. *Numa* 18. 3, where we read that in the calendar of Numa a month of 22 days was intercalated every other year after February, and called Μερκηδίνος (-δόνιος in Plut. *Caes.* 59, perhaps through an identification or confusion with the adjective *mercedonius* (Paul ex F. 124 M.), a view which seems to have been adopted at all events by Cincius ap. Lyd. *de Mensibus* 4. 92, though he gives the form as -δίνος).

Page 130. **132 bis.** Von Planta publishes for the first time (II. 164 *a*) an insc. in Osc. αβ "on a small object of terracotta in the shape of one half of a hollow finger which has been bisected along its length."

perkium | púiiehsúm

Page 131. **133.** Von Planta (ib. 165) follows Fröhner *Rh. Mus.* 47. 297 in reading **vibis úrúfiis**, comparing the common *gens Orfia, Orbia.*

Page 134. **137 *c*, *f* and *g*.** Von Planta on a second reading of the fragments at Naples (ibidem II. 119) has made a number of minor corrections in the text which he published in 1894 (in nearly all of them[1]

---

[1] His variants in *a, b, d* and *e* are:

a 8	ḵulu	4	pakulliis 1̱
9	m̱a̱	5	velehi
b 2	gṉa̱	6	....ẖẖiis
3	luvḵ	12	....is e..
d 1	He omits v̱	*e* 3	....s̱ niir
2	ṉ...ṯ illis		

agreeing with the text given in this edition); and he has also made the important discovery that the fragments (c) and (f) fit together if (g) be inserted between them in ll. 2—4; the second word in each of these lines he therefore now reads as **fuvfdis, buttis** and **rahiis** respectively. In the last word of (f) he conjectures [s]**ullas**, no doubt rightly, though still reading the preceding word as **sullud̦**, which seemed to me less likely than **sullum** in 1894; the latter is now clearly confirmed by the sense 'aduocati(?) et testes[1] omnes et horum uoluntates (**uhftis** is a fem. subst. nom. pl. = L. *opti- in optio) omnium omnes.'

The only other points in which his reading of (c) and (f) varies from the text to be obtained by combining the two directly as given on p. 134 are that in l. 4 he would read **marahi[e]is niir**, adding that **niir** follows the **is** "wohl unmittelbar." I noted however a distinct gap in the plate, as did Von Planta in his first reading; and though of course this gap may have never contained any letters, I do not feel as confident as Von Planta does now that **niir** is a complete word, as I could not detect the interpunct before it which he now reads (or conjectures?) in e 3 (v. p. 681 footn.). l. 6 ad fin. **papeis** had become clear. l. 8 **rufriis** (**maris** in my text on p. 134 is an unhappy misprint for **maras**). l. 9 **rahiieis uppiieis**.

Page 151. Add to Vesūuīus the modern name *M. Vesůvio.*

ib. Add to Sŏbŏthus Σεπειθος nm. of Naples, *Beschr. Berl.* p. 125.

Page 183—4. The capture of "Bovianum" by Sulla in 89 B.C. (App. *B. C.* 1. 51) might have been mentioned, and its recapture by Silo in the following year (Jul. Obsequens, *Prodig.* cxvi.)[2]; Mommsen (*C. I. L.* IX. p. 239, *Hist. of Rome* [Eng. Tr.] 3. pp. 252, 255) refers these events to Bovianum Undecimanorum, I suppose because it is the nearest of the two towns to the Hirpini whom Sulla had just left.

Page 193. **176.** The correction **mz** was made independently both by Mr Walter Dennison and Von Planta (II. p. 642).

Page 196. **183** c. By an unfortunate oversight I omitted Friedländer's reading of the only two specimens of this didrachma (*Osk. Münz.* 26), in which the sign before the *h* appears as Ϙ, a representation which he expressly describes as exact. Compare with this the S = f of Vibo and Fensernum (**6, 7, 143**), and note that this fits very well with the suggestion as to the origin of the Osc. **8** made on p. 463.

Page 201. **187 A.** Sabelli. I owe the following note to Prof. Sonnenschein's kindness. (I am bound to say, however, that passages like *Aen.* 8. 510, where Evander's wife is called *Sabella*, leave me still doubtful

---

[1] Skutsch in a communication to Von Planta (ib. p. 621) ingeniously justifies this rendering by the conjecture that the whole curse refers to a lawsuit.

[2] This reference I owe to the kindness of Mr R. D. Hicks.

whether the meaning can be always confined to Samnium in the strict geographical sense.)

July 9, 1897.

"The passages quoted in all dictionaries in which the word *Sabellus* is supposed to have the meaning 'Sabine' fall into two classes: (1) those which are quite indecisive, i.e. in which it might equally well mean 'Samnite'; e.g. *Sabellis ligonibus* Horace, *Od.* III. 6. 38, *pubem Sabellam* Vergil, *Georg.* II. 167, Columella, *De R. R.* x. 137 : (2) those in which it would be more correctly interpreted as meaning 'Samnite'—the meaning which it is admitted to have in Livy VIII. 1, Pliny III. 12. 107 (*Samnitium quos Sabellos et Graeci Saunitas dixere*). To this class belongs Hor. *Sat.* II. 1. 36 *pulsis, vetus est ut fama, Sabellis* (referring to the foundation of Venusia after the last Samnite war), *Epist.* I. 16. 49 *renuit negitatque Sabellus* (referring to Horace himself—not, I think, as the possessor of an estate in the Sabine country, but rather as born on the confines of the Samnite country, and probably descended from a family which was of Samnite blood and was enslaved during the Samnite wars). The *anus Sabella* of *Sat.* I. 9. 30 is clearly better located in the neighbourhood of Venusia than in Sabina. That *Sabellus* meant 'Samnite' to Varro is clearly shown by *Sat. Men.* 17 (ed. Bücheler) *Terra culturae causa attributa olim particulatim hominibus, ut Etruria Tuscis, Samnium Sabellis* (quoted by Junius Philargyrius on Verg. *Georg.* II. 167). The whole question will be discussed by me in greater detail in a forthcoming number of the *Classical Review.*"

E. A. S.

Page 201 ff. **187.** The following accents on the modern names in this section, which reached me too late for insertion in proof, I owe, like the rest, to Prof. A. Sogliano.

On p. 201	*Telése*	*Bifërno f.*
	Boiáno	*Isérnia*
	Fogliantse	*S. M. a Faifoli*
	Alife	*Monte Caracéno*
	Voltúrno f.	*Alfedéna*
	Sepino	*Trivénto.*

On p. 202	*Cerréto Sannita*
	Montáquila
	Duróne f.
	Calvisi
	Carife.

On p. 203	*Montágna del Matése*	*Vándra f.*
	Scápoli	*Cérro al Voltúrno*
	Molise	*Limosáno*
	Tappino f.	*Agnóne.*

Page 212 f. **197.** The following accents also reached me after the sheet was printed off:

On p. 212   *Laríno*

On p. 213   *Lanciáno*   *Fresa*
            Ortóna a máre   *Sinéllo f.*
            Sángro f.   *C. di Láma*
            Trigno f.   *Atéssa*
            Pagliéta   *Osénto f.*
            Casacalénda   *Orsógna*
            Térmoli   *Vásto.*
            Pálmoli

Page 216. It should have been added that many, if not most, of the types of these coins of the Allies were taken directly from Roman coins (denarii of the Servilia, Veturia and other gentes, in circulation at the time); even the well-known picture of the warriors (in varying number), swearing alliance above a pig whose sacrifice is to ratify the treaty, is imitated from a coin of the gens Veturia; Friedländer and Dressel ll. cc. give full details.

200. Mommsen (*Hist. of Rome*, 3. p. 253 footn.) infers from **safinim** that this coin belongs to the later period of the war when only the Samnites remained in arms, and therefore substituted their name for *Italia*, *Vítelliú* of the coins of 90 B.C.

Page 217. Note xxi. It should perhaps have been explicitly stated that the signs in (*a*) and (*b*) belong respectively to series of coins in which the sign for 5 is (*a*) upright as in Latin, and (*b*) reversed as in these examples. The direction is the same, namely retrograde, in both series.

Page 222. **205 C. 2.** Add to *asisua* the glosses from Goetz *Corp. Gl. Lat.* II. pp. 496, 568: *assua*: πέταυρον. *asisua*: foueo deceptionis anima (!).

Page 229. Rem. 9 (2). Add: cf. L. *turunda* = Gr. τυροῦντα.

Page 235. **206 bis.** Found at Sulmo in March 1897, by De Nino, to whom I owe two excellent impressions, whence the text.

brata poef sa | anacta ceri

In Gracchan Lat. *αβ* (N, P, T, but ||=*e*); the content is clearly parallel to that of **206**, and the omission of the *e* of *anaceta* may be either an example of 'syllabic writing' (v. 272 n.) or a mere abbreviation, as *poef-* is for some nomen whose Latin form would begin with *Pub-*, and probably *ceri* for *Ceria*.

ADDENDA. 685

Page 236. **208 bis**. The word *hospus* is now explained by Von Planta (II. p. 656), clearly rightly, as standing for *hospo(t)s, the Pael. nom. sg. masc. corresponding to L. *hospes* for *hospe(t)s*, with the meaning 'passer-by, friend,' which *hospes* frequently has in Latin epitaphs.

Page 249. **241**. The following accents reached me after the sheet was printed off:

Sulmóna
Atérno f.
Castél Vécchio Subéquo
Scánno
M. Morróne
Pacéntro
Pettoráno sul Gízio
Péntima

Prátola Pelígna
Prèzza
Pópoli
Tremónti
Tócco da Casáuria
Molína
Acciáno.

Page 256. **245**. The following accents reached me after the sheet was printed off:

Manoppéllo,
Alénto f.
Fóro f.
Arielli f.
Bucchiánico,
Móro f.

Page 260. **249 bis**. *pumula*, uitis Amiternino agro peculiaris, Plin. 14 § 37.

Page 294 f. The reading *atolero* was first suggested by Garrucci (see Zvet. *It. Med.* p. 82).

Page 297. Add to 270 C: Ἴσσα an island in L. Fucinus, Dion. Hal. 1. 14, assigned by him to the Aberrigines, cf. 310 C (where for 'a lake,' read 'L. Fucinus'); with this Büch. compares Mars. *esalicom*, see the Glossary.

Page 330. Thurneysen (*Kuhn's Ztschr.* 35. 193) has added another to the long list of interpretations of this insc. He reads *duenoi ne* in the third line, so that "*dze noine*" would seem now to be abandoned generally; but his fresh conjectures (e.g. that *oites iai*=*utens eis*) are far from convincing.

Page 356. **309 A** s.v. *Nerio*. The passage from Ennius, *Nerienem Mauortis et Herclem*, should have been quoted, as in it the first *e* of *Nerienem* may be scanned as short by nature and the second as long if the *i* be made consonantal; not so however the iambic of Imbrex, *Nolo ego Neaeram te uocent sed Nerienem* (? leg. *sed Nerienem te uocent*).

Page 362. **309 D**. Add: *uinaciola*, genus uitis ('soli nouerunt Sabini'), Plin. 14 § 38.

ADDENDA.

Page 463. See the addendum to page 196.

Page 518 f. Syntax § 73. There should have been mentioned in this section the traces which the dialects afford of the originally **voiceless** and **timeless** use of the participles in *-to-*, i.e. the traces of their earlier purely **adjectival** and, in the neuter, **substantival** meaning. Brugmann has analysed their development in Latin in *Indog. Forschungen* 5. 87 ff., an essay which is a masterpiece of fine syntactical discrimination. From it I take the following examples;

(1) of the **indifference of the suffix to the distinction of active and passive**: (*a*) with **active** meaning beside active verbs, Umb. *śersnatur=cenati* beside *cenare*, *taśez=tacitus* beside *tacere*, *sesust* (i.e. **sessos est* or *erit*, v. p. 485 footn.) 'sēderit' beside *sedere* (compare Lat. *pōtus, ausus*, Gr. τλητός 'enduring' etc.); (*b*) with **passive** meaning beside deponent verbs, Umb. *mefa*=Lat. *mensa* (v. Glossary, and cf. Lat. *ēmensus, adeptus* etc. in pass. sense), Pg. *oisa aetate* probably =*usa aetate*, i.e. *consumpta*.

(2) of its **indifference to distinctions of time**; Umb. *taśez* like Lat. *tacitus* has no notion of past time, nor have the neuter nouns quoted in the next paragraph (compare Lat. *amatus* 'beloved,' *laudatus* 'praiseworthy,' Gr. ξυνετός, κλυτός, Lat. *inclutus* etc.). Yet the compound perfect in the dialects has developed not merely the pure perfect uses (Osc. *scriptasset* 28 25, Umb. *screihtor sent* VI *a* 15), but also the aoristic use (Umb. *emps et termnas* 355) of the Lat. perfect.

(3) The use of the neuter as an abstract noun appears in Osc. *censtom*, Umb. *vasetom* (*-e fust* v. p. 494); cf. Lat. *in occulto, ad imperatum* etc.

Page 529. Von Planta 289 *a* quotes from Lattes, *Rendiconti d. Reale Accad. dei Lincei* II. fasc. 10—12, and III. fasc. 1—2, a transcription of another long inscription of this 'Sabellic' class recently found in Novilara near Pesaro.

Page 530. Von Planta (II. p. 597) compares with Τουτς or Τουτι- the cognomen *Tutus, C. I. L.* IX. 380, X. 1403. He counts the whole insc. as Oscan, explaining ποτερεμ in the same way as is suggested in the text.

Page 532. *46. Von Planta (II. p. 665) has discovered this 'lost' insc. in the Naples Museum, so that one of the reasons for counting it a forgery has disappeared. Von Planta apparently has no suspicions at all.

Published by the Cambridge University Press.

The Restored Pronunciation of Greek and Latin: with Tables and Practical Explanations. By EDWARD VERNON ARNOLD, M.A., Professor of Latin at the University College of North Wales, late Fellow of Trinity College, Cambridge; and ROBERT SEYMOUR CONWAY, M.A., Professor of Latin at the University College of South Wales and Monmouthshire, late Fellow of Gonville and Caius College, Cambridge. Second Edition. 1s.

"We must congratulate the authors and their colleagues upon the boldness of their enterprise and express a hope that Wales will show the way to England in adopting the reformed system thoroughly, not as an alternative, or in parts."—*Academy*, Nov. 23, 1895.

"Alles kurz und zuverlässig und durchaus geeignet den Zweck zu fördern welchem es dienen soll."—*Deutsche Litteraturzeitung*, May 23, 1896.

Published by Kegan Paul, Trench, Trübner & Co.

Verner's Law in Italy, 1887. By R. S. CONWAY, M.A. 8vo., 120 pp. 5s.

"The essay deserves a cordial welcome, not only for what it contains but also as a promise of excellent work in the future."—Prof. A. S. WILKINS in the *Academy*, Feb. 4, 1888.

"A most important contribution to the history of the Italic Dialects. The book is full of fruitful suggestions upon a wide range of topics."—New York *Nation*, May 17, 1888.

"Au point de vue de la conscience et de la méthode, de l'étendue et de la variété des connaissances, peu d'essais de linguistique indo-européenne méritent plus d'attention et d'éloges que celui de M. Conway."—VICTOR HENRY in the *Revue Critique*, April 2, 1888.

Published by the Cambridge University Press.

Relliquiae Philologicae: or, Essays in Comparative Philology. By the late HERBERT DUKINFIELD DARBISHIRE, M.A., Fellow of St John's College, Cambridge. Edited by R. S. CONWAY, M.A., late Fellow of Gonville and Caius College, Cambridge, Professor of Latin in University College, Cardiff; with a Biographical Notice by J. E. SANDYS, Litt.D., Fellow and Tutor of St John's College and Public Orator in the University of Cambridge. Demy 8vo., 279 pp., 7s. 6d.

"Der stattliche Band, ein Denkmal pietätvoller Freundschaft, birgt die Ernte eines Menschenlebens....Wir können nur ahnen was der spurende Scharfsinn, der unruhig vorwärts drängende Wagemut und die ehrliche Entschlossenheit des früh Verstorbnen unsrer Wissenschaft hätte schenken können."—Prof. STREITBERG in *Indog. Anzeiger* VI. 3.

"The exceptional honour paid to H. D. Darbishire's memory by the Cambridge Philological Society participating in the issue of this memorial volume is amply justified by the contents. The bright and strong personality of the brave young scholar whose brilliant promise was so suddenly blighted by death sparkles throughout his essays."—*Athenaeum*, May 23, 1896.

www.ingramcontent.com/pod-product-compliance
Lightning Source LLC
Chambersburg PA
CBHW021803230426
43669CB00008B/612